T&T CLARK HANDBOOK OF ANALYTIC THEOLOGY

Forthcoming titles in this series include:

T&T Clark Handbook of Colin Gunton,
edited by Myk Habets, Andrew Picard, and Murray Rae

T&T Clark Handbook of Theological Anthropology,
edited by Mary Ann Hinsdale and Stephen Okey

T&T Clark Handbook of Christology,
edited by Darren O. Sumner and Chris Tilling

T&T Clark Handbook of Christian Prayer,
edited by Ashley Cocksworth and John C. McDowell

Titles already published include:

T&T Clark Handbook of Pneumatology,
edited by Daniel Castelo and Kenneth M. Loyer

T&T Clark Handbook of Ecclesiology,
edited by Kimlyn J. Bender and D. Stephen Long

T&T Clark Handbook of Christian Theology and the Modern Sciences,
edited by John P. Slattery

T&T Clark Handbook of Christian Ethics,
edited by Tobias Winright

T&T Clark Handbook of Thomas F. Torrance,
edited by Paul D. Molnar and Myk Habets

T&T Clark Handbook of Christian Theology and Climate Change,
edited by Ernst M. Conradie and Hilda P. Koster

T&T Clark Handbook of Edward Schillebeeckx,
edited by Stephan van Erp and Daniel Minch

T&T Clark Handbook of Political Theology,
edited by Rubén Rosario Rodríguez

T&T Clark Companion to the Theology of Kierkegaard,
edited by Aaron P. Edwards and David J. Gouwens

T&T Clark Handbook of African American Theology,
edited by Antonia Michelle Daymond, Frederick L. Ware, and Eric Lewis Williams

T&T Clark Handbook of Asian American Biblical Hermeneutics,
edited by Uriah Y. Kim and Seung Ai Yang

T&T Clark Handbook to Early Christian Meals in the Greco-Roman World,
edited by Soham Al-Suadi and Peter-Ben Smit

T&T CLARK HANDBOOK OF ANALYTIC THEOLOGY

Edited by
James M. Arcadi and James T. Turner, Jr.

LONDON • NEW YORK • OXFORD • NEW DELHI • SYDNEY

T&T CLARK
Bloomsbury Publishing Plc
50 Bedford Square, London, WC1B 3DP, UK
1385 Broadway, New York, NY 10018, USA
29 Earlsfort Terrace, Dublin 2, Ireland

BLOOMSBURY, T&T CLARK and the T&T Clark logo are trademarks of
Bloomsbury Publishing Plc

First published in Great Britain 2021
Paperback edition published 2022

Copyright © James M. Arcadi, James T. Turner, Jr., and contributors, 2021

James M. Arcadi and James T. Turner, Jr. have asserted their right under the Copyright, Designs and Patents Act, 1988, to be identified as Editors of this work.

For legal purposes the Acknowledgments on p. x constitute an extension of this copyright page.

Cover design: Terry Woodley
Cover image: *Shepherd King* © Tanja Butler/tanjabutler.com

All rights reserved. No part of this publication may be reproduced or transmitted in any form or by any means, electronic or mechanical, including photocopying, recording, or any information storage or retrieval system, without prior permission in writing from the publishers.

Bloomsbury Publishing Plc does not have any control over, or responsibility for, any third-party websites referred to or in this book. All internet addresses given in this book were correct at the time of going to press. The author and publisher regret any inconvenience caused if addresses have changed or sites have ceased to exist, but can accept no responsibility for any such changes.

A catalogue record for this book is available from the British Library.

A catalog record for this book is available from the Library of Congress.

ISBN: HB: 978-0-5676-8129-4
PB: 978-0-5677-0101-5
ePDF: 978-0-5676-8130-0
eBook: 978-0-5676-8133-1

Series: T&T Clark Handbooks

Typeset by Newgen KnowledgeWorks Pvt. Ltd., Chennai, India

To find out more about our authors and books visit www.bloomsbury.com and sign up for our newsletters.

*To those who first taught us to think analytically and theologically.
From James Arcadi to Fred Sanders, John Mark Reynolds, and Jack Davis.
From J. T. Turner to Thom Provenzola and Ed Martin.*

CONTENTS

ACKNOWLEDGMENTS	x
Introduction *James M. Arcadi*	1
Part I Methods and Sources	7
1 The Importance of Model Building in Theology *Oliver D. Crisp*	9
2 Modeling Inspiration: Perspicuity after Pentecost *Adam Green*	21
3 Religious Epistemology in Analytic Theology *Tyler Dalton McNabb and Erik Baldwin*	33
4 *Norma Normata*: The Role of Tradition in Analytic Theology *R. Lucas Stamps*	45
5 Analytic Theology and Philosophy of Science: Toward an All-Encompassing Theory of God, the World, and Human Life *Benedikt Paul Göcke*	55
6 The Fellowship of the Ninth Hour: Christian Reflections on the Nature and Value of Faith *Daniel Howard-Snyder and Daniel J. McKaughan*	69
Part II Doctrine of God	83
7 Classical Theism *R. T. Mullins*	85
8 An Anselmian Approach to Divine Omnipotence *Katherin Rogers*	101
9 Maximal Greatness and Perfect Knowledge *Benjamin H. Arbour*	113
10 Retrieving Divine Immensity and Omnipresence *Ross D. Inman*	127

11 Divine Goodness and Love 141
    Jordan Wessling

12 Providence 155
    David Fergusson

13 Divine Aseity and Abstract Objects 165
    Lindsay K. Cleveland

14 The Trinity 181
    Thomas H. McCall

Part III Person and Work of Christ 195

15 The Incarnation 197
    Timothy Pawl

16 Christ's Impeccability 215
    Johannes Grössl

17 Philosophical Issues in the Atonement 231
    William Lane Craig

18 Election, Grace, and Justice: Analyzing an Aporetic Tetrad 243
    James N. Anderson

Part IV Pneumatology 255

19 The Indwelling of the Holy Spirit 257
    Adonis Vidu

20 Deification and Union with God 269
    Carl Mosser

21 Toward an Analytic Theology of Charismatic Gifts: Preliminary Questions 281
    Joanna Leidenhag

Part V Creation and Humans 295

22 *Creatio Ex Nihilo* 297
    Andrew Ter Ern Loke

23 The Soul as *Imago Dei*: Modernizing Traditional Theological Anthropology 311
    Joshua R. Farris

24 The Fall and Original Sin 325
    Olli-Pekka Vainio

25 Sin as Self-Deception 335
    William Wood

26 Analytic Theological Ethics *Kent Dunnington*	347
27 Willie Jennings on the Supersessionist Pathology of Race: A Differential Diagnosis *Sameer Yadav*	357
28 Goodness, Embodiment, and Disability: Lessons from Then for Now *Hilary Yancey*	369
29 Gender and Justice: Human and Divine Gender in Analytic Theology *Michelle Panchuk*	381
30 Analytic Theology and Animals *Faith Glavey Pawl*	395
31 Analytic Theology and the Sciences *Aku Visala*	407
32 The *End* of Things: Resurrection and New Creation *James T. Turner, Jr.*	423
Part VI Experiences and Practices	437
33 Analytic Spirituality *David Efird*	439
34 Christian Baptism: A Reformed Account *Nathaniel Gray Sutanto*	451
35 On the Intelligibility of Eucharistic Doctrine(s) in Analytic Theology *James M. Arcadi*	463
36 Analytic Theology and Liturgy *Joshua Cockayne*	477
37 Prayer *Scott A. Davison*	489
A COMPREHENSIVE CATEGORIZED BIBLIOGRAPHY OF ANALYTIC THEOLOGY *Jesse Gentile*	499
NOTES ON CONTRIBUTORS	521
INDEX	525

ACKNOWLEDGMENTS

All Scripture quotations are referenced in the footnotes to individual chapters, where relevant. The editors would like to give full acknowledgments to the following versions of the Bible here:

All Scripture quotations footnoted as "New International Version" are taken from the Holy Bible, New International Version®, NIV®, copyright ©1973, 1978, 1984, 2011 by Biblica, Inc.™ Used by permission of Zondervan. All rights reserved worldwide. www.zondervan.com. The "NIV" and "New International Version" are trademarks registered in the United States Patent and Trademark Office by Biblica, Inc.™

All Scripture quotations footnoted as "New Revised Standard Version Bible" are from New Revised Standard Version Bible, copyright © 1989 by National Council of the Churches of Christ in the United States of America. Used by permission. All rights reserved worldwide.

All Scripture quotations footnoted as "English Standard Version" are from the ESV® Bible (The Holy Bible, English Standard Version®), copyright © 2001 by Crossway, a publishing ministry of Good News Publishers. Used by permission. All rights reserved.

All Scripture quotations footnoted as "New American Bible, revised edition" are from *New American Bible, revised edition*, copyright © 1970, 1986, 1991, and 2010 by Confraternity of Christian Doctrine, Washington, DC, and are used by permission of the copyright owner. All rights reserved. No part of the New American Bible may be reproduced in any form without permission in writing from the copyright owner.

All Scripture quotations footnoted as "Revised Standard Version" are taken from the Revised Standard Version of the Bible, copyright © 1946, 1952, and 1971 by National Council of the Churches of Christ in the United States of America. Used by permission. All rights reserved worldwide.

All Scripture quotations footnoted as "New American Standard Bible" are taken from the New American Standard Bible® (NASB), copyright © 1960, 1962, 1963, 1968, 1971, 1972, 1973, 1975, 1977, and 1995 by The Lockman Foundation. Used by permission. www.Lockman.org.

Introduction

JAMES M. ARCADI

I. ANALYTIC THEOLOGY: WHENCE

The term "analytic theology" comes from the 2009 Oxford University Press publication *Analytic Theology: New Essays in the Philosophy of Theology* edited by Oliver D. Crisp and Michael C. Rea.[1] However, the editors of this volume hold analytic theology to be simply a contemporary instantiation of an enduring relationship between theology and philosophy in the Christian tradition. Not only does this relationship go back millennia, but the relationship between theology and analytic philosophy—the origin of the "analytic" in analytic theology—also predates the publication of the volume with this movement's name in the title. In this introductory essay, I first sketch a brief history of analytic theology, finding it as but another version of a long-standing methodological approach. This will be followed by a portrayal of analytic theology as an intellectual culture in which certain sensibilities, tools, and characteristics are borrowed from analytic philosophy for properly theological ends.

I.1 An Ancient Handmaiden

Within the study of religion—and religious beliefs in particular—often it is not easy to demarcate clearly the boundary line between philosophy and theology. One must not forget that an Athenian jury convicted none other than the quintessential philosopher, Socrates, on the very *theological* charge of impiety toward the gods. When one reads such medieval thinkers as the Christian Thomas Aquinas, the Muslim Avicenna, or the Jewish Maimonides, one sees that this boundary line frequently is artificial. Within the Christian tradition, one can point to the second-century church father, Clement of Alexandria (1979: 305), as the scholar who first characterized the relationship between philosophy and theology as one of a handmaiden—philosophy as the aid and assistant to the theological task. This aiding and assisting role of philosophy pervades the Christian theological project throughout the centuries, even as the particular philosophical school serving as handmaiden may change. Hence, whether the philosophical school was Neoplatonism with Clement or Augustine, Aristotelianism with Thomas Aquinas or Peter Martyr Vermigli, or phenomenology with Edward Schillebeeckx or Jean-Luc Marion, theology always has been done in some kind of conversation with philosophy. Analytic theology is no different in this overall methodological approach to philosophy. Its

---

[1] For further introductory material, see McCall (2015).

difference lies simply in that the philosophical dialogue partner is analytic philosophy—a dialogue partner often found absent from the major theological conversations of the twentieth century.

I.2 The Strands of St. Basil and St. Alvin

William Abraham (2013) demarcates the development of specifically analytic theology as emerging independently along two main strands, with two key players. From the middle of the twentieth century onward, Basil Mitchell and Alvin Plantinga serve as paradigm examples of analytic philosophy being pressed into the service of theology. Mitchell represents an Oxbridge approach to philosophy of religion that renewed Christian theism as a viable component of philosophical inquiry. In North America, the strand of St. Alvin centers on Plantinga, the philosophy department of the University of Notre Dame, and the Center for Philosophy of Religion that resides therein.[2] Like Mitchell, Plantinga's work created space within analytic philosophy for theism to be taken seriously. One might be inclined to place Richard Swinburne within the strand of St. Basil, for he succeeded Mitchell as the Nolloth Chair at Oriel College. These three philosophers, along with Thomas V. Morris, Nicholas Wolterstorff, William Alston, Norman Kretzmann, Eleonore Stump, and Marilyn McCord Adams, might all be considered the first generation of—anachronistically named—analytic theologians. These initial practitioners of what would come to be called analytic theology were mostly analytic philosophers attempting to build a bridge toward Christian theology by addressing topics typically considered under the heading of "theology." This still takes place. However, in the second and third generations of analytic theologians, there are more and more scholars with theology and divinity training building the bridge between theology and philosophy from the theological side. Here is where the work of seminary and divinity school professors such as Alan Torrance, Sarah Coakley, Oliver Crisp, Thomas McCall, Kevin Hector, and Adonis Vidu come to the fore. McCord Adams is perhaps a paradigm example of an analytic theologian, one with specialized training in both philosophy and theology, and having taught in appointments in both philosophy and theology departments, most notably as the Regius Professor of Divinity at Oxford University.

II. ANALYTIC THEOLOGY: WHAT

Rather than seeing analytic theology as bound by hard and strict guidelines, we here follow Crisp (2017) in holding analytic theology to be most akin to a MacIntyrian intellectual culture. Crisp defines this as "a rough grouping within a particular intellectual discipline ... that identifies itself as having a distinctive approach to its subject matter" (163). As an intellectual culture, and not a rigid methodology, it is at times difficult to outline analytic theology definitively.[3] Nevertheless, following William

---

[2] Recently, the Logos Institute for Analytic and Exegetical Theology at the University of St. Andrews has been inaugurated, perhaps merging these two streams and becoming the global center of the analytic theology movement.

[3] Ironic, we realize, for a movement that is often concerned with definitional clarity. This state of affairs is not due to lack of trying, see, e.g.: the aforementioned Abraham (2013), Cortez (2013), Baker-Hytch (2016), Wood (2016), and Crisp, Arcadi, and Wessling (2019).

Wood, we hold that this intellectual culture can be marked by formal and substantive characteristics.[4]

II.1 Formally

Formally, analytic theology tends to follow the, almost canonical, prescriptions laid down by Michael Rea in the original *Analytic Theology* volume. These prescriptions (not restrictions) include:

P1. Write as if philosophical positions and conclusions can be adequately formulated in sentences that can be formalized and logically manipulated.
P2. Prioritize precision, clarity, and logical coherence.
P3. Avoid substantive (non-decorative) use of metaphor and other tropes whose semantic content outstrips their propositional content.
P4. Work as much as possible with well-understood primitive concepts and concepts that can be analyzed in terms of those.
P5. Treat conceptual analysis (insofar as it is possible) as a source of evidence. (2009: 4–5)

These prescriptions are drawn largely from the ambitions and style of analytic philosophy and have been discussed extensively in the literature. We simply offer these as a brief description of the formal shape of the analytic theological intellectual culture. Formally, there is nothing about analytic theology that limits it to any one substantive theological tradition. The Tillichian, Torrancian, or Thomist might all follow Rea's prescriptions and hence could do analytic theology in this formal sense. Moreover, in fact, there seems nothing about analytic theology formally that would preclude scholars of other religions engaging in the same project. To wit, there have been some recent attempts at offering instantiations of analytic Jewish theology and analytic Islamic theology.[5]

II.2 Substantively

However, in addition to these formal characteristics, the recent analytic theological literature in the Christian tradition typically has evinced some key substantive components to this theological intellectual culture as well. The substantive theological commitments of the analytic theological research program tend to include commitment to (a) some form of theological realism, (b) the truth-apt and truth-aimed nature of theological inquiry, and (c) the importance of providing theological arguments for substantive doctrinal positions. This has brought about the tendency among analytic theologians to discuss, explicate, and defend largely traditional positions within the history of Christian theological reflection including Trinitarianism, Chalcedonian Christology, and Classical Theism.

III. THIS VOLUME: WHENCE AND WHAT

One does not usually start building a bridge from the middle. Rather from one shore to another does the span come to completion. In early (anachronistically named) analytic theology, the bridge was clearly built from the coast of philosophy toward the coast of

---

[4] See Wood (2016).
[5] See, for instance, Sztuden (2018) and Saeedimehr (2018).

theology. Plantinga, Mitchell et al. were philosophers reaching across a divide toward topics typically under the purview of systematic theology. But, as noted, the past twenty years or so have shown that this is not the only direction from which the analytic theology bridge-building goes.

The structure of this volume attempts to demonstrate a bridge-building from the shores of theology. If one compares the list of topics in this volume's table of contents with such standard reference works of systematic theology as *The Cambridge Companion to Christian Doctrine*, *The Oxford Handbook of Systematic Theology*, or any number of standard single-author comprehensive works of systematic theology, then one ought to notice a symmetry of topics. One should notice this because this is precisely what we editors did when roughing up the topic list. As such, this volume follows a fairly standard list of topics as one comes across in systematic theology. That list is, of course, not without contention, and no doubt there will be some contention with the topics we have or have not included. Nevertheless, we hope most scholars familiar with the tradition of Christian theological reflection will find familiar topics, albeit discussed from an analytic theological perspective.

The audience we have in mind for the volume is the student or scholar who is working on a particular theological topic, be it for a term paper or a scholarly article, who asks themselves, "I wonder what analytic theologians have said about X?" Hence, we have asked our contributors to provide both a "lay of the land" survey of their topic as well as a constructive offering of their own perspective on said topic. This latter task is in service of demonstrating to the reader what analytic theology is and how it can be done. Therefore, rather than being the conclusion of the research for the student or scholar, we hope the chapters in this volume will be the beginning. To this end, we have also included an extensive bibliography in this volume. Like the list of topics in the volume, what is included in the bibliography and what is not will likely be a source of contention. It is not always clear what is "in" or "out" as regards to analytic theology. Hence, we hope this bibliography will be received not as a clear demarcation of an analytic *nihil obstat* but in the spirit in which it is offered: a starting point for future research. Therefore, the entries are categorized according to rough conceptual groupings for ease of reference. We hope researchers will see the chapters in this volume as windows, roadmaps, or portals into fields fertile with reflection on some of the core issues in Christian thought that have animated theological reflection for centuries and received analytic treatment more recently.

In conclusion, we wish to offer thanks to those who have helped to make this volume possible. We are first and foremost grateful to our wives and families for their love and constant support. We are very thankful to Anna Turton, Veerle Van Steenhuyse, and the staff at T&T Clark for their work in bringing this volume to fruition. Parker Settecase assisted greatly in compiling the index. A thanks in no small part goes to the John Templeton Foundation for a couple reasons: first, because the Foundation was an early supporter of initiatives connected to the budding field of analytic theology from which we have benefited by getting to know a number of our contributors through Templeton-connected events. Second, Templeton funded a three-year project from 2015 to 2018 at Fuller Theological Seminary in Pasadena, California. This was how the editors of this volume connected and where the idea for this volume first was planted. The "Fuller AT Team" of Crisp, Allison Wiltshire, Jordan Wessling, Christopher Woznicki, Jesse Gentile, and Steven Nemeş, along with the editors of this volume, cultivated an approach to analytic theology (ripened in the Southern California sun) that is reflected in this volume.

Finally, this volume is dedicated to our first theological and philosophical mentors. Without them, we would not be in the position to edit this volume, and we offer it to them as a small token of our appreciation.

References

Abraham, W. J. (2013), "Turning Philosophical Water into Theological Wine," *Journal of Analytic Theology* 1: 1–16.

Baker-Hytch, M. (2016), "Analytic Theology and Philosophy of Religion: What's the Difference," *Journal of Analytic Theology* 4: 347–61.

Clement of Alexandria (1979), "Stromata," in A. Roberts and J. Donaldson (eds.), *The Ante-Nicene Fathers: Translations of the Writings of the Fathers down to AD 325*, vol. 2, 299–567, Grand Rapids, MI: Eerdmans.

Cortez, M. (2013), "As Much As Possible: Essentially Contested Concepts and Analytic Theology: A Response to William J. Abraham," *Journal of Analytic Theology* 1: 17–24.

Crisp, O. D. (2017), "Analytic Theology as Systematic Theology," *Open Theology* 3: 156–66.

Crisp, O. D., J. M. Arcadi, and J. Wessling (2019), *The Nature and Promise of Analytic Theology*, Leiden: Brill.

Crisp, O. D., and M. C. Rea, eds. (2009), *Analytic Theology: New Essays in the Philosophy of Theology*, Oxford: Oxford University Press.

McCall, T. H. (2015), *An Invitation to Analytic Christian Theology*, Downers Grove, IL: IVP Academic.

Rea, M. C. (2009), "Introduction," in O. D. Crisp and M. C. Rea (eds.), *Analytic Theology: New Essays in the Philosophy of Theology*, 1–32, Oxford: Oxford University Press.

Saeedimehr, M. (2018), "Divine Knowledge and the Doctrine of Badā'," *TheoLogica: An International Journal for Philosophy of Religion and Philosophical Theology* 2 (1): 23–36.

Sztuden, A. (2018), "Judaism and the Euthyphro Dilemma: Towards a New Approach," *TheoLogica: An International Journal for Philosophy of Religion and Philosophical Theology* 2 (1): 37–50.

Wood, W. (2016), "Trajectories, Traditions, and Tools in Analytic Theology," *Journal of Analytic Theology* 4: 254–66.

PART I

Methods and Sources

CHAPTER ONE

The Importance of Model Building in Theology

OLIVER D. CRISP

Analytic theologians have become known for their use of theological model building.[1] There are other modern nonanalytic theologians who use the language of models, for example, the constructive feminist theologian Sally McFague (1982), or, in the religion and science literature, Ian Barbour (1997). Yet it is true to say that one important way in which analytic theologians have approached the constructive task of theology involves setting forth particular models for given doctrines as a way of "picturing" the view clearly so that it may then be subjected to criticism. But what is meant by a theological model in the analytic literature, and why should we think that models are an appropriate way to think about going about the task of setting out constructive versions of a given doctrine?

This chapter addresses these questions in the following way. In the first section, I give some account of what I mean by a model in this context, drawing on some of the recent literature in philosophy and analytic theology. Armed with this information, the second section focuses on the different sorts of models used in theology. These include instrumentalist, anti-realist, realist, and arealist accounts. The third section briefly considers two case studies of models in analytic theology: the Trinity and the incarnation. Finally, the conclusion draws together the different threads of the foregoing and offers some reflection on how this analytic penchant for model building may be of use to systematic and constructive theology more broadly.

I. MODELS

In this chapter I am particularly concerned with conceptual models, though of course there are physical models as well (a point to which we shall return shortly). So we may begin by distinguishing between a *model* as a kind of conceptual structure or framework for understanding a particular thing and its *target phenomena*.

As an initial pass at giving a rough and ready account of what models are—one that is relevant to the theological task—we might say that they are *simplified conceptual frameworks or descriptions by means of which complex sets of data, systems, and processes may be organized and understood*. Call this rough and ready account MODEL.[2] On the

---

[1] See, e.g., Wood (2016). He also discusses this in the broader context of analytic theology in Wood (2021).
[2] This way of thinking about models in theology is an account I have borrowed from Crisp (2019: 89).

basis of MODEL, we might then describe some of the most important characteristics such models possess. They are representational, analogous, hermeneutical in nature, have a certain fidelity to aspects of the thing they represent, and take different forms. Let us consider each of these characteristics in turn. Often models are used to *represent* some aspect of another thing, simplifying a more complex entity or system in such a way that the model is a kind of *analog* to the phenomena it represents, being both like and unlike it.[3] Consider the example of a model aircraft made of wood. It has a shape that is recognizably that of an airplane. We see it and immediately think of it in terms of the thing the wood models: an aircraft. However, we do so knowing that it is also significantly unlike a real aircraft, not just in scale but also in many other respects (e.g., it is made of solid wood, does not fly, has no moving parts, etc.).

There is an important sense in which the manner in which models represent a given thing is a hermeneutical decision made by those formulating the model. We must understand how the model in question is being used to represent the phenomena of which it is a simpler description in order to grasp in what way it is a model and what phenomena it is modeling. This is sometimes referred to as the *fidelity* of the model to the thing represented. For instance, if the model aircraft is a child's toy, we know that its role dictates what aspects of a real aircraft it models. It looks like an airplane, having a fuselage, wings, and a tailplane. But the likeness is limited to certain superficial physical characteristics because it is a toy, not, say, a working scale model of an aircraft (so it has no engine, is incapable of flight, etc.). This is a point that has been made elsewhere in the recent philosophical and theological literature.[4]

But models need not be of concrete items in the world around us. We can also model imaginary things, like a model of the Millennium Falcon. The model itself does not need to be some physical artifact either. It can be conceptual, like the model of an atom in a physics textbook or a mathematical model like a graph of an asymptote. It may be an idealized picture of some phenomena such as a frictionless plane, or it may be a toy model, like the toy airplane—one that is simplified, limiting fidelity to certain stripped-down aspects of the phenomena in view. Thus, models have different forms or can be expressed in different ways, whether physical, conceptual, fictional, ideal, or some combination thereof.

Second, and more briefly, a word about the *target* of a particular model. The target is the particular phenomena or thing that the model is supposed to help clarify. So, in the case of, say, the scale model of a car that is used to test aerodynamics in a wind tunnel for a proposed new model vehicle, the car is the model, and the proposed new vehicle is the target.

The hermeneutical function of models, and the fact that the model and target phenomena can both be real or imaginary, is not formally expressed by MODEL but is commensurate with it. In fact, MODEL is a fairly conceptually "thin" description, and deliberately so. It is consistent with a range of different views about the nature and purpose of models as these things have been understood in recent theology. For theologians have rather different accounts of the sort of things models are (where they are willing to countenance such conceptual structures) and what the target of such models should be.

---

[3] A similar point is made by Roman Frigg and Stephan Hartmann (2020). And Wood (2016) observes, "In a sense, all models are analogies—or, more precisely, all models represent their targets in virtue of analogical relations" (45).

[4] Thus, philosopher Michael Weisberg (2013: 15) says that a model is "an interpreted conceptual structure that can be used to represent real or imagined phenomena." Cited in Wood (2016: 45).

II. THEOLOGICAL MODELS

It might seem obvious that theologians should adopt the language of models that has been so successful in the natural sciences. But not everyone sees things that way. Some theologians are hostile to what they regard as a kind of Trojan horse—bringing in ways of thinking alien to theology, or that may somehow assimilate theology to a kind of philosophical project—perhaps even a kind of rationalism. (Some, motivated by Barthian concerns about the shape and place of theology, might have this worry.) Others think that the purpose of theological statements is distorted or mischaracterized if we adopt the language of models. (Here I have in mind theologians who think that theology is primarily concerned with producing a coherent grammar for Christian praxis, which is a view often associated with postliberalism. On this view, models might be thought of as a distortion of theology—a kind of category mistake, if you will.) Still others may be concerned that models simply fail as conceptual tools in theology because the target of theological statements, namely, the Deity, is not accessible to human ratiocination in a way that would be necessary for us to be able to construct a model. (For instance, one might think that God is not a being that can be modeled by creatures, or that we know too little about the divine nature to model it, or that model-making is a kind of incipient idolatry because all it can hope to achieve is the formation of a kind of golem, rather than a verisimilitude of the divine. Theologians who are drawn to strong versions of apophatic theology might think something like this.)

There are various reasons for these worries. One might be to do with *the cognitive function of models* in relation to their targets, which is an epistemic concern.[5] Here the objection might be: What do models in theology actually deliver? What help can they provide us in making theological statements? What is their cognitive value? And does the cognitive value of the model track some value in the target? (In other words, is the cognitive value we ascribe to the model a value to be found in the target as well, or only in the model?) Another concern might have to do with the *ontological status* of the model in relation to its target. Then the worry might be: What do we think our models commit us to (if anything), theologically speaking? Do they actually map onto reality in some way so that we may track things about the divine, or do they have a merely instrumental value? Perhaps they are fictions of a sort along the lines of fictional characters like Sherlock Holmes and the worlds they inhabit. Here, too, we can distinguish between the ontological commitments entailed by the model and the extent to which these ontological commitments track some property of the target. For instance, suppose I favor a social model of the Trinity that entails that in God there are three centers of consciousness and will. Does this imply that there *really are* three centers of consciousness and will in God's nature, which is the target of this model? Is the relation of the model to the target isomorphic in this respect or is the model merely a kind of approximation to its target in this respect and therefore does not require strict fidelity?[6]

With these semantic, cognitive, and ontological concerns in mind, let us consider three broad theological approaches to models construed along the lines of MODEL, finessed with the comments we have culled from Weisberg (2013) concerning the interpretive

---

[5] For discussion of this point, see Frigg and Hartmann (2020).
[6] For instance, is the model a fictional one? It models an imaginary entity, rather than a real one—much as one might offer a model of a Greek god, or a member of the Asgardian pantheon. Theological fictionalists might take this sort of view. See, e.g., Le Poidevin (2019).

aspect of models and the fact that they may target real or imagined phenomena. The three principle ontological commitments in this context are: *instrumentalism*, *anti-realism*, and *realism*. These I take to be broad categories that include a range of different possible options. They may not be the only logically possible options. But they do represent what I take to be some of the most important live options (to borrow William James's famous phrase) that are the subject of theological discussion and that are relevant to analytic theologians.

To begin, let us consider the prospect of adopting MODEL along with an instrumental view of theological statements. On an instrumental view, as with instrumentalism in the philosophy of science, one is not committed to the reality of the entities posited in the model. It is merely a useful way of conceiving the matter that has a certain instrumental value—that is, as a means to some further end, such as the construction of a coherent grammar by means of which churches and Christians may govern their liturgies and praxis. Such instrumentalism may be anti-realist in nature. That is, it may bottom out as a way of thinking about models that does not commit the theologian to the existence of the target entities posited in the model. For, according to theological anti-realism, such entities do not actually refer to anything that is mind-independent.[7] On one way of reading her work, this appears to be how McFague thinks about models. They are, on her view, extended metaphors. But they are metaphors all the way down, so to speak.[8] Of course, one can have a realist account of metaphors. But often in theological discourse the use of metaphorical language has been opposed to realist language (and that is often how it seems McFague uses such language). Those who think of models in instrumentalist terms may take this way of thinking in an anti-realist direction. Then, the entities posited in the model are literally constituents of a mental world built by the theologian. Gordon Kaufman is one recent theologian who seems to think that such imaginative ways of thinking about doctrine are the right way to conceive of the theological task and of model building in theology. He writes,

> Theologians should attempt to construct conceptions of God, humanity, and the world appropriate for the orientation of contemporary human life. As we have been observing, these notions are (and always have been) human creations, human imaginative constructions; they are our ideas, not God's. What is needed in each new generation is an understanding of God adequate for and appropriate to human life in the world within which it finds itself, so that human devotion and loyalty, service and worship, may be directed toward God rather than to the many idols that so easily attract attention and interest. (Kaufman 1993: 31)

Allowing that doctrines are human constructions does not necessarily imply anti-realism. Many theological realists would claim that all doctrine is the product of human creativity, being ectypal. The difference is such theologians would also want to say that such theological creations should be modeled as far as possible after the divine archetype given in revelation. By contrast, Kaufman seems to be committed to a kind of anti-realism: human conceptual constructions in theology, and theological model building, are brought forth anew for each generation in pictures and metaphors that communicate religious truth in changing circumstances. Although this too might be understood along

---

[7] For a discussion of this, see Plantinga (1983), Rea (2007), and Keller (2014).
[8] "Models are dominant, comprehensive metaphors with organizing, structural potential" (McFague 1982: 193).

critically realist[9] lines, it appears, as a matter of fact, that Kaufman was more of a thoroughgoing anti-realist.

There is more than one way to be an anti-realist about model building in theology, however. One could also be a fictionalist about the entities posited in a given model.[10] As Robin Le Poidevin (2019) has recently characterized it, according to the religious fictionalist, "religious statements are propositional, and so evaluable as true or false. But they are only true within a fiction—the Christian fiction, or Buddhist fiction, and so on. Insofar as they are fact-stating, they are only fictional fact-stating, and so not answerable to a reality which is independent of our beliefs, attitudes or conventions" (25).

Le Poidevin is concerned with religious belief and religious doctrine, as well as religious practice. But we can extend his point to theological model building was well. On this way of thinking, anti-realism is consistent with propositional attitudes towards the content of theological models, provided one thinks of the entities posited in the model as being part of a fiction. In a similar manner, one might adopt propositional attitudes towards models of, say, the metaphysics of Star Wars, whilst acknowledging that the entities treated by such models are themselves aspects of a fiction, in this case, the science-fiction world first imagined by George Lucas.

However, theological world-building need not be anti-realist or even instrumental in nature. I take it that many theologians think that there is a mind-independent world, that we can successfully refer to that world in our theology, and that theological model building is consistent with these theologically realist commitments. This may be true even if, as I think is the case, theological models are merely proxies for the truth of the matter. One can be committed to the (mind-independent) truth of, say, the Trinity, and yet think that at best our theologizing about the Trinity will inevitably yield models that are approximations to the truth of the matter rather than the truth plain and simple. On this way of thinking, theological models point toward something that is true.[11] There may be principled theological reasons for thinking this is the case, reasons having to do with commitments that are, at root, realist in nature. For instance, one might think that the Trinity is a mystery that no created intellect can penetrate and that our theologizing should be done apropos of this assumption. One way in which the theologian might build a model of the Trinity on this basis is to begin with the supposition that all our theologizing about the Trinity is fallible, fragile, and liable to fail and fall conceptually

---

[9]By "critical realism" I mean (very roughly) the notion that there is some mind-independent entity to which particular human conceptualizations point, although no one conceptual picture gets at the whole truth of the matter. Imagine several viewers of a sculpture reporting their views of the work. The particular vantage they have will shape their view of the artwork in important respects and (plausibly) no one vantage yields a complete account of the work of art though each offers some partial account of it. Critical realism (as I am using the term here) presumes something like this picture is true with respect to different accounts of a given entity—in this case, theological entities like the Trinity or incarnation, and the doctrines that express these truths.

[10]There is a lively debate about fictionalist accounts of models in the philosophy of science literature. See, e.g., Salis (2020).

[11]Compare Barbour:

> Models and theories are abstract symbol systems, which inadequately and selectively represent particular aspects of the world for specific purposes. This view preserves the scientist's realistic intent while recognizing that models and theories are imaginative human constructs. Models, on this reading, are to be taken seriously but not literally; they are neither literal pictures nor useful fictions but limited and inadequate ways of imagining what is not observable. They make tentative ontological claims that there are entities in the world something like those postulated in the models. (1997: 115)

short in significant respects.[12] We are, so it might be thought, fallen human beings incapable of apprehending God. Yet we can approach God, so to speak, by attempting to provide constructive approximations to the truth of the matter that reflect the teaching of Holy Writ and other sources of theological authority, such as conciliar and creedal pronouncements. Much Trinitarian model building in recent analytic theology attempts to do just that (Swinburne 1994; McCall and Rea 2009; McCall 2010; Hasker 2013).[13]

So commitment to MODEL is consistent with instrumentalism in theological model building, anti-realism in theological model building, and realism in theological model building. These are not necessarily all the logically possible options. For instance, one might think that some sort of theological arealism is the right approach to such meta-theological matters. In this context, arealism involves the refusal to make metaphysical commitments one way or another on whether the entities posited in a particular theological model are, in fact, mind-independent or not. Some traditional theologians seem to speak of the divine nature in a way that suggests such an approach. One example of this is the sort of high-octane apophaticism one finds in much of the Christian tradition, which maintains that fallen human beings are incapable of apprehending the divine essence and can only fallibly and incompletely theologize about the nature of God, or about how God appears to us—how he is mediated by means of revelation or signs, such as the burning bush, or the words of a prophet, or by means of the incarnation.[14]

III. TWO CASE STUDIES: TRINITY AND INCARNATION

This completes our overview of theological models. I now want to illustrate the points made in the previous section with two examples of how models have been used in recent analytic theology. For it is one thing to consider how models function at the meta-theological level. It is another to see whether that actually maps onto how things actually work in a given literature. Thus far, I have argued that models are simplified conceptual frameworks or descriptions by means of which complex sets of data, systems, and processes may be organized and understood. They have an important hermeneutical function. Moreover, the model and target phenomena can both be real or imaginary. I have indicated that there is a cognitive and epistemic aspect to understanding models, and an ontological aspect as well. And I have attempted to give a rough-and-ready taxonomy of different options consistent with this account of models in Christian theology. This includes instrumentalist, anti-realist, realist, and arealist approaches.

Now, in principle, an analytic theologian could take any one of these approaches because (in my view, at least) analytic theology does not commit its practitioners to any substantive theological views. It is a set of methodological commitments, or a sensibility of a sort, supported by a particular intellectual culture.[15] There are analytic theologians from most of the different strands of the Christian tradition. In this respect, it is an ecumenical enterprise—perhaps because its methodological commitments are so open-textured. Nevertheless, it transpires that there are very few analytic theologians who are anything other than theological realists. The vast majority of analytic theologians are, in

---

[12] I have attempted to do something like this in Crisp (2019: ch. 4). This approach has been recently critiqued in Yadav (2020).
[13] See also the relevant essays in Rea (2009).
[14] See, e.g., Pseudo-Dionysius (1987) and Aquinas (1948: Supp.Q92.a1).
[15] For a discussion of this, see Crisp, Arcadi, and Wessling (2019).

fact, traditional theists who maintain that God is a mind-independent reality, the creator and sustainer of the world.[16]

This is reflected in the sort of models analytic theologians have developed in their work to date. Two notable examples in the literature of the last two decades is the work that has been done on the Trinity and on the incarnation, two central and defining Christian dogmas. I will touch briefly on each in turn.[17]

There has been work on a number of different accounts of the Trinity among analytic theologians, as well as helpful work done in classifying various extant views of the Trinity (see McCall and Rea 2009). Unlike recent nonanalytic systematic theology, much of the focus of this work has been on how to understand the relation between the divine unity and triunity—what is often referred to as the threeness-oneness problem. It is usually thought to be the sign of a successful research program that it generates new ways of thinking about old problems. Analytic theology has already generated new models of the Trinity. This is no mean feat, given the number of minds that have tackled the dogma of the Trinity and the length of time that it has been the subject of intellectual inquiry. One particularly striking example of such new model building is the *constitution account* of the Trinity that has been put forward by Michael Rea and Jeff Brower (2005), building on some earlier work in relative identity and the Trinity by Peter van Inwagen (1981) and Peter Geach (1980), among others. Rea and Brower (2005) suggest that we apply a version of Aristotelian hylomorphism to the Trinity so that the divine persons of the Trinity are "constituted" by the "stuff" of divinity, rather like an Aristotelian form relative to some parcel of matter. They use the example of a block of marble fashioned into a statue that is also a pillar in a building. There is the marble stuff that composes each of these items, and then there are the "forms" of the block, the pillar, and the statue that organize the same parcel of matter in three distinct ways. Thus, we have sameness and difference in a way that is relevant to the dogma of the Trinity. Three distinct "forms," one parcel of matter that is composed by these forms, and each form having different persistence conditions. For instance, if the statue is effaced, the block may still stand as a pillar. Apply this to the doctrine of the Trinity. The marble stuff is like the divine nature, the different "forms" like the divine persons each of whom is distinct and yet "composed" by the same divine stuff. We have sameness of substance, but difference of persons.

---

[16]*Caveat lector*: some analytic theologians are theistic personalists. They think God is a maximal person, on analogy with human persons. Other analytic theologians are what we might call classical theists, such as Thomists. For many Thomists, theistic personalism may be a species of theism but it is also a kind of idolatry because its practitioners imagine that God is an individual person like created persons, only perfect and unlimited in power and knowledge. But, say the Thomists, God is not in a genus, he is not a being like creatures, and there are no distinctions to be had between his essence and his attributes. Thus, theistic personalism rests on a grave theological mistake. For their part, theistic personalists are quick to point out the fact that there seem to be serious conceptual problems with aspects of Thomistic classical theism (e.g., divine simplicity, the pure act account of the divine nature) that are not easily resolved. Thus, when I say that most analytic theologians are traditional theists, I mean by this that most presume God is a mind-independent reality, the creator and sustainer of the world. There are still significant differences of view on how these claims should be construed, as the recent debate between theistic personalists and classical theists among analytic theologians attests. For a classic theistic personalist account of the divine nature, see Swinburne ([1977] 1993). For a contemporary version of classical theism of the Thomist variety, see Stump (2003).

[17]There are other places in the recent analytic theology literature that discuss these issues, and that are relevant here. See Wood (2016), who does a terrific job of assessing the merits of the constitution model of the Trinity; and Arcadi (2018), who provides an overview of recent work on the incarnation.

Inevitably, this view has come in for some criticism, but we need not pursue that here. What is important for our purposes is that we can see in this example how the application of a new model of the Trinity to a long-standing fundamental problem in the doctrine of the Trinity may help illuminate important issues about the divine nature that are the mark of a vibrant research program.[18] Although Rea and Brower are theological realists, one could take their model and adapt it to the needs of an instrumentalist, an anti-realist, a fictionalist, or even an arealist.[19] (I leave this task as homework for the reader.)

The doctrine of the incarnation has been another topic that has exercised analytic theologians. Here, too, a number of different models of the incarnation have been mooted, most of which are explicitly attempts to express the teaching of classical Christology, as summarized in the two natures doctrine of the Council of Chalcedon of AD 451. On this way of thinking, Christ is the divine person of God the Son, subsisting in two natures: his divine nature, which he has essentially, and his human nature, which he assumes at the first moment of incarnation. One recent model of the incarnation that has been developed by analytic theologians is the compositional account. There is more than one way to construe the compositional account. Here is one of them.[20]

Suppose we think of Christ as composed of different "parts." He has his human nature and his divine nature. And yet there is only one person "in" Christ, so to speak, that is, the person of God the Son. How are we to make sense of this? Perhaps we should think of Christ as a concrete particular, with a concrete human nature that comprises a human body and soul rightly related. This human nature is assumed at the incarnation by God the Son. Thus, we have a view according to which in Christ there are the following concrete parts: his human nature, comprising his human body and soul, rightly related; and the person of God the Son, who is hypostatically united to this particular concrete human nature. One oddity of this view is that *Christ* is a name that refers to the mereological whole comprising these various parts. A second oddity is that God the Son is not identical with his human nature. Having said that, one potential advantage of this view is that it doesn't necessarily compromise divine simplicity, for no substantive change occurs to God the Son at the first moment of incarnation. What is more, it doesn't mean that God the Son is encumbered by physical parts that are somehow "part" of him either.

The analytic theologians associated with this view seem to think of it in a theologically realist sense, as an attempt to track with fidelity central claims concerning the metaphysical relation between the divinity and humanity of Christ.[21] But one need not construe it in this way. With some minor adjustments it could be used by an instrumentalist, anti-realist, or arealist. As with the constitutional account of the Trinity, there have been objections to this version of the compositional view of the incarnation. But, once again, we need not pursue those worries here. It is sufficient that we have drawn attention to one important use of theological modeling in the recent discussions of the incarnation in the analytic theological literature that is illuminating and that helps illustrate how analytic discussion of this topic has borne fruit.

---

[18]Editor's note: for more on this research program, see Thomas McCall's chapter in this volume.
[19]An option that may be worth further consideration in this regard: combine the constitution account of the Trinity with the kind of theological arealism expressed by Jonathan Jacobs (2015), an Orthodox Christian philosopher.
[20]See, e.g., Leftow (2002) and Crisp (2007).
[21]Editor's note: for more on these sorts of things, see Timothy Pawl's chapter in this volume.

IV. THE VALUE OF THEOLOGICAL MODELS

What, then, is the value of theological models as I have outlined them here? What is achieved in the use of such models? To my way of thinking, the use of models in theology is similar to the use of models in the sciences. That is, theological models provide us with helpful ways of making sense (to the extent that we can make sense[22]) of complex material, so that we can use this material in hypotheses, constructive argument, and theorizing. I have suggested we think of theological modelling along the lines of

> MODEL: a simplified conceptual framework or description by means of which complex sets of data, systems, and processes may be organized and understood.

This may be construed in various ways as we have seen, because MODEL is metaphysically underdetermined. But that reflects how models are used in theology. I have also suggested that models, including theological models, are representational, analogous, hermeneutical in nature, have a certain fidelity to aspects of the thing they represent, and take many forms. I suggest that much of the unhappiness about the use of models in theology stems from a rather flat-footed way of thinking about models, which does not take into sufficient account the different ways in which models are understood and construed in the current literature. In the case of the two sorts of theological models I have considered from recent analytic theology, I was careful to note that these are only two of a range of different models that have been put forward, and that these models may also be thought of as underdetermined in important respects that bears upon the question of the fidelity of these models to their target phenomena.

There is nothing to stop a particular theologian from taking the constitutional model of the Trinity and thinking of it in, say, fictionalist terms as a model that clearly articulates an account of the dogma consistent with the letter of Nicene orthodoxy so that its fidelity is to the propositional content of the creed as traditionally understood. But, being a fictionalist account, it would not make the additional claim that the bare propositional commitments of Nicene orthodoxy expressed in the creed refers to some mind-independent phenomenon. It is an open question why someone might approach matters in this way, and it is certainly true to say that very few analytic theologians working today would be sympathetic to such a move. As I have already said, the intellectual culture of analytic theology is broadly traditional and orthodox in its theological commitments—including commitment to some sort of theological realism. Still, that is not to say a fictionalist interpretation of these things cannot be had; it can. The more important question is whether such an account is the best approximation to the truth of the matter. For the vast majority of analytic theologians, the answer to that question will be in the negative. But, in a way, the use of doctrinal models makes that judgment easier to arrive at by clarifying some of its central conceptual commitments. That, it seems to me, is one good reason to think the use of models in theology has an important, and helpful, place.

References

Aquinas, St. T. (1948), *Summa Theologica*, trans. Brothers of the English Dominican Province, New York: Benzinger Brothers.

---

[22] As Wood (2016) and Yadav (2016), among others, have argued, model building in theology is consistent with a high tolerance for apophaticism.

Arcadi, J. M. (2018), "Recent Developments in Analytic Christology," *Philosophy Compass* 13 (4): 402–12.
Barbour, I. G. (1997), *Religion and Science: Historical and Contemporary Issues*, San Francisco: HarperCollins.
Crisp, O. D. (2007), *Divinity and Humanity: The Incarnation Reconsidered*, Cambridge, Cambridge University Press.
Crisp, O. D. (2019), *Analyzing Doctrine: Toward a Systematic Theology*, Waco: Baylor University Press.
Crisp, O. D., J. M. Arcadi, and J. Wessling (2019), *The Nature and Promise of Analytic Theology*, Leiden: Brill.
Frigg, R., and S. Hartmann (2020), "Models in Science," in E. N. Zalta (ed.), *Stanford Encyclopedia of Philosophy*. Available online: https://plato.stanford.edu/entries/models-science/ (last accessed May 13, 2020).
Geach, P. (1980), *Reference and Generality*, 3rd ed., Ithaca: Cornell University Press.
Hasker, W. (2013), *Metaphysics and the Tripersonal God*, Oxford: Oxford University Press.
Jacobs, J. (2015), "The Ineffable, Inconceivable, and Incomprehensible God: Fundamentality and Apophatic Theology," in J. L. Kvanvig (ed.), *Oxford Studies in Philosophy of Religion 6*, 158–76, Oxford: Oxford University Press.
Kaufman, G. D. (1993), *In the Face of Mystery: A Constructive Theology*, Cambridge: Harvard University Press.
Keller, J. A. (2014), "Theological Anti-Realism," *Journal of Analytic Theology*, 2 (2014): 13–42.
Leftow, B. (2002), "A Timeless God Incarnate," in S. T. Davis, D. Kendall SJ, and G. O'Collins (eds.), *The Incarnation*, 273–302, Oxford: Oxford University Press.
Le Poidevin, R. (2019), *Religious Fictionalism*, Cambridge: Cambridge University Press.
McCall, T. H. and M. C. Rea, eds. (2009), *Philosophical and Theological Essays on the Trinity*, Oxford: Oxford University Press.
McCall, T. H. (2010), *Which Trinity? Whose Monotheism? Philosophical and Systematic Theologians on the Metaphysics of Trinitarian Theology*, Grand Rapids, MI: Eerdmans.
McFague, S. (1982), *Metaphorical Theology: Models of God in Religious Language*, Minneapolis: Fortress Press.
Plantinga, A. (1983), "How to Be an Anti-Realist," *Proceedings of the American Philosophical Association*, 80 (1983): 47–70.
Pseudo-Dionysius (1987), *Pseudo-Dionysius: The Complete Works*, ed. Colm Lubheid, Mahwah: Paulist Press.
Rea, M. C., and J. Brower (2005), "Material Constitution and the Trinity," *Faith and Philosophy*, 22 (1): 57–76.
Rea, M. C. (2007), "Realism in Theology and Metaphysics," in C. Cunningham and P. Candler (eds.), *Belief and Metaphysics*, 323–44, London: SCM Press.
Rea, M. C., ed, (2009), *Oxford Readings in Philosophical Theology: Volume 1: Trinity, Incarnation, and Atonement*, Oxford: Oxford University Press.
Salis, F. (2020), "The New Fiction View of Models," *British Journal for the Philosophy of Science*: 1–28.
Stump, E. (2003), *Aquinas*, New York: Routledge.
Swinburne, R. ([1977] 1993), *The Coherence of Theism*, 2nd ed., Oxford: Oxford University Press.
Swinburne, R. (1994), *The Christian God*, Oxford: Oxford University Press.
van Inwagen, P. (1981), "And Yet They Are Not Three Gods But One God," in T. V. Morris (ed.), *Philosophy and the Christian Faith*, 241–78, Notre Dame: University of Notre Dame Press.

Weisberg, M. (2013), *Simulation and Similarity: Using Models to Explain the World*, Oxford: Oxford University Press.
Wood, W. (2016), "Modeling Mystery," *Scientia et Fides*, 4 (1): 39–59.
Wood, W. (2021), *Analytic Theology and the Academic Study of Religion*, Oxford: Oxford University Press.
Yadav, S. (2016), "Mystical Experience and the Apophatic Attitude," *Journal of Analytic Theology*, 4: 17–43.
Yadav, S. (2020), "The Mystery of the Immanent Trinity and the Procession of the Spirit," in O. D. Crisp and F. Sanders (eds.), *The Third Person of the Trinity: Explorations in Constructive Dogmatics*, 102–19, Grand Rapids, MI: Zondervan Academic.

CHAPTER TWO

Modeling Inspiration: Perspicuity after Pentecost

ADAM GREEN

Popular debates about the inspiration of Scripture tend to make a simplifying assumption about *what* is inspired and ignore the question of *who* the text is inspired *for*.[1] The simplifying assumption is that inspiration is all and only a matter of providing epistemic backing for each member of a body of assertions. When the text says *x*, we debate whether *x* should be thought of as the testimony of God, a human agent, or a human community. If human testimony is at issue, we then move to the question of whether a twenty-first-century person can also believe *x* in virtue of the competence and sincerity of testifiers at such a great sociohistorical remove from us. That the text could ever have a function other than or in addition to asserting propositions and eliciting belief in them does not tend to come up.

Similarly, if we think about Scripture as testimony, a focus on the epistemic backing provided by the testifier ignores something very interesting about the recipient of testimony in this case. This library of ancient texts we call the Bible is supposed to speak in a way that isn't just inspired for the original audience but which, in principle, lends itself to speaking in an inspired way into any context and to all audiences. There is, of course, a term for this topic, the perspicuity of Scripture, but this topic is typically discussed as a downstream implication of one's model of inspiration. If we are to emphasize the divinity of inspiration, then the text must be clear. If (and to the extent that) the text is unclear, the explanation must be that the text is more human than some care to admit.[2] If, however, we keep squarely in mind the need to reach "the ends of the earth," we should ask how any text, no matter how clear for the original audience, could be clear to all the peoples that Scripture is supposed to reach.

---

[1] It is not just popular debates that make these simplifying assumptions. For instance, in a critical survey of the philosophical theology of revelation and inspiration, Stephen Davis defines biblical inspiration as "that influence of the Holy Spirit on the writing of the Bible that ensures that the words of its various texts are appropriate both for the role that they play in Scripture and for the overall salvific purpose of Scripture itself" (2009: 48). This definition points obliquely to the diversity within Scripture as well as the telos of Scripture as a text meant to be apt for being lived out, yet because of the nature of the literature Davis is canvassing, the discussion of the article is almost entirely devoted to the first twelve words of this definition.

[2] For a classic, yet not unqualified, statement of the perspicuity of Scripture, it is hard to do better than the Westminster Confession:

> All things in Scripture are not alike plain in themselves, nor alike clear unto all; yet those things which are necessary to be known, believed, and observed; for salvation, are so clearly propounded and opened in some place of Scripture or other, that not only the learned, but the unlearned, in a due use of ordinary means, may

In order to lay a foundation for addressing these two puzzles, we now turn to a curious overlap among five authors with very different assumptions, methods, and ends. Unlike nearby topics such as the nature of revelation (cf. Swinburne 1992), the inspiration and perspicuity of Scripture is surprisingly little discussed in the budding field of analytic theology. Thus, at least four of the five scholars discussed below would neither think of themselves as analytic theologians nor think of their projects as analytic ones.

I. STRANGE BEDFELLOWS

In his book *Inspiration and Incarnation*, Old Testament scholar Peter Enns is concerned that evangelicals sacrifice the humanity of Scripture and endanger the faith of their members in the process due to a simplistic perspective on what it means for Scripture to be divinely inspired (2015: 15). The humanity of the text can't be wished away, however. The text borrows from other material in the ancient world to express its message (cf. 13–60). There is theological diversity within the Scriptures (cf. 61–102), and New Testament authors take significant liberties in how they use the Old Testament (cf. 103–56).

For Enns, none of these features of the text need be problematic once one places Scripture in its human context. That God would draw upon the social imaginary of the ancient near east to speak to an ancient near eastern audience is not surprising. Moreover, different messages or emphases might be necessary as time moves forward. Given human finitude, the message for different times and places might produce some cognitive tension for us, especially when we compare them in a decontextualized way. Likewise, Enns thinks it understandable that the way that New Testament authors use the Old requires situating their hermeneutic practice within the interpretive traditions and precedents of Second Temple Judaism (cf. 142ff). The New Testament too is written in a human context, and a divine message would have to be expressed within the cognitive constellations of the people of the time to be properly understood.

Just as Christians affirm that Jesus is fully human and fully divine, so too, for Enns, Scripture is fully human even if divinely inspired (cf. 17). The divine intent of Scripture opens up for us as we become students of the humanity of the text. One might, though, be forgiven for thinking that Enns's work militates against the perspicuity of Scripture. Divine communicative intent is incarnated in the world of the original audience for the sake of the original audience. Though we might seek to isolate the meaning of past revelation and recontextualize the divine message for our own day, it is hard to resist the thought that we've not been given much reason to hope for a perspicuous text.

If Enns is intent on giving the evangelical reader a way of thinking of modern biblical scholarship as friend rather than foe, philosopher Merold Westphal in his little book *Whose Community? Which Interpretation?* strives to do the same for postmodern hermeneutics. Just as Enns is intent to ward off the inference "if human, then not divine" as applied to Scripture, so too is Westphal concerned to block the inference "if interpreting is perspectival, then anything goes" (2009: 15). For Westphal, the theological promise of postmodern hermeneutics lies in its acknowledgement of the fact that we are not God. Because we do not have access to God's all-encompassing meta-perspective, we have to own our limitations and our situatedness when we interpret anything, including Scripture.

---

attain unto a sufficient understanding of them. (As quoted on Callahan 2001: 10, which also serves as a useful entrée into contemporary engagement with the topic.)

That does not mean that "anything goes." To use one of Westphal's illustrations, the same figure can look like a duck or a rabbit depending on how one attends to it without also looking like a moose or a spider (24).

Similarly, Westphal is anxious to walk back rhetoric in the postmodern tradition about the death of the author (57ff). Instead, for him the meaning of the text is a co-creation of author and reader. One might say that what is co-created is not so much the meaning of the text as such but the meaning of the text for the reader. Until the reader has taken the communicative potential of the text and met it halfway by engaging with it from the reader's distinctive perspective, it cannot be received by the reader as having a determinate application to the reader's world and perhaps not as having a determinate content period. That said, for Westphal, the author constrains what a reader may legitimately do with the text, and these constraints can be greater or lesser depending on such factors as genre and the clarity of the author's writing.

The reader is subject to many influences that shape the interpretation and application of the text. These influences need not simply be lenses through which we see the text that we can never critically engage (cf. 73). Westphal, instead, has it that they are voices that address us with putative authority. These influences include interpretive traditions that make claims on us in the name of the text. It is to some extent up to the reader whether she will defer to, ignore, or dialogue with the influences that together give shape to her perspective, and the meaning we find in a text is in no small part a matter of which interpretive voices are available to us and what we do with them.

If Enns is, at least in part, trying to stick up for the humanity of Scripture and Westphal for the humanity of interpretation, Reformed systematic theologian Kevin Vanhoozer, in his book *Biblical Authority after Babel*, has the opposite kind of project. Vanhoozer wants to reimagine and reappropriate the solas of the Reformation, including *sola scriptura*, in the face of the charge, informed by post-Reformation history, that biblical interpretation is "human, all too human" (2016: cf. 65). The solas allow us to keep biblical interpretation from being a merely human enterprise.

The solas, for Vanhoozer, are interconnected, and they are not so much negative rights (e.g., freedom from tradition) so much as they are regulative ideals that allow one to orient oneself appropriately within the economy of grace and thereby live out the Gospel. *Sola gratia* reminds one that the diverse voices of Scripture all have in common that they witness to the gracious self-revelation of God (62–3) and that, whatever else biblical interpretation may involve, it is, fundamentally, a matter of putting oneself in position to receive God's gracious self-revelation in Scripture (64). *Sola fide* requires that one interpret Scripture from a position of confidence in God's ability to do efficacious work not only in one's own life but in that of others, which encompasses their interpretive efforts. Thus, since the interpretation of Scripture is not independent of *sola gratia* and *sola fide*, "biblical interpreters believe that they will have a better understanding of what God is saying in Scripture by attending to the work of other interpreters" (105).

In keeping with *sola scriptura*, the words of Scripture have primacy as God's primary vehicle of self-giving revelation. Because we are to acknowledge God's work in other believers and the church generally, while also respecting our individual and collective fallibility, one should read Scripture in the light of how other believers read Scripture, which includes an attentiveness to diverse theological traditions. "*Sola scriptura* is not a recipe for sectarianism, much less an excuse for schism, but rather a call to listen for the Holy Spirit speaking in the history of Scripture's interpretation in the church" (145). Because we are fallible, however, one should expect differences in interpretation, which should elicit continuing dialogue "generated and governed by Scripture, and guided by a convictional conciliarism that unites diverse churches in a transdenominational communion" (211). Thus, there is a curious convergence between Vanhoozer and Westphal here on the need to read in dialogue with interpretive traditions, for Westphal because we are human and for Vanhoozer out of respect for the working of God's grace in more lives than just our own.

Vanhoozer's intersecting solas make room for a restricted version of the perspicuity of Scripture. One should expect there to be difference in the interpretation of Scripture. We're all sinners holding onto God's gracious self-revelation as best we can through faith. He claims, however, that "for those who have been enlightened, it is impossible to miss the light (meaning) of the gospel shining out from [Scripture's] pages" (113). This is not a claim that all assertions contained in holy writ are perfectly clear. It's a restricted claim. His contention is that, whatever else may be subject to debate and discussion, the perspicuity of the Gospel can be used as a litmus test for dividing appropriate Christian interpretation from that which is beyond the pale.

The Reformed philosopher Nicholas Wolterstorff uses speech act theory to sensitize us to the multiple kinds of speech we find in Scripture in his classic *Divine Discourse* (1995: cf. 13). In Scripture, we find threats, promises, apologies, expostulations, words of comfort, and much more. Thus, if we are, following Vanhoozer, to listen for the Holy Spirit in Scripture and in the history of interpretation, Wolterstorff would draw our attention to the fact that the Holy Ghost's chosen instrument doesn't just play in an assertoric key. This raises the important question of whether a divinely inspired speech act that is not an assertion is inspired *qua* promise, warning, exhortation, and so on, or whether what is inspired is just the nearby assertion that a promise was once extended, a warning was given, an exhortation was made, and so on.[3]

Genre is relevant here. A speech act in a historical narrative is more plausibly restricted in its scope to the relating of facts about past happenings. Perhaps one can without loss translate, say, Jesus's cry of dereliction into a divinely inspired claim that Jesus asked this question upon the cross. There are other genres, however. Should the source for the cry of dereliction in the psalms be similarly relativized to "It is a fact that the psalmist once asked, 'My God, my God, why have you forsaken me?'"? As a reading of what God meant us to take away from the opening of Psalm 22, it's not very plausible. Even as regards historical narrative, the church has traditionally used allegorical or typological readings of historical narratives so as to suggest that when Scripture reports what God and others said or did, it doesn't merely do that.

J. L. Austin (1962) launched speech act theory with a book entitled *How to Do Things with Words*. For Wolterstorff, it is important to note that one can sometimes do things with someone else's words. One can, for instance, do so through deputized speech in which a representative conveys a message they were given, perhaps in her own words, and one can do so through authorized speech where someone is authorized within limits to speak in a way that the authorizer is thereby committed to, even if the genesis of the words lies in the representative (cf. Wolterstorff 1995: 42ff). Likewise, words expressed by one person can be appropriated by another for a different communicative intent (cf. 51ff). In fact,

---

[3]This distinction, I take it, is related to Wolsterstorff's concern to distinguish revelation from divine discourse (1995: cf. 19). The latter but not the former presumes the sort of interpersonal space in which perlocutionary acts can be performed vis-à-vis the human subject, thus allowing the divine to do more than simply inform the human hearer through the divine's special attentions.

sometimes one can aptly convey one's meaning by appropriating two different texts and playing them off of each other so as to convey a message that goes beyond either taken in isolation (205).[4] Wolterstorff thinks we see all of this in Scripture.

Moreover, God can use Scripture to address modern readers in new illocutionary acts much like Antony, the desert father, took himself to be addressed by a text about giving up one's possessions originally addressed to someone else (189). Furthermore, the divine reappropriation of the text need not restrict itself to assertions. In Antony's case, it was a command. Thus, in the communication of God's word, we make Scripture available to address each new generation with promises, warnings, exhortations, laments, and so on that can count as continuing divine speech (cf. Green and Quan 2012). The diversity of these speech acts is relevant because we are not meant only to know specially revealed facts. When it comes to how one is to live now, a continuing promise is more relevant than the fact that a promise was once given to a near eastern audience.

In his book *Scripture in Tradition*, John Breck is not concerned with squaring the human production of Scripture with divine inspiration so much as with the tension between Scripture and tradition. He diagnoses the rift between Catholics and Protestants as, in no small part, a squabble over a false choice between the two (2001: 3). By way of contrast, Breck identifies the Orthodox tradition as being that Scripture is both "a part of Tradition and its normative element" (4). Scripture doesn't exist as Scripture apart from the history and continuing life of the church, and yet it also is supposed to act as a rule of proper belief and practice helping to ensure the fidelity and thus continuity of the church.

Breck emphasizes that "inspirational work involves what we term a synergy, a cooperative effort between, on the one hand, the Holy Spirit and, on the other, the human instrument who receives divine revelation and translates it into the gospel proclamation" (9). This synergy characterizes not just the writing of Scripture but also its continuing life within the church. Tradition is the "living memory" of the Church, and the Scriptures are part of this living memory (9). Yet, this living memory doesn't record just anything. Rather, the purpose of all of Scripture is the revelation of Christ, and the revelation of Christ comes to us not simply as the bequeathing of abstract theological insights about the God-man but as an act of grace with pragmatic import, "the gospel proclamation."

A distinctive emphasis in Breck, as an Orthodox author, is on "anamnesis" (12), the idea that the use of Scripture, especially in the liturgy, should not simply bring to mind God's great actions but, in some sense, should allow one to relive them. Thus, while Wolterstorff might emphasize God's continuing to speak and Westphal would emphasize the need to keep interpreting and dialoguing with Scripture, this same theme of the continuing work of Scripture takes on a more embodied dimension for Breck. He also insists, in good patristic fashion, that enacting a faithful life is necessary to understand spiritual things. As Athanasius famously ends *On the Incarnation*, "without a pure mind and a life modeled on the saints, no one can comprehend the words of the saints" (2011: 110). Or, as Breck puts it relating the idea specifically to Scripture, "one cannot interpret the Scriptures faithfully or accurately unless one lives in accordance with them" (2001: 31).

The difference with our other authors, however, is one of emphasis and, to some extent, means. Breck critiques our use of Scripture generally, saying, "We have restricted ourselves to interrogating the biblical text, rather than allowing ourselves to be addressed

---

[4]How "appropriation" works can be debated. William Lane Craig's Molinist theory of inspiration is, in a way, a novel theory of how God appropriates texts (Craig 1999) but not the hands-on intervention that most of us would associate with appropriation.

and challenged by the living and life-giving Word of God" (17). This quotation could have easily been spliced into Wolterstorff or Vanhoozer without anyone being the wiser. Even Westphal's emphasis on the need to dialogue with different interpretive lenses is close to the spirit of what Breck claims here. The idea in common is that Scripture is the kind of text in the light of which we are to interrogate our own lives thereby allowing God to speak into them. Scripture is not simply a set of validated assertions to be accepted; it is an inspired instrument for viewing one's life with eyes of faith and for encountering God in the process. As Breck puts it, "through the working of the Holy Spirit in the interplay between text and reader, it can become … a medium for communion with the God who reveals himself in and through it" (21).

Thus, we see philosophers, theologians, and biblical scholars across a variety of traditions and with a variety of projects who all want us not to see Scripture as simply making assertions that we predicate of either human or divine authors and thence accept or reject. Instead, papering over significant differences in emphasis, they all bring out the idea that Scripture cannot fill the role of inspired speech for a particular reader unless that reader (1) actively engages and contextualizes the text (2) into an individual and collective life of faith (3) for the purpose of more deeply receiving and embodying the grace of God (4) with the help of interpretive communities that own their historical continuity with, as well as their distance from, the original audience.

In the next section, I will develop a model that will help us make sense of this convergence.

II. HOLY SPIRIT AS MAP MAKER

Maps represent. As with photographs or paintings, one might describe what a map represents using propositions, but maps do not represent by way of propositions. This is true of other kinds of models as well, but maps prove an especially instructive example for our purposes.[5] A map of a national park, for instance, represents by translating the spatial relationships of the terrain into discernibly similar spatial relationships on a flat surface. Symbols can then be placed within this spatial translation schema so as to indicate where the things symbolized are. Maps, as it turns out, have many of the features that the authors from the previous section were converging on in their accounts of the inspiration of Scripture. I do not claim to be the first person ever to think of comparing Scripture and the cartographic arts, but a closer look at how maps represent allows us to make progress on our topic.

Maps are perspectival, and they represent in a way that has in mind the perspectives of particular kinds of people, people using the map for particular ends. For example, a hiking map typically will assume that a hiker will start from one of a small set of points on the map (e.g., parking lots) and then will prioritize the representation of established trails that fork off from those points. It will include those features of the terrain that are most salient to hikers—ranger stations, waterfalls, mountains, perhaps slope gradients. Maps carried by employees of the gas company would ignore waterfalls. A treasure map would restrict the paths it depicts to the one or two that get one to the booty rather than including any pleasant jaunt in the region.

---

[5]For an important exploration of the role that models play as representational vehicles in science, see Giere (2006). The discussion here is deeply indebted to Giere's trailblazing work in the philosophy of science.

There is a sense in which, even if one understands the conventions of maps, one has not fully unlocked the representational potential of a map until one has fitted it to the terrain it is meant to depict. The map does not have usable content without a competent act of fitting the map to what it is a map of and the intended use of the map may require not just accurate cognition but embodied action.[6] Similarly, a hiking map may present options that shape a hiker's choice of trail, but it does not dictate where one should go until one brings one's intentions into dialogue with it.

A map's usability is partly a function of strategic simplifications. Although it has more information in it than a map might, an aerial photograph is less inherently usable because of the cognitive noise that comes with every wrinkle of the terrain being represented equally. In contrast, the power of a map is just as much a function of what is strategically left out as what is included. As a result, there is a potential tension built into the comparing of maps. If two maps of the same terrain prioritize and simplify the representation of the terrain in the exact same way, they are for all intents and purposes the same map. Yet it is clear that, though bad maps exist, it is also possible to produce good maps of the terrain that are different. The difference could be a function of their being intended for different uses (e.g., the hiking map versus the treasure map) or different contexts of use (e.g., summer hiking versus winter hiking). Usability can sometimes be enhanced by distorting what one is depicting strategically, such as when one represents landmarks as bigger than they are to draw out their salience or simplifies the zigzags of a trail to depict its approximate route. The strategic simplifications of one context of use might not fit another context of use, however. The terrain might also change in relevant ways such that a good map could be outdated in part though still counting on the whole as a good map.

Even though difference among maps of the same terrain may introduce some novel challenges for integration, having multiple (good) maps of the same terrain can also be very useful. Having multiple maps provides one a composite understanding of the terrain and how to navigate it under a variety of conditions. Furthermore, one might have some maps designed for beginners while having progressively more demanding maps that become more usable as one gains experience.

Map use is a social practice. Though the ability to use basic spatial relationships to represent is a fairly universal capacity, the interpretation of more specialized maps and the discernment of the proper contexts of their use are socially mediated practices that one can grow in. To the extent, for example, that the navigation of terrain is difficult or the cost of failing to achieve a goal is high, it behooves one to have a realistic sense of one's own abilities and the humility to seek out experienced guides or at least experienced map readers.

So much for the extended metaphor.[7] If we turn, then, to Scripture, it is instructive to think of this library of ancient texts as a series of remappings of God's work in the world. Some genres are stripped down to elements that readily lend to their reapplication to different people in different times, such as, to a large extent, wisdom literature or

---

[6] There is a certain resonance between the point expressed here and the oft repeated claim in Paul Moser's work that God would not give us "spectator evidence" but rather "authoritative evidence," in other words, evidence that is essentially linked to the call to live out agape (cf. Moser 2008: 10). Yet, the account in this chapter allows for more to be cognitively available prior to action than Moser seems to countenance when he makes this point.
[7] In a forthcoming essay, Sameer Yadav uses "signposts" as a guiding metaphor for a perceptual model of discerning meaning within and living in light of Scripture. His project has some differences from what we are up to here, but I take his model to be highly consonant with this one with large areas of overlap at both the levels of mechanism and application.

the psalms. Many a city slicker has been able to imaginatively identify with the idea that "The Lord is my shepherd" (Ps. 23:1).[8] Other genres might show the same relational dynamics replaying across different characters and situations such that the common spiritual denominators shine through the differences of detail from scenario to scenario. Think, for instance, of the endless cycle of disobedience, punishment, and deliverance in the book of Judges.

Whether it be the exceptionless moral logic of Proverbs in comparison to the disconcerting subtlety of Ecclesiastes or the cleaned up portrait of King David in Chronicles as contrasted with the David of Kings, some of these mappings overlap in ways that reveal some maps to be simpler than if not outright different from others. Yet the impulse to preserve such differences in a single tradition makes some sense if we think of them as models that use strategic simplifications of the messy story of God's relation to humanity in general and Israel in particular for different kinds of situations—for instance, Kings as a charting of the moral frailty that led to a people's experience of exile and Chronicles for a people returning to the promised land who needed to hear that God had preserved for them a legacy still worth cherishing. Yet the tradition chooses to preserve maps that are in tension with each other well beyond the times of the original audiences of either. One wonders if it might not be because there was a need to have both.

Scripture does not answer every theological or philosophical question one might want answered. What one might think, however, is that it maps out what life has looked like given varying levels of faith and fidelity. Moreover, both within Scripture itself and within the traditions of different churches, we are given examples of how to make sense of one's circumstances in light of Scripture. Tradition does not simply preserve theological claims in excess of the claims of Scripture; it fosters sensibilities and supports practices that grow one's knowledge of how to use the common story to navigate life. And, indeed, in this kind of context the prevalence of narrative genres in Scripture takes on special significance.[9]

A model-based picture of divine inspiration does not give up on truth. Far from it! Maps are useful only if they accurately depict the terrain. The level of accuracy required depends on the intended use, but verisimilitude is still a requirement of a good map. Maps can even be dogmatic (e.g., "According to the map, this path will take us to the Falls, not that one"). What the account does do is make more room for the relevance of things other than assertions. Promises, exhortations, and warnings are intended, of course, to shape behavior. If God uses these speech acts to help one orient oneself correctly to the task of faithful living, then I don't see a reason not to call the promises, exhortations, and warnings themselves inspired. Moreover, these speech acts more directly guide behavior than assertions about what promises or warnings have been made in the past. More subtly, a question, a lament, or an unresolved tension might properly orient one's living by providing examples of how to live out faith under conditions of uncertainty or distress or by identifying values that must be held onto even though we are not in a cognitive position to give a pat answer as to how they can coexist.

In short, thinking of Scripture as a series of remappings of the divine-human relationship puts one in a new position to make sense of how one can allow Scripture to be human and messy in one sense, while preserving a high view of what it means

---

[8] All Scripture quotations in this chapter are taken from the New International Version of the Bible.
[9] For a well-regarded extended discussion of the importance of narrative and an object lesson in using the distinctive vehicle of biblical narrative to do theological work, see Stump (2010).

for Scripture to be divinely inspired. Human beings aren't very good at taking general theological assertions and living them out. God condescends to address us at our level, in our narrow, culture-bound hardheadedness. The human details may change, but God and the human condition are shown afresh from each new angle. A composite picture of God and the possibilities for relating to God comes through as we see remappings of the same relationship and as we see various attempts to enact that relationship in and through both the people of Israel and the community of the church.

Let us turn, finally, to the perspicuity of Scripture in light of the preceding discussion. Testimony, even credible testimony to a belief reliably arrived at by a testifier, does not do a hearer any good unless it is communicated so as to be clear to the hearer. In the Christian tradition, God's message is not supposed to be restricted to just the original audience. It is supposed to go to the "ends of the earth" (Acts 1:8). Thus, the testimony contained in Scripture must meet a very demanding standard of clarity to be up to its function. Even if one were somehow to argue that each member of the original, historical audience was in an epistemic position such that each sentence of Scripture would have been clear to them, a dubious claim already, the same clearly does not hold for all human audiences past, present, and future. Thus, without some way of delimiting the scope or function of inspired speech, it seems clear that Scripture is not clear and thus fails to be exemplary *qua* testimony.

Following the suggestion we took from Vanhoozer, one might suppose, however, that the kind of perspicuity that is important is the ability of Scripture to guide someone into their next steps in the life of grace, a life with God in community. To put it more squarely in Vanhoozer's terms, it is the Gospel that must shine in the pages of Scripture not necessarily what it was like living in first-century Palestine (though a sense of the latter no doubt helps). Through our discussion, we can translate this into the following formulation of the perspicuity of Scripture. In order for Scripture to count as perspicuous, it needs to be the case that for any person in any social location, it is in principle possible for Scripture to show up as inspired for them in the sense that an individual map or set of maps of the human condition is available that is usable by them to guide them in their next steps in individual and corporate life in God. The "in principle" qualifier covers the usual ways in which we can subvert our own epistemic status, but it is also intended to draw attention to the fact that Scripture is supposed to be wedded to the life of the church. The church should foster an understanding of how to live guided by Scripture, though, of course, it can get in the way as well. One need not think of a text showing up as inspired for a person as being a function simply of human agency whether individual or collective, however. Just as one should preserve a place for the Holy Spirit in the production and curation of the inspired text, so too one should expect the Holy Spirit to be intimately involved in bridging the gap between the text to be read and the life to be lived out in light of the text. Likewise, to harken back to Breck, a life lived in, with, and by the Spirit should in turn inform how the text shows up for one.

Thinking of perspicuity in terms of usability, on the one hand, allows us to make an even more robust claim than is typical about the clarity of Scripture because it highlights the importance of epistemic states other than propositional knowledge, such as knowledge-how and acquaintance knowledge. For instance, a testifier attempting to convey how to ride a bicycle, in a sense, takes on more than a testifier looking to impart a correct belief about the way people ride bicycles, though conveying the former will typically result in conveying the latter as a by-product. Likewise, a testifier trying to facilitate acquaintance knowledge is not successful in virtue of her sentences being understood. Rather, she must put the hearer in a position to experience something.

On the other hand, thinking of the perspicuity of Scripture in this way allows the text to be clear in one way while being unclear in others. Perspicuity matters because of the way Scripture is supposed to link up with living, which certainly includes the life of the mind but extends well beyond it. If that's true, though, then a series of narratives that show how God interacts with us in our embodied and socially embedded existence might produce greater clarity in how to use the text for life, especially when taken as a whole, even though the cultural particularity of the narratives might include details not completely clear to each and every reader. This is familiar from great works of literature generally. There is something moving about *The Odyssey* or the *Brother's Karamazov* that is conveyed partly through the concrete details of their telling even though many of those details may be unclear to the reader. In the successive remappings of Scripture and the retellings of tradition, however, the essentials for navigating one's own life and for recontextualizing the essentials of the faith are nonetheless conveyed and cultural distance mitigated. Thus, this way of thinking about inspiration makes it clearer both why the perspicuity of Scripture is important and how the narrative dense diversity of Scripture could be an apt tool for the kind of perspicuity that matters, namely, a perspicuity that promotes perspicacity in Christian living.

III. CONCLUSION

In conclusion, Vanhoozer draws on the story of the tower of Babel as an apt metaphor for his project of grappling with differences in Biblical interpretation. I don't think Vanhoozer goes far enough. We need not only a vision of "biblical authority after Babel" but of "perspicuity after Pentecost." In the story of Babel, we see the hubris of humankind punished with an inability to speak and mean as one. In the book of Acts, we see that God's plan for the Gospel is that it immediately accommodate itself to a diverse audience and that its ability to do that is received as a sign that it is inspired speech. In Pentecost, we have a typological transfiguration of Babel. The Babel story only works, though, if the cursed lack translators. Likewise, Pentecost only works because translating the work of God into diverse cultural contexts provides a better composite vision of God's presence in history than otherwise.[10]

References

Athanasius (2011), *On the Incarnation*, trans. J. Behr, Yonkers: St Vladimir's Press.
Austin, J. L. (1962), *How to Do Things with Words*, Oxford: Clarendon Press.
Breck, J. (2001), *Scripture in Tradition*, Yonkers: St Vladimir's Press.
Callahan, J. (2001), *The Clarity of Scripture*, Downers Grove, IL: InterVarsity Press.
Craig, W. L. (1999), "'Men Moved by the Holy Spirit Spoke from God': A Middle Knowledge Perspective on Biblical Inspiration," *Philosophia Christi*, 1 (1): 45–82.
Davis, S. (2009), "Revelation and Inspiration," in T. Flint and M. Rea (eds.), *The Oxford Handbook of Philosophical Theology*, 30–53, New York: Oxford University Press.

---

[10] I gratefully acknowledge the helpful insights of Steven Nemes, Rico Vitz, Teri Merrick, and Bill Yarchin as well as the editors of this volume, James Arcadi and J. T. Turner, on previous drafts of this chapter.

Enns, P. (2015), *Inspiration and Incarnation*, Grand Rapids, MI: Baker Academic.
Giere, R. (2006), *Scientific Perspectivism*, Chicago: University of Chicago Press.
Green, A., and K. Quan (2012), "More than Inspired Propositions: Shared Attention and the Religious Text," *Faith & Philosophy*, 29 (4): 416–30.
Moser, P. (2008), *The Elusive God*, New York: Cambridge University Press.
Stump, E. (2010), *Wandering in Darkness*, New York: Oxford University Press.
Swinburne, R. (1992), *Revelation*, New York: Oxford University Press.
Vanhoozer, K. (2016), *Biblical Authority after Babel*, Grand Rapids, MI: Brazos Press.
Westphal, M. (2009), *Whose Community? Which Interpretation?*, Grand Rapids, MI: Baker Academic.
Wolterstorff, N. (1995), *Divine Discourse: Philosophical Reflections on the Claim that God Speaks*, New York: Cambridge University Press.
Yadav, S. (forthcoming), "Scripture as Signpost," in F. Aquino and P. Gavrilyuk (eds.), *Sensing Things Divine*, New York: Oxford University Press.

CHAPTER THREE

Religious Epistemology in Analytic Theology

TYLER DALTON MCNABB AND ERIK BALDWIN

Can we know that God exists? Is it rational to believe that God revealed Himself through scripture? Do pragmatic reasons play a role in whether one's belief about a religious text is justified? These are the type of questions that religious epistemologists seek to answer. Religious epistemology then, roughly, is the study of knowledge, rationality, justification, and warrant as it pertains to religious belief and practice. There isn't, of course, just one approach to epistemology. Similarly, there isn't just one approach to religious epistemology. Philosophers of religion and analytic theologians differ widely with respect to how to analyze the epistemic status of a religious belief. For example, Roman Catholics, being committed to the infallibility of sacred tradition and an infallible magisterium, have generally emphasized the community's role in one's religious doxastic process (Zagzebski 2015). Whereas, perhaps due to the influence of the doctrine of *sola scriptura*, Protestants have traditionally emphasized the individual and scripture in developing their epistemological commitments (Plantinga 2000). There are, of course, instances in which those in the higher church traditions endorse epistemologies that emphasize the individual (Swinburne 2014), and there are Protestants who endorse epistemologies that emphasize the community (Meek 2011). Nonetheless, these generalities do seem to fit our knowledge of the literature.

In this chapter, we will separate the field of religious epistemology into epistemologies that emphasize the individual and those epistemologies that emphasize the community. We will give two examples of each in turn. First, we will discuss Alvin Plantinga's and Richard Swinburne's religious epistemologies.[1] Then, we turn to discussing Linda Zagzebski's religious epistemology and a broadly Thomistic one inspired by Alasdair MacIntyre's rationality of traditions. After we survey the aforementioned religious epistemologies, we will argue that the various epistemologies can be synthesized.

---

[1] While we think these epistemologies emphasize the individual more than her community, it doesn't follow that there is no role for the community in the respective epistemologies. Obviously, Plantinga's epistemology does require that some community exists in order to make sense of the testimony of scripture. There is simply a greater emphasis on the individual in comparison to the individual's community, at least, as the epistemologies were originally glossed with respect to religious knowledge.

I. ALVIN PLANTINGA'S REFORMED EPISTEMOLOGY

Traditionally, philosophers considered knowledge to be justified true belief. That is to say, they maintained that if a subject affirmed a true proposition, and if she was within her right in affirming the proposition, we rightly attribute knowledge to her. Edmund Gettier, in his 1963 article, "Is Justified True Belief Knowledge?," gives various counterexamples to the idea that knowledge is merely justified true belief (Gettier 1963). Since then, numerous Gettier-style counterexamples have been developed. Take the following example as a sample: Judas has a bad problem with lying. In fact, Judas is known for making things up all the time. Peter doesn't know this, however. Peter asks Judas if the local basketball team won the game. Judas, having no idea about basketball, tells Peter very confidently that the local basketball team won. Unbeknownst to Judas, the local basketball team did actually win. Peter believes Judas and possesses a justified, true belief. Something about this seems very lucky, lucky enough that we shouldn't consider Peter's belief to constitute knowledge.

There are typically three responses to Gettier-styled counterexamples. The primary initial response to Gettier-styled counterexamples is to add a fourth condition to the traditional tripartite analysis of knowledge (Pappas and Swain 1978). This approach, however, hasn't been met with too much success (Moreland and Craig 2008). A more recent approach argues that knowledge is not analyzable (Williamson 2000). Rather, knowledge is seen as a mental state. A third approach, that of Alvin Plantinga, differs from both of these; he argues that knowledge is warranted, true belief. Warrant, here, is the key ingredient that turns mere true belief into knowledge.

Plantinga develops a theory of warrant known as proper functionalism (Plantinga 1993; Baldwin and McNabb 2018; McNabb 2018). Roughly, S's belief that p is warranted if and only if

(1) The belief in question is formed by way of cognitive faculties that are properly functioning.
(2) The cognitive faculties in question are aimed at the production of true beliefs.
(3) The design plan is a good one. That is, when a belief is formed by way of truth-aimed cognitive proper function in the sort of environment for which the cognitive faculties in question were designed, there is a high objective probability that the resulting belief is true.
(4) The belief is formed in the sort of environment for which the cognitive faculties in question were designed (Boyce 2016).

In his account of warrant, Plantinga denies what is known as epistemic internalism. While there are various strands of internalism, the most popular version is known as access internalism. Access internalism is the view that, in order for S to have a justified or warranted belief, S needs to have access to good reasons that support the belief in question. Contrarily, Plantinga endorses what is called epistemic externalism, which is just the denial of the internalist thesis. This means that in order for a belief to be warranted, the subject doesn't need to have access to reasons that enable her belief to be warranted.

Plantinga employs proper functionalism to argue for the thesis of reformed epistemology, namely, that religious belief can be justified or warranted, apart from argumentation. Plantinga first argues that it is epistemically possible (i.e., as far as we know, it could be the case) that a general theistic belief can be warranted apart from argument. Following John Calvin (Calvin 1960: 44), Plantinga postulates the possibility of humans possessing a *sensus divinitatis* (SD) (Plantinga 2000: 179). The SD is a faculty aimed toward producing beliefs about God and His activities. For example, imagine picking up a flower and you notice all of the intricate texture it possesses. You form an immediate belief that there is a transcendent creator responsible for this flower's existence. This belief wasn't arrived at by way of induction or abduction but rather was a natural doxastic response to experience. Plantinga argues that if the SD meets the proper functionalist constraints when it produces this belief, the belief would be warranted.

Plantinga doesn't stop at arguing for general theistic belief, however. Plantinga argues that specifically Christian belief can be warranted. Plantinga thinks that, while the SD works sufficiently well in most people, because sin has damaged the SD, it no longer works optimally. In response to this problem, Plantinga argues that it could be the case that the Holy Spirit exists and is responsible for conveying the Great Truths of the Gospel in Holy Scripture. (Roughly, we take it that the Great Truths of the Gospel are what is found in something like the Nicene Creed.) If the Spirit testifies to a subject about the Great Truths of the Gospel and the Spirit moves the subject to believe these truths as the Spirit repairs or improves the SD, assuming the subject responds positively to these truths and the proper functionalist constraints are in place, her belief in the truths will be warranted (Plantinga 2000: 241–89).

Notice that, for Plantinga, the design plan of a subject's faculty could be to produce a belief "that p" even if there are no communities that affirm that p. A subject's confidence level needn't change just because there is genuine epistemic peer disagreement. All that is needed for warranted, Christian belief is the testimony and instigation of the Spirit, and the subject possessing cognitive proper function. Following Athanasius's famous statement, "Athanasius Contra Mundum" (Athanasius Against the World, a phrase used to express Athanasius's fierce and unshakeable commitment to his convictions), a subject under the right conditions can properly move forward arguing for her religious belief against all other communities. Perhaps we can say, "Plantingians Contra Mundum."

II. RICHARD SWINBURNE'S BAYESIAN EVIDENTIALISM

Swinburne is an epistemic internalist about justification. Specifically, Swinburne uses Bayesian probability theorem to determine if a belief is justified. Using Bayes' Theorem, we assess the prior probability (which considers simplicity and how the relevant theory fits with our background knowledge) of a hypothesis, with the explanatory power of the hypothesis. A standard formula goes as follows:

$$P(h/e \& k) = \frac{P(h/k)P(e/h \& k)}{P(e/k)}$$[2]

---

[2] Roughly, it can be understood as follows:

k = general background knowledge
e = phenomena to be explained
h = the hypothesis
P(e/h & k) = the explanatory power of a hypothesis
P(h/k) = prior probability of a hypothesis
P(e/k) = the likelihood of the evidence independent of theory

For those who are less acquainted with probability calculus, see Swinburne (2014: 66–7).

With respect to the hypothesis that theism is true (HT), Swinburne takes it that P(h/k) will be high. A hypothesis that postulates one maximally great immaterial mind is a simple hypothesis. This seems especially so, in comparison to a rival hypothesis concerning the existence of our world, viz., one that postulates a countless number of universes. Given this, most of Swinburne's project is an attempt to show that we would expect certain features in our universe on HT that we wouldn't expect given not-HT.

Take for example the evidence that we have moral knowledge. Would we expect this on HT? We imagine most would be inclined to think that we would. But, would we expect moral knowledge on not-HT? Swinburne argues that natural selection is likely to give us the right sort of beliefs about what sort of actions we should take, but it isn't likely that unguided natural selection should lead to moral awareness (Swinburne 2014: 116–18). For example, tigers have to have certain beliefs in order to obtain food and cooperate with fellow tigers; however, they needn't have beliefs about what is objectively good or what is binding upon them. Swinburne puts it this way: "A tiger may desire and so believe it a good thing to help one particular fellow tiger in distress without believing it to be of overriding importance to help any other tiger in distress, when he did not wish to do so" (2014: 217). So, it seems like we should expect moral awareness on HT, at least, more so than not-HT. And given that this is the case, we have a good c-inductive argument for theism. A c-inductive argument is an argument that adds to the probability of a hypothesis, in this case, the hypothesis that theism is true (Swinburne 2014: 13). If one has enough c-inductive arguments, one has a successful p-inductive argument (Swinburne 2014: 14, 17). That is, you have an argument that shows that the hypothesis in question is overall more probable than not. In making the case that there is a strong p-inductive argument for theism, Swinburne looks at the apparent evidence for God in the fine-tuning of the universe, the existence of a complex universe, the existence of beauty, and the existence of human consciousness.

Swinburne extends this basic strategy to defend particular substantive doctrines about God. For instance, he employs Bayesian strategies in support of the doctrine of the incarnation and when countering proposed defeaters to rational belief in God stemming from the problem of evil (Swinburne 1998, 2008). A Swinburnian can use confirmation theory to argue for specific Christian traditions too. We now move to give a test case for how a Swinburnian would argue for a specific religious tradition. Doing this not only will elucidate how a Swinburnian approaches religious epistemology but also will help make clear how other religious epistemologies address important questions.

Perhaps the central distinction between Roman Catholic and Reformational Christianity is the Roman Catholic Church's endorsement that Jesus created an office for Peter and his successors, and, the *telos* of this office is to infallibly protect the morals and faith of the Church. This endorsement would be part of what we will call the Roman Catholic hypothesis. Roughly, the Roman Catholic hypothesis is the hypothesis that the essential claims of the Roman Catholic Church are true. Essential to the Roman Catholic faith, then, is whether there was a special bishop in Rome who succeeded Peter. This bishop would have ultimate authority of other bishops, even those bishops in his own city. Call this bishop a monarchial bishop. In *Roman but Not Catholic* (2017), Kenneth Collins and Jerry Walls argue that the probability that there would be evidence of a monarchical papacy in the early patristic sources is very high. And yet, according to Collins and Walls, there is no evidence in the early patristic sources for a monarchial papacy.

Collins and Walls look to the following four key figures to help make plausible their claim that there was no monarchial bishop in early Christian history: Clement of Rome,

Ignatius, Hermas, and Justin Martyr. One would expect Clement to address the concept of a monarchial bishop in Rome, given that he was an elder within the Roman Church. Yet, as Collins and Walls note, Clement continually refers to the leadership in the church in the plural. Similarly, one would expect both Hermas and Justin Martyr to mention a monarchial bishop in Rome since they were members of the Roman community, but they fail to do so as well. With respect to Ignatius, while he was not a member of the Roman Christian community, he does spend a lot of time talking about the bishop's role in the ecclesiastical structure of the church in every letter he writes, besides one, namely, his letter to the Roman community.

Contrary to what one might initially expect if the Roman Catholic hypothesis were true, these patristic writers make no mention of a monarchial bishop in Rome and it is precisely because of this that most Roman Catholic historians agree with the Protestant and Orthodox consensus that there was no monarchial bishop in Rome in the early Roman Church (Eno 2008; Duffy 2014). Questions relevant to Collins and Walls's hypothesis arise: What's the probability that each writer would have known of a monarchial bishop in Rome, would have recorded it, and the record would have survived, given that there was in fact such a monarchial bishop? Collins and Walls put the probability for Clement at 0.44, Hermas at 0.53, Ignatius at 0.33, and Justin at 0.27 (2017: 248–9). After establishing this much, Collins and Walls move on to calculate that the probability that at least one of these authors would have known about a monarchial bishop of Rome, would have written about the monarchial bishop in Rome, and that the record would have survived, is about 0.87 (2017: 249).[3] Overall, then, Collins and Walls think that the likelihood of one of these patristic writers mentioning a monarchial bishop in Rome is extremely high if there were in fact such a bishop. As they put it, "the fact that none of them did is a powerful argument from silence, and a striking result given the stringent standards for such arguments" (Collins and Walls 2017: 249–50).

To make their argument go through, Collins and Walls accept particular background knowledge claims. Other Swinburnians will begin with different background knowledge claims. Some will assign different likelihoods regarding whether the church fathers would explicitly mention a monarchial/special bishop in Rome and propose alternative explanations for their silence on the issue. As such, the relevant Bayesian probability judgments and their evidential force will vary.

While not explicitly Bayesian, John Henry Newman employed probabilistic reasoning in his defense of the reasonability of Christianity as well as specifically Roman Catholic beliefs and doctrines (Newman 1978, 2011). Newman held that the antecedent probability of the development of the doctrine of Papal Supremacy was very high. He writes,

> In proportion to the probability of true developments of doctrine and practice in the Divine Scheme, so is the probability also of the appointment in that scheme of an external authority [the Pope and the magisterium] to decide upon them, thereby

---

[3] In articulating the key equation to calculate this probability, Collins and Collins (2017: 249) state the following:

$1 - P(\sim CR\ \&\ \sim HR\ \&\ \sim IR\ \&\ \sim JR) = 1 - [P(\sim CR) * P(\sim HR) * P(\sim IR) * P(\sim JR)]$
Since $P(CR) = 0.44$, and $P(CR\ or\ \sim CR) = P(CR) + P(\sim CR) = 1$
we know that
$P(\sim CR) = 1 - P(CR) = 1 - 0.44 = 0.56$
and we can conclude that
$P(CR\ or\ HR\ or\ IR\ or\ JR) = 1 - [(0.56) * (0.47) * (0.67) * (0.73)] = 1 - 0.1287 = 0.87$.

> separating them from the mass of mere human speculation, extravagance, corruption, and error, in and out of which they grow. (Newman 1978: 78–9)

And,

> must be viewed in the light of the general probability ... that doctrine cannot but develop as time proceeds and need arises, and that its developments are parts of the Divine system, and that therefore it is lawful, or rather necessary, to interpret the words and deeds of the earlier Church by the determinate teaching of the later. (Newman 1978: 78–9)

What, then, of Ignatius's silence? Newman reminds us that Ignatius's aim was to address disagreements so as to secure the unity of the Church of his day. Early on, the apostles and their successors had secured such a unity. As time went on, the need officially to recognize church structures and hierarchies in order to secure unity became evident. In light of this, Newman maintains that Ignatius's silence on the subject of the Pope's authority doesn't count against the doctrine. He continues,

> When the Church ... was thrown upon her own resources, first local disturbances gave exercise to Bishops, and next ecumenical disturbances gave exercise to Popes; and whether communion with the Pope was necessary for Catholicity would not and could not be debated till a suspension of that communion had actually occurred. It is not a greater difficulty that St. Ignatius does not write to the Asian Greeks about Popes, than that St. Paul does not write to the Corinthians about Bishops. And it is a less difficulty that the Papal supremacy was not formally acknowledged in the second century, than that there was no formal acknowledgment on the part of the Church of the doctrine of the Holy Trinity till the fourth. No doctrine is defined till it is violated. (Newman 1978: 151)

A follower of Newman, then, would think that one of the bishops in Rome, at least implicitly, was recognized as possessing ultimate authority in some sense. And it wasn't until disputes arose that the implicit recognition became more explicit.

We do not here take a stand here on whether Collins and Walls have got things right or whether Newman's view is correct. Rather, our intention is to provide an example of how Swinburnian evidentialism can be employed by different individuals in ways that provide rational support for different religious doctrines and traditions. A Swinburnian relies on her individual probabilistic assessments in order to figure out what is rational to believe. However, as Newman illustrates, not all epistemologists are convinced that this is the best route to take when it comes to the epistemic evaluative process.

III. LINDA ZAGZEBSKI'S EPISTEMIC AUTHORITY

In *Epistemic Authority*, Zagzebski begins by arguing that one is rational in trusting one's own cognitive equipment. Moreover, if one is rational to trust one's own cognitive faculties, one is normally rational in trusting the cognitive faculties of other sincere epistemic agents. This leads Zagzebski to endorse epistemic universalism. As she puts it, epistemic universalism is the view that "the fact that another person has a certain belief always gives me *prima facie* reason to believe it" (Zagzebski 2015: 58). She then argues that one is justified in accepting the testimony of S if by trusting S's testimony one is more likely to get to truth than if one does not trust S's testimony. She formulates her view in the following theses:

Justification Thesis 1 for Authority of Testimony (JAT 1)

The authority of a person's testimony for me is justified by my conscientious judgment that I am more likely to satisfy my desire to get true beliefs and avoid false beliefs if I believe what the authority tells me than if I try to figure out what to believe myself.

Justification Thesis 2 for the Authority of Testimony (JAT 2)

The authority of another person's testimony for me is justified by my conscientious judgment that if I believe what the authority tells me, the result will survive my conscientious self-reflection better than if I try to figure out what to believe myself.

Third-person JAT thesis 1

The authority of a person's testimony for me is justified by the fact that I am more likely to satisfy my desire to get true beliefs and avoid false beliefs if I believe what the authority tells me than if I try to figure out what to believe myself.

Third-person JAT thesis 2

The authority of a person's testimony for me is justified by the fact that I am more likely to get a belief that will survive my future conscientious self-reflection if I believe what the authority tells me than if I try to figure out what to believe myself (Zagzebski 2015: 137–38).

Zagzebski goes on to argue that in the same way that an agent's testimony can be justified, so too can a community's testimony be justified. That is, S is justified in accepting a community's testimony if accepting the community's testimony will put S in a better epistemic position to believe truth. Seeking to believe true propositions, S should attach herself to a community (Zagzebski 2015: 188). A truth conducive community would develop a structure to preserve and transmit the practices that define the community for future members of the community (191). And likely, S will want to attach herself not just to any community but to one that has been around for hundreds or thousands of years; for, other things being equal, traditions that have deep roots into the past are more likely to be truth conducive, particularly so given that the current generation isn't privy to all of the evidence and ideas that other generations have had (199). Finally, it seems likely that a community that doesn't adopt a democratic structure will be more conducive to truth since democratic structures privilege the present rather than the past. Communities with democratic structures are prone to use only the evidence we currently have and they are more susceptible to neglecting the evidence that the community's forefathers had (156). It would be rational, then, for S to accept the testimony and authority of a community with a long-standing tradition and one that lacks a democratic structure for carrying out its doxastic responsibilities. Zagzebski applies her view to religious belief in the following thesis:

Justification of Religious Authority Thesis

The authority of my religious community is justified for me by my conscientious judgment that if I engage in the community, following its practical directives and believing its teachings, the result will survive my conscientious self-reflection upon my total set of psychic states better than if I try to figure out what to do and believe in the relevant domain in a way that is independent of Us. (Zagzebski 2015: 122)

How would a Roman Catholic Zagzebskian respond to the Swinburnian-styled argument against the papacy? She would argue that the non-Roman Catholic Swinburnian is blinded by her own time period and lacks access to evidence of which those who lived over a millennium ago had access to. This especially seems so given that the sources that we have access to from that time period are severely limited. And assuming that the papal doctrine hadn't been substantially developed by the end of the first century, there is not a lot of reason to think that we now are in an epistemic position to judge the likelihood of there being a monarchial bishop in Rome in the late first century.[4] Perhaps things are as the Roman Catholic tradition maintains; perhaps there was a special bishop in Rome who had more authority than other bishops (including those other bishops in Rome) in the same way that Peter had more authority than the other apostles.[5] Just as Peter was slow to realize the extent of his office, and just as it wasn't visibly obvious that Peter possessed special authority that the other apostles lacked, the same could be said of Peter's immediate successors in the Diocese of Rome. The Roman Catholic Zagzebskian will trust the authority of the Roman Catholic Church when it comes to these matters. And the justification for trusting the Roman Catholic Church is based on her religious beliefs having a higher probability of being true if she submits to the Roman Catholic Church's teaching.

In addition to developing a thorough religious epistemology, Zagzebski has developed an argument for theism that is based in part on her commitment to epistemic universalism. The argument goes as follows:

1. I must have a general attitude of self-trust in my epistemic faculties as a whole. This trust is both natural and shown to be rational by philosophical reflection.
2. The general attitude of epistemic self-trust commits me to a general attitude of epistemic trust in the faculties of all other human beings.
3. So the fact that someone else has a belief gives me a *prima facie* reason to believe it myself.
4. Other things equal, the fact that many people have a certain belief increases my *prima facie* reason to believe it, and the reason is strong when the beliefs are acquired independently.
5. The fact that other people believe in God is a *prima facie* reason to believe that God exists, and the fact that many millions of people constituting a very high majority believe or have believed in prior ages that God exists increases my *prima facie* reason to believe in God myself. Even though many of those beliefs were acquired from others, I have reason to trust the beliefs of trusted others who acquired their beliefs from persons they trust. That is, I have reason to trust their trust. Furthermore, even if we completely discount for dependence, there are still many millions of people who independently believe or have believed in past ages in the existence of God (Zagzebski 2015: 186).

---

[4] For more on this point, see Blado (forthcoming).
[5] See Mt. 16:19 in light of Isa. 22:22. Also, see Peter opening the gates of heaven for the Jews in Acts 2, for the Samaritans in Acts 8, and for the Gentiles in Acts 10.

Roughly, the basic idea is that since the vast majority of people in the world believe that God exists, one has *prima facie* reason to believe that God exists. Of course, the argument can be rejected on various grounds. The most obvious way to respond to the argument is to reject epistemic universalism and thus reject the first premise. One could also run a *reductio* against the argument. For example, one might think that Christians shouldn't endorse this argument; for what happens if Islam becomes the biggest religious tradition in the world? Would we then have *prima facie* reason to accept the core tenets of Islam? Perhaps the Christian Zagzebskian will bite the bullet and agree that we would. However, this argument would just be one piece of evidence that should be considered and the overall evidential considerations point in the direction of Christianity, not Islam. But then, should the Christian look to see which Christian tradition has the most believers and then convert to that specific tradition? In this case, it seems like all Christians should affirm Roman Catholicism, Eastern Orthodoxy, or Anglicanism. Roman Catholicism, Eastern Orthodoxy, and Anglicanism seem to be in the best position given the number of followers each tradition possesses.

IV. A BROADLY THOMISTIC APPROACH

According to Thomas Aquinas, going about acquiring religious knowledge is a third-person activity. That is, each of us is but one inquirer among many. It follows that self-knowledge must be, "integrated into a general account of souls and their teleology" (MacIntyre 2006: 149). Insofar as one moves toward truth successfully, one's intellect becomes adequate to the objects it knows and one consequently "responds to the object as the object is and as it would be, independently of the mind's knowledge of it" (MacIntyre 2006: 149). Jacques Maritain sums things up thus:

> Aquinas makes knowledge *absolutely dependent* upon what is. To know, in fact, is essentially to know *something*, and something which ... measures it and governs it, and thus possesses its own being, independent of my knowledge ... the object of knowledge ... must, by its very nature of known object, be that which a thing is—a thing other than myself and my subjective activity ... The entire specification of my act of intelligence comes, therefore, from the object *as something other*, as free from me. In knowing, I subordinate myself to a being independent of me; I am conquered, convinced and subjugated by it. And the truth of my mind lies in its conformity to *what* is outside of it and independent of it. (Maritain 1958)

For Thomists, inquiry is a social affair. Unpacking this notion, Alasdair MacIntyre maintains that individual inquirers find themselves already having been shaped by traditions of inquiry. Following Jennifer Herdt's characterization, a tradition of inquiry is a group of people "engaged in a common conversation on a set of topics over an extended period of time, groups that may overlap and have fuzzy edges and whose set of topics is constantly evolving" (Herdt 1998: 544).

MacIntyre maintains that the goal of philosophical inquiry is to discover tradition-transcendent truths; we can't come to know them without relying on the resources of some particular tradition(s) of inquiry or other. Epistemological theorizing about religious matters relies on conceptual resources, tools, and methods that are products of traditions of inquiry. While our inquiries into truth must rely on tradition-based resources, truth remains tradition-independent. MacIntyre's epistemological approach endorses Thomas

Aquinas's realist view that truth is the conformity of the intellect to things (*adaequatio intellectus ad rem*) in a world that exists independent of human cognition. MacIntyre writes,

> One of the great originating insights of tradition-constituted enquiries is that false beliefs and false judgments represent a failure of the mind, not of its objects. It is mind which stands in need of correction. Those realities which mind encounters reveal themselves as they are, the presented, the manifest, the unbidden. So the most primitive conception of truth is of the manifestness of the objects which present themselves to mind; and it is when mind fails to represent that manifestness that falsity, the inadequacy of mind to its objects, appears. (MacIntyre 1988: 357)

V. PHILO-SYNTHESIS

Having now laid out various individual-centered and community-centered epistemologies, we move to synthesize a Plantingian approach to religious epistemology with a broadly Zagzebskian approach. We will use these two specific epistemologies as representatives of other individual-centered and community-centered epistemologies. These two epistemologies, at first glance, seem to be the furthest apart. It seems plausible, then, that if these two epistemologies are compatible, other individual-centered and community-centered epistemologies are likely compatible as well. On the other hand, one might object that any attempt to synthesize an individual-centered epistemology with a community-centered epistemology merely yields one more community-centered epistemology. Briefly, the contention might be that our proposed synthesis is unstable and collapses into a community-centered epistemology. To deal with this objection, we clarify our terms. By "compatible" we just mean that these two overall epistemological frameworks can both be consistently held. Of course, our synthesized model possesses important features that proponents of individual-centered models want to capture as well as features that proponents of community-centered models would want to capture. And that is why we think our proposed model will be attractive to epistemologists from both camps.

Let's return to the Zagzebskian religious authority thesis:

> The authority of my religious community is justified for me by my conscientious judgment that if I engage in the community, following its practical directives and believing its teachings, the result will survive my conscientious self-reflection upon my total set of psychic states better than if I try to figure out what to do and believe in the relevant domain in a way that is independent of Us.

Perhaps, after reflecting on how a community has a much better track record at getting religious doctrines correct, it is part of the subject's design plan to produce the belief that she needs to accept the authority of a specific religious community. It's the rational thing to do if the subject is convinced that by accepting the community's authority, she is likely to have more true religious beliefs and less false ones. In this case, the subject's warranted belief that she should accept the authority of the religious community can lead to other warranted beliefs. If the community testifies about p, assuming that p is part of a warranted testimonial chain, S's acceptance of p could be warranted.

Can S's belief that the community's testimony is true be defeated? It seems so. Perhaps she obtains new information that the community that she has attached herself to actually has a very bad track record or that she was mistaken about her own track record. In this case, if the design plan is such that she should doxastically move away from the community, her belief that she should detach herself from the community would be warranted, and her initial belief would be defeated.

Continuing to use Collins and Walls's probabilistic defeater against the papacy as a test case for how certain epistemologists should engage defeat, we can now ask how a Roman Catholic who endorses this Plantingian and Zagzebskian hybrid approach would respond to their attempted defeater. On reflection, it seems that the Roman Catholic could do one of two things. First, reflecting on the argument might lead one to question the track record of the Roman Catholic institution altogether. After all, so much of what the Roman Catholic Church testifies to assumes the authority of the papacy. But if that assumption is unjustified, would it be rational for Roman Catholics to believe that the institution as a whole is reliable? This way of thinking about things suggests, therefore, that, in accordance with the design plan, Roman Catholics ought to discount the authority of the papacy. On the other hand, perhaps the Roman Catholic in question reflects on how she doesn't think that she is in a position to judge the historicity of the papacy and that the Roman Catholic Church overall has a great track record of getting things right. On this way of thinking about the proposed defeater, there is no good reason for the Roman Catholic not to continue to trust in the authority and testimony of the Roman Catholic Church, and hence no good reason for her to discount the authority of the papacy. We won't endorse which route is the right action to take here. Rather, we have merely offered this scenario up to help show that individual-centered epistemologies and community-centered epistemologies are compatible.

References

Baldwin, E., and T. D. McNabb (2018), *Plantingian Religious Epistemology and World Religions: Prospects and Problems*, Lanham: Lexington Press.

Blado, J. (forthcoming), "On the Plausibility of the Papacy: Scaling the Walls of Contemporary Criticisms," *The Heythrop Journal*.

Boyce, K. (2016), "Proper Functionalism," *Internet Encyclopedia of Philosophy*. Available online: https://www.iep.utm.edu/prop-fun/ (accessed January 7, 2020).

Calvin, J. (1960), *Institutes of the Christian Religion*, trans. F. L. Battles, ed. J. T. McNeill, Philadelphia: Westminster Press.

Collins, K., and J. Walls (2017), *Roman but Not Catholic: What Remains at Stake for 500 Years after the Reformation*, Grand Rapids, MI: Baker Academic.

Duffy, E. (2014), *Saints & Sinners: A History of the Popes*, New Haven: Yale University Press.

Eno, R. B. (2008), *Rise of the Papacy*, Eugene, OR: Wipf and Stock.

Gettier, E. (1963), "Is Justified True Belief Knowledge?," *Analysis*, 23 (6): 121–3.

Herdt, J. (1998), "Alasdair Macintyre's 'Rationality of Traditions' and Tradition-Transcendental Standards of Justification," *Journal of Religion*, 78 (4): 524–46.

McNabb, T. D. (2018). *Religious Epistemology*, Cambridge: Cambridge University Press.

MacIntyre, A. (1988), *Whose Justice? Which Rationality?*, Notre Dame: University of Notre Dame Press.

MacIntyre, A. (2006), "First Principles, Final Ends, Contemporary Issues," in *The Tasks of Philosophy*, vol 1, Cambridge: Cambridge University Press.

Maritain, J. (1952), *The Range of Reason*, The Jacques Maritain Center, University of Notre Dame. Available online: https://maritain.nd.edu/jmc/etext/range01.htm (accessed January 7, 2020).

Meek, E. L. (2011), *Loving to Know: Introducing Covenant Epistemology*, Eugene: Cascade Books.
Moreland, J. P., and W. L. Craig (2008), *Philosophical Foundations for a Christian Worldview*, Downers Grove, IL: InterVarsity Press.
Newman, J. H. (1978), *An Essay on the Development of Christian Doctrine*, London: Basil Motagu Pickering.
Newman, J. H. (2011), *An Essay in the Aid of a Grammar of Assent*, Cambridge: Cambridge University Press.
Pappas, G. S., and M. Swain, eds. (1978), *Essays on Knowledge and Justification*, Ithaca, NY: Cornell University Press.
Plantinga, A. (1993), *Warrant and Proper Function*, New York: Oxford University Press.
Plantinga, A. (2000), *Warranted Christian Belief*, New York: Oxford University Press.
Swinburne, R. (1998), *Providence and the Problem of Evil*, Oxford: Oxford University Press.
Swinburne, R. (2008), *Was Jesus God?* New York: Oxford University Press.
Swinburne, R. (2014), *The Existence of God*, 2nd ed., Oxford: Clarendon Press.
Williamson, T. (2000), *Knowledge and Its Limits*, Oxford: Oxford University Press.
Zagzebski, L. T. (2015), *Epistemic Authority: A Theory of Trust, Authority, and Autonomy in Belief*, New York: Oxford University Press.

CHAPTER FOUR

Norma Normata: The Role of Tradition in Analytic Theology

R. LUCAS STAMPS

One of the common complaints leveled against the emerging discipline of analytic theology (AT) is the allegedly tenuous relationship it enjoys with the history of scriptural interpretation and the history of Christian doctrine. Both critics and proponents of AT have highlighted the ahistorical character of some of the projects being carried out under the analytic banner. At the same time, some practitioners of AT have been keenly sensitive to the historical contexts within which certain Christian doctrines have developed. So sweeping generalizations are unwarranted on this front. In this chapter, I propose a theological framework for thinking about the role of tradition in AT. It begins by suggesting that the Wesleyan quadrilateral still serves as a useful rubric for thinking about doctrinal formulation (at least in its Protestant mode). As the divinely inspired, written revelation of God, Scripture is the *norma normans* ("the rule that rules"), which serves to regulate all other sources for doing theology. But under Scripture's supreme authority, there are other norms that serve as derivatively authoritative guides to interpreting, synthesizing, and explicating Holy Scripture, namely, tradition, reason, and Christian experience. AT has been especially interested in the role of reason in theological methodology, but deference to the consensual tradition of the church—the *norma normata* ("the ruled rule") for Christian theology—has not been uniform across the discipline. Herein, I will also examine the use of the Christian tradition by some key practitioners of AT, suggesting that approaches to tradition fall along a spectrum of views: from what we might call *maximalist* approaches to *minimalist* approaches. I will further suggest that maximalist approaches stand the best chance to keep AT from becoming ghettoized by bringing it into closer dialogue with other modes of theological discourse.

I. THEOLOGICAL METHODOLOGY

Questioning the role that tradition plays in theology is not unique to the discipline of AT. All theologizing from a Christian perspective must give some account of the place of tradition in the theological task. So this question points up the broader considerations of theological method. Among Protestant reflections on this front, the famous Wesleyan quadrilateral remains a helpful approach to these issues. While John Wesley himself never explained his theological method in quite these terms, Wesleyan thinkers such as Albert Outler (1985) have summarized his approach in terms of the supreme authority of Holy Scripture with tradition, reason, and experience as useful and indispensable guides to interpreting the Scriptures.[1] To appeal to the quadrilateral should not be mistaken for a kind of methodological naïveté, as if theology can be reduced to a formula in which we simply "crunch the numbers" to arrive at the desired "right answer." Theological formulation is often complicated and nuanced, as Wesleyan analytic theologian William Abraham notes when he derides the "lazy and dogmatic use of the so-called Wesleyan quadrilateral" (2009: 67). Still, the quadrilateral provides something like an initial framing to the theological task that more granular reflections can then fill in. Obviously Roman Catholic theologians will have a different accounting of these issues, given the role of the magisterium as the living voice of the Church and the custodian of the truth contained in the Scriptures. Despite these fundamental differences, there is a kind of differentiated consensus we may speak of when comparing the methodologies of Protestants and Catholics (and Orthodox Christians as well). So, the reflections that follow are not meant to be sectarian in nature. Instead, they are offered as a way of thinking about the task of theology from a broadly catholic perspective.

Since my aim in this chapter is to explain the role of tradition in AT, reflections on the other three legs of the stool, so to speak, will be relatively brief. I take it that for all theologies that can classified as meaningfully Christian, the Holy Scriptures serve as the *principium*, the source and fount, of all true theology. The Scriptures have pride of place because of their inspired nature, as the divinely given revelation of God that testify to the Father's creating and saving works in his Son and Spirit. Protestants cash out this commitment to Scripture's supremacy in terms of *sola scriptura*: the Bible and the Bible alone is the sole written revelation of God by which all other sources of theology must be measured. But among the Protestant Reformers and the best of their theological heirs, this commitment to Scripture's supreme authority was never meant to reduce theology to privatized scriptural interpretation. Tradition still served an integral role in Protestant interpretation, as we will see. And among Roman Catholics, the foundational status of Scripture is plainly taught in the *Catechism of Catholic Church*: "Since therefore all that the inspired authors or sacred writers affirm should be regarded as affirmed by the Holy Spirit, we must acknowledge that the books of Scripture firmly, faithfully, and without error teach that truth which God, for the sake of our salvation, wished to see confided to the Sacred Scriptures" (1995: 107, cited from *Dei Verbum* 11).

Demonstrating reason's role in theology is one of the central burdens of the AT project. Reason functions as a kind of negative test for the truth of a theological proposition.[2] Logical coherence does not necessarily prove the truth of a theological argument, but logical *incoherence* would count against its truth. Likewise, conceptual clarity does not necessarily demonstrate the preferability of a theological model, but conceptual ambiguity might be a strike against it. Scripture and reason work hand in hand precisely because theology is, as John Webster argued, "an activity of the created intellect, judged,

---

[1] It is not my intention to enter into intramural debates among Wesleyans about the quadrilateral. As a Baptist theologian, I find the quadrilateral a helpful rubric for thinking about Protestant theological method more generally, regardless of its provenance.

[2] This use of reason corresponds to what Paul Helm calls "procedural reason," as opposed to "substantive reason," which sees reason alone as capable of delivering truths about reality (1997: 5-6). Crisp points out that AT has aspects of both uses of reason within its purview (2009b: 35).

reconciled, redeemed, and sanctified through the redemptive works of the Son and the Spirit" (2008: 733). Human reason is a divine gift, which was corrupted but not obliterated by the fall into sin and which is being renewed by the saving activity of God. Christian experience, as well, has a role to play in the theological task, not so much as a source of theology but as the stage, so to speak, on which theology carries out its speaking and acting role. There is a sense in which Christian doctrine is demanded by Christian experience, in that Christianity is primarily an encounter, enabled by the person of the Holy Spirit, with the person of the Incarnate Son, who reveals to believers the person of the Father. Thus, doctrine seeks to give an account of the God we meet in conversion to Christ. But then doctrine returns once again to experience as the loving response to the fundamental beliefs expressed in the church's doctrinal affirmations. Which brings us then to the role of tradition in the theologian's work. The term "tradition"derives from the Latin *tradere*, which means to hand over or to deliver. Appeal to the apostolic tradition finds an early exemplar in the great second-century father, Irenaeus, who viewed the traditions handed on from the apostles and passed down through the succession of bishops as a hermeneutical key that preserves Scripture's true meaning (1997: 42).

But some terminological clarification is necessary in order to explicate precisely what is meant by the tradition of the church. Some have questioned whether or not we can meaningfully speak of *the* tradition of Christian doctrine, given the multiplicity of perspectives on offer in the history of Christian reflection. On certain doctrines, this warning is apt. What, we might ask, is the *traditional* understanding of Christ's atonement? In this case, it is perhaps better to speak of *traditions*, plural, that have sought to understand Christ's reconciling work of atonement, rather than *the* tradition, singular, that provides a definitive account. On other doctrines, however, we can detect a consensus of judgments that evince a profound consistency over time. For example, there is remarkable unanimity among Christian theologians on the core elements of the doctrine of the Trinity, from the late fourth century through the medieval and Reformation eras to the eve of modernity.[3] Yes, the conceptual terms and certain metaphysical commitments may vary, but the doctrinal judgments rendered by those varying concepts is noticeably consistent. The evangelical Methodist theologian Thomas Oden spoke of a "consensual" tradition on these matters: that is, the church as a whole, across space and time, has reached a kind of lay consensus on the cardinal doctrines of the faith (1992: xii). It is in this sense that "the tradition" serves as the *norma normata* (the ruled rule), which

---

[3] On the consistency of what we can call the "classical doctrine" of the Trinity, see Holmes (2012). Many contemporary theologians, including some analytic theologians, have sought to draw a fairly sharp distinction between the so-called Latin Trinity of the West, exemplified chiefly in St. Augustine, and the Eastern Trinity of, say, the Cappadocian Fathers. But recent patristic scholarship has demonstrated that these attempts to draw a wedge between Eastern and Western trinitarianisms are overwrought. The famous de Regnon thesis—which posits that the Western theologians began with divine unity and worked toward the personal distinctions, while the Eastern theologians began with the three persons and worked toward their unity—simply cannot be borne out by the historical evidence. Certainly there were some differences, with the filioque controversy of the medieval period serving as the principle distinction. But the consensus between East and West is more conspicuous: both regions of Christendom affirmed the absolute equality of the divine persons in the numerically singular divine essence and distinguished the persons only in terms of the eternal relations of origin. Both East and West were committed to the notion that there is only one power and will in the Godhead and that the persons are to be distinguished, not as discrete centers of consciousness and will, but only in terms of their personal modes of being in the divine essence, that is, the relations of origin. There were some differences in the metaphysical commitments of East and West, but only in a narrow sense, namely, the question of whether or not the divine essence should be considered a universal or a particular. On this last point, see Cross (2009).

is subservient to the *norma normans non normata* (the ruling rule that cannot itself be ruled) of Holy Scripture.

II. CLARIFYING THE ROLE OF TRADITION IN THE THEOLOGICAL TASK

But even if we can discern something like *the* tradition on a given doctrine, the question remains as to how this tradition ought to function in the theological task. Reformation historian Heiko Oberman suggests that there are at least two major understandings of tradition on offer in the history of Christian theology. According to one view, which Oberman calls "Tradition I," tradition is seen as an exegetical guide to interpreting the singular revelation of God in Holy Scripture (1966: 58). Tradition, on this view, does not so much give the church new doctrines, beyond what is taught in Scripture, which the faithful are now bound to believe, as it reveals to the church the authoritative way in which Scriptures are to be interpreted. This view seems to be the primary understanding of tradition in the earliest centuries, and it is certainly the view of the Protestant Reformers. The Magisterial Reformation doctrine of *sola scriptura* did not cast off all traditional claims in favor of a radically individualized form of interpretation. The Reformers were not, for example, theological iconoclasts on the doctrines of the Trinity and the Incarnation. They were, in the main, theological conservatives on these cardinal Christian doctrines, despite their sometimes heated polemic against "popes and councils." And in their writings, the Reformers made copious appeals to influential church fathers and conciliar opinions. But they viewed these traditional ways of interpreting Scripture as subordinate to the supreme authority of Scripture itself.

Oberman's second category, which he calls (cleverly enough) "Tradition II," sees the tradition of the church in a different manner. On Tradition II, the tradition is seen as a second source of revelation alongside Scripture (Oberman 1966: 58). Even if Scripture retains its pride of place, there are subsequent doctrines, perhaps only hinted at in Scripture, that are taught by the church's magisterium and which are equally binding on the faithful. This view was the understanding of tradition under the crosshairs of the Reformers' critique of the late medieval church. Doctrines that cannot be clearly demonstrated from Scripture (such as, according to Protestants, the doctrine of purgatory or Mary's assumption to heaven) are not to be seen as binding simply because they belong to the church's tradition. Tradition, in such cases, is no longer playing a ministerial role in the task of biblical exegesis but is giving new doctrine, as it were, yielding a two-source theory of divine revelation. Contemporary Roman Catholics may complain that this two-source view of revelation is not the position to be found in the documents of the Second Vatican Council or in the *Catechism of the Catholic Church*, which speaks of "one source" in two "modes of transmission," but this debate need not deter us. The important point for our purposes is to note that this second category, Tradition II, is not the only one that has been defended in the history of Christian thought. It is possible to appeal to a robust understanding of tradition as a derivative authority for Christian theology, without surrendering the Reformation commitment to Scripture's supreme and underived authority as the written revelation of God.[4]

---

[4]Reformed theologian Keith Mathison has quipped, following the assessment of the Anabaptists by Alister McGrath, that many evangelicals effectively practice "Tradition 0."

But what exactly is the "tradition" to which Christian theologians, including analytic theologians, might appeal in their work? We have already distinguished between certain doctrines that lend themselves more readily to a consensus view in the Christian tradition and other doctrines that are more open-ended. But with all doctrines, there is a necessity to distinguish further what we might consider a hierarchy of authorities that constitute the tradition(s) as a whole.[5] At the top of this hierarchy, underneath the ultimate authority of Scripture, are, first, the *ecumenical creeds and councils*. The three creeds recognized as ecumenical—the Apostles', the Nicene, and the so-called Athanasian Creeds—summarize the consensual tradition of the Christian church on the chief doctrines of the Trinity and the Incarnation of the Son of God for the salvation of the world. The seven ecumenical councils give fuller shape to this consensual tradition and represent the essentials of the faith of the undivided church bequeathed from the patristic era.

Embedded within these Trinitarian and Christological guidelines are, second, certain *classical doctrines* that are implied by them. Revisionist analytic theologians may balk at this suggestion, but I believe that the doctrines associated with classical Christian theism are either necessary consequences or else presuppositions of the creedal/conciliar pronouncements. At least historically, it is very difficult to conceive of the classical doctrines of the eternal generation of the Son, the consubstantiality of the divine persons, or the hypostatic union without accounting for the key role that doctrines like divine simplicity and divine impassibility played in their historical development. To wrench these classical doctrines from the development of Trinitarian and Christological orthodoxy is to dehistoricize the conciliar doctrines to such a degree that they become unintelligible.[6] So it seems to be the case that espousing creedal/conciliar Christian doctrine also commits one to a certain set of classical doctrines implied in it. Something similar could be said for the doctrines of sin and grace, which (despite their various understandings in the history of doctrine) are presupposed by creedal lines such as "for us and for our salvation" and "I believe ... in the forgiveness of sins." Additionally, the conciliar doctrines provide at least some basic parameters for analytic theologians wishing to explicate the doctrine of theological anthropology for today. Even, say, materialist anthropologies must give some account of how these formulations fit with Chalcedon's insistence upon the Son's assumption of a "body and a reasonable soul."[7]

Third, on a more local level, church and denominational *confessions of faith* further delimit the parameters within which analytic theologians ought to exercise their craft. These confessions often reiterate the essentials of the creedal/conciliar faith but spell out further the doctrinal distinctives of the ecclesiastical bodies that adopt them and should serve as guardrails for individual theologians operating in those ecclesial contexts. So, for example, a Reformed analytic theologian seeking to spell out the dynamics of divine providence or of human freedom would do so within the constraints of the Westminster Standards, to the degree that those confessional symbols are accepted as binding in his or her ecclesiastical context. These confessional constraints do not rise to the level of creedal

---

[5] The hierarchy detailed here bears resemblance to the ones offered by Thomas McCall and Oliver Crisp. The only significant difference is that I have had more explicit a middle category between creeds and confessions, namely, the classical doctrines implied in the creedal and conciliar formulations. See McCall (2015) and Crisp (2009a).
[6] So, a trinitarian model that simply dispenses with divine simplicity begs the question as to whether or not it is *the* doctrine of the Trinity as it was historically formulated. For similar observations about the dangers of dehistoricizing Christian doctrines, see Branson (2018).
[7] Oliver Crisp explores the possibility of developing a materialist anthropology in light of classical Christology (2009a: 137–54).

commitments; other Christian traditions are welcome to work out Christian doctrine in their own contexts. But they do serve as binding guardrails for those who have accepted their ecclesial authority.[8]

Fourth, we can speak of certain *theological luminaries* as comprising part of the tradition of Christian theology. The great works of Athanasius, the Cappadocian Fathers, Augustine, Maximus the Confessor, Anselm, Thomas Aquinas, Martin Luther, and John Calvin are not on the same plane of authority as creeds, classical doctrines, or confessions. Quite obviously one could not simply embrace all of the theologoumena from all of these authors *in toto*, since, given their divergences, such an attempt would produce inconsistencies. But the theological giants of the past have, in many ways, set the agenda for the ongoing theological conversations that comprise the Christian theological task, and contemporary analytic theologians would be remiss to ignore their contribution. On this front, it is a welcome sign that so much recent analytic theology has been engaged in what Webster (2007) called "theologies of retrieval."

III. TRADITION IN ANALYTIC THEOLOGY

So, with these categories of tradition in place, we are now in a position to consider how analytic theologians have interacted with the role of tradition in their various works. Many of the programmatic statements about the analytic project have taken head-on the potential objection that theology in the analytic mode runs the risk of dehistoricizing the doctrines under analysis. McCall admits that this criticism of analytic theology is sometimes warranted: "Analytic theologians may be quick to isolate a particular text and try to break it down to find the real 'core' of the doctrine, or they may find the historical context of little relevance to the sober truth" (McCall 2015: 84). Another practitioner of AT, Beau Branson, draws attention to two different approaches to the AT task: (1) the "virtue approach," which distills the supposedly essential core of a doctrine, treating it as a kind of "metaphysical puzzle," and seeks to demonstrate that it has certain theoretical virtues, principally the virtue of being logically consistent, and (2) the "historical approach," which gives primary consideration to the doctrine as it was historically developed (Branson 2018). For Branson, part of the problem with the first approach is that it begs the question regarding whether or not the distilled version of the doctrine is in fact *the* doctrine, as it was historically conceived. Absent some convincing "consistency transferring relation" (2018: 10) between the doctrine under analysis and *the* historic doctrine, the analysis becomes dehistoricized and thus undermines its intended logical aims. Indeed, some analytic theologians, such as Dale Tuggy (2003), have happily admitted that the historical contexts within which Christian doctrines were developed are more of an encumbrance to theological analysis than a help. Tuggy writes that a "focus on the most difficult philosophical problems" facing the doctrine of the Trinity are "often obscured by historical concerns" (2003: 165). So, he contents himself with focusing on the problems of "inconsistency, intelligibility, and poor fit with the Bible," rather than carefully attending to, say, the arguments of the all-important fourth century, when the key tenets of the historic doctrine of the Trinity were hammered out (165–6).

---

[8] This does not mean that minority reports within a confessional tradition should be silenced. For a nuanced example of retrieval in the Reformed tradition, see Crisp (2014).

But if certain AT practitioners have either self-consciously bracketed out historical considerations or else neglected their significance, McCall maintains that there is nothing about the analytic project that necessitates this ahistorical approach, and he notes many "happy exceptions" to the criticism (2015: 29).[9] McCall spells out an approach to theological authority similar to the one defended above. Scripture is the "norming norm" of Christian theology, but underneath its ultimate authority stands the interpretive guides of the creeds, theological confessions, and "prominent theologians of the church catholic" (88–9). Similarly, Crisp has spoken of a "weighting" of theological authorities with Scripture at the top of the hierarchy and creeds, confessions, and individual theologians cascading from there (2009a: 9–20). Crisp conceives of the analytic project as an iteration of the venerable Christian tradition of faith seeking understanding (2009b: 51).

While particular analytic theologians may have stricter or looser commitments to the authority of certain traditional doctrines, there is nothing intrinsic to the analytic project that necessitates a more revisionist approach to the Christian tradition. An analytic theologian is within her rights to accept a particular conciliar doctrine by faith and from that posture of faith to seek to demonstrate and to explicate its logical coherence by the tools of the analytic method. Not that AT is primarily apologetic in its aims; instead, AT may serve as an exercise—even a holy and prayerful exercise—of created and redeemed reason to explore the metaphysical dimensions of Christian belief. But neither should AT projects of a more "conservative" orientation be seen as simply repeating the theological findings of the Christian past. Retrieval is not repristination. AT also aims to be theology in a constructive mode, analyzing the formulations of the past with humility and deference, but at times seeking creative new ways of accounting for the metaphysical and epistemological commitments implied in Christian doctrine. Traditions are dynamic, not static. As Alasdair MacIntyre has defined it, a tradition is "an historically extended, socially embodied argument, and an argument precisely in part about the goods which constitute that tradition" (1981: 222). Thus, deference to tradition need not be interpreted as some kind of reactionary *traditionalism*.[10] Still, analytic theologians committed for theological reasons to the *sensus fidelium*, the notion that God has providentially illumined the collective mind of the universal church, will wish to frame any new proposals as developments from within rather than departures from the Christian tradition.

In another apologia for AT, Abraham casts the discipline as a particular way of doing systematic theology, one "attuned to the deployment of the skills, resources, and virtues of analytic philosophy" (2009: 59). Framing AT in terms of Christian systematic theology quite obviously places the discipline in direct conversation with the tradition of the church, since the sources and methods of systematic theology and the loci themselves have taken shape in the context of Christian history. In Abraham's terms, systematic theology—including by implication systematic theology done in an analytic mode—is made necessary by the fundamental Christian experiences of baptism and conversion.

---

[9] Perhaps this phrase, "happy exceptions," concedes too much. Indeed, we should note that many of the early practitioners of AT were historians of philosophy, who wrote seminal works on various medieval figures. We might think of Eleonore Stump's work on Thomas Aquinas, Marilyn McCord Adams's work on William Ockham, and Richard Cross's work on Duns Scotus.

[10] Jaroslav Pelikan's quip is worth remembering: "Tradition is the living faith of the dead, traditionalism is the dead faith of the living. And, I suppose I should add, it is traditionalism that gives tradition such a bad name" (1984: 65).

The creeds of the church emerged in a context of wrestling with the implications of Christian faith and worship. As such, they constitute the nonnegotiable parameters within which AT must operate, if it is to be considered meaningfully Christian. "If the deep truths of the Gospel and the central elements of the Nicene Creed are constitutive of the Christian faith, then much modern and contemporary theology is really the invention of various forms of post-Christian religion" (Abraham 2009: 57). Abraham, like Crisp, sees the AT project as an exercise in faith seeking understanding. As such, it begins "by standing inside the circle of Christian faith and seeking to articulate the deep contours of the vision of God that is to be found in the Church" (60). In this way, AT can serve as an aid to the church: "We need the help of analytic theology to do justice to the God we meet in the worship of the Church" (61). So far from standing in opposition to the tradition of the church, AT, according to Abraham, is well positioned to defend the tradition. For Abraham, one of the virtues of analytic philosophy is that it can be utilized to clarify and argue for "the truth of the Christian Gospel taken up in the great themes of the creeds of the Church" (69).

If McCall, Crisp, and Abraham are in any sense representative of the discipline of AT, it simply cannot be argued that the AT project is by some logical necessity antithetical to the Christian tradition. Even if they are "happy exceptions," to use McCall's phrase, they are not insignificant ones nor the only ones. In addition to the historically sensitive scholars McCall cites in his 2015 introduction to AT (including Richard Cross, Eleonore Stump, Jeffrey Bower, and J. T. Paasch), one could add more recent AT works, such as Timothy Pawl's impressive two volumes in defense of conciliar Christology and its entailments (Pawl 2016 and 2019).[11]

Pawl's work draws attention to one final clarification needed on the role of tradition in AT. Even for analytic theologians committed to some level of deference to Christian tradition, there is a spectrum of views on how far this commitment goes. Drawing on an analogy to "strict" and "loose" confessional subscription, McCall suggests that there are stricter and looser commitments to Christian tradition among analytic theologians. We might also conceive of this spectrum in terms of a traditional *maximalism* and a traditional *minimalism*. Pawl's work certainly constitutes a version of the former, in that he accepts the entirety of the seven ecumenical councils (including all of their canons and accepted documents and letters) as authoritative in his attempt to demonstrate the logical consistency of the church's two-natures Christology. Other AT projects dealing with the doctrine of the incarnation take a more minimalist approach. Here, we might think of Garett DeWeese's rejection of the classical dyothelite (two-wills) understanding of the incarnation or Peter van Inwagen's attempt to defend a materialist understanding of human persons in light of the ancient creeds (DeWeese 2007; van Inwagen 1995). These minimalist analytic theologians are not necessarily rejecting the important role that tradition plays in the development of Christian doctrine, as Tuggy does. Instead, they are often attempting to show that certain entailments of Christian doctrine that we might assume at first blush are not actually borne out by the doctrine as such. In some cases, perhaps especially among Protestant analytic theologians, who may attribute less binding

---

[11]It should be noted that there is a difference between analytic theologians committed to taking the *history* of doctrine seriously and those committed to embracing that history as a norm for theology, that is, as the *tradition*. Some historically sensitive analytic theologians may be quite revisionist in their own constructive proposals. But certainly any AT practitioners committed to the tradition will also of necessity be concerned with the historical development of doctrine.

authority to creeds and councils in favor of some form of biblicism, the minimalist's methodology may be an example of cherry-picking. So, for example, analytic theologians who reject dyothelitism seem to privilege the first four ecumenical councils ending with Chalcedon, and thus sense a lesser burden to defend the Sixth Ecumenical Council.

In short, there seems to be a spectrum of approaches to the history of doctrine in AT. Some take a maximalist view, treating doctrinal development as a true norm for theology (such as Pawl). Others engage the history of doctrine and even show some deference to it but feel less committed to embracing it *en toto* (such as DeWeese). Still others show less concern with the history of doctrine and may even see it as an encumbrance to the AT task (such as Tuggy). At times, the lines between the minimalist approach and the ahistorical approach can become blurred, especially when conciliar judgments are summarily dismissed for failing some other privileged test, such as the clear teaching of Scripture.[12]

IV. CONCLUSION

Some AT projects have either consciously or unconsciously given insufficient weight to the place of tradition in the theological task. But not all. And among the "happy exceptions" are many of the leaders in the field. A spate of historically sensitive, analytic treatments of Christian doctrine have been published in recent years, which ought to allay the fears of the many critics of the movement. Classic Christian systematic theology has sought to account not only for the foundational status of Holy Scripture in the church's theological reflection but also for the role of tradition, reason, and, experience as interpretive guides. Much of modern theology lost sight of the traditions of the church in favor of theological iconoclasm, innovation, and revisionism. But in more recent years, the church has witnessed several movements from across the theological spectrum that are seeking for a greater rootedness in the Christian tradition. These theologies of retrieval include movements as diverse as the *Nouvelle Théologie* within Roman Catholicism and *ressourcement* efforts within evangelicalism. Some analytic theologians have been among those engaged in theological retrieval as well, which again should be a welcome sign to the critics accusing the movement of an ahistorical bent. If AT is to be constructive theology, then it may need to question, critique, or seek to advance upon certain traditional formulations. But if AT is to remain a serious player in the grand historical sweep of Christian theology, including its more recent gestures toward retrieval, then hewing closer to the maximalist approach to tradition seems the more promising course.

References

Abraham, W. J. (2009), "Systematic Theology as Analytic Theology," in O. D. Crisp and M. C. Rea (eds.), *Analytic Theology: New Essays in the Philosophy of Theology*, 54–9, Oxford: Oxford University Press.

Branson, B. (2018), "Ahistoricity in Analytic Theology," *American Catholic Philosophical Quarterly*, 92 (2): 195–224.

Catechism of the Catholic Church (1995), New York: Image.

---

[12] But, of course this scriptural test may beg the question regarding the particular doctrine in question, since many of the voices from the Christian past were also committed to a high view of Scripture.

Crisp, O. D. (2009a), *God Incarnate: Explorations in Christology*, London: T&T Clark.
Crisp, O. D. (2009b), "On Analytic Theology," in O. D. Crisp and M. C. Rea (eds), *Analytic Theology: New Essays in the Philosophy of Theology*, 33–53, Oxford: Oxford University Press.
Crisp, O. D. (2014), *Deviant Calvinism: Broadening Reformed Theology*, Minneapolis: Fortress.
Cross, R. (2009), "Two Models of the Trinity?," in M. Rea (ed.), *Oxford Readings in Philosophical Theology, Volume 1: Trinity, Incarnation, and Atonement*, 107–26, Oxford: Oxford University Press.
DeWeese, G. (2007), "One Person, Two Natures: Two Metaphysical Models of the Incarnation," in F. Sanders and K. Issler (eds.), *Jesus in Trinitarian Perspective*, 114–53, Nashville: B&H Academic.
Helm, P. (1997), *Faith and Understanding*, Grand Rapids: Eerdmans.
Holmes, S. R. (2012), *The Quest for the Trinity: The Doctrine of God in Scripture, History, and Modernity*, Downers Grove, IL: InterVarsity Press.
Irenaeus. (1997), *On the Apostolic Preaching*, trans. J. Behr, Crestwood: St Vladimir's Seminary Press.
MacIntyre, A. (1981), *After Virtue: A Study in Moral Theory*, 2nd ed., Notre Dame, IN: Notre Dame University Press.
McCall, T. H. (2015), *An Invitation to Analytic Christian Theology*, Downers Grove, IL: IVP Academic.
Oberman, H. A. (1966), *Forerunners of the Reformation: The Shape of Late Medieval Thought*, Cambridge: James Clarke.
Oden, T. C. (1992), *Classic Christianity: A Systematic Theology*, New York: Harper Collins.
Outler, A. (1985), "The Wesleyan Quadrilateral in John Wesley," *Wesleyan Theological Journal*, 20 (1): 7–18.
Pawl, T. (2016), *In Defense of Conciliar Christology: A Philosophical Essay*, Oxford: Oxford University Press.
Pawl, T. (2019) *In Defense of Extended Conciliar Christology: A Philosophical Essay*, Oxford: Oxford University Press.
Pelikan, J. (1984), *The Vindication of Tradition*, New Haven: Yale University Press.
Tuggy, D. (2003), "The Unfinished Business of Trinitarian Theorizing," *Religious Studies*, 39 (2): 165–83.
van Inwagen, P. (1995), "Dualism and Materialism: Athens and Jerusalem?," *Faith and Philosophy*, 12 (4): 475–88.
Webster, J. (2007), "Theologies of Retrieval," in J. Webster, K. Tanner, and I. Torrance (eds.), *The Oxford Handbook of Systematic Theology*, 583–99, Oxford: Oxford University Press.
Webster, J. (2008), "Biblical Reasoning," *Anglican Theological Review*, 90 (4): 733–51.

CHAPTER FIVE

Analytic Theology and Philosophy of Science: Toward an All-Encompassing Theory of God, the World, and Human Life

BENEDIKT PAUL GÖCKE

Analytic theology is theology that is based on the assumption that God revealed Himself to humanity, and that deploys the methods of analytic philosophy to establish an all-encompassing theological theory of God, the world, and human life. Philosophy of science analyzes the presuppositions, aims, limits, methods, and the historicity of a scientific understanding of reality. Analytic theology and philosophy of science therefore refer to each other: on the one hand, because it is the aim of analytic theology to establish an all-encompassing theory of God, the world, and human life, analytic theology needs to engage in philosophy of science to account for this possibility. On the other hand, because the presuppositions, aims, limits, and methods of a scientific understanding of reality may well depend on metaphysical and theological presuppositions, philosophy of science should take account of analytic theology. I argue that based on recent debates in the philosophy of science, the attempt to develop an all-encompassing theological theory of God, the world, and human life that deploys the means of analytic philosophy not only coheres with the historicity, presuppositions, aims, limits, and methods of science but also is a genuine task of the scientific account of reality itself.

I. WHAT IS ANALYTIC THEOLOGY?

Analytic theology is theology that deploys the methods of analytic philosophy. To clarify the concept of analytic theology, in what follows, I will clarify the purpose of theology and I will clarify the methods of analytic philosophy.

I.1 What Is the Purpose of Theology?

The purpose of theology is to provide an all-encompassing metaphysical and theological theory of God, the world, and human life.[1] An all-encompassing theological theory of God, the world, and human life is a metaphysical system of theology that, by including non-epistemic values and norms, provides epistemologically reflected answers to philosophical and theological questions concerning the existence and essence of God, the fundamental nature of the world, and the purpose and goal of human life. In contrast to secular attempts to provide an all-encompassing metaphysical theory, theology is based on the assumption that, in addition to reason and experience, divine revelation and its understanding in the tradition of the church is an essential source of knowledge, where divine revelation is understood as leading to insights into the fundamental nature of reality that unaided human reason is incapable of establishing itself.[2] Theology thus claims that understanding God, the world, and human life, based on reason, experience, and a particular understanding of divine revelation, is understanding them adequately. An all-encompassing theological theory, on its own understanding, therefore, is the right perspective from which to engage God, the world, and human life; it unlocks truths and insights into the nature of reality that cannot be adequately seen from another perspective.[3]

Although the goal of theology is to provide a single all-encompassing theory, theology as a discipline *sui generis* is constituted of several theological subdisciplines. Each of the theological disciplines has its own domain of discourse but nevertheless is essentially related to the other theological disciplines and contributes to the overall theological theory. For instance, in the case of Roman Catholicism, the Apostolic Constitution *Sapientia Christiana* specifies the following theological disciplines: "Holy Scripture: Introduction and Exegesis; ... fundamental theology ...; ... dogmatic theology; ... Moral theology and spirituality; ... pastoral theology; ... Liturgy; ... church history, patristics and archeology; ... Church Law." From a systematic point of view, however, the most important theological disciplines are dogmatic theology and fundamental theology. Their purpose is to establish and formulate the all-encompassing theological theory by uniting and synthesizing the insights of the various other theological disciplines. In this respect, the task of dogmatic theology is to show, *ad intra*, the coherence of theology as a discipline *sui generis* by showing that the insights of all theological disciplines form a coherent theory that is faithful to Sacred Scripture and the tradition of the church. Correspondingly, it is the task of fundamental theology, *ad extra*, that is, in dialogue with philosophy and the natural sciences, to show that there is warrant that the all-encompassing theological theory is true.

---

[1] Because God is both the proper object of theology and a metaphysical entity, a theological account of reality *eo ipso* is a metaphysical account of reality. Van Inwagen (2002: 1) is right in arguing that "metaphysics is the study of ultimate reality." As Chalmers (2009: 1) states, "metaphysics is concerned with the foundations of reality." According to Loux (2002: 10–11), "traditional metaphysicians ... insist that we manage to think and talk about things—things as they really are and not just things as they figure in the stories we tell." Cf. also Göcke (2019c) and Göcke (2019d).
[2] The classical understanding of revelation is presupposed here in which there cannot be a contradiction between divine revelation and reason. See Morerod (2016: 13). Cf. also Göcke 2019a.
[3] This is in harmony with Wolterstorff's (2005: 91–92) advice to theologians:

> Do not be ersatz philosophers, do not be ersatz cultural theorists, do not be ersatz anything. Be genuine theologians. Be sure-footed in philosophy ... But then: be theologians ... What we need to hear from you is how things look when seen in light of the triune God ... who creates and sustains us, who redeems us, and who will bring this frail and fallen, though yet glorious, humanity and cosmos to consummation.

Together, dogmatic and fundamental theology thus have to show (1) that the suggested all-encompassing theological theory is hermeneutically faithful to Sacred Scripture, (2) that nothing in the natural sciences contradicts theological teachings, (3) that nothing in philosophy contradicts theological teachings, (4) that the insights of the natural sciences and of philosophy in fact cohere with theological doctrine and thus with hermeneutically reflected divine revelation, (5) that the theological theory in question provides the best systematic unification and coherent ultimate explanation of the insights of the natural sciences, and (6) that because of (1) to (5) there is a rational claim to be made that the theological theory at hand is true. Dogmatic and fundamental theology hence have to show that the divinely inspired theological perspective on reality provides the best system of knowledge into which all the sciences can be synthesized and understood as part of the all-encompassing system of theology. That theology, in principle, can succeed in this task, is expressed in the claim that theology is the queen of the sciences—*regina scientiae*.[4]

The purpose of theology as a discipline *sui generis* is to establish an all-encompassing theological theory of God, the world, and human life that, based on reason, experience, and divine revelation, accounts for the unity of the sciences. However, such a theory, and the development thereof, by no means must be misunderstood as an end in itself, that is, as an exercise in pure θεωρέειν. Instead, the purpose of theology is to develop an all-encompassing theological theory *because* this is an essential contribution to the good life and to the salvation of souls. Far from being in opposition to practical concerns, theory is the *conditio sine qua non* for the good life. The purpose of theological θεωρία therefore, ultimately, is found in its implications for the πρᾶξις of the Christian life. The purpose of theology hence is to establish an all-encompassing theory that is both faithful to Sacred Scripture, philosophy, and the natural sciences and, only because of this, is able to provide warranted orientation for the life of the faithful that contributes to the salvation of souls.

I.2 *What Is Analytic Philosophy?*

Analytic philosophy is based on the assumption of a legitimate division between the genesis and the plausibility of a philosophical position, with a concomitant emphasis on the greater relevance of the plausibility of philosophical theses.[5] A first feature of analytic philosophy therefore consists in this: it is primarily concerned with the truth or rational acceptability of philosophical theses.[6] An analysis of the truth or rational acceptability of a philosophical thesis has to be informed by historical developments only in so far as it is necessary to arrive at a systematically clear formulation of a thesis. The reason is that further knowledge regarding the genesis of a philosophical thesis is strictly irrelevant to its truth or rational acceptability.[7] A second feature of analytic philosophy consists in its

---

[4] Cf. *Veritatis Gaudium*.
[5] By the concept of the genesis of a philosophical thesis I refer to the diachronic process which leads to a theory's development and formulation. The analysis of the genesis of a philosophical thesis makes it possible to explain why a thesis was developed by its representatives and for what reasons it was understood in which way. The concept of the validity of a philosophical thesis expresses its claim to truth or rational acceptability. The analysis of the validity of a philosophical thesis is interested in the grounds that speak systematically for or against the truth or rational acceptability of a thesis.
[6] Since the 1950s, the concept of analytic philosophy has been used to denote the world's leading philosophical research program. See Beaney (2013a: 3): "Over the course of the twentieth century analytic philosophy developed into the dominant philosophical tradition in the English-speaking world, and it is now steadily growing in the non-English-speaking world."
[7] See Beaney (2013b: 58). See also Frege (1884: VII).

executing the analysis of the truth or rational acceptability of a thesis in at least three stages. The first priority of analytic philosophy is achieving the greatest possible conceptual precision. It tries to analyze the concepts which are decisive for the question at hand, by providing necessary and sufficient conditions for the fulfillment of those concepts, in a clear, comprehensible manner. Based on conceptual analysis, analytic philosophy tries, in a second step, to formulate as precisely as possible philosophical theses which it understands as claims to truth, and therefore as factual or normative theses about reality and our place in it. Based on the clarification of the concepts involved, it attempts to clarify as clearly as possible what a particular philosophical thesis asserts about reality and our place in it, which other theses are sufficient for the thesis examined, and what the truth or falsehood of this thesis logically implies. After conceptual analysis, and the clarification of the philosophical thesis under examination, the work of the analytic philosopher turns to the core of analytic philosophy: the argument. The argument is the decisive instance of the work of the analytic philosopher for, in an argument, either the reasons that speak for or against the truth or rational acceptability of a thesis are comprehensibly formulated or else the alleged best explanation of the truth of a set of premises is stated explicitly, in order to make possible, in addition to the desired conceptual precision, the greatest possible argumentative and explanatory transparency.[8]

Because there are two ways that premises of an argument can transfer truth or rational acceptability to the conclusion of an argument, and because the alleged best explanation of a set of premises traditionally is understood to be a thesis the truth of which would entail the truth of the premises and in this sense would explain their truth, there are three corresponding kinds of argument: deductive, inductive, and abductive arguments. Deductive arguments on the one hand, and inductive and abductive arguments on the other, differ in terms of the logical relation between the truth of the premises and the truth of the conclusion. Whereas for a deductively valid argument it is impossible that the premises are true and the conclusion false, inductive and abductive arguments can have true premises but a false conclusion. Although it may seem that inductive and abductive arguments thus defined are of little use, they are very useful whenever a general conclusion has to be derived from a finite set of data, as in the case of inductive arguments, or when the best explanation for the truth of a set of premises is looked for, as in the case of abductive arguments.[9]

In the analysis of deductive and inductive arguments, on the one hand, premises are given as reasons for the truth of a conclusion, before the logical form of the argument is examined by analyzing the relation between the alleged truth of the premises and the truth of the conclusion. The analysis of the validity of deductive and inductive arguments therefore examines whether, based on the assumption of the truth of the premises, it is reasonable to proceed to the truth of the conclusion. The analysis of the soundness of deductive and inductive arguments further asks whether the premises are true and how their truth may be epistemologically captured. In the case of a valid argument, its very validity provides the reasons the truth of the premises entails the truth of the conclusion. Whereas the truth of the premises of deductively valid arguments entails the truth of the conclusion, the analysis of inductive arguments needs to specify which evidence is enough evidence to bestow rational acceptability to the conclusion of the argument.[10]

---

[8] See Parsons (2013: 247–8).
[9] See, e.g., the entry on abduction in the *Stanford Encyclopedia of Philosophy* by Douven (2017).
[10] Often Bayes' theorem is used to specify the probability of a particular hypothesis in light of the evidence. For further discussion, see Swinburne (2002).

The analysis of abductive arguments, on the other hand, is concerned with the question whether the suggested conclusion really is the best explanation of the truth of the premises, and therefore has to provide an account of what explanation consists in, and with the question whether there are reasons for the truth of the suggested explanation independent from the fact that its truth would explain the truth of the premises.[11]

Against the background of this analysis, the defining characteristic of analytic philosophy consequently consists in stressing the analysis of the truth or rational acceptability of philosophical theses using the three steps: (1) conceptual analysis, (2) thesis specification, and (3) analysis of the philosophical strength of deductive, inductive, and abductive arguments. Although, until the middle of the last century, analytic philosophy was empirical, materialistic, or influenced by the linguistic turn, according to which philosophical problems are merely linguistic illusions, today it is no longer *de facto* true that the concept of analytic philosophy is used to characterize certain positions, but a method, and a style for approaching genuine philosophical questions.[12]

I.3 What Is Analytic Theology?

Based on experience, reason, and divine revelation, analytic theology attempts to establish an all-encompassing theological theory of God, the world, and human life to contribute to the salvation of souls. In order to develop this theory, analytic theology deploys the tools of analytic philosophy: It strives for clear and precise conceptual analysis, which it uses to formulate clear descriptive and normative theses about the existence and essence of God, the fundamental nature of the world, and the purpose and goal of human life. It then strives for the formulation of sound deductive, and strong inductive, and abductive arguments to justify the truth and rational acceptability of its account of reality. It uses reason, experience, and a hermeneutic of divine revelation to show that together these sources of human knowledge provide the most adequate perspective on the nature of God, the world, and human life that is able to synthesize the insights of the humanities and the natural sciences into a coherent whole.[13] Analytic theology, by its very nature, therefore is interdisciplinary and must engage the humanities and the sciences.

II. WHAT IS PHILOSOPHY OF SCIENCE?

Philosophy of science is the reflection on the presuppositions, aims, limits, methods, and the historicity of science. Although "science" in English is often understood narrowly as referring to the natural sciences only, it is more adequate to understand "science" analogous to the German "Wissenschaft," which refers both to the natural sciences and the humanities.[14]

---

[11]As Gensler (2017: 106) says,

> The general form of the inference to the best explanation raises some issues. On what grounds should we evaluate one explanation "better" than another? Should we accept the *best possible* explanation (even though no one may yet have thought of it) or the *best currently available* explanation (even though none of the current explanations may be very good)? And why is the best explanation most likely to be true?

[12]See Beaney (2013a: 26); cf. Papineau (2012).
[13]For more on this, see Crisp (2011: 38), McCall (2015: 178), and Arcadi (2016: 5).
[14]Although to many it seems obvious that a scientific approach to reality is "better" than a nonscientific approach, there is no unanimity about what "science" actually is. The following considerations therefore cannot claim universality but can only aim to specify a general concept of science that is both systematically interesting and

II. 1 What Is the Aim of Science?

The aim of science understood as "Wissenschaft" is to provide reliable theoretical and practical orientation concerning the nature of reality and our place in it, based on our pre-theoretical experience of reality. Science provides *theoretical* orientation because it explains what is given in our experience of reality in terms of not necessarily observable entities that account for the fact that we experience reality as we do. Science provides *practical* orientation because the knowledge it generates enables us to act in the world in a controlled and reliable way. Practical orientation is a form of art, that is, τέχνη. Theoretical science and applied science therefore are two sides of the same coin.

Science provides theoretical and practical orientation in the form of scientific theories. A scientific theory, roughly, is a system of propositions some of which function as the *explanans* and some of which are the *explanandum* of the theory in question. The *explanans* of scientific theories is what provides answers to questions about the respective domain of discourse, for instance, its structure, its causal history and development, or its metaphysical constitution. Depending on the domain of discourse, scientific theories account for the past, the present, the future, for single events or general features of a domain of discourse.[15]

The aim of science is to develop *true* theories where a theory is true if and only if it corresponds to the way things really are (cf. Schurz 2014: 23).[16] True theories, for conceptual reasons, provide the most reliable theoretical and practical orientation concerning reality and our place in it. The aim for truth, metaphorically, is the epistemological glue that ties science and reality together. The aim of science is reached when science provides an all-encompassing scientific theory of reality that enables optimal theoretical and practical orientation concerning the nature of reality and our place in it, where optimal orientation entails that there is no alternative theory that coheres better with our experience of reality and of our place in it.

II.2 What Are the Methods of Science?

There is no categorical difference between ordinary knowledge and scientific knowledge.[17] The methods used to justify our claims to ordinary knowledge are not different in kind from the methods used in the sciences: These are deduction, induction, and abduction. Neither are the methods to approach a particular domain of discourse to collect data and gain evidence. The difference between ordinary knowledge and scientific knowledge therefore is a relative one: A scientific approach to reality uses deductive, inductive, and abductive reasoning with greater awareness of the logical structure of these kinds of reasoning, with a greater emphasis on logical and mathematical rigor, and with more sophisticated means to collect data and evidence, to achieve a degree of argumentative precision,

---

historically adequate. Cf. Hoyningen-Huene (2013: 6): "It is no exaggeration to state that although we are familiar today with the phenomenon of science to a historically unparalleled degree, we do not really know what science is."

[15]Cf. Weingartner (1971: 38).

[16]For further discussion of the aim of science cf. Laudan (1984), van Fraassen (1980), and Reeves (2019).

[17]Cf. van Huyssteen (1999: 132): Both ordinary and scientific knowledge are subject to the following demand: "to be rational we have to believe on the basis of some form or appropriate and carefully considered evidence, which thus makes our beliefs more rational than nonrational or irrational beliefs."

systematicity, and adequacy to the data that is not needed for ordinary knowledge.[18] Although the justification of a scientific theory proceeds by deductive, inductive, or abductive reasoning, and is based on different kinds of data collection and evidence, the work of the scientist is not restricted to the use of arguments and the collection of data and evidence. Scientists also work with different heuristics to gain insights regarding the corresponding domain of discourse. For instance, thought experiments and models are heuristic means that can help to understand a domain of discourse and hence to build a scientific theory by understanding features of the model or the thought experiment that are transferred back to the domain of discourse in question. Based on different sources of knowledge and different heuristics, the scientific account of reality and our place in it thus uses deductive, inductive, and abductive reasoning to develop scientifically justified theories that explain what is identified in need of explanation. Once a theory is developed, the scientific account continuously checks whether the developed theory holds up under scrutiny when considered in light of other relevant sources of knowledge. In case a scientific theory does not correspond to reality, for instance, by failing to predict future events accurately, by failing to be adequate for new data or evidence, or by failing to account for a new *explanandum*, it will be adapted, as long as the adaption still seems reasonable to the scientific community, or overthrown, if there is an alternative theory with greater explanatory power.

II.3 *What Are the Presuppositions of Science?*

One's conceptual scheme or framework *a priori* frames the overall interpretation of reality as one experiences it. A conceptual scheme hence constitutes the core of a worldview.[19] Because a scientific account of reality is always embedded in a particular worldview and its overall interpretation of reality, the scientific account of reality and our place in it is of necessity and *a priori* determined by the overall interpretation of reality as it is provided by the worldview in which it is embedded. Hence, science does not have an epistemologically innocent eye on reality. It cannot provide an account of reality in itself, that is, as it would, epistemologically, appear to a view from nowhere. Instead, science is based on presuppositions that constitute the core of the worldview of which it is part.[20] A first presupposition that constitutes the worldview of which science is part is that our experience of reality is not self-explanatory. The world we experience is in need of explanation in terms of not necessarily observable entities that account for the fact that, relative to our conceptual scheme, we experience the world as we do. Without this presupposition, science would be superfluous. A second presupposition of science is that reality itself can adequately be grasped by scientific theories in such a way that, based on the conceptual scheme of the worldview they are part of, they actually can cohere with and correspond to reality. Without this presupposition concerning the principal intelligibility of reality, science could not account for the nature of reality. Reality has to be able to meet the scientific approach halfway. A third and related presupposition is that scientific methods and heuristics of

---

[18] I agree with Hoyningen-Huene (2013: 24): "Our thesis only asserts that given some scientific knowledge about some subject and some extra-scientific knowledge about the same subject matter, then scientific knowledge will exhibit a higher degree of systematicity." Cf. also Hoyningen-Huene (2013: 14).
[19] For further analysis of the concept of a worldview, cf. Göcke (2016) and Göcke (2018).
[20] Cf. Reeves (2019: 20): "Scientific research constructs the world as well as redescribes it and so is a kind of practical activity that bears strong affinities to other types of craft knowledge."

justifying theories, as well as our methods to collect data and to sort the evidence, are reliable methods to provide theoretical and practical orientation regarding the nature of reality and our place in it. Without this presupposition, science could not explain the reliability of its theories.[21]

II.4 What Are the Limits of Science?

Against the background of the aforementioned presuppositions of science, principal limitations regarding the ability of the scientific approach to reality can be identified. Because science is embedded and predetermined by the conceptual scheme or framework of the worldview from which it emerges, science can only provide theoretical and practical orientation concerning reality and our place in it *relative to* the conceptual scheme of the worldview in question. The scientific approach to reality therefore, regarding its logical structure, claims that *if* one assumes a particular conceptual scheme and its presuppositions concerning our experience of reality, and *if* one assumes that our sources of knowledge provide reliable information concerning reality that can be explained in scientific theories by deductive, inductive, and abductive reasoning, *then* reliable theoretical and practical orientation with respect to a particular domain of discourse is specified in the corresponding scientific theory. Science thus provides a particular perspective on reality that is already predetermined by the metaphysical presuppositions that constitute the worldview in which it is embedded.

Because of this structural feature of the scientific approach to reality, a second limitation of science is this: There may be more than one scientific theory regarding a particular domain of discourse. If a scientific theory T_1 and a scientific theory T_2 both are set to explain the same domain of discourse, then both will provide a different *explanans* for the *explanandum* that will differ in respect to the theory-relative *a priori* conceptual scheme used to account for the scientific problem in question. T_1, structurally, will claim that if one assumes particular presuppositions $P_1, \ldots, P_n$ about the domain of discourse and the methods to approach it, then conclusions $C_1, \ldots, C_n$ can be justified scientifically. Correspondingly, T_2 will claim that if one assumes particular presuppositions $Q_1, \ldots, Q_n$ about this domain of discourse and the methods to approach it, then conclusions $D_1, \ldots, D_n$ can be justified scientifically. Which theory coheres better with reality and thus provides the more reliable theoretical and practical perspective on the interpretation of our experience of reality may, *ceteris paribus*, only be seen in the long run of human history that continues to check which of these scientific theories corresponds better to reality. Although, then, the aim of science is to develop true theories, it can only provide scientific theories about our experience of reality and our place in it relative to the conceptual scheme or framework of the worldview of which they are part, where the reliability of the developed theories may only be seen in the long run of human history. Truth as the aim of science hence is a regulative idea of the scientific account to reality and our place in it.

---

[21]Koperski (2015: 26–7) refers to these presuppositions as "metatheoretic shaping principles (MSP's) of science": "This is the region where the philosophy of science and science proper blend into one another. There is no sharp line between the two. MSP's help to determine what good theories, laws, and models look like as well as how one should proceed in their discovery and development."

II.5 What Is the Historicity of Science?

Science is no natural kind, but a contingent cultural institution that might not have developed.[22] The development of science is thus a contingent historical reality. It began when humanity started to engage in philosophical reflections concerning the *αἰτία* of things and started to use intersubjectively traceable methods of justification that related empirical insights with insights of reason to provide reliable theoretical and practical orientation relative to the conceptual scheme deployed. Our predecessors made a historically and systematically astonishing discovery that increasingly reinforced relying on the scientific account of reality. This discovery was that relying on a particular perspective of experienced reality, and relative to a conceptual scheme, deductive, inductive, and abductive reasoning in fact led to theoretical and practical orientation with a degree of reliability previously unheard of. If the scientific approach to reality had not been so successful, then science as a cultural institution would have long vanished. However, although the methods and presuppositions of science have shown themselves to be reliable, the attempt to provide reliable theoretical and practical orientation concerning reality and our place in it does not, of necessity, proceed toward truth by way of linear accumulation of scientific knowledge.[23] Although some scientific theories provide an accumulation of knowledge, in so far as they are able to account for their respective domain of discourse in increasing details of explanation and prediction, this seems to be the exception rather than the rule. Instead, more often than not, the history of science is the history of new and discontinuous scientific perspectives on a particular domain of discourse, where these new perspective also can be addressed as new paradigms, research programs, or research traditions.[24] Sometimes a new perspective is elaborated because the old paradigm fails to be empirically adequate in light of new evidence, sometimes a change in the theory-relative *a priori* assumptions necessitates the development of a new scientific theory, and sometimes human beings follow their inspiration regarding how things might be better explained by a new theory. Because the historicity of science, *cum grano salis*, is no linear accumulation of scientific knowledge, but the search for the best perspective from which to understand reality and our place in it, progress in science consists in the elaboration of perspectives that lead to scientific theories with an increasing theoretical and practical reliability concerning reality and our place in it.[25] The aim of science thus is the search for the best perspective on reality and our place in it. This process, in due course of history, also can have a drawback on the conceptual scheme or framework of the worldview that provides the background assumptions on which the scientific theory in question was developed in the first place. There is the possibility that the advance of science that started based on certain assumptions of a particular worldview leads to changes in the overall interpretation of reality as we experience it.

---

[22]Cf. Harrison (2015) for further analysis.
[23]Philosophy of science therefore has to reflect on the normative implications of the concept of science as well as on the history of science. As Lakatos (1970: xx) states, "Philosophy of science without history of science is empty; history of science without philosophy of science is blind."
[24]For further discussion, see Fleck (1980), Kuhn (1996), and Lakatos (2001).
[25]Cf. Koperski (2015: 256). For further discussion, cf. Kitcher (1993).

III. TOWARD AN ALL-ENCOMPASSING THEORY OF GOD, THE WORLD, AND HUMAN LIFE

Based on the specified concept and purpose of analytic theology and the reflections on the aims, presuppositions, limits, methods, and the historicity of science, analytic theology turns out to be a scientific discipline.

III.1 Analytic Theology and Philosophy of Science

1. The aim of science: The aim of science is the aim of analytic theology. Analytic theology aims to provide the best all-encompassing scientific perspective on reality and our place in it, where the three most important features of reality are assumed to be God, the world, and human life. Analytic theology is aware that the aim of science is a regulative idea of reason.
2. The methods of science are the methods of analytic theology. Analytic theology attempts to develop an all-encompassing theological theory based on a whole variety of data and evidence and, for this reason, deploys deductive, inductive, and abductive reasoning as well as heuristic means, such as models and thought experiments.[26] Because the domain of discourse of theology as a discipline *sui generis* contains different objects of investigation—including objects of study as diverse as God, the universe, rites, models, normative texts, historical texts, buildings, artefacts, the human person, and so forth, it operates with a huge variety of scientific methods. For instance, theology uses philological and hermeneutical methods to analyze the proper understanding of God's revelation as witnessed by the authors of the Holy Bible understood as *norma normans non normata*. The investigation of the history of the Church deploys methods of historical studies; the analysis of Christianity's impact on society operates with methods also found in the social sciences, and the discussion of the right form of Catechesis deploys methods of education science.[27]
3. Analytic theology is fully aware of the presuppositions regarding the necessary conditions for the possibility of science. It does not aim or claim to provide an all-encompassing theological theory from the point of nowhere but based on the perspective of Christian faith. It aims to develop its all-encompassing perspective relative to the conceptual scheme of Christian faith and assumes (but also: argues) that a hermeneutically reflected account of divine revelation as described in Sacred Scripture is a warranted source of knowledge in addition to empirical, social, or *a priori* knowledge. In fact, analytic theology has the resources to justify the metaphysical presuppositions of science—that reality is open to scientific investigation—by pointing out that these presuppositions in fact are due to God's intention to create a reliable world for human beings to live in.[28]
4. Analytic theology, in its attempt to provide an overall perspective of reality against the background of Christian faith, is fully aware of the limits of science and the fact that there are other perspectives on reality, for instance, a naturalistic one. It is also aware that currently it might not be clear whether analytic theology's theory or naturalism's

---

[26]Editor's note: See Oliver Crisp's contribution to this volume.
[27]For an analysis of the philosophy of science of each discipline of Roman Catholic theology cf. the contributions in Göcke and Ohler (2019b).
[28]Cf. McGrath (2006: 240). See Göcke (2017) for further discussion.

theory provides a more reliable theoretical or practical orientation concerning reality and our place in it. It can accept that this could be something that becomes apparent only in the long run of human history. But that does not make it unscientific.
5. Analytic theology fully coheres with the historicity of science. It is aware that, like all scientific reflections, theological reflections are engaged with by human beings and therefore are embedded in historical contexts. Hence, theological theories are able to change. New perspectives can replace old ones, although there are some core assumptions like the existence of God and the Incarnation of the second person of the Trinity that are constitutive of theology. These assumptions would be given up only if there was sound argument against their rational acceptability, that is, if there was sound argument entailing that reliable theoretical and practical orientation concerning reality and our place in it is rationally inacceptable based on the assumption that God exists and became incarnate in Jesus of Nazareth.

III.2 Toward an All-Encompassing Theory of God, the World, and Human Life

Analytic theology is not only a scientific discipline itself. Analytic theology is one way of realizing the ultimate purpose inherent in the scientific account to reality itself. Because science aims to provide theoretical and practical orientation concerning reality and our place in it, science *eo ipso* aims to provide an overall—that is, an all-encompassing—perspective on reality and our place in it. Because a presupposition of science is that reality itself is a coherent and consistent whole that at least in principle can be grasped by scientific theories that have a rational claim to being true, and because truth does not contradict truth, there has to be a perspective on reality and our place in it that unites and synthesizes the different sciences into an all-encompassing theory that provides the most reliable theoretical and practical orientation humanity can obtain. Analytic theology aims to offer such a perspective on God, the world, and human life, based on experience, reason, and divine revelation. It, therefore, participates in the genuine task of the scientific account to reality itself. Whether it is any good for the good life or the flourishing of humanity, only time can tell. This, though, is the fate of any scientific account of reality.

References

Arcadi, J. M. (2016), "Analytic Theology as Declarative Theology," *TheoLogica*, 1: 1–16.
Beaney, M. (2013a), "What is Analytic Philosophy?," in M. Beaney (ed.), *The Oxford Handbook of The History of Analytic Philosophy*, 3–29, Oxford: Oxford University Press.
Beaney, M. (2013b). "The Historiography of Analytic Philosophy," in M. Beaney (ed.), *The Oxford Handbook of The History of Analytic Philosophy*, 30–60, Oxford: Oxford University Press.
Chalmers, D. (2009), "Introduction: A Guided Tour of Metametaphysics," in D. Chalmers, D. Manley, R. Wasserman (eds.), *Metametaphysics: New Essays on the Foundations of Ontology*, 1–37, Oxford: Oxford University Press.
Crisp, O. D. (2011), "On Analytic Theology," in O. D. Crisp and M. C. Rea (eds.), *Analytic Theology: New Essays in the Philosophy of Theology*, 33–53, Oxford: Oxford University Press.
Douven, I. (2017), "Abduction," in E. N. Zalta (ed.), *The Stanford Encyclopedia of Philosophy*. Available online: https://plato.stanford.edu/entries/abduction/.
Fleck, L. (1980), *Entstehung und Entwicklung einer wissenschaftlichen Tatsache: Einführung in die Lehre vom Denkstil und Denkkollektiv*, Frankfurt am Main: Suhrkamp.

Frege, G. (1884), *Die Grundlagen der Arithmetik. Eine logisch mathematische Untersuchung über den Begriff der Zahl*, Breslau: Koebner.
Gensler, H. J. (2017), *Introduction to Logic*, New York: Routledge.
Göcke, B. P. (2016), "Overview: Worldviews." Available online: https://sda.bodleian.ox.ac.uk/sda/#!/themes/article/86.
Göcke, B. P. (2017), "A Scientific Theology? A Programmatic Account of the Problems and Prospects for a Confessional and Scientific Theology," *TheoLogica*, 1 (1): 53–77.
Göcke, B. P. (2018), "Theologie als Wissenschaft. Allgemeine wissenschaftstheoretische Grundlagen der Diskussion der Wissenschaftlichkeit christlicher Theologie," in B. P. Göcke (ed.), *Die Wissenschaftlichkeit der Theologie. Historische und systematische Perspektiven*, 7–X44, Münster: Aschendorff.
Göcke, B. P. (2019a), "Theologie als Regina Scientiae," in B. P. Göcke and T. Schärtl (eds.), *Freiheit ohne Wirklichkeit? Anfragen an eine Denkform*, 375–405, Münster: Aschendorff Verlag.
Göcke, B. P. and L. Ohler, eds. (2019b), *Die Wissenschaftlichkeit der Theologie. Band 2: Katholische Disziplinen und ihre Wissenschaftstheorien*, Münster: Aschendorff.
Göcke, B. P. (2019c), "Alter Wein in neuen Schläuchen: Analytische Philosophie als *Ancilla Theologiae*," in M. Blay, T. Schärtl, C. Tapp, and C. Schröer (eds.), *Stets zu Diensten? Welche Philosophie braucht die Theologie heute?*, 227–58, Münster: Aschendorff.
Göcke, B. P. (2019d), "Transhumanism, Panentheism, and the Problem of Evil," *European Journal for Philosophy of Religion*, 11 (2): 65–89.
Harrison, P. (2015), *The Territories of Science and Religion*, Chicago: University of Chicago Press.
Hoyningen-Huene, P. (2013), *Systematicity: The Nature of Science*, Oxford: Oxford University Press.
Kitcher, P. (1993), *The Advancement of Science: Science without Legend, Objectivity without Illusions*, Oxford: Oxford University Press.
Koperski, J. (2015), *The Physics of Theism: God, Physics, and the Philosophy of Science*, Oxford: Wiley Blackwell.
Kuhn, T. S. (1996), *The Structure of Scientific Revolutions*, Chicago: University of Chicago Press.
Lakatos, I. (1970), "History of Science and Its Rational Reconstructions," *PSA: Proceedings of the Biennial Meeting of the Philosophy of Science Association*: 91–136.
Lakatos, I. (2001), *The Methodology of Scientific Research Programmes*, Cambridge: Cambridge University Press.
Laudan, L. (1984), *Science and Values: The Aims of Science and Their Role in Scientific Debate*, Berkeley: University of California Press.
Loux, M. (2002), *Metaphysics: A Contemporary Introduction*, London: Routledge.
McCall, T. H. (2015), *An Invitation to Analytic Christian Theology*, Downers Grove, IL: IVP Academic.
McGrath, A. E. (2006), *A Scientific Theology: Nature*, London: T&T Clark.
Morerod, C., O.P. (2016), "All Theologians Are Philosophers, Whether Knowingly or Not," in M. L. Lamb (ed.), *Theology Needs Philosophy: Acting Against Reason is Contrary to the Nature of God*, 3–18, Washington, DC: Catholic University of America Press.
Papineau, D. (2012), *Philosophical Devices: Proofs, Probabilities, Possibilities, and Sets*, Oxford: Oxford University Press.
Parsons, K. M. (2013), "Perspectives on Natural Theology from Analytic Philosophy," in R. R. Manning (ed.), *The Oxford Handbook of Natural Theology*, 247–61, Oxford: Oxford University Press.
Rea, M. C. (2011), "Introduction," in O. D. Crisp and M. C. Rea (eds.), *Analytic Theology: New Essays in the Philosophy of Theology*, 1–32, Oxford: Oxford University Press.

Reeves, J. (2019), *Against Methodology in Science and Religion: Recent Debates on Rationality and Theology*, London: Routledge.
Schurz, G. (2014), *Einführung in die Wissenschaftstheorie*, Darmstadt: WBG.
Swinburne, R., ed. (2002), *Bayes's Theorem*, Oxford: Oxford University Press.
Van Fraassen, B. (1980), *The Scientific Image*, Oxford: Clarendon Press.
Van Huyssteen, W. (1999), *The Shaping of Rationality*, Grand Rapids, MI: Eerdmans.
Van Inwagen, P. (2002), *Metaphysics*, Boulder, CO: Westview Press.
Weingartner, P. (1971), *Wissenschaftstheorie I. Einführung in die Hauptprobleme*, Stuttgart: frommann-holzboog.
Wolterstorff, N. (2005), "To Theologians: From One Who Cares About Theology but Is Not One of You," *Theological Education*, 40 (2): 79–92.

CHAPTER SIX

The Fellowship of the Ninth Hour: Christian Reflections on the Nature and Value of Faith

DANIEL HOWARD-SNYDER AND DANIEL J. MCKAUGHAN

It is common for young Christians to go off to college assured in their beliefs but, in the course of their first year or two, they meet what appears to them to be powerful defenses of scientific naturalism and crushing critiques of the basic Christian story (BCS), and many are thrown into doubt. They think to themselves something like this:

> To be honest, I am troubled about the BCS. While the problem of evil, the apparent cultural basis for the diversity of religions, the explanatory breadth of contemporary science, naturalistic explanations of religious experience and miracle reports, and textual and historical criticism of the Bible, among other things, don't make me believe the BCS *is false*, I am in serious doubt about it, so much so that I lack belief of it. In that case, how can I have Christian faith? And if I don't have faith, how can I keep on praying, attending church, affirming the creed, confessing my sins, taking the sacraments, singing the hymns and songs, and so on? I can't, unless I'm a hypocrite. So integrity requires me to drop the whole thing and get out.

Of course, our student is not alone. Many Christians find themselves for some portion of their lives somewhere on the trajectory from doubt to getting out. Indeed, Christians in the West struggle with intellectual doubt more than they used to, especially university-educated Christians.[1] What should we say to them? Some will say "Get out!", welcoming the development as a path to liberation. We'd like to explore a different response.

We begin by affirming the integrity these Christians display by aiming to live in accordance with their best judgment. Further, we can address the basis of their doubt. But we suspect that many of them—perhaps quite rightly—will still be in enough doubt to cancel belief. They have a problem, a practical problem: should I sacrifice my integrity

---

[1] See, e.g, Fisher (2017); Kosmin and Keysar (2009); Krause (2006); and The Pew Forum on Religion & Public Life (2015).

to stay in, or should I preserve my integrity and get out? Call this *the problem of the trajectory from doubt to getting out*.

Christians generally have an interest in responding to this problem, not least because of the plummeting population of youth in western churches, many of whom leave precisely because of their doubt. For those of us who are not in doubt and who deem the grounds for the BCS adequate for belief, there is still the matter of relating well to those who think otherwise. We suspect that a satisfying response will require Christian communities to rethink what authentic participation requires cognitively, and to find ways to encourage doubters—young and old—to participate with integrity despite their doubt.

Notice that the problem presupposes that *if you have enough doubt to cancel belief, then you can't have faith*. We propose to examine this presupposition. Toward that end, we will assess three theories of faith, plump for one of them, and then apply it to the problem of the trajectory.

I. BELIEF-ONLY

According to the first theory:

> Belief-Only. For you to put or maintain faith in someone, in some capacity, is for you to believe that they will come through for you in that capacity.

So on Belief-Only, for you to put your faith in Dr. Huber, as a dentist, is for you to believe that she will come through for you as a dentist, and for you to put your faith in Jesus, as your Savior and Lord, is for you to believe that he will come through for you as Savior and Lord. Belief-Only is often qualified; for example, the belief must be based on testimony or insufficient evidence, or it must be accompanied by certainty or caused by an act of will. Since these qualifications have no bearing on our concerns, we set them aside.

We have three worries about Belief-Only.

First, you can believe that someone will come through in some capacity even if you oppose it or regard it as bad or undesirable; but you can't have faith in that case. That's why you would never have faith in Timothy McVeigh, as a terrorist, even though you believed that he will come through as one. That's why you wouldn't have faith in Satan, as a devil, even if you believed that he delivers all too well on that score. You oppose terrorism and devilry; you regard them as bad or undesirable. Faith, instead, involves (1) a positive evaluation of their coming through, regarding it as good or desirable, as well as (2) a positive conative posture toward their coming through, being for it, in favor of it, wanting it to be so, or even wanting to want it to be so—anything in virtue of which you care with positive valence about whether they come through—where the conative includes desire, will, and the emotions.

Second, you can believe that someone will come through for you in some capacity, and even want them to, without being disposed to rely on them in that capacity; but you cannot have faith in that case. Imagine Jesus calling someone to follow him. Suppose they want to follow him. Yet, due to the demands of discipleship—for example, giving up attachment to wealth, status, autonomy, and the like—they are conflicted and so, perhaps due to weakness of will, they walk away. They lack faith in Jesus *as Lord* since they are not disposed to rely on him in a way that is appropriate to putting faith in him *as Lord*. In short, if you have faith in someone, in some capacity, then you will be *disposed to rely on them* in that capacity. (For our theory of relying, see Howard-Snyder and McKaughan, unpublished b.)

A third worry arises when we reflect on what makes faith valuable, notably the role that it plays in forming and maintaining relationships of *mutual faith and faithfulness*. Ryan Preston-Roedder (2018) observes three sources of value. First, when you put your faith in someone, as a spouse, or a friend, or the like, you are more likely to see and appreciate their potential and value in these capacities. Second, when you put your faith in someone, in a certain capacity, they are more likely to live up to your favorable view of them because your approval of and reliance on them gives them additional reason to come through for you in that capacity. Third, when you put your faith in someone, there's a sense in which you cast your lot with them; you make yourself vulnerable to them and you rely on them to respond faithfully. If they do respond faithfully, the result is a sort of solidarity, a solidarity that can increase when they reciprocate the faith you have put in them by putting their faith in you, and you respond faithfully. These observations make sense of Teresa Morgan's claim that, in the ancient Greco-Roman world, faith played a crucial role in forming and maintaining relationships of mutual faith and faithfulness "at every socio-economic level," "relationships of wives and husbands, parents and children, masters and slaves, patrons and clients, subjects and rulers, armies and commanders, friends, allies, fellow-human beings, gods and worshippers, and even fellow-animals" (2015: 120).

Now to our worry. Putting your faith in someone can help to promote and sustain valuable relationships in these three ways *only if* your faith is at least somewhat resilient in the face of challenges of various sorts. By way of illustration, unless the faith you put in your spouse can withstand the strains of marriage, your faith in them won't make these valuable things more likely. If you are disposed to pack your bags and head out the door at the first sign of them not coming through as a spouse, your "faith" in them will not make it more likely that you will see them as a spouse favorably, or that they will see themselves as a spouse favorably and act accordingly, or that you both experience marital solidarity. Nor will the relationship benefit from ways that resilient reliance itself contributes to stability and security (McKaughan 2017; Howard-Snyder and McKaughan unpublished a).

II. RESILIENT RELIANCE

A second theory of faith, which we regard as a plausible understanding of faith as it is exhibited in *The Gospel According to Mark* (GMark), avoids all three worries about Belief-Only. According to our second theory:

> Resilient Reliance. For you to put or maintain faith in a person in some capacity is (i) for you to have a positive evaluative-conative posture and a positive cognitive attitude toward their coming through in that capacity, and (ii) for you, in light of your posture and attitude, to be disposed both to rely on them to come through in that capacity and to overcome challenges to relying on them in this way.

(We distinguish faith from trust in McKaughan and Howard-Snyder, unpublished.) We defend our reading of GMark elsewhere (Howard-Snyder 2017), but here's a taste of the argument for it.

In the world of Mark's narrative, Jesus explicitly commends someone's faith three times, and on each occasion their most salient feature is *resilient reliance*, a disposition to overcome challenges to relying on Jesus and/or God to be or do something that is important to them.

Consider the woman with a hemorrhage (Mk 5:21-34) whom we will call "Veronica," in accordance with tradition. A synagogue leader named "Jairus" begs Jesus to come to his home to heal his dying daughter (v. 22).[2] Jesus consents and, as they walk together, a "large crowd" follows (v. 24). At the rear of the crowd is Veronica, who suffers from "a flow of blood" (continuous uterine bleeding), unable to find a cure, and getting worse (vv. 25-26). Mark says that "she had heard about Jesus" and that she knew of his ability to heal (v. 27). So she weaves her way through the crowd, which is "pressed in on him" (v. 31) trying to get close. When she does, she secretly touches his cloak from behind (v. 28). Immediately, she is healed (v. 29). Jesus senses that "power [has] gone forth from him," stops, pivots, and asks who touched his cloak (v. 30). The disciples balk at the question, given the size and nearness of the crowd (v. 31). Jesus persists. Eventually Veronica falls down before Jesus, "in fear and trembling", and tells him "the whole truth" (v. 33). As she finishes, he says, "Daughter, your faith has made you well; go in peace, and be healed of your disease" (v. 34).

The narrative emphasizes how she relied on Jesus to heal her despite numerous obstacles to her acting on her faith in him. Mark says, "She had endured much under many physicians, and had spent all that she had; and she was no better, but rather grew worse" (5:26). Her condition, her feeling of hopelessness induced by twelve years of medical failure, her getting worse, and her anemia-burdened struggle to approach Jesus through the "large crowd" were all obstacles she overcame to get to Jesus. Moreover, the purity laws prohibited an unclean woman from mixing with the crowd and from touching nonfamilial men. In reaching out to Jesus, relying on him to heal her, she overcame her internalization of these prohibitions and fear of reprisal, and she may have even overcome a Torah-inspired fear that in touching a holy man she would die.

Now Jesus knew of her resilient reliance when, as she finished her story, he commended her faith. Indeed, resilient reliance seems the most evident fact about her. So it seems plausible that Jesus fastened on it when he commended her faith. The same goes for the characters in two other stories in which Jesus commends someone's faith: blind Bartimaeus (Mk 10:46-52) and the friends of the paralytic (Mk 2:1-12).

Very briefly, here are six considerations that underscore the centrality of resilient reliance to faith in GMark. First, as we just indicated, in three stories in which Jesus commends someone's faith, he fastens on their resilience in the face of challenges to relying on him to heal on their behalf. Second, in no other story does Jesus commend someone's faith; resilient reliance always attends commendation. Third, on four other occasions that Mark uses the Greek words for faith, he twice associates resilient reliance with faith—in the story of Jairus (Mk 5:21-24, 35-43) and the father of the demon-possessed son (Mk 9:14-29)—and he twice associates lack of resilient reliance with a lack of faith—in the disciples' lack of faith in him on the stormy sea (Mk 4:40) and their lack of faith in God to heal the demon-possessed boy (Mk 9:19). Fourth, in two other stories—the Syrophoenician woman (Mk 7:24-30) and the woman who anoints Jesus at Bethany (Mk 14:3-9)—Mark does not use the Greek words for faith but

---

[2] Biblical quotations in this chapter are from the New Revised Standard Version of the Bible.

when Matthew and Luke, who relied on GMark as a source, retell these stories (the first in Mt. 15:21-28, the second in Lk 7:36-50), they see them as exemplars of faith, having Jesus explicitly commend them for their faith and, when he commends them, he plausibly fastens on their resilient reliance on him. Fifth, Mark encourages us to view Jesus as a role-model and, when we do, we see him as modeling a faith closely associated with resilient reliance, especially in his prayer in Gethsemane (Mk 14:32-42) and his execution on Golgotha (Mk 15:21-37), but also in the faith he maintains in his disciples. Sixth, as Teresa Morgan argues, in the Greco-Roman world surrounding the early churches, faith centrally involved resilient reliance in the face of challenges—especially, she repeatedly notes—in the face of fear, doubt, and skepticism. As such, faith held together relationships in times of crisis and, as such, it was considered a virtue (Morgan 2015: 7, 117, 120, 121).

These six points together strongly suggest that "without doubt, the leading characteristic of Markan faith is sheer dogged perseverance" in the presence of challenges to relying on Jesus and and/or God, as Christopher Marshall, the foremost expert on faith in GMark, puts it (1989: 237).

III. BELIEF-PLUS

Consider now a third theory, which includes all the components that we think are needed for faith but adds a restriction on the positive cognitive attitude. Rather than saying that faith in someone, in some capacity, requires *some positive cognitive attitude or other* toward their coming through for you in that capacity, this third theory requires that the positive cognitive attitude in question is *belief* that that they *will* come through for you in that way. So we have

> Belief-Plus. For you to put or maintain faith in a person in some capacity is (i) for you to have a positive evaluative-conative posture toward their coming through in that capacity and *believe* that they *will* come through in this way, and (ii) for you, in light of your posture and belief, to be disposed both to rely on them to come through in that capacity and to overcome challenges to relying on them in this way.

While Belief-Plus improves on Belief-Only, we suspect that its belief-condition goes too far. There are several reasons for this. We mention five.

Reason 1. The faith exhibited in GMark does not require such belief. Consider Veronica again. Although in the world of the story it was common knowledge that Jesus was *able* to heal, it was not a foregone conclusion that he *would* heal. Indeed, Veronica had plenty of evidence that counted against Jesus healing her. She had suffered medical failure for twelve long years and was only getting worse, despite expert treatment; moreover, by her lights, there was a very good chance that if she touched Jesus, a holy man, she would die, or be stoned for violating the purity laws. To suppose that in the face of such evidence Veronica nevertheless *believed* that Jesus *would* heal her is to uncharitably impute to her an irrational degree of credulity, especially when, in the world of the story, there is a semantically and culturally attuned option available (Morgan 2015): faith in Jesus to heal her without belief that he would heal her.

The same can be said about Jairus. In the world of the story, he has too much counterevidence to sensibly *believe* that his daughter *is* alive and so a candidate for healing. Mark highlights this fact repeatedly. First, the messengers come from Jairus's house to inform him that "Your daughter is dead" (Mk 5:35). Second, when they arrive at his home, they are met by "a commotion, people weeping and wailing loudly" (v. 38), a ritual mourning for the dead. Third, after Jesus asserts that she is only sleeping, the ritual mourners laugh at the suggestion (v. 40). Fourth, Jairus then "went in where the child was" and sees her with his own eyes (v. 40). Perhaps his wife cradled his daughter in her arms, crying while she stroked her hair; perhaps when their eyes met, she conveyed to him the hopelessness of the situation: it's too late, she's dead. In his telling of the story, Mark explicitly calls our attention to this incrementally mounting counterevidence. It seems uncharitable to attribute to Jairus the belief that his daughter is alive, especially when there is another reading available, one that ascribes no intellectual deficiency to Jairus and one that is well within the semantic space and first-century cultural understanding of *faith*: Jairus retains his faith in Jesus, to heal his daughter, from the beginning of the story until the end, even though just prior to the vindication of his faith, he lacks both the belief that she *is* alive and the belief that Jesus *will* heal her.

The faith of other minor characters in GMark seem plausibly seen in this light, too; especially Bartimaeus and the father of the demon-possessed son.

Reason 2. Some exemplars of faith lack the required belief or anything like it; indeed, some even lack belief that God exists.

Consider a Christian exemplar: Saint Teresa of Calcutta. In 1942, after what she took to be a call from the Lord, she vowed to give her life completely to him, no matter what, and to serve him in the poorest of the poor. At the time, she did not expect that the "no matter what" clause of her vow would include five decades of belief-canceling doubt. It appears from her private writings that she not only experienced the felt absence of God during that period but also experienced doubt so severe that she lacked belief. "*There is no One* to answer my prayers," she wrote, "So many unanswered questions live within me—I am afraid to uncover them—because of the blasphemy.—*If there be God*, please forgive me" (Kolodiejchuk 2007: 186–8, emphasis added). Later she wrote,

> In my soul I feel just that terrible pain of loss—of God not wanting me—of God not being God—*of God not really existing (Jesus, please forgive my blasphemies*—I have been told to write everything). The darkness that surrounds me on all sides—I can't lift my soul to God—no light or inspiration enters my soul.—I speak of love for souls—of tender love for God—words pass through my lips—and *I long with a deep longing to believe them*.—What do I labour for? If there be no God—there can be no soul.—If there is no soul then Jesus—You also are not true. (192–3, emphasis added)

This was not a single occurrence but an experience that lasted from her late thirties until her death in her late eighties, the five-decade long crucible in which her sainthood was formed. In her retreat notes from 1959 she wrote,

> Do I value the salvation of my soul? I don't believe I have a soul. There is nothing in me. Am I working in earnest for the salvation of the souls of others? There was a burning zeal in my soul for souls from childhood until I said "yes" to God & then all is gone. *Now I don't believe*. (349, emphasis added)

In 1965, she wrote, "And because *I want to believe*, I accept the darkness of faith with greater joy and confidence" (253, emphasis added). Her condition is such that, with respect to whether there are souls or whether there is a God, she can say only "Now I don't believe," "I want to believe," and "I long with a deep longing to believe them."

How are we to understand Saint Teresa? Early on, she described herself as having lost her faith (187). However, under the supervision of her spiritual director, she came to a more mature understanding when she described her faith in Jesus with nine short words: "to live by faith and yet not to believe" (248). If we follow Saint Teresa in her later self-understanding, then we can see her as an exemplar of faith, resolving to act on the assumption that the BCS is true—and keeping her vow to serve Jesus despite her belief-canceling doubt.

Let us be clear. Even if Saint Teresa's faith in the Christian God did not include belief that the BCS is true, she could not have had such faith while *dis*believing the BCS. *Dis*belief is too negative a cognitive attitude for faith. Rather, you can have faith in the Christian God only if you have *some positive cognitive attitude or other* toward the BCS, something belief-*like*. Of course, belief itself is a belief-like attitude. Early on in her life, Saint Teresa believed that *the BCS is true*. But as her doubt grew and crowded out her belief, perhaps another belief replaced it; perhaps she believed that *the BCS is more likely than not*, or perhaps she believed that *the BCS is more likely than any credible alternative worldview*. Alternatively, perhaps another kind of positive cognitive attitude toward the BCS replaced it, a *beliefless* positive cognitive attitude.

In this connection, many people say that belief is not the only positive cognitive attitude one can take toward a proposition; for example they distinguish believing something from accepting it, trusting that it is true, imaginatively assenting to it, hoping that it is true, and giving it some degree of credence (Alston 1996; Audi 2011; McKaughan 2013; Schellenberg 2016; Buchak 2018). We suggest that we might usefully distinguish *believing* something from *belieflessly assuming* it. We develop this suggestion elsewhere (Howard-Snyder 2019a, 2019b; McKaughan and Howard-Snyder forthcoming); here we merely illustrate. Consider the following case:

> An army general faces enemy forces. She needs to act. Her scouts give some information about the disposition of the enemy but not nearly enough to settle whether they are situated one way rather than several others. So she assumes that they are situated in the way that seems the least false of the credible options given her information, say, that they are scattered throughout the boulder field near the mountain peak. Then, acting on that assumption, she disperses her forces in the way that seems most likely to thwart the enemy if they are situated in the boulder field, say, a pincer movement with mortar shelling.

Notice that we can easily imagine that, although the general is in doubt about the enemy's position, and although she neither believes nor disbelieves that they are positioned in any particular way, she *acts on the assumption* that they are in the boulder field. That is, she *assumes*—*belieflessly* assumes—that the enemy is in the boulder field, and so she acts accordingly.

Perhaps something similar was true of Saint Teresa. She was in doubt about the BCS, and so she neither believed nor disbelieved it. Even so, we can easily imagine that she acted on the *beliefless* assumption that it was true, and so she acted accordingly: she maintained her faith in God despite her doubt, she remained committed to her vows to serve Jesus in the poorest of the poor, and she continued to pray, to confess her sins, to take the sacraments, and so on, relying on God—if such there be, as she would say—to save souls and redeem sinners, herself included.

Faith Glavey Pawl (2018) suggests that there is a better way to understand Saint Teresa's situation, one that sees her as an exemplar of Christian faith but *not* an exemplar of *beliefless* Christian faith. Suppose we agree, says Pawl, that (1) Saint Teresa is an exemplar of Christian faith and that (2) she experienced unbelief of the BCS for most of her adult life. Nevertheless, (3) she might also have still believed the BCS. True enough, this is a paradoxical situation, but it is not impossible. More importantly, it follows that, on Belief-Plus, she had faith in the Christian God. After all, she satisfied the belief condition in addition to the other conditions for faith, even though she also experienced unbelief of the BCS for most of her adult life. Consequently, the exemplar-status of Saint Teresa's faith does not favor Resilient Reliance over Belief-Plus.

To get a better understanding of Pawl's proposal, let's consider different things she might mean by her claim that (2) Saint Teresa experienced "unbelief" during most of her adult life.

First, by "unbelief" Pawl might mean *dis*belief. In that case, the suggestion is that Saint Teresa both believes the BCS and disbelieves the BCS for most of her adult life; since she believed, she satisfied the belief condition of Belief-Plus. We have two concerns about this suggestion: One concern is that if you believe that p you'll possess a tendency to inwardly assent to p when p comes to mind, and a tendency to outwardly assent to p when asked whether p. But if you disbelieve that p, you'll lack both of those tendencies. You can't both possess and lack the same tendencies, and so you can't both believe p and disbelieve that p, not even if you are a saint. Another concern is that Saint Teresa did not disbelieve the BCS. That's because she had faith in the Christian God, and no one can have faith in the Christian God while *dis*believing that the Christian God exists.

Second, by "unbelief" Pawl might mean "lack of belief." In that case, the suggestion is that Saint Teresa both had and lacked belief of the BCS for most of her adult life; since she had belief, she satisfied the belief condition of Belief-Plus. We have one concern about this suggestion: it asserts a logical contradiction.

Third, by "unbelief" Pawl might mean "doubt." In that case, the suggestion is that Saint Teresa both believes and doubts the BCS for most of her adult life; since she believed, she satisfied the belief condition of Belief-Plus, despite her doubt. Before we assess this suggestion, we need to say a word or two about doubt.

We must distinguish *having doubts* about p, *being in doubt* about p, and *doubting that* p. For one to have doubts about p—note the "s"—is for one to have what appear to one to be grounds to believe not-p and, as a result, for one to be at least somewhat less inclined to believe p. For one to be in doubt about p is for one neither to believe nor disbelieve p as a result of one's grounds for p seeming to be roughly on a par with one's grounds for not-p. One can *have doubts* without *being in doubt*, and one can *be in doubt* without *having doubts*. We must distinguish *having doubts* and *being in doubt* from *doubting that*. If one *doubts that* p, one is at least strongly inclined to disbelieve p; *having doubts* and *being in doubt* lack that implication.

With this threefold distinction in hand, we return to the third interpretation of Pawl (3), according to which unbelief is doubt. One concern is that if "doubt" means "doubt that," then the suggestion is that Saint Teresa both believes and doubts that the BCS is true. Doubting that the BCS is true neighbors disbelieving it, and so our two concerns about disbelief above apply to this suggestion as well. A second concern is that if "doubt" means "has doubts"—*mere* doubts, not doubts whose cumulative force results in being in doubt or doubting that—then the suggestion is that Saint Teresa both believes and has some doubts about the BCS. Our concern about this suggestion is that it misrepresents Saint Teresa. She did not simply have mere doubts about the BCS. Her doubt was belief-canceling doubt. What is our evidence for this? Our evidence is her own self-description, quoted above. She says that she lacks belief. She says that she desperately wants to believe. Moreover, these are not things she writes casually, in passing, or in a dark moment;

rather, they are her considered view of herself, expressed to her confessors and spiritual directors. She worries over a prolonged period that it is blasphemous even to confess her doubts, which she would not have done if her doubt was not belief-canceling. We submit that it would be uncharitable to deny her self-description. A third concern is that if "doubt" means "in doubt," then the suggestion is that Saint Teresa both believed and was in doubt about the BCS. Our concern with this suggestion is that if you are in doubt about whether p, then you will lack two tendencies that you will possess if you believe that p, namely a tendency to inwardly assent to p when p comes to mind and a tendency to outwardly assent to p when asked whether p. Since no one can both possess and lack the same tendencies, Saint Teresa did not believe the BCS while being in doubt about it. Hence, while we are grateful to Pawl for her proposal regarding Saint Teresa, it does not appear to hold up to scrutiny.

Before leaving Saint Teresa, notice that, if she is an exemplar of Christian faith, and if she nevertheless suffered from belief-canceling doubt about the BCS, she exhibits a chief value of the resilience of faith: it can counteract the doubt that might otherwise end a valuable relationship of mutual faith and faithfulness.

Let's consider a nonreligious exemplar of faith. In Homer's *Odyssey*, the hero Odysseus tries to return to his wife Penelope after the decade-long Trojan War, but he is prevented from doing so for another ten years. Imagine what that was like for Penelope. When Odysseus departs, she has faith in him, as her husband. Naturally enough, she also believes that he exists.

But now fast-forward twenty years. Does her faith in him require belief that he will come through for her as a husband? Does it require belief that he exists? Penelope is not naïve. Perhaps Odysseus has betrayed her. Is it likely that a strapping champion such as him could resist the siren calls of beautiful young maids and goddesses all that time? Perhaps he's not even alive. Might he have been killed? Imagine that she receives reports of his capture, reports that raise considerably the likelihood that he is dead, reports that put her in considerable doubt about whether he is alive. Can she nevertheless persevere in her faith in him?

Clearly enough, she could still regard it as a good thing if he is still alive, and she could long for it to be true with all her heart. Moreover, she could still act on the (beliefless) assumption that he is alive, continuing to rely on him to keep his husbandly promises and to make every effort to return. And she could exhibit resilience in the face of challenges to living in light of her reliance on him, turning away suitors and expressing her resolve to remain committed to him by, for example, setting a place for him at the table each evening and entreating the gods for his safe return.

Of course, Penelope's doubt may present motivational challenges or temptations that she would be less inclined to face if she believed. And maybe it would take heroic grit for her to persevere in the face of such challenges. But none of that implies that she cannot retain her faith in Odysseus in the absence of belief that he is alive. Moreover, there is nothing about the noncognitive components of faith that require that she believes that he is alive; nor does there seem to be anything else that requires it. What, then, would keep us from attributing faith to her?

Upshot: exemplars of faith seem to pose a difficulty for Belief-Plus.

Reason 3. A third reason to think that the belief-condition of Belief-Plus goes too far observes that types of positive cognitive attitude other than belief can play the same role in faith that Belief-Plus assigns to belief alone. According to Belief-Plus, you have faith in someone, in some capacity, only if you *believe* that they will come through in that way.

No other type of attitude will do. Not seeming, not credence, not trust, not acceptance, not hope, not beliefless assuming. Only belief is allowed, even though other attitude-types can play any role that belief plays in faith.

Reason 4. According to Belief-Plus, when belief is the positive cognitive attitude that you have while you have faith in someone, in some capacity, the content of that belief must be that *they will come through* in that capacity. No "thinner" content will do: not that *it's likely that they will come through*, not that *it's more likely than not*, not *that there's a good enough chance to risk relying on them*, and so on for a long list of ineligible "thinner" propositions. Only the "thickest" proposition that they *will* come through is allowed, even though "thinner" contents can suffice to play the role that the "thickest" one does in faith.

Reason 5. Faith can't play the role that it is supposed to play in a well-lived life—particularly in moments of crisis and doubt—unless we back off the thickest belief condition that Belief-Plus lays down. The role of faith is to render you resilient in the face of challenges to relying on its object for something that matters to you, and it serves this role partly by responding to new counterevidence. While new counterevidence might induce doubt about whether someone will come through for you, faith tends to help keep you behaviorally on track, to help keep you from being deterred or disheartened into inaction. Due to its belief-condition, Belief-Plus cannot account for faith's role when counterevidence comes in or one runs into other obstacles—just the circumstances in which it is most needed.

By way of illustration, consider a case of faith in oneself. Imagine "a first-generation college student—a child of Mexican immigrants—who discovers, upon entering college, that many of her classmates and teachers hold rather dim views of Hispanic students' drive and intellectual ability" (Preston-Roedder 2018: 175). Suppose these dim views constitute new counterevidence to her belief that she will succeed as a student, so much so that they induce in her belief-canceling doubt about whether she will come through. However, if she has faith in herself, as a student, her resilience in the face of this counterevidence might help her to overcome the debilitating effects of her belief-canceling doubt, for example, by helping her to keep her nose in the books and motivating her to say "no" to extracurricular temptations. Her faith in herself, as a student, would not help her overcome her doubt if it required her to believe that she *will* succeed.

IV. REVISITING THE PROBLEM OF THE TRAJECTORY

Having argued for Resilient Reliance and having raised several objections to Belief-Plus, let's return to the problem with which we began. What might the Resilient Reliance view of faith counsel us to say to our struggling Christian treading the path from doubt to getting out? Perhaps it would counsel something like this:

> Do not give up your concern for the truth or your aim to live with integrity. There seems, however, a way for you to remain a practicing Christian without giving up either of them.
>
> First it is obvious that you care about whether the BCS is true; your distress makes that clear. Moreover, it is obvious that you want to live in light of the BCS, although you are struggling with a serious intellectual challenge on that score. Further, it is obvious that you are resilient in the face of this challenge. In fact, it's amazing how you have hung in there despite your doubt. But here's the good news: those three

things about you are exactly what faith looks like in the circumstances that you now find yourself. In fact, you not only do not *lack* faith; you are one of its exemplars. The place you are in right now—exhibiting resilience in the face of intellectual challenges to living in light of your faith—that is exactly where Saint Teresa found herself, and it is arguably where Jesus found himself on the cross, feeling abandoned by God and in serious doubt about God's faithfulness and love, "teetering on the edge between disillusionment and faith," as Father John Neuhaus put it (2000). The main question is whether you can find a way to follow their example, and in your case that boils down to whether you can make peace with your doubt while living with integrity.

Perhaps you can. That's because, although believing the BCS right now is out of the question for you, your doubt need not prevent you from resolving to act on the assumption that the BCS is true. That's the sort of thing spouses do when things are going especially badly, that's what parents do when their children go through a rough adolescence, that's what friends do when changes threaten to tear them apart. In fact, it's what many people do in all kinds of situations in a well-lived life. We retain our faith in another, despite our doubt about whether they will come through, or even whether they exist, and we do so by acting on the assumption that things will turn out all right in the long run. And you can do the same: despite your doubt, you can act on the assumption that the BCS is true and, on the basis of that assumption, you can continue to follow Jesus, by beliefless faith and not by sight. Moreover, you can do it with integrity because you are not believing against your evidence.

So if what is really tearing you up is that you are in doubt and so you lack the faith required to live with integrity, we suggest that you need a better understanding of faith: one according to which faith is compatible with serious doubt, even belief-canceling doubt; one that allows you to own your doubt, to struggle with it in all honesty, while you continue to practice with integrity.

That is how Resilient Reliance solves the problem of the trajectory from doubt to getting out.

Of course, the friend of Belief-Plus will respond differently to the problem. Faith Glavey Pawl (2018) rightly noticed that the Resilient Reliance solution presupposes that Christian practice with integrity and sincerity requires Christian faith. That's not so obviously true, however. A fair bit of Christian practice—for example, attending church services, petitionary prayer, pitching in here and there in the parish, church-related social justice activism, and so on—can be grounded in something other than faith, without a lack of integrity or sincerity. For example, couldn't someone align themselves with the Christian community and practice with integrity and sincerity even if they simply open themselves to experiencing God or had the thinnest of hope in God? Couldn't such openness or thin hope motivate that alignment and practice? If so, Christian practice with integrity does not require Christian faith.[3]

Perhaps that's right. However, we suspect that there is more at stake here for the Christian community. We want to make three points in this connection.

First, there are norms in the Church according to which—even if one opens themselves to experiencing God or puts thin hope in God, and even if their openness or thin hope motivates their alignment and practice—so long as one lacks *faith* in God or *faith* that the BCS is true, one is prohibited from full participation. For example, in

---

[3] See Cuneo (2017a,b); Muyskens (1979).

many denominations, those who lack faith and so cannot sincerely confess faith, are not permitted to be baptized, affirm the creeds, practice the liturgy, complete confirmation, become members, take the Eucharist, be married in the church, or serve as leaders. Faith plays a role in Christian theology and practice that openness and thin hope do not. This is not the place to explain why. We only note that the Church picks out faith, and not openness or thin hope, as the central response God desires of humans, and that, in the New Testament, faith, and not openness or thin hope, is closely associated with salvation; moreover, people are rebuked for their lack of faith.[4]

Second, suppose we affirm these faith-requiring norms for full participation. Then, if we also insist, along with Belief-Plus, that people cannot have faith in God unless they *believe* that God *will* come through for them with respect to what they are relying on God for, and if we also insist that people cannot have faith that the BCS is true unless they *believe* that the BCS *is* true, our faith-requiring norms will preclude from full participation people who struggle with belief-canceling doubt. At best, such people will be declared to have only "pretend faith," not "genuine faith."

Third, if those faith-requiring norms rest on misunderstandings of the nature of faith, and if faith is compatible with belief-canceling doubt, then, unless the Church reforms its view of faith, it will continue to contribute needlessly to a problem about full participation and belonging in the Church that is increasingly being addressed in the West by walking out the door.

For this reason, we submit that the Church today would do well to take with utmost seriousness the idea of beliefless Christian faith of the sort we have plumped for in these pages.

V. EPILOGUE

One final thought. During his first Roman imprisonment, Paul suffered just as you might expect. What's more, he had taken quite a fall. Once a Hebrew of Hebrews, an esteemed rabbinic scholar, maximally zealous, and with respect to living the law, faultless—now he sat in a Roman prison. That's when he wrote these words to the church at Philippi:

> But whatever was to my profit I now consider loss for the sake of Christ. What is more, I consider everything a loss compared to the surpassing greatness of knowing Christ Jesus my Lord, for whose sake I have lost all things. I consider them rubbish, that I may gain Christ and be found in him, not having a righteousness of my own that comes from the law, but that which is through faith in Christ—the righteousness that comes from God and is by faith. I want to know Christ and the power of his resurrection and the fellowship of sharing in his sufferings, becoming like him in his death, and so, somehow, to attain to the resurrection from the dead. Not that I have already obtained all this, or have already been made perfect, but I press on to take hold of that for which Christ Jesus took hold of me. (Phil. 3:7-12)

Among other things, Paul says here that he wants to know "the fellowship of sharing in [Christ's] sufferings, becoming like him in his death." This suggests that there's a fellowship whose members draw near to the Lord *through sharing in his suffering, becoming like him*

---

[4] Jn 3:16, 5:24, 11:25, 20:31; Rom. 1:16, 10:9-10; 1 Pet. 1:9; Eph. 1:13.

in his death. This may involve the suffering of a body broken by disease, injury, or age; or it may involve the suffering of ridicule, ostracism, or martyrdom.

But Jesus knew another kind of suffering. Hear again a crucial part of the Great Passion: "At the ninth hour he cried with a loud voice ... 'My God, my God, why have you forsaken me?'" We can easily imagine that, for Jesus, these words expressed, among other things, the suffering of doubt about God's love and faithfulness, perhaps even God's existence. Either way, we submit that if there is such a thing as "the fellowship of sharing in [Christ's] sufferings, becoming like him in his death," and if one way to become like him in his death is to be in belief-canceling doubt, then we should expect to find among ourselves some—perhaps even many—who are called to become like Jesus in his death, in this specific way.

Of course, suffering in this or any other way is not to be sought for its own sake. Even so, some of the New Testament authors speak of Christ's followers finding a kind of union, fellowship, and purpose in persevering through suffering in the shared faith that the ninth hour will be followed by the third day.[5] We find it interesting that, at the same retreat in 1959 where Saint Teresa confessed "Now I don't believe," she also affirmed a readiness to accept her suffering out of love for Jesus. Elsewhere she wrote, "You have tasted the chalice of His agony—and what will be your reward my dear sister? More suffering and a deeper likeness to Him on the Cross" (Kolodiejchuk 2007: 155–6).

Far from being on their way out of the Church, those on the trajectory from doubt to getting out may well be members of a fellowship that draws near to the Lord through experientially identifying with his suffering doubt. If there is such a fellowship, what should we call it? Perhaps we should call it *The Fellowship of the Ninth Hour*.[6]

References

Alston, W. P. (1996), "Belief, Acceptance, and Religious Faith," in J. Jordan and D. Howard-Snyder (eds.), *Faith, Freedom, and Rationality*, 3–27, Lanham: Rowman & Littlefield.

Audi, R. (2011), *Rationality and Religious Commitment*, New York: Oxford University Press.

Buchak, L. (2018), "When is Faith Rational?," in G. Rosen, A. Byrne, J. Cohen, E. Harman, and S. Shiffrin (eds.), *The Norton Introduction to Philosophy*, 2nd ed. 115–27, New York: W. W. Norton.

Cuneo, T. (2017a), "Aligning with Lives of Faith," *International Journal for Philosophy of Religion*, 81 (1–2): 83–97.

Cuneo, T. (2017b), "The Inaccessibility of Religion Problem," *Ergo: An Open Access Journal of Philosophy*, 4 (23): 669–91.

Fisher, A. R. (2017), "A Review and Conceptual Model of the Research on Doubt, Disaffiliation, and Related Religious Changes," *Psychology of Religion and Spirituality*, 9(4): 358–67.

Howard-Snyder, D. (2016), "Does Faith Entail Belief?," *Faith and Philosophy*, 33 (2): 142–62.

---

[5]Rom. 5:1-5, 8:17-21, and 12:12; 2 Cor. 1:3-4, 4:17, 8:1-2, and 12:10; Phil. 1:29-30 and 3:10; Mt. 5:10-12, 10:38; Lk. 6:22-23; Acts 5:41, 9:16, 14:22; Col. 1:24; 2 Tim. 3:12; Jas. 1:2-3, 12; 1 Pet. 1:6-9, 2:19, 2:20-21, 3:14, 4:12-14, and 5:9-10; Rev. 2:10.

[6]Acknowledgements: This publication was made possible through the support of a grant from the John Templeton Foundation. The opinions expressed in this publication are those of the author(s) and do not necessarily reflect the views of the John Templeton Foundation. We also thank Faith Glavey Pawl for her comments presented at the Society of Christian Philosophers 40th Anniversary Conference, Calvin College, Grand Rapids MI, September 2018, and the audience members who participated.

Howard-Snyder, D. (2017a), "Markan Faith," *International Journal for the Philosophy of Religion*, 81 (1–2): 31–60.
Howard-Snyder, D. (2017b), "The Skeptical Christian," in J. L. Kvanvig (ed.), *Oxford Studies in Philosophy of Religion*, vol. 8, 142–67, Oxford: Oxford University Press.
Howard-Snyder, D. (2019a), "Can Fictionalists have Faith? It All Depends," *Religious Studies*, 55 (4): 447–68.
Howard-Snyder, D. (2019b), "Three Arguments to Think that Faith Does *Not* Entail Belief," *Pacific Philosophical Quarterly*, 100 (1): 114–28.
Howard-Snyder, D., and D. J. McKaughan (unpublished a), "How is Faith Related to Faithfulness?"
Howard-Snyder, D., and D. J. McKaughan (unpublished b), "Relying on Someone for Something."
Marshall, C. (1989), *Faith as a Theme in Mark's Narrative*, New York: Cambridge University Press.
Kolodiejchuk, B., ed. (2007), *Mother Teresa: Come Be My Light: The Private Writings of the "Saint of Calcutta"*, New York: Doubleday.
Kosmin, B. A., and A. Keysar (2009), "American Religious Identification Survey (ARIS 2008): Summary Report," 1–24. Available online: http://commons.trincoll.edu/aris/files/2011/08/ARIS_Report_2008.pdf.
Krause N. (2006), "Religious Doubt and Psychological Well-Being: A Longitudinal Investigation," *Review of Religious Research*, 47: 287–302.
McKaughan, D. J. (2013), "Authentic Faith and Acknowledged Risk: Dissolving the Problem of Faith and Reason," *Religious Studies*, 49 (1): 101–24.
McKaughan, D. J. (2016), "Action-Centered Faith, Doubt, and Rationality," *Journal of Philosophical Research*, 41 (supplement): 71–90.
McKaughan, D. J. (2017), "On the Value of Faith and Faithfulness," *International Journal for the Philosophy of Religion*, 81: 7–29.
McKaughan, D. J. (2018), "Faith through the Dark of Night: What Perseverance Amidst Doubt Can Teach Us About the Nature and Value of Religious Faith," *Faith and Philosophy*, 35 (2): 195–218.
McKaughan, D. J., and D. Howard-Snyder (forthcoming), "Faith," in S. Goetz and C. Taliaferro (eds.), *The Encyclopedia of Philosophy of Religion*, Hoboken: Wiley-Blackwell.
McKaughan, D. J., and D. Howard-Snyder (unpublished), "How Does Trust Relate to Faith?."
Pawl, F. G. (2018), "Comments on Daniel Howard-Snyder and Daniel McKaughan, 'The Fellowship of the Ninth Hour'," The Society of Christian Philosophers 40th Anniversary Conference, Calvin College, Grand Rapids, MI.
Rath, B. (2017), "Christ's Faith, Doubt, and the Cry of Dereliction," *International Journal for the Philosophy of Religion*, 81 (1–2): 161–9.
Morgan, T. (2015), *Roman Faith and Christian Faith: Pistis and Fides in the Early Roman Empire and Early Churches*, New York: Oxford University Press.
Muyskens, J. (1979), *The Sufficiency of Hope*, Philadelphia: Temple University Press.
Neuhaus, R. J. (2000), *Death on a Friday Afternoon: Meditations on the Last Words of Jesus from the Cross*, New York: Basic Books.
Preston-Roedder, R. (2018), "Three Varieties of Faith," *Philosophical Topics*, 46 (1): 173–99.
Schellenberg, J. L. (2016), "Working with Swinburne: Belief, Value, and the Religious Life," in M. Bergmann and J. Brower (eds.), *Faith and Reason: Themes from Swinburne*, 26–45, Oxford: Oxford University Press.
The Pew Forum on Religion & Public Life (2015), "America's Changing Religious Landscape: Christians Decline Sharply as Share of Population; Unaffiliated and Other Faiths Continue to Grow," 1–200. Available online: http://www.pewforum.org/2015/05/12/americas-changing-religious-landscape/.

PART II

Doctrine of God

CHAPTER SEVEN

Classical Theism

R. T. MULLINS

Contemporary scholarship proffers many models of God such as classical theism, neoclassical theism, open theism, panentheism, and pantheism (Diller and Kasher 2013; Mullins 2016b). In order to distinguish a model of God from its rivals, a model of God must say something unique about the divine nature that is not captured in other models. Theists of various stripes affirm that God is a necessary being who is omnipotent, omniscient, morally perfect, and perfectly free (Swinburne 2016). An affirmation of these divine attributes does not say anything particularly unique about God and thus fails to distinguish one model of God from others. What distinguishes classical theism from its rivals is its commitment to a God who is timeless, immutable, simple, and impassible (Williams 2013: 95–7). Classical theists claim that these attributes are mutually entailing (McCann 2012: 12–14). Of course, it is contentious if these attributes are in fact mutually entailing, but for present purposes I shall assume that they are (Mullins 2018).

In this chapter, I shall offer a brief exploration of the systematic connections between these four classical attributes and highlight some of the underlying philosophical commitments that classical theists have used to develop their concept of God and the God-world relationship. After articulating the classical concept of God, I shall consider two problems that have plagued classical theism over the centuries and consider some possible responses to these problems: first, the problem of creation *ex nihilo* for timelessness and immutability, and, second, the problem of a modal collapse for divine simplicity.

I. HOW TO DEVELOP THE CLASSICAL DOCTRINE OF GOD

Classical theists employ different methods for developing their model of God. The main methods seem to be a combination of perfect being theology, natural theology, and reflections on Holy Scripture. It is not clear how these different methods fit together in order to develop a model of God, but that is not a unique problem for classical theism. Perhaps, one might see classical theism as engaged in a continual hermeneutical process of reflective equilibrium in which one is considering insights from each method in order to arrive at a conception of God (Leftow 2011; Göcke 2018: 167). This is an interesting suggestion, but such a patchwork approach might face some difficulties for the classical theist because it is not clear that each method independently or jointly leads to the God of classical theism.

For example, the support classical theism gets from scripture might be dubious in light of contemporary biblical scholarship. Some proponents of classical theism say that their model of God is underdetermined by the biblical evidence (Helm 2010:11;

Dolezal 2011: 67; Stump 2016). However, many scholars today think that the Bible teaches a very different conception of God than that of classical theism (Boyd 2000; Sanders 2007; Fretheim 2015). These critics of the classical view maintain that classical theism contradicts the biblical claims about God, especially since divine suffering and change are major biblical themes (Fretheim 1984; Moberly 2013: 108–37). Moreover, various classical theists admit that certain attributes, such as timelessness, are not taught in scripture (Charnocke 1682: 181–6). What classical theists often say is that we need philosophy in order to arrive at the classical doctrine of God (Berkhof 1984: 60). This has led critics of classical theism to say that debates over the classical doctrine of God are really debates about metaphysics and not about the Bible (Ward 2015: 26).

If the classical theist cannot gain support from scripture, perhaps one might think that she can derive her model of God from natural theology. This is not immediately obvious because some versions of the arguments for the existence of God do not lead to the God of classical theism (Swinburne 2004). Yet other versions of these arguments do lead to a being who is simple, timeless, immutable, and impassible (Feser 2017). The plausibility of those particular arguments is controversial but not indefensible. Thus, the classical theist can maintain some support for her model of God from natural theology.

What about support from perfect being theology? Most theists agree that God is a perfect being, or the being than which none greater can be conceived (Morris 1991; Speaks 2018). The claim that God is the greatest means that God essentially has all of the great-making properties. Great-making properties are properties that are intrinsically better to have than not have.

The claim that God is perfect is typically associated with the divine attributes of aseity and self-sufficiency. To say that God has the attribute of aseity is to claim that God's existence does not depend on, nor is derived from, anything *ad extra* to God. To say that God has the attribute of self-sufficiency is the claim that God's perfect nature is in no way dependent on, nor derived from, anything *ad extra* to the divine nature. Many theists wish to add a further claim to these two divine attributes. They say that God is the ultimate source of existence and perfection such that God is responsible in some sense for the existence of anything else apart from Himself (Feser 2017: 170; Bohn 2018).

These claims about divine perfection leave it somewhat ambiguous as to which attributes God in fact has. Typically, a theist will say that God is a necessarily existent being who possesses certain essential properties such as maximal power, maximal knowledge, maximal goodness, and perfect freedom (Nagasawa 2017). Notice that this does not give us the four unique attributes of classical theism: timelessness, immutability, simplicity, and impassibility. How does one arrive at those classical attributes?

As noted before, classical theists typically say that one must rely on philosophy in order to justify the classical conception of God. It is worth noting that the method of perfect being theology relies on different defeasible intuitions about perfection. One's intuitions about perfection are often tied to an assortment of philosophical assumptions. This is not a defect within the method of perfect being theology. If having defeasible intuitions and philosophical assumptions is a defect, then every method in every discipline is doomed. Rather, my claim is more modest. My claim is that, in order to arrive at the four unique classical attributes, one must add further philosophical assumptions that are not contained within scripture, natural theology, or perfect being theology. This need not be seen as a defect of classical thinking since all models of God need to bring in further philosophical assumptions to fill out their model of God. Throughout the discussion on the four classical divine attributes, I shall note different assumptions that classical theists use to help them fill out the notion that God is perfect.

II. TIMELESSNESS, IMMUTABILITY, AND SIMPLICITY

I start by focusing on the claim that God is timeless. For classical theists, to say that God is timeless is to say that God necessarily exists (1) without beginning, (2) without end, (3) without succession, (4) without temporal location, and (5) without temporal extension (Mullins 2016a: chapter 3). Conditions (1)–(2) seem obvious as conditions for an eternal being and follow straightforwardly from God's necessary existence. Yet, conditions (3)–(5) need more unpacking.

In order to understand condition (3), one must be aware of some metaphysical commitments amongst classical theists. Most classical theists affirm a relational theory of time where time exists if and only if change or succession occurs. As Rory Fox notes, succession and change serve as the fundamental basis for determining whether or not something is temporal or non-temporal (Fox 2006: 226–7). According to classical theism, God is timeless, and as such must exist without succession. Hence, the affirmation of condition (3).

How does the classical theist justify condition (3)? The classical theist will appeal to divine immutability. God is immutable in that God does not and cannot undergo any intrinsic or extrinsic change (Lombard 2007: Distinctions VIII and XXXVII.7). The denial of intrinsic change in God is well understood in contemporary literature, but the denial of extrinsic change is often not appreciated. Extrinsic changes are sometimes referred to as relational changes or mere Cambridge changes. This is a change that an object undergoes in relation to something else. Often times, contemporary theists think that immutability does not require denying that God undergoes extrinsic relational changes. However, as Paul Helm makes clear, the denial of extrinsic, or mere Cambridge, change is crucial for justifying (3) (Helm 2010: 19–20, 81–7). If God were only immutable with regards to intrinsic change, God would still undergo succession as He changes extrinsically in relation to other things, thus, contradicting condition (3) (Deng 2018: 36, Zimmerman and Chisholm 1997).

In order to deny that God undergoes extrinsic or relational changes, and thus succession, classical theists deny that God is really related to the universe (Augustine 1991: V.17; Lombard 2007: XXX.1; Aquinas 1934: II.12). According to Boethius (1918), the category of relation does not apply to God at all (IV). The claim that God is not really related to creation is a complicated matter. Later, I shall say more about it. What matters at the moment is that, on classical theism, God is immutable such that God cannot undergo any kind of change, be it intrinsic or extrinsic. (Dolezal 2017: 97). This is systematically connected to condition (3), the affirmation that a timeless God exists without succession.

What justifies the classical theist in affirming immutability? In order to arrive at immutability, one must understand a classical assumption about value, called the Platonic assumption (Mullins 2016a: 48–9). This assumption asserts that there are no value-neutral changes because all change is for the better or worse (Rogers 2000: 47). Given this assumption, if God is perfect, then God cannot change. If God changed, God would either become better or worse. The classical theist says that God cannot become better because God is already perfect. She also says that God cannot become worse because a perfect being cannot become less than perfect. Thus, she says that God must be immutable.

With this justification for immutability, one might think that the classical theist has secured condition (3). However, classical theists traditionally say that more is needed to secure condition (3). To further help one understand condition (3), it is worth saying something about the doctrine of divine simplicity. On the classical understanding of God, all of God's essential attributes are identical to each other, and identical to the divine nature, which is identical to the divine existence (Dolezal 2017: 41–2). For example, God's attribute of omniscience is identical to God's omnipotence, and these in turn are identical to the divine nature and existence. With creatures like you and me, we are substances that possess properties like knowledge and power. With the simple God, this is not the case. The simple God does not possess any properties, forms, immanent universals, or tropes (Bergmann and Brower 2006: 359–60). Instead, there is the simple, undivided substance that we call God. This simple substance does not have any intrinsic or extrinsic properties because it does not possess any properties at all (Rogers 1996: 166).

Moreover, a simple God is purely actual. This means that the simple God does not possess any potential whatsoever (Rogers 1996; Dolezal 2011). On classical theism, it is assumed that to possess potentiality implies mutability since going from potential to actual entails undergoing a change, and thus undergoing succession. Classical theism has already ruled out any kind of change in God, so a simple God must be purely actual. The claim that God is pure actuality and simple has further entailments. It entails that all of God's actions are identical to each other such that there is only one divine act. Further, this one divine act is identical to the divine substance, and thus identical to God's existence (Aquinas 1934: II.10). In other words, God is an act (Rogers 2000: 27).

What justifies the doctrine of divine simplicity? It is often asserted that simplicity is entailed by divine aseity (Brower 2009; Duby 2016: 121–31). However, this alleged entailment is a hotly contested issue (Fowler 2015; Baddorf 2017). What is needed to justify divine simplicity is another set of metaphysical commitments about composition. The classical tradition affirms that genus, differentia, forms, accidental properties, essence, and existence are metaphysical parts (Hughes 2018: 2). On this understanding, if a being is not identical to its properties or its existence, and so forth, then this being will be a composite object. To be sure, some contemporary metaphysicians will find it curious that "existence" could be a proper part of an object, but this claim is needed to help justify divine simplicity (Hughes 2018: 11–13).

To help one draw the connections between simplicity, immutability, and timelessness, recall the fact that the simple God does not have any properties at all. Classical thinkers claim that a simple God has no properties, not even accidental Cambridge properties like *being referred to* as *Creator, Redeemer, Lord,* or *Judge of All Men*.[1] To be sure, classical theists claim that it is true that God is the creator, but they claim that what makes this true is something in reference to the creature, and not any property that God possesses. This is because even referring to God in this way would make God temporal and mutable (Wolterstorff 2010: 153). Thus, simplicity rules out any kind of intrinsic or extrinsic change in God, and thus rules out any succession in God. Hence, the affirmation of condition (3).

---

[1] This is a fairly traditional claim that is often not well appreciated in contemporary literature. Cf. Augustine (1991: V.17), Boethius (1918: IV), Lombard (2007: XXX.1), Aquinas (1934: II.12), Arminius (1986: 116).

At this point, the reader should have a better grasp on the claim that the timeless, immutable, and simple God exists without succession. However, conditions (4)–(5) still need explication—the claims that God exists without temporal location and without temporal extension. In order to maintain that God exists without temporal location and extension, classical theists affirm that God exists as a whole, or all at once, in a timeless present that lacks a before and after (Aquinas 1936: I.Q10; Oresme 1968: 163–5). This is sometimes referred to as God's atemporal duration (Stump and Kretzmann 1981; Leftow 1991). Can the classical theist coherently speak of God's timelessness as a present or as a duration?

In contemporary discussions, the notion of God's timeless duration has been charged with obvious incoherence by proponents and critics of classical theism (Smith 1989: 323; Rogers 1994: 6; Craig 2001: 11–12). The charge is that duration involves a succession of moments, and a timeless present explicitly denies a succession of moments. Thus, an atemporal duration is self-contradictory since it affirms and denies succession. Moreover, one might complain that the notion of a timeless present is incoherent because the present is an inherently temporal notion (Deng 2018: 27–9). Hence, it might seem that the classical theist cannot coherently maintain that God endures in a timeless present. This leaves the classical theist with little means to articulate conditions (4)–(5).

I think that these objections are interesting, but I find them unpersuasive because they are missing some important metaphysical assumptions within the classical tradition. There is another set of metaphysical commitments that will help one understand the classical doctrine of divine timelessness. The majority of classical theists have affirmed a presentist ontology of time and an endurantist account of persistence through time.[2] On presentism, only the present moment of time exists. The past no longer exists, and the future does not yet exist. On endurantism, an object persists through time by existing as a whole, or all at once, at all times at which it exists. Since the present is the only moment of time that exists, the object exists as a whole at the present.

Knowing this commitment to presentism and endurantism will help one understand various classical statements about God's eternal present and atemporal duration, and thus conditions (4)–(5). I will start with the notion of a timeless present. Is it possible to coherently speak of a timeless present? I say yes. As I understand it, a moment of time is the way things are but could be subsequently otherwise. A timeless moment cannot be subsequently otherwise since a timeless moment, by definition, exists without a before and after. Yet a moment of time and a timeless moment share the same feature of *being the way things are*. To understand this, consider what Ulrich Meyer calls the property-time link. According to Meyer, there is an intrinsic conceptual link between predication and a moment of time (Meyer 2013: 37–9). Whenever we predicate a property of something, we intuitively say that this object has a property at a particular moment of time. The classical theist can make a similar claim about God's timeless moment.

Meyer's property-time link is not far off from the way Brian Leftow understands God's timeless present. Leftow suggests that God's timeless present functions logically as a date in that one can index propositions to it (Leftow 1991: 54). Classical theists have traditionally made claims of this nature. For example, classical theists will say that from all eternity God is predestining the salvation of the elect (Couenhoven 2018: 11). In these

---

[2] There are some contemporary classical theists who affirm alternative ontologies of time and theories of persistence over time. I will discuss these below. For a full discussion, see Mullins (2016a: chapters 4 and 6).

sorts of statements, classical theists are predicating things of God, and indexing them to God's eternal present. In order to maintain condition (4)—the claim that God does not have temporal location—the classical theist will insist that anything one predicates of God must only be indexed to God's timeless present, and not to any temporal present.

That is how the classical theist can attempt to speak coherently of God's timeless present. What about God's atemporal duration? The classical theist says that God has the perfection of existing as a whole, or all at once (Anselm 2008a: 21–2 and 24; 2008b: 13, 19, and 22). The classical theist is saying that God is an endurant being, not that God has successive duration (Pasnau 2011b).

To get a better handle on this, it will be helpful to understand a distinction often made in the Middle Ages. During the Middle Ages, it was common to distinguish between an endurant object and the life of the object. Classical theists, like Nicole Oresme and Anselm, say that an object endures through time and can be properly said to exist as a whole, or all at once, in the present. The present is the only moment that exists, so an endurant object does not have parts lying about at other times. It exists wholly and entirely in the present. Yet, classical theists say that we can draw a conceptual distinction such that the endurant object has a before and after in its life. In other words, the life of the endurant object can be conceptually divided up into temporal parts because the endurant object has temporal location and extension (Cross 2005: 122; Pasnau 2011a: chapter 18). Classical theists maintain that conceptual distinctions are perfectly appropriate to predicate of creatures, but not so for a simple and timeless God. This is because the classical theist says that even conceptual distinctions count as metaphysical parts, and a simple God does not have any metaphysical parts (Hasker 2016: 701–4).

For classical theists, conceptual distinctions are repugnant to divine simplicity and must be denied of God. In arguing for God's timelessness, Anselm draws upon the denial of conceptual distinctions. He (2008b) says that, "whatever is made up of parts is not absolutely one, but in a sense many and other than itself, and it can be broken up either actually or *by the mind*—all of which things are foreign to" God.[3] Anselm makes it clear that God is a "unity itself not divisible by any mind" (18). Thus, God's life is identical to God's attributes, which are identical to God. Anselm then goes on to say of God, "Since then, neither You nor Your eternity which You are have parts, no part of You or of Your eternity is anywhere or at any time, but You exist as a whole everywhere and Your eternity exists as a whole always" (18).

When classical theologians deny that God has temporal parts, they are denying that God has the sorts of conceptual distinctions that apply to the lives of endurant temporal creatures. They are asserting that God has no before and after in His life because He has no distinct moments in His life at all. He is not spread out through time like temporal creatures are. Thus, classical theism affirms that God lacks temporal location and extension.

III. THE EMOTIONAL LIFE OF THE ETERNAL GOD

Thus far, I have discussed the attributes of timelessness, immutability, and simplicity. What about the doctrine of divine impassibility? There are three claims that make up the core of impassibility. First, it is metaphysically impossible for God to suffer (Helm 1990: 120–1).

---

[3]Emphasis mine.

Second, it is metaphysically impossible for God to be moved, or acted upon, by anything outside of God (Arminius 1986: 117; Creel 1997: 314). Third, God lacks passions. Yet this third claim needs to be nuanced since it is sometimes mistakenly thought to imply that the impassible God lacks emotions.

Anastasia Scrutton suggests that we can place the classical understanding of emotions on a continuum. On one side of the continuum are passions that are involuntary, arational, and physical. On the other side of the continuum are what we today would call the cognitive emotions, which are voluntary, potentially rational, and nonphysical (Scrutton 2011: 53). Part of the claim from classical theists, then, is that the impassible God only has cognitive emotions whilst lacking passions.

This notion of a continuum helps gain some traction on understanding the classical doctrine of God, yet there is more to the story. For example, Rogers denies that God has any passions; but she does not say that God cannot have any cognitive emotion whatsoever. She holds that the impassible God only has positive emotions like love and joy (Rogers 2000: 51). The impassible God cannot be subject to negative emotions such as sadness or suffering. This is why classical theists deny that God has any empathy or compassion (McCabe 1987: 44; Davies 2006: 234). If God empathizes with creatures, God will be subject to negative emotions like sadness or suffering. That is incompatible with impassibility (Zagzebski 2013: 44).

How do classical theists justify the claim that God only has positive emotions like love and joy? As I have explained elsewhere (2018), there are three criteria that classical theists use to discern which emotions can literally be attributed to the impassible God.[4] The first criterion is that God cannot have any emotion that is inconsistent with God's moral perfection. The second says that God cannot have any emotion that is inconsistent with God's perfect rationality.

Nonclassical theists who reject impassibility are quite happy to accept these two criteria for God's emotional life (Taliaferro 1989; Scrutton 2011). Thus, there is nothing in these two criteria that justifies impassibility. In order to justify impassibility, one must understand another assumption that classical theists use to articulate their doctrine of God—divine blessedness. Classical theists affirm a third criterion, which says that any emotion that entails a disruption of God's happiness cannot literally be attributed to God.

How do classical theists justify this third criterion? Classical theism affirms that God is perfectly blessed or happy in Himself, and His happiness is in no way dependent upon anything external to the divine nature. One common argument for divine blessedness is that God is perfectly acquainted with the Good. In order to be happy, one must have a proper emotional evaluation of the greatest good and be intimately related to the greatest good. Given divine simplicity, God is identical to the Good. Given God's omniscience, He cannot possibly fail to evaluate that He is the greatest good. Thus, classical theism affirms that God is necessarily, perfectly happy (Silverman 2013: 168).

Classical theists use this sort of argument to draw a connection between all three of these criteria. The claim is that it would be immoral and irrational for God to be moved by creatures from His perfect bliss. Why? The idea is that a perfectly rational God knows that He is the greatest good. If He were to be moved by something external to the divine nature, God would be giving a false emotional evaluation of that external thing. This is

---

[4] Readers should note that literal predication is compatible with both univocal and analogical predication. Analogical predication is not a metaphorical usage of language (Muis 2011). Further, classical theism is compatible with both univocal and analogical predication (Cross 2008; Williams 2005).

because God would be valuing this external thing as greater than Himself. According to the classical theist, such a false emotional evaluation would be both irrational and immoral (Wittmann 2016: 145). Hence, they say God must be impassible and in a state of pure, undisturbed bliss.

In what follows, I will consider two objections to classical theism, and some of the kinds of responses that classical theists offer. The following discussion is by no means exhaustive. In exploring these objections, my aim is to offer readers an insight into the kinds of debates that are taking place about classical theism.

IV. THE PROBLEM OF CREATION *EX NIHILO* FOR TIMELESSNESS AND IMMUTABILITY

The doctrine of creation *ex nihilo* became robustly articulated in the early days of the Christian church. As classical theists reflected on this doctrine, they affirmed that there is a state of affairs such that God exists without creation, and a state of affairs such that God exists with creation (Broadie 2010: 53). This is because God lacks a beginning, whereas creation has a beginning. As John of Damascus explains, "it is not natural that that which is brought into existence out of nothing should be co-eternal with what is without beginning and everlasting" (Damascus 1898: I.7). According to Damascene, there are different kinds of ages, some of which are temporal, and one of which is non-temporal. Damascene explains that there is a timeless age prior to creation that lacks measure and division (Damascus 1898: II.1). To be clear, what we have here in Damascene is the claim that there is a state of affairs such that God exists without creation.

The notion that there is a state of affairs where God exists without creation is typically connected to God's freedom and impassibility. Classical theists maintain that God is free to create or not to create, and that God would be just as perfectly blissful without creation (Creel 1986: 159; Kretzmann 1991: 208; Webster 2010: 12; Burrell 2013: 5; McFarland 2014: 43). The classical theist's affirmation of divine freedom to exist without creation is also motivated by the felt need to distinguish the doctrine of creation *ex nihilo* from other cosmogonies that teach that the universe necessarily and eternally emanates from God (Garcia 1992: 192; Blowers 2012: 186). These other creation doctrines are more at home within panentheism than they are with classical theism because panentheism denies creation *ex nihilo* (Göcke 2013).

A. W. Pink elaborates on God's precreation existence because he thinks it is important for understanding the solitary greatness and self-sufficiency of God's perfection. Pink explains as follows:

> "In the beginning, God" (Gen. 1:1). There was a time, if "time" it could be called, when God, in the unity of His nature (though subsisting equally in three Divine Persons), dwelt all alone. "In the beginning, God." There was no heaven, where His glory is now particularly manifested. There was no earth to engage His attention. There were no angels to hymn His praises; no universe to be upheld by the word of His power. There was nothing, no one, but God; and *that*, not for a day, a year, or an age, but "from everlasting." During a past eternity, God was alone: self-contained, self-sufficient, in need of nothing. (Pink 1975: 9)

With the classical theist's affirmation that there is a state of affairs in which God exists without creation and a state of affairs in which God exists with creation, one can develop a problem that creation *ex nihilo* causes for timelessness and immutability. There are many ways to develop this kind of problem. Here is one way to develop the objection. Call it the Creation Objection.

C1. If God begins to be related to creation, then God changes.
C2. God begins to be related to creation.
C3. Therefore, God changes.
C4. If God changes, then God is neither immutable nor timeless.
C5. Therefore, God is neither immutable nor timeless.

Classical theists have been deeply aware of this sort of problem. The traditional move is to deny (C2). As mentioned above, the classical theist denies that God is really related to creation. She says that God cannot be related to anything *ad extra* to the divine nature. Thus, God cannot begin to be related to creation (Dodds 2008: 165–9; cf. McWhorter 2013).

A real relation involves substances having an accidental property associated with the relation. For example, when a man begets a son, the man acquires the accidental property *father*, and the child acquires the property *son*. One would naturally think that when God creates a universe, God would acquire the accidental property *creator*, and the universe would have the property *creation*. This is because the property *creator* is not some pseudo-Cambridge property because it is grounded in God's free intentional act to create a universe (Mawson 2018: 54). Intentional actions are intrinsic to agents, and thus cannot be extrinsic, or merely Cambridge, properties. Yet, traditional classical theists maintain that a simple God cannot have any accidental properties, nor any properties at all. The property *creator*, is an accidental property, and thus must be denied of the simple God (Augustine 1991: V.17). When the classical theist considers the universe coming into existence, she says that God does not begin to be related to the universe because God cannot be related to anything *ad extra* to the divine nature on pain of God having an accidental property and undergoing change (Lombard 2007: XXX.1).

Critics of classical theism will say that this response is deeply *ad hoc*. A critic will also say that it is unintuitive to claim that God is not really related to creation. The critic thinks it quite obvious that God's act of creating and sustaining a universe implies that God is really related to the universe (Craig 2001: 61–78).

Some contemporary classical theists agree that this is deeply unintuitive, and thus affirm that God is really related to creation (Rogers 2009: 336). These classical theists try to deny (C2) in a different way. The strategy here is to deny the classical assumptions of presentism and God's precreation state of affairs. Instead of affirming presentism, this view affirms an eternalist ontology of time whereby all moments of time eternally exist. On eternalism, no moments of time ever come into existence, and no moments of time ever cease to exist. Instead, all moments of time coeternally exist with God. The payoff for this strategy is that there is no state of affairs where God exists without creation, and thus no sense in which God begins to be related to creation. Rather, God is eternally related to creation (Rogers 2006; Mawson 2008; Helm 2010).

Critics of classical theism will reject this reply to the Creation Objection. For example, William Lane Craig says that adopting eternalism completely destroys the doctrine of creation *ex nihilo*. This "emasculated doctrine of *creatio ex nihilo* does not do justice to the biblical data, which give us clearly to understand that God and the universe do not timelessly co-exist, but that the actual world includes a state of affairs which is God's existing alone without the universe" (Craig 2001: 254). Whether or not the doctrine of creation *ex nihilo* can be made sense of on an eternalist ontology of time is up for debate since it looks remarkably like the panentheist's denial of creation *ex nihilo*.

V. THE PROBLEM OF MODAL COLLAPSE FOR SIMPLICITY

Many contemporary theists struggle to accept the identity claims of divine simplicity because it sounds incoherent on the surface. They wonder how attributes like *power*, *knowledge*, and *existence* can be identical (Morris 1987: 98–122; cf. Hughes 2018; Tapp 2018; Hasker 2016). Various kinds of responses have been offered to remove the incoherence, but there is no agreed upon solution at this time (Leftow 2006; Brower 2008; Saenz 2014). I wish to highlight a serious problem with saying that God's action is identical to God's existence. Call it the Modal Collapse Objection.

To start, note that classical theists affirm the infallibility of omnipotence. God's causal power is infallible in that, if God intentionally acts to bring about some state of affairs x, then it is not possible for x to fail to obtain (Frost 2015: 46). This gives us the first premise in the Modal Collapse Objection.

> M1. If God intentionally acts to actualize this world, then this world cannot possibly fail to obtain.

A worry from classical theists is that if God's act to actualize a world is absolutely necessary, then everything that occurs in the world occurs of absolute necessity as well. Why? The source of the universe's contingency is grounded in the free and contingent will of God (Frost 2015). If God's intentional act to actualize the world is absolutely necessary, and thus not contingent, then the grounds for the contingency of the world will disappear. This worry can be stated as follows:

> M2. If God's intentional act to actualize this world is absolutely necessary, then this world exists of absolute necessity.

In order to avoid this worry, classical theists maintain that God's act to actualize a world is contingent, and thus the world only exists of hypothetical necessity. Hypothetical necessity is when some state of affairs must follow from a prior state of affairs, yet that prior state of affairs need not have obtained. Classical theists maintain that God did not have to create the universe. God is free to create or not create the universe (Leftow 2016: 152; Pruss 2017: 213–14; Skrzypek 2017: 148). Thus, His intentional act to actualize this world is contingent, giving the world a merely hypothetical necessity.

The problem with this classical affirmation of the contingency of divine acts is that it contradicts other things that the classical theist says about the simple God. In particular:

> M3. God's existence is absolutely necessary.
> M4. Anything that is identical to God's existence must be absolutely necessary.
> M5. All of God's intentional actions are identical to each other such that there is only one divine act.
> M6. God's one divine act is identical to God's existence.

(M3) is uncontroversial among classical theists (Rogers 2000: 40). (M4) is true on pain of violating identity. (M5) and (M6) are explicitly stated in the doctrine of divine simplicity (Rogers 1997: 35–41; Dolezal 2017: 59). Therefore,

> M7. God's one divine act is absolutely necessary.

With (M7) one can derive a modal collapse. A modal collapse occurs when the typical modal distinctions between necessity and contingency are all collapsed into one category. In this case, all of the modal distinctions are collapsed into absolute necessity. One way to understand a modal collapse is that it says that there is only one possible world—the actual world. According to this, God could not have actualized another world on pain of violating divine simplicity.

In order to derive a modal collapse, notice that (M5) says that all of God's intentional actions are identical to each other such that there is only one divine act. Thus, God's intentional act to actualize this world is going to be identical to this one divine act and have the same modal status as this one divine act. According to (M7) this one divine act is absolutely necessary. Thus,

M8. God's intentional act to actualize this world is absolutely necessary.

From (M2) and (M8), we get:

M9. This world exists of absolute necessity.

(M9) is the modal collapse that the classical theist wishes to avoid.

At this point, one might say that the argument is making some invalid inferences because of an ambiguity in the phrase "God's intentional act." In particular, one might say that 'God's intentional act' designates, or refers to, God's effects instead of God Himself (Tomaszewski 2019: 280). However, this is an implausible reading of 'God's intentional act.' God's intentional acts quite clearly refer to the cause (i.e., God), and not the effect. As mentioned before, intentional acts are intrinsic to agents. In the case of the simple God, His intentional acts are not merely intrinsic to Him, they are identical to Him.

Moreover, divine simplicity explicitly endorses the claim that 'God's act' refers to God because God's act is identical to God's existence. This is why classical theists often say that God is simply act, or God is His act, or God is Pure Act. As Rogers explains, "All the terms we correctly use to describe God refer to this one act" (Rogers 1997: 40). In other words, 'God's act' rigidly designates God on pain of violating the identity claims of divine simplicity. To say otherwise is to abandon divine simplicity.

What this means is that God's actions are identical to God's existence, and thus it is not possible for God to have done otherwise. To say that God could have done otherwise is to say that God could have existed otherwise because God's act is identical to God's existence. But divine simplicity explicitly denies that God could have existed otherwise (Rogers 1997: 45–7; Dolezal 2011: 198–200). Thus, these divine actions are performed of absolute necessity, which entails a modal collapse. This is because the entire way that things are is the only way that things could be. This is a very serious problem for classical theism.

One option is to just bite the bullet on the modal collapse. Some classical theists are willing to bite the bullet, and admit that this is the only way the world could be (Rogers 1997: 68–9; McCann 2012: 170; 2016: 249–50). Yet, most seem to find the modal collapse a deeply dissatisfying bullet to bite (Garcia 1992; Skrzypek 2017). In general, most classical theists claim that God could have refrained from creating, and thus could have existed without actualizing any world (Kretzmann 1991: 208).

Another strategy is to try to weaken the doctrine of divine simplicity (Stump and Kretzmann 1985, 1987; Crisp 2019: 54–75). Perhaps someone attracted to this strategy could try to deny (M5) and (M6) by saying that God's acts are not identical to each other, and not identical to God's existence. This would avoid the conclusion in (M7), thus blocking the inference to (M8) and (M9). However, in weakening divine simplicity in this way, one will not only have abandoned the classical doctrine of divine simplicity, but one will also have introduced complexity, potentiality, and accidental properties into God in a way that undermines timelessness and immutability (Dolezal 2011: 198–9; Duby 2016: 50–1). Hence, classical theists ought to avoid this strategy for fear of losing the entire classical understanding of God.

By far, the most common response from classical theists is to appeal to ineffable mystery. One version of the appeal to mystery says that God's freedom and the contingency of the world are mysteries beyond our ken (Dolezal 2011: 206–12; Feser 2017: 224–6). According to Timothy Pawl (2016), one can appeal to mystery in theology when one is asked to give a positive account of something that is beyond one's ken. However, one cannot appeal to mystery when one is faced with a derived contradiction because one's beliefs have been shown to entail a contradiction (89–90). This is because contradictions are not mysterious; they are necessarily false. In the case of the Modal Collapse Objection, the classical theist has a contradiction on her hands because, contrary to (M8) and (M9), she wishes to maintain the contingency of God's intentional actions and the contingency of the world. Appealing to mystery here fails to identify which premise of the argument one is rejecting and leaves the problem in place.

In another appeal to mystery, one might try to deny (M4) by saying that there are different kinds of necessity in God. On this strategy, one says that God's act of actualizing the world is a different kind of necessity from God's absolutely necessary existence (Duby 2016: 120). For example, one might say that God's existence is of absolute necessity whereas God's act of actualizing the world is of hypothetical necessity. This approach admits that God's act is identical to God's existence, but it maintains that it is a mystery as to how the act and existence do not share the same kind of necessity (Levering 2017: 103–5). This approach, however, is implausible because it is impossible for two things to be strictly identical and have different kinds of necessity. It is, however, possible for two things to be in a *constitution* relation and have different modal properties. A constitution relation is a kind of sameness without identity, but simplicity demands identity. Thus, this will not help the classical theist avoid the Modal Collapse Objection.

References

Anselm (2008a), "Monologion," in B. Davies and G. Evans (eds.), *Anselm of Canterbury: The Major Works*, New York: Oxford University Press.

Anselm (2008b), "Proslogion," in B. Davies and G. Evans (eds.), *Anselm of Canterbury: The Major Works*, New York: Oxford University Press.

Aquinas, T. (1934), *Summa Contra Gentiles*, trans. English Dominican Fathers, London: Burns, Oates, and Washbourne.

Aquinas, T. (1936), *Summa Theologiae*, trans. English Dominican Fathers, London: Burns, Oates, and Washbourne.

Arminius, J. (1986), *The Works of James Arminius*, vol. 2, trans. J. Nichols, London: Baker Book House Company.

Augustine (1991), *The Trinity*, trans. E. Hill, Hyde Park: New City Press.

Baddorf, M. (2017), "Divine Simplicity, Aseity, and Sovereignty," *Sophia*, 56: 403–18.

Bergmann, M., and J. Brower (2006), "A Theistic Argument against Platonism (and in Support of Truthmakers and Divine Simplicity)," in D. W. Zimmerman (ed.), *Oxford Studies in Metaphysics*, vol. 2, 357–86, Oxford: Oxford University Press.

Berkhof, L. (1984), *Systematic Theology*, Edinburgh: The Banner of Truth Trust.
Blowers, P. M. (2012), *Drama of the Divine Economy: Creator and Creation in Early Christian Theology and Piety*, Oxford: Oxford University Press.
Boethius (1918), *The Trinity is One God Not Three Gods*, trans. H. Stewart, London: G.P. Putnam's Sons.
Bohn, E. D. (2018), "Divine Foundationalism," *Philosophy Compass*, 13 (10): 1–11.
Boyd, G. A. (2000), *God of the Possible: A Biblical Introduction to the Open View of God*, Grand Rapids, MI: Baker Books.
Broadie, A. (2010), "Scotistic Metaphysics and Creation Ex Nihilo," in D. B. Burrell, J. M. Soskice, and W. R. Stoeger (eds.), *Creation and the God of Abraham*, 53–64, Cambridge: Cambridge University Press.
Brower, J. E. (2008), "Making Sense of Divine Simplicity," *Faith and Philosophy*, 25 (1): 3–30.
Brower, J. E. (2009), "Simplicity and Aseity," in T. P. Flint and M. C. Rea (eds.), *The Oxford Handbook of Philosophical Theology*, 105–28, Oxford: Oxford University Press.
Burrell, D. B. (2013), "Creatio Ex Nihilo Recovered," *Modern Theology*, 29 (2): 5–21.
Charnocke, S. (1682), *Several Dischourses upon the Existence and Attributes of God*, London: Newman.
Couenhoven, J. (2018), *Predestination: A Guide for the Perplexed*, London: T&T Clark.
Craig, W. L. (2001), *God, Time, and Eternity*, London: Kluwer Academic.
Creel, R. E. (1986), *Divine Impassibility: An Essay in Philosophical Theology*, Cambridge: Cambridge University Press.
Creel, R. E. (1997), "Immutability and Impassibility," In P. L. Quinn and C. Taliaferro (eds.), *A Companion to Philosophy of Religion*, Malden: Blackwell.
Crisp, O. D. (2019), *Analyzing Doctrine: Toward a Systematic Theology*, Waco: Baylor University Press.
Cross, R. (2005), *Duns Scotus on God*, Burlington, VT: Ashgate.
Cross, R. (2008), "Idolatry and Religious Linguange," *Faith and Philosophy*, 25: 190–6.
Damascus, J. o. (1898), "Exposition of the Orthodox Faith," In P. Schaff and H. Wace (eds.), *A Select Library of the Nicene and Post-Nicene Fathers of the Christian Church*, vol. 9, trans. S. Salmond, 546–777, Edinburgh: T&T Clark.
Davies, B. (2006), *The Reality of God and the Problem of Evil*, London: Continuum International.
Deng, N. (2018), *God and Time*, Cambridge: Cambridge University Press.
Diller, J. and A. Kasher, eds. (2013), *Models of God and Alternative Ultimate Realities*, New York: Springer.
Dodds, M. J. (2008), *The Unchanging God of Love: Thomas Aquinas and Contemporary Theology on Divine Immutability*, 2nd ed., Washington, DC: The Catholic University of America Press.
Dolezal, J. E. (2011), *God without Parts: Divine Simplicity and the Metaphysics of God's Absoluteness*, Eugene, OR: Pickwick Publications.
Dolezal, J. E. (2017), *All That Is in God: Evangelical Theology and the Challenge of Classical Christian Theism*, Grand Rapids, MI: Reformation Heritage Books.
Duby, S. J. (2016), *Divine Simplicity: A Dogmatic Account*, London: Bloomsbury.
Erickson, M. J. (2004), *Christian Theology*, 2nd ed., Grand Rapids: Baker Books.
Feser, E. (2017), *Five Proofs of the Existence of God*, San Francisco: Ignatius Press.
Fowler, G. (2015), "Simplicity of Priority?," in J. Kvanvig (ed.), *Oxford Studies in Philosophy of Religion*, vol. 6, Oxford: Oxford University Press.
Fox, R. (2006), *Time and Eternity in Mid-Thirteenth-Century Thought*, Oxford: Oxford University Press.

Fretheim, T. E. (1984), *The Suffering of God: An Old Testament Perspective*, Philadelphia: Fortress Press.

Fretheim, T. E. (2015), *What Kind of God? Collected Essays of Terence E. Fretheim*, ed. M. J. Chan and B. A. Strawn, Winona Lake: Eisenbrauns.

Frost, G. (2015), "Aquinas and Scotus on the Source of Contingency," in R. Pasnau (ed.), *Oxford Studies in Medieval Philosophy*, vol. 2, 46–66, Oxford: Oxford University Press.

Garcia, L. L. (1992), "Divine Freedom and Creation," *The Philosophical Quarterly*, 42 (16): 191–213.

Göcke, B. P. (2013), "Panentheism and Classical Theism," *Sophia*, 52 (1): 61–75.

Göcke, B. P. (2018), *The Panentheism of Karl Christian Friedrich Krause*, Oxford: Peter Lang.

Hasker, W. (2016), "Is Divine Simplicity a Mistake?," *American Catholic Philosophical Quarterly*, 90: 699–725.

Helm, P. (1990), "Impossibility of Divine Passibility," in N. M. Cameron (ed.), *The Power and Weakness of God*, Edinburgh: Rutherford House Books.

Helm, P. (2010), *Eternal God: A Study of God without Time*, 2nd ed., Oxford: Oxford University Press.

Hughes, C. (2018), "Aquinas on the Nature and Implications of Divine Simplicity," *European Journal for Philosophy of Religion*, 10 (2): 1–22.

Kretzmann, N. (1991), "A General Problem of Creation: Why Would God Create Anything at All?," in S. MacDonald (ed.), *Being and Goodness: The Concepts of the Good in Metaphysics and Philosophical Theology*, 208–28, London: Cornell University Press.

Leftow, B. (1991), *Time and Eternity*, Ithaca, NY: Cornell University Press.

Leftow, B. (2006), "Divine Simplicity," *Faith and Philosophy*, 23 (4): 365–80.

Leftow, B. (2011), "Why Perfect Being Theology?," *International Journal for Philosophy of Religion*, 69 (2): 103–18.

Leftow, B. (2016), "Two Pictures of Divine Choice," in H. J. McCann (ed.), *Free Will and Classical Theism: The Significance of Freedom in Perfect Being Theology*, 152–73, Oxford: Oxford University Press.

Levering, M. (2017), *Engaging the Doctrine of Creation: Cosmos, Creatures, and the Wise and Good Creator*, Grand Rapids, MI: Baker Academic.

Lombard, P. (2007), *The Sentences Book 1: The Mystery of the Trinity*, trans. G. Silano, Ontario: Pontifical Institute of Mediaeval Studies.

Mawson, T. (2008), "Divine Eternity," *International Journal for the Philosophy of Religion*, 64: 35–50.

Mawson, T. (2018), *The Divine Attributes*, Cambridge: Cambridge University Press.

McCabe, H. (1987), *God Matters*, London: Cassell.

McCann, H. J. (2012), *Creation and the Sovereignty of God*, Bloomington: Indiana University Press.

McCann, H. J. (2016), "Free Will and the Mythology of Causation," in A. A. Buckareff and Y. Nagasawa (eds.), *Alternative Concepts of God: Essays on the Metaphysics of the Divine*, 234–54, New York: Oxford University Press.

McFarland, I. A. (2014), *From Nothing: A Theology of Creation*, Louisville: Westminster John Knox Press.

McWhorter, M. R. (2013), "Aquinas on God's Relation to the World," *New Blackfriars*, 94 (1049): 3–19.

Meyer, U. (2013), *The Nature of Time*, Oxford: Oxford University Press.

Moberly, R. (2013), *Old Testament Theology: Reading the Hebrew Bible as Christian Scripture*, Grand Rapids, MI: Baker Academic.

Morris, T. V. (1987), *Anselmian Explorations: Essays in Philosophical Theology*, Notre Dame, IN: University of Notre Dame.

Morris, T. V. (1991), *Our Idea of God: An Introduction to Philosophical Theology*, Downers Grove, IL: InterVarsity Press.

Muis, J. (2011) "Can Christian Talk About God Be Literal?," *Modern Theology*, 27: 582–607.

Mullins, R. (2016a), *The End of the Timeless God*, Oxford: Oxford University Press.

Mullins, R. (2016b), "The Difficulty of Demarcating Panentheism," *Sophia*, 55: 325–46.

Mullins, R. (2018), "Why Can't the Impassible God Suffer?," *TheoLogica*, 2: 3–22.

Nagasawa, Y. (2017), *Maximal God: A New Defense of Perfect Being Theism*, Oxford: Oxford University Press.

Oresme, N. (1968), *Le Livre du ciel et du monde*, London: University of Wisconsin Press.

Pasnau, R. (2011a), *Metaphysical Themes: 1274–1689*, Oxford: Oxford University Press.

Pasnau, R. (2011b), "On Existing All at Once," in C. Tapp and E. Runggaldier (eds.), *God, Eternity, and Time*, 11–28, London: Routledge.

Pawl, T. (2016), *In Defense of Conciliar Christology: A Philosophical Essay*, Oxford: Oxford University Press.

Pink, A. W. (1975), *The Attributes of God*, Grand Rapids, MI: Baker Books.

Pruss, A. R. (2017), "Divine Creative Freedom," in J. L. Kvanvig (ed.), *Oxford Studies in Philosophy of Religion*, vol. 7, 213–38, Oxford: Oxford University Press.

Rogers, K. A. (1994), "Eternity Has No Duration," *Religious Studies*, 30 (1): 1–16.

Rogers, K. A. (1996), "The Traditional Doctrine of Divine Simplicity," *Religious Studies*, 32 (2): 165–86.

Rogers, K. A. (1997), *The Anselmian Approach to God and Creation*, Lewiston: Edwin Mellen Press.

Rogers, K. A. (2000), *Perfect Being Theology*, Edinburgh: Edinburgh University Press.

Rogers, K. A. (2006), "Anselm on Eternity as the Fifth Dimension," *The Saint Anselm Journal*, 3: 1–8.

Rogers, K. A. (2009), "Back to Eternalism: A Response to Leftow's 'Anselmian Presentism'," *Faith and Philosophy*, 26 (3): 320–38.

Saenz, N. B. (2014), "Against Divine Truthmaker Simplicity," *Faith and Philosophy*, 31 (4): 460–74.

Sanders, J. (2007), *The God Who Risks: A Theology of Divine Providence*, Downers Grove, IL: InterVarsity Press.

Scrutton, A. (2011), *Thinking through Feeling: God, Emotion and Passibility*, New York: Continuum International.

Silverman, E. (2013), "Impassibility and Divine Love," in J. Diller and A. Kasher (eds.), *Models of God and Alternative Ultimate Realities*, 165–74, New York: Springer.

Skrzypek, J. W. (2017), "A Better Solution to the General Problem of Creation," *European Journal for Philosophy of Religion*, 9 (1):147–62.

Smith, Q. (1989), "A New Typology of Temporal and Atemporal Permanence," *Nous*, 23 (3): 307–30.

Speaks, J. (2018), *The Greatest Possible Being*, Oxford: Oxford University Press.

Stump, E. (2016), *The God of the Bible and the God of the Philosophers*, Milwaukee: Marquette University Press.

Stump, E., and N. Kretzmann (1981), "Eternity," *Journal of Philosophy*, 78 (8): 429–58.

Stump, E., and N. Kretzmann (1985), "Absolute Simplicity," *Faith and Philosophy*, 2 (4): 353–82.

Stump, E., and N. Kretzmann (1987), "Simplicity Made Plainer," *Faith and Philosophy*, 4 (2): 198–201.

Swinburne, R. (2004), *The Existence of God*, Oxford: Oxford University Press.
Swinburne, R. (2016), *The Coherence of Theism*, Oxford: Oxford University Press.
Taliaferro, C. (1989), "The Passibility of God," *Religious Studies*, 25 (2): 217–24.
Tapp, C. (2018), "Utrum Verum Et Simplex Convertantur: The Simplicity of God in Aquinas and Swinburne," *European Journal for Philosophy of Religion*, 10 (2): 23–50.
Tomaszewski, C. (2019), "Collapsing the Modal Collapse Argument: On an Invalid Argument Against Divine Simplicity," *Analysis*, 79 (2): 275–84.
Ward, K. (2015), *Christ and the Cosmos: A Reformulation of Trinitarian Doctrine*, Cambridge: Cambridge University Press.
Webster, J. (2010), "Trinity and Creation," *International Journal of Systematic Theology*, 12: 4–19.
Williams, T. (2005), "The Doctrine of Univocity is True and Salutary," *Modern Theology*, 21: 575–85.
Williams, T. (2013), "Introduction to Classical Theism," in J. Diller and A. Kasher (eds.), *Models of God and Alternative Ultimate Realities*, 95–100, New York: Springer.
Wittmann, T. (2016), "The Logic of Divine Blessedness and the Salvific Teleology of Christ," *International Journal of Systematic Theology*, 18 (2): 132–53.
Wolterstorff, N. (2010), *Inquiring About God*, ed. T. Cuneo, Cambridge: Cambridge University Press.
Zagzebski, L. (2013), *Omnisubjectivity: A Defense of a Divine Attribute*, Milwaukee: Marquette University Press.
Zimmerman, D. W., and R. M. Chisholm (1997), "Theology and Tense," *Nous*, 31 (2): 262–5.

CHAPTER EIGHT

An Anselmian Approach to Divine Omnipotence

KATHERIN ROGERS

How are you [God] omnipotent, if you cannot do all things? Or at least, if you are not able to be corrupted or to lie or to make what is true to be false, as for example what is done not to be done, and many similar things: how are you able to do all things?

—Anselm, *Proslogion* 7

St. Anselm of Canterbury can be seen as the unofficial patron saint of contemporary analytic theology and philosophy of religion. He approaches difficult religious issues logically, sets out his arguments clearly, and holds that many thorny dilemmas can be solved through the careful definition of terms and analysis of concepts. He is often cited by contemporary philosophers and theologians, and the label "Anselmian" is given to discussions involving a being than which a greater cannot be conceived. But Anselm's own views are often ignored or misunderstood. Here I hope to correct this situation as it bears on a central concept in analytic theology, divine omnipotence.

Analyzing omnipotence raises numerous questions: Must an omnipotent being be able to do *anything*? Change the past? Make a round square? Make a stone too heavy for it to lift? Do evil? Make factual errors? Commit suicide? Bring about any possible state of affairs, such as some free agent *freely* choosing X over Y? At least since St. Augustine's day it has been clear that we cannot understand "omnipotence" as "the ability to do everything that all possible beings can possibly do."[1] There are things only an essentially limited being can do (using "do" broadly), such as make a stone too heavy for it to lift, since something can be "too heavy" only for a corporeal being (corporeality is a limitation) of limited strength. And there seem to be things that only an essentially unlimited being—unlimited at least in some ways—can do. Always knowing everything that can possibly be known would be an example. Since no possible being can be both essentially limited and essentially unlimited simultaneously, no possible being can do everything that all possible beings can possibly do. That "omnipotence" means the ability to do *anything* may figure in the folk understanding, but among philosophers it has been off the table for roughly two millennia.

Philosophers take two main approaches to omnipotence. One, perhaps the more popular method recently, is labeled the "secular" approach. It proposes a definition

---

[1] Augustine writes that God can do anything he should will to do, and there are many things he "cannot" do: "He cannot die, He cannot sin, He cannot lie, He cannot deceive. So much He cannot do, because if He were able to do them, He would not be omnipotent" *Sermo* CCXIII (from notes by Schmitt (Anselm 1938e, 1: 106)).

of "omnipotence" for "some being x", setting aside other attributes we might want to ascribe to God. The proponent of this approach often appeals to his intuitions and commitments concerning actions, powers, and abilities, perhaps including a nod to the "folk" understanding. Sometimes it is then asked how this definition fits with some view of God, and often puzzles arise in trying to square this "omnipotence" with other divine attributes. The other approach starts by setting out a view of God and then considers what "omnipotent" might mean, given that understanding. It is this latter method that seems to me most perspicuous.

In this chapter, I first look briefly at some examples of the former method and problems that it engenders. Then I turn to an example of the latter method. I sketch St. Anselm of Canterbury's basic understanding of the divine nature, his analysis of omnipotence, and how this analysis deals with some of the standard puzzles of omnipotence. This approach is useful for several reasons. Anselm's theory is philosophically and theologically powerful, it is historically interesting, and it involves assumptions that are different from those standard in the contemporary literature. It is helpful for philosophers and theologians to evaluate the assumptions that constitute the "common wisdom" of their day and circle, and one aid in that job is to appreciate that different assumptions can ground different, but plausible, conclusions regarding the perennial questions of philosophy and theology. Anselm's understanding of "omnipotence" is far from that of many contemporary philosophers and theologians and *very* far from any "folk" understanding (assuming there is such a thing). But that does not undermine its philosophical and theological power and gives us all the more reason to consider it.

Graham Oppy discusses three recent attempts to produce a secular definition of "omnipotence" and raises problems with them (2005: 58–84). A quick look at this discussion illustrates not only difficulties defining "omnipotence" having bracketed views of the divine but also common contemporary assumptions that the tradition of Anselm (and Augustine and Thomas Aquinas) finds unacceptable—because they conflict with divine omnipotence! These efforts at definition are detailed and complex, attempting to rule out certain "powers", like the ability to change the past or control a free being. But, as Oppy argues, these definitions invite criticisms including undermining counterexamples.

First, Oppy reviews a definition of "omnipotence" offered by Joshua Hoffman and Gary Rosenkrantz (Hoffman and Rosenkrantz 2002a,b):

> Def: x is *omnipotent at t* iff [if, and only if] for all suitable states of affairs that s, if it is possible for some agent to bring it about that s, then at t x has it within its power to bring it about that s. [Oppy adds "suitable" to capture states of affairs (henceforth SOAs) that Hoffman and Rosenkrantz define but do not label.] (Oppy 2005: 62, bracketed insert added)

Unpacking this definition would be a lengthy process, but to get an idea of Oppy's criticisms it is enough to say a little about a "suitable" SOA, s: either s is unrestrictedly repeatable, and of the form "in n minutes, p," or s is of the form, "q forever after" where q is unrestrictedly repeatable. Hoffman and Rosenkrantz construct the definition including "unrestricted repeatability" to rule out the possibility of their omnipotent being being able to change the past. But this allows Oppy to propose examples of SOAs that appear "suitable," yet an omnipotent being cannot bring them about, or SOAs that presumably an omnipotent being could bring about, but which the definition rules out. He (2005: 70) writes,

First, that a certain state of affairs is unrestrictedly repeatable at some moments in the history of the universe does not guarantee that that state of affairs is unrestrictedly repeatable at other moments in the history of the universe. ... *Second*, that a certain state of affairs is unrestrictedly repeatable at some moments in the history of the universe does not guarantee that there is more than one agent for whom it is logically possible to bring about that state of affairs. [It is logically possible for a particular libertarian free agent to bring about a repeatable SOA, but not for anyone else to do so.] ... *Third*, there are states of affairs that an omnipotent being ought to be able to bring about that seem likely to resist any analysis in terms of unrestricted repeatability: e.g., bringing time to an end.

Oppy (2005: 70–1) also addresses a definition offered by contemporary Molinists Thomas Flint and Alfred Freddoso:

Def: S is *omnipotent* at t in W iff for any state of affairs p and world type for S, Ls, such that p is not a member of Ls, if there is a world W* such that: (1) Ls is true in both W and W*; and (2) W* shares the same history with W at t; and (3) at t in W* someone actualizes p; then S has the power at t in W to actualize p.

Again, unpacking the definition would be a serious undertaking, but we can say enough to appreciate problems. A "world-type" is "a consistent set of propositions such that exactly one of each counterfactual of freedom and its negation are the members of the set." A Molinist "counterfactual of freedom" "is a proposition of the form: if individual essence P were instantiated in circumstances C at time t and its instantiation were left free with respect to action A, then the instantiation of P would freely do A" (71). That is, there are true propositions about what any possible free agent *would* freely choose in any possible situation. One motivation for this definition is to capture the thought that human agents can have libertarian free will, but nonetheless God, knowing all these counterfactuals, can actualize the possible world in which the choices that He *wants* to be made *are* made.

The inclusion of counterfactuals of freedom is one difficulty for this definition. Another is the assumption that time is essentially tensed; the omnipotent being acts "at t," suggesting that it is time-bound. (The Anselmian account rejects both of these problematic concepts.) Oppy poses several other difficulties. For example, Molinists distinguish between the ability to "strongly" actualize an SOA or to "weakly" actualize it; roughly the difference between S's bringing about the SOA itself or S's bringing it about by actualizing another being, T, in a situation such that when T is in that situation it brings about the SOA. Molinists make this distinction in attempting to preserve divine sovereignty and human libertarian freedom, but, as Oppy points out, Flint and Freddoso's definition allows that an omnipotent being, S, be able only to *weakly* actualize some SOA that other agents could *strongly* actualize, even setting aside situations involving free agency. And that, Oppy opines, suggests that S is not omnipotent.

Oppy offers a further criticism of the Flint and Freddoso definition that, while it may connect with their approach, rests on an assumption that Anselm denies. The definition includes S at t actualizing an SOA at t. He writes, "At time t, no one has—nor can have—the power to bring about states of affairs that obtain at t; it is already too late for that!" (2005: 77).

Oppy cites a third definition proposed by Edward Wierenga (1983, 1989):

> a being x is omnipotent in a possible world w at time t *iff* it is true in w both that (i) for every [SOA] that p, if it is logically possible for the history of the world to be as it is until t and for x to strongly actualise the [SOA] that p at t, then x has it within its power to strongly actualise the [SOA] that p at t; and (ii) there is at least one [SOA] that x has within its power to strongly actualise at t. (77)

Oppy notes that objections usually point out that x may be essentially limited such that there are SOAs x cannot actualize but other beings, not so essentially limited, may be able to actualize. This raises the specter of the, by definition, omnipotent Mr. McEar who is essentially limited to one ability—he can scratch his ear.[2] Even if Mr. McEar and his kindred are not really possible beings, the definition is still open to a severe general problem that Oppy develops: Hypothesize a being, O, which is essentially limited in the SOAs it can actualize, and another being that is not thus essentially limited which can do all the things O can, but more besides. This other being is more powerful than O, and O is not omnipotent since "it is simply an analytical truth that nothing can be more powerful than an omnipotent being" (2005: 78).

As Oppy points out, on many standard monotheisms, the divine creator is like O in being essentially limited, for example, in being essentially perfectly good. Then, suggests Oppy, we can posit a being that can do everything that O can do but, not confined to doing good, can do more besides (2005: 82).[3] Thus, O is not omnipotent and "omnipotence" should not be ascribed to God on standard monotheism. He writes, "We should draw a careful line between the (secular) idea of *omnipotence*, and the (religious) idea of *divine power* ... if the (secular) idea of omnipotence is capable of coherent explanation, then it will turn out to be quite distinct from the (religious) idea of divine power." The religious idea of divine power should not be allowed to claim the label of "omnipotence" since "there is by now a fairly well-established use of the word 'omnipotence' in the philosophical literature that does not conform to [the religious account]" (2005: 82–3).

It seems correct that elaborations of secular "omnipotence" are unlikely to capture what the philosophically and theologically informed religious believer understands God's power to entail. I am loathe, though, to relinquish the term "omnipotence." What Oppy takes to be "fairly well-established" has a history of only several decades, while "omnipotence" as the label for divine power is *better* established. Its history goes back close to two millennia and includes seminal and towering figures such as Augustine, Anselm, and Aquinas. The terminological dispute is easily resolved. Those working on the secular concept can refer to their subject as "secular omnipotence," and we who are attempting to understand the power of God can (as in the title of this chapter) refer to "divine omnipotence." In what follows, "omnipotence" will refer mainly to Anselm's understanding of divine omnipotence.

Although Anselm addresses several puzzles of omnipotence, he does not offer a definition. In Anselm's day, among intellectuals, there was at least rough agreement on what the core of divine omnipotence consists in. This core is expressed early in Anselm's

---

[2] Mr. McEar was first hypothesized by Alvin Plantinga (1967) and named by Richard LaCroix (1975).
[3] For other analyses arguing that being essentially morally perfect is a limitation on omnipotence, see Loke (2010) and Morriston (2001: 156–7). Kenneth Pearce and Alexander Pruss focus on freedom of will and distinguish between a *limitation* that does not interfere with a being's freedom and a *constraint* (2012: 403–14). It is not clear that their definition can survive the sort of attack that Oppy levels against Wierenga.

Monologion, chapters 1–4: there is a "highest being," the source of all other beings. Ultimately he identifies this being with God. God's causing all other beings from nothing constitutes the most fundamental divine power. All non-divine existents exist "through" God. God causes them by having them "participate" in His existence. "Participation" is the absolutely unique relationship where God makes things *ex nihilo* such that they "reflect" Himself, each thing in its own limited way. "Reflect" is the standard, and perhaps the best, metaphor for a causal relationship that has no analogue among created beings. Created things never bring anything into being from nothing. Your parents put together stuff that was already there in order to conceive you. The most creative novelist combines concepts already extant to produce the world of the novel. God's causing creation, which can be called "primary causation," causes whatever exists to exist at the moment it exists. Creatures are "secondary causes" that interact with what is already there in creation, and all creatures with all their properties and their causal powers are caused by God to be from nothing immediately and simultaneously with their existence.

This conception of divine causation has deep historical roots stretching back through Neoplatonism to Plato. But Aquinas, usually considered more Aristotelian than platonic, adopts the platonic language when expressing this most fundamental exercise of divine power. He writes in *Summa Theologica* (1948: Ia.q44.a1), "Therefore all beings other than God are not their own being, but are beings by participation. ... All things which are diversified by the diverse participation of being, so as to be more or less perfect, are caused by one First Being, Who possesses being most perfectly." For scriptural support, Thomas quotes Rom. 11:36 (as it appeared in the version of the Vulgate he used), "Of Him, and by Him, and in Him are all things." He could also have quoted Acts 17:28, beloved by Christian Neoplatonists, where Paul explains to the Athenians that it is in God that we live, and move, and have our being.

On this conception of God and creation, the way that omnipotence has often been spelled out in the contemporary literature misses the mark. The question is usually posed in terms of what possible worlds or what possible SOAs God can actualize. The ontological status of possible worlds and SOAs is debated among philosophers, but many hold that, even rejecting Lewis's thought that all possible worlds have the same ontological status as our actual world, we should nevertheless grant them existence, perhaps as platonic abstracta (Menzel 2016: 2.2.1). The form in which issues regarding omnipotence are posed could suggest God surveying a series of possible worlds or SOAs existing outside of Him and then choosing which to actualize. The Flint and Freddoso Molinist definition, employing "counterfactuals of freedom," clearly presents this view. According to Flint (1998: 123–4), these counterfactuals depend neither upon God nor upon any actual agents actually choosing. God surveys possible worlds existing outside of Him and chooses what world best suits His purposes. The Anselmian rejects Molinism. It is not possible for *anything* to exist independently of God. The most fundamental exercise of divine power is creation *ex nihilo*, and that means that God is not confronted with anything outside of Himself which He uses to create.[4]

It seems a significant limitation on "some being x" that it must use things such as possible worlds or SOAs understood as platonic abstracta existing outside of it and

---

[4] Aquinas analyzes *possibilia* as God's understanding how His nature can be imitated (1948: Ia.q25.a6). Brian Leftow, agreeing that all non-divine existents come from God, holds that "talk about possible worlds is a useful fiction" to be parsed in terms of divine powers that operate on two levels, a natural, non-chosen level and a nonnatural level at which God gives Himself certain powers (2012: 41, 261–3).

independently of it to achieve its desired results. Anselm's God, who is the source of all that is not Himself, looks to be far more powerful. From the Anselmian perspective, the way in which the question of omnipotence is often expressed in the contemporary literature entails that the proposed omnipotent "being x" will fall short.

Anselm's God is both ubiquitous and eternal. True, He cannot leave Ohio, but this is because He is not *confined* to this or that patch of space. Nor is He limited to existing at some instantaneous present moment. Anselm (on my interpretation) is an isotemporalist (Rogers 2008: 176–84). Isotemporalism, sometimes called "eternalism," is the view that all times are equally existent. God, being eternal, "sees" all times as equally and immediately present to Him. What to the temporally limited perceiver appears to be past, present, and future is subjective, indexed to that perceiver at a given time. God, in one act, is immediately causing all space and time and everything in them. Being eternal renders Anselm's God more powerful than "some being x" that exists and acts only at some absolute present moment. Causing everything, everywhere, at all times, is more powerful than causing just what is here now to be here now. Knowing all of time, God, in His one, eternal act, can set in motion events to occur before a particular time to produce results at that time. God cannot *change* what is, from our perspective, the past ... nor our present, nor our future. He cannot do other than He actually does in His one eternal act.

Many of the criticisms and counterexamples aimed at recent definitions of "omnipotence" ask us to imagine a being that can do everything the "omnipotent" being in question, x, can do, but that can do more besides, proving x to fail in omnipotence. This is a legitimate move regarding "some being x", but it is difficult to mount against Anselm's understanding of God and the relationship of God to creation. The core of divine power is the ability to make all the actual existent beings there are *ex nihilo*, and it is not clear what a being just like Anselm's God, but who can make *more* beings *ex nihilo* would be. (We will address the related question of whether or not God could fail to create or could create a different universe below.) This sort of criticism is usually raised when those presenting a definition of "omnipotence" assume that the attribute can be properly applied to God on some traditional understanding of God. So a common example of a being who can do everything that x can do, but more, is a being who fits the proposed definition of "omnipotence" but—contrary to what motivated the definition—this other being can also do evil: A being, x, that is essentially morally perfect is thereby limited and cannot be omnipotent. The phrasing "a being, x, that is essentially morally perfect" seems to portray a being that, by nature, always conforms to the moral rules. This suggests something existing outside of x to which x must conform to be what it is, essentially morally perfect.

This is not the Anselmian view. In the *Monologion* 1, even before the argument to show there is a "highest" Being, the source of all other beings, Anselm offers a parallel argument to show that there is a "highest" Good, the source of all goods. Anselm's universe is imbued with value. All existents are good by participating in the Good.[5] God Himself is the standard for all good. He is simple, so the "properties" and the actions, which *quoad nos* look to be diverse—God's being, His power, His goodness, His thinking, His making, His willing—are one and identical in God. Anselm often characterizes being morally

---

[5]The common wisdom of modernity has managed to leech the value out of things, but the natural attitude of small children, and scientists when they are doing science, is that things—sand, bugs, the moons of Jupiter, et al.—are wonderful and worth attending to. It is not clear that the common wisdom is correct. See also Davison (2012).

good, for created agents, as conforming to the will of God. He is careful to note that this is not what we today call "divine command theory"—in its purest form that would be the view that the right thing for human agents to do is whatever God commands *and God can command anything logically possible* (Anselm 1938a: Book 1, chapter 12). (More below on the "primacy" of the divine will.) A being that can do everything God can do vis-à-vis value must be the absolute source and standard for all value in creation, including moral goodness. Anselm's definition of sin is to will what God wills that you not will. God cannot possibly sin, or even cause the created agent to sin (1938c: chapter 8). He cannot produce evil. The claim that we can imagine a being like Anselm's God who can also do evil is incoherent.

Another way to dismiss the thought that we can imagine some being x more powerful than Anselm's God because x can do everything God can do and can also do evil proceeds by considering why and how any agent chooses what it chooses. Anselm holds that agents do not choose something unless they desire it, and they do not desire it unless they believe it will produce happiness. Since Socrates, many of the world's great philosophers have held the view that the key to happiness is behaving well. In the long run, being wicked harms oneself and so one is wicked out of ignorance. Anselm, Augustine, and Aquinas certainly agree. The "ability" to desire and pursue some wrong, and ultimately harmful, object requires that the agent be ignorant. So, again, a being that can do everything God can do, and also do evil, is incoherent. In answer to the question "How is God omnipotent when there are all sorts of things he cannot do, such as lie …?," Anselm writes,

> Is it that being able to do these things is not power but impotence? For someone who can do these, does what does not benefit him and what he ought not to do. The more one is able to do these, the more adversity and perversity have power over him, and the less he has power against them. So who is able to do these, is not able due to power, but due to impotence. (1938e: chapter 7)

Anselm holds that "power follows will," and since God cannot *will* evil, He cannot *do* evil (1938a: Book 2, chapter 10).

But the point about God's essential goodness introduces a perennial issue regarding the scope of God's power. Should we say that, although God necessarily wills the best, God confronts genuinely open options such that the divine willing the best could issue in a different creation or no creation at all? The question is often phrased the way Gottfried Leibniz put it: "Must God create the best of all possible worlds?" And this is acceptable in the present, pre-Leibnizian, discussion so long as one does not suppose that possible worlds are platonic abstracta existing independently of God. Aquinas insists that God must have open options. God knows all the ways His infinite nature can be reflected in a well-ordered, created world, but there is no "best" world and God's necessarily willing the best could have issued in a different creation from the actual world, or in no creation at all. If one holds that divine freedom must entail open options, then one will answer the Leibnizian question in the negative: God does not need to create the best of all possible worlds, and divine omnipotence includes the power to create myriad good worlds or (at least according to Aquinas) no created world at all.

When the issue is omnipotence, this view has the advantage of proposing that God is free under a libertarian conception of freedom and could have produced all sorts of different worlds. And if libertarian freedom is necessary for great power, then allowing libertarian freedom to God is to be preferred. This is not the Anselmian approach, however. Anselm holds that *created* agents must be free under a libertarian description since, with everything about us coming from God, it is only by being able to choose between open options and from ourselves that we can be praiseworthy or blameworthy. More fundamentally, we need libertarian freedom in order to engage in the project for which God made us rational animals, that is to help in the construction of our characters as oriented toward the good (1938d: chapter 68; Rogers 2008: 56–60). (More on whether divine omnipotence includes being able to control the free choices of created agents below.) God, Anselm holds, is perfectly free by the appropriate definition—He is able to will justice (in this case, Himself) for its own sake. But there is a best to will and God inevitably wills it (Rogers 2008: 185–205). In Anselm's system, there is no value to supposing that God might be doing other than He is doing and hence no motivation for ascribing libertarian freedom to God. Unlike us, God exists absolutely *a se*. He is the ultimate source of all value. It would undermine His power to suppose that He is like us and needs open options to bear moral responsibility or to help in orienting his character toward the good. And there are disadvantages to holding that God has libertarian freedom. As Anselm notes discussing created free choices, and as critics always point out, on libertarianism one cannot give a decisive reason or explanation for the agent choosing this over that (1938b: chapter 27). If God might just as well have opted for a different creation or no creation at all, we cannot explain His creating *our* world as the manifestation of His perfect goodness. On the Anselmian view, ours is the best world God can make, taking into account the libertarian free choices of created agents.

This leads to the question of whether or not divine omnipotence entails the power to see to it that a created agent *freely* chooses as God would have it choose. The Molinist approach to reconciling created freedom with divine omnipotence fails because it posits "counterfactuals of freedom," abstracta outside of God that He must deal with in order to create (Flint 1998: 123–4). This undermines His omnipotence. (A further problem for the Molinist is that the "counterfactuals of freedom" necessitate the actual choices of actual agents, so it is difficult to see how Molinism preserves meaningful, libertarian free will (Rogers 2015: 109–16).) Anselm is clear that God does not cause human, morally significant choices. Indeed, as noted above, it is just logically impossible for God to cause sin, since to sin is to will what God wills that you not will. And, were God to necessitate a created agent's choices, the agent could not choose *a se*, and aseity is required for the created agent to be morally responsible and contribute to its own orientation toward the good. So the Anselmian answer to the puzzle concerning free will and omnipotence is, "No. God cannot see to it that the created agent *freely* chooses as He would have it choose."

But this generates a new puzzle. If the core of divine omnipotence is God's primary causation of the existence of everything that exists, how can He *not* be the cause of created agents' choices? Aren't those choices "things"? Aquinas says "Yes" and concludes that God is the primary cause of the act of sin (1948: I.Q83.a1, ad3). This does not entail that God willed evil, since the evil of the sin is a privation and what exists in the sin is part of the divine plan to be used for good (Aquinas 1948: Ia.q19.a9). Anselm (as I interpret him) opts for a different approach, a "parsimonious agent causation"; God causes every *thing* but does not cause the choice to sin … or the choice to resist sin. God causes the conflicting desires that produce the situation in which the created agent can make a libertarian free choice. But the choice is the agent, *from himself*, continuing to desire one of these to the point of intention, such that the competing desire becomes no longer viable. This choice has no new ontological status beyond the being of the continued desire (Rogers 2015: 81–100). God knows what the agent chooses, not because the agent exercises any causal power toward God, but because He knows which of the competing desires He continues to sustain (Rogers 2019: 96–7). Yes, there is something in the universe that is "up to" the agent in a way that God permits, but does not control. And this may seem to conflict with omnipotence. But the alternative is to hold that God causes sin. Moreover, unlike theories that include independently existing abstracta, God Himself is the source of the situation. And if this Anselmian picture of a free created agent's choices, and relationship to the *creator omnium* is logically possible, then it would undermine divine omnipotence to hold that God cannot make a robustly free agent whose choices He does not control.

Throughout this chapter, I have assumed that God "cannot" do the logically impossible. And this claim is supported by the quotation with which I began: Anselm says to God, "You are not able to be corrupted or to lie or to make what is true to be false, as for example what is done not to be done." We have already discussed the point that God, though perfectly free, cannot do evil, so He cannot lie. But Anselm includes "to make what is true to be false" in the same breath as lying. Regarding the possible, the impossible, and the necessary, Anselm makes a radical and provocative claim,

> God is improperly said to be unable to do something or to do something by necessity. This is because all necessity and impossibility is subject to His will; while His will is not subject to any necessity or impossibility. Indeed, nothing is necessary or impossible unless because He wills it; but for Him to will or to not will something on account of necessity or impossibility is far from the truth. Wherefore, He does everything that He wills, and only because He wills. Just as no necessity or impossibility precedes His willing or not willing, or His doing or not doing, nevertheless He immutably wills and does many things. And just as when God does something, after it is done, now He is not able to make it not to be done, but it is always true that it is done, still it is not right to say that it is impossible for God to make what was the case in the past not to have been in the past—truly there is at work here no necessity for not doing it, or impossibility for doing it, but only God's will, ... when God is said not to be able, no power is denied in Him, rather his insuperable power and strength is signified. Nothing other should be understood than that no thing is able to bring it about that He should do what He is *said* not to be able to do. (1938a: Book 2, chapter 17; emphasis added)[6]

The necessary and the possible depend upon the *will* of God. Does this entail that God *creates* logical truths, such that in His own nature He transcends them?[7] Could God, then, have created other rules of logic? This seems radically incoherent and prohibits us from saying or thinking anything meaningful about God's nature. But this appearance is rooted in the assumption that God can will other than He is willing and that God's will is something other than His nature. God, as perfect Good, wills Himself and so what is necessary and possible *even for God* can flow from God's willing without the unwholesome consequences mentioned above. God's will is absolutely independent, and it is identical to the divine nature, which just *is* God. God's will, then, is the source of all that is not God.[8] Working this concept into a careful, analytic definition of divine omnipotence might be hard or impossible. For example, the sort of source that God is

---

[6] I take Anselm's talk of the "past" to be *quoad nos*.
[7] Possibly René Descartes says this (Rogers 2000: 94–6).
[8] See note 4 on other ways of analyzing possibilia while maintaining that God makes *everything* that is not God.

has no analogue in creation, making it difficult to express in nonmetaphorical terms. But the requirement that the human knower should be able to grasp the nature of divine power with analytic clarity seems misplaced. If we can wrap our minds around the power and activities of "some being x," that is a sure sign that "x" is not the God of Anselm (or Augustine or Aquinas). As Anselm writes of the soul attempting to "see" God, "It is both obscured by its own smallness and overwhelmed by Your immensity. Truly it is limited by its own narrowness and conquered by Your greatness" (1938e: chapter 14). The power of God is so great that we must expect that human concepts cannot fully encompass it. If we are able to make enough sense of divine omnipotence to deal with the perennial dilemmas it raises, we have accomplished something. The contemporary analytic theologian would do well to consider Anselm's approach to divine omnipotence and the tradition in which it is grounded.

References

All translations in this chapter are my own.

Anselm (1938a), *Cur deus homo*, in F. S. Schmitt (ed.), *Opera Omnia*, 6 vols., Rome: Friedrich Frommann Verlag.

Anselm (1938b), *De casu diaboli*, in F. S. Schmitt (ed.), *Opera Omnia*, 6 vols., Rome: Friedrich Frommann Verlag.

Anselm (1938c), *De libertati arbitrii*, in F. S. Schmitt (ed.), *Opera Omnia*, 6 vols., Rome: Friedrich Frommann Verlag.

Anselm (1938d), *Monologion*, in F. S. Schmitt (ed.), *Opera Omnia*, 6 vols., Rome: Friedrich Frommann Verlag.

Anselm (1938e), *Proslogion*, in F. S. Schmitt (ed.), *Opera Omnia*, 6 vols., Rome: Friedrich Frommann Verlag.

Aquinas, T. (1948), *Summa Theologica*, in A. Pegis (ed.) *Basic Writings of St. Thomas Aquinas*, New York: Random House.

Davison, S. (2012), *On the Intrinsic Value of Everything*, New York: Continuum.

Flint, T., and A. Freddoso (1983), "Maximal Power," in A. Freddoso (ed.), *The Existence of God*, 81–113, Notre Dame: Notre Dame Press.

Flint, T. (1998), *Divine Providence: The Molinist Account*, Ithaca, NY: Cornell University Press.

Hoffman, J., and G. Rosenkrantz (2002a), *The Divine Attributes*, Oxford: Blackwell.

Hoffman, J., and G. Rosenkrantz (2002b), "Omnipotence," in E. N. Zalta (ed.), *Stanford Encyclopedia of Philosophy*, Available online: https://plato.stanford.edu/entries/omnipotence/.

LaCroix, R. (1975), "Swinburne on Omnipotence," *International Journal for Philosophy of Religion*, 6: 251–5.

Leftow, B. (2012), *God and Necessity*, Oxford: Oxford University Press.

Loke, A. T. E. (2010), "Divine Omnipotence and Moral Perfection," *Religious Studies*, 46: 525–38.

Menzel, C. (2016), "Possible Worlds," in E. N. Zalta (ed.), *Stanford Encyclopedia of Philosophy*. Available online: https://plato.stanford.edu/entries/possible-worlds/.

Morriston, W. (2001), "Omnipotence and Necessary Moral Perfection: Are they Compatible?," *Religious Studies*, 37: 143–60.

Oppy, G. (2005), "Omnipotence," *Philosophy and Phenomenological Research*, 71: 58–84.

Pearce, K., and A. Pruss (2012), "Understanding Omnipotence," *Religious Studies*, 48: 403–14.

Plantinga, A. (1967), *God and Other Minds*, Ithaca, NY: Cornell University Press.

Rogers, K. (2000), *Perfect Being Theology*, Edinburgh: Edinburgh University Press.

Rogers, K. (2008), *Anselm on Freedom*, Oxford: Oxford University Press.
Rogers, K. (2015), *Freedom and Self-Creation: Anselmian Libertarianism*, Oxford: Oxford University Press.
Rogers, K. (2019), "Foreknowledge, Freedom, and Vicious Circles," in B. Arbour (ed.), *Philosophical Essays against Open Theism*, 93–109, New York: Routledge.
Wierenga, E. (1983), "Omnipotence Defined," *Philosophy and Phenomenological Research*, 43: 363–75.
Wierenga, E. (1989), *The Nature of God: An Inquiry into Divine Attributes*, Ithaca, NY: Cornell University Press.

CHAPTER NINE

Maximal Greatness and Perfect Knowledge

BENJAMIN H. ARBOUR

Analytic theologians spill plenty of ink about the nature of the discipline and the methodologies employed by its practitioners. Those familiar with the history of the relationship between philosophy and theology sometimes joke that analytic theology is really just medieval scholasticism warmed over; some of us wonder why that would be bad. Proceeding by way of Anselmian perfect being theology,[1] in what follows, I offer an attempt at an overview of an analytic theological approach to the doctrine of divine omniscience. I hope that those interested in theology proper might see how analytic philosophy assists theologians in properly interpreting what Scripture teaches about God's knowledge.

I. ON PERFECT BEING THEOLOGY

The possession of certain properties is valuable. We intuitively know that being knowledgeable and being powerful count as great-making attributes, and without a strong argument that our intuitions are misleading on these matters, we have good reason to trust our intuitions. Thomas Morris explains, "Most practitioners of perfect being theology take our intuitions about matters of value, as they do most other intuitions, to be innocent until proven guilty, or reliable until proven deceptive. The alternative is a form of skepticism with few attractions" (1991: 39).

Being knowledgeable and being powerful are not merely instrumentally valuable; rather, they are intrinsically valuable. That is, to possess knowledge is good in and of itself, not merely because one can use such knowledge for some other purpose. The same holds for power. However, not all good properties are intrinsically valuable. Consider the property of being wealthy. Having money isn't valuable in and of itself; instead, having money is valuable because it enables one to make purchases or contribute to causes. Presumably, some purchases or contributions make one happy, and happiness is intrinsically good (Morris 1991: 35–9).

Perfect being theologians confess that God is omnipotent, omniscient, and morally perfect. Virtually no debate exists among analytic theologians concerning the great-making

---

[1] Space constraints preclude extended defenses of perfect being theology, but Anselmian intuitions seem eminently reasonable to me and have been ably defended elsewhere. Cf. Morris (1987); Rogers (2000); Hill (2005: especially 1–26); Leftow (2011); and Wierenga (2011).

status of these three attributes, even if scholars disagree about how to properly understand them. Power, knowledge, and righteousness contribute to a being's overall greatness; accordingly, a perfect being enjoys these properties maximally. Moreover, a truly perfect being would possess these great-making attributes in the most perfect mode, which means that such a being couldn't fail to possess these attributes. It follows that God should be understood to possess omnipotence, omniscience, and moral perfection essentially and not contingently. Philosophers can logically deduce that if God exists, and if God is perfect, then God possesses the maximal amount—an omni-amount—of any great-making attribute. Therefore, we conclude that God is omnipotent, omniscient, and morally perfect unless we have some good reason to think that the upper limit of what is possible with respect to power, and/or knowledge, and/or righteousness is something less than omnipotence, omniscience, and moral perfection, respectively.

Yujin Nagasawa offers a taxonomy of arguments against perfect being theology, suggesting that there are three kinds of such arguments (2017: 79–120). First, there are arguments purporting to show the impossibility of any single divine attribute, such as the paradox of the stone with regard to omnipotence. Either God can create a stone so heavy that not even God can lift it, or God cannot create such a stone. Either way, there is something God cannot do, so omnipotence is impossible (or so those who argue thusly contend). Second, there are arguments purporting to show that two or more attributes are not composible. Some argue that since an omnipotent being could sin, and because a morally perfect being cannot sin, it is therefore impossible for any being to be both omnipotent and morally perfect at the same time. Finally, consider arguments purporting to show the incompatibility of one or more divine attributes with some contingent fact about the universe. Problems of evil and/or divine hiddenness paradigmatically express this type of argument.

Nagasawa's reformulation of Anselmian theism opens the door to the idea that God might be something less than omni-perfect, if being omni-perfect turns out to be logically impossible (cf. Todd 2015). He argues that there must be some upper limit to what is possible; so even if that upper limit turns out to be something other than the conjunction of omnipotence, omniscience, and moral perfection (and any other great-making attributes), this doesn't undermine the analytic theologian's confidence in the existence of a maximally great being. Nagasawa's strategy forestalls atheistic arguments that might stem from issues concerning the coherence of omniscience, by offering perfect being theologians a way out by reconceiving divine omniscience as maximally great knowledge (even if that turns out to be something less than omniscience, strictly speaking). However, giving up omniscience before one makes an effort to defend the doctrine would be unwise. Punting is an acceptable defensive strategy, but only on fourth down. Moreover, efforts to show that omniscience, omnipotence, and moral perfection aren't jointly composible have been shown unsuccessful (Swinburne 2016; Bernstein 2018). With all this in mind, let's turn our attention to see how analytic philosophy can assist theologians to understand better the claims of Scripture regarding the nature and scope of divine knowledge.

II. DEFINING OMNISCIENCE IN LIGHT OF MAXIMAL GREATNESS

Although philosophers agree that knowledge is a great-making attribute, are there any theological reasons for thinking that God is omniscient? Yes. Consider the following passages from the Scriptures of the three main Abrahamic faiths:

Say: Would you appraise Allah of your religion? and Allah knows all that is in the heavens and all that is in the earth; and Allah is All-Aware of everything. (Qur'an 49:16)

For truly my words are not false; one who is perfect in knowledge is with you. (Job 36:4); and Do you know the balancings of the clouds, the wondrous works of him who is perfect in knowledge? (Job 37:16)[2]

for whenever our heart condemns us, God is greater than our heart, and he knows everything. (1 Jn 3:20)

Christians, Jews, and Muslims confess that God's knowledge is perfect and that God is all-knowing. Whereas many biblical theologians are content to rely on special revelation, analytic theologians make use of analytic philosophy to understand better the content of special revelation.

We have seen that if God is the greatest of all possible beings, then God possesses maximally great knowledge. Presumably, maximally great knowledge entails omniscience. Therefore, if omniscience is possible, then God must be omniscient, and essentially so. Unfortunately, this brief argument doesn't prove that omniscience is possible, nor does it provide a properly nuanced definition of omniscience. How, then, should theologians formulate the doctrine of divine knowledge? Analytic Anselmianism helps. In showing how, I proceed in two parts. I begin with remarks on the *nature* of divine knowledge, then I turn to the *scope* of divine knowledge.

III. ON THE NATURE OF DIVINE KNOWLEDGE

Whereas some consensus exists about the nature of human knowledge (e.g., properly justified true belief, or warranted true belief), little work has been done recently on the nature of divine knowledge. Because contemporary thinkers haven't said much about what it means for God to know something, it's unclear if they think divine knowledge requires justification and/or warrant, or whether God has beliefs. Moreover, it's difficult to answer questions about *how* God knows something without antecedently understanding *what* it is for God to know something. Let's consider whether truth is a necessary condition for divine knowledge, whether God has belief(s), and whether divine knowledge requires justification.

III.1 Truth as a Component of Divine Knowledge

Standpoint epistemology, along with objections against the existence of objective truth commonly found in continental philosophy, might undermine the idea that truth is a necessary condition for divine knowledge. Thankfully, there does seem to be a broad consensus among analytic epistemologists that knowledge is factive. Regardless of which theory of truth one defends, analytic epistemologists maintain that, if anyone knows that p, it follows that p is true. Analytic theologians generally agree that even God cannot know that which is false; so truth is a necessary condition for knowledge, even for God. Therefore, in order for God to know that p, p must be true.

Some epistemologists defend fallibilism, whereupon either knowledge itself is fallible, or one or more epistemic property is fallible (e.g., beliefs, cognitive faculties, justification) (Dougherty 2011b). Fallibilism comes in both strong and weak forms. According to

---

[2]Biblical quotations in this chapter are from the English Standard Version of the Bible.

strong fallibilism, all human knowledge is fallible. It's important to note that a generally fallibilist approach to epistemology does not entail that every instance of knowledge is fallible. Because fallible knowledge is clearly inferior to infallible knowledge, and because any divine being would enjoy maximally great knowledge, perfect being theology entails divine infallibility. Those who deny fallibilism will see no problem with divine infallibility. Anselmians who adopt fallibilist approaches to epistemology in general can maintain even strong fallibilism about human knowledge while taking divine infallible knowledge as a special species of knowledge.

Another difference between human epistemology and divine epistemology emerges when considering that truth isn't a sufficient condition for human knowledge, since there are undoubtedly a great many truths that humans have yet to discover. For those who affirm that God has beliefs, divine knowledge obviously requires not only truth but also belief. But it's disputed as to whether or not God has beliefs. If God lacks beliefs, it's not clear that anything beyond truth is necessary for divine knowledge. This becomes clearer when we consider the mode of divine knowledge.

III.2 Divine Beliefs or Lack Thereof

St. Thomas Aquinas discusses the nature of divine knowledge at length in both the *Summa Theologiae* as well as the *Summa Contra Gentiles*. He argues that God enjoys immediate knowledge, rather than discursive knowledge, of all things. William Alston summarizes Aquinas nicely, suggesting that because

> the divine essence contains the likeness of all things, God, in knowing Himself perfectly, thereby knows everything. Now since God is absolutely simple His knowledge cannot involve any diversity. Of course what God knows in creation is diverse, but this diversity is not paralleled in His knowledge of it. Therefore, "God does not understand by composing and dividing." His knowledge does not involve the complexity involved in propositional structure any more than it involves any other kind of complexity.
> But although God's knowledge, in itself, consists wholly of His simple intuition of His own essence, nevertheless He does not thereby miss anything, including whatever can be "enunciated," i.e., formulated in propositions. (Alston 1989: 180; cf. Aquinas 1975: I.58; and Aquinas 2012: Ia.Q14.aa5-6)

All this follows from the doctrine of divine simplicity (DDS). However, DDS is controversial; so consider another motivation for non-propositional divine knowledge.

> It seems plausible to suppose that the propositional character of human knowledge stems from our limitations. Why is our knowledge parceled out in separate facts? For two reasons. First, we cannot grasp any concrete whole in its full concreteness; at most we cognize certain abstract features thereof, which we proceed to formulate in distinct propositions. Second, we need to isolate separate propositions in order to relate them logically, so as to extend our knowledge inferentially. Both these reasons are lacking in the divine case. God can surely grasp any concrete whole fully, not just partial aspects thereof. And God has no need to extend His knowledge, inferentially or otherwise, since it is necessarily complete anyway. Hence there would be no points in God's carving up His intuition of reality into separate propositions. We have to represent divine knowledge as the knowledge of this or that particular fact; but this is only one of the ways in which we are forced to think of God's nature and doings in terms of our own imperfect approximations thereto. (Alston 1989: 183)

A properly Anselmian motivation of immediate knowledge parallels an argument concerning divine power. If two beings have the ability to lift the same heavy weight, but the task proves difficult for one being while the other accomplishes the task with relative ease, we deduce that the latter being is superior to the former with respect to strength. Similarly, consider two people who each get a perfect score on an exam, but one person found the exam to be easy, whereas the other person toiled. Maximal greatness implies perfect cognitive powers, so the first person has a superior intellect. However, we should not conclude mistakenly that maximal epistemic greatness is a mere *ability* to know (e.g., omniscient-able), but rather the actual possession of knowledge.

Consider asking two people how they know that the interior angles of an equilateral triangle measure sixty degrees. One person reasons from knowledge that the sum of the interior angles of any triangle are 180 degrees and then infers that the angles of an equilateral triangle must all be identical. Having deduced as much, this person divides 180 degrees by three and concludes that each interior angle must be exactly sixty degrees. The second person responds that, by definition, the interior angles of any equilateral triangle are each sixty degrees. The second person's knowledge, because it's non-inferential, and therefore not discursive, is superior to the first person's. Accordingly, maximally great knowledge would be immediate in all cases where immediate, nondiscursive knowledge is possible.

There are three possibilities concerning the nature of immediate divine knowledge: either all divine knowledge is immediate, or some (but not all) divine knowledge is immediate, or all divine knowledge is discursive. There are no good reasons to think that *all* divine knowledge is discursive, since divine knowledge of at least some things could be properly basic in the following sense: some instances of divine knowledge might be of God's rationally believing "that *p*" without reasons. However, some argue that there are good reasons to think that at least some of what God knows is necessarily discursive, because non-inferential knowledge of some truths is impossible. We will consider this further when we turn to discuss the scope of divine knowledge.

So, even apart from the DDS, there are Anselmian motivations for rejecting the idea that God's knowledge is propositional in nature, and this has implications for the question about whether God has beliefs. Alston suggests why:

> Whatever else a belief may be, it is obviously a *propositional* attitude, a psychological state that involves the structural complexity of some proposition. We have no inkling of how some psychological state could be a belief without being a belief that *p*, where "*p*" stands for a sentence that expresses a proposition. Hence a being whose knowledge involves no propositional structure or complexity has no beliefs as part of its knowledge. On any nonpropositional conception of divine knowledge there can be no case for supposing that God's knowledge involves beliefs. (Alston 1989: 183)

Alston's analysis poses a problem for any definition of omniscience that entails beliefs about propositions. Unless we can articulate an adequate response to Alston, definitions of omniscience that involve discussions of beliefs and/or propositions need to be modified accordingly.[3]

Of course, there are some philosophers and theologians who dispute this, since they don't take beliefs to be necessarily propositional. Trent Dougherty denies that God has

---

[3] To consider one important response, see Hasker (1988).

beliefs (plural) but thinks God does have a single belief, which he takes to mean that God takes the world to be a certain way.[4] It's not obvious that this is propositional and may be compatible with the view that God enjoys knowledge by acquaintance with the world (cf. Dickinson 2019).

III.3 Divine Knowledge and Epistemic Justification

Assuming divine infallibility, for anything that God believes or cognizes immediately, divine knowledge doesn't require any justification or warrant as a necessary condition for such beliefs or cognitions to count as divine knowledge, at least not as though God might be subject to any potentially undermining epistemic defeaters. With respect to justification, for any divine beliefs/cognitions, God wouldn't ever need to explain the basis of such knowledge. In fact, all divine knowledge might be properly basic, especially for those inclined to think that all divine knowledge is immediate and nondiscursive. This holds regardless of whether someone thinks all divine knowledge is known immediately by God through acquaintance, or immediately believed, or perhaps known immediately through some other mode.

However, some epistemologists defend evidentialism, which is an epistemology whereupon, roughly, people's beliefs are rational in proportion to their evidence for their beliefs.[5] So, committed evidentialists insist that knowledge that p requires that one's relevant background evidence sufficiently explains why one knows that p (tipping the hat at the no-false-lemma view). The same holds for those who think knowledge entails belief, and beliefs are properly based if and only if one's background beliefs serve to explain properly why one believes that p, or believes that p. Given that all God's knowledge is complete, infallible, and monotonic, God's beliefs are never subject to revision since there are no additional considerations that could possibly be given to motivate overturning any divine knowledge.[6]

Moreover, one of two options exist for contemporary perspectives on warrant. Some epistemologists take warrant to be whatever property that, in sufficient quantity, serves to turn true belief into knowledge. Although these accounts of warrant block Gettier objections from undermining "justified true belief" as the proper definition of knowledge, they are perfectly compatible with accounts of proper justification. Therefore, on such an account of warrant, we have no reason to discredit previously stated evidentialist accounts of divine knowledge—at least for those who think God has belief(s). Alternatively, other epistemologists take warrant to be something that requires properly functioning cognitive faculties alongside an appropriate design plan (e.g., Plantinga 2000). However, it's not obvious that God has faculties (especially for those who defend classical theism and the DDS). Moreover, given that God exists *a se*, necessarily and eternally, it's impossible that any design plan could provide the necessary conditions for divine warrant concerning any divine belief/cognition. Accordingly, either divine knowledge does not require warrant, or warrant reduces to proper justification for divine knowledge.

---

[4] Trent Dougherty, personal correspondence, April 26, 2020.
[5] Perhaps the most historically significant defense of evidentialism as it concerns religious issues comes from Clifford (2001). For more contemporary discussions of evidentialism, see Dougherty (2011a).
[6] Thanks to Trent Dougherty for several helpful conversations regarding the relationship between evidentialism and divine epistemology.

It's important to note that on some particularly strict formulations of DDS, God's knowledge is identical with His existence. On these formulations of DDS, whenever we speak of God knowing anything, we are speaking analogically. But, as aforementioned, DDS is controversial, and one needn't depend on DDS in order to defend the idea that God doesn't have belief(s). Nonetheless, we conclude as follows regarding the *nature* of divine knowledge. For those who don't think God has belief(s), for anything known by God immediately, and non-propositionally, truth alone is sufficient for divine knowledge. For those who think God does have belief(s), two options are available depending on what one thinks about evidentialism: either truth plus belief is sufficient such that epistemic justification isn't necessary for divine knowledge, or contemporary articulations of knowledge (properly justified true belief) adequately capture the nature of what it is for God to know p in virtue of the monotonicity of divine knowledge.

IV. ON WHAT GOD DOES (AND DOESN'T) KNOW

Common sense leads us to suppose that any omniscient being knows 100 percent of all truths—that's what the "omni-" is supposed to convey. However, some analytic theologians argue that knowledge of 100 percent of all truths is impossible, even for God, despite the assertions of perfect knowledge (Job 37:16) or that God knows everything (Qur'an 49:16; and 1 Jn 3:20) in the Scriptures of Abrahamic faiths. Those who deny that God knows 100 percent of all truths either defend aberrant, heterodox definitions of omniscience in an effort to preserve omniperfect construals of perfect being theology or suggest that something less than absolute omniscience is the right way to understand maximally great knowledge. Debate about how to construe omniscience is controversial, and it involves various puzzles related to set theory, personal indexicals, temporal indexicals, future contingents, and epiphenomenal qualia. Each puzzle requires increasingly nuanced definitions of omniscience.[7] In an effort to provide a roadmap, I'll attempt to explain each puzzle and then sketch various responses one might take, given one's intuitions about the variables in the respective puzzles.

IV.1 Set Theory

In an exchange with Alvin Plantinga, Patrick Grim offers an argument against the coherence of omniscience by way of set theory (Plantinga and Grim 1993). Utilizing Cantor's power set theorem, Grim demonstrates that there is no set of all truths, because any power set will necessarily be larger than the original set, and therefore the power set will contain truths *about* the set of all truths that aren't contained *within* the set of all truths, which is absurd. Grim argues that it's impossible for God to know all truths since it's impossible for there to be a set of all truths in the first place. Daniel Hill effectively responds by noting that there is no property of being true *simpliciter*, so there cannot be a set of all truths, because "if there were [a set of all truths], there would be the property of being a member of that set, which would be equivalent to the property of being true *simpliciter*," (Hill 2005: 32). One might be inclined to think that for every proposition, p, if p is true, then an omniscient being knows p. But, as Hill notes, in order for "every"

---

[7] Due to space constraints, I'm unable to pay appropriate homage to numerous articles and books on omniscience that have helped me think through the puzzles concerning the doctrine of maximally great knowledge, but I'm especially indebted to Hill (2005: 27–124) and Wierenga (2009).

to quantify, we need a set of every proposition. Alternatively, one might think that if any being is omniscient, "then every instance of the following schema is true: if Φ is true the x knows that Φ" (Hill 2005: 32). Hill's penetrating analysis is worth quoting at length:

> Here, "Φ" is a dummy sentence letter, not a variable. The problem with [this account of omniscience], however, is that there are propositions that are not expressible in natural language. This is easy to see: every natural language has a finite vocabulary. Although a sentence may be arbitrarily long, it also must be finite. Hence, the set of possible sentences is denumerable. The set of true propositions is indenumerable, however; this may be proved directly, using the Cantorian-style arguments that Grim employs, or indirectly, by pointing out that there are indenumerably many sets, and, for every set, a true proposition that it is indeed a set. (Hill 2005: 32)

This all suggests, again, that there is no property of truth *simpliciter*, which requires a very nuanced definition of omniscience.

> For every being, x, if x is omniscient then for every proposition, p, if p is true $_n$, then x knows$_n$ p, and if p is *false*$_n$ then x does not *believe*$_n$ p. (Hill 2005: 33)[8]

Hill's definition solves the problem at the cost of complicating our understanding of omniscience. Having antecedently discussed whether or not God's knowledge is propositional, or whether belief(s) are constituent of divine knowledge, I'll leave it to readers to modify definitions accordingly since these reformulations will prove to be overly repetitive as we consider additional puzzles. Following Hill's lead, I will ignore the orders of propositions and subscript numerals for the sake of simplicity. For those concerned about Grim's paradox, feel free to supplement these accordingly.

IV.2 Indexicals: Personal and Temporal

Philosophers debate about whether propositions containing indexicals reduce to non-indexed propositions (Perry 1993). Indexicals are words that index ideas to particular people, places, or times. How one responds to issues concerning indexicals has significant ramifications for analytic understandings of omniscience and/or maximal knowledge.

To see more clearly the nature of these problems, let's take up the issue of personal indexicals first. Consider the following pair of sentences:

Ben Arbour is Ben Arbour.
I am Ben Arbour.

Does the second sentence express any new information not contained in the first? Hill thinks yes, and he defends his view with a thought experiment (2005: 46). Suppose I have amnesia and a doctor is trying to discern the severity of my condition. When asked, "Do you believe that Ben Arbour is Ben Arbour?" I respond, "Well, of course—that's just the law of identity!" Knowing my background in philosophy, the doctor is pleased with my response, so he asks the follow-up question, "Are you Ben Arbour?" Upon being asked, suppose I respond, "I don't know who I am." This thought experiment suggests that what is expressed by the locution "Ben Arbour is Ben Arbour" is not perfectly identical to what is express by the locution "I am Ben Arbour." On this account, there's a difference

---

[8]In a footnote, Hill explains, "n" is not a variable but a schematic letter, which will be replaced by specific numerals for specific instances of the schema.

between knowing *that* I am Ben Arbour (*de re*) compared to *de se* knowledge of the proposition <I am Ben Arbour>. If this account is correct, it's difficult to see how anyone other than Ben Arbour—including God—can know the truth known by Ben Arbour when he knows the truth expressed by the locution "I am Ben Arbour."

A similar puzzle concerns temporal indexicals. Any statements involving specific time(s) are bound to be caught up with indexicals. Consider:

It is presently 7:00 a.m., CST.

Debates about the metaphysics of time suggest that there are two ways of interpreting this sentence. On any A-theoretic understanding of time, there is something privileged about the present such that tense is an objective reality that doesn't reduce to something more fundamental such as before-than, after-than, or simultaneous-to relations. B-theoretic approaches to time take the opposite view, denying the objective reality of the present. This entails that sentences like "It is presently 7:00 a.m., CST," that contain temporal indexicals (e.g., now, today, in five minutes) don't express any new information not already contained in propositions such as "The moment of time identified as 7:00 a.m., CST, precedes the later moment identified as 7:01 a.m., CST."

William Lane Craig argues that those who defend an A-theoretic approach to tense ought to not also defend divine timelessness, because these two positions together entail problems for divine omniscience (Craig 2009: 160). If God is in time, then God can know truths expressed by propositions containing non-reductive temporal indexicals. Of course, because one man's *modus ponens* is another man's *modus tollens*, defenders of divine timelessness can parry by denying that the temporal indexicals in such propositions are essentially non-reductive. Alternatively, advocates of divine timelessness might take this argument to be a good reason for rejecting A-theoretic approaches to tense.

In responding to the problem of indexicals, one can take any of three basic approaches. One can defend the view that indexicals are reductive, and therefore that there are no essentially indexed propositions to be known. Alternatively, one can defend the view that, because God knows 100 percent of all truths, it must be the case that God somehow knows even truths containing essentially non-reductive indexicals. Finally, one can defend the view that it's impossible for anyone to know 100 percent of all irreducibly indexical propositions. Obviously, if there are no essentially indexed propositions to be known, there's no problem that analytic theologians need to solve to preserve Anselmian intuitions that divine omniscience entails knowledge of 100 percent of all truths.

The existence of non-reductively indexed propositions only poses a problem for defenders of omniscience who believe that God's knowledge is propositional in nature. Even if some propositions are essentially indexed, if God's knowledge isn't propositional, then God's inability to know those propositions doesn't count against conceptions of omniscience whereupon God knows 100 percent of all truths. This is because God's immediate knowledge of all the facts about the relevant propositions is enough to preserve omniscience. One might defend this account by way of the DDS the way Aquinas does, or along the lines proposed by Alston. Alternatively, one might follow David Lewis in taking properties to be the objects of belief rather than propositions (Lewis 1979). Admittedly, this idiosyncratic view solves the problem but for some philosophers goes too far astray of epistemic intuitions that propositions are the objects of belief (cf. Hill 2005: 54–9). Because some analytic theologians believe both that God's knowledge is propositional in nature and that at least some propositions are essentially indexed, we will consider a few strategies that have been proposed to solve the problem that essentially indexed propositions pose for conceptions of omniscience that requires divine knowledge of 100% of all truths.

IV.3 Castañeda's Principle P

Hector-Neri Castañeda (1967) offered what he called "Principle P" as a solution to the problem that essentially indexed propositions poses for omniscience. Principle P states that, roughly, if a person Y knows that p, and if person X knows that person Y knows that p, then X knows that p. Daniel Hill notes that "a very similar principle was discussed and rejected by William of Ockham in his commentary on Peter Lombard's *Sentences*" (Hill 2005: 41). Hill goes on to explain why he believes Castañeda's solution fails, but it seems that this discussion misses an important distinction between knowledge *de re* and knowledge *de se*.[9]

Hill argues as follows. Suppose that we substitute for p some sufficiently difficult mathematical theorem, perhaps a proof of Goldbach's conjecture. Suppose also that I am not a mathematician who knows this proof. Now suppose that Alexander Pruss does know that there is such a proof, and that I know that Pruss knows that there is such a proof. According to Castañeda's Principle P, if I know that Pruss knows that there is a proof of Goldbach's conjecture, then I know that there is a proof of Goldbach's conjecture. Hill rightly points out that Pruss's knowledge of the proof doesn't entail that I know the proof, but it would be a mistake to dismiss Principle P on such grounds. Castañeda does not assert that "if X knows that Y knows p, then X knows p." This would be false for the reasons Hill points out, as discussed above. But Principle P isn't about knowledge *de se*, but rather knowledge *de re*, and hinges upon the idea that knowledge is factive. Therefore, if I know that Pruss knows a proof of Goldbach's conjecture, it doesn't follow that I know the proof. What does follow, from Castañeda's Principle P, is more modest. If I know *that* Pruss knows *that* a mathematical theorem proves Goldbach's conjecture to be true, then I know *that* a mathematical theorem proves Goldbach's conjecture true. Unfortunately, this doesn't solve our problem concerning essentially indexed propositions, because what we are concerned about is the mode by which someone apprehends knowledge *de se* rather than knowledge *de re* (Nagasawa 2003). In the hypothetical example of Pruss's knowledge of some proof, and my knowledge that Pruss knows some proof, I do not have *de se* knowledge of some proof but rather only *de re* knowledge of some proof.

IV.4 Relative Truth versus Absolute Truth

In *Divinity and Maximal Greatness*, Hill discusses the strategy of proposing the relativity of truth. I cannot improve on his summary, so I quote from him at length:

> One is tempted in exasperation to say, when asked whether an omniscient being can know what I know when I know that I am Daniel Hill, "Of course not—it's not true for the omniscient being!" The spirit behind this approach is that indexical propositions

---

[9] The distinction between *de re* and *de se* originates in the Latin, "of the thing" compared against "of oneself". So understood, knowledge *de re* amounts to knowledge *that*, whereas knowledge *de se* involves the mode of knowing, including first-person apprehension of truths involving the knower. To better understand why puzzles about knowledge *de se* are controversial for defenders of divine omniscience, see Nagasawa (2003) and Zagzebski (2008: 232–7).

are true at some times and false at others, true at some places and false at others, true for some people and false for others. If this approach could be made to work then it would solve all our problems. I fear, however, that it cannot be made to work: the notion of relative truth—true for you, but not for me—I find baffling. ... I cannot understand what relative truth is if it does not thus collapse into absolute truth, and so fear that this approach cannot help us. (Hill 2005: 50)

IV.5 Modal Reformulations of Omniscience

Some scholars surmise that it is simply impossible for anyone, including God, to know 100 percent of all truths. These thinkers suggest that maximal epistemic greatness turns out to be something less than knowledge of 100 percent of all truths. It's difficult to see how anything less than knowledge of 100 percent of all truths counts as perfect knowledge, instead of something like the property "being as close to perfect knowledge as possible." Moreover, it's hard to see how a being that doesn't know everything genuinely counts as omniscient, since "omni" implies all. This point stands despite efforts to redefine omniscience along modal lines.

Richard Swinburne suggests that "a being is omniscient if he knows at each time all true propositions which it is logically possible that he entertain" (1993: 172). We should take it as trivially true that only what it is logically possible to know can be known, even by an omniscient being. Therefore, of course we conclude that Swinburne is correct that a being can only know what it is logically possible for an omniscient being to know. But this is an insufficient definition of omniscience. To see why, consider the case of McStupid, who always knows who he is but knows nothing else. In fact, suppose further that it's impossible for McStupid to know anything else (Hill 2005: 44). On Swinburne's definition, McStupid counts as omniscient, but this is obviously inadequate for perfect knowledge. William Hasker suggests that omniscience means that "it is impossible that God should at any time believe what is false, or fail to know any true proposition such that his knowing that proposition at that time is logically possible" (Hasker 1998: 187). Interestingly, both Hasker and Swinburne, along with Peter van Inwagen (2008), defend a version of open theism that I call "limited foreknowledge open theism" where God lacks knowledge of the truth-values of propositions concerning future contingents (PCFC), and some PCFCs are true. Limited foreknowledge open theism requires that God lacks knowledge of 100 percent of all truths, whereas alternative versions of open theism don't necessarily entail this untoward conclusion.[10] Moreover, there are several reasons why we would be mistaken to conclude that an omniscient being could fail to know any truth.

First, there are good arguments for the claim that all truths are knowable in principle and that all truths are known by at least one person even if it's not the case that any single person knows 100 percent of all truths (Kvanvig 2006). Given this, it's impossible that any truth exists that is completely unknown. However, some might argue that there might be some truth known by at least one person but unknown by God. Others will counter that this is impossible, given God's necessary existence along with the fact that God is essentially omniscient. However, this counter presupposes a definition of maximal

---

[10] Of course, there are biblical texts that undermine open theism, such as Isa. 42:9, 44:7, and 48:5–6 (cf. Hill 2005: 88–9). Unfortunately, space constraints preclude a more detailed analysis of issues related to the dilemma of freedom and foreknowledge. For a more detailed analysis of versions of open theism and the relationship between these and definitions of omniscience, see Arbour (2018: especially 1–10 and 60–2) and Rhoda (2008).

epistemic greatness, which is exactly what is under investigation and therefore begs the question.

If it is possible that some truth is unknown by God, then maximal epistemic greatness doesn't entail divine knowledge of 100 percent of all truths. But this all runs contrary to what we take to be the most natural interpretation of plain readings of the Scriptures of all three Abrahamic faiths. However one conceives of the relationship between philosophy and special revelation in analytic theology, at minimum, we must insist that information runs both ways. Yes, philosophy can inform theology; but theology can also inform, and perhaps constrain, what is allowed by philosophy. Also, aside from concerns stemming from special revelation, it's difficult to see how anything less than knowledge of 100 percent of all truths counts as *perfect* knowledge, rather than something like nearly perfect, or "as close to perfect as possible." Additionally, it's hard to see how a being that doesn't know everything genuinely counts as omniscient, since "omni" implies all. This point stands despite efforts by many to redefine omniscience along modal lines. Those who want to insist that knowledge of 100 percent of all truths is impossible should opt for a term other than omniscience, because, technically speaking, maximal epistemic greatness doesn't yield a divine being that is all-knowing.

V. A DEFINITION OF OMNISCIENCE

In conclusion, I'd like to offer two possible definitions of omniscience. Consider Hill's definition, which avoids all the pitfalls we have considered.

> For every being, x, x is omniscient if and only if, for every type of belief state, B, if x is in a token of B then x's token of B has as object a true proposition, and if x is not in a token of B then if x were in a token of B then x's token of B would have as object a false proposition. (Hill 2005: 64)

This definition does not relativize truth, nor does it fail to account for indexicals. Moreover, it explains why God might lack a belief state in a way that preserves an important aspect of perfect knowledge by pointing out that the object of the belief state that God lacks would have as object a false proposition.

While I find Hill's definition to be adequate for anyone inclined to think that God has beliefs and/or that God's knowledge is necessarily propositional in nature, I propose two changes to this definition. The first change is more inclusive in accommodating those who think God's knowledge is not, or might not, be propositional in nature, and that belief(s) might not be constituent of divine knowledge. The second change stipulates infallibility so as to preserve divine epistemic perfection insofar as Anselmian considerations are concerned. So understood, I suggest that

> for every being, x, x is omniscient if and only if, for every type of knowledge state, B, if x is in a token of B then x's token of B has as an object a truth, and if x is not in a token of B then if x were in a token of B then x's token of B would have as an object a falsehood; and, x enjoys all cognitive perfections such that everything known by x is known perfectly and, therefore, infallibly.

No doubt, there are other puzzles that need to be solved concerning the nature of divine knowledge. I hope that we now see that explaining carefully how theologians should understand divine omniscience isn't as easy as one might initially think it is. My goal has been to inspire those interested in omniscience to see the value of analytic philosophy in clarifying what is (and isn't) entailed by the claim that God enjoys perfect knowledge. In hopes that some readers have enjoyed something akin to a whetting of their intellectual appetites, I'll look forward to continued study of the subject as others ensure that no stone is left unturned in analytic contributions to the subject of divine knowledge and its relationship to perfect being theology.

References

Alston, W. P. (1989), *Divine Nature and Human Language: Essays in Philosophical Theology*, Ithaca: Cornell University Press.
Arbour, B. H., ed. (2018), *Philosophical Essays against Open Theism*, New York: Routledge.
Aquinas, T. (1975), *Summa Contra Gentiles: Book One: God*, trans. A. C. Pegis, South Bend: University of Notre Dame Press.
Aquinas, T. (2012), *Summa Theologica*, ed. The Aquinas Institute, Steubenville: Emmaus Academic.
Bernstein, C. (2018), "Is God's Existence Possible?" *Heythrop Journal*, 59 (3): 424–32.
Castañeda, H-N. (1967), "Omniscience and Indexical Reference," *Journal of Philosophy*, 64: 203–10.
Clifford, W. (2001), "The Ethics of Belief," in M. Peterson, W. Hasker, B. Reichenbach, and D. Basinger (eds.), *Philosophy of Religion: Selected Readings*, New York: Oxford University Press.
Craig, W. L. (2009), "Divine Eternity," in T. P. Flint and M. C. Rea (eds.), *The Oxford Handbook of Philosophical Theology*, 145–66, New York: Oxford University Press.
Dickinson, T. M. (2019), "God Knows: Acquaintance and the Nature of Divine Knowledge," *Religious Studies*, 55 (1): 1–16.
Dougherty, T., ed. (2011a), *Evidentialism and its Discontents*, New York: Oxford University Press.
Dougherty, T. (2011b), "Fallibilism," in S. Bernecker and D. Pritchard (eds.), *The Routledge Companion to Epistemology*, 131–43, New York: Routledge.
Hasker, W. (1988), "Yes, God Has Beliefs!," *Religious Studies*, 24 (3): 385–94.
Hasker, W. (1998), *God, Time and Knowledge*, Ithaca: Cornell University Press.
Hill, D. J. (2005), *Divinity and Maximal Greatness*, New York: Routledge.
Kvanvig, J. (2006), *The Knowability Paradox*, New York: Oxford University Press.
Leftow, B. (2011), "Why Perfect Being Theology?," *International Journal for Philosophy of Religion*, 69 (2): 103–18.
Lewis, D. (1979), "Attitudes *De Dicto* and *De Se*," *Philosophical Review*, 88: 513–43.
Morris, T. V. (1987) *Anselmian Explorations*, Notre Dame: University of Notre Dame Press.
Morris, T. V. (1991), *Our Idea of God*, Notre Dame: University of Notre Dame Press.
Nagasawa, Y. (2003), "Divine Omniscience and Knowledge *De Se*," *International Journal for Philosophy of Religion*, 53 (2): 73–82.
Nagasawa, Y. (2017), *Maximal God*, New York: Oxford University Press.
Perry, J. (1993), *The Problem of the Essential Indexical and Other Essays*, New York: Oxford University Press.
Plantinga, A. (2000), *Warranted Christian Belief*, New York: Oxford University Press.
Plantinga, A., and P. Grim (1993), "Truth, Omniscience, and Cantorian Arguments: An Exchange," *Philosophical Studies*, 71: 267–306.
Rhoda, A. R. (2008), "Generic Open Theism and Some Varieties Thereof," *Religious Studies*, 44: 225–34.

Rogers, K. (2000), *Perfect Being Theology*, Edinburgh: Edinburgh University Press.
Swinburne, R. (1993), *The Coherence of Theism*, rev. ed., New York: Oxford University Press.
Todd, P. (2015), "The Greatest Possible Being Needn't Be Anything Impossible," *Religious Studies*, 51 (4): 531–42.
Van Inwagen, P. (2008), "What Does an Omniscient Being Know About the Future?" *Oxford Studies in Philosophy of Religion*, 1: 216–30.
Wierenga, E. (2009), "Omniscience," in T. P. Flint and M. C. Rea (eds.), *The Oxford Handbook to Philosophical Theology*, 129–44, New York: Oxford University Press.
Wierenga, E. (2011), "Augustinian Perfect Being Theology and the God of Abraham, Isaac, and Jacob," *International Journal for Philosophy of Religion*, 69: 139–51.
Zagzebski, L. (2008), "Omnisubjectivity," *Oxford Studies in Philosophy of Religion* 1: 231–47.

CHAPTER TEN

Retrieving Divine Immensity and Omnipresence

ROSS D. INMAN

Immensus Pater, immensus Filius, immensus Spiritus Sanctus
—Athanasian Creed (Burn 1918: 101)

The divine attributes of immensity and omnipresence have been integral to classical Christian confession regarding the nature of the triune God. Divine immensity and omnipresence are affirmed in doctrinal standards such as the Athanasian Creed (c. 500), the Fourth Lateran Council (1215), the Council of Basel (1431–49), the Second Helvetic Confession (1566), the Westminster Confession of Faith (1647), the Second London Baptist Confession (1689), and the First Vatican Council (1869–70). In the first section of this chapter, I offer a brief historical overview of divine immensity and divine omnipresence in the Christian tradition. I then offer a brief taxonomy of contemporary models of divine omnipresence in the philosophical and theological landscape. In the more constructive section, I aim to gesture toward the retrieval of several classical insights regarding immensity and omnipresence that remain unexplored in contemporary analytic work.

I. DIVINE IMMENSITY AND OMNIPRESENCE: HISTORICAL LANDSCAPE

In the Christian theological tradition, divine immensity and omnipresence have largely been understood to be distinct yet intimately related divine attributes. Divine immensity has been closely associated with divine infinity, where divine infinity has traditionally been understood in negative terms as God's being without limitation of any kind, whether in essence, power, knowledge, wisdom, goodness, and so on (Eph. 3:20; Isa. 40:12, 15, 17). In positive terms, God is understood to be qualitatively infinite in that the divine nature is intrinsically full and complete in the eternal, divine processions of paternity, filiation, and spiration. It is precisely because of the absolute fullness and plenitude of the triune God *ad intra* (Ps. 145:3) that there are no finite bounds to the range of God's gratuitous relations to creatures *ad extra* (Job 11:7-8; Isa. 40:12, 15; Dan. 4:34; Eph. 1:19, 2:7).

To say that God is immense, then, is to say that the divine nature is without limitation, particularly as it pertains to the limitations of space; the divine nature is uncircumscribable, immeasurable, and incapable of being contained or bound by space. Being qualitatively and positively infinite, God categorically transcends—and is entirely unconditioned by—spatial limitations and boundaries due to the intrinsic fullness of the divine life (correlatively, divine eternity has been classically understood as the infinity of the divine nature with respect to time or duration).[1] Hillary of Poitiers (AD 300–368) summarizes this close connection between divine infinity and immensity as follows: God is "infinite, for nothing contains Him and He contains all things; He is eternally unconditioned by space, for He is illimitable" (Poitiers 1994: 2.6).[2]

As a corollary of divine infinity, and in contrast to divine omnipresence, immensity has been taken to be an *absolute*, that is, non-relational, divine attribute. God *ad intra*, apart from his relation to creation, is immense in his essence.[3] Divine immensity entails that not only is the triune God not conditioned or limited by space, but also that this fact positively indicates "the boundless liberty of God to be and act as he determines in relation to space. Immensity concerns the plenitude, richness, sufficiency and effectiveness of God and so of God's disposition of himself in relation to creaturely space" (Webster 2016a: 93). The attribute of divine omnipresence, however, has historically been understood to be a *relative* divine attribute predicated on God's works *ad extra* in relation to created space and its occupants; God is omnipresent purely in relation to created, spatial reality (Bavinck 2004: 168).

Common scriptural passages cited in favor of divine immensity and omnipresence include Ps. 139:7-10, Jer. 23:24, 1 Kgs 8:23, 27, Acts 17, and Isa. 66:1. These scriptural texts emphasize both *divine ubiquity*, that the divine essence itself is everywhere present throughout space, as well as *divine immensity*, that the divine essence cannot be contained or limited by space.

The immensity of God is underscored in Solomon's theologically rich prayer at the temple dedication, "O Lord, God of Israel, there is no God like you, in heaven above or on earth beneath ... But will God indeed dwell on the earth? Behold, heaven and the highest heaven cannot contain you; how much less this house that I have built" (1 Kgs 8:23, 27).[4] The contrast between the immense, Holy One of Israel and the circumscribed gods of the nations is clear and deliberate; it is impossible for any created place to contain the true and living God of Israel. God, as immense and the ultimate source of all non-divine reality, is Lord of all spatial reality and thus cannot be contained by space (Isa. 66:1). Along similar lines, and perhaps echoing Solomon's prayer of dedication, the Apostle Paul weds the sheer plenitude of God as the limitless creator and sustainer of all with God's inability to be contained by place, "The God who made the world and everything in it, being Lord of heaven and earth, does not live in temples made by man,

---

[1] Arminius (1986: IV, XV–XVI) summarizes the classic view nicely: "From the simplicity and infinity of the divine essence, arise infinity with regard to *time*, which is called 'Eternity'; and with regard to *place*, which is called 'Immensity.'"
[2] For a sampling of patristic authors on immensity, see Clement of Alexandria (1885: 2.2); Athanasius (1982: 17); Cyril of Alexandria (1874: 1.9); John of Damascus (1958: 1.13); Augustine (1961: 7.20.26) and (1994: 4.4.5). For a sampling of medieval authors, see Anselm, *Monologion* (2007: chs. 14, 22); Aquinas (2012: Ia, qq. 7–8).
[3] See Turretin (1992); Muller (2003: 335–45); Webster (2016a: 93.). Leibniz (1989: 106), in his rich correspondence with Samuel Clarke on immensity and space, underscores this traditional idea as follows: "It is true that the immensity and eternity of God would subsist though there were no creatures, but those attributes would have no dependence either on times or places. If there were no creatures, there would be neither time nor place, and consequently no actual space. The immensity of God is independent of space."
[4] All Biblical quotations in this chapter are from the English Standard Version of the Bible.

nor is he served by human hands, as though he needed anything, since he himself gives to all mankind life and breath and everything" (Acts 17:24-25).

Perhaps the most commonly cited scriptural text in the Christian dogmatic tradition in support of God's ubiquitous presence is Psalm 139: 7-10:

> 7 Where shall I go from your Spirit?
> > Or where shall I flee from your presence?
> 8 If I ascend to heaven, you are there!
> > If I make my bed in Sheol, you are there!
> 9 If I take the wings of the morning
> > and dwell in the uttermost parts of the sea,
> 10 even there your hand shall lead me,
> > and your right hand shall hold me.

The Psalmist proceeds to recount that neither deep darkness (139: 11-12) nor the hidden place of a mother's womb can escape the divine presence (vv. 13-16). Through the prophet Jeremiah, God addresses the deceptive prophets of Israel who attempt to remove themselves from the council of the Lord by saying, "Am I a God at hand, declares the Lord, and not a God far away? Can a man hide himself in secret places so that I cannot see him? declared the Lord. Do I not fill heaven and earth? declares the Lord" (Jer. 23:23-24).

Historically, dogmatic reflection on divine omnipresence in the Christian tradition has taken the form of the following threefold schema: God is everywhere by (1) *essence*, (2) *power*, and (3) *presence*.[5] This threefold schema has been central to patristic, medieval, post-Reformation, and early modern Christian theological inquiry concerning divine omnipresence.[6] In his *Sentences*, what was once the standard university text in Western medieval theology, Peter Lombard synthesized previous theological work on divine omnipresence as follows: "And so it is to be known that God, existing ever unchangeably in himself, by presence, power, and essence is in every nature or essence without limitation of himself, and in every place without being bounded, and in every time without change" (Lombard 2007: bk. 1, d. 37, ch. 1). While there have been a variety of ways of explicating this threefold schema in the history of Christian dogmatics, one standard way to gloss tenets (2) and (3) has been in terms of God's being everywhere by way of divine activity and operation, that is, (1), and everywhere by way of divine knowledge, that is, (3), respectively. That is, God is everywhere by his power and operation insofar as God creates, sustains, and governs all spatial creatures (Acts 17:28). Moreover, God is also everywhere by presence, that is, (3), precisely because God is directly cognitively aware of each and every spatial creature and creaturely event (Heb. 4:13).[7] Here it is important to underscore that tenet (1), God's ubiquitous presence by essence, has traditionally been distinguished from tenets (2) and (3), that is, God's ubiquitous presence by power and knowledge. The divine essence or substance *itself*, not merely the divine power or the divine knowledge, is present to each and every place in space.

---

[5] The schema is often thought to originate with Peter Lombard (2007: bk. 1, d. 17, ch. 1), but Lombard himself points out that it extends back to Gregory the Great's Commentary on the Song of Songs. See also Turretin (1992) and Aquinas (2012: Ia.Q8.a3) in particular.
[6] See Fuerst (1951) and Reynolds (1992).
[7] See Fuerst (1951) for a thorough treatment of how this threefold schema has been understood in the Christian tradition.

Patristic, medieval, and post-Reformation theologians were largely in agreement about the precise mode of presence at work in divine omnipresence, *how* the divine essence is present at every point in space, that is, tenet (1). Classical theologians commonly distinguished three ways in which a being could be in or present at a place, whether a material being (e.g., body) or an immaterial being (e.g., God, angels, human souls). A clear statement of these various modes of presence—*circumscriptive, definitive,* and *repletive*—is offered (and endorsed) by Francis Turretin, in explicit reliance on the received medieval theological inheritance:[8]

> Three modes of being in a place are commonly held: (1) *circumscriptively*—attributed to bodies because they are in a place and space so as to be commensurate with parts of space; (2) *definitively*—applicable to created spirits and incorporeal substances (which are defined by certain places, and are so here as not to be anywhere else); (3) *repletively*—which is ascribed to God because his immense essence is present with all and, as it were, completely fills all places. (Turretin 1992, my emphasis)

The core idea behind *circumscriptive presence*, a mode of presence that belongs exclusively to material beings, is that material beings are both composed of proper parts (and thus not mereologically simple) and are extended throughout a particular place by way of their having distinct proper parts "spread out" across the place in question. My body, for example, is circumscriptively present at a place P in virtue of its having distinct proper parts (head, hands, heart, etc.) that are themselves present at the distinct sub-places, ps, of P. While my entire body is wholly present at P, my body is *partly* located where my right arm is, and *partly* located where my head is, and so on. More carefully, following William of Ockham (1991), "What is *circumscriptively* in a place is a thing which is such that (i) a part of it is in a part of the place and (ii) the whole of it is in the whole of the place" (my emphasis). In this way, that which is circumscriptively present at a place is *circumscribed by* and *contained in* the place in question; while my body can be *partly* present at distinct places at the same time, it is incapable of being *wholly* present (without remainder) at distinct places at one and the same time (it cannot simultaneously be *wholly* multi-located).

Definitive presence is the mode of presence that uniquely characterizes spiritual creatures, both angels and human souls, insofar as they are both non-composite (and thus mereologically simple) and limited in nature; what is devoid of proper parts cannot be circumscriptively present at a place and thus cannot be *partly* present at distinct places at the same time.[9] Rather, angels and humans souls can be said to be at a place in virtue of being *wholly* present at a place P as well as *wholly* present at every distinct sub-place, ps, of P. Where material beings are capable of being wholly present at only a single place at a time, immaterial beings are able to be *wholly* present at distinct places at the same time. Again, as Ockham (1991) puts it, "a thing is *definitively* in a place when (i) the whole of it is in the whole place and not outside the place and (ii) the whole of it is in each part of

---

[8]The distinction between circumscriptive, definitive, and repletive presence was a staple of patristic, medieval, and post-Reformation reflection on the relationship between spiritual and material creation. See John of Damascus (1958: 1, c.13); William of Ockham (1991); Augustine (2004: 187, 4.11); Lombard (2007: bk. 1, d. 37 n. 6); and Anselm (2007: ch. 21) for a concise statement of each of these modes of spatial presence in the Latin West, and Turretin (1992) for a representative work in the post-Reformation period.

[9]Robert Pasnau (2011a: 18) uses the terms "meremeric existence" and "holenmeric existence" in the place of the more traditional terminology of circumscriptive and definitive presence, respectively.

the place." However, like created material beings, created spiritual beings like angels and human souls are *bound* and *contained* by the places where they are present insofar as their natures are finite and limited. Spiritual creatures, as Turretin puts it above, "are defined by certain places, and are so here as not to be anywhere else." While my immaterial soul, for example, can be wholly present in the whole of my body and wholly present in each part of my body, it cannot be wholly present at some distinct place where my body is not present (e.g., a white sandy beach in Bermuda).

Finally, God alone is *repletively present* in so far as the divine essence, being spiritual, infinite, and immense, is capable of being *wholly present at each and every place at the same time*.[10] As a mereological simple, the ubiquity of the divine essence, that is, tenet (1) of the threefold schema, is not to be glossed in terms of circumscriptive presence. Yet as infinite, immense, and neither contained nor bound by any place whatsoever, the ubiquitous presence of the divine essence is not to be glossed in terms of definitive presence either; the divine essence is wholly present to each existing place at the same time, yet bound by none. Augustine (2004) articulates and contrasts this unique mode of ubiquitous divine presence—repletive presence—with circumscriptive and definitive presence as follows:

> Yet he is not spread out in space like a mass such that in half of the body of the world there is half of him and half of him in the other half, being in that way whole in the whole. Rather, he is whole in the heavens alone and whole on the earth alone and whole in the heavens and in the earth, contained in no place, but whole everywhere in himself. (*Letter* 187, 4.11).)

Note that the differences between the above modes of presence concern a difference in *kind* as well as *degree*. In contrast to definitive and repletive presence, circumscriptive presence is a distinct kind of presence at a place insofar as it is defined in terms of mereological extension, having proper parts distributed across distinct places. Definitive and repletive presence, however, arguably differ only in degree.[11] Thomas Aquinas, for instance, states that both the human soul and God are similarly present in the places where they are located, "just as the soul is whole in each part of the body, so God is whole in all things and in each thing" (2012: Ia.Q8.a2.ad3).[12]

II. DIVINE OMNIPRESENCE: CONTEMPORARY LANDSCAPE

With the above historical framework in place, I now want to present a brief taxonomy of contemporary models of divine omnipresence as found in recent analytic philosophical and theological literature. At the very least, extant theological and philosophical models of divine omnipresence agree on the following: to say that God is omnipresent is to say

---

[10] Thomas Aquinas (2012: Ia, q. 8, a. 4) would qualify this by saying that God alone is repletively present both *primarily* (the divine nature itself is *wholly* present everywhere and not some proper part of the divine nature) and *per se* (i.e., God "is not everywhere accidentally, on the basis of an assumed condition").

[11] This is not to say that the *metaphysical grounds* in virtue of which God is repletively present, viz. God's immensity (a corollary of divine infinity), does not differ qualitatively from the grounds in virtue of which created spirits are definitively present. My point here is that repletive presence *per se* differs from definitive presence only in degree, not kind.

[12] See also William T. Shedd (2003: 278), "The omnipresence of God is not by extension, multiplication, or division of essence. He is all in every place, similarly as the soul is all in every part of the body. The whole essence of God is here, is there, and everywhere."

that God is present to or located at each and every place. The individual models differ in how they characterize the precise nature of ubiquitous divine presence.

In a previous work (2017), I characterized two distinct notions of location or presence—derivative and fundamental—and defined two general models of divine omnipresence accordingly.[13] Here I want to modify slightly those previous definitions to make them conducive to those with more classical theistic sensibilities concerning the divine nature.[14] Taking "is present at" as primitive, we can explicate these two varieties of presence as follows (where "p" stands for some place):

> *Fundamental Presence*: x is present at p fundamentally $=_{df}$ x is present at p but not solely in virtue of standing in causal and/or epistemic relation(s), R(s), to some distinct entity, y, that is present at p.
>
> *Derivative Presence*: x is present at p derivatively $=_{df}$ x is present at p solely in virtue of standing in some causal and/or epistemic relation(s), R(s), to some distinct entity, y, where y is present at p fundamentally.

Material objects, for example, are plausibly construed as being present at their respective places in the fundamental sense. Trees, tables, and tigers are present at a place, but not simply in virtue of being causally related to something that is itself present at a place. However, something may be present to a place by way of standing in some causal or epistemic relation to something that is itself present at a place, for example, my being cognitively aware of or in causal contact with things and events at a place.

It is important to note that a thing's being derivatively present at a particular place is *nothing more* than its standing in some causal and/or epistemic relation(s) to a distinct thing that is itself present at a place in the fundamental sense. By contrast, a thing's being present at a place in the fundamental sense amounts to the claim that its being present somewhere cannot be reduced to its standing in a causal and/or epistemic relation R to a distinct thing y that is present at a place in the fundamental sense.

With the above definitions of fundamental and derivative presence in hand, we can define two general models of divine omnipresence as follows. Let "P_d" stand for derivative presence, "P_f" for fundamental presence, and read "P(God, p)" as "God is present at p" (Inman 2017):

> (DO) *Derivative Omnipresence*: $(\forall p)(p$ is a place $\rightarrow P_d(God, p))$
> For every place, p, God is derivatively present at p.
> (FO) *Fundamental Omnipresence*: $(\forall p)(p$ is a place $\rightarrow P_f(God, p))$
> For every place p, God is fundamentally present at p.

On a DO model, God is omnipresent by being derivatively present at each and every place. An FO model, by contrast, maintains that God is omnipresent by being fundamentally present at each and every place; the divine nature is everywhere present but not solely in virtue of causal and/or epistemic contact with things present at a place

---

[13] My (2017) paper on divine omnipresence was accepted for publication in 2014 but was widely circulated as "forthcoming" for several years until its 2017 publication in the eighth volume of *Oxford Studies in Philosophy of Religion*.

[14] The prior formulation of fundamental presence entailed that God's fundamental ubiquitous presence is intrinsic to God (God being present to every place in his own right, i.e., non-relationally), which cuts against a robust understanding of divine aseity and simplicity, the latter affirming that God is strictly identical to whatever God is intrinsically.

in the fundamental sense. A rough and informal test for distinguishing a DO from an FO model would be if the model entails that God, considered apart from his bearing causal and/or epistemic relations to things that are themselves present at *p* fundamentally, could nevertheless be present at *p*. If so, then you have an FO model; if not, then a DO model.

It is an oft-repeated claim in the contemporary literature that DO is arguably *the* classical model of divine omnipresence in the Christian tradition (Jedwab 2016). Individual DO models differ with respect to how they construe the particular causal and/or epistemic relations (R or Rs) in which God stands to entities that are present at a place in the fundamental sense. A widespread interpretation of Anselm of Canterbury (albeit incomplete, by my lights) characterizes R exclusively in epistemic or cognitive terms, namely, God's immediate knowledge or cognitive awareness of the goings on at every place.[15] Likewise, many interpret Aquinas as explicating divine omnipresence principally in terms of God's directly causally sustaining in existence each and every creature at a place (Swinburne 1993; Cross 2003; Wainright 2010; Wierenga 2010). It is difficult to see how, on a DO model, omnipresence is a distinct divine attribute over and above divine omniscience, omnipotence, or God's providential and causal activity in creation. Consequently, the proponent of a DO model might think that divine omnipresence is ultimately reducible to or simply "nothing over and above" a range of distinct divine attributes or divine actions in relation to creatures.

The vast bulk of contemporary work on divine omnipresence in analytic philosophy and theology aims to explicate and defend a variant of DO. The likes of Richard Swinburne (1993), Charles Taliaferro (1994), Joshua Hoffman and Gary Rosenkrantz (2002), William Lane Craig and J. P. Moreland (2003), Edward Wierenga (2010), William Wainwright (2010), Joseph Jedwab (2016), James Arcadi (2017) and George Gasser (2019) all unpack Rs in terms of God's standing in immediate (basic) causal relations and/or his immediate knowledge of the goings on at every place.[16]

Be that as it may, there are a handful of contemporary philosophers and theologians who favor a variant of an FO model of omnipresence, including Luco J. Van Den Brom (1993), Hud Hudson (2009, 2014), Robert Oakes (2006), Alexander Pruss (2013), Richard Cross (2016), Ross Inman (2017), and James Gordon (2018). Some have even argued that FO models have greater historical prominence than is standardly acknowledged.[17] What unifies various FO models is that each affirms that God is present at every place but not simply in virtue of his standing in causal and/or epistemic relations to objects that are present at a place fundamentally. On an FO model, while God does indeed stand in causal and epistemic relations to spatial creatures that are present in the fundamental

---

[15] See Wierenga (1988), Blount (1997), and Hudson (2009). Although see Conn (2011), Leftow (1989), Pasnau (2011a), and Zagzebski (2013) for an alternative reading of Anselm on omnipresence.

[16] Although J. P. Moreland has expressed in personal conversation that he is inclined to adopt an FO model of omnipresence where God is wholly present at each region of space, akin to the way in which the immaterial human soul is wholly present at each part of the human body. The recent work of Eleonore Stump (2010, 2013, 2018) on divine omnipresence is a bit harder to classify. On the one hand, Stump appeals to the notion of shared or joint attention as a more fine-grained epistemic condition on divine presence, in addition to God's immediate causal activity and cognitive awareness. Yet Stump regularly speaks as if there are independent conditions that must obtain in order for God to stand in these epistemic relations to creatures. For example, Stump (2010: 117) says, "In order for God to be omnipresent, that is, in order for God to be always and everywhere present, it also needs to be the case that God is always and everywhere *in a position to share attention* with any creature able and willing to share attention with God" (my emphasis). The notion of being in a position to share attention with God suggests that omnipresence is not to be analyzed, at bottom, in terms of a DO model.

[17] See Pasnau (2011b), Cross (2016), and Inman (2017), in particular.

sense, these relations are not exhaustive of nor most fundamental to the nature of divine omnipresence. Consequently, for those who defend a variant of FO, omnipresence is a distinct divine attribute and thus irreducible to omnipotence, omniscience, or God's providential and causal activity in creation (or a combination thereof). It is also important to note that the primary issue distinguishing FO and DO models is not whether God's ubiquitous presence is best understood in spatial or nonspatial terms. Indeed, one could adopt a DO model and maintain that the immediate causal relations in virtue of which God is everywhere present constitutes a genuine mode of spatial presence.[18] Likewise, one could in principle adopt an FO model and hold that God is strictly aspatial, yet affirm that the way in which God is everywhere present is not exclusively constituted by causal and/or epistemic considerations.[19]

III. TOWARD A RETRIEVAL OF DIVINE IMMENSITY AND OMNIPRESENCE

In this next, more constructive section, I want to gesture toward the retrieval of several classical tenets of divine immensity and omnipresence in the Christian tradition. Though strictly distinct attributes, divine immensity and omnipresence have been traditionally thought to be closely connected in the following sense: it is precisely *because* the divine essence is infinite and immense *ad intra* that the divine essence is repletively present to each and every place *ad extra*, as per tenet (1) of the above threefold schema. On this classical picture, then, divine immensity is *explanatorily prior* to divine omnipresence; divine immensity is the principal *metaphysical ground* of God's repletive presence in creation. Along these lines, Turretin (1992: 197) states that repletive presence "is ascribed to God because his immense essence is present with all and, as it were, completely fills all places." Similarly, in his *Public Disputations,* Jacob Arminius (1986: IV, XV–XVI) summarizes this classical insight as follows: "Immensity is a pre-eminent mode of the Essence of God, by which it is void of place according to space and limits ... After creatures, and places in which creatures are contained, have been granted to have an existence, from this Immensity follows the Omnipresence or Ubiquity of the Essence of God."

Moreover, it is interesting to note that Aquinas treats omnipresence immediately after he discusses divine perfection and infinity in his *Summa Theologiae*. In his preliminary remarks to question 7 on "Divine Infinity," which immediately precedes the question "God's existence in things," Aquinas notes the explanatory ordering between divine infinity and omnipresence: "After considering divine perfection, the next topic that ought to be considered is God's infinity and God's existence in things, for it is said that God is everywhere and in all things in so far as God is unbounded and infinite" (Aquinas 2012: Ia.q.7). Perhaps the clearest articulation of the classical relationship between immensity and omnipresence is Turretin (1992: 201), echoing the medieval scholastics:

---

[18] Harm Goris (2009: 42), who interprets Aquinas's along the lines of what I am calling a DO model, states, "The only way spiritual beings can be in a place is by way of causality: by bringing about an effect in a body, they become located in space." Jeffrey Brower (personal correspondence) has also suggested a reading of Aquinas on omnipresence along the lines of DO, yet one where God's ubiquitous presence is strictly spatial.

[19] One option here, taken by Turretin (1992: 198) and other Reformed Scholastics, is by way of *via negativa*, that the precise manner in which the divine essence is everywhere present is ultimately not "in the multiplication of the divine essence ... in the extension and diffusion of any corporeal mass ... or in physical contact."

Although the immensity and the omnipresence of God are always connected together, yet they admit of distinction. The former indicates an absolute property belonging to him from eternity; the latter, based upon it, denotes a habitude to place existing in time. They are related to each other as a first and second act or a principle (*principia*) and a principiate (*principiati*). For out of immensity arises omnipresence, which supposes immensity as its foundation. God is therefore omnipresent because he is immense.

Consequently, failing to note the explanatory posteriority of God's ubiquitous presence *ad extra* to the full and immense life of the triune God *ad intra* yields a theologically truncated model of divine omnipresence.[20]

Second, despite its widespread acceptance among contemporary philosophers and theologians, there is significant historical precedent for rejecting the view that divine omnipresence is "nothing over and above" God's ubiquitous (direct) causal activity and/or knowledge. There is strong representation in the Christian tradition for the view that divine omnipresence is not exhausted by tenets (2) and (3) of the classical threefold schema, that is, divine power and presence (i.e., knowledge).[21] So much so that Francisco Suarez can summarize the preceding consensual Christian tradition regarding divine omnipresence (including immensity as the principal metaphysical ground of omnipresence) in the following manner: "God is intimately present to this corporeal universe, not just by presence (that is, cognitively) and by power or action, but also by his essence or substance, just as all the theologians teach, as certain to the faith, on account of divine immensity."[22]

This fuller account of divine omnipresence within the Christian tradition stands in sharp contrast to the near universal bent in the contemporary literature to characterize omnipresence as "nothing over and above" God's immediate causal activity or knowledge. Consequently, in explicating divine omnipresence in this reductive manner, the majority of contemporary models have contracted divine omnipresence to tenets (2) and/or (3) of the classical, threefold schema. But this is to neglect an integral and essential part of a much fuller, historically entrenched account of divine omnipresence, viz., tenet (1), that God is everywhere present by way of the divine essence itself being repletively present at each place. And, arguably, it is God's repletive presence by essence, that is, tenet (1) of the classical threefold schema, which is most fundamental to divine omnipresence *per se*.[23] As Turretin (1992: 198) notes, "The orthodox believe and confess the immensity and omnipresence of God, not only as to virtue and operation, but principally as to essence."

There have, moreover, been a host of theologically motivated *epistemic grounds* cited in favor of tenet (1) of the classic threefold schema that remain largely overlooked or unexplored in the contemporary literature. Historically, in addition to Scripture as a source of warrant, there have been three primary theological reasons cited in favor the ubiquity of the divine essence in particular, that is, tenet (1): divine simplicity, immediate

---

[20]See Webster (2016a: 87–107) and (2016b: 115–26) for a fuller treatment of this line of thinking concerning immensity and omnipresence in particular, as well as "well-ordered thought about the divine perfections" (2016a: 97) in general.
[21]See Turretin (1992: 197) and Lombard (2007: bk. 1, d. 37).
[22]I owe this citation to Pasnau (2011b: 303).
[23]As Petrus van Mastricht (2019: 197, 198, my emphasis) underscores, "But as this immensity and omnipresence of God, *first and foremost*, concerns the essence of God, it thus also, through his essence, considers his knowledge … and also his operation and providence," and "And when that infinity has been taken away, the omnipresence built upon cannot but fail."

divine causal action at every place, and divine immensity. First, regarding divine simplicity, since the divine essence is devoid of metaphysical complexity, and if the divine power is universally operative at each place (a tenet of classical theism), then the divine essence itself is therefore wholly present at each place.[24] Second, since God is immediately causally active at each place, sustaining created beings in existence, and since immediate causal action at a distance is thought to be impossible, the divine essence is therefore said to be present at each place where God is immediately causally active.[25] Indeed, it is often claimed in the tradition that God's immediate causal action at a place *presupposes* (and thus cannot be solely constitutive of) God's presence at that place.[26] Third, and what is perhaps the most commonly cited theological reason for divine omnipresence, is that divine immensity precludes the divine essence from being limited or bound to a particular locale in space. The immensity of the divine essence *ad intra* yields the ubiquity of the divine essence *ad extra*.

It is vitally important to distinguish the claim that immediate causal and epistemic relations play a crucial *epistemic* role in demonstrating the ubiquity of the divine essence, tenet (1) of the threefold schema, from the further claim that immediate causal relations *metaphysically constitute* the ubiquity of the divine essence. Many contemporary analytic philosophers and theologians who adopt a DO model of omnipresence do so on the grounds that causal and epistemic considerations have played an integral role in historical dogmatic reflection on omnipresence. While it is certainly the case that causal and epistemic relations have played an integral role in providing *epistemic grounds* for affirming the ubiquity of the divine essence, this does not warrant the more substantive claim that these relations *metaphysically ground* the ubiquity of the divine essence. This very point was underscored by Turretin (1992: 201) within the polemical context of Socinianism (whose adherents denied divine immensity as well as God's ubiquitous presence by essence, tenet (1) in favor of tenets (2) and (3)):

> It is one thing to declare and demonstrate *a posteriori* the presence of God through the external operation; another thing to define *a priori* the presence of God by that operation or to maintain that God is not present except by power and operation. The former we acknowledge can rightly be done, but the latter we deny because the operation of God supposes his presence, and he must first be conceived to be and to exist before he can be conceived of as acting. Certain more modern thinkers (who limit the omnipresence of God by his operation), may be allowed their opinion if they understand it in the former sense for its manifestation *a posteriori*; but if they refer it to its constitution *a priori*, it is deservedly rejected as contrary to Scripture and approaching too near the error of the Socinians.[27]

Consequently, for Turretin, while it is reasonable to *infer* the ubiquity of the divine essence from God's immediate and universal causal operation in creation, it is problematic to *define* such presence solely in causal terms as this would be to omit an essential and

---

[24] For a clear example of this line of thinking in the medieval and Protestant scholastic periods see Anselm (2007: 225–6) and Mastricht (2019: 199).

[25] See Anselm (2007: 225–6). Aquinas argues that the principle of no immediate action at a distance applies to all agents, spiritual or corporeal, no matter how powerful (2012: Ia.Q8.a1.ad3). See also Aquinas (1975: bk.II, 68.3). Although, as Cross (2003, 2016) points out, this widespread principle was challenged by Duns Scotus.

[26] See Wesley (1991: 525) and Turretin (1992: 199, 201).

[27] See also Trueman (2007: 39–42) for an explication of John Owen's defense of God's ubiquitous presence by essence within the same polemical context against Socinianism.

arguably more fundamental aspect of divine omnipresence. While it remains to be seen whether the fuller account of divine omnipresence in terms of the classical threefold schema is defensible, contemporary analytic theologians do well to consider its historical and theological merits.

References

Anselm (2007), *Anselm: Basic Writings*, trans. and ed. T. Williams, Indianapolis: Hackett.
Aquinas, T. (1975), *Summa Contra Gentiles*, trans. and ed. A. C. Pegis, Notre Dame: University of Notre Dame Press.
Aquinas, T. (2012), *Summa Theologiae*, trans. Fr. L. Shapcote, O.P., ed. J.Mortensen and E. Alarcón, Lander: The Aquinas Institute.
Arcadi, J. M. (2017), "God is Where God Acts: Reconceiving Divine Omnipresence," *Topoi*, 36 (4): 631–9.
Arminius, J. (1986), *Public Disputations*, in *The Works of James Arminius*, London edition, trans. J. Nichols, Kansas City: Beacon Hill Press.
Athanasius (1982), *On the Incarnation of the Word*, Crestwood: St. Vladimir's Seminary Press.
Augustine (1961), *Confessions*, trans. R. S. Pine-Coffin, New York: Penguin Books.
Augustine (1994), *Sermons 273-305A: On the Saints*, vol. III/8, trans. E. Hill, ed. J. E. Rotelle, Hyde Park: New City Press.
Augustine (2004), *Letters 156–210*, vol. II/3, trans. R. Teske, ed. B. Ramsey, Hyde Park: New City Press.
Bavinck, H. (2004), *Reformed Dogmatics Vol 2: God and Creation*, ed. John Bolt, trans. John Vriend. Grand Rapids, MI: Baker Academic.
Blount, D. K. (1997), "An Essay on Divine Presence," PhD diss., University of Notre Dame, Notre Dame.
Burn, A. E. (1918), *The Athanasian Creed*, 2nd ed., London: Rivingtons.
Clement of Alexandria (1885), *The Stomata, or Miscellanies. Ante-Nicene Fathers: The Writings of the Fathers down to a.d. 325*, trans. A. Roberts and J. Donaldson, Grand Rapids, MI: Christian Classics Ethereal Library.
Conn, C. H. (2011), "Anselmian Spacetime: Omnipresence and the Created Order," *Heythrop Journal*, 52 (2): 260–70.
Craig, W. L., and J. P. Moreland (2003), *Philosophical Foundations for a Christian Worldview*, Downers Grove, IL: InterVarsity Press.
Cross, R. (2003), "Incarnation, Omnipresence, and Action at a Distance," *Neue Zeitschrift fur Systematische Theologie und Religionsphilosophie*, 45 (3): 293–312.
Cross, R. (2016), "Duns Scotus on Divine Immensity," *Faith and Philosophy*, 33 (4): 389–413.
Cyril of Alexandria (1874), *Commentary on the Gospel According to St. John*, vol. 1, in *A Library of Fathers of the Holy Catholic Church* 43, London: Walter Smith.
Damascus, St. J. (1958), *The Orthodox Faith*, in *Writings, The Fathers of the Church*, vol. 37, trans. F. H. Chase, Washington, DC: The Catholic University of America Press.
Fuerst, A. (1951), *An Historical Study of the Doctrine of the Omnipresence of God in Selected Writings between 1220–1270*, Washington DC: Catholic University of America Press.
Gasser, G. (2019), "God's Omnipresence in the World: On Possible Meanings of 'en' in Panentheism," *International Journal for Philosophy of Religion*, 85 (1): 43–62.
Gordon, J. R. (2018), "Rethinking Divine Spatiality: Divine Omnipresence in Philosophical and Theological Perspective," *Heythrop Journal*, 59 (3): 534–43.

Goris, H. J. M. J. (2009), "Divine Omnipresence in Thomas Aquinas," in H. J. M. J. Goris, H. Rikhof, and J. M. Schoot (eds.), *Divine Transcendence and Immanence in the Work of Thomas Aquinas: A Collection of Studies Presented at the Third Conference of The Thomas Instituut Te Utrecht, December 15–17, 2005*, 37–58, Leuven: Peeters.

Hoffman, J., and G. S. Rosenkrantz (2002), *The Divine Attributes*, Malden: Blackwell.

Hudson, H. (2009), "Omnipresence," in T. P. Flint and M. C. Rea (eds.), *The Oxford Handbook of Philosophical Theology*, 199–216, Oxford: Oxford University Press.

Hudson, H. (2014), *The Fall and Hypertime*, Oxford: Oxford University Press.

Inman, R. (2017), "Omnipresence and the Location of the Immaterial," in J. L. Kvanvig (ed.), *Oxford Studies in Philosophy of Religion*, vol. 8, Oxford: Oxford University Press.

Jedwab, J. (2016), "God's Omnipresence: A Defense of the Classical View," *European Journal for Philosophy of Religion*, 8 (2): 129–49.

Leftow, B. (1989) "Anselm on Omnipresence," *New Scholasticism*, 63 (3): 326–57.

Leibniz, G. W. (1989), *Philosophical Papers and Letters*, a selection translated and edited, with an introduction by L. E. Loemker, Dordrecht: Kluwer Academic.

Lombard, P. (2010), *The Sentences: The Mystery of the Trinity*, trans. G. Silano, Toronto: Pontifical Institute of Mediaeval Studies.

Muller, R. (2003), *Post-Reformation Reformed Dogmatics*, 2nd ed., Grand Rapids, MI: Baker Academic.

Oakes, R. (2006), "Divine Omnipresence and Maximal Immanence: Supernaturalism versus Pantheism," *American Philosophical Quarterly*, 43 (2): 171–9.

Ockham, W. (1991), *Quodlibetal Questions*, trans. A. J. Freddoso and F. E. Kelly, New York: Yale University Press.

Pasnau, R. (2011a), "On Existing All at Once," in C. Tapp and E. Runggaldier (eds.), *God, Eternity, and Time*, 11–29, Burlington: Ashgate.

Pasnau, R. (2011b), *Metaphysical Themes 1274–1671*, Oxford: Clarendon Press.

Poitiers, H. (1994), *On the Trinity*, in *Hillary of Poitiers: Select Works*, trans. E. W. Watson and L. Pullan, Grand Rapids, MI: Christian Classics Ethereal Library.

Pruss, A. (2013), "Omnipresence, Multilocation, the Real Presence and Time Travel," *Journal of Analytic Theology*, 1: 60–73.

Reynolds, P. L. (1992), "The Essence, Power, and Presence of God: Fragments of the History of an Idea, from Neopythagoreanism to Peter Abelard," in H. J. Westra (ed.), *From Athens to Chartes: Neoplatonism and Medieval Thought: Studies in Honor of Edouard Jeauneau*, 351–80, Leiden: Brill.

Shedd, W. G. T. (2003), *Dogmatic Theology*, ed. A. Gomes, Phillipsburg, NJ: P&R.

Stump, E. (2010), *Wandering in Darkness*, New York: Oxford University Press.

Stump, E. (2013), "Omnipresence, Indwelling, and the Second Personal," *European Journal for Philosophy of Religion*, 4 (4): 29–53.

Stump, E. (2018), *Atonement*, New York: Oxford University Press.

Swinburne, R. (1993), *The Coherence of Theism*, New York: Oxford University Press.

Taliaferro, C. (1994), *Consciousness and the Mind of God*, Cambridge: Cambridge University Press.

Trueman, C. (2007), *John Owen: Reformed Catholic, Renaissance Man*, Burlington: Ashgate.

Turretin, F. (1992), *Institutes of Elenctic Theology*, vol. 2, trans. G. M. Giger, ed. J. T. Dennison, Jr., Phillipsburg: P&R.

Van Den Brom, L. J. (1993), *Divine Presence in the World: A Critical Analysis of the Notion of Divine Omnipresence*, Kampen: Kok Pharos.

Van Mastricht, P. (2019), *Theoretical-Practical Theology: Faith in the Triune God*, vol. 2, ed. J. R. Beeke and M. T. Spangler, Grand Rapids, MI: Reformation Heritage Books.

Wainwright, W. J. (2010), "Omnipotence, Omniscience, and Omnipresence," in C. Taliaferro and C. Meister (eds.), *The Cambridge Companion to Christian Philosophical Theology*, 46–65, Cambridge: Cambridge University Press.
Webster, J. (2016a), *Confessing God*, London: T&T Clark.
Webster, J. (2016b), *God without Measure: Working Papers in Christian Theology*, vol. 1, London: T&T Clark.
Wesley, J. (1991), *John Wesley's Sermons: An Anthology*, ed. A. C. Outler and R. P. Heitzenrater, Nashville: Abingdon Press.
Wierenga, E. (1988), "Anselm on Omnipresence," *New Scholasticism*, 62 (1): 30–41.
Wierenga, E. (2010), "Omnipresence," in C. Taliaferro, P. Draper, and P. L. Quinn (eds.), *A Companion to Philosophy of Religion*, 2nd ed., 258–62, Malden, MA: Blackwell.
Zagzebski, L. (2013), *Omnisubjectivity: A Defense of a Divine Attribute*, Milwaukee: Marquette University Press.

CHAPTER ELEVEN

Divine Goodness and Love

JORDAN WESSLING

Theists affirm that God is necessarily omnipotent, omniscient, and perfectly good. While some theists deny that God is good in the strict moral sense of the term, since it is said that God does not possess moral virtues and is not subject to obligations (e.g., Morris 1991: 47–64; Davies 2004: chapter 10), most theists would probably agree that God enjoys some perfection that is at least analogous to moral goodness. Minimally, God possesses character traits that are similar to human moral virtues and God is praiseworthy for the intentional acts He performs for excellent reasons. This chapter concerns God's moral goodness, or at least that which many will conclude is analogous to moral goodness. (For ease of expression, I drop the qualification of *analogous* to moral goodness hereafter.)

Contemporary discussions of God's perfect moral goodness tend to focus on formal characterizations of that goodness as well as the examination of certain apparent implications that follow from it. Such contemporary discussions include investigations into the following questions:

- What is God's relation to moral values, and might some creaturely character traits, acts, or states of affairs have their moral status in virtue of some relation they bear to some feature of the divine nature and/or exercise of the divine will (e.g., Adams 1999; Zagzebski 2004; Murphy 2017)?
- Is God's moral goodness best modeled after virtue theory, deontology, consequentialism, or some combination thereof (e.g., Hoffman and Rosenkrantz 2002; Garcia 2009)?
- Must God create the best on account of His perfect goodness (e.g., Rowe 2004)?
- Can God be perfectly good yet significantly free (e.g., Timpe 2013: 103–18)?
- What conceptions of perfect divine moral goodness, if any, are compatible with the reality of divine hiddenness and the existence of creaturely evil and suffering (e.g., Stump 2010; Schellenberg 2015; Rea 2018)?

These are important issues that merit the attention they have received. Nevertheless, it is quite possible to answer these questions in ways that do not grant one much insight into the content of the divine moral character as that character is presented within one significant theistic tradition, namely Christianity. Within Christian scripture, and to a lesser degree Christian tradition, we find little by way of direct address of the listed questions. Instead, we find a God who is specifically identified with love (e.g., Mt. 5:43-48; Jn 17:1-26; Eph. 5:1-2; 1 Jn 4:7-21) and who dramatically demonstrates the depth of His love by becoming human and dying a brutal criminal's death to free humans from their sins and make them His sons and daughters. So, if the goal is to understand the nature of God's moral goodness from a Christian perspective, rather than merely treat the significant issues listed, then one should perhaps seek to provide some sort of account of perfect divine love. This is the track that is taken in the present chapter; the interrelation between God's love and His moral goodness more generally will be considered after topics related to divine love are treated.

I. THE NATURE OF DIVINE LOVE

I.1 Modeling Love

Analytic theologians and philosophers of religion regularly use models or accounts of divine attributes as a means of conceptually simplifying and organizing the mystery of the divine, for the purpose of coming to a greater understanding of the relevant divine attribute and for making progress on a range of affiliated issues. The aim of such models often (though not always) is to approximate the truth of the matter by analogously representing salient features of the divine attribute at issue (Wood 2016). When it comes to modeling God's moral goodness, it is often assumed that God and humans are similar in such a manner that conceptions of divine goodness can be reasonably modeled after conceptions of human goodness (Garcia 2009: 221; cf. Murphy 2017: 23–9). Models of divine love are not typically different in this respect, and several such models have been proposed. We shall consider just two in their basic form.

I.2 The Benevolence Account

Central to most models of God's love is the idea that God loves by desiring and/or willing a person's good for her own sake. From the Christian point of view, this emphasis on benevolence should come as no surprise. If nothing else, benevolence explains God's self-sacrificial death in Christ, which provides a standard for human love (e.g., Jn 3:16, 15:9-12; Eph. 5:1-2; 1 Jn 4:11). Some Christian theorists maintain, however, that benevolence is not only necessary for a model of divine love but also jointly necessary and sufficient for it—or at least benevolence plus some minor additions, usually the accompaniment of certain feelings or emotions (e.g., Hill 1984: 55–72; Creel 1986: 117–21; Oord 2010: 19–30). Call this the *benevolence account* of divine love.

It is unlikely that the benevolence account provides a full account of God's love (cf. Adams 1980 and Wessling 2017a). One reason to think this comes from the worry that benevolence by itself (or benevolence plus the minor additions often provided in benevolence accounts) does not adequately capture the biblical witness to God's love as intimately personal. The limited glimpses we see of the love between the Father and Son, for example, reveal a life of glory (Jn 17:5), sharing (Jn 17:1-10), joy (Jn 15:1-11), communion (1 Jn 4:4-21), and unity (Jn 17:20-25). It is doubtful, though, that the richness of this love is best captured *exclusively* by benevolence. Something similar could be said of God's deification of humans (e.g., 2 Pet. 1:4; Jn 17:26), Christ's preparation of the Church as His bride (Eph. 5:25-27), or Jesus's calling His disciples "friends" (Jn 15:15).[1]

---

[1] Biblical quotations in this chapter are from the New Revised Standard Version of the Bible.

Hence God's love, at least when other-directed, appears to contain some kind of intimate relational or interpersonal component alongside benevolence.

I.3 The Value Account

Perhaps sensing that benevolence by itself does not (absent the perception of need) sufficiently motivate one to be personally involved with the beneficiaries of one's benevolence, many Christians, both presently and historically, have maintained that God's love must include some kind of desire for union alongside benevolence (see, e.g., Barth 1957: 276; Adams 1980; Stump 2010). While it is not always clear to what the inclusion of the desire for union within one's conception of divine love is supposed to amount, many would agree that this divine unitive desire, when directed at humans, inclines God to indwell beloved individuals and make them more like Himself (think here of the doctrine of deification) and to engage them in some interpersonal and intimate way (think of the beatific vision as the face-to-face fulfillment of Moses's mere glance at God's back—Exod. 33:18-20; cf. 1 Cor. 13:12). Given limitations of space, the desire for union within divine love must be left without much by way of further analysis. Nevertheless, readers are likely able to discern how the inclusion of the desire for union within one's model of divine love has the potential of rectifying the noted shortcoming with the benevolence account. Be that as it may, the defender of the notion that God's love contains both benevolence as well as the desire for union presumably should explain how these two components of love fit together, so as not to give the impression that benevolence and the unitive desire merely happen to coexist and perhaps sometimes even have conflicting aims. My own way of making sense of these and other desiderata is embedded in what I call the *value account* of God's love (Wessling 2020).

According to the value account, "to value" something, and like cognates, is to perceive or experience as good the realization of P, where P refers to some state of affairs (Oddie 2005: 28–82). Here the perception or experience of P's goodness is construed along non-doxastic lines in that to perceive P as good is the not same as believing that P is good, though the perception of P's goodness might be the basis of such a belief. Instead, the relevant perception of P's goodness concerns representing P as good, analogous to the way in which someone who sees that something is red represents it as such. With that admittedly rough understanding of an agent valuing something in place, the defender of the value account maintains that for God to love P is for God to respond to P's intrinsic goodness by valuing P's existence and flourishing as well as union with P.

Within the value account, one may distinguish between love that is directed at nonpersonal beings and that which is directed toward personal beings, where the latter kind of love is something like the species of the former, which is the genus. Both the species and the genus versions of the value account concern responding to the intrinsic goodness of the beloved individual according to the kind of entity that the beloved individual is. One benefit of this genus-species distinction is that it allows for the idea that God can love all of creation, the personal and nonpersonal alike. However, in order to streamline the discussion of the value account, we will focus exclusively on God's love as directed toward personal beings, most centrally humans.

So, to grasp the way in which the proponent of the value account conceives of God's person-directed love, consider a case in which God loves a human person. According to the value account, God loves a human person when He responds to her *dignity* by valuing (1) her existence, (2) her flourishing, and (3) union with her. The nature and place of dignity within the value account merit comment as well as each member of the valuing-trio.

To unpack the idea of dignity, it is helpful to borrow from Immanuel Kant's well-known distinction between dignity and price. Everything, we are told by Kant, has either a dignity or a price. "If it has a price, something else can be put in its place as an equivalent; if it is exalted above all price and so admits of no equivalent, then it has a dignity" (Kant 1958: 77). Applied to human persons, who each enjoy dignity, this means that humans possess a high kind of value that makes them entirely irreplaceable. Unlike items that have a price, one cannot substitute the loss of one human person with anything else, including another human, to replace that value.[2] If the value account is true, God loves a human by responding to a human's dignity with the noted valuing-trio.

Why maintain that God views humans as possessing dignity, as opposed to some other kind of worth, and that God responds to the perception of this dignity with love? While our thinking about such matters is largely provisional given divine transcendence, the Christian teaching that God became a human and died for humans motivated by love arguably provides considerable evidence for the claim that God sees humans as possessing dignity, or something very close, and that God loves them for this dignity. *Pace* Anders Nygren and his followers (Nygren 1982: 75–9), it does not seem particularly rational, after all, to go to such great lengths to redeem humans if God does not regard them to be extraordinarily valuable and if He could replace the value of each human with a simple creative act of will. But God is supremely rational and He did, motivated by love, go to these tremendous lengths in Christ to save humans, which, it seems, furnishes at least some support for the notion that God sees humans as dignified, or something very close, and that this dignity factors into the way that God loves humans.

Notice, though, that couching God's love in terms of a response to value can be seen to set certain limits, even if very high ones, on God's love of humans. Assuming that God calibrates or in some way matches the strength of His love to the intrinsic value of that which is loved, God will love the human more than tadpoles, mountain ranges, or anything that has less value than the dignified human; but God will love the human much less than He loves Himself—given the obvious value disparity. It follows that the individual who renders the value account in this way will not agree with Thomas F. Torrance's claim that the cross demonstrates "that God loves us more than he loves himself" (1996: 244). No, the cross reveals that God judges that humans are worth dying for; it would be perverse, on the present value account, to suppose that God loves anything as much as or more than He who is the fount of all truth, beauty, and goodness. The fact that the value account has such natural resources for explaining God's deep yet sensible love of humanity once again provides some evidence for the relevant components of the value account.

Turn, finally, to the noted valuing-trio of the value account. God values a human's existence and flourishing by perceiving the existence of His image-bearer as good, and by wanting this human to live well, ultimately by reaching her *summum bonum*. Here we find the incorporation of benevolence into the value account. The addition is that God not only wants goodness *for* the beloved human (i.e., benevolence) but also values the instantiation of the goodness *of* this human (i.e., values her existence). In valuing union, furthermore, God values the goodness of being *with* that individual in the sense that God

---

[2] That said, the concept of human dignity, as presently utilized, does not include the notion that there is no greater value. It is apparently possible, after all, for something to be high in value and irreplaceable, yet be surpassed by the value of something else.

affirms the goodness of being in a certain kind of deifying and intimate interpersonal relationship with the beloved human.

Notice that certain members of the valuing-trio often entail one another (cf. Stump 2010: 91, 101). If God values a human's highest good, then (plausibly, given omniscience) God also values union with that human, since the highest good of all humans is union with God (or, if you like, a union with God that God values). Conversely, if God values union with a human, God (given omniscience) also values that human's highest good, since, again, the highest good of all humans is union with God. Moreover, it is plausible that God cannot value someone's highest good and union with her unless God also values her existence. Thus, the valuing-trio forms a tightly integrated, appreciative response to the intrinsic worth of the one loved.

What has been stated about God's love of humans can be applied, *mutatis mutandis*, to God's love of other personal beings. For example, God can love an angel, say Gabriel, by adopting the attitudes toward Gabriel found in the value account, although there might be differences between God's love of Gabriel and some human, given the differences between these kinds of personal beings. Similarly, God can love Himself in accordance with the value account. In intra-trinitarian love, for instance, the divine persons can perceive each other's magnificent worth and value the existence and good of one another as well as a kind of union with each other. Indeed, it is not unreasonable to maintain that part of what makes God's intra-trinitarian life truly blessed is valuing each other in this way and receiving the joyous emotions that perhaps spring from such valuing.

The value account of divine love has a number of virtues (see Wessling 2020 for a detailed defense). Although multifaceted, the value account points to an integrated response to goodness that corresponds to one common way of understanding God's love, namely, as possessing both benevolence plus some kind of desire for union, and the value account readily makes sense of God's strong yet measured love of humanity as well as the joy of intra-trinitarian love. In light of such virtues, the value account of divine love merits serious consideration.

II. MAXIMAL LOVE

In the eyes of many Christians, God is not simply the most loving being that exists; rather, God is the most loving being that possibly could be—and necessarily so. In short, God is maximally loving. It is unclear, however, what it might mean to suppose that God is maximally loving—and some have denied that we can make much sense of the claim (Murphy 2017: 22–66; Rea 2018: 63–89; cf. Trakakis 2016 and Yadav 2019). In this section, two understandings of God's maximal love are considered (which I stipulate as mutually exclusive, given the presence of certain value-assumptions that will soon become clear enough), one of which is suggested to provide the beginnings of a plausible conception of this love.

II.1 The Ultimate Degree View

First, maximal love might be understood as equivalent to the claim that God exemplifies love to the *ultimate degree* (cf. Murphy 2017: 34–42; Rea 2018: 63–89). Stressing the idea that God's love can never be surpassed on account of its perfection, the proponent of the ultimate degree view of God's maximal love submits that God's love must be of the greatest possible scope and depth: God must love every lovable person and thing, and, for each person or thing that God loves, God must love that person or thing to a degree that could not possibly be exceeded. Suppose that my Boston terrier, Hugo, constitutes an appropriate creature for God to love. According to the ultimate degree view of God's maximal love, God must then love Hugo as much as *any* being could possibly be loved. Thus, if God loves some human, or even Himself, more than He does Hugo, God fails to exemplify love to the ultimate degree, and, hence, *ex hypothesi*, fails to qualify as a maximally loving being.

The idea that maximal love requires the instantiation of love to the ultimate degree is implausible. Arguably, the degree to which God loves someone or something should in some way track with the inherent intrinsic value of that which is loved. Indeed, it seems plain enough that to love everyone and everything at the same unsurpassably deep level, irrespective of its intrinsic value, would be a defect, not a great-making feature of love, and thus beneath maximally perfect love. After all, it seems that it would be a moral defect on God's part to regard the death of a cockroach to be as grievous as the death of some beloved human. Yet if God loves *all* creatures equally, then God would regard the noted deaths equally as far as His love is concerned. It seems similarly untoward for God to love humans as much as He loves Himself. What such implications reveal is that if God is maximally loving, He in some sense calibrates the degree to which He loves to the value of the object loved.

II.2 The Optimal Level View

A more promising understanding of God's maximal love is what might be called the *optimal level view* (cf. Murphy 2017: 42–3). Unlike the ultimate degree view, which conceives of God's love as insensitive to gradations of value, on the optimal level view, God's maximal love is cashed out by way of the best and highest *fit* between the divine affection and value of the object loved. That which is loved sets parameters, in some way, on the manner and strength by which it should be loved. The optimal level understanding of maximal love meshes nicely with the value account of divine love, whereby God's love is a kind of appreciation of someone or something's intrinsic worth, and where the worth determines how the object of affection should be loved.

Nevertheless, characterizing God's maximal love in terms of the optimal level is not without its challenges. Perhaps the most severe challenge is that it is incredibly difficult to specify what the appropriate fit between God's love and that which is loved might be. One promising approach to this matter is to think of God loving each thing He loves to the highest possible degree that matches the intrinsic inherent worth of that which is loved (although see Leftow 2017). It is not unreasonable to assume that, for any entity that might be loved, there is a discrete corresponding range of strength between N_A and N_Ω by which that entity can be properly or aptly loved. (Accordingly, it could be said that plants have a distinct corresponding range of N_A–N_Ω—say, Np_A–Np_Ω—by which they can be aptly loved, as do humans—say, Nh_A–Nh_Ω—and so on.) To have an attitude of affection for some entity at any node below N_A would be too weak to count as love, though it might superficially look like love. To love some entity at any level above N_Ω would be to love that entity too much or perversely, or perhaps not true love at all.[3] Any levels between

---

[3] In the case of God-directed love, it is plausible to maintain that one could never surpass an upper limit that would make love of God perverse or too strong, since God is maximally perfect.

N_A and N_Ω would be genuine instances of love, even though there might be room for improvement.

The God of maximal love, given the optimal level view, loves each entity at strength N_Ω, the highest appropriate strength given the inherent intrinsic worth of the kind of entity under consideration (where the relevant kind of strength might be Np_Ω, or Nh_Ω, etc.). For if it is true that it is a nonnegotiable feature of God's maximal perfection that He must possess love in the very best and highest form (i.e., God must be maximally loving), and if it is true that there exists the relevant kinds of N_A–N_Ω ranges (which seems reasonable given that there exists the phenomena of loving certain kinds of beings too much or too little), then something like the claim that God must love each appropriate entity with the relevant kind of optimal strength (or strength N_Ω) appears fairly plausible.

However, there remains the difficult issue of providing an analysis of what it means to love some entity at the highest relevant *strength*. Should this strength of love, for instance, be cashed out in terms of some kind of intensity of feeling, disposition toward certain actions, or something else? This matter cannot be considered in detail presently, but the relevant form of strength can be reasonably understood to include both an affective component as well as an action component. For those who maintain that God undergoes affective experiences, it can be said that God is disposed to experience the best, most fitting emotional response to beloved entities as determined by the kind of entity at issue plus the surrounding circumstances. Obviously, those who deny that God undergoes emotional experiences in response to creation are not likely to affirm the noted affective component as a means of unpacking the strength of Gods maximal love. Nonetheless, they can affirm the action component of such strength: a disposition or inclination to perform actions to bring about a beloved individual's highest good and union with her. What this disposition comes to will need to be negotiated on a case by case basis, depending upon the value of the being that is proposed as a candidate for love plus the relevant circumstances. But, generally, something like the following rough-and-ready characterization of the matter seems right, at least when the entity in question is an immensely valuable creature: for any given subject that God as a maximally loving being loves, God does all that can be done to bring about that subject's highest good and union with that subject, provided that there is neither (1) a competing greater good (or, if one prefers, a competing and more weighty reason) that renders this course of action inappropriate, nor (2) a competing equal good (or, if one prefers, a competing and equally weighty reason) that renders it permissible not to engage in this course of action. Add to this, as a kind of side-constraint, that a maximally loving being would never intentionally act in a manner that makes impossible the fulfillment of a beloved subject's highest good, when that subject enjoys dignity or some other high level of value. To act in such a manner would be intrinsically unloving and thus beneath maximal love.

There is much to be said on behalf of this rendering of the optimal strength of God's maximal love. Among other things, it makes sense of the idea that God, on account of His maximal perfection, must respond to each entity by loving it as much as it possibly or properly could be loved, given its worth. At the same time, it does not absurdly imply that God loves each entity as much as He could possibly love any being (it does not imply, for instance, that God loves Himself and humans equally). Still, many of the details of the optimal strength view remain to be worked out, making it an area of research that requires additional attention by analytic theologians and philosophers of religion.

III. LOVE AMONG GOD'S MORAL ATTRIBUTES

III.1 The Identity Thesis

Thus far, we have been examining God's love as a way of understanding God's moral goodness. But what is the relationship between God's love and His moral nature more generally? Is God's moral goodness identical to His love, such that God possesses no moral attribute that is not essentially and most fundamentally a matter of love (or loving), or does God have other moral attributes that are distinct from and not reducible to love? Following an adaptation of an essay by Frances Howard-Snyder, let us agree that God's love is identical to His moral goodness if a complete understanding of God's love, plus a complete description of the relevant circumstances (excluding additional moral premises), would in principle enable one to determine each actual or possible item of behavior (including behaviors of thought and character) that God would judge that He should do, is acceptable to do, or should not do (2005: 3–4). Call this claim the "Identity Thesis."

Apart from certain considerations having to do with divine simplicity (see, e.g., Radde-Gallwitz 2009: 6–7), two leitmotifs from the New Testament provide some evidence for the Identity Thesis. Consider, first, that Jesus, as well as various New Testament authors, teach that love fulfills the law (e.g., Mt. 22:34-40; Rom. 13:8-10; Gal. 5:14; perhaps Lk. 10:25-37, 18:18-23; perhaps Mk 12:29-33; perhaps Jn 13:34-35; and maybe 1 Jn 4:16-21). Certainly, there is debate about what love as the fulfilment of the law might mean (and there might be differences of understanding among the relevant biblical figures), but it may be reasonably supposed (even if contentiously supposed) that it means that love *completes* human morality. Once again, following Howard-Snyder, let us agree that love completes human morality if loving each relevant individual in the highest most valuable feasible way entails "for each bit of behavior or possible bit of behavior (including behaviors of saying or thinking or being a certain way) ... that the behavior ought to be done or that it is not the case that the behavior ought to be done" (2005: 3–4). So understood, the way in which love is thought to *complete* human morality bears a striking resemblance to the Identity Thesis. Similar to the way the Identity Thesis implies that there is no divine moral action nor moral virtue that is not fundamentally a way of loving, there is no ideal human moral action nor ideal moral virtue that is not fundamentally a way of loving. Second, Jesus, as well as certain biblical authors, ground this completed human ethic of love within God's nature (e.g., Mt. 5:43-48; Lk. 6:28-36; Jn 13:31-35, 15:9-12; Eph. 5:1-2; 1 Jn 4:7-21). That is to say, according to these persons, the love to which Christians are called reflects, or closely resembles, God's character of love (cf. Borg 1998: 125–43). Taken together, these two biblical teachings (or the interpretations thereof) support, even if by no means entail, the Identity Thesis. For if humans are called to love in a manner that completes morality, and this completed morality closely resembles the character of God, then it stands to reason that there is no divine moral action nor moral virtue that is not fundamentally a way of loving. But if this is so, then it looks as if the Identity Thesis is true.

Whatever the apparent biblical plausibility of the Identity Thesis, the thesis faces a number of challenges. One such challenge is that scripture indicates that God performs wrathful acts that ostensibly cannot be understood as acts of love. Another challenge to the Identity Thesis comes from the idea that love by itself does not determine what one should do when the interests of two or more people conflict. However, since God plausibly must decide what to do when such conflicts arise, there must be some other moral principle apart from love that God uses in these circumstances. Let us consider these challenges to the Identity Thesis in reverse order.

III.2 The Problem of Conflicts of Interest

There are many ways in which the interests of beings might conflict, each of which potentially demands specific treatment by the proponent of the Identity Thesis. To list just a few examples, there can conceivably be conflicts of interests between two beings of unequal value, between beings of equal value, between a large group of creatures with low value and a very small numbers of creatures with high value, and more besides. In addition, and once again just to scratch the surface, there are cases where some good can be divided to fulfill partially the interests of two or more parties, cases where the good at issue cannot be split up effectively, and cases where the relevant interests are more or less important. Such issues cry out for examination, and yet very little work has been done on them as they relate to the Identity Thesis.

The value account of divine love has inbuilt resources for dealing with at least some of these challenges to the Identity Thesis. If the value account is true, and God proportions the strength of His love according to the intrinsic value of that which is loved, then, in cases of conflict of interests, God's love will generally dispose Him to favor the interests of that being, or group of beings, that is more valuable—at least this seems to be the case when all other things are equal and when the good in question cannot be fruitfully divided and shared among the relevant parties. Call this proportioning of the strength of love the "Favoring Principle."

It might be thought that the fact that God in Christ died for humans obliterates the Favoring Principle. For God's value far outstrips the value of the collection of all humans that will ever come to be, yet God set aside His interests unto death for the salvation of the world. But if this is so, we are without grounds for supposing that the Favoring Principle is true—or so it might be thought.

There are a number of ways in which the proponent of the Favoring Principle might respond. For instance, one might claim that given the unitive nature of the value account, God's interests and human interests are intertwined in such a way that overcomes the notion that God in Christ choose to give at long-term cost to Himself. To see the point, suppose that, subsequent to God's decision to create, part of what is in God's interest is to be united with holy, or fully sanctified, humans whom He loves, and that one of the best means for God to achieve the fulfillment of this interest is to endure death in Christ. If so, then Christ's death is a way of procuring God's ultimate interests as well as the ultimate interests of humans, not clearly an instance in which God completely sacrificed the interests of a being with maximal value (namely Himself) for the sake of beings with considerably less value (namely humans). More generally, the idea that the ultimate interests of people dovetail on account of the ways in which they ideally should love perhaps provides resources for resolving many cases of apparent conflicts of interests.

Another option for the defender of the Favoring Principle is to propose some additional principle that springs from love according to which God favors certain kinds of interests over others. For example, because fallen humans require Christ's sacrifice (or so it might be maintained) to have the opportunity for eternal life, it might be thought that God's love should predispose God to favor the fulfillment of the more fundamental interests of humans over the satisfaction of His own interests in the life of Christ, given that Christ's sacrifice does not ultimately or permanently preclude God from flourishing. Roughly and generally, the thought would be that God, *ceteris paribus*, would be inclined to promote those interests of a being that are most fundamental to its flourishing over those interests that are not equally fundamental to a being. So far as I am aware, however, no one has explicated and defended such a principle.

But even if the Favoring Principle and accompanying principles are true, these principles alone do not protect the Identity Thesis from various ways in which conflicts of interest might be thought to undermine that thesis. For the protection of the Identity Thesis against such challenges, Howard-Snyder may yet again prove helpful. She has defended a number of principles according to which one can apparently resolve many-person conflicts by acting exclusively in accordance with the ethic that one must love all persons equally (Howard-Snyder 2005). These principles include dividing and equally sharing the good for each individual when doing so is fruitful, dividing and sharing the good unequally when doing so would be most beneficial overall, and choosing at random and "blindly" whom one will benefit when only a single individual (or subset of the whole) can be benefited. To this we might add the idea that when a person must benefit some individuals at the expense of others, that person should do what she subsequently can to compensate those not benefited. Howard-Snyder's concern is with human morality, but reformulated versions of such principles perhaps can be utilized in defense of the Identity Thesis. Whatever the case, more work could certainly be done on the plausibility of the Identity Thesis in light of conflicts of interests. Meanwhile, it is far from clear that there are not resources for treating conflicts of interest in accordance with the Identity Thesis.

III.3 *The Problem of Divine Wrath*

Scripture presents God as expressing wrath in at least two general ways that pose distinct problems for the Identity Thesis. First, God is said to visit calamity on individuals or entire people groups irrespective of individual moral wrongdoing, and, second, God is described as punishing individuals with severe punishments that seem irredeemable. Examples of the former are the killing of the firstborn children of Egypt or the Israelite conquest of Canaan, whereas examples of the latter are punishments via death or consignment to hell. Either expression of wrath is problematic for the Identity Thesis for the obvious reason that they seem incompatible with, or at least unmotivated by, perfect love for the subjects involved. We shall discuss these two kinds of expressions of divine wrath in turn.

Theologians have developed a number of strategies for treating texts in which God is depicted as bringing destruction on people regardless of individual wrongdoing. Three basic prominent strategies (which are not necessarily mutually exclusive) include what might be called the *dismissal procedure*, the *recognition procedure*, and the *affirmation procedure* (for a recent survey of procedures, see Seibert 2016 and Boyd 2017: 335–462). Advocates of the dismissal procedure claim that texts which portray God as performing the relevant wrathful acts are not in fact products of divine inspiration and so need not be affirmed. Should this strategy succeed, the Identity Thesis will likely emerge unscathed—although the task of defending a theologically viable version of the dismissal procedure arguably remains largely incomplete. Defenders of the recognition procedure maintain that it must be recognized that the relevant texts exaggerate or symbolically represent executions of divine wrath, which may or may not have happened, in a manner that entails that scripture does not intend to teach that God commands genocide or is otherwise involved in the apparently immoral killing of innocents. Examples of this procedure include the ancient notion that the violent texts at issue should be interpreted allegorically as well as the more contemporary notion that these violent texts represent forms of ancient Near Eastern hyperbole. Again, either version of this procedure is likely to insulate the Identity Thesis from much challenge, though it is unlikely that *all* the relevant depictions of divine wrath can be dealt with according to the recognition procedure. Finally, those who defend the affirmation procedure contend that scripture in fact teaches that God performs wrathful acts of the relevant kinds and that this should be affirmed as an accurate description of divine behavior. Often the affirmation procedure is accompanied by some kind of explanation as to why God might be justified in performing these terrible acts. However, it is extraordinarily difficult to see how the affirmation procedure might be rendered compatible with the Identity Thesis, or, for that matter, with any plausible conception of God's moral goodness. Perhaps the best route for the defender of the Identity Thesis who simultaneously adopts the affirmation procedure is to provide reason for thinking that there is always some many-person conflict of interests at work in cases where God brings calamity on people irrespective of individual moral wrongdoing, and that one of more of the previously discussed ways of dealing with many-person conflicts can be marshaled on behalf of the Identity Thesis. Whether such a method has any hope of saving the Identity Thesis is likely to remain a matter of much dispute.

Turn, next, to the issue of divine punishments for individual wrongdoing that appear to be incompatible with the Identity Thesis. Typically, what rests behind the notion that certain divine punishments are incompatible with the Identity Thesis is the idea that God sometimes intentionally punishes in ways that are positively and irredeemably bad for those punished. Call the thesis that God punishes severely in this way the "Severe Retribution Thesis."

While some biblical passages can be interpreted in a manner that supports the Severe Retribution Thesis, it is not indisputably incumbent upon the theologian to hold that the Severe Retribution Thesis is true. A predominant way in which theologians deny that God punishes with Severe Retribution might be called the *natural consequences view*. According to it, God is too loving to impose external penalties on wrongdoers through special divine action; so, instead, God allows sinful humans to experience the awful yet eventually inevitable consequences of their own behavior. As an example as to how this might work, God's wrath can be expressed toward an egoist not by imposing external punishment upon him but by allowing him to persist in his self-centered ways until his selfishness repels all companions, leaving him miserably alone. More generally, the natural penalty of a vicious life is becoming a vicious person, and the vicious person ultimately cannot flourish. It is said that this more "removed" divine approach to dealing with human sin not only is biblically preferable to the Severe Retribution Thesis but also is befitting of God's love since it manifests a way in which God respects the choices of even His most wayward creatures. If the natural consequences view is true and compatible with scripture, then the challenge to the Identity Thesis derived from the Severe Retribution Thesis rests upon a mistaken interpretation of scripture.

The problem with the natural consequences view, however, is that it appears to be at odds with the plain teaching of various biblical texts. Consider Acts 12:20-25. There we are told that King Herod refused to give glory to God, and, "immediately" as a result, "an angel of the Lord struck him down, and he was eaten by worms and died" (12:23). At an earlier stage within the same book, something similar is said to happen to Ananias and Sapphira. "Immediately" after receiving the apostolic judgment that they lied not merely to the Church but to God about a certain sum of money, they fall to the floor and die

(Acts 5:1-11). Luke does not explicitly say that they were killed by God, but the narrative leaves the implication unambiguous. Thus, A.T. Hanson, one of the foremost defenders of the natural consequences view, admits that "the death of Ananias and Sapphira appears to be an instance of direct divine punishment" of the kind that is incompatible with the natural consequences view (1957: 131). Although it may be possible to interpret passages such as these in a manner that is compatible with the natural consequences view, that view certainly does not sit well with these texts and others like it (e.g., 1. Cor. 27-31; 2 Pet. 2:1-16; Rev. 16). This mismatch has led some theologians to contend that whenever a biblical passage strongly implies that God performs abrupt retributive actions of the kind that do not mesh with the natural consequences view, we should suppose that the human authors of scripture are wrongly interpreting the events of history (cf. Hanson 1957: 157–8). However, all other things being equal, it is better to have a theory of divine wrath that does not require one to cut out the bits of scripture that collide with that theory. One need not be an advocate of biblical infallibility to suppose as much.

Fortunately for the defender of the Identity Thesis, there is another theory of divine punitive wrath that does not require one to deny that God punishes out of love in an immediate, and in some sense a retributivist, fashion. According to a theory that might be called *divine communicative punishment*, God's punishment aims to communicate to offenders the censure they deserve, with the purpose of trying to persuade these individuals to start down the path of spiritual transformation. So understood, God's punitive wrath, though sometimes frightful, is at root an expression of God's love, intent on revealing to sinful creatures the error of their ways, so that they might repent, be reformed, and be reconciled to the God who never stopped loving them. Elsewhere I have argued that divine communicative punishment has biblical, theological, and theoretical benefits in its favor and that it can account for damnation and immediate killings by God, provided that one is willing to allow for postmortem opportunities for salvation in hell and otherwise (Wessling 2017b, 2019, and 2020). We cannot examine that case here. But should it succeed, the defender of the Identity Thesis has resources for assuaging the worry that God's punishments of individuals are sometimes not fundamentally expressions of love.

IV. CONCLUSION

Throughout this chapter we have been examining God's love as a way of understanding God's moral goodness; indeed, we have entertained the idea that the two are ultimately identical. But even if it should turn out that God's moral goodness is broader than His love, it likely that a God whose character ought to be predominantly understood in terms of love will have a number of implications for many of the questions concerning divine goodness listed in the introductory section of this chapter. For instance, conceiving of God's moral goodness largely or exclusively in terms of love may suggest that God's moral nature is better modeled after virtue theory than it is consequentialism or deontology (see, e.g., Garcia 2009: 230–5), and it likely that the greater the emphasis placed on God's love, the more difficult the problems of evil and divine hiddenness become (see, e.g., Yadav 2019). Whatever the case, there remain many stimulating avenues of research upon which the analytic theologian might embark that will hopefully help the Church know and worship Her God as good in the face of many contemporary questions and challenges.

References

Adams, R. (1980), "Pure Love," *Journal of Religious Ethics*, 8: 83–99.
Adams, R. (1999), *Finite and Infinite Goods: A Framework for Ethics*, New York: Oxford University Press.
Barth, K. (1957), *Church Dogmatics* II/1, ed. G. W. Bromily and T. F. Torrance, trans. A. T. Mackay, T. H. L. Parker, W. B. Johnston, Harold Knight, and J. L. M. Haire, London: T&T Clark.
Borg, M. (1998), *Conflict, Holiness and Politics in the Teachings of Jesus*, 2nd ed., Harrisburg: Trinity Press International.
Boyd, G. (2017), *The Crucifixion of the Warrior God: Interpreting the Violent Old Testament Portraits in Light of the Cross*, Minneapolis: Fortress Press.
Creel, R. (1986), *Divine Impassibility: An Essay in Philosophical Theology*, Cambridge: Cambridge University Press.
Davies, B. (2004), *Introduction to Philosophy of Religion*, 3rd ed., New York: Oxford University Press.
Garcia, L. (2009), "Moral Perfection," in T. P. Flint and M. C. Rea (eds.), *The Oxford Handbook of Philosophical Theology*, 217–35, New York: Oxford University Press.
Hanson, A. T. (1957), *The Wrath of the Lamb*, London: S.P.C.K.
Hill, W. (1984), "Does Divine Love Entail Suffering in God?" in B. Clarke and E. Long (eds.), *God and Temporality*, 55–72, New York: New Era Books.
Hoffman, J., and G. Rosenkrantz (2002), *The Divine Attributes*, Malden, MA: Blackwell.
Howard-Snyder, F. (2005), "On These Two Commandments Hang All the Law and the Prophets," *Faith and Philosophy*, 22 (1): 3–20.
Kant, I. (1958), *Groundwork of the Metaphysics of Morals*, trans. H. J. Paton, New York: Hutchinson's University Library.
Leftow, B. (2017), "Two Pictures of Divine Choice," in H. McCann (ed.), *Free Will and Classical Theism: The Significance of Freedom in Perfect Being Theology*, 152–74, Oxford, Oxford University Press.
Morris, T. (1991), *Our Idea of God: An Introduction to Philosophical Theology*, Vancouver: Regent College.
Murphy, M. (2017), *God's Own Ethics: Norms of Divine Agency and the Argument from Evil*, New York: Oxford University Press.
Nygren, A. (1982), *Agape and Eros*, trans. P. Watson, Chicago: Chicago University Press.
Oddie, G. (2005), *Value, Reality, and Desire*, Oxford: Oxford University Press.
Oord, T. (2010), *Defining Love: A Philosophical, Scientific, and Theological Engagement*, Grand Rapids, MI: Brazos.
Radde-Gallwitz, A. (2009), *Basil of Caesarea, Gregory of Nyssa, and the Transformation of Divine Simplicity*, Oxford: Oxford University Press.
Rea, M. (2018), *The Hiddenness of God*, New York: Oxford University Press.
Rowe, W. (2004), *Can God Be Free?* New York: Oxford University Press.
Schellenberg, J. (2015), *The Hiddenness Argument: Philosophy's New Challenge to Belief in God*, New York: Oxford University Press.
Seibert, E. (2016), "Recent Research on Divine Violence in the Old Testament (with Special Attention to Christian Theological Perspectives)," *Currents in Biblical Research*, 15: 8–40.
Stump, E. (2010), *Wandering in Darkness: Narrative and the Problem of Suffering*, New York: Oxford University Press.
Timpe, K. (2013), *Free Will in Philosophical Theology*, New York: Bloomsbury.

Torrance, T. F. (1996), *The Christian Doctrine of God: One Being, Three Persons*, Edinburgh: T&T Clark.

Trakakis, N. (2016), "The Hidden Divinity and What It Reveals," in A. Green and E. Stump (eds.), *Hidden Divinity and Religious Belief: New Perspectives*, 192–209, New York: Cambridge University Press.

Wessling, J. (2017a), "Benevolent Billy: A Thought Experiment to Show that Benevolence is Insufficient for Christian Love," *Philosophia Christi*, 19: 181–91.

Wessling, J. (2017b), "How Does a Loving God Punish? On the Unification of Divine Love & Wrath," *International Journal of Systematic Theology*, 19 (4): 421–43.

Wessling, J. (2019), "A Love that Speaks in Harsh Tones: On the Superiority of Divine Communicative Punishment," in J. M. Arcadi, O. D. Crisp, and J. Wessling (eds), *Love, Divine and Human: Contemporary Essays in Systematic and Philosophical Theology*, London: T&T Clark.

Wessling, J. (2020), *Love Divine: A Systematic Account of God's Love for Humanity*, Oxford: Oxford University Press.

Wood, W. (2016), "Modeling Mystery," *Scientia et Fides*, 4: 1–21.

Yadav, S. (2019), "The Hidden Love of God and the Imaging Defense," in J. M. Arcadi, O. D. Crisp, and J. Wessling (eds.), *Love, Human and Divine: Contemporary Essays in Systematic and Philosophical Theology*, London: T&T Clark.

Zagzebski, L. (2004), *Divine Motivation Theory*, New York: Cambridge University Press.

CHAPTER TWELVE

Providence

DAVID FERGUSSON

I. INTRODUCTION

The term for "providence" seldom appears in scripture. The Greek *pronoia* and the Latin *providentia* have a much richer provenance in classical philosophy, though these terms were soon used to express themes embedded in the stories of the Bible and the doctrinal tenets of Christian theology. In the early church, theologians assumed at least a partial alliance with the providential philosophies found in Stoic and Platonist philosophers (Bergjan 2002; Elliott 2015). Providence is about both divine foresight and provision. Nature and history are ruled by God, whether according to general principles or particular determinations. Like a wise ruler, God attends not only to the general terms of governing the cosmos but also to the specificities of human affairs. The appearance of Christ came at the right time for the commencement of the gospel in the Gentile world; this was confirmed by the subsequent growth of the church, which provided a further sign of divine foresight. Our actions have outcomes that are providentially ordered, particularly with respect to eschatological rewards and punishments. In these ways, philosophical notions of providence were adapted to distinctively Christian purposes. The main difference that emerged was one that tended to separate the churches of the Greek east from the Latin west. "Fate" was a Stoic notion that was held in the Christian east to compromise our divinely bestowed freedom—it was insisted by Orthodox theologians that some things are genuinely up to us—whereas in the west, "fate" tended to be affirmed as the servant of divine providence (Louth 2007).

Although the theology of providence was largely an occasional theme in early Christian thought, perhaps an exercise in "irregular dogmatics," it was treated more systematically in the writings of the scholastics. For Thomas Aquinas, everything happens in accordance with the will of God. This is understood through a distinction between primary and secondary causality, which yielded a form of double agency. If the primal will of God is the first cause of every event, this is mediated by secondary causes. These are the created and intermediate forms by which the divine will is exercised. This distinction could conveniently preserve the integrity of human freedom and the order of natural causes, while ensuring that God could not be considered the author of sin and evil. Though with distinctive emphases upon scripture, faith, and divine sovereignty, a structurally similar account of providence reappears in John Calvin and the later Reformed tradition, again with recourse to the same philosophical tools, especially the distinction between primary and secondary causality, the latter appearing as subordinate to the former. The position is expressed succinctly by Heinrich Bullinger in the Second Helvetic Confession

(1566): "For God, who has appointed to everything its end, has ordained the beginning and the means by which it reaches its goal" (Cochrane 1966: 233).

The theology of providence was a dominant theme through much of modernity. Even in revisionist theologies not noted for their dogmatic convictions, providence often survived in an inflected form. Charles Taylor describes the ways in which the theologies of the Enlightenment could be cast as forms of "providential deism" (Taylor 2007: 221–69). The confidence surrounding this providentialism is apparent in much of the literature until the traumas of the Great War (1914–18) shattered the imperial optimism of the previous century. Thereafter traditional approaches were increasingly questioned, revised, deflated, or articulated in a more defensive mode. In particular, more synergist accounts have been ventured, which slacken the grip of a meticulous providence upon nature and history without abandoning scriptural emphases upon a benevolent divine rule. Analytic philosophers of religion have been prominent in these experiments with the result that their work has moved on to more overtly theological terrain. This has both enriched the exploration of newer models of providence while reinvigorating the assessment of classical approaches. In what follows, I shall examine recent discussion of the standard Thomist-Calvinist model and its Molinist revision, before exploring some alternative proposals.

II. THE CLASSICAL MODEL

The classical model of providence, at least in the Latin west, is dominated by a commitment both to divine sovereignty and to the integrity of creaturely causes. Everything that happens is determined by the primal will of God but mediated through the secondary causes that we see at work in the material world. Divine sovereignty entails that nothing can occur that is not willed by God. Hence, the exercise of divine rule requires more than a foreknowledge of events—God must ordain, concur, and will that these take place, not simply "by a bare permission" (Westminster Confession V. 4). This position is sustained by a succession of arguments based on considerations around the divine being and the sufficiency of explanation, and buttressed by examples from scripture. In articulating a maximalist doctrine of providence, theologians claimed that anything less would be unfitting for God and contrary to the teaching of scripture. While this theology of providence was intensely debated and defended in the age of Reformed orthodoxy (Goudriaan 2006: 143–232), it would be a mistake to regard it as a Reformed invention. Its roots can be found in medieval scholasticism as the Reformed orthodox themselves had no difficulty in recognizing.

In expounding this theology of providence, Paul Helm has advanced several considerations in its favor (Helm 1993). These tend to focus on the coherence of the position and the scriptural support that it commands. In addition, much attention is devoted to refuting contrary positions in such a way that the field is cleared of all but one possibility. It is argued that "risky" views of providence that accord too much scope to creaturely autonomy tend to compromise the sovereign rule of God as this is attested in scripture. These views also lead to unwelcome assumptions about the loss of divine omniscience and eternity, and uncertainty around final outcomes. If God can be frustrated or compromised by human freedom or chance events, then this must weaken God's providence. A timeless, omniscient, and sovereign God becomes temporally bound, fallible in belief, and unable fully to secure an original intent (Helm 1993: 54–5). Here we see how discussions of providence inevitably engage wider issues in the doctrine of God and, in particular, the coherence of classical theism. We should not be surprised therefore to find opponents of classical theism also advancing revisionist accounts of providence (Lucas 1976 and 1989).

The classical position continues to have an impressive list of defenders (Jensen 2014; White 2015). Strenuous efforts have been made to rebut objections concerning the theodicy problem and the charge of determinism. Although God cannot be presented as the author of sin and evil, God's rule extends over these in such a way that there is a permissive willing or concurring with creaturely causes. These are willed, but only in the sense that they are intended in the long run to serve both the glory and redemptive purposes of God. If we describe such causes as outside the will of God or unintended by-products of another process, then we merely generate some intractable problems. If God foresees what will happen, then God must in some way decree that this will take place unless we assume that there are events that God cannot control or rule. A bare permission is not coherent unless we view this as foreseen and willed. The world cannot surprise God or throw up unintended consequences without compromising divine sovereignty. It is for this reason that providence has sometimes been located within the doctrine of God—it is a necessary corollary of the divine attributes.

In this context, the classical distinction between primary and secondary causation continues to be expounded. Emerging in the Neoplatonism of Proclus, this already had a long history in Islamic thought from the ninth century (Taylor 2016). The differentiation of forms or levels of causality has at least five benefits for the theological metaphysician:

1. It protects the integrity of the system of natural causes—these can be described by the methods of the natural sciences and the social historian without reference to the supernatural as one among many forces at work.
2. Within this scheme, there remains scope for miraculous events that do not cohere with normal patterns of secondary causation—these can be attributed to the particular will of God in respect of their exceptional character.
3. The counterintuitive assumptions of occasionalism in which God is the hidden cause of every event to the extent that natural causes are apparent rather than real can be avoided. Secondary causes are genuine—they do not deceive us.
4. Primary causality enables the theologian to understand the total system of secondary causes as willed and ruled by God and therefore serving a providential purpose.
5. The distinction also allows a construction of human freedom as compatible with a form of divine determinism. The exercise of divine and human agency is neither a competition nor a zero-sum game. One form of agency does not recede in order that the other may flourish. These work together but at different levels; they are complementary rather than competitive.

In addition to its attractions, this scheme can draw upon scriptural support from those passages that speak of God working through creaturely agencies but overruling them to fulfill a more primal intention. For example, the Joseph story (Genesis 37–50) could be interpreted along those lines. His brothers do evil in selling Joseph into slavery, but some deeper purpose ordained by God is thereby enacted. This does not abrogate the human agencies involved—the brothers act of their own volition and are held culpable—but with foresight God works in and through these to establish a higher purpose. Joseph's sojourn in Egypt eventually saves his people back in Canaan at a time of prolonged famine.

Given its explanatory power, seeming simplicity, and apparent fit, why have so many theologians demurred at this account, particularly in recent times?

Three fundamental problems can be identified with the classical view. The first is the free will objection. If God decrees and knows from all eternity what I shall do, then how is my decision to act free at the time immediately before that action? In what sense could I have done otherwise under the same conditions? Exponents of the classical view have often appealed to a compatibilist view of human freedom. If, for example, my free action is one that is determined by the condition of my mind and will prior to acting, then God can both know and determine this condition. On this view, there is no incompatibility between divine determinism and human freedom; indeed, the former is the guarantee of the latter. Critics of the classical view of providence, however, tend to favor a stronger libertarian account of freedom. If my action is genuinely undetermined at the time immediately prior to my decision to act in this way, so that I could have done otherwise, then my choice cannot be decreed from some timeless realm inhabited by God. In making this strong libertarianism an axiom for the theology of providence, the critic may then be faced with some adjustments to the traditional view of divine timelessness. A second problem concerns the problem of evil. According to the classical view, God ordains everything that happens. This generates a meticulous providence that consolidates the connection between the divine will and manifold evils such as disease, natural catastrophe, malicious deeds, and tragic accidents. Theologians such as John Calvin were willing to embrace this view on the basis that it was scripturally warranted and ineluctable given the difficulties generated by its negation. But more recent work on the problem of evil has been reluctant to affirm this tight connection between the divine will and everything that happens. A stronger distinction between divine permission and willing is often introduced in this context, though as a historical note it is worth recalling that this has generally been maintained within Eastern Orthodoxy. A third difficulty with the classical view is its religious adequacy. The dynamic and interactive relationship between God and the world that is integral to prayer, worship, and service appears to be threatened by the view that the course of the future is determined fully by the primal will of God. The more cooperative and reactive elements of divine providence, which appear throughout scripture, are not captured by the classical approach. Indeed, many people may have quietly defected from this mainstream view or privately harbored their doubts (Wood 2008: 65). If we are to embrace a stronger sense of God's wrestling with recalcitrant creaturely material and improvising to bring about God's ends, then an alternative account will be needed. For these reasons, recent scholarship has experimented with a variety of models that are preferred to the standard position of Thomists and Calvinists.

III. THE REVIVAL OF MOLINISM

One way in which these criticisms can be accommodated without undue disturbance to the classical view is to revive the Molinist position with its appeal to middle knowledge (Flint 1998; Craig 1999). On this account, we can distinguish three forms of divine knowledge. There is God's natural knowledge of necessary truths (e.g., $2+2 = 4$) and there is God's knowledge of what God decrees shall happen (e.g., the fall of Adam and Eve). Additionally, there is God's middle knowledge of counterfactual possibilities, which includes many conditional truths. For example, God knows what would happen in all the possible worlds in which free creatures exercised their libertarian freedom differently. The basic advantage of this position is that it enables full providential control to be maintained alongside creaturely freedom. In actualizing this world (Plantinga 1977: 38–9) from among all the possible options, God knows exactly what free creatures will do under all the circumstances that will arise. With this knowledge, God can then exercise providence to ensure all the desired outcomes. Yet what we do is genuinely up to us, rather than determined by God. The appeal to middle knowledge ensures that our free acts are protected and that God is no longer cast as the author of sin. Yet God's omniscience, sovereign will, and providential control can all be maintained by the Molinist. More controversially, a Christological defense of middle knowledge has recently been articulated. The middle knowledge of God can guarantee that the human Jesus exercises true libertarian freedom but does so impeccably (Flint 2001).

Despite its initial appeal, there are formidable problems facing the exponent of middle knowledge. Does this really protect libertarian freedom? Critics have argued that if I am genuinely free at the moment of decision then God cannot know how I will act on the basis of all the antecedent conditions. In selecting this world for creating, therefore, God cannot know which of the many possible worlds has been actualized since its initial conditions cannot guarantee future outcomes. It seems that God must await our free decisions to learn which of many possible worlds this one will be, an outcome that will have consequences for the exercise of divine providence. According to this criticism, future conditionals are ungrounded and therefore indeterminate; for this reason, there is nothing that can be known until these are actualized (Hasker 2004: 155). A further problem is that God's sovereignty seems to be modified by the need for God to consult an array of possible worlds before selecting one of these. Like an interior decorator flicking through samples of paint color before making a selection, God is determined by a set of possibilities that are given and presented rather than willed. This loss of sovereignty in the appeal to middle knowledge was already noted in the seventeenth century—God was likened to Jupiter consulting the Fates before deciding what to do (van Asselt 2001: 167).

Owing to these difficulties, a middle knowledge approach to providence tends to be squeezed by the classical view on one side and more revisionist approaches on the other. Either God determines this world more strongly than via middle knowledge or else God's accommodation of human freedom requires a more open approach to the exercise of providence. A variety of "openist" or "interactive" proposals can be discerned in the literature.

IV. INTERACTIVE APPROACHES

Although the revisionist view has been closely associated with the movement known as "open theism," this was already evident in the work of analytic philosophers in the 1970s. Peter Geach once suggested that divine providence might be constructed on the model of God as a grand master of chess. No matter what moves the opponent makes, God can realize the divine intention by accommodating these in a strategy that will eventually result in a checkmate (Geach 1977: 58). The parameters and the outcome are fixed, though the moves that will be made are in part conditional upon the decisions of the opponent. Hence, God remains in control even while ceding some autonomy to creaturely agencies. J. R. Lucas (1976) advocates an improvised version of divine providence that is reactive but always successful by virtue of God's love, patience, and resourcefulness. God does not have one best plan but an infinity of best plans capable of accommodating our mistakes. Lucas is ready to affirm divine temporality as well as an abridged account of omniscience in order to secure the coherence of his position. But these departures from classical theism are presented as gains in retrieving a more scripturally adequate account of divine-human relations. Passages that refer to God's change of mind or conditionality in dealing with human beings are read, *contra* Calvin, not as metaphorical accommodations to our human mode of understanding but as genuine depictions of divine reactivity. Lucas offers the more personal analogy of the Persian carpet maker who can accommodate the mistakes of his apprentice children in weaving a new design through a seemingly inexhaustible creativity (Lucas 1976: 39). A similar accommodation of libertarian freedom is also evident in Richard Swinburne's adjustment of the traditional account of omniscience. God's foreknowledge cannot include an infallible awareness of the outcome of free decisions. To this extent, human freedom entails that divine foreknowledge is not incorrigible (Swinburne 1998: 133). It seems that we add to the stock of God's true beliefs only as and when we make these decisions.

The more recent cluster of proposals described as "open theism" has developed this approach, mainly within evangelical circles. Several strands of this more relational understanding of divine providence can readily be identified. The stress on human freedom is paramount to the extent that some outcomes are genuinely up to us. God may influence and cooperate with us in manifold ways, but the act of faith is one in which we freely assent to God. This is our decision, not God's. One consequence of this is that the construction of divine omniscience has to accommodate the openness of the future. Given creaturely freedom, the future is indeterminate. It is not so much that it is unknowable, but that there is nothing yet available to be known, even by God. So divine providence must find its way in a world (ordained by God) that is neither wholly knowable nor controllable.

Here open theism can make a virtue out of a necessity. A world characterized by creaturely autonomy and indeterminacy is part of the divine design. In the act of creation, God lets the world be. In this context, the concept of *kenosis* is sometimes employed. In conferring freedom and openness upon an evolving world, God resolves not to determine everything that happens by an act of primal will. There is a stepping back from a maximal providence that decrees each event. Yet, for the open theist, this does not signal a reversion to deism. God remains deeply involved in the life of the world but in modes of action that respect the conditions of creation. Hence, instead of determinism, there is influence, interaction, improvisation, and other forms of divine activity that are intended to coordinate with creatures rather than to control them. It is also argued that this makes better sense of the Bible, divine suffering, and the lives of the faithful. God is depicted in the stories of scripture as engaging in multiple forms of interaction with God's people. Some biblical scholars have inclined to this approach, recognizing that it captures the more relational and anthropopathic imagery of scripture than classical theism does (Fretheim 2005). And in the practice of petitionary prayer, we assume that we make requests of God, seek guidance and inspiration, and orient ourselves under God's direction toward the future (Tiessen 2000). To present this as the unfolding of what is already decreed and fixed in every detail seems to make a charade of our lives as we move into the future. As an accompaniment to the divine involvement in creation, the doctrine of God's timelessness is also abandoned in favor of a temporal God who can work in, with, and through the creation. Finally, in its eschatological focus, open theism seeks to avoid the apparent unfairness of predestined outcomes by positing a salvation that is the result of our free assent to the work of God's grace in our lives. What is on offer here is not so much the revisioning of divine providence but a different theological scheme.

Though it reflects multiple historical and contemporary influences, much notable work in open theism has originated from within analytic philosophy of religion (Sanders 1998; Hasker 2004). At the same time, its exponents have typically sought to distance themselves from process thought that is generally adjudged more heterodox in its doctrinal revisionism. Within much of open theism, there remains a strong account of divine action, of creation out of nothing, and a robust eschatology. In relation to theodicy, it offers some possible gains. Evil is the by-product of a creation that possesses the stability and lawlike structure necessary for creatures to exercise their freedom responsibly. We need a predictable but not wholly pliable world in which to grow and develop. The possibilities of sin and accident cannot be excluded from such a creation. How far this can be pressed into a theodicy is not always clear, but most open theists seem to assume that this is a better response to the problem of evil than anything that is available on the classical account (Oord 2016).

Open theism has produced an intense and frequently hostile debate that has sometimes resulted in pronounced division within evangelical circles, though patient dialogue has also proved possible (Hall and Sanders 2003). Leaving aside its obvious departure from key elements of the classical tradition, we can identify the following problems. If God lacks complete foreknowledge of human choices, in what ways can providence be effectively exercised? Here the open theist can claim that God knows a great deal about the future by virtue of an awareness of antecedent conditions, of causal regularities, and of human character. Although this does not amount to full omniscience in the traditional sense, God has sufficient knowledge of the world to influence it effectively. This seems about right, though when pressed it might slide in either of two directions. If God knows almost everything about us and is only rarely surprised by our free choices, then the overall position is not much different from the classical view with respect to the exercise of providence. In addition, it can be argued that divine permission and divine willing must be closely connected to the extent that what God permits are circumstances that God does not prevent. Here some form of divine concurrence and double agency begins to reemerge though there may be ways in which this can be distinguished from the classical view (Fergusson 2018: 217–40). Yet, on this construction, the differences appear less stark. Alternatively, if God's foreknowledge is significantly curtailed by the openness of the future, then we might ask how much control God can really exercise, particularly if God is ontologically bound by kenotic constraints (Oord 2016). Might God in the end be powerless to realize God's primary intention? This is probably the most unnerving feature of open theism for its critics. Instead of affirming key aspects of faith and trust in God, it seems to undermine these by weakening God's capacities and generating human anxiety as to the eventual future. Can we really be sure that all will be well, if the conditions governing God's action are restricted in this way? Coupled with its sharp departure from a centuries-old tradition of providential theology, the claims of open theism appear too disconcerting for its critics. Some have argued in this context that a slide toward a more radical process theology is all but inevitable within this paradigm. And, from a more theological perspective, one might wonder whether its model of a divine-human partnership is too symmetrical, perhaps even anthropomorphic, thus threatening the core conviction that we are saved and transformed only by the mystery of an all-prevailing love. These debates will surely continue.

V. CONCLUSION

Several concluding observations are in order. First, the disputes between the classical, Molinist, and openist positions may prevent a more nuanced theology of providence from emerging. The multiple forms of divine action in scripture are not reducible to one single model, whether of control, of activating middle knowledge, or entering into a partnership with free creatures. In the interests of a more adequate account of the God-world relationship, the modes of God's action need to be narrated and clearly distinguished (Fergusson 2018). Accounts of divine action also suffer from an abstract quality or the search for the Grail of the "causal joint." Little attention is devoted to the actual uses of providentialism in the history of Christian theology and the practices of the church. William Abraham has challenged this narrowing of focus by seeking a richer account more fully informed by doctrinal convictions that "reach for the full wealth of divine action showered upon us in the Son and in the Holy Spirit" (Abraham 2018: 155).

Second, greater attention needs to be devoted to the question of how one can arrive at a lively belief in providence. In this context, Eleonore Stump has made a pertinent contribution in her identification of a personal knowledge that emerges only in encounter, relationship, and a first-person narrative. This is set apart from the more standard and impersonal form of knowledge represented in analytic philosophy (Stump 2010: 40–63). The personal knowledge that arises in relational contexts cannot be obtained except from its being lived and appropriated in a practical setting. This is of relevance to providentialism. Why would one believe in the efficacy of God's providence? It seems hard to deduce this on the basis of a more detached natural theology, though eighteenth-century versions of the design argument often attempted to do so. But as a practical orientation, informed by prayer and scripture, it can make sense of one's life in relation to the world, to other people, and to God. A conviction about providence can thus be represented as a way of responding to a narrative account of the world that sets our lives in a particular perspective and enables us to act accordingly. It must be inhabited and lived in order to be believed. John Cottingham writes of an "epistemology of involvement," though making it clear that this does not imply an uncritical submission that suspends rational objections (Cottingham 2014: 23).

Finally, we should note that the role of analytic theology in these discussions is not easily delineated. This suggests that analytic techniques and approaches have been incorporated, often to good effect, in these debates, but that they cannot be isolated or pursued apart from other forms of enquiry. In particular, the need to interact with exegetical work and the history of dogma inevitably results in engagement with a range of different methodologies. Such blending of skills and disciplinary strengths is to be welcomed.

References

Abraham, W. J. (2018), *Divine Agency and Divine Action: Systematic Theology, Volume III*, Oxford: Oxford University Press.

Bergjan, S-P. (2002), *Der Fürsorgende Gott*, Berlin: De Gruyter.

Cochrane, A. C. (1966), *Reformed Confessions of the Sixteenth Century*, London: SCM Press.

Free Church of Scotland (1860), "The Confession of Faith," in *The Subordinate Standards, and Other Authoritative Documents of the Free Church of Scotland*, 1–100, Edinburgh: Johnston, Hunter.

Cottingham, J. (2014), *Philosophy of Religion: Towards a More Humane Approach*, Cambridge: Cambridge University Press.
Craig, W. L. (1999), *The Only Wise God: The Compatibility of Divine Foreknowledge and Human Freedom*, Eugene: Wipf and Stock.
Elliott, M. (2015), *Providence Perceived: Divine Action from a Human Point of View*, Berlin: De Gruyter.
Fergusson, D. (2018), *The Providence of God: A Polyphonic Approach*, Cambridge: Cambridge University Press.
Flint, T. P. (1998), *Divine Providence: The Molinist Account*, Ithaca: Cornell University Press.
Flint, T. P. (2001), "The Possibilities of Incarnation: Some Radical Molinist Suggestions," *Religious Studies*, 37 (3): 125–39.
Fretheim, T. (2005), *God and World in the Old Testament*, Nashville: Abingdon Press.
Geach, P. (1977), *Providence and Evil*, Cambridge: Cambridge University Press.
Goudriaan, A. (2006), *Reformed Orthodoxy and Philosophy, 1625–1750*, Leiden: Brill.
Hall, C. A., and J. Sanders (2003), *Does God Have a Future? A Debate on Divine Providence*, Grand Rapids, MI: Baker Academic.
Hasker, W. (2004), *Providence, Evil and the Openness of God*, London: Routledge.
Helm, P. (1993), *The Providence of God*, Leicester: Inter-Varsity Press.
Jensen, A. S. (2014), *Divine Providence and Human Agency: Trinity, Creation and Freedom*, Aldershot: Ashgate.
Louth, A. (2007), "Pagans and Christians on Providence," in J. H. D. Scourfield (ed.), *Texts and Culture in Late Antiquity: Inheritance, Authority, and Change*, 279–98, Swansea: Classical Press of Wales.
Lucas, J. R. (1976), *Freedom and Grace*, London: SPCK.
Lucas, J. R. (1989), "Foreknowledge and the Vulnerability of God," in G. Vesey (ed.), *Royal Institute of Philosophy Lecture Series: 25, The Philosophy in Christianity*, 119–28, Cambridge: Cambridge University Press.
Oord, T. J. (2016), *The Uncontrolling Love of God: An Open and Relational Account of Providence*, Downers Grove, IL: IVP Academic.
Plantinga, A. (1977), *God, Freedom and Evil*, Grand Rapids, MI: Eerdmans.
Sanders, J. (1998), *The God Who Risks: A Theology of Providence*, Downers Grove, IL: IVP Academic.
Stump, E. (2010), *Wandering in the Darkness: Narrative and the Problem of Suffering*, Oxford: Oxford University Press.
Swinburne, R. (1998), *Providence and the Problem of Evil*, Oxford: Clarendon.
Taylor, C. (2007), *A Secular Age*, Cambridge: Harvard University Press.
Taylor, R. C. (2016). "Primary and Secondary Causality," in R. C. Taylor and L. X. López-Farjeat (eds.), *The Routledge Companion to Islamic Philosophy*, 225–35, London: Routledge.
Tiessen, T. (2000), *Providence & Prayer: How Does God Work in the World?*, Downers Grove, IL: IVP Academic.
Van Asselt, W. J. (2001), *The Federal Theology of Johannes Cocceius (1603–1669)*, Leiden: Brill.
White, V. (2015), *Purpose and Providence: Taking Soundings in Western Thought, Literature and Theology*, London: T&T Clark.
Wood, C. (2008), *The Question of Providence*, Louisville: Westminster John Knox Press.

CHAPTER THIRTEEN

Divine Aseity and Abstract Objects

LINDSAY K. CLEVELAND

Central to the traditional Jewish, Christian, and Islamic understanding of God is the view that God does not depend upon anything apart from Himself for His existence. God is self-existent, which is to say that God exists in and of Himself, independently of everything else. This attribute of God is called *aseity* from the Latin *a se*, which means *of itself* or *through itself*. Some traditional theists regard divine aseity as one of the most fundamental aspects of our understanding of God. Thomas Aquinas, for example, sought in his famous "five ways" to establish the existence of a self-existent God (1920: I.2.3). Aquinas's arguments appeal to the necessity of a first cause that is itself uncaused, unchanging, necessary in and of itself, greatest of all things in perfection, or the source of the order according to which things act for the sake of an end. Other traditional theists, such as Augustine and Anselm, regard goodness or perfection as God's most fundamental feature and, assuming that dependence on another is always an imperfection, argue that divine aseity follows directly from God's perfection (Brower 2009). Despite differences in how traditional theists argue for divine aseity, they share the view that God is self-existent.

The traditional understanding of God's aseity is closely related to the traditional doctrine of creation—the view that everything other than God is created by God. Given this traditional doctrine of creation, it follows that God alone is self-existent. Christians have traditionally understood this view of creation to be expressed by biblical passages, such as the prologue to the Gospel of John. John says, concerning the Word who "was in the beginning with God," that "all things came to be through him, and without him nothing came to be" (Jn 1: 2-3).[1] Christians have traditionally taken the "all things" there to mean that literally all things other than God came to be through the Word, who is one with God, such that nothing other than God exists through itself.

The view that God alone is self-existent is challenged by various versions of the philosophical view called *platonism*.[2] While there are important differences between the classical Platonism put forward by Plato and contemporary versions of platonism, they have in common the view that there exist entities other than God that are uncreated, necessary, and eternal and that exist independently of God. Plato held that such entities do not exist in the physical world but in a transcendent, conceptual realm that Plato

---

[1] All biblical quotations in this chapter are taken from the New American Bible, revised edition.
[2] I do not capitalize "platonism" in order to include views that are not intended to represent the view of the historical Plato.

referred to as the realm of Ideas or Forms. On classical Platonism, such entities include mathematical objects like numbers and perfect geometrical shapes as well as perfect exemplars of qualities that particular things instantiate to an imperfect degree. On contemporary platonism, such entities include additional mathematical objects like functions and sets, properties (understood by platonists as universal qualities exemplified by particulars), propositions (i.e., the information content of declarative sentences), or possible worlds (i.e., alternative ways the actual world might have been). Contemporary platonists call such entities *abstract* to distinguish them from the concrete entities in our experience.[3] Insofar as such entities are taken to be uncreated, they conflict with the view that God alone is self-existent.

I explain and briefly assess the various options for addressing the conflict between platonism and the traditional understanding of divine aseity after first clarifying some relevant terms and discussing some motivations for platonism.

I. TERMINOLOGY

It is necessary to clarify some terms used in the debate regarding divine aseity and abstract objects. William Lane Craig, the most prominent contemporary scholar on the topic, has given a helpful account of the relevant terms, which I follow here (2016, 2017). First, it is important to distinguish between two general versions of platonism regarding abstract objects, since only one is incompatible with divine aseity. The two are what have been called *heavyweight* or *robust platonism* and *lightweight platonism*. The respective weights of the platonism pertain to the degree of metaphysical commitment involved in the affirmation of abstract objects. Heavyweight platonists affirm that abstract objects are real entities whose existence is as robust as the ordinary concrete entities in our everyday experience. Peter van Inwagen is the most prominent heavyweight Christian platonist in contemporary philosophy.[4] Lightweight platonists, on the other hand, seem to regard abstract objects as mere semantic objects. Bob Hale, one contemporary lightweight platonist, compares abstract objects to grammatical objects: just as something can be the direct object of a sentence without thereby really existing (e.g., "The whereabouts of the President"), so abstract objects are simply what we are talking about when we use terms like "5" or "The square root of 25" (1987: 4). Given that lightweight platonism does not involve commitment to the real existence of abstract objects, it does not threaten the traditional understanding of divine aseity (and really seems to be just a version of anti-realism). So, only heavyweight platonism conflicts with divine aseity. Henceforth, I use "platonism" to refer to heavyweight platonism.

A second important set of terminological distinctions is that between platonism/anti-platonism and realism/anti-realism. Platonism is the view that abstract objects exist, while *anti-platonism* is the view that abstract objects do not exist. Anti-platonists

---

[3]While stating precisely what the distinction between abstract and concrete objects consists in is controversial, the most successful account of the distinction with respect to accurately sorting the examples typically given for abstract and concrete objects is the account of abstract objects as being causally impotent and concrete objects as being causally potent (Rosen 2018).

[4]While van Inwagen is a heavyweight platonist with respect to the ontological status of abstract objects (including properties), he has also been described as a lightweight (or "ostrich") platonist with respect to the degree of ontological explanation he thinks one type of abstract object, namely properties, yields (Pruss 2016). For van Inwagen denies that platonic properties provide any metaphysical explanation.

may nevertheless be realists about the objects (e.g., mathematical objects, properties, propositions, or possible worlds) that platonists take to be abstract, but by taking such objects to be concrete rather than abstract. So, *realism* is best characterized as the view that mathematical objects, properties, propositions, or possible worlds exist, whether concretely or abstractly. *Anti-realism* is the view that no such objects exist at all, whether abstractly or concretely. So, anti-realism entails anti-platonism, while anti-platonism is compatible with both realism and anti-realism.

A final terminological clarification is needed, for, in the relevant literature, both anti-realism and anti-platonism have been labeled *nominalism*. Furthermore, the term "nominalism" has been used in two distinct philosophical debates for at least three different views.[5] First is the classic debate over the existence of universals. In the medieval period, the term "nominalism" was first used to denominate the view that the general terms we use to categorize or describe things (e.g., "human," "dog," "brown") are mere names applicable to many particular things that neither instantiate a universal property nor are represented by universal concepts. In contemporary philosophy, the term "nominalism" is used more broadly to denominate the view that universal properties do not exist. It is worth noting that it is consistent to be a nominalist in the contemporary sense, because one denies the existence of universal properties, while not being a nominalist in the medieval sense, because one affirms the existence of universal concepts.[6] The second debate in which the term "nominalism" is used in yet another sense is a more recent debate centered in the philosophy of mathematics. Here "nominalism" is a synonym for anti-platonism regarding abstract mathematical objects, that is, the view that such objects do not exist. It is consistent to be a nominalist in this final sense, while not being a nominalist in the former senses, and vice versa. Given the ambiguity in the usage of the term "nominalism," I avoid the use of the term altogether.

II. MOTIVATIONS FOR PLATONISM

There are two main arguments for platonism. First is the classic *one over many argument*, which was first expressed by Plato and which is an argument for the existence of properties and relations only. The one over many argument may be understood as an inference to the best explanation. The fact to be explained is that multiple distinct things resemble one another in particular ways. For example, Socrates, Plato, and Aristotle resemble one another with respect to their each being human. A red rose, fire truck, and cardinal resemble one another with respect to their color. The main claim in the argument is that what best explains the relevant resemblances is that the particular things share something in common, which is a universal property: the property *being human* in the first case and the property *being red* in the second. This basic one over many argument is an argument

---

[5]Craig discusses only two views that have been called "nominalism." He neglects the distinctively medieval sense of the term.
[6]By "universal concepts," I mean concepts whose content is universal in the sense that it abstracts from the particularities of concrete things and so is representative of an indefinite number of concrete things. Thomas Aquinas and John Duns Scotus are examples of medieval philosophers who are nominalists only in the contemporary sense, but not in the medieval sense. For an articulation of this view, see Brower (2015). I critique and modify Brower's account of Aquinas's view in Cleveland (2018). For more on the distinctively medieval problem of universals, see Klima (2017).

for the existence of universal properties (and of relations, by extension) but not for the specifically platonist view that universal properties are abstract objects.

Platonists have argued further that such properties must be necessarily existent mind-independent abstract objects, for it seems that what a given property consists in (e.g., say *being human* consists in being a rational animal) does not depend on there actually being instances of that property and, relatedly, it seems there are more possible properties (e.g., *being a unicorn*) than those that are actually instantiated. The one over many argument is regarded by many as a poor argument for platonism because the claim that universal properties, conceived of as abstract objects, are the best explanation of the resemblances between things is thought to be implausible. For it is difficult to understand how concrete things acquire their characteristics by standing in the mysterious *exemplification relation* to nonspatial, noncausal abstract objects.

The second main argument for platonism, namely the *indispensability argument,* is the dominant argument for platonism. While the *indispensability argument* has roots in Plato's works, the first clear articulation of the argument was given by Gottlob Frege (1884) and there have been many articulations of the argument since. The *indispensability argument* may be used to support the existence of any of the various kinds of supposed abstract objects. The main claim of the *indispensability argument* is that we are committed to the existence of abstract objects by many of the statements we take to be true. Given this, abstract objects are taken to be indispensable. Mark Balaguer (2016) summarizes the *indispensability argument* as follows:

1. If a simple sentence (i.e., a sentence of the form "a is F," or "a is r-related to b," or …) is literally true, then the objects that its singular terms denote exist. Likewise, if an existential sentence is literally true, then there exist objects of the relevant kinds; e.g., if 'There is an F' is true, then there exist some Fs.
2. There are literally true simple sentences containing singular terms that refer to things that could only be abstract objects. Likewise, there are literally true existential statements whose existential quantifiers range over things that could only be abstract objects.
3. Therefore, abstract objects exist.

Premise (1) states a *criterion of ontological commitment*, which is a principle that states when we are committed to believing in certain kinds of objects in virtue of our affirmation of the truth of certain sentences. The criterion expressed by premise (1) is claimed to be the standard view in philosophy. It includes the qualification that we are ontologically committed by singular terms and existential quantifiers only when we think the relevant singular term or existential quantifier cannot be paraphrased away. Since premise (1) is generally accepted and premise (3) follows trivially from premises (1) and (2), platonists seek to motivate premise (2) by providing examples of different kinds of such sentences to establish the existence of abstract objects.[7]

There are several ways of resisting the indispensability argument. Craig discusses in detail various arealist and antirealist critiques (2016, 2017). Such critiques involve rejecting one or the other of the two premises of the argument. Some reject the criterion of ontological commitment assumed in premise (1). Craig (2016) himself challenges the criterion, arguing that it is contrary to common sense to assume that mere linguistic

---

[7] For a detailed summary of such examples, see Balaguer (2016).

analysis entails significant metaphysical conclusions. Further, since it seems there are no arguments in support of the truth of the criterion, but only of its supposed usefulness, he concludes that it is far from incumbent upon us to give it our assent.

III. OPTIONS FOR ADDRESSING THE CONFLICT BETWEEN PLATONISM AND DIVINE ASEITY

There are three main options for addressing the conflict between platonism and divine aseity. One involves rejecting platonism as it is standardly conceived and attempting to modify platonism to make it compatible with divine aseity. Another option involves rejecting platonism altogether and adopting a realist or anti-realist alternative to platonism. The final option, which few theists find attractive, is to embrace platonism and deny that God alone is self-existent. I'll discuss the last option first.

III.1 Platonism without Divine Aseity

Peter van Inwagen, based on his own indispensability argument for a platonic conception of properties, reluctantly embraces platonism regarding properties and so abandons God's unique self-existence (2004). Keith Yandell advocates a view he calls *theistic propositionalism*, which is a form of platonism regarding propositions, according to which both God and propositions are self-existent entities (2014). Platonists like van Inwagen and Yandell who seek to be biblically faithful must endorse an alternative to the traditional, *prima facie* interpretation of biblical passages, such as the prologue to the Gospel of John, according to which literally all things other than God depend upon God for their existence. Platonists must say that John is not really talking about everything other than God but only about a subset of such things that excludes the abstract objects that platonists take to be self-existent.

In the technical terms of logic, platonists must embrace the view that John intended a *restricted domain of quantification*, meaning that the relevant class of things the statement concerns is not all things in existence, but some subset. In contrast, Christians have traditionally interpreted texts like the one from the Gospel of John as having an *unrestricted domain of quantification* (though without using this technical term). Craig, who discusses in detail the biblical and patristic basis for the doctrine of divine aseity and opposes the restricted view, argues persuasively that the "crucial point here is that the unrestrictedness of the domain of quantification is based, not in what kinds of objects were thought to lie in the domain, but rather in the Jewish doctrine of God as the only being which exists eternally and *a se*. It is who or what God is that requires that the domain of quantification be unrestricted, whatever beings might be discovered to lie in the domain" (2016: 17). Given this, in order to affirm the unrestricted view, it is not necessary that John or any other early Christian writer, whose language is most naturally read as expressing the unrestricted view, had in mind the relevant abstract objects when they claimed that all things other than God are created by God, but only that all things other than God, whatever they may be, are created by God.

III.2 Modified Platonism to Secure Divine Aseity

Next, I discuss some attempts to modify platonism to reconcile it with God's unique self-existence. One general strategy for such reconciliation is to maintain that abstract objects are created by God. The view, given by Thomas Morris and Christopher Menzel, that God creates abstract objects, specifically through His intellective activity, has been called both *theistic activism* and *absolute creationism* (1986).[8] On this view, which I call *theistic activism*, properties are identified with divine concepts and propositions with divine thoughts, where thoughts are made up of concepts. Craig discusses in detail the ambiguity present in Morris and Menzel's work as well as in other relevant literature regarding whether the relevant contents of God's mind are taken to be abstract (thus preserving platonism) or concrete (thus eliminating abstract objects and so abandoning platonism) (2017: 124–8). Given Morris and Menzel's stated intention to reconcile platonism and divine aseity, I follow Craig in taking theistic activism to be platonist and I discuss the anti-platonist reduction of abstracta to concrete contents of God's mind in the next section. While Morris and Menzel locate created platonic abstracta "inside" of God as parts of God, another option is to locate created platonic abstracta "outside" of God.[9] However, there is a significant philosophical problem with both strategies.

The philosophical problem with the notion that God creates platonic abstracta is that it seems to be viciously circular and, thus, incoherent. This is known as the bootstrapping objection, which is given in terms of God's creation of properties. Assuming God's own properties are exemplifications of platonic properties, it follows, on theistic activism, that God creates His own properties. But God would have to exemplify at least some platonic properties, such as the property *being powerful*,[10] before He could create any properties and that is incoherent.[11] While Morris and Menzel (1986) defend theistic activism against another bootstrapping worry regarding logical priority, this bootstrapping objection concerning the causal prerequisites of an action, which I call the *causal bootstrapping objection*, is decisive against theistic activism, given a platonist view of property exemplification.

The only ways to escape the causal bootstrapping objection are to maintain that God's properties are uncreated (and so exempt God's properties from the view that properties are created), to abandon the platonic understanding of property exemplification, or to embrace divine simplicity. But the first option is also incoherent, and the others are likely to be objectionable to the platonist. First, if God's properties are uncreated and they are not identical to God, then, given a platonic view of property exemplification, regardless of whether God's properties are taken to be thoughts in the mind of God or entities

---

[8] Morris and Menzel's article is entitled "Absolute Creation," but the term they use to denominate their view is *theistic activism*. Because they suggest that *theistic activism* includes a modal component, Craig uses *absolute creationism* for the view that God creates abstract objects and *theistic activism* for the view that, in addition, God is the source of modality, i.e., of what is necessary, possible, and impossible (2016: 55). But Morris and Menzel affirm only that modal truths depend on God in the sense that He creates them (along with the other platonic abstracta), while they deny that God could have not created them or made such modal truths different. So, Morris and Menzel's claim about modality is simply an application of the view that God creates abstract objects to propositions regarding modality.

[9] The spatial terms of being inside or outside of God are, of course, metaphorical since God does not occupy space. The distinction between what is "inside" or "outside" of God most naturally concerns what is either identical to or a proper part of God, or neither identical to nor a proper part of God.

[10] The property *being able to create a property* is given by Michael Bergmann and Jeffrey Brower in their well-known version of the bootstrapping objection (2006). However, as Craig has recently noted, the platonist may deny that *being able to create a property* is a genuine property, whereas *being powerful* is clearly a genuine property (2018).

[11] It is worth noting that I agree with Craig that Menzel's recent attempt to refute Bergmann and Brower's bootstrapping objection fails and seems to be based on a misinterpretation (Craig 2018; Menzel 2016).

"external" to God, a new bootstrapping problem, which I call the *metaphysical priority bootstrapping objection*, follows and renders the view incoherent. The metaphysical priority bootstrapping objection concerns the incompatibility of both God's mind being metaphysically prior to His concepts and God's concept/property *having a mind* being metaphysically prior to God's mind (Cleveland 2018). Second, most platonists regarding properties account for the characteristics of things in terms of their exemplification of platonic properties and to abandon that view would diminish much of the motivation for platonism regarding properties. Third, despite its venerable tradition, the doctrine of divine simplicity is typically denied by theistic platonists due to their assumption that properties are abstract. For, given divine simplicity, God is identical to His properties, but if properties are abstract, then God is identical to an abstract object, which is absurd. Further, the theistic activist specification of God's creation of abstract objects in terms of the contents of God's intellect is already incompatible with divine simplicity, since it assumes that God is composed of both uncreated and created parts.

Another strategy for reconciling platonism and divine aseity to some extent is to identify platonic abstracta with God's *uncreated* thoughts, which are taken to be nonidentical to God.[12] Since, on such a view, God's thoughts must be *proper parts* of God, it follows that God is not uniquely self-existent, but so too are His thoughts.[13] But as I mentioned above, given a platonic view of property exemplification, the view that God's properties are identical to God's thoughts is rendered incoherent by the *metaphysical priority bootstrapping objection*. This problem also applies to some realist versions of divine conceptualism to which I now turn.

III.3 Anti-Platonist Divine Conceptualism

The traditional Christian response to platonism is some form of anti-platonist *divine conceptualism*, which is the view that there are no platonic abstracta, whether created or uncreated, and that the roles taken to be played by at least some platonic abstracta are fulfilled by God's uncreated concepts, also referred to as "ideas." The prominent patristic, medieval, and early modern accounts of divine conceptualism are anti-realist with respect to God's concepts, which is to say that while God's concepts are taken to fulfill certain roles, they are not taken to have robust existence. In contrast, though there are contemporary defenders of the traditional anti-realist view of God's concepts, the contemporary debate concerning divine aseity and abstract objects focuses on recent forms of divine conceptualism that tend to be realist in the sense that God's concepts are taken to be concrete entities that are proper parts of God. I begin by discussing realist forms of divine conceptualism and then contrast them with the main traditional anti-realist forms of divine conceptualism, including the view I take to be most promising.

III.3.1 Realist Divine Conceptualism
The late-twentieth-century renaissance of Christian philosophy brought with it a revival of divine conceptualism as an account of supposed abstract objects. Philosophers such as Robert Adams and Alvin Plantinga have proposed that at least some supposed abstract objects may be construed as divine ideas or concepts, though neither have developed

---

[12] The *modified theistic activism* of Paul Gould and Richard Brian Davis is an example (2014).
[13] In contemporary philosophy, *proper parts* are parts that are nonidentical to the whole, while *improper parts* are parts that are identical to the whole.

a full account (Adams 1983; Plantinga 1993, 2011, 2013). Plantinga suggests we construe propositions as divine thoughts, properties as divine concepts, and sets as divine collections. Plantinga clearly proposes a realist form of divine conceptualism, for he claims that such contents of God's minds are caused by God and thus are entities that are non-identical to God. Plantinga doesn't address the causal bootstrapping objection, which seems to apply to his view, since he conceives of properties as caused by God and he does not exempt God's properties.

The most developed realist forms of divine conceptualism are given by Brian Leftow and Greg Welty. On Welty's *theistic conceptual realism* (TCR), God's ideas are necessarily existent concrete (as opposed to abstract) mental entities, some of which function as abstract objects, including properties, propositions, and possible worlds (2000, 2014). Because Welty exempts God's own attributes from being divine ideas, he escapes both the causal and the metaphysical bootstrapping objections. It is unclear exactly how he conceives of the relationship between the attributes/properties of creatures and God's ideas of such properties. Since Welty notes that he conceives of property possession in terms of *falling under a concept*, such that what it means to possess a property is to fall under the relevant (presumably divine) concept of that property, his view of properties seems almost the same as Leftow's *theistic concept nominalism*.

Leftow develops his *theistic concept nominalist* view of universals in one context (2006) and a related divine conceptualist view of modality in another (2012).[14] He characterizes his view as concept nominalist in the sense that he rejects universal and particular properties and instead accounts for the attributes of created things in terms of their falling under God's concept of the relevant attribute. The *falling under* relation of concept nominalism replaces the *exemplification relation* of realist views of universal properties. Leftow takes God's concepts to be reducible to concrete divine mental events and divine powers, which he thinks can also fulfill the role of possible worlds.[15] Leftow argues that modality, that is, what is necessary and possible, is chosen by God in virtue of His unconstrained imagination; thus, for Leftow, God causes at least some of His mental content, in virtue of which He creates.

While Leftow rightly seeks to preserve God's ultimacy in the explanation of all things, he eliminates too much for the sake of ontological simplicity. Leftow's theistic concept nominalist view of properties amounts to occasionalism with respect to formal causation. Contrary to the common sense view that there is, in technical terms, formal causation such that, for example, cats bring into existence other cats and something hot causes other things to become hot (though not without God's sustaining power), Leftow's view is that it is God's cat-concept that causes the existence of the cat and God's concept of heat that causes things to become hot. It seems to me much more plausible (and beautiful) that God creates things with their own formal causal powers, so they can imitate God to limited degrees in bringing about the relevant effects. With respect to modality, Leftow thinks God chooses what is possible because He does not think God's nature yields the full range of creaturely kind-concepts. But it seems to me much more plausible (and beautiful)

---

[14]Craig classifies Leftow's divine conceptualist view of modality as a theistic activist view, presumably because Leftow thinks God causes modality. But Leftow is clear that he opposes theistic platonism and thus conceives of the divine mental entities that play the role of supposed abstract objects as concrete.

[15]Because Leftow seems to take divine mental events and powers to be nonidentical to God, he seems to be a realist regarding those entities that he takes to fulfill the roles of properties and possible worlds.

that God's infinite perfection does yield the full range of creaturely kind-concepts, which are conceived by God in terms of limited degrees of perfection, as I explain more below.

Although Welty and Leftow are both careful to exempt God's attributes from their views of properties/attributes as divine concepts, it is worth noting that realist divine conceptualist views are subject to bootstrapping objections (even though in the literature bootstrapping objections have only been directed to theistic activism). Such views fail due to bootstrapping if they include the view that things, including God, have their characteristics in virtue of having properties as distinct constituents or in virtue of exemplifying properties. This is so whether God's thoughts are taken to be caused by God or uncaused and whether they are taken to be abstract or concrete. If God's thoughts are taken to be caused by God, then the causal bootstrapping objection concerning the properties God must possess in order to cause properties applies. If God's thoughts are not taken to be caused by God, but to be self-existent, then the metaphysical priority bootstrapping objection concerning the incompatibility of both God's mind being metaphysically prior to His concepts and God's concept/property *having a mind* being metaphysically prior to God's mind applies (Cleveland 2018). In short, any view, whether platonist or anti-platonist realist, according to which properties are identified with God's concepts, God's concepts are proper parts of God, and God has His characteristics in virtue of having properties as constituents or exemplifying properties, is incoherent due to divine bootstrapping.

III.3.2 Limited Anti-Realist Divine Conceptualism

The traditional Christian response to (classical) platonism is anti-platonism (i.e., it involves the rejection of self-existent abstract objects) and may be characterized as limited anti-realist divine conceptualism. It is anti-realist with respect to the ontological status of the divine ideas/concepts, which are taken to fulfill at least some of the roles of supposed platonic abstracta. The traditional view that God's ideas do not have robust existence is compatible with realism regarding non-divine concrete entities, which may be taken to fulfill other roles of supposed platonic abstracta. Given this, I say "limited" to qualify the extent to which divine concepts that do not have robust existence are taken to fulfill the roles of supposed platonic abstracta. The view I favor, and which combines ideas from Aristotle, Aquinas, and Leibniz, is a combination of anti-realism regarding the divine ideas and realism regarding non-divine, property-like, particular forms. I summarize my favored view after first briefly explaining Augustine's anti-realist divine conceptualist view upon which it builds.

III.3.3 Augustine's Anti-Realist Divine Conceptualism

Augustine of Hippo directly confronted the question of how to reconcile, in some sense, Plato's theory of the Forms with the Christian view of God as the only self-existent being. Augustine's solution was to "locate" the Forms in the mind of God. Given this, contemporary theistic activists and realist divine conceptualists have characterized their views as developments of Augustine's. However, they often do so without explicitly acknowledging the significant differences between their view and Augustine's with respect to the motivation for appealing to God's ideas, the theoretical work that God's ideas do, or the ontological status of God's ideas. Whereas these contemporary philosophers seem largely motivated by realist indispensability arguments and so take God's ideas to have robust existence (whether abstract or concrete), Augustine was principally motivated to account for the rationality of God's creation and the intuition that there are, in some sense, perfect exemplars of what God has created, neither of which require God's ideas to have robust existence. Given Augustine's assumptions that God creates in accordance with a rational plan and that God's rational plan for one kind of entity, for example, a human being, is distinct from that of his rational plan for another kind of entity, for example, a horse, Augustine concludes that "individual things are created in accord with reasons unique to them."[16] Given God's unique aseity, Augustine argues further that these reasons "must be thought to exist nowhere but in the very mind of the Creator" (2010).

Augustine's view is obscured by the theistic activist and (some) realist divine conceptualist construals of God's ideas as universal properties that created things exemplify. While Augustine (2010) says, "It is by participation in these [ideas] that whatever is exists in whatever manner it does exist," there is no good reason to construe this participation relation as the exemplification relation that is thought by platonists to obtain between particulars and universal properties. Not only did Augustine never explicitly affirm that entities other than God exemplify any properties that are numerically the same as God's attributes or ideas, but he never affirmed that God's attributes are exemplifications of universal properties. Augustine could not have coherently affirmed either of these claims, which assume there is a real multiplicity of universal properties, given his commitment to divine simplicity, which entails that God's ideas do not have robust existence. The same is true for Thomas Aquinas and so Nicholas Wolterstorff (1970) is mistaken to claim that both Augustine and Aquinas conflate divine ideas as exemplars and as universal properties. For Augustine and Aquinas, divine ideas are exemplars but not universal properties.

There are, thus, in the relevant contemporary philosophical literature, not only misleading endorsements of Augustine's divine conceptualism but also mistaken criticisms of his and other medieval views due at least in part to a neglect of the significance of divine simplicity to the relevant views. Though divine simplicity has been dismissed by some as incoherent, many such objections have been directly, and in my mind, successfully, addressed. Thus, philosophers and theologians engaged in this debate would do well to interact with more recent defenses of divine simplicity.[17]

III.3.4 *An Aristotelian-Thomistic-Leibnizian Anti-Realist Divine Conceptualism*

Augustine's general divine conceptualist view was followed by other medievals and developed most notably by Aquinas and the early modern philosopher, Gottfried Leibniz. Aquinas's explanation of how a multiplicity of divine ideas is compatible with divine simplicity yields an account of how God's ideas (in conjunction with God's infinite power and perfection) explain not only the rationality of God's act of creation but also, in the most fundamental way, the possibility of any possible characteristic, including those that are merely possible since they'll never be actualized.

Like Augustine, Aquinas assumes that God's creating is rational, that God's ideas for what He creates derive wholly from Himself, and that God is simple. Given this and Aquinas's conception of God as unlimited in and thus, as the fullness of being and perfection, it is plausible that God's perfect knowledge of Himself entails knowledge of all possible limited forms of being and perfection. Aquinas explains this with an arithmetical analogy taken from Aristotle's *Metaphysics* VIII: Aquinas compares the forms of things and the definitions that signify them with numbers. Just as the subtraction

---

[16] Augustine explains that the term "reasons" (*rationes*) is synonymous with "forms" (*formae*), "species" (*species*), and "ideas" (*logoi*).

[17] See Leftow (1990, 2009); Vallicella (1992); Grant (2003, 2012); Pruss (2008).

of a unit changes the number, so the subtraction of one difference/perfection changes the form/species. Aquinas explains that what is one reality can be conceptually distinguished when at least one of the elements of one thing is not included in the notion of the other (1955: I.54.3). For example, assuming a human being is a rational animal, the notion of a human being yields the notion of an irrational animal. Because we can conceptually distinguish rationality and animality (since neither entails the other), there is within the notion of a human being the content of what it is to be an irrational animal, namely, animality without rationality. Assuming with Aquinas that God possesses within Himself all perfections and all non-divine beings possess only some perfections to a limited degree, it follows that God can consider all beings less perfect than Himself through considering His own essence (1955: I.54.4).[18] Thus, we need not think God's ideas have robust existence.

Given that God's perfection is infinite, He is omnipotent, and each thing that God could create is and possesses a subset of God's perfections in a limited way, it is plausible to think that there are more kinds and characteristics of things that God could create beyond those that are actually instantiated. So, the divine ideas account for our intuition that, and our speaking as though, there are more kinds and characteristics of things that could exist beyond those that are or will be instantiated. This does not commit us to the robust existence of God's ideas. I reject the criterion of ontological commitment assumed in indispensability arguments for platonism for reasons given above. Instead, I think what Aquinas seemed to assume is right, namely, that quantification over any entity in a meaningful statement need not entail the existence of that entity, but only that that entity is a human concept, that is, an object of thought, where objects of thought considered in themselves do not exist but are simply the information content of human acts of thought. So, quantification over any entity in a meaningful statement only entails the existence of some particular act of human thought (Klima 1993).[19]

I have sketched how, from Aquinas's perspective, God's ideas fulfill some of the roles of supposed abstract objects: they serve as the exemplars of all created things and they, together with God's infinite perfection and power, account for the intuition that there are more possible characteristics than those that have been or will be actualized. It does not follow that God's ideas explain related but distinct issues relevant to supposed abstract objects, such as the actuality of a given attribute, what the actuality of a given attribute consists in, and the relation that obtains between distinct instances of the "same" attribute.

Aquinas's own view of attributes is notoriously controversial. Elsewhere I have given what I take to be the best account of Aquinas's view, according to which there are no universal properties, but only particular, simple, property-like *forms* in Aquinas's terms. Such forms are created in accord with, but are ontologically distinct from, God's ideas of them, and they inhere in relevant "matter" to either compose a substance or characterize a given substance in nonessential ways. Those forms that are of the same species as one another (e.g., my form of humanity and your form of humanity) bear to one another a relation of *internal sameness*, which is less than the numerical sameness of universal properties but greater than the mere resemblance of particular

---

[18]Although we may speak of the subtraction or negation of perfections from God's idea of Himself resulting in the content of concepts of creatures, we need not think God literally subtracts perfections to compose concepts of creatures. We can maintain, with Aquinas, that God has knowledge in the most perfect way, which is immediate and without succession, composition, or division (1955: I.54.55-8).

[19]Although is some cases it will also entail the existence of some extramental entity.

tropes (Cleveland 2018).[20] In virtue of this internal sameness and God's creation of humans with the immaterial power of abstraction, humans can abstract from their experience of particular things a universal kind-concept, which is universal in the sense that it represents an unlimited number of particulars of the given kind and so can yield cognition of relevant necessary truths.

It is beyond the scope of this chapter to give a complete account of each of the roles taken to be played by abstract objects, each of which has its own philosophical literature. So, I will simply point the reader to some promising non-platonist views of some such roles that are compatible with anti-realist divine conceptualism. Above I've given a partial summary of my Thomistic account of supposed property roles (developed more fully in Cleveland 2018). Just as there are several related though distinct issues regarding properties, so there are several related though distinct issues regarding modality: accounting for possible worlds, grounding modal claims, and accounting for global possibilities. Unlike the main alternatives, Alexander Pruss's Aristotelian-Leibnizian theory of modality (2011) addresses each of these issues and is compatible with the views inspired by Aquinas that I've expressed. By endorsing a Leibnizian view of propositions as divine ideas and possible worlds as maximal collections of compossible propositions,[21] Pruss provides a response to the problem of the intentionality of propositions and an account of possible worlds.[22] By endorsing the Aristotelian view of possibilities as grounded in the causal powers and dispositions of things together with a necessary First Cause, Pruss accounts for the grounds of modal claims and global possibilities.

As for the objects of mathematics, Armand Maurer (1993) has a helpful account of Aquinas's view that reconciles apparently contrary interpretations. Maurer argues that, for Aquinas, mathematical objects are mental entities, namely, the content of some human concepts, which have a remote foundation in the real world of sensible qualities, while their proximate foundation is in the constructive activity of the human intellect that gives them their formal character. Just as universal-kind concepts can yield cognition of relevant necessary truths in virtue of the God-given immaterial abstractive power of the human mind, so mathematical concepts can yield cognition of relevant necessary truths.[23]

---

[20] It seems to me that Robert Koons's (2018) recent Aristotelian account of the same species relation in terms of the more fundamental relations of formal causation and potentiality is compatible with and promising as a more complete account of the internal sameness relation that I propose. Koons also helpfully explains the philosophical superiority of such a view to the dominant contemporary forms of realism and nominalism.

[21] Pruss explains, "A collection of propositions is compossible provided there is something that can initiate a causal chain leading to its being the case that they are all true" (2011: 221).

[22] From Aquinas's perspective, propositions are subject-predicate structured entities that only exist contingently as the content of human acts of intellectual judgment. While God's knowledge is thus not propositionally structured, it is still true from Aquinas's perspective that God knows the content of all possible propositions, which He knows in a simple act (1920: Ia.Q14.a14; Frost 2017).

[23] It is worth noting that there is a form of divine conceptualism that misunderstands Augustine's and Aquinas's views and that has been officially condemned by the Roman Catholic Church as heretical. This view, called *ontologism*, is the view that humans innately intuit God's presence in their minds and that human concepts have the characteristics of necessity, universality, and eternity because they consist in direct knowledge of God's essence as the archetype of all things (Sauvage 1911). Instead, at least from Aquinas's perspective, God has created the human intellect with the capacity to possess universal concepts that yield cognition of some necessary and eternal truths whose foundation is in God but the cognition of which cannot be equated with or thought to entail complete knowledge of God's essence.

IV. CONCLUSION

I have outlined and briefly assessed the various options for addressing the conflict between platonism and the traditional understanding of divine aseity, according to which God alone is self-existent. Because there is good reason to accept this understanding of divine aseity and to reject the main arguments for platonism, I reject versions of platonism that abandon the traditional notion of divine aseity and views that modify platonism in order to secure divine aseity. Because there is good reason to favor limited anti-realist divine conceptualism over realist versions of divine conceptualism, I advocate a recovery of the traditional Christian response to platonism, which is limited anti-realist divine conceptualism. On such a view, while the divine ideas/concepts are taken to fulfill at least some of the roles of supposed platonic abstracta, they are not taken to have robust existence. As I summarized above, I favor a combination of ideas from Aristotle, Aquinas, and Leibniz into a view that is anti-realist regarding the divine ideas that play some of the roles of supposed abstract objects and realist regarding non-divine, property-like, particular forms that play other roles of supposed abstract objects. On such a view, not only is God alone self-existent but God is also ultimate in the explanation of all things in plausible (and beautiful) ways.[24]

References

Adams, R. M. (1983), "Divine Necessity," *Journal of Philosophy*, 80 (11): 741–52.
Aquinas, T. (1920), *Summa Theologiae*, 2nd, rev. ed., trans. Fathers of the English Dominican Province, New Advent online edition.
Aquinas, T. (1955), *Summa Contra Gentiles*, trans. Pegis, New York: Hanover House.
Augustine (2010), "Q. 46 On the Ideas," in *Eighty-Three Different Questions*, trans. by D. Mosher, Washington, DC: Catholic University of America Press.
Balaguer, M. (2016), "Platonism in Metaphysics," in E. N. Zalta (ed.), *The Stanford Encyclopedia of Philosophy*. Available online: https://plato.stanford.edu/archives/spr2016/entries/platonism/.
Bergmann, M., and J. E. Brower (2006), "A Theistic Argument Against Platonism (and in Support of Truthmakers and Divine Simplicity)," in D. Zimmerman (ed.), *Oxford Studies in Metaphysics*, vol. 2, 357–86, Oxford: Oxford University Press.
Brower, J. E. (2009), "Simplicity and Aseity," in T. P. Flint and M. C. Rea (eds.), *The Oxford Handbook of Philosophical Theology*, 105–28, Oxford: Oxford University Press.
Brower, J. E. (2015), "Aquinas on the Problem of Universals," *Philosophy and Phenomenological Research*, 92 (3): 715–35.
Cleveland, L. K. (2018), "Groundwork for a Thomistic Account of Contemporary Property Roles," PhD diss., Baylor University, Baylor.
Craig, W. L. (2016), *God over All: Divine Aseity and the Challenge of Platonism*, Oxford: Oxford University Press.
Craig, W. L. (2017), *God and Abstract Objects*, New York: Springer.
Craig, W. L. (2018), "In Defense of Absolute Creationism," *The Review of Metaphysics*, 71 (3): 445–67.

---

[24] I am grateful to James Arcadi, J. T. Turner, and Jeremy Skrzypek for helpful comments.

Frost, G. (2017), "Aquinas on Propositions," in J. Haldane and J. P. O'Callagahn (eds.), *Bloomsbury Companion to Aquinas*, London: Continuum.

Gould, P., ed. (2014), *Beyond the Control of God?: Six Views on the Problem of God and Abstract Objects*, New York: Bloomsbury.

Gould, P. M., and R. B. Davis (2014), "Modified Theistic Activism," in P. M. Gould (ed.), *Beyond the Control of God?: Six Views on The Problem of God and Abstract Objects*, 51–64, New York: Bloomsbury.

Gould, P. M., and R. B. Davis (2017), "Where the Bootstrapping Really Lies: A Neo-Aristotelian Reply to Panchuk," *International Philosophical Quarterly*, 57 (4): 415–28.

Grant, W. M. (2003), "Aquinas, Divine Simplicity, and Divine Freedom," *Proceedings of the American Catholic Philosophical Association*, 77: 129–44.

Grant, W. M. (2012), "Divine Simplicity, Contingent Truths, and Extrinsic Models of Divine Knowing," *Faith and Philosophy*, 29 (3): 254–74.

Hale, B. (1987), *Abstract Objects (Philosophical Theory)*, Oxford: Basil Blackwell.

Van Inwagen, P. (2004), "A Theory of Properties," in D. Zimmerman (ed.), *Oxford Studies in Metaphysics*, vol. 1, 107–38, Oxford: Oxford University Press.

Klima, G. (1993), "The Changing Role of Entia Rationis in Mediaeval Semantics and Ontology: A Comparative Study with a Reconstruction," *Synthese*, 96 (1): 25–58.

Klima, G. (n.d.), "The Medieval Problem of Universals," in E. N. Zalta (ed.), *The Stanford Encyclopedia of Philosophy*. Available online: https://plato.stanford.edu/archives/win2017/entries/universals-medieval/>.

Koons, R. C. (2018), "Forms as Simple and Individual Grounds of Things' Natures," *Metaphysics*, 1 (1): 1–11.

Leftow, B. (1990), "Is God an Abstract Object?," *Noûs*, 24 (4): 581–98.

Leftow, B. (2006), "God and the Problem of Universals," in D. Zimmerman (ed.) *Oxford Studies in Metaphysics*, vol. 2, 325–56, Oxford: Oxford University Press.

Leftow, B. (2009), "Aquinas, Divine Simplicity and Divine Freedom," in K. Timpe (ed.), *Metaphysics and God: Essays in Honor of Eleonore Stump*, 21–38, London: Routledge.

Leftow, B. (2012), *God and Necessity*, Oxford: Oxford University Press.

Maurer, A. (1993), "Thomists and Thomas Aquinas on the Foundation of Mathematics," *Review of Metaphysics*, 47 (1): 43–61.

Menzel, C. (2016), "Problems with the Bootstrapping Objection to Theistic Activism," *American Philosophical Quarterly*, 53 (1): 55–68.

Morris, T. V., and C. Menzel (1986), "Absolute Creation," *American Philosophical Quarterly*, 23 (4): 353–62.

Plantinga, A. (1993), *Warrant and Proper Function*, Oxford: Oxford University Press.

Plantinga, A. (2011), *Where the Conflict Really Lies: Science, Religion, and Naturalism*, Oxford: Oxford University Press.

Plantinga, A. (2013), "Response to William Lane Craig's review of *Where the Conflict Really Lies*," *Philosophia Christi*, 15 (1): 175–82.

Pruss, A. R. (2008), "On Two Problems of Divine Simplicity," in J. L. Kvanvig (ed.), *Oxford Studies in Philosophy of Religion*, vol. 1, 150–67, Oxford: Oxford University Press.

Pruss, A. R. (2011), *Actuality, Possibility, and Worlds*, New York: Continuum.

Pruss, A. R. (2016), "Divine Aseity and Light-Weight Platonism," *Alexander Pruss's Blog*, July 21. Available online: https://alexanderpruss.blogspot.com/2016/07/divine-aseity-and-light-weight-platonism.html.

Rosen, G. (2018), "Abstract Objects," in E. N. Zalta (ed.), *The Stanford Encyclopedia of Philosophy*. Available online: https://plato.stanford.edu/archives/spr2020/entries/abstract-objects/.

Sauvage, G. (1911), "Ontologism," in *The Catholic Encyclopedia*, vol. 11, New York: Robert Appleton. Available online: https://www.newadvent.org/cathen/11257a.htm.
Vallicella, W. F. (1992), "Divine Simplicity: A New Defense," *Faith and Philosophy*, 9 (4): 508–25.
Welty, G. (2000), "An Examination of Theistic Conceptual Realism as an Alternative to Theistic Activism," MPhil diss., Oriel College, Oxford.
Welty, G. (2014), "Theistic Conceptual Realism," in P. M. Gould (ed.), *Beyond the Control of God?: Six Views on the Problem of God and Abstract Objects*, 81–96, New York: Bloomsbury.
Wolterstorff, N. (1970), *On Universals*, Chicago: University of Chicago Press.
Yandell, K. (2014), "God and Propositions," in P. M. Gould (ed.), *Beyond the Control of God?: Six Views on the Problem of God and Abstract Objects*, 21–35, New York: Bloomsbury.

CHAPTER FOURTEEN

The Trinity

THOMAS H. MCCALL

I. INTRODUCTION

The Athanasian Creed states,

> This is the catholic faith, that we worship one God in Trinity, and the Trinity in unity, without either confusing the persons or dividing the substance. For the Father's person is one, the Son's another, the Holy Spirit's another; but the Godhead of the Father, the Son, and the Holy Spirit is one, their glory equal, their majesty co-eternal. Such as the Father is, such is the Son, such also is the Holy Spirit ... Thus the Father is God, the Son God, and the Holy Spirit God; and yet there are not three Gods but there is one God. Thus the Father is Lord, the Son Lord, and the Holy Spirit Lord; and yet there are not three Lords but there is one Lord ... Because just as we are obliged by Christian truth to acknowledge each person separately both God and Lord, so we are forbidden by the catholic religion to speak of three Gods or Lords. (Kelly 1964: 17–20)

The doctrine of the Trinity, as summarized here, is at once both a core Christian doctrine and something that is very mysterious. This doctrine was forged in the fires of very heated controversy (especially in the fourth century).[1] Throughout the centuries, it has often been the subject of intense interest and the object of criticism. Both critics and defenders of the doctrine have been interested in questions about the logical coherence of the core doctrinal claims, they have argued about the theological grounding of the doctrine, they have wondered if the classical doctrine is of any practical or moral relevance, and they have argued over disputed points of higher resolution detail. In what follows, I shall first offer an overview of the "threeness-oneness problem" and some extant proffered solutions to it. I shall conclude with some observations about the prospects for further work. The focus here is on contemporary work in analytic theology (although, as we shall see, further developments are now better positioned to build upon helpful historical work).

II. THE THREENESS-ONENESS PROBLEM

Concerns about logical coherence are embedded deeply within traditional discussions of the doctrine, and these concerns have again come to the forefront in recent treatments of the doctrine within analytic philosophy of religion and theology. Several models or

---

[1] For helpful studies of these debates, see especially Barnes (2001), Ayres (2004, 2010), Beeley (2008), and Anatolios (2011). The older studies of Hanson (1988) and Gregg and Groh (1981) remain helpful as well.

theories have arisen, some of which are self-consciously committed to the retrieval of older approaches.

II.1 The Logical Problem

Just what is the logical problem? It arises from the conjunction of three important claims:

(T1) There is exactly one God;
(T2) Father, Son, and Holy Spirit are not identical;
(T3) Father, Son, and Holy Spirit are consubstantial (or *homoousios*).[2]

The challenge is obvious even on brief reflection: the conjunction of (T1)–(T3) appears to be inconsistent. Perhaps one could hold with consistency to any two of (T1)–(T3), but the acceptance of a third introduces inconsistency and incoherence. To spell this out a bit further, consider:

(LPT1) There is exactly one God, the Father Almighty (from T1);
(LPT2) The Father is God (from (LPT1));
(LPT3) The Son is consubstantial with but not identical to the Father (and Spirit) (from (T2) and (T3));
(LPT4) If there are x and y such that x is a God, x is not identical to y, and y is consubstantial with x, then it is not the case that there is exactly one God (premise);
(LPT5) Therefore: it is not the case that there is exactly one God (from (LPT2), (LPT3), and (LPT4)).

But of course (LPT5) contradicts (LPT1).

To avoid the contradiction, one could reject any of (T1), (T2), or (T3). But to do so is to reject theological orthodoxy. Or one could reject the premise contained in (LPT4). But this strikes many as a very steep price to pay; for many analytic theologians, such a move would be akin to philosophical heterodoxy. Orthodox Christians then have a problem, and it is a serious one. Or so it seems.

II.2 Social Trinitarianism

Some of the responses to the logical problem fly under the banner of "Social Trinitarianism" (ST). Unfortunately, the term "Social Trinitarianism" has become used for a very wide variety of purposes; it has acquired a broad semantic range in contemporary theology. So perhaps it will help to get clear on the meaning of the term (as employed here). In some cases of late-twentieth and early-twenty-first-century theology, the label "Social Trinitarianism" has come to stand for various efforts to "apply" the doctrine to a wide range of socio-political and ethical concerns. Some of these efforts are vigorous, but in many cases the connections seem to be stretched rather thin. Some of these attempts at drawing out the "implications" of the doctrine for purposes of pastoral, political, and moral theology are quite "conservative" in nature; while in other cases they are much more revisionist and "progressive." There is much more to be said about such efforts, and this is one area of theology where further doctrinal analysis could be very helpful. For present purposes, however, I simply note that this is *not* the meaning of ST; as I am using

---

[2] This summary of the problem draws from McCall and Rea (2009: 1) and Rea (2009: 404–7).

the label, it does not refer to the attempts to draw some practical or social implications from the doctrine.

In other cases, the label ST is loaded with historical meaning. In these cases, the claim is usually that the "Greek" or "Eastern" theology of the fourth century (and especially the "Cappadocian" theologians Basil of Caesarea, his brother Gregory of Nyssa, and their friend Gregory of Nazianzus) is opposed to the "Western" or "Latin" theology that is exemplified by Augustine (and then later Anselm and Thomas Aquinas). In contrast to this "Latin" theology that is dominated by impersonal categories of substance metaphysics, the "Greek" theology is said to be much more personal and social in nature—and the term is then employed to signal retrieval from and continuity with this older patristic tradition. This historically oriented account of ST has been the subject of much criticism (and even derision) on historical grounds; it simply is not so easy to pit the so-called "relational" and "dynamic" theology of the Greek fourth century against the allegedly "static" and "impersonal" theology of the Latin tradition. This is simply not an adequate understanding of ST, and it is not what is at work here.

A related approach is to think of ST as any doctrine of the Trinity that makes positive use of the so-called social analogy. Famously, Gregory of Nyssa made very cautious use of the analogy of Peter, James, and John for the Trinity, and Gregory of Nazianzus employed the analogy of Adam, Eve, and Seth. But such an approach is also insufficient for present purposes, for the mere employment of an analogy does not bring us to any substantive theological positions; one could take a very "social" account of the Trinity (along the lines of a proper definition) without using a social analogy, or one could perhaps use a social analogy without being a proponent of ST. So the use of the analogy is neither necessary nor sufficient, and it will not concern us further.

Sometimes it is said—usually, it seems, by the critics of ST—that ST is any account of the Trinity that uses a distinctly "modern" notion of personhood as applied to the Trinity. Often the claim is pejorative: whether intentionally or unwittingly, ST "imports" a modern account of "person"—often labeled further as "Cartesian" or "Lockean"—into the traditional doctrine. This distinctly ST move is often contrasted with older or "classical" notions of personhood (those that are not concerned with psychological distinctness or relationships between self-conscious agents). And this distinctly ST move is then often criticized for being not only obviously revisionist but also implicitly tritheistic. Again, for our purposes we can set this aside (as a definition of ST). This critical account of ST makes some interesting historical claims and raises some important theological issues. These claims deserve to be taken seriously, but a set of historical claims about a doctrine do not, in this case at least, amount to a definition of a doctrinal claim. And there are many counterexamples that would undercut any effort to define ST along these lines. For some of the staunchest defenders of ST disavow modern notions—in point of fact, they wish to draw upon ST as a resource from which to retrieve older and more properly theological understandings of what a person is (e.g., LaCugna 1991). Moreover, some of the fiercest *critics* of ST make explicit use of distinctly modern accounts of personhood—Brian Leftow (2007), for example, is sharply critical of ST but then employs the notion of "Locke-persons" for his positive account of "Latin Trinitarianism" (357–75). So for present purposes, this account of ST need not distract us further.

Other approaches to the meaning of the ST label come closer and are more promising but are still not quite sufficient. Some contemporary theologians associate ST with any doctrine according to which the divine persons share in mutual love; on this account, just any doctrinal formulation that posits love of the Father for the Son (*ad intra*) would count as ST. Similarly, any doctrine according to which the divine persons have distinct agency (in any sense) is also said to be ST. Such approaches come closer to the mark, for at least they contain more substantive claims about the content of the doctrine (rather than merely making contestable and overly simplistic observations about historical provenance). But these approaches are also less than adequate for our purposes. For just *any* doctrine of the Trinity—at least one that is grounded in scripture and informed by the Christian tradition—should affirm that the Father loves the Son and the Son loves the Father. After all, in Jesus's "high priestly" prayer to his Father, he refers to the love that is shared between them "before the world began" (Jn 17:5, 24).[3] And even Aquinas, who is sometimes taken to be the zenith of the Latin tradition, affirms that the Father and Son love one another within the inner life of the Trinity (ST 1948: Ia.Q37.a2).[4] So if mutual love within the Trinity is enough to qualify as ST, then all theologians should be defenders of it.[5] We could say similar things about agency.[6]

Having cleared away some common misunderstandings of ST, we can now offer an account that is somewhat more precise. Consider ST as the conjunction of:

(ST1) The Father, the Son, and the Holy Spirit are "of one essence" but are not numerically the same substance. The divine persons are, then, consubstantial or homoousios only in the sense that they share a divine generic or kind-essence.

(ST2) Properly understood, the central claim of monotheism is the claim that there is only one divine generic or kind-essence. This does not include or entail the claim that there is only one divine substance.

(ST3) The divine persons must each be in full possession of the divine nature and in some particular relation R to one another for Trinitarianism to count as monotheism. (McCall and Rea 2009: 3).

Exactly what that particular relation R amounts to is important. It is also the point of much debate. Some proponents of ST take that R to be something like perfect love and harmony of will. Others add to this (or perhaps clarify it further) by insisting that the R is (or entails) mutually interdependence, so that no one divine person can even possibly exist apart from the other divine persons. Still others take the R of ST to be the relation of proper parts (or something closely akin to proper parts) to a whole.

Cornelius Plantinga Jr. (1989) conceives of the Trinity as "a divine, transcendent society or community of three fully personal and full divine entities: the Father, the Son, and the Holy Spirit. These three are wonderfully united by their common divinity, that is, by the possession of each of the whole generic divine essence ... [and] the divine persons are also unified by their joint redemptive purpose, revelation, and work" (27–8). He holds this view because he takes it to be "an ally with the best-developed biblical presentation on the issue and with three-quarters of the subsequent theological tradition" (34). He argues that his view avoids Arianism (which he takes to be "Exhibit A" in the catalog of tritheisms), and he affirms that the divine persons are interdependent. So if "belief

---

[3] Biblical quotations in this chapter are taken from the New International Version of the Bible.
[4] See further the illuminating discussions in Emery (2007: 106) and Emery (2003: 155, 216–17).
[5] This is not to deny that there are outliers, e.g., Rahner (1997: 106) and Ward (2015: 242).
[6] Traditionally, the *opera ad extra* are undivided, yet such actions do not rule out some distinction of agency and may reach their *terminus* on one or another of the divine persons. Thus, only the Son becomes incarnate, only the Holy Spirit descends at Pentecost, etc. With respect to the *opera ad intra,* on the other hand, the situation is different. Only the Father generates the Son.

in three *autonomous* persons or three *independent* persons amounts to tritheism," then his position fails to qualify (37). For the divine persons are "essentially and reciprocally dependent" (37). Richard Swinburne's avowedly ST position is similar in many respects. He is sure that the divine persons are three individual souls, for a person—rather human or divine—is "simply a rational individual" (1994: 182). Each is a center of consciousness who is in full possession of the divine kind-essence. Possessing the full divine essence, each person has "all the divine properties of omnipotence, omniscience, perfect freedom and perfect goodness" (Swinburne 2016: 302). But Swinburne's account emphasizes the priority of the Father in the Trinity; while it is true that the Son and Spirit "exist as necessarily as does the Father," nonetheless it is also true that the Father is the cause of the Son and Spirit in a unique way (302).

William Lane Craig labels his view ST but takes a different approach and comes to a rather different conclusion. He suggests that the Triune God of the Christian faith is composed of the three divine persons in a way that is (admittedly, remotely) analogous to the existence of Cerberus, the three-headed watchdog of Hades in Greek mythology. He takes the divine persons to be "three centers of consciousness, intentionality, and volition," but he also insists that God is exactly one soul—"a soul which is endowed with three complete sets of rational cognitive faculties, each sufficient for personhood" (Craig 2009: 99). So on Craig's account, the claim to monotheism is secured by the recognition that there is one God who has parts: "we could think of the persons of the Trinity as divine because they are parts of the Trinity, that is, parts of God" (Moreland and Craig 2003: 591). The divine persons are (or, minimally, are relevantly like) parts—in this case, personal parts of an interpersonal whole.

As we have seen, there are different versions of ST.[7] What these versions of ST—ST properly so-called—have in common is their commitment to

(1) the thesis that the divine persons are genuinely and robustly distinct (as persons who know and love one another while acting in perfect cooperation in relation to all that is not God)

along with

(2) the thesis that the divine essence is rightly understood as a generic or kind-essence.

These versions keep (1) and (2) closely linked and then accept and defend both. But other analytic theologians keep them closely linked and then reject both, while still others uncouple them and keep (1) while rejecting (2).

II.3 Anti-Social Trinitarianism

Many philosophers of religion and theologians are less than satisfied with ST; the underlying and very deep worry is that ST simply does not do enough to ward off charges of tritheism. Indeed, some critics aver that ST just *is* a version of polytheism; the sophisticated arguments and clever analogies simply cannot secure monotheism, and we are left with tritheism (or perhaps with a theology that entails that there are four deities). Leftow (1999) argues forcefully that ST "cannot be both orthodox and a version of monotheism" (203). In place of ST he defends what he refers to as "Latin Trinitarianism."

---

[7]Other interesting possibilities from proponents of ST include Brown (1985), Davis (2006: 60–78), Mcintosh (2016: 167–86), and especially Yandell (2009: 151–68).

Leftow insists that we think of God as exactly one substance and of the persons as distinct but not discrete. He offers an analogy drawn from time-travel:

> You are at Radio City Music Hall, watching the Rockettes kick in unison. You notice that they look quite a bit alike. But (you think) they just must be made up to look that way. After all, they came on-stage at once, each from a different point backstage, they put their arms over each others' shoulders for support, smile and nod to each other, and when the number is over, they scatter offstage each in her own direction. So they certainly seem to be many different women. But appearances deceive. Here is the true story. All the Rockettes but one, Jane, called in sick that morning. So Jane came to work with a time machine ... ran on-stage to her position at the left of the chorus line, kicked her way through the number, then ran off. She changed her makeup, donned a wig, then stepped into her nephew's Wells-omatic, to emerge from a point to the right of her first entry, stepped into the line second from the chorus line's left, smiled and whispered a quip to the woman on the right, kicked her way through the number, then ran off. She then changed her makeup again. (Leftow 2004: 307)

The point should be plain: there is no doubt that there is only one Jane, but there is also no doubt that she is present several times over in the chorus line. There is one trope of Jane-ness that is simultaneously present in leftmost-Jane, center-Jane, and rightmost-Jane. Similarly, in one strand God lives the Father's life, in one the Son's, and in one the Spirit's. The events of each strand add up to the life of a Person. "The lives of the Persons add up to the life God lives *as* the three Persons." He concludes that "there is one God, but he is many in the events of his life, as Jane was in the chorus line: being the Son is a bit like being the leftmost Rockette" (Leftow 2004: 312). The three persons are thus three "parts" of God's life.

Leftow's proposal is fascinating and ingenious, but it is not free of criticisms. At one level, it has been observed that, despite the label of "Latin Trinitarianism," the view sits at some distance from the mainstream Latin tradition; it does, after all, posit that God has parts, and it is not at all easy to see how this might be compatible with the ubiquitous traditional claim that God is simple.[8] Michael Rea argues that Leftow's account is "imprecise at a crucial juncture" and incomplete (Rea 2009: 410). What is the relation between leftmost-Jane, center-Jane, and rightmost-Jane? Are they—"they"—identical? Or are they distinct? If distinct, are they consubstantial? Rea worries that the account is underdeveloped and yet inadequate (he suggests that it be augmented and bolstered by what he calls the "Constitution Theory") (Rea: 2009: 417–18). More worrisome yet are the concerns that Leftow's view entails a fourth person or super-person (thus leaving us with a quaternity) or defaults to a version of modalism.[9] These concerns are related to the distinct agency and consciousness of the divine persons. As we have seen, Leftow insists that any acceptable, monotheism-securing doctrine of the Trinity must reject (2) and instead hold to a single divine substance. But he also recognizes that the divine persons are portrayed in scripture as agents who interact with one another (as well as what is not God); in short, it appears that the Father, Son, and Spirit are personal entities who know and love one another. Leftow thus introduces the notion of "Locke-persons." Taking a cue from John Locke's theory, Leftow says that persons are "identical over time just as far

---

[8] See the discussion in McCall (2009: 113–14).
[9] See Hasker (2009: 162–4), McCall (2009: 115–22).

as a single 'consciousness' extends;" a person begins to exist when a consciousness begins, and a person ceases to exist when that same consciousness ends (Leftow 2007: 367). Of course God is eternal, and there is nothing intermittent in the divine life. Nonetheless, Leftow finds the notion useful:

> My Lockean "mode"-based suggestion about the Trinity, then, is this. Perhaps the triune Persons are event-based persons founded on a generating substance, God ... these streams are mental streams, and each such stream is the life of a Locke-person. God never exists save *in* the Persons ... there is just one God who generates and lives as the three Persons, by generating and living in three distinct mental streams. (374)

Whether or not the notion of Locke-persons can do enough work for Leftow's proposal remains a matter of further debate.[10] But what should be clear is that Leftow forcefully rejects (2) while remaining somewhat ambiguous about (1).

In contrast, Keith Ward's proposal contains no such ambiguity. He clearly keeps (1) and (2) coupled together—and he just as clearly and very forcefully rejects both. Indeed, he is critical of Leftow for being too much "like a social theorist," for if the "life-streams" of the Father and Son do not share first-person access and "think and act" distinctly, then this "is all you want (and probably more than you want) for a social view" (Ward 2015: 240–1). He denies that the Father and Son are distinct persons in any recognizable sense of the term "person," and he likewise denies that there is mutual love between Father and Son (242). There indeed is love between the man Jesus Christ and the Father, but this is only "mutual love between Father and the human aspect of the incarnate Son" (242).

So Ward is highly critical of ST, and he even rejects Leftow's explicitly *anti-ST* theology as too much like ST. But what does he propose? In his theology, the divine persons are three "aspects" or "forms of being" of "one divine consciousness and will, one personal being" (247). He denies that this counts as a form of modalism, for on his view God is *essentially* threefold. God is only contingently Triune in the sense that the forms of being are only contingently denominated "Father, Son, and Holy Spirit," but God would be threefold in any case and being non-threefold is not an option for God (246–56). For while "the specific modalities of Father, Son, and Spirit are appearances to us in our world," nonetheless these modalities "manifest an essential threefoldness of the divine, an 'immanent Trinity' which belongs to Being itself" (253).

Interlocutors point out that Ward's proposal is very thorough-going in its rejection of commitments often associated with ST. Indeed, it is so very thoroughgoing that it departs from the Christian tradition much more broadly. Thus, Dale Tuggy (2016) notes that Ward's theology is not "a reformulation of either a late fourth-century catholic view of the Trinity, or of a modern Protestant view of the Trinity" but instead "is a different animal entirely," one that "is neither a biblical nor a creedal doctrine, but a new, speculative one" (365). Defenders of ST argue, contra Ward, that his criticisms of their positions are far from decisive, and critics raise several probing objections to Ward's proposal (e.g., Davis 2016; Hasker 2016). They argue that his doctrine falls well outside the boundaries established by the ecumenical creedal statements (and thus should be a complete nonstarter for any Christian committed to confessional orthodoxy) (Swinburne 2016). They probe more deeply; they make a case that his proposal runs afoul of the very biblical witness that generated and supports the creedal statements (Davis

---

[10]For a sampling of such debate, see Hasker (2012) and Leftow (2012a,b).

2016: 310–11; Hasker 2016: 336–8). In addition, the critics are concerned about the theological entailments of Ward's doctrine. Davis is concerned that Ward's view does not escape the "specter of modalism," and Tuggy concludes that Ward does not do enough to "turn back a charge of modalism" (Davis 2016: 311; Tuggy 2016: 367). And, perhaps surprisingly, it turns out that Ward's theology might be open to the charge of polytheism. For on his view, God is said to be omnipotent while Jesus, who is also said to be divine "in some sense," is said to be non-omnipotent.[11] But how many senses of "divinity" are there if there is only one God? How many can there be? If God has an omnipotence-rich divine essence (call it the O-positive divine essence) while Jesus has an omnipotence-deprived divine essence (call it the O-negative divine essence), then we have two divine essences. And if these are instantiated (in Ward's case, one by God and the other by the divine Son), then how do we not have two gods? And, for a strict monotheist such as Ward (who thinks that ST is tritheistic), is not this one god too many (McCall 2016: 321–22)?

II.4 Relative Identity and Numerical Sameness without Identity

To this point, we have seen that the advocates of ST (on the definition I have offered) are committed to both

(1) the divine persons are genuinely and robustly distinct (as persons who know and love one another while acting in perfect cooperation in relation to all that is not God);

and

(2) the divine essence is rightly understood as a generic or kind-essence.

Meanwhile, critics of ST such as Ward also hold (1) and (2) together—but then reject them together. But other approaches do not take them as a package deal; some analytic theologians hold fast to (1) while rejecting (2) (or, minimally, holding it at arm's length). They take different routes to this end, but in doing so they hold to (what is sometimes called) numerical sameness without identity.

Peter van Inwagen is clearly committed to (1). He plainly states that persons—whether human or divine—

> are those things to which personal pronouns are applicable: a person can use the word "I" and be addressed as a "thou" … [and] it is evident that the Persons of the Trinity *are* in this sense "persons," *are* someones: if the Father loves us, then someone loves us, and if the Son was incarnate by the Holy Ghost of the Virgin Mary, then someone was incarnate by the Holy Ghost of the Virgin Mary. (van Inwagen 1995: 264–5)

He understands the divine persons to be fully and relationally personal; the divine persons know and love one another in the intra-divine life, and it is their mutual relationships that make them the distinct persons they are. So far, his view is hard to distinguish from the robust versions of ST.

But van Inwagen does not rest content with the common ST appeals to (2), and he does not retreat to the other ST strategies that rely upon some relation R that is supposed to secure monotheism for ST. Instead, he appeals to the logic of relative identity. According to the logic of relative identity (at least as articulated by a theorist such as Peter Geach), absolute identity is not expressible, and it is a mistake to presume that classical

---

[11]Compare Ward (2015: 164–5) with Ward (2015: 81).

(or "absolute") accounts of identity are correct (Geach 1980: 238–49). Where classical accounts hold that identity is an equivalence relation that is reflexive, transitive, and symmetric, the logic of relative identity insists that all equivalence and identity statements are relative. On relative identity, a question such as "is x the same as y?" is ill-formed. The proper question is "is x the same F as y?" Proponents of the logic of relative identity hold that objects may be identical under one sortal concept but distinct under another (e.g., Noonan 1997). Thus things can be said to be the same relative to one kind of thing, but distinct relative to another kind of thing. Applied to the doctrine of the Trinity, the result is both predictable and theologically orthodox: the Father, Son, and Holy Spirit are distinct persons while also being the same God. So van Inwagen: if we are counting "divine beings by beings, there is one; counting divine Persons by beings, there is one; counting divine Beings by persons, there are three; counting divine Persons by persons, there are three" (van Inwagen 1995: 250). So if we express the core theological claims of the doctrine of the Trinity in terms of relative identity, these core claims "can be shown to be mutually consistent" (van Inwagen 2003: 97).

But if theologically orthodox, the solution is found to be philosophically heterodox by many theorists. And in addition to the basic objections to the logic of relative identity, there are several distinctly theological worries.[12] Rea, for instance, is concerned that leaving the philosophical objections unaddressed actually reopens the door to the theological troubles. More specifically, committed to what Rea refers to as a "pure" doctrine of relative identity (that both maintains that some doctrine of relative identity is in fact true and that the way to make sense of the claims of Trinitarian theology is with relativized identity claims rather than absolute identity claims) makes it difficult to rule out both theological anti-realism and modalism (Rea 2003: 431–6).

In place of a "pure" doctrine of relative identity, Rea and Jeffrey E. Brower offer what Rea refers to as an "impure" account. More specifically, they appeal to the analogy of material constitution. Of course they know that it is *only* an analogy (and not a metaphysical description of God's inner life), and they are quick to point out the limitations and disanalogous elements, but they offer it as a helpful way to account for the key claims to Trinitarian theology. When we say that each of the divine persons *is* God, we do not intend the "is" of predication (as in ST). Instead, we mean the "is" of numerical sameness. But in this case, the "is" of numerical sameness is not the "is" of identity. But—and here the theological account readily takes leave of the more familiar and mundane illustrations—neither is it the "is" of accidental sameness; instead it is the "is" of essential sameness. Drawing an analogy with form-matter compounds such as statues, they argue that "the Persons of the Trinity can also be conceived of in terms of hylomorphic compounds," and we "can think of the divine essence as playing the role of matter" while regarding "the properties *being a Father, being a Son,* and *being a Spirit* as distinct forms instantiated by the divine essence, each giving rise to a distinct Person" (Brower and Rea 2005: 68). They conclude that if we think about the Trinity this way, "the problem of the Trinity disappears." For

> according to the Aristotelian solution to the problem of material constitution, a statue and its lump are *two* distinct hylomorphic compounds; yet they are numerically one material object. Likewise, then, the Persons of the Trinity are *three* distinct Persons but

---

[12]On the philosophical worries, see Wiggins (2001). Swinburne (1994) endorses and echoes Wiggins's criticisms (14–16, 187–8).

numerically one God, [and] there will be three distinct Persons, each Person will be God (and will be the same God as the other Persons), and there will be exactly one God. (69)

What we need, they insist, is numerical sameness without identity. And this is just what their model provides; they conclude that it is "the most philosophically promising and most theologically satisfying solution on offer" (70).

William Hasker takes a rather different route to a similar conclusion. He offers an enthusiastic endorsement and energetic defense of (1). Labeling this position "ST," he maintains that the divine persons are "distinct centers of knowledge, will, love, and action."[13] Not content with mere affirmations and assertions, he offers rigorous defense of this claim on both biblical and traditional grounds. Biblically, he notes that "ST" (again, on his account, ST = (1)) is admitted by virtually everyone at the level of the "economic" Trinity while also being evident in Johannine theology at the level of the "immanent" Trinity.[14] He also finds a basis for belief in (1) to be widespread within patristic theology, and here he appeals not only to the "Greek" or "Cappadocian" theologians but also to Augustinian theology (Hasker 2013: 26–49). Hasker is convinced that the mutual love of the three divine persons—their perichoretic communion—is essential to the intra-Trinitarian divine life, and that nothing is or could be more basic or fundamental to the divine being. Hasker does not, however, endorse (2). In considering what it means to say that the three divine persons share the divine nature, he argues that the claim "does not mean merely that they share a common generic essence" (226). Instead, he deliberately follows patristic (again, on his reading, both Greek and Latin) teaching in his conviction that "the three persons share a single concrete nature, a single instance or trope of deity" (226; cf. 50–67). At the same time, however, Hasker is also critical of other strategies that attempt to hold to (1) without the corresponding commitment to (2). In particular, he weighs in the balances and finds wanting van Inwagen's use of relative identity, Leftow's creative employment of time-travel analogies, and the material constitution strategy of Rea and Brower. Following the work of Lynne Rudder Baker, he proposes an alternative account of constitution as the way forward. Constitution, he says, is "very definitely a kind of sameness, even though it does not amount to identity" (245). The constituting kind is the single and concrete divine nature (of which there is only one trope that is shared between the persons), the constituted kind is the divine persons, and "the divine nature constitutes the divine trinitarian persons when it *sustains simultaneously three divine life-streams,* each life-stream including cognitive, affective, and volitional states" (243).[15] Thus we have three divine persons, and exactly one God.

Such commitments to (1) that remain leery of—or flatly deny—(2) are common to the broader tradition of Latin theology. This is not to say that the various analogies related to numerical sameness without identity are common; they are not, some theologians (e.g., Abelard) make positive use of the analogy, but many other theologians do not. The basic commitment to a robust understanding of the distinctness of the persons within

---

[13] Hasker (2013) notes that "this is a claim that has been argued for, indirectly but also at times directly, throughout the book to this point" (193).
[14] It should be obvious that Hasker's account of what qualifies as "ST" departs from my own narrower definition. As I noted earlier, the term "ST" admits of many uses. Of course Hasker is free to use the term as he wishes; I only point this out in an effort to be clear.
[15] Cf. Anderson (2007) and Tuggy (2011).

their mutual relations of loving communion, coupled with an insistence on numerical sameness, is very widespread.

II.5 Mystery and Mysterianism

One may wonder about the place of mystery in these doctrinal formulations and accompanying theories and models. It is important to note that these analytic endeavors are not (at least in most cases) an attempt to dispel all mystery or remove all mysterious elements. To the contrary, many of these analytic theorists are explicit that they are not trying to fully explain God's own inner life. They are (often) keenly aware that the doctrine likely exceeds the limits of human comprehension. What they are doing is, minimally, more akin to "playing defense" against the common charges that the doctrine is inherently contradictory and thus necessarily false. Those who are more positive or confident offer something a bit more optimistic, but even then they are aware that they are offering only the faintest reflections of the Trinity.

It might help to think more clearly about what "mystery" actually amounts to in this context. Oliver D. Crisp suggests that we think of the doctrine along these lines: a proper theological mystery is "a truth that is intelligible in principle but that may not be entirely intelligible to human beings in their current state of cognitive development" (2019: 99). He draws upon Edwin Abbott's novel *Flatland* to help illustrate the point: as sentient plane beings who live in a two-dimensional world might not be able to conceive adequately of a three-dimensional world, so also we might struggle to conceive adequately of a Triune God. But of course such struggle is only a testament to the inability of the inhabitants of the two-dimensional world—it says nothing about the possibility or reality of the three-dimensional world. Crisp's observations about mystery do not, of course, in any way discredit or devalue the work of analytic theologians on the doctrine, but they might serve to better contextualize such work.

III. ANALYTIC TRINITARIAN THEOLOGY THEN, NOW, AND LATER

Contemporary work in Trinitarian theology stands to benefit greatly from the efforts at *ressourcement*. The complexities and rich intellectual resources of the Christian traditions (both Latin and Eastern) are being mined, and newer developments seek to learn from and build upon the advances of older (and oft-forgotten) theologians. Various patristic and medieval theologians have become mentors and guides for a younger generation (e.g., Friedman 2010; Paasch 2012; Thom 2012; Williams 2017). Moreover, recent developments in the "theological interpretation of Scripture" are bringing theologians into closer contact with the Bible and into conversation with biblical scholarship.[16] Further engagement with the so-called Early High Christology Club and recent developments in "prosoponic exegesis" hold great promise for the future of analytic theology of the Trinity.[17]

Other doctrinal matters also await future analytic engagement. The venerable doctrine of the eternal generation of the Son and the more distinctly modern debates over the

---

[16] For an accessible introduction, see Treier (2008).
[17] For examples of the "Early High Christology Club," see Hurtado (2003), Fee (2007), Bauckham (2008), and Wright (2013). For examples of "prosoponic exegesis," see Bates (2015), Hill (2015), and Pierce (2020).

subordination of the Son to the Father would benefit from closer analytic scrutiny.[18] Recent discussions of the proper relation of the doctrine of election to the doctrine of the Trinity have largely been located in the house of Barth studies, but these too could use a dose of analytic clarity. Perhaps more importantly, the relation of the doctrine of divine simplicity to the doctrine of the Trinity deserves more attention, for while there has been considerable work devoted to the doctrine of simplicity as well as significant treatment of the doctrine of the Trinity, not much has drawn the various elements of the discussions together. Finally, issues related to gender and the doctrine of the Trinity would seem to have room for further analytic theological engagements; to this point, many of the critiques and proposals coming from feminist thought and queer theory do not employ analytic tools and resources, while much of the work in analytic theology has not paid a lot of attention to the concerns that come from these quarters. The time may be ripe for further *rapprochement*.[19]

IV. CONCLUSION

Analytic theologians have had a lot to say about the doctrine of the Trinity. Much of the work has been devoted to the "logical" or "threeness-oneness problem." Such work has become increasingly sophisticated and more deeply informed by the theological resources of the Christian traditions. It has also begun to branch out into other areas of doctrine, and analytic tools are now being used on a variety of topics. It is not a stretch to predict that future work will make further strides.

References

Anatolios, K. (2011), *Retrieving Nicaea: The Development and Meaning of Trinitarian Doctrine*, Grand Rapids, MI: Baker Academic.
Anderson, J. (2007), *Paradox in Christian Theology: An Analysis of Its Presence, Character, and Epistemic Status*, Milton Keynes: Paternoster.
Aquinas, T. (1948), *Summa Theologica*, trans. Fathers of the English Dominican Province, New York: Benzinger Bros.
Ayers, L. (2004), *Nicaea and Its Legacy: An Approach to Fourth-Century Trinitarian Theology*, Oxford: Oxford University Press.
Ayres, L. (2010), *Augustine and the Trinity*, Cambridge: Cambridge University Press.
Barnes, M. R. (2001), *The Power of God: Δύναμις in Gregory of Nyssa's Trinitarian Theology*, Washington, DC: Catholic University of America Press.
Bates, M. (2015), *The Birth of the Trinity: Jesus, God, and Spirit in New Testament and Early Christian Interpretations of the Old Testament*, Oxford: Oxford University Press.
Bauckham, R. (2008), *Jesus and the God of Israel: God Crucified and Other Studies on the New Testament's Christology of Divine Identity*, Grand Rapids, MI: William B. Eerdmans.
Beeley, C. A. (2008), *Gregory of Nazianzus on the Trinity and the Knowledge of God: In Your Light We Shall See Light*, Oxford: Oxford University Press.
Brower, J. E., and M. C. Rea (2005), "Material Constitution and the Trinity," *Faith and Philosophy*, 22 (1): 57–76.

---

[18] On eternal generation, see Makin (2017: 243–59).
[19] Sarah Coakley's important work (2013) in analytic feminist Trinitarian theology is groundbreaking.

Brown, D. (1985), *The Divine Trinity*, LaSalle: Open Court.
Coakley, S. (2013), *God, Sexuality, and the Self: An Essay "On the Trinity"*, Cambridge: Cambridge University Press.
Craig, W. L. (2009), "Toward a Tenable Social Trinitarianism," in T. H. McCall and M. C. Rea (eds.), *Philosophical and Theological Essays on the Trinity*, 89–99, Oxford: Oxford University Press.
Crisp, O. D. (2019), *Analyzing Doctrine: Toward a Systematic Theology*, Waco: Baylor University Press.
Davis, S. T. (2006), *Christian Philosophical Theology*, Oxford: Oxford University Press.
Davis, S. T. (2016), "Comments on Keith Ward's *Christ and the Cosmos*," *Philosophia Christi*, 18 (2): 307–12.
Emery, G. (2003), *Trinity in Aquinas*, Ypsilanti: Ave Maria.
Emery, G. (2007), *The Trinitarian Theology of St. Thomas Aquinas*, Oxford: Oxford University Press.
Fee, G. D. (2007), *Pauline Christology: An Exegetical-Theological Study*, Grand Rapids, MI: Baker Academic.
Friedman, R. (2010), *Medieval Trinitarian Thought from Aquinas to Ockham*, Cambridge: Cambridge University Press.
Geach, P. (1980), *Logic Matters*, Berkeley: University of California Press.
Gregg, R. C., and D. E. Groh (1981), *Early Arianism: A View of Salvation*, Philadelphia: Fortress Press.
Hanson, R. P. C. (1988), *The Search for the Christian Doctrine of God: The Arian Controversy 318–381 AD*, Edinburgh: T&T Clark.
Hasker, W. (2009), "A Leftovian Trinity?," *Faith and Philosophy*, 26 (2): 154–66.
Hasker, W. (2012), "Dancers, Rugby Players, and Trinitarian Persons," *Faith and Philosophy*, 29 (3): 325–33.
Hasker, W. (2013), *Metaphysics and the Tri-Personal God*, Oxford: Oxford University Press.
Hasker, W. (2016), "A Cosmic Christ?," *Philosophia Christi*, 18 (2): 333–41.
Hill, W. (2015), *Paul and the Trinity: Persons, Relations, and the Pauline Letters*, Grand Rapids, MI: William B. Eerdmans.
Hurtado, L. W. (2003), *Lord Jesus Christ: Devotion to Jesus in Earliest Christianity*, Grand Rapids, MI: William B. Eerdmans.
Kelly, J. N. D. (1964), *The Athanasian Creed*, London: Adam and Charles Black.
LaCugna, C. M. (1991), *God for Us: The Trinity and Christian Life*, New York: HarperCollins.
Leftow, B. (1999), "Anti Social Trinitarianism," in S. T. Davis, D. Kendall, SJ, and G. O'Collins, SJ (eds.), *The Trinity: An Interdisciplinary Symposium on the Trinity*, 203–50, Oxford: Oxford University Press.
Leftow, B. (2004), "A Latin Trinity," *Faith and Philosophy*, 21 (3): 304–33.
Leftow, B. (2007), "Modes without Modalism," in P. van Inwagen and D. Zimmerman (eds.), *Persons, Human and Divine*, 357–75, Oxford: Oxford University Press.
Leftow, B. (2012a), "On Hasker On Leftow On Hasker On Leftow," *Faith and Philosophy*, 29 (3): 334–9.
Leftow, B. (2012b), "Time, Travel, and the Trinity," *Faith and Philosophy*, 29 (3): 313–24.
Makin, M. (2017), "Philosophical Models of Eternal Generation," in F. Sanders and S. R. Swain (eds.), *Retrieving Eternal Generation*, 243–59, Grand Rapids, MI: Zondervan Academic.
McCall, T. H. (2009), *Which Trinity? Whose Monotheism? Philosophical and Systematic Theologians on the Metaphysics of Trinitarian Theology*, Grand Rapids, MI: William B. Eerdmans.
McCall, T. H. (2016), "Professor Ward and Polytheism," *Philosophia Christi*, 18 (2): 313–22.

McCall, T. H., and M. C. Rea (2009), "Introduction," in T. H. McCall and M. C. Rea (eds.), *Philosophical and Theological Essays on the Trinity*, 1–18, Oxford: Oxford University Press.

McIntosh, C. A. (2016), "God of the Groups," *Religious Studies*, 52 (2): 167–86.

Moreland, J. P., and W. L. Craig (2003), *Philosophical Foundations for a Christian Worldview*, 1st ed., Downers Grove, IL: InterVarsity Academic.

Noonan, H. (1997), "Relative Identity," in B. Hale and C. Wright (eds.), *A Companion to Philosophy of Language*, 634–52, Oxford: Blackwell.

Paasch, J. T. (2012), *Divine Production in Late Medieval Trinitarian Theology: Henry of Ghent, Duns Scotus, and William Ockham*, Oxford: Oxford University Press.

Pierce, M. (2020), *Divine Discourse in the Epistle to the Hebrews: The Recontextualization of Spoken Quotations from Scripture*, Cambridge: Cambridge University Press.

Plantinga, C. (1989), "Social Trinity and Tritheism," in R. J. Feenstra and C. Plantinga Jr. (eds.), *Trinity, Incarnation, and Atonement: Philosophical and Theological Essays*, Notre Dame, IN: University of Notre Dame Press.

Rahner, K. (1997), *Trinity*, trans. J. Donceel, New York: Crossroad.

Rea, M. C. (2003), "Relative Identity and the Doctrine of the Trinity," *Philosophia Christi*, 5 (2): 431–45.

Rea, M. C., (2009), "The Trinity," in T. P. Flint and M. C. Rea (eds.), *The Oxford Handbook of Philosophical Theology*, 403–29, Oxford: Oxford University Press.

Swinburne, R. (1994), *The Christian God*, Oxford: Oxford University Press.

Swinburne, R. (2016), "Response to Keith Ward, *Christ and the Cosmos*," *Philosophia Christi*, 18 (2): 297–305.

Thom, P. (2012), *The Logic of the Trinity: Augustine to Ockham*, New York: Fordham University Press.

Treier, D. J. (2008), *Introducing Theological Interpretation of Scripture: Recovering a Christian Practice*, Grand Rapids: Baker Academic.

Tuggy, D. (2011), "On Positive Mysterianism," *International Journal for Philosophy of Religion*, 69 (3): 205–26.

Tuggy, D. (2016), "Some Objections to Ward's Trinitarian Theology," *Philosophia Christi*, 18 (2): 363–73.

van Inwagen, P. (1995), *God, Knowledge, and Mystery: Essays in Philosophical Theology*, Ithaca, NY: Cornell University Press.

van Inwagen, P. (2003), "Three Persons in One Being: On Attempts to Show That the Doctrine of the Trinity is Self-Contradictory," in M. Y. Stewart (ed.), *The Trinity: East/West Dialogue*, Dordrecht: Kluwer Academic.

Ward, K. (2015), *Christ and the Cosmos: A Reformulation of Trinitarian Doctrine*, Cambridge: Cambridge University Press.

Wiggins, D. (2001), *Sameness and Substance Renewed*, Cambridge: Cambridge University Press.

Williams, S. (2017), "Unity of Action: A Latin Social Model of the Trinity," *Faith and Philosophy*, 34 (3): 321–46.

Wright, N. T. (2013), *Paul and the Faithfulness of God*, Minneapolis: Fortress Press.

Yandell, K. E. (2009), "How Many Times Does Three Go Into One?," in T. H. McCall and M. C. Rea (eds.), *Philosophical and Theological Essays on the Trinity*, 151–68, Oxford: Oxford University Press.

PART III

Person and Work of Christ

CHAPTER FIFTEEN

The Incarnation

TIMOTHY PAWL

I. INTRODUCTION

The Christian doctrine of the incarnation is the claim that the Second Person of the Blessed Trinity, the Son, the Word, became incarnate of the Virgin Mary. In the technical language, he *assumed* human nature from the *theotokos*—the God-bearer. This initial chapter of the part of this book on the person and work of Christ will focus on the metaphysics of the incarnation, and, in particular, the metaphysical issues at the center of the current, analytic discussion of the incarnation. These issues include: the ontological category under which the assumed, human nature of Christ is to be subsumed; the number and type of the components or parts of that nature; the appropriate understanding of the union between the two natures; and the main metaphysical objection to the incarnation—that it implies that one person had two contradictory attributes.[1]

II. THE ONTOLOGY OF THE HUMAN NATURE OF CHRIST

What sort of entity is Christ's assumed human nature? Is it something that you and I have, too—a shareable thing, such as a Platonic form? Or is it something individual and particular, causally efficacious and locatable in space and time? The first sort of thing is typically called an *abstract* entity, standard examples of which include sets, numbers, properties, and propositions. The second sort of thing is typically called a *concrete* entity, standard examples of which include plants, animals, stars, and cars. This divide between the abstract and the concrete is often presented as the most general ontological distinction between varieties of entities. It is a testament to the lack of consensus in the current Christological debate, then, that the two main theories of Christ's assumed human nature disagree about whether that nature is abstract or concrete.[2] In fact, the two theories have the now-standard titles of the *abstract nature view* and the *concrete nature view*.[3]

On the abstract view, the human nature assumed by Christ is a property or group of properties: the property (or group of properties) both necessary and sufficient for

---

[1] The work of this chapter builds upon and sometimes borrows from book-length treatments I've written of this subject. See Pawl (2016d, 2019b, 2020a).
[2] These are not the only two views in the current debate, though. See the work of Edwin Chr. van Driel (2008: 104) and Michael Rea (2011: 149) for other theories.
[3] For discussions of these two views of nature, see Crisp (2007b: 41), Dalmau (2016: IIA:68), Dubray (1911), and Plantinga (1999: 184). For discussions of the ontology of Christ's assumed human nature in a historical context, see Adams (1999), Cross (2005), and Pawl (2016d: chapter 2 section II.b; 2019b: chapter 1 section IV.b).

being a human. Anything that *instantiates* this property (or ...) is human, and anything human instantiates this property. You and I instantiate this one universal property. On the concrete view, by contrast, the human nature assumed by Christ is an individual, particular instance of human nature. It is a concrete thing, locatable in time and space.

Which type of nature did the Second Person of the Trinity assume: abstract or concrete? Different philosophical milieus have yielded different answers to this question. According to Marilyn McCord Adams (1999) and Richard Cross (1996: 115; 2002: 265; 2005: 26; 2019), the Medievals and early Reformation thinkers typically took the nature to be a concrete entity.[4] On the other hand, much of the analytic work on the incarnation that is not explicitly building off the medieval tradition has taken an abstract view of the nature.[5] What explains this difference?

I venture two explanatory hypotheses. First, the Medievals had a standard understanding of "nature" on which a nature is an acting thing. As Kenneth Baker writes, "A nature is understood by philosophers and theologians to be a principle of operation. A nature then is active through its powers—it causes things to happen in the real world" (2013: 37). Similarly, Thomas Aquinas in *De ente et essentia* discusses the views of Aristotle and Boethius in affirming that one usage of the term "nature" (or, better, the Greek and Latin terms we translate as "nature") is to refer to a substance, since substances are the origin or principle of their actions.

Unlike the Medievals, contemporary analytic philosophers do not typically have a notion of nature such that a nature is a substance with causal powers. Rather, the common contemporary analytic notion of nature sees natures as essential properties. As such, since the contemporary analytic discussion lacked an interpretation of "nature" such that it is concrete, the contemporary philosophers did not see such a reading as a live option, and instead focused on the more familiar abstract reading.

A second explanatory hypothesis has to do with how steeped in the history of the doctrine the philosophical and theological interlocutors are. Texts accepted at the third ecumenical council, the Council of Ephesus (AD 431) paraphrase reference to Christ's human nature as "flesh enlivened by a rational soul," and a "holy body rationally ensouled" (Tanner 1990: 41, 44). Likewise, the councils predicate terms such as "pierced" and "wills" of the human nature of Christ (Tanner 1990: 80–1, 129).[6] Such paraphrases and predications make no sense when said of an abstract, shareable object.

Even though there is an ontological gulf between these two theories of the human nature of Christ, in a real sense there is very little fundamental disagreement between the two views.[7] For any traditional Christology will require there to be a flesh and blood thing that the Word is specially related to, and in virtue of which it is true to say things like "the Word was born" and "the Son suffered on the cross." We might call that thing, as I have elsewhere, *Christ's human element*.[8] There is disagreement about whether we identify

---

[4]Additional resources on the Medieval and Reformation acceptance of the concrete nature view include Bavinck (2006: 304–8), Chemnitz (1971: 30, 58), Crisp (2007b: 133), Freddoso (1986: 30–2), Hipp (2001: 481), Pohle (1911: 222), Stump (2004: 206–7; 2005: 409), Wellum (2016: 451).

[5]See, for instance, Moreland and Craig (2003: 606), Morris (1987: 38–9; 2002: 164–5), and Senor (2011: 88). Moreland and Craig, it should be said, do distinguish between human nature and an *individual* human nature, which maps on to the abstract and concrete natures, respectively.

[6]I discuss both these reasons in much greater detail elsewhere; see Pawl (2016d: chapter 2 section II.b; 2019b: chapter 1 section IV.b).

[7]Brian Leftow (2004: 279) makes a similar point; see also Hasker (2017a: 434–5) and Marmodoro and Hill (2008: 101).

[8]See Pawl (2020a,b).

Christ's human element with his assumed human nature or not. That disagreement, though, is a matter of labeling. Much more substantive is the question to which we turn now: What are the number and types of components in that human element?

III. THE NUMBER AND TYPE OF THE COMPONENTS OR PARTS OF CHRIST'S ASSUMED HUMAN NATURE

In what follows, I will assume the concrete view of natures, and so will use "Christ's human nature" and "Christ's human element" synonymously. The final paragraph of the previous section made it clear that such an assumption is not metaphysically untoward.

The question of the number and type of parts of the assumed human nature of Christ is closely related to a different debate in the current literature, between two-part and three-part compositional Christologies. This debate concerns the number of parts—or, better, part-like things—in the incarnate Word. *Two-part compositional Christology* typically claims that the Word has the divine nature and the human body as parts, where the role of the human soul is played by the Word himself. *Three-part compositional Christology* typically claims that the soul must be a distinct, created entity, and so Christ has three part-ish things: (1) the divine nature, and the human nature, which is itself composed of two parts; (2) the body; and (3) the soul.[9] Since one can agree on the number of parts but disagree on which parts there are, the question of the number of part-like things in the composite Christ and the ontological components of the human nature are not the exact same question.

We can divide between theories of the human nature that take it not to be identical to the Word or the divine nature, and those that do take the human nature to be identical to the Word or the divine nature. Following the work of Jonathan Hill (2011) and James Arcadi (2018: 4), we might distinguish transformational from relational views of the human nature. On a *transformational* view, the Son himself transformed into a human.[10] On the view of Kevin Sharpe, "the Son's becoming human was a matter of his being transformed into a human and not merely his assumption of a concrete human nature" (2017: 118). On the *relational* view, in becoming incarnate, the person is not *changed into* something else, but rather, comes to relate to something else in a special way. That special mode of union, in which the two natures are united in the one divine person, is traditionally called the *hypostatic union*. Of these two theories, the relational view is by far the majority report. The transformational view is beset by multiple difficulties, presented by Leftow (2015) and others, and is inconsistent with the teachings of the Council of Ephesus:

> For we do not say that the nature of the Word was changed and became flesh, nor that he was turned into a whole man made of body and soul. Rather do we claim that the Word in an unspeakable, inconceivable manner united to himself hypostatically flesh enlivened by a rational soul, and so became man and was called son of man. (Tanner 1990: 41)[11]

---

[9] Arcadi (2018: 5–7) has provided a helpful delineation of these different compositional christologies. See also the discussion by Crisp (2007b: 41–5).
[10] For discussion of this view, see Merricks (2007), Crisp (2009: chap. 7), van Horn (2010), Leftow (2015), Sharpe (2017), Turner (2017), and Lim (2019). For related discussion, see Jaeger (2017).
[11] For more discussion of the transformational view, see Pawl (2020a).

As such, transformational views have found very few defenders in historic or analytic debates.

In addition to dividing transformational from relational views of the incarnation, we can also divide views based on whether they posit a body, a soul, or both in Christ, and whether they claim that any of those things can have their role played by the person of the Word. The traditional view, as evidenced by the quotations marshalled from the Council of Ephesus at the end of Part 2, is that Christ's human nature was composed of both a body and a rational soul. As such, Christian thinkers accepted that there is a body and a rational soul in Christ, though there have been differences in opinion of what exactly a soul is (e.g., a subsisting form of the body; a substance in its own right, etc.), and whether the Word could play the role of the soul.

Those who affirm that the assumed human nature of Christ lacked a created soul are referred to as *Apollinarians*, after an early bishop of Laodicea who endorsed a similar view. One finds this view endorsed by Moreland and Craig (2003: 611), where they note that the ecumenical councils preclude it. Craig has called his view "Neo-Apollinarianism," though there's good reason to doubt its novelty: one finds the same view anathematized in a synod of Rome in 382.[12]

IV. THE APPROPRIATE UNDERSTANDING OF THE UNION

Concerning the union, there are disagreements concerning just what is united and just what results from the union. These debates all take place within the relational framework of Part 3; it proves difficult to understand a *union* in the incarnation if the divine person *changes into* the human nature.

Thomas Flint (2011: 71–9) provides two ways of understanding the Hypostatic Union in compositional terms, which he calls "Model T" and "Model A."[13] On Model T,

> In becoming human, the Son or Word of God (whom I'll label W) takes on CHN [that is, Christ's human nature] as a part. This assumption results in a Son who combines both his original divine substance (D) and his created human nature (CHN). (Flint 2011: 71. Bracketed insert added.)

On Model A,

> the Son unites himself to CHN in the incarnation. But the composite thus formed is not the Son. The Son remains simply one part of the composite entity that results from his assuming a human nature. That composite entity, which (following Scotus and Leftow) we can call Christ, is a contingent thing, composed of another contingent entity (CHN) and of a necessary one (the Son). (Flint 2011: 79)

On Model T, the Word comes to have an additional nature part (or part-like thing). On Model A, the Word begins to be a part of a larger whole, which has CHN as its other part. That whole, on Model A, is Christ.

---

[12]We pronounce anathema against them who say that the Word of God is in the human flesh in lieu and place of the human rational and intellective soul. For, the Word of God is the Son Himself. Neither did He come in the flesh to replace, but rather to assume and preserve from sin and save the rational and intellective soul of man. (As quoted in Sollier 1907)

[13]For discussion of these two compositional models of the incarnation, see Crisp (2011; 2016: chap. 6), Flint (2015), Hasker (2015), Leftow (2011: 321), and Turner (2019: n. 5).

The traditional view, espoused in the early ecumenical councils, is that Jesus Christ is one person "of" or "in" two natures. For instance, "a union of two natures took place," and "one and the same Christ, Son, Lord, only-begotten; acknowledged in two natures," and "two different natures come together to form a unity, and from both arose one Christ, one Son" (Tanner 1990: 70, 86, 41, respectively). Two natures united in the person of the Word. Model A, then, is on shaky ground, since it misidentifies the things united together, claiming that one of them is the Word himself.

Model A is also in a tricky position insofar as it requires a larger whole to have a person part. On the traditional view of personhood, a person is a supposit of a rational nature.[14] A supposit, though, cannot be a part of something larger. Thus, Model A has problems with the traditional notions of personhood and supposit. Finally, Model A denies that the Word suffered. True, Christ did, and the Word is a part of Christ. But the Word himself did not suffer. It is for reasons such as these that the person in the current literature who christened the Model A composite "Jesus Christ," Brian Leftow, has recanted of that naming.[15] These arguments have not gone unanswered, however. Oliver Crisp (2011: 52–6) has replied to some of them in print.

Another debate concerning the union has to do with which analogies work to explain it best. One traditional analogy employed in the Athanasian Creed (Denzinger 2002: para 40) and the Council of Ephesus (Tanner 1990: 52) is that as a man's soul indwells his body, so likewise the Word indwells the human nature. One recent analogy used by Kathryn Rogers (2010, 2013) is that just as a boy might play a video game, and so enter into and act in the game world through his character, so likewise the Son can enter into and act in the created world through taking up a human nature. Another analogy from William Hasker (2017b) claims that the incarnation can be understood in terms of the sci-fi movie *Avatar*. In the movie, a human person can enter a machine and have his consciousness transferred to an alien biological organism. So likewise, the Word, through the hypostatic union, can enter the biological human nature.

V. THE FUNDAMENTAL PHILOSOPHICAL OBJECTION TO THE INCARNATION

Much of the discussion of the incarnation in analytic theology has focused on what has been termed the "Fundamental Philosophical Problem for the Incarnation." As Richard Cross puts the objection,

> The fundamental philosophical problem specific to the doctrine is this: how is it that one and the same thing could be both divine (and thus, on the face of it, necessary, and necessarily omniscient, omnipotent, eternal, immutable, impassible, and impeccable)

---

[14] See Geddes (1911) and Pawl (2016d: 30–4) for more on supposit and person.

[15] Leftow (2011: 321) writes,

> Though I have argued that GS + B + S [the composite of God the Son, Christ's Body, and Christ's Soul] is *personal*, there is no person with which it is identical ... I slipped up because in the paper to which Senor responds, I needed a term to refer to what I have been calling GS + B + S, and had the bright idea of using "Jesus Christ," a personal name. This let me fool myself. I've switched to "GS + B + S" here because it does not appear to be a personal name.

and human (and thus, on the face of it, have the complements of all these properties)? (Cross 2011: 453)[16]

The idea is that anything divine has what we might call, for ease of reference, *the allegedly divine predicates* (e.g., essential omnipotence; immutability), whereas anything human has *the allegedly human predicates* (e.g., limited power; mutability). No one thing can have both the divine and the human predicates at the same time and in the same respect; thus, Christ is not both God and man.[17]

There are various types of solutions to the Fundamental Problem. One variety revises logic in order to avoid the apparent contradiction. The remaining varieties employ classical logic (which, for our purposes, might be understood as logic with a non-relative identity relation and the law of non-contradiction). A second variety revises our conceptions of divinity and humanity, aiming to show that for every pair of allegedly divine and human predicates (e.g., limited in power and omnipotent; mutable and immutable), it is false that both are *really* predicates of divinity or humanity. A third variety of response to the Fundamental Problem accepts that the allegedly divine and human predicates must really be apt of divine and human things (respectively), but denies that these predicates must be apt of Christ *at the same time*. A fourth variety of response again accepts that the alleged predicates are really apt of divine and human things (respectively), and accepts that they are had at the same time, but denies that they are had *in the same respect*. A fifth and final (at least, for our purposes) variety of response denies a tacit assumption of all the previous solutions. Each previous solution has accepted the assumption that the alleged divine and alleged human predicates are complements, as Cross claimed they are in the quotation above. That is, each previous solution has accepted that it would be contradictory for one and the same thing to be both mutable and immutable, or limited in power and omnipotent, and so forth, at the same time in the same respect. The fifth variety of solution breaks company with the previous four in rejecting that assumption. In what follows, I will briefly canvas the subspecies of these types of options.

Consider the first variety of response: modifying logic. This variety comes in two forms in the contemporary discussion: employing a relative identity relation rather than absolute identity; truncating (from the perspective of classical logic) the rules of logic. I will consider them in turn.

First, one might relativize identity. On a relativized identity view, claims such as "Fr. James is Dr. Arcadi" are incomplete. An identity claim requires a type (called a *sortal*) to be included. Fr. James is *the same human as* Dr. Arcadi. Or Fr. James is *the same person as* Dr. Arcadi. Importantly, on this view, it is possible that two things, A and B, be the same x, but not be the same y. Moreover, it follows, on relative identity, as Peter van Inwagen (1998) notes, that A can be the same x as B, and A have some feature, without B having

---

[16]For a selection of recent discussions of this problem, see: Adams (2006: 121–3; 2009: 242–3), Arcadi (2018), Bäck (1998: 84; 2008), Bartel (1995: 155), Davis (2006: 116), Dawson (2004: 161–2), Evans (2006: 13), Feenstra (2006: 142–4), Geisler and Watkins (1985), Gordon (2016: 64), Gorman (2000; 2011; 2014; 2016; 2017: chapter 6), Guta (2019), Hebblethwaite (2008: 60), Hick (1989: 415; 2006: 66–70), Hill (2012: 3), Kelly (1994), Klima (1984), Labooy (2019), Leftow (2011: 316), Le Poidevin (2009b: 704), Loke (2009: 51; 2011: 493–4), Macquarrie (1990), Moreland and Craig (2003: 597), Morris (1987: chapter 1; 2009), Moulder (1986: 290–8), Pawl (2014a; 2015; 2016b; 2016d: chapters 4–7; 2018), Riches (2016: 5, 166), Senor (2002: 221), Spence (2008: 16), Stump (1989; 2004; 2005: chapter 14), Sturch (1991: chapters 2, 12), Vallicella (2002), van Inwagen (1998: sections 2–4), Ware (2013: 16), and Wellum (2016: 446–55).

[17]I have discussed this argument, its formulations, and potential responses in great detail elsewhere. See Pawl (2014a; 2015; 2016b; 2016d, chapters 4–7; 2018; 2019b; 2020a).

that feature. Put otherwise, on relative identity, the Indiscernibility of Identicals—which says that if A = B then anything true of A is true of B and vice versa—is false. So, given relative identity, the human-natured thing can be the same person as the divine-natured thing, and the human natured thing can be mutable, without it being true that the divine-natured thing is mutable. As a consequence, we cannot derive that there is one thing, the person, that is both mutable and immutable. A revision of logic has kept us from deriving a contradiction.[18]

Second, one might truncate the entailment rules that are licit in theological discussion, as Jc Beall does.[19] Beall accepts that Christ has contradictory features—that, for instance, it is true that Christ is immutable and, at the same time, in the same way, that very same proposition is also false. The main danger of accepting a contradiction on Classical Logic is that it leads to what is called *explosion*. The idea is that from a contradiction, anything at all follows. In brief: suppose that P is true and also that ~P is true. Since P is true, P or Q is also true (by a rule called *Disjunctive Introduction*). But since P or Q is true, and ~P is true, it follows that Q is true (by a rule called *Disjunctive Elimination* or *Disjunctive Syllogism*). So we've derived the truth of Q, where Q *could be anything at all*.[20] Beall's preferred account of logic quarantines the contradictory explosion by denying the logical validity of certain inference forms required to derive the contradiction. For instance, his view denies the logical validity of *Disjunctive Syllogism*. On Beall's view, yes, there is a contradiction, but it doesn't explode.

Consider next the second variety of response to the fundamental problem. This response reenvisions divinity and/or humanity, denying that some set of features *really* belong to either type of entity. This is often done in tandem, with some allegedly divine predicates being denied as well as some allegedly human predicates.

Concerning the allegedly divine predicates, some argue that the classical conception of God, which Cross references in his explication of the Fundamental Problem, is faulty. Perhaps we are wrong to think that God must be impassible, immutable, atemporal, and simple. As such, no instance of the fundamental problem that includes those features will be sound. The opponent of Classical Theism will deny the opening claim in each case—the claim that God must be immutable, or that God must be impassible, and so forth.

Others, rather than denying the truth of classical theism, instead revise our understanding of classical theism. For instance, Michael Gorman, in a move isomorphic to the merely/fully move discussed below, writes,

> My suggestion is that it is enough to give us a form of classical theism, one claiming not that every divine being is immaterial, but, more carefully, that every *solely* divine being is immaterial. (Gorman 2016: 283)

Here, the idea is that Classical Theism is true, but not every divine being must be immaterial on Classical Theism. The same move can apply to other allegedly divine predicates.

Considering the allegedly human predicates, the most common strategy in the current debate begins by making a distinction between things that are merely human

---

[18] For more on relative identity with respect to the incarnation, see Conn (2012) and Jedwab (2015, 2018). My thanks to Joseph Jedwab for his patient help in understanding the relative identity response to the Fundamental Problem.
[19] See Beall (2019).
[20] I discuss this in more detail in Pawl (2016d: 84–5).

and those that are fully human.[21] Something is *fully human* if it is a complete instance of humanity. Something is *merely human* if it is a complete instance of humanity *and* it is not an instance of any other natural kind. All humans except for Jesus (on the traditional Christian picture) are both fully and merely human. But Jesus (and only Jesus) is fully human but not merely human. Rather, he is fully human and fully God, not merely either.

To see how this distinction helps, consider the instance of the Fundamental Problem that focuses on power. Such an argument claims that all humans are limited in power in some way. The proponent of the merely/fully distinction will note that that claim admits of an ambiguity. Does it mean that anything *fully* human is limited in power, or that anything *merely* human is limited in power? If understood the first way, the proponent of this distinction will deny the premise. If understood the second way, the proponent can concede the truth of the premise but deny its relevance to the case of Christ—perhaps all *mere* humans are limited in power; since Christ is no mere human, such a conditional will not apply to him. As such, reasoning to Christ's limitation in power from this premise is invalid. On neither interpretation, then, will the argument be sound.

The proponent of this second variety of response hopes that together, these two moves concerning the alleged predicates of divine and human things serve to eliminate at least one predicate from each candidate pair of predicates (e.g., eliminate *limited in power*, eliminate *immutable*, etc.).[22]

Consider the third variety of response. This response accepts classical logic, accepts the inconsistency of claiming the candidate pairs of Christ at the same time, in the same respect, but denies that they are said *at the same time*. The most common version of this response is called *Kenotic Christology*, based on its scriptural motivation from Phil. 2:6–8, where Paul talks of Christ emptying himself, taking the form of a slave. The main idea here is that Christ has the alleged divine predicates apt of him while preincarnate, but that he *gives up* those features while incarnate. As such, while non-incarnate, he has the divine features; while incarnate, he has the human ones, at no time does he have both incompatible predicates apt of himself.[23] Since contradictions require the truth of both a proposition and its negation *at the same time*, we have not derived a contradiction here. Problem solved.[24]

Consider the fourth variety of response. This response admits classical logic, admits the inconsistency of claiming the candidate pairs of Christ at the same time, in the same respect, admits that they are said at the same time, but denies that they are said *in the same respect*. This approach most often employs *qua locutions*—statements of the form "Christ is immutable *qua divine*" and "Christ is mutable *qua human*." The idea here is to find some way of claiming that there is no contradiction, owing to the fact that a necessary condition for a contradiction—the proposition being both true and false at the same time *in the same respect*—goes unsatisfied.

This variety of response has fallen on hard times in the literature, in large part because it often is not elaborated. One is told that Christ is immutable as God and mutable as man,

---

[21]This distinction is often traced back to Thomas Morris (1987: 65–7), but one finds it at least as far back as John of Damascus (2000: 283) in the eighth century AD.
[22]I have argued that such a strategy will fail to be consistent with Conciliar Christology; see (Pawl 2016d: 97–104).
[23]For more on Kenosis, see Archer (2017), Crisp (2007b: chapter 5), Davis (2011), Evans (2006), Le Poidevin (2009b: section 6), Senor (2011), and Thompson (2006).
[24]I have argued elsewhere that Kenotic Christology fails to be consistent with Conciliar Christology; see Pawl (2016d: 104–16).

but one isn't told how this is supposed to show the contradiction to be thwarted.[25] There are no fewer than six ways of interpreting how these qua locutions work, depending on which portion of the predications is modified by the "qua," and on whether that modification includes a variable or not.[26] For example, one might think that the modifier is attached to the predicate itself, such that Christ isn't impassible and passible *simpliciter* but rather is impassible-*as-God* and passible-*as-man*. In such a case, this response claims, when properly understood with the "qua" additions, the predicates *really* said of Christ are not incompatible. Likewise, using the same example, one might distinguish between theories that claim that the predicate has "built-in" types and those that have variables for the types. Are there various predicates—mutable-as-man; mutable-as-canine; mutable-as-bovine, and so forth—or is there only one predicate that includes an embedded variable—mutable-as-x?[27]

Finally, consider the fifth variety of response to the Fundamental Problem. This response accepts classical logic, unlike the relative identity response and Beall's response. In addition, it denies the incompatibility of the allegedly divine and human predicates, unlike every other response. Even said at the same time, in the same respect, of one and the same thing, these predicates do not yield a contradiction. How could such a response go?

I have argued for one such response elsewhere (Pawl 2014a; 2016d: chapter 7). Using the example of impassibility and passibility, I have argued that when properly understood, one and the same thing can be impassible and passible at the same time, in the same respect. What is the proper understanding of the terms that safeguards their consistency in the case of Christ?

Does being impassible require that a thing have no nature that is causally affectable? Or does it require instead that it have at least one nature that is not causally affectable? Where does one put the negation: out front, as in the first case, or more narrowly, in the second case. If we understand impassibility in the second way, then to be impassible and passible is to have a nature that can be causally affected and also a (different) nature that cannot be causally affected. Christ, on this view, fulfills both of those conditions, and so Christ is both passible and impassible.[28] You and I are passible and not impassible; the Father and Holy Spirit are impassible and not passible. But in the unique case of Christ, owing to the hypostatic union of two natures in one person, the truth conditions for being both passible and impassible can be satisfied. The same reasoning—moving the negation from the outside to the inside—can work for the other allegedly incompatible pairs of predicates.

One might wonder here: in what sense are these allegedly incompatible divine and human predicates said in the same respect of Christ? In reply, Christ is said to be passible in exactly the same way that you are: you and Christ both have natures that are causally affectable. And he is said to be impassible in exactly the same way that the Father is: they both have a nature that is not causally affectable. Those two predicates would imply a

---

[25] For this variety of objection, see Morris (1987: 48–9), van Inwagen (1998: section 4) and Holland (2012: 74).
[26] See Pawl (2016d: chapter 6) for an in-depth discussion of them all.
[27] See Gorman (2014; 2016; 2017: chapter 6) and Labooy (2019) for a recent sympathetic discussion of these "qua" clause strategies. The view under discussion differs from the relative identity view, insofar as this view adds a modification to the predication, whereas the relative identity view adds the modification to identity claims.
[28] As it happens, one can find the view spelled out by Gabriel Biel (died 1495) hundreds of years ago. I thank Richard Cross for pointing this out to me.

contradiction were they both said of you (owing to the fact that you have but a single nature). Since they would be contradictory when said of you, they must be said in the same respect of you in such a case. But they are said in those very same senses of Christ as they would be of you. So they are said in the same respect of Christ as well.

VI. CONCLUSION

There are other areas of debate in the contemporary discussion in analytic theology that do not fit neatly into the previous sections. Some discuss whether multiple incarnations are possible.[29] Some discuss whether Christ's wills could contradict one another, or whether his having two wills or two consciousnesses implies that there are two persons in the incarnation.[30] There is discussion of whether Christ's wills are free.[31] About whether Christ is impeccable, or merely sinless.[32] About what Christ knew, and when Christ knew it.[33] There is discussion of the ontology of Christ's human nature with respect to his death.[34] Some discuss the relation between modern biology and the incarnation.[35] In this brief chapter, I have outlined the recent discussions concerning the incarnation in the analytic theology literature. I grouped the topics under the headings of the ontology of the human nature of Christ, the number and type of components of Christ's assumed human nature, the understanding of the hypostatic union, and the fundamental philosophical objection to the incarnation.[36]

References

Adams, M. M. (1985), "The Metaphysics of the Incarnation in Some Fourteenth-Century Franciscans," in W. A. Frank and G. J. Etzkorn (eds.), *Essays Honoring Allan B. Wolter*, 21–57, New York: Franciscan Institute.

---

[29]For multiple incarnations, see Adams (1985; 2006: 198–9; 2009: 241), Adams and Cross 2005), Baker (2013: 47), Bonting (2003), Brazier (2013), Craig (2006: 63), Crisp (2008; 2009: chapter 8), Cross (2005: 230–2), Davies (2003), Fisher and Fergusson (2006), Flint (2001b: 312; 2012: 192–8), Freddoso (1983; 1986), George (2001), Hebblethwaite (2001; 2008: 74), Jaeger (2017), Kereszty (2002: 382), Kevern (2002), Mascall (1965: 40–41), Morris (1987: 183), Pawl (2016a; 2016c; 2019: chapters 2 and 3), Le Poidevin (2009a: 183; 2011), O'Collins (2002: 19–23), Sturch (1991: 43, 194–200), and Ward (1998: 162).

[30]See Moreland and Craig (2003: 611–13) and Wessling (2013). Concerning consciousnesses, see Arcadi (2016) and Loke (2017, 2018).

[31]See Flint (2001a), Gaine (2015: chapter 7), Hebblethwaite (2008: 68), Hick (1989: 442; 2006: 56), Kereszty (2002: 392–6), Moloney (2009), McFarland (2007), McKinley (2015), Morris (1987: 153), Pawl (2014c; 2014b; 2019: chapters 5–6), Pawl and Timpe (2016), Rogers (2016), and Sturch (1991: 29, 167).

[32]See Arendzen (1941: 181–4), Banks (1973: 50–5), Canham (2000: 95), Couehoven (2012: 406–7), Crisp (2007a,c), Davidson (2008: 395), Dahms (1978: 373), Erickson (1996: 562), Fisk (2007), Gaine (2015: 168–72), King (2015: 73–6), Knox (1967: 47–52), Morris (1987: chapter 7), Murray and Rea (2008: 82–90), O'Collins (1995: 283–4), Pelser (2019), Sturch (1991: 19–20), Swinburne (1994: 204–7), Ware (2013: chapter 5), Wellum (2016: 459–65), and Werther (1993: 2012).

[33]See Archer (2017), Gaine (2015: chapter 6), Loke (2013), de Margerie (1980), Moloney (2000), Pawl (2019b: chapters 7, 8), Rosenberg (2010), Scarpelli (2007), Speer (1993), and Wellum (2016: 454–9).

[34]See Jaeger (2017), Jaeger and Sienkiewicz (2018), and Nevitt (2016).

[35]See, for instance, Dumsday (2017).

[36]I thank the John Templeton Foundation, which funded some research time for this chapter with an Academic Cross Training grant: ID#61012. I also thank the Logos Institute for Analytic and Exegetical Theology for a Senior Research Fellowship, during which I wrote this chapter.

Adams, M. M. (1999), *What Sort of Human Nature? Medieval Philosophy and the Systematics of Christology*, Milwaukee: Marquette University Press.

Adams, M. M. (2006), *Christ and Horrors: The Coherence of Christology*, 1st ed., Cambridge: Cambridge University Press.

Adams, M. M. (2009), "Christ as God-Man, Metaphysically Construed," in M. C. Rea (ed.), *Oxford Readings in Philosophical Theology*, 239–63, Oxford: Oxford University Press.

Adams, M. M. and R. Cross. (2005), "What's Metaphysically Special About Supposits? Some Medieval Variations on Aristotelian Substance," *Aristotelian Society Supplementary Volume*, 79 (1): 15–52.

Arcadi, J. M. (2016), "Andrew Ter Ern Loke: A Kryptic Model of the Incarnation," *Journal of Analytic Theology* 4 (1): 459–63.

Arcadi, J. M. (2018), "Recent Developments in Analytic Christology," *Philosophy Compass*, 13 (4).

Archer, J. (2017), "Kenosis, Omniscience, and the Anselmian Concept of Divinity," *Religious Studies*, 54 (2): 201–13.

Arendzen, J. P. (1941), *Whom Do You Say-?: A Study in the Doctrine of the Incarnation*. New York: Sheed and Ward.

Bäck, A. T. (1998), "Scotus on the Consistency of the Incarnation and the Trinity," *Vivarium*, 36 (1): 83–107.

Bäck, A. T. (2008), "Aquinas on the Incarnation," *The New Scholasticism*, 56 (2): 127–45.

Baker, K. (2013), *Jesus Christ – True God and True Man: A Handbook on Christology for Non-Theologians*, South Bend: Saint Augustine's Press.

Banks, W. L. (1973), *The Day Satan Met Jesus*, Chicago: Moody Press.

Bartel, T. W. (1995), "Why the Philosophical Problems of Chalcedonian Christology Have Not Gone Away," *The Heythrop Journal*, 36 (2): 153–72.

Bavinck, H. (2006), *Reformed Dogmatics, Vol. 3: Sin and Salvation in Christ*, Grand Rapids, MI: Baker Academic.

Beall, J. (2019), "Christ – a Contradiction: A Defense of Contradictory Christology," *Journal of Analytic Theology*, 7: 400–33.

Bonting, S. L. (2003), "Theological Implications of Possible Extraterrestrial Life," *Zygon*, 38 (3): 587–602.

Brazier, P. (2013), "C. S. Lewis: The Question of Multiple Incarnations," *The Heythrop Journal*, 55 (3): 391–408.

Canham, M. M. (2000), "Potuit Non Peccare Or Non Potuit Peccare: Evangelicals, Hermeneutics, and the Impeccability Debate," *The Master's Seminary Journal*, 11 (1): 93–114.

Chemnitz, M. (1971), *The Two Natures in Christ*, Saint Louis: Concordia.

Conn, C. H. (2012), "Relative Identity, Singular Reference, and the Incarnation: A Response to Le Poidevin," *Religious Studies*, 48 (1): 61–82.

Couenhoven, J. (2012), "The Necessities of Perfected Freedom," *International Journal of Systematic Theology* 14 (4): 396–419.

Craig, W. L. (2006), "Flint's Radical Molinist Christology Not Radical Enough, *Faith and Philosophy*, 23 (1): 55–64.

Crisp, O. D. (2007a), "William Shedd on Christ's Impeccability," *Philosophia Christi*, 9 (1): 165–88.

Crisp, O. D., (2007b), *Divinity and Humanity: The Incarnation Reconsidered*, Cambridge: Cambridge University Press.

Crisp, O. D. (2007c), "Was Christ Sinless or Impeccable?," *Irish Theological Quarterly*, 72 (2): 168–86.

Crisp, O. D. (2008), "Multiple Incarnations," in M. W. F. Stone (ed.), *Reason, Faith and History: Philosophical Essays for Paul Helm*, 219–38, Aldershot: Ashgate.

Crisp, O. D. (2009), *God Incarnate: Explorations in Christology*, New York: T&T Clark.

Crisp, O. D. (2011), "Compositional Christology without Nestorianism," in A. Marmodoro and J. Hill (eds.), *The Metaphysics of the Incarnation*, 45–66, Oxford: Oxford University Press.

Crisp, O. D. (2016), *The Word Enfleshed: Exploring the Person and Work of Christ*, Grand Rapids, MI: Baker Academic.

Cross, R. (1996), "Alloiosis in the Christology of Zwingly," *Journal of Theological Studies*, 47 (1): 105–22.

Cross, R. (2002), "Individual Natures in the Christology of Leontius of Byzantium," *Journal of Early Christian Studies*, 10 (2): 245–65.

Cross, R. (2005), *The Metaphysics of the Incarnation: Thomas Aquinas to Duns Scotus*, New York: Oxford University Press.

Cross, R. (2011), "The Incarnation," in T. P. Flint and M. C. Rea (eds.), *The Oxford Handbook of Philosophical Theology*, 452–75, New York: Oxford University Press.

Cross, R. (2019), *Communicatio Idiomatum: Reformation Christological Debates*. Oxford: Oxford University Press.

Dahms, J. V. (1978), "How Reliable Is Logic," *Journal of the Evangelical Theological Society*, 21 (4): 369–80.

Dalmau, J. (2016), *On the One and Triune God*, trans. Kenneth Baker, vol. IIA, Sacrae Theologiae Summa IIA, Saddle River: Keep the Faith.

Davidson, I. J. (2008), "Pondering the Sinlessness of Jesus Christ: Moral Christologies and the Witness of Scripture," *International Journal of Systematic Theology* 10 (4): 372–98.

Davies, P. (2003), "ET and God," *The Atlantic Monthly*, 292 (2): 112–18.

Davis, S. T. (2006), "Is Kenosis Orthodox," in C. S. Evans (ed.), *Exploring Kenotic Christology*, 112–38, Oxford: Oxford University Press.

Davis, S. T. (2011), "The Metaphysics of Kenosis," in A. Marmodoro and J. Hill (eds.), *The Metaphysics of the Incarnation*, 114–33, New York: Oxford University Press.

Dawson, S. (2004), "Is There a Contradiction in the Person of Christ? The Importance of the Dual Nature and Dual Consciousness of Jesus Christ," *Detroit Baptist Seminary Journal*, 9: 161–81.

de Margerie, Bertrand (1980), *Human Knowledge of Christ: The Knowledge, Fore-Knowledge and Consciousness, Even in the Pre-Paschal Period, of Christ the Redeemer*, Boston: Pauline Books & Media.

Denzinger, H. (2002), *The Sources of Catholic Dogma*, Fitzwilliam: Loreto Publications.

Dubray, C. (1911), "Nature," in *The Catholic Encyclopedia*, vol. 10, New York: Robert Appleton Company. Available online: http://www.newadvent.org/cathen/10715a.htm.

Dumsday, T. (2017), "How Modern Biological Taxonomy Sheds Light on the Incarnation," *Journal of Analytic Theology*, 5: 163–74.

Erickson, M. J. (1996), *The Word Became Flesh: A Contemporary Incarnational Christology*, Grand Rapids, MI: Baker Academic.

Evans, C. S. (2006), *Exploring Kenotic Christology: The Self-Emptying of God*, Oxford: Oxford University Press.

Feenstra, R. (2006), "A Kenotic Christology of Divine Attributes," in C. S. Evans (ed.), *Exploring Kenotic Christology*, 139–64, Oxford: Oxford University Press.

Fisher, C. L., and D. Fergusson. (2006), "Karl Rahner and The Extra-Terrestrial Intelligence Question," *The Heythrop Journal*, 47 (2): 275–90.

Fisk, P. J. (2007), "Jonathan Edwards's Freedom of the Will and His Defence of the Impeccability of Jesus Christ," *Scottish Journal of Theology*, 60 (3): 309–25.

Flint, T. P. (2001a), "'A Death He Freely Accepted': Molinist Reflections on the Incarnation," *Faith and Philosophy*, 18 (1): 3–20.

Flint, T. P. (2001b), "The Possibilities of Incarnation: Some Radical Molinist Suggestions," *Religious Studies*, 37 (3): 307–20.

Flint, T. P. (2011), "Should Concretists Part with Mereological Models of the Incarnation?," in A. Marmodoro and J. Hill (eds.), *The Metaphysics of the Incarnation*, 67–87, New York: Oxford University Press.

Flint, T. P. (2012), "Molinism and Incarnation," in K. Perszyk (ed.), *Molinism: The Contemporary Debate*, 187–207, Oxford: Oxford University Press.

Flint, T. P. (2015), "Is Model T Rattle-Free?," *Faith and Philosophy*, 32 (2): 177–81.

Freddoso, A. (1983), "Logic, Ontology and Ockham's Christology," *The New Scholasticism*, 57 (3): 293–330.

Freddoso, A. (1986), "Human Nature, Potency and the Incarnation," *Faith and Philosophy*, 3 (1): 27–53.

Gaine, S. F. (2015), *Did the Saviour See the Father?*, London: T&T Clark.

Geddes, L. (1911), "Person," in *The Catholic Encyclopedia*, vol. 11, New York: Robert Appleton Company. Available online: http://www.newadvent.org/cathen/11726a.htm.

Geisler, N. L., and W.D. Watkins. (1985), "The Incarnation and Logic: Their Compatibility Defended," *Trinity Journal*, 6 (2): 185–97.

George, M. I. (2001), "Aquinas on Intelligent Extra-Terrestrial Life," *The Thomist* 65 (2): 239–58.

Gordon, J. R. (2016), *The Holy One in Our Midst: An Essay on the Flesh of Christ*, Minneapolis: Fortress Press.

Gorman, M. (2000), "Personal Unity and the Problem of Christ's Knowledge," *Proceedings of the American Catholic Philosophical Association*, 74: 175–86.

Gorman, M. (2011), "Incarnation," in B. Davies and E. Stump (eds.), *The Oxford Handbook of Aquinas*, 428–35, Oxford: Oxford University Press.

Gorman, M. (2014), "Christological Consistency and the Reduplicative Qua," *Journal of Analytic Theology*, 2: 86–100.

Gorman, M. (2016), "Classical Theism, Classical Anthropology, and the Christological Coherence Problem," *Faith and Philosophy*, 33 (3): 278–92.

Gorman, M. (2017), *Aquinas on the Metaphysics of the Hypostatic Union*, Cambridge: Cambridge University Press.

Guta, M. P. (2019), "The Two Natures of the Incarnate Christ and the Bearer Question," *TheoLogica: An International Journal for Philosophy of Religion and Philosophical Theology*, 2 (3): 1–31.

Hasker, W. (2015), "Getting That Model T Back On the Road," *Faith and Philosophy*, 32 (2): 172–6.

Hasker, W. (2017a), "A Compositional Incarnation," *Religious Studies*, 53 (4): 433–47.

Hasker, W. (2017b), "Incarnation: The Avatar Model," in J. Kvanvig (ed.), *Oxford Studies in Philosophy of Religion*, vol. 8, 118–41, Oxford: Oxford University Press.

Hebblethwaite, B. (2001), "The Impossibility of Multiple Incarnations," *Theology*, 104 (821): 323–34.

Hebblethwaite, B. (2008), *Philosophical Theology and Christian Doctrine*, Oxford: John Wiley & Sons.

Hick, J. (1989), "The Logic of God Incarnate," *Religious Studies*, 25 (4): 409–23.

Hick, J. (2006), *The Metaphor of God Incarnate: Christology in a Pluralistic Age*, 2nd ed., Louisville: Westminster John Knox Press.

Hill, J. (2011). "Introduction," in A. Marmodoro and J. Hill (eds.), *The Metaphysics of the Incarnation*, 1–19, Oxford: Oxford University Press.

Hill, J. (2012), "Incarnation, Timelessness, and Exaltation," *Faith and Philosophy*, 29 (1): 3–29.

Hipp, S. (2001), *"Person" in Christian Tradition and in the Conception of Saint Albert the Great*, Münster: Aschendorff.

Holland, R. A. (2012), *God, Time, and the Incarnation*, Eugene: Wipf and Stock.

Jaeger, A. (2017), "Hylemorphic Animalism and the Incarnational Problem of Identity," *Journal of Analytic Theology*, 5: 145–62.

Jaeger, A. J., and J. Sienkiewicz (2018), "Matter without Form: The Ontological Status of Christ's Dead Body," *Journal of Analytic Theology*, 6: 131–45.

Jedwab, J. (2015), "Against the Geachian Theory of the Trinity and Incarnation," *Faith and Philosophy*, 32 (2): 125–45.

Jedwab, J. (2018), "Timothy Pawl. In Defense of Conciliar Christology," *Journal of Analytic Theology*, 6: 743–47.

Kelly, C. J. (1994), "The God of Classical Theism and the Doctrine of the Incarnation," *International Journal for Philosophy of Religion*, 35 (1): 1–20.

Kereszty, R. A. (2002), *Jesus Christ: Fundamentals of Christology*, revised and updated 3rd ed., Staten Island: Alba House.

Kevern, P. (2002), "Limping Principles A Reply to Brian Hebblethwaite on 'The Impossibility of Multiple Incarnations'," *Theology*, 105 (827): 342–47.

King, R. (2015), "Atonement and the Completed Perfection of Human Nature," *International Journal of Philosophy and Theology*, 76 (1): 69–84.

Klima, G. (1984), "Libellus Pro Sapiente," *New Scholasticism*, 58 (2): 207–19.

Knox, J. (1967), *The Humanity and Divinity of Christ: A Study of Pattern in Christology*, Cambridge: Cambridge University Press.

Labooy, G. H. (2019), "Stepped Characterisation: A Metaphysical Defence of qua-Propositions in Christology," *International Journal for Philosophy of Religion*, 86 (1): 25–38.

Le Poidevin, R. (2009a), "Identity and the Composite Christ: An Incarnational Dilemma," *Religious Studies*, 45 (2): 167–86.

Le Poidevin, R. (2009b), "Incarnation: Metaphysical Issues," *Philosophy Compass*, 4 (4): 703–14.

Le Poidevin, R. (2011), "Multiple Incarnations and Distributed Persons," in A. Marmodoro and J. Hill (eds.), *The Metaphysics of the Incarnation*, 228–41, Oxford: Oxford University Press.

Leftow, B. (2004), "A Timeless God Incarnate," in S. T. Davis, D. Kendall, and G. O'Collins (eds.), *The Incarnation*, 273–99, Oxford: Oxford University Press.

Leftow, B. (2011), "Composition and Christology," *Faith and Philosophy*, 28 (3): 310–22.

Leftow, B. (2015), "Against Materialist Christology," in C. P. Ruloff (ed.), *Christian Philosophy of Religion: Essays in Honor of Stephen T. Davis*, 65–94, Notre Dame, IN: University of Notre Dame Press.

Lim, J. (2019), "In Defense of Physicalist Christology," *Sophia*, Available online: https://doi.org/10.1007/s11841-019-0718-5.

Loke, A. (2009), "On the Coherence of the Incarnation: The Divine Preconscious Model," *Neue Zeitschrift Für Systematische Theologie Und Religionsphilosophie*, 51 (1): 50–63.

Loke, A. (2011), "Solving a Paradox against Concrete-Composite Christology: A Modified Hylomorphic Proposal," *Religious Studies*, 47 (4): 493–502.

Loke, A. (2013), "The Incarnation and Jesus' Apparent Limitation in Knowledge," *New Blackfriars*, 94 (1053): 583–602.

Loke, A. (2017), "On the Use of Psychological Models in Christology," *The Heythrop Journal* 58 (1): 44–50.

Loke, A. (2018), "On the Two Consciousnesses Model: An Assessment of James Arcadi's Defense," *Journal of Analytic Theology*, 6: 146–50.

Macquarrie, J. (1990), *Jesus Christ in Modern Thought*, London: SCM Press.

Marmodoro, A., and J. Hill (2008), "Modeling the Metaphysics of the Incarnation," *Philosophy and Theology*, 20 (1/2): 99–128.

Mascall, E. L. (1965), *Christian Theology and Natural Science: Some Questions in Their Relations*, Hamden: Archon Books.

McFarland, I. (2007), "'Willing Is Not Choosing': Some Anthropological Implications of Dyothelite Christology," *International Journal of Systematic Theology*, 9 (1): 3–23.

McKinley, J. E. (2015), "A Model of Jesus Christ's Two Wills in View of Theology Proper and Anthropology," *Southern Baptist Journal of Theology*, 19 (1): 69–89.

Merricks, T. (2007), "The Word Made Flesh: Dualism, Physicalism, and the Incarnation," in P. van Inwagen and D. Zimmerman (eds.), *Persons: Human and Divine*, 281–301, Oxford: Oxford University Press.

Moloney, R. (2000), *Knowledge of Christ*, London: Bloomsbury Academic.

Moloney, R. (2009), "The Freedom of Christ in the Early Lonergan," *Irish Theological Quarterly*, 74 (1): 27–37.

Moreland, J. P., and W. L. Craig (2003), *Philosophical Foundations for a Christian Worldview*, Downers Grove, IL: IVP Academic.

Morris, T. V. (1987), *The Logic of God Incarnate*, Ithaca, NY: Cornell University Press.

Morris, T. V. (2002), *Our Idea of God: An Introduction to Philosophical Theology*, Vancouver: Regent College.

Morris, T. V. (2009), "The Metaphysics of God Incarnate," in M. C. Rea and T. P. Flint (eds.), *Oxford Readings in Philosophical Theology*, 211–24. Oxford: Oxford University Press.

Moulder, J. (1986), "Is a Chalcedonian Christology Coherent?," *Modern Theology*, 2 (4): 285–307.

Murray, M. and M. C. Rea. (2008), *An Introduction to the Philosophy of Religion*, Cambridge: Cambridge University Press.

Nevitt, T. C. (2016), "Aquinas on the Death of Christ," *American Catholic Philosophical Quarterly*, 90 (1): 77–99.

O'Collins, G. (1995), *Christology: A Biblical, Historical, and Systematic Study of Jesus Christ*, Oxford: Oxford University Press.

O'Collins, G. (2002), "The Incarnation: The Critical Issues," in S. T. Davis, D. Kendall, and G. O'Collins (eds.), *The Incarnation*, 1–30, Oxford: Oxford University Press.

Pawl, T. (2014a), "A Solution to the Fundamental Philosophical Problem of Christology," *The Journal of Analytic Theology*, 2: 61–85.

Pawl, T. (2014b), "The Freedom of Christ and Explanatory Priority," *Religious Studies*, 50 (2): 157–73.

Pawl, T. (2014c), "The Freedom of Christ and the Problem of Deliberation," *International Journal for Philosophy of Religion*, 75 (3): 233–47.

Pawl, T. (2015), "Conciliar Christology and the Problem of Incompatible Predications," *Scientia et Fides*, 3 (2): 85–106.

Pawl, T. (2016a), "Brian Hebblethwaite's Arguments against Multiple Incarnations," *Religious Studies*, 52 (1): 117–30.

Pawl, T. (2016b), "Temporary Intrinsics and Christological Predication," in J. L. Kvanvig (ed.), *Oxford Studies in Philosophy of Religion*, vol. 7, 157–89, Oxford: Oxford University Press.

Pawl, T. (2016c), "Thomistic Multiple Incarnations," *The Heythrop Journal*, 57 (2): 359–70.
Pawl, T. (2016d), *In Defense of Conciliar Christology: A Philosophical Essay*, Oxford: Oxford University Press.
Pawl, T. (2018), "Conciliar Christology and the Consistency of Divine Immutability with a Mutable, Incarnate God," *Nova et Vetera*, 16 (3): 913–37.
Pawl, T. (2019a), 'Explosive Theology: A Reply to Jc Beall's 'Christ – a Contradiction'," *Journal of Analytic Theology*, 7: 440–51.
Pawl, T. (2019b), *In Defense of Extended Conciliar Christology: A Philosophical Essay*, Oxford : Oxford University Press.
Pawl, T. (2020a), *The Incarnation*. Cambridge: Cambridge University Press.
Pawl, T. (2020b), "The Metaphysics of the Incarnation: Christ's Human Nature," in T. Marschler and T. Schärtl (eds.), *Herausforderungen des klassischen Theismus*, Bd. 2: Inkarnation, 131–48, Münster: Aschendorff.
Pawl, T., and K. Timpe. (2016), "Freedom and the Incarnation," *Philosophy Compass*, 11 (11): 743–56.
Pelser, A. (2019), "Temptation, Virtue, And The Character Of Christ," *Faith and Philosophy*, 36 (1): 81–101.
Plantinga, A. (1999), "On Heresy, Mind, and Truth," *Faith and Philosophy*, 16 (2): 182–93.
Pohle, J. (1911), *The Divine Trinity: A Dogmatic Treatise*, St. Louis: B. Herder.
Rea, M. (2011), "Hylomorphism and the Incarnation," in A. Marmodoro and J. Hill (eds.), *The Metaphysics of the Incarnation*, 134–52, Oxford: Oxford University Press.
Riches, A. (2016), *Ecce Homo: On the Divine Unity of Christ*, Grand Rapids, MI: Eerdmans.
Rogers, K. A. (2010), "Incarnation," in C. Taliaferro and C. V. Meister (eds.), *The Cambridge Companion to Christian Philosophical Theology*, 95–107, Cambridge: Cambridge University Press.
Rogers, K. A. (2013), "The Incarnation as Action Composite," *Faith and Philosophy*, 30 (3): 251–70.
Rogers, K. A. (2016), "Christ's Freedom: Anselm vs Molina," *Religious Studies*, 52 (4): 497–512.
Rosenberg, R. S. (2010), "Christ's Human Knowledge: A Conversation with Lonergan and Balthasar," *Theological Studies*, 71 (4): 817–45.
Scarpelli, T. (2007), "Bonaventure's Christocentric Epistemology: Christ's Human Knowledge as the Epitome of Illumination in De Scientia Christi," *Franciscan Studies*, 65 (1): 63–86.
Senor, T. D. (2002), "Incarnation, Timelessness, and Leibniz's Law Problems," in G. E. Ganssle and D. M. Woodruff (eds.), *God and Time: Essays on the Divine Nature*, 220–35, Oxford: Oxford University Press.
Senor, T. D. (2011), "Drawing on Many Traditions: An Ecumenical Kenotic Christology," in A. Marmodoro and J. Hill (eds.), *The Metaphysics of the Incarnation*, 88–113, Oxford: Oxford University Press.
Sharpe, K. W. (2017), "The Incarnation, Soul-Free: Physicalism, Kind Membership, and the Incarnation," *Religious Studies*, 53 (1): 117–31.
Sollier, J. (1907), "Apollinarianism," in *The Catholic Encyclopedia*, New York: Robert Appleton. Available online: http://www.newadvent.org/cathen/01615b.htm.
Speer, A. (1993), "The Certainty and Scope of Knowledge: Bonaventure's Disputed Questions on the Knowledge of Christ," *Medieval Philosophy & Theology*, 3: 35–61.
Spence, A. (2008), *Christology: A Guide for the Perplexed*, London: T&T Clark.
St. John of Damascus (2000), *Saint John of Damascus: Writings*, trans. F. H. Chase, Washington, DC: Catholic University of America Press.

Stump, E. (1989), "Review of Morris' The Logic of God Incarnate," *Faith and Philosophy*, 6: 218–23.
Stump, E. (2004), "Aquinas's Metaphysics of the Incarnation," in S. T. Davis, D. Kendall, and G. O'Collins (eds.), *The Incarnation*, 197–218, Oxford: Oxford University Press.
Stump, E. (2005), *Aquinas*, New York: Routledge.
Sturch, R. (1991), *The Word and the Christ: An Essay in Analytic Christology*, Oxford: Oxford University Press.
Swinburne, R. (1994), *The Christian God*, Oxford: Oxford University Press.
Tanner, N. P. (1990), *Decrees of the Ecumenical Councils*, Washington, DC: Georgetown University Press.
Thompson, T. R. (2006), "Nineteenth-Century Kenotic Christology: The Waxing, Waning, and Weighing of a Quest for a Coherent Orthodoxy," in C. S. Evans (ed.), *Exploring Kenotic Christology*, 74–111, Oxford: Oxford University Press.
Turner, J. T. (2017), "On Two Reasons Christian Theologians Should Reject The Intermediate State," *Journal of Reformed Theology*, 11 (1–2): 121–39.
Turner, J. T. (2019), "Hylemorphism, Rigid Designators, and the Disembodied 'Jesus': A Call for Clarification," *Religious Studies*, online first, 1–16. Available online: https://doi.org/10.1017/S0034412519000040.
Vallicella, W. F. (2002), "Incarnation and Identity," *Philo*, 5 (1): 84–93.
van Driel, E. C.. (2008), *Incarnation Anyway: Arguments for Supralapsarian Christology*, Oxford: Oxford University Press.
Van Horn, Luke. (2010), "Merricks's Soulless Savior," *Faith and Philosophy*, 27 (3): 330–41.
van Inwagen, P. (1998), "Incarnation and Christology," in E. Craig (ed.), *Routledge Encyclopedia of Philosophy*, London: Routledge.
Ward, K. (1998), *God, Faith, and the New Millennium: Christian Belief in an Age of Science*, Oxford: Oneworld.
Ware, B. A. (2013), *The Man Christ Jesus: Theological Questions on the Humanity of Christ*, Wheaton: Crossway.
Wellum, S. J. (2016), *God the Son Incarnate: The Doctrine of Christ*, Wheaton: Crossway.
Werther, D. (1993), "The Temptation of God Incarnate," *Religious Studies*, 29 (1): 47–50.
Werther, D. (2012), "Freedom, Temptation, and Incarnation," in D. Werther and M. Linville (eds.), *Philosophy and the Christian Worldview: Analysis, Assessment and Development*, 252–64, New York: Continuum.
Wessling, J. (2013), "Christology and Conciliar Authority," in O. D. Crisp and F. Sanders (eds.), *Christology: Ancient & Modern*, 151–70, Grand Rapids, MI: Zondervan.

CHAPTER SIXTEEN

Christ's Impeccability

JOHANNES GRÖSSL

I. INTRODUCTION: THE IMPECCABILITY PARADOX

The letter to the Hebrews states that Christ has been tempted "in every respect [we are]...yet without sin" (4:15).[1] For the author, it is crucial that Christ could empathize with our weakness, even that, like us, he "learned obedience" (5:8). If being without sin is solely understood as the retrospective observation that Jesus, living an exemplary human life, did not sin, there seems to be no theological challenge. However, if Christ is understood as possessing a divine nature or even being identical to the second person of the Trinity, he is not only contingently sinless but essentially unable to sin, i.e., impeccable. As Eleonore Stump writes: "Just as it is part of orthodox Christianity that Christ has two natures, one fully divine and one fully human, so it is part of orthodox Christianity both that Christ was really tempted and that Christ was unable to sin" (Stump 2018: 242).

How can an impeccable person be tempted? How can an impeccable person be truly free? Among many others, Stump answers these questions by rejecting the principle of alternate possibilities as a requirement for an agent possessing free will: "Christ could freely refuse Satan's temptations even if it is not true that he could accept them" (242). However, ordinary libertarians will reject such a solution, since they regard the ability to choose between good and evil as an essential attribute of human nature. If being truly human, following this premise, implies the ability to sin and being truly divine implies the inability to sin, a being that possesses both a human and a divine nature cannot be logically conceived. Chalcedonian Christology would either lead us to accept a logical paradox or would need to be rejected.

In this contribution, I will analyze and present possible solutions to this apparent inconsistency. It will be shown that this discussion is closely related to philosophical controversies on the nature of humanity and the nature of free will. If being human does entail free will and if possessing free will entails the ability to choose between morally significant options, one needs to develop more complex Christological models to explain how the two-natures-view is tenable. I will present and evaluate various adoptionist (section 2), unitive (section 3), and disjunctive (sections 4 and 5) Christological attempts to solve the impeccability paradox.

---

[1] Biblical quotations in this chapter are taken from New Revised Standard Version of the Bible.

II. THE EASY WAY OUT: ADOPTIONISM

Some contemporary exegetes argue that the doctrines of Christ's sinlessness and impeccability are only results of "retrospective theologizing," but not based upon historic facts (Siker 2015). The evaluation that Christ was indeed peccable and possibly even sinned is often associated with a rejection of Conciliar Christology, with the consequence that Christ's divinity is either interpreted as a metaphor or described as an *acquired* attribute. Already in the second century, Theodotus of Byzantium claimed that Christ was adopted at his baptism to be God's son. In his theory, Christ was a mere human, possibly a very special human, who, at some time in his life, reached a state in which he was ready to be adopted.[2] Later Adoptionists, such as Paul of Samosata, argue that Christ was a human who, by his own power, kept himself from sinning, which is why he got anointed by the Spirit and given the title "Christ." For most adoptionists, Christ was thus sinless but not impeccable: he did not sin, but could have sinned. He was adopted by God because he did not sin. A more moderate version could even accept that Christ did sin earlier in his life but has developed his character in a way such that he reached a state of sinlessness or even impeccability. Accordingly, different types of Adoptionism with respect to Christ's ability to sin can be discussed:

(A1) Christ could sin, did not sin, and was thus adopted to be Son of God (and made impeccable as a consequence).
(A2) Christ could sin, did sin, and reached a state of sinlessness and was thus adopted to be Son of God (and made impeccable as a consequence).
(A3) Christ could sin, did sin, and reached a state of impeccability by forming perfect virtues and was thus adopted to be Son of God.

These theories are not in conciliar tradition, because the Council of Nicaea rejected all types of Adoptionism and Subordinatianism, for they are incompatible with Christ's true divinity.[3] If a human person becomes deified, as an Irenaean soteriology proposes for all of saved humanity, she does not literally become God: she becomes God*like* or joins into full union with God. But in the conciliar tradition, it is a crucial axiom that Christ enabled human salvation, thus there must be a difference between Christ's divinity and human "divinity." A Preexistence Christology, as defended by the Evangelist John or the Letter to the Philippians, cannot be maintained in an adoptionist setting.

If adoptionism is excluded as a possibility and Christ's preexistence and divinity is defended in a nonmetaphorical way, one needs to discuss how these attributes are compatible with Christ's possessing a human nature and a human (free) will.

III. UNITIVE SOLUTIONS WITH ONE CENTER OF ACTION

The famous theologian and historian, Alois Grillmeier (1982), proposed to distinguish two schools of thought within Christianity in Late Antiquity: one being connected to

---

[2] Theodotus referred to the story of Christ's baptism in Mark 1, where God says, "You are my Son, whom I love. With you I am well pleased." The verb εὐδόκησα can be translated as "have become pleased" or "am pleased," the former points to adoption, the second is compatible with God's "being pleased" from the beginning of Christ's life.
[3] However, Adoptionists are not necessarily Pelagian, as it might seem, since there is plenty of room for requiring God's grace in the redemption process: Christ's being free of original sin could be a work of God; Christ's effort to remain sinless or forming perfect virtues could be assisted by the Holy Spirit.

the city of Alexandria, the other to the city of Antioch. In short, an Alexandrian—or "unitive"—Christology focuses on the unity of Christ's divine and human nature (with Monophysitism being the associated christological heresy), while an Antiochene—or "disjunctive"—Christology emphasizes the distinction between the natures (with Nestorianism being the associated christological heresy). In the two centuries after the Council of Chalcedon, the Alexandrian school dominated, which resulted in a one-sided compromise between the schools, stating that Christ only had one divine energy (*Monenergism*) or will (*Monothelitism*). Even still, the Council of Constantinople in 680/81 rejected both doctrines, claiming that Christ had two wills, one divine and one human; they are intertwined in such a way that the human will necessarily subordinates to the divine will (δεῖ ὑποταγῆναι). Most systematic theologians thus interpret Constantinople III as claiming that Christ had a human "will of the flesh" and a "will to do what God wills" but was not free in a libertarian sense regarding his second-order will to let the divine will prevail over the will of the flesh. It is disputed, however, whether this second-order will belongs to Christ's divine or human nature and whether Christ is free to choose this second-order will. In opposition to the Antiochians, Alexandrian Christologies claim that there is only one center of action in Christ, which determines his higher-order desires, namely, the center of action of the Second Divine Person: The freedom of Christ *is* the freedom of the Logos (Essen 2001: 291; cf. Grillmeier 1982: 625). But, if this is true, what kind of freedom is attributed here?

III.1 Compatibilist Views

If one overviews the history of theology regarding the relationship between Christ's human and divine will, one finds that Christ was not thought to have the power to choose between opposites, especially not the power to act against God's will. Up to today, most theologians concur with Maximus the Confessor's view, which highly influenced the official doctrine of dyothelitism: The Third Council of Constantinople taught that Christ has two wills, one divine and one human. According to Maximus, Christ is fully human, including a creaturely free will, but without having a power to choose evil (Bausenhart 1989: 51). Such a statement is possible only if one accepts a compatibilist view of free will, i.e., that having free will does not entail the power to choose between opposites.

Several variants of compatibilist views can be identified throughout the Christian tradition and within contemporary analytic theology: Semi-compatibilists reject free will but think that moral responsibility is compatible with determinism. Genuine compatibilists believe that free will is, in some cases, compatible with determinism: "Hierarchical compatibilists" believe that a person is free when her first-order desires align with her second-order desires. "Reason-view compatibilists" believe that a person is free when she acts according to reasons instead of inclination or habit (cf. McKenna and Coates 2015: section 4.3). So-called source incompatibilists believe that a person is free when she acts according to her true character (cf. Timpe 2007). These variants can be applied to Christology. One can hold respective views regarding Christ's pre-glorification freedom:

(C1) Christ had no free will and no power to choose, but was able to earn merit for his actions, and also for his not-sinning. *(semi-compatibilism)*
(C2) Christ did not suffer from weakness of will and was therefore free to align his first-order-will with his fixed second-order-desires. *(hierarchical compatibilism)*

(C3) Christ was perfectly reasonable and did not err regarding any information relevant for his moral decisions, thus he was not able to sin. *(reason-view compatibilism)*

(C4) Christ did not suffer from weakness of will or psychological instability, such that he always acted according to his impeccable character. *(source incompatibilism)*

Proponents of C1 are incompatibilists regarding the compatibility of free will and determinism, but compatibilists regarding the compatibility of moral responsibility and determinism, following John Martin Fischer (2009). If moral responsibility attributed to a human being is all that is needed to give a proper account of the atonement, this approach would suffice. However, there are serious doubts about whether semi-compatibilism can account for genuine moral responsibility and accountability. In order to give credit to someone or regard someone as guilty of something, we intuitively require that this person either have the power to do otherwise or at least have had this power in the past.[4]

According to C2, Christ, unlike other human beings, possesses full *freedom of action*: no weakness of will and no conflicting desires. This, however, does not answer to the problem of whether Christ can choose his higher-order desires. Furthermore, it conflicts with the doctrine of the true humanity of Christ, or at least with his true embodiment, because weakness of will is an essential part of our physical existence, at least for the *fallen* human being. But even the un-fallen Christ found himself, according to Scripture at least once (but probably regularly), in a situation when his "will of the flesh" was not aligned to his higher order desires, for example, the wish to do what God wills him to do. A better and moderate version of C2 would thus claim that Christ's willpower was merely sustained or strengthened by the Holy Spirit in morally significant situations, especially during the final temptation in Gethsemane (Stump 2018: 277; cf. Lk. 22:43).

According to the intellectualist position, C3, Christ is prevented from ignorance or error at least in all those of his convictions upon which morally significant decisions are based (cf. White 2008). Adherents of this position claim that no human being can freely act contrary to his intellectual desires. If C3 is combined with moderate C2 (cf. Henderson 2017: 263), one can further preclude weakness of will as a reason for why Christ acts against his better judgment, leading to Christ possessing perfect virtue. Or, reversely, one can follow Leftow's "restricted temptation" view (2014: 14–16) and argue for Christ's being truly, yet blamelessly, tempted due to his natural lack of willpower and knowledge.

However, the intellectualist position would require us to reconsider fundamental ethical assumptions, because in the Western moral and judiciary system, it makes a big difference whether a morally wrong action is committed because of weakness of will, because of ignorance or error, or *despite* sufficient willpower and better knowledge. Accounting for this difference is the strength of a moderate voluntarist position: in order to be morally responsible, one needs to have the power to favor an irrational over a rational option, or at least to choose the less rational of two non-irrational options. Applied to Kantian ethics, one could say that if a person acts arbitrarily and without any

---

[4]According to regular compatibilist positions, Christ had free will and the ability to choose between opposites, but he was in some way hindered in exercising this ability, either by internal or external conditions. If it were sufficient to be truly tempted and to earn merit for withstanding temptations by not knowing about one's immunity to sin (McKinley 2009: 219–43), Christ would suffer the same way we do when we are tempted, but it is hard to conceive how an impeccable Christ could earn merit for not falling into temptation. Brian Leftow (2014: 21–3) discusses the possible solution that Christ's merit for resisting temptation is based on the Logos' decision to become incarnate in the first place.

reasons, she is not considered to be free and responsible; however, if she chooses non-universalizable principle of actions (maxims) over universalizable principle of actions, she is free and morally blameworthy for her choice.

Similarly, position C4 does not solve the problem, at least not at first glance, because it lacks the requirement of having power to choose or at least change one's habits or desires (cf. Leftow 2014: 8, 20). However, there is a very important insight that has been emphasized by so-called restrictive libertarians: our actions are strongly influenced by our character, which is again strongly influenced by our genes, our upbringing, our environment, and culture (cf. Kane 1985; van Inwagen 1989). If we have free will, we can only slightly shift our character in little steps toward good or evil, either according to Kane by rare "self-forming actions," or in Aristotelian tradition by slowly acquiring and developing virtues and overcoming vices. If an impeccable or morally perfect character with completely developed virtues is logically conceivable (Henderson 2017), the power to choose is not essential to the agent (because otherwise no one could ever possess an impeccable character); rather, having such a power is a *property of the character*. A "fully" developed character, whether good or evil, is irreversibly formed; thus it does not allow the agent to change it. A not fully developed character, on the other hand, allows the possessing agent to change it. Thus, libertarian freedom is not a *power to do otherwise,* but only a disposition to do otherwise. This disposition is actualized not only by sufficient cognitive, emotional, and physical capacities, but also by one's character, which determines the scope of possible actions and the scope of possible change in character.

Most patristic models to explicate Christ's inability to sin presume a compatibilist account of free will. Either Christ is impeccable because of his inherent impeccability (McKinley 2009: 97–102), or Christ's human nature is deified and thus made impeccable by the Logos (102–16), or Christ's humanity is directed by the impeccable Logos "in sinless action by his prevailing divine will" (117–31), or alternatively by the Holy Spirit or empowering grace (131–43). According to the pneumatological solution, Christ is prevented from sinning by the Spirit as an external non-compelling influence; this approach may be explicated in a dispositional or libertarian instead of a compatibilist account of free will.

III.2 Dispositional Views

Compatibilist views require that a person can be free without possessing the power to choose between alternate possibilities. When discussing the essential attributes of human nature, it is, however, reasonable to distinguish between the potential to develop a power, the potential to exercise a power, and the actual ability to exercise a power. For example, a 2-year-old can only be regarded as a human if being human does not require possessing morally significant free will. Most people would, however, in accordance with a Christian or Kantian anthropology, attribute being human also to children, the comatose, and strongly disabled or mentally impaired adults, since they all have the *potential* to be or become moral agents. Therefore, "dispositional compatibilists" claim that a person is free when she has the power to do otherwise now or in some possible future, or if a counterfactual analysis shows that she could have done otherwise in certain possible situations.

In order to actualize an ability, one needs to find oneself in a situation in which this ability can be actualized. If one has the ability to swim, but never experiences being located in water, one cannot actualize the disposition. If Christ has morally significant freedom as a power to choose between obligation and inclination, but never finds himself in a situation in which an inclination is strong enough to motivate him to an immoral decision, he could be counted as free and contingently impeccable. A counterfactual analysis would, however, show that he would have been forced to make a morally significant decision if he had found himself in different circumstances. The open question here is whether Christ had the power to bring about such freedom-enabling circumstances. Two options are available:

(D1) Christ had the ability to sin, but never experienced a situation when he could exercise this ability as a power; however, he had the power to bring about such a situation.

(D2) Christ had the ability to sin, but never experienced a situation when he could exercise this ability as a power; he did *not* have the power to bring about such a situation.

Restrictive libertarians can agree with D1: one is culpable even if one does not have the power to act differently than one does in case one has culpably done something or neglected some action in the past that would have given one the power to act differently now. For example, a lack of willpower does not count as an excuse if one has the chance to exercise one's willpower but culpably chooses not to. When one knows about one's weakness of will, one also is responsible to avoid situations of irresistible temptation. According to D2, however, Christ never had the power to bring himself into a situation in which he can sin. Here, it is hard to tell what could prevent him from making such a choice. One needs to postulate a power that guides him not to fall into any real temptation, either by one of the presented compatibilist strategies or by meticulous providence or divine intervention. This, however, very likely entails an infringement not only on Christ's freedom, but on the freedom of all agents surrounding him. Furthermore, it seems plausible that controlling circumstances in order to preclude opportunities for sin does not constitute genuine virtue (Pawl and Timpe 2009: 403).

In order to avoid the question about what prevented Christ from actualizing his ability to sin, one can go further and postulate that he never even developed the ability to sin, thus never became a moral agent, but is nevertheless fully human because he could have developed this ability if he had grown up in different circumstances:

(D3) Christ had the potential to develop the ability to sin; he did not have the power to bring about a situation which would have initiated the development of this ability.

The situation D3 describes is similar to that of a child who has been indoctrinated all of her life and trained to be a child soldier: she is not a moral agent, but could have become one. The same holds for disabilities that result from, for example, lack of oxygen at birth. While some humans are, because of unactualized potential, not able to choose the good, a contingently impeccable Christ is not able to choose evil. Here, the question arises whether Christ still had the power to develop the ability to sin, since this power is not in itself morally reprehensible. One could thus argue that choosing to remain impeccable is a supererogatory work:

(D4) Christ had the potential and the power to develop the ability to sin but chose not to.

With D4, we have integrated a libertarian element into Christ's impeccability, without attributing to him the power to do evil. This strategy will now be further explicated.

III.3 Libertarian Views

Proponents of a *Kenotic Christology* emphasize the preexistence of the Second Divine Person and the identity of the *logos asarkos* with the *logos ensarkos*. In a classical conception of God as morally perfect or benevolent, God can only be attributed libertarian free will in the sense that he can choose to perform or omit to perform supererogatory acts, but not to do evil (Swinburne 1994: 204–7). For example, it is accepted by many Christians that God could have refrained from creating the world. If one applies this conception of supererogatory libertarian free will to Christ, one can deny his moral perfection without denying his impeccability:

(L1) Christ had free will, but no power to choose evil—only to choose less than the best. *(Free will entails the power to choose between morally significant alternatives)*

Critics of such "supererogatory solutions" often refer to Jas 4:17, which says that "anyone who knows the right thing to do and fails to do it, commits sin." Avoiding this distinction, more radical kenoticists could argue that by becoming human, the Logos temporarily withdrew his impeccability, in order to become compatible with human nature (McKinley 2009: 205–17):

(L2) Christ had free will and the power to choose evil. *(Free will entails the power to choose between good and evil)*

L2 contradicts traditional kenoticists who generally claim that neither omnipotence nor omniscience, but rather love or moral perfection, are essential divine attributes (Breidert 1977). Radical kenoticism would, in my evaluation, inevitably lead to tritheism, since the Son could potentially reject the Father. For Kenotic Social Trinitarians (Davis 2011), it is foremost the perichoresis of the divine wills that grounds the unity of the three divine persons.

As indicated above, a dispositional account can be combined with the theory of supererogation as presumed in L1. It is not necessary to defend Christ's power to give in to Satan's temptations or to run away in Gethsemane in order to maintain his freedom. Similar to A1–3, one can hold that an always-impeccable Christ acquired perfect virtue over time, which eventually led him to obey God's will even in a state of extreme distress, and that he could have omitted those supererogatory acts that are necessary for such character formation. For clarification, it might be helpful to extend the meaning of the term "sin" to include the rejection of supererogatory requests by God (or deeds that prevent one to enter into full union with God). In this terminology, Christ can be morally perfect—in the sense that he cannot commit any evil act—but not impeccable, because he has libertarian free will to not give his life for the salvation of the world.

IV. DISJUNCTIVE SOLUTIONS WITH ONE CENTER OF ACTION

Classical theists, who endorse God's atemporality and immutability, often reject unitive Christologies for they entail a change in God, or at least in the Divine Word. However, a growing number of theologians, among those not only open theists and process theologians, are reevaluating divine immutability in order to preserve God's personhood and relationality.

The previously discussed unitive strategies also threaten Christ's true humanity: if being a person entails possessing one consciousness and one center of action, and if Christ is merely one person, he can, so it seems, only possess either solely a divine consciousness or solely a human consciousness.[5] This is why some authors, especially in the liberal theological traditions, claim that Christ possesses not a humanized divine consciousness but a divinized human consciousness. Accordingly, his divinity is not marked by having a second consciousness or range of consciousness, but by a special way in which his human consciousness is configured. This strategy has its roots implicitly in Irenaeus of Lyon but is explicit in Schleiermacher who claimed that Christ's divinity is a metaphor for his having a so-called God-consciousness (Stefano 2015).

The impeccability problem can be solved easily using this strategy: The Logos is not a person in a univocal sense, only a "power" influencing created persons (Gregersen 2015). If Christ is a person in which the divine power is maximally effective (cf. Rahner 1976: 216), it might prevent him from doing evil acts, that is, make him impeccable. Accordingly, impeccability itself cannot be ascribed to God, because God has no consciousness and no will—these terms cannot be attributed to an apersonal or transpersonal Godhead. However, a new problem arises: Why is the divine power more or less effective in some people? Can human beings reject grace? Could Christ have rejected the power of the Logos that transformed him into a morally perfect and impeccable character? To answer this, parallel to the Alexandrian solutions, either a compatibilist, dispositionalist, or libertarian strategy can be applied:

(UC) The union with the Logos prevents Christ from sinning.
(UD) The union with the Logos deifies Christ's human nature, making him impeccable.
(UL1) The union with the Logos would never have existed if Christ freely chose to sin.
(UL2) The union with the Logos could break apart if Christ freely chooses to sin.

In UC–UL2, Christ's possessing a divine nature in some way depends on the acceptance of grace by his human nature. UC is taught by early medieval scholars such as Peter Abelard who claimed that the ability to sin and the ability not to sin are essential to human nature and necessary for moral virtue (McKinley 2009: 161). Versions of UD were taught by Bonaventure, Duns Scotus, and Thomas Aquinas. Bonaventure claimed that the hypostatic union transformed Christ's soul to be impeccable. According to Scotus and Aquinas, the beatific vision causes this transformation (161); if reason-view compatibilism (cf. C3) is true, perfect knowledge can make a peccable human person unable to sin. Likewise, but in a Calvinist tradition, Oliver Crisp (2007a: 175) affirms that "by virtue of being united to the Son, this human nature (*his* [by itself peccable] human nature) is rendered incapable of sin." Here, the "capacity to sin" remains, but the circumstances (being united to the Son) make Jesus "incapable of exercising this capacity" (Ibid.).

By teaching that Christ is a composite between Logos, human mind, human body (cf. Pawl 2016: 43; 207–9), Aquinas and other medieval theologians can maintain the immutability of the Logos while attributing all change in Christ to his human nature.

---

[5] If it is a sole divine consciousness, it is either the consciousness of the Logos according to Social Trinitarianism or the consciousness of God according to Latin Trinitarianism. If such a divine consciousness is only "humanized," i.e., altered in order to be very similar to a human consciousness, it is disputable whether an actual human nature is assumed; rather only all essential attributes of humanity are shared (abstract nature view). Cf. Crisp (2007b: 41–49).

However, the union either controls (UC) or changes (UD) human nature in such a way that there is no real possibility of sinning left. The state of Christ's glorified soul can be compared to the eschatological state of our souls; in Heaven, we cannot sin but still count as human beings (Gaine 2003: 11; Pawl and Timpe 2009; Turner 2020). Christ, according to this view, exemplifies in advance the eschatological state of all saved human beings. Here one can object that there is a difference between whether a person has freely contributed to her impeccable character (for example, by not rejecting divine grace transforming her character) or whether a person never had this choice.

If one wants to defend a libertarian free will of the human nature, the union needs to be in some way *dependent* on Christ's decisions. The problem is that, according to conciliar tradition, Christ cannot exist independent of the union with the Logos (*doctrine of anhypostasis* as defended by Leontius of Byzantium and Constantinople II), thus he can neither acquire his divine nature nor lose it. In order to explain the dependence explicated in UL1, one needs to refer to God's foreknowledge of free contingent actions, as William of Ockham did. In an Ockhamist tradition, one can claim that God made his decision to become unified with a particular human nature dependent on his foreknowledge that this particular human nature would freely accept this union (and thus his impeccability). Here, the problem is that simple foreknowledge does not suffice for such a counterfactual dependence: God needs to know what a certain possible human person that is not unified with the Logos would freely do in order to use this knowledge to unite himself with the nature of this possible person. There are serious doubts about (1) whether such middle knowledge—God's prevolitional knowledge of counterfactual free decisions as introduced by Luis de Molina—is at all possible and (2) whether trans-world identity between the incarnated Logos and the possible merely human Jesus can be maintained. Accordingly, Ryan Mullins (2015) evaluates Thomas Flint's (2011) Molinist Christology as being incompatible with the conciliar tradition.

Thomas Schärtl (2017) tries to defend UL1 within an eternalist framework but acknowledges that if this strategy fails, "you cannot avoid the risk of breaking up the hypostatic union in Christ if you cannot rule out Christ's possibility to sin" (Schärtl 2019: 182). The theological options would be reduced to UL2 or a rejection of libertarianism. Many traditional theologians would argue that it is impossible that the hypostatic union can break apart, thus compatibilism must be true. But is the hypostatic union truly indissoluble? The Franciscan William of Ware argued in the late thirteenth century that "if that [human] nature were laid aside by the Word, it would immediately make a person, or be a person" (In *Sent.* 171; cf. Cross 2002: 283). It is hard to conceive the scenario that Christ, once he starts sinning, loses his divine nature because Christ *is* the incarnated divine person. A model UL2 would need to postulate that Christ ceases to exist once he by his human will chooses to sin. He would be replaced by a then newly created person Jesus of Nazareth, an ordinary human, who shared all memories of the human nature of Christ. A moderate version of UL1 could use Stump's theory of the fragmentation of the psyche through sin (2018: 125; 147) in order to argue that the hypostatic union depends on the psychologically fully integrated state of the human psyche of Christ. This raises the question whether the union was still established during the crucifixion (163). Possibly, it is necessary for Christ to not only feel, but actually be abandoned by God, and thus being "made sin" (2 Cor. 5:21), as Paul writes, in order to take up the sins of the world. This, however, still does not answer the question whether in such a state Christ could have rejected God and, if a temporary separation from God is necessary for human salvation, whether Christ could have done anything to avoid this separation.

There are good historic arguments to interpret the conciliar tradition in a way that reads the *two-will-thesis* as the ultimate rejection of Docetism, but not as a defense of two subjects or centers of willing (Bathrellos 2004: 182; Loke 2016). Christ's possessing a human will may only mean that Christ was not only hungry, thirsty, and experienced pain but also had a first-order desire to eat, drink, and avoid suffering. Because as an ordinary human being, Christ must have suffered from weakness of will, he probably found himself in situations in which he could not control these human first-order desires. But this does not establish a second center of action in him, it only shows that his one existing free will is restricted by psychological factors as it applies to all humans. William Lane Craig, for these reasons, concedes that his Christology implies monothelitism and argues that a will must always be attributed to a person, and not to a nature. His interpretation of what the doctrine of dyothelitism is about says that Christ exercises his one single will "through both the human nature and the divine nature" (Craig 2008; cf. Craig and Moreland 2003: 597–614).

If the one center of action of Christ is divine, as defended by Alexandrian/unitive solutions, Christ seems to be not fully human, only psychologically very similar to us. If this one center of action is human, as defended by Antiochene/disjunctive solutions, it is hard to rule out that the hypostatic union could break apart. The only tenable way here is to reinterpret the divinity of Jesus as a mere configuration of his humanity, a special state of grace, which does not impair his free will and thus can be lost. Because few Christian theologians are willing to accept this consequence, alternative theories have been developed in the past decades, which try to interpret dyothelitism as stating that Christ had two centers of actions: two wills in a contemporary understanding of the word 'will'.

V. DISJUNCTIVE SOLUTIONS WITH TWO CENTERS OF ACTION

A second type of Antiochene strategy challenges the premise that one person can only have one consciousness or one center of action. If "will" is equated with "willing subject of action" (which is clearly not the theory defended by Maximus the Confessor who largely influenced the conciliar view), Christ must have a human *and* a divine center of action. If possessing a human will entails possessing a human consciousness, and if possessing a divine will entails possessing a divine consciousness, the two-wills-view entails a two-consciousness-view. The major challenge of such theories is to show why possessing two consciousnesses does not entail being two separate persons. Historically, it was in the fifth century when Nestorius supposedly advanced the view that in Christ there was a separate human person and a divine person in a mere "moral union." Nestorianism was rejected by the Council of Ephesus in 431 with the Cappadocian argument that only a human nature that was fully assumed can be healed (Gregory of Nazianzus 1837: Ep 101, 32). Since all proponents of what is often called two-minds-view reject the existence of two separate consciousnesses, it is better to use the terminology of speaking of two "ranges of consciousness."

This view is inspired by the scholastic reduplication strategy to solve logical paradoxes about the incarnation. According to this strategy, Christ can be attributed F-ness *qua* divine nature, but at the same time not-F-ness *qua* human nature (Cross 2009: 455–57; Pawl 2016: 117–51). Applied to peccability, this leads to the following thesis:

(RS) Christ was peccable *qua* human nature but impeccable *qua* divine nature.

This thesis can be explicated either in a dispositionalist view as presented earlier in this chapter: Christ would be peccable if he were not united with the Logos. But it can also be explicated referring to a two- or divided-consciousness-view (Swinburne 1994: 197–203; Cross 2009: 466–71):

(DC) Christ had free will and the power to choose evil in his human range of consciousness but had no free will and no power to choose evil in his divine range of consciousness.

The advantage of such views is that only they can explain why Christ had full beatific vision (as Scotus and Aquinas claim) and was at the same time ignorant of things or even mistaken about certain beliefs:

> The second person of the Trinity is essentially omniscient. But the Gospels present Jesus as ignorant and mistaken. So, minimally, we need a subject for this lack of knowledge. It cannot be the second person of the Trinity on pain of contradiction. So it must be the assumed nature. (Cross 2002: 315)

Let us assume that it is possible that there are two ranges of consciousness within one person. Does this solve the impeccability paradox? If the human range of consciousness has its own center of action, it needs to be autonomous: "The Word, as Scotus points out, does not exercise direct causal control over the human nature, which thus has a degree of psychological and causal autonomy" (Ibid.: 319). There are different ways to portray such an autonomy without risking that the two consciousnesses split apart:

(N1) Christ had two separate but interconnected ranges of consciousness.
(N2) Christ had two ranges of consciousness, while the human consciousness is embedded into the divine consciousness.
(N3) Christ had one human consciousness and one divine preconscious.

N1 entails that there are two centers of actions and two wills in Christ. There needs to be a mechanism that hinders the human will from acting against the divine will; here again, a compatibilist view of free will is unavoidable. Alternatively, one could argue that the union of the natures is contingent upon Christ's actions. According to such a reverse adoptionism, human nature would become a separate, merely human person if he had started to develop a character incompatible with mutual indwelling with God—very similar to approach UL2 discussed above.

A version of N2 is famously defended by T. V. Morris (1986): The divine consciousness can fully access the human consciousness, but not reversely. Morris calls this an "asymmetric accessing relation" (105). Regarding the impeccability problem, Morris claims that peccability is only an essential attribute of "mere humanity," but not of human nature in general (66; 137–62). This assumption, in my opinion, seems to be an *ad hoc* solution, because there is no other reason to make this distinction besides solving the impeccability paradox. Furthermore, the theory needs to address the criticisms against compatibilism and explain why God did not simply create all humans as non-mere humans and thus as impeccable.

N3 was introduced into the Christological discussion by Andrew Loke (2009): When becoming incarnate, the Logos changed into a human-like consciousness by transferring all those divine attributes incompatible with humanity into a pre-conscious. While the unconscious is the part of the mind which is not directly accessible by the consciousness, the preconscious is accessible; it contains "mental contents that are not currently in consciousness but are accessible to consciousness by directing attention to them" (52). The Logos then chooses not to access his preconscious, or only in a way that is compatible with being human. Therefore, Christ can learn obedience and become increasingly secure about his special relationship with God, moral teachings or his mission on earth. In Loke's view, there is a major difference between our (ordinary human) consciousness and Christ's consciousness: the latter is controlled by Christ's impeccable preconscious. Thus, Christ is prevented by his divine preconscious from sinning without being fully aware of this process. It is ensured "that He would always choose to rely on the Holy Spirit and the Word of God to overcome temptation." (62, footnote 51). He is truly tempted, because he does not know about his impeccability, and therefore feels exactly what mere humans feel when they are tempted.[6]

Although integrating some Antiochene intuitions, Loke agrees with Alexandrians that the Logos is personally identical to the incarnated Christ. If this is true, Christ can only be peccable if the Logos itself became peccable. If the kenosis of divine attributes includes a suspension of divine benevolence and moral perfection, these attributes would not be essential divine attributes. But rejecting God's necessary moral perfection is not an attractive solution for Christian theists, probably not for any theist, although there have been voices that argued that impeccability is incompatible with moral perfection (Martin 1962; Pike 1969). If the Christian tradition is correct and any divine person is *necessarily* good, it seems that both N2 and N3 fail to maintain a human free will in Christ.

VI. FINAL CONSIDERATIONS

Charles Hodge summarizes the motivation for a libertarian Christology adequately: "If He was a true man he must have been capable of sinning. ... Temptation implies the possibility of sin. If from the constitution of His person it was impossible for Christ to sin, then His temptation was unreal and without effect, and He cannot sympathize with his people" (Hodge [1871] 1960: 457; cf. Crisp 2007a: 169). Unfortunately, all libertarian attempts to defend a human will in Christ and ascribe to him some form of peccability have major disadvantages. Character Forming Adoptionism (*acquired impeccability*) conflicts with a traditional Christian soteriology. A Molinist strategy struggles with the grounding of counterfactuals of creaturely freedom. Radical Kenotic strategies, which teach that the Logos has divested his impeccability when becoming human, not only challenge perfect being theology, but also entail monothelitism. Liberal christological models manage to maintain a genuine human will in Christ but regard his divinity either as a gradual or as a losable attribute, which also seems to conflict with a traditional Christian soteriology.

---

[6]Loke anticipates the objection "that Jesus would not be fully human according to this model, for humans cannot have a preconscious that is divine." He believes, however, that possessing a divine preconscious is "not necessarily contrary to the essential property of being human" (2009: 57).

The most prominent way among Christian theologians to deal with the impeccability paradox is to defend a compatibilist account of free will, or at least a so-called libertarian view without the power to choose between alternatives, as William Lane Craig claims when defending God's impeccability: "Libertarian freedom of the will does not require the ability to choose other than as one chooses." (2001: 262) In my opinion, the most promising attempt is less radical than Craig's: libertarian freedom can be defined as the power to choose between morally significant options, which is usually, but not necessarily actualized in a power to do evil. While free will is a disposition essential to human nature, the scope of one's freedom is determined by one's upbringing and surrounding. Because Christ was brought up in an ideal situation (which was brought about by free decisions of many humans in many generations) and guarded by the Holy Spirit, he has actualized his freedom only as a power to accept or reject his mission to give his life for humanity, but not as a power to sin. Christ can therefore be free such that he can acquire merits for his deeds and at the same time be impeccable.

References

Bathrellos, D. (2004), *The Byzantine Christ: Person, Nature, and Will in the Christology of St Maximus the Confessor*, Oxford: Oxford University Press.

Bausenhart, G. (1989), "Einheit als Freiheitsgeschehen. Die Christologie des 7. Jahrhunderts an der Grenze substanzmetaphysischen Denkens," in D. Hattrup and H. Hoping (eds.), *Christologie und Metaphysikkritik*, Münster: Aschendorff.

Breidert, M. (1977), *Die Kenotische Theologie des 19. Jahrhunderts*, Gütersloh: Gütersloher Verlagshaus Mohn.

Craig, W. L. and J. P. Moreland (2003), *Philosophical Foundations of a Christian Worldview*, Downers Grove, IL: InterVarsity Press.

Craig, W. L. (2008), "Monotheletism." Available online: www.reasonablefaith.org/writings/question-answer/monotheletism/.

Craig, W. L. (2001), *Time and Eternity: Exploring God's Relationship to Time*, Wheaton, IL: Crossway Books.

Crisp, O. D. (2007a), "Was Jesus Sinless or Impeccable," *Irish Theological Quarterly*, 72: 168–86.

Crisp, O. D. (2007b), *Divinity and Humanity. The Incarnation Reconsidered*, Cambridge: Cambridge University Press.

Cross, R. (2002), *The Metaphysics of the Incarnation: Thomas Aquinas to Duns Scotus*, Oxford: Oxford University Press.

Cross, R. (2009), "The Incarnation," in: T. P. Flint and M. C. Rea (eds.), *The Oxford Handbook of Philosophical Theology*, 452–75, Oxford: Oxford University Press.

Davis, S. T. (2011), "The Metaphysics of Kenosis," in A. Marmodoro and J. Hill (eds.), *The Metaphysics of the Incarnation*, 114–33, New York: Oxford University Press.

Essen, G. (2001), *Die Freiheit Jesu. Der neuchalkedonische Enhypostasiebegriff im Horizont neuzeitlicher Subjekt- und Personphilosophie*, Regensburg: Pustet.

Fischer, J. M. (2005), "Frankfurt-Type Examples and Semi-Compatibilism," in R. Kane (ed.), *The Oxford Handbook of Free Will*, 243–65, New York: Oxford University Press.

Flint, T. (2011), "Molinism and Incarnation," in: K. Perszyk (ed.), *Molinism: The Contemporary Debate*, 187–226, Oxford: Oxford University Press.

Gaine, O. P. (2003), *Will There Be Free Will in Heaven*, London: T&T Clark.

Gregersen, N. H. (2015): "The Extended Body of Christ: Three Dimensions of Deep Incarnation," in N. H. Gregersen (ed.), *Incarnation: On the Scope and Depth of Christology*, 225–54, Minneapolis: Fortress Press.

Gregory of Nazianzus (1837), "Epistola 101, ad Cledonium presbyterum contra Apollinarum," in: *Opera quae exstant omnia*, ed. J. P. Migne, Patrologiae Graeca 37: 175–94, Paris: J. P. Migne.

Grillmeier, A. (1982), *Jesus der Christus im Glauben der Kirche*, vol. 1, Freiburg: Herder.

Henderson, K. (2017), "Impeccability and Perfect Virtue," *Religious Studies*, 53 (2): 261–80.

Hodge, C. ([1871] 1960), *Systematic Theology*, vol. 2, London: James Clarke.

Kane, R. (1985), *Free Will and Values*, Albany: SUNY Press.

Leftow, B. (2014), "Tempting God," *Faith and Philosophy*, 31 (1): 3–23.

Loke, A. (2009), "On the Coherence of the Incarnation: The Divine Preconscious Model," *Neue Zeitschrift für Systematische Theologie und Religionsphilosophie*, 51: 50–63.

Loke, A. (2016), "On Dyothelitism Versus Monothelitism: The Divine Preconscious Model," *The Heythrop Journal*, 57 (1): 135–41.

Martin, C. B. (1962), *Religious Belief*, Ithaca, NY: Cornell University Press.

McKenna, M., and D. J. Coates (2015), "Compatibilism," in E. N. Zalta (ed.), *The Stanford Encyclopedia of Philosophy* (Winter 2018 edition). Available online: https://plato.stanford.edu/archives/win2018/entries/compatibilism/.

McKinley, J. (2009), *Tempted For Us, Theological Models and the Practical Relevance of Christ's Impeccability and Temptation*, Eugene, OR: Paternoster.

Morris, T. V. (1983), "Impeccability," *Analysis*, 43: 106–12.

Morris, T. V. (1986), *The Logic of God Incarnate*, Ithaca, NY: Cornell University Press.

Mullins, R. T. (2015): "Flint's Molinism and the Incarnation is too Radical," *Journal of Analytic Theology*, 3: 109–21.

Pawl, T., and K. Timpe (2009), "Incompatibilism, Sin, and Free Will in Heaven," *Faith and Philosophy*, 26 (4): 398–419.

Pawl, T. (2014), "The Freedom of Christ and the Problem of Deliberation," *International Journal for Philosophy of Religion*, 75 (3): 233–47.

Pike, N. (1969), "Omnipotence and God's Ability to Sin," *American Philosophical Quarterly*, 6 (3), 208–16.

Rahner, K. ([1976] 2008), *Grundkurs des Glaubens: Einführung in den Begriff des Christentums*, Freiburg i.Br.: Herder.

Schärtl, T. (2017), "Die Freiheit Jesu. Vorschläge zur metaphysischen Modellierung der Christologie Raymund Schwagers," in J. Niewiadomski (ed.), *Das Drama der Freiheit im Disput: Die Kerngedanken der Theologie Raymund Schwagers*, Freiburg i.Br.: Herder.

Schärtl, T. (2019), "The Burden of Freedom: The Interference of Libertarian Freedom and Philosophical Theology," in K. v. Stosch, S. Wendel, M. Breul and A. Langenfeld, *Streit um die Freiheit: Philosophische und theologische Perspektiven*, 161–92, Paderborn: Schöningh.

Siker, J. (2015), *Jesus, Sin and Perfection in Early Christianity*, New York: Cambridge University Press.

Stefano, T. (2015), "Christology from Lessing to Schleiermacher," in F. Murphy (ed.), *The Oxford Handbook of Christology*, 347–61, Oxford: Oxford University Press.

Stump, E. (2018), *Atonement*, New York: Oxford University Press.

Swinburne, R. (1994), *The Christian God*, Oxford: Clarendon Press.

Timpe, K., and T. Pawl (2009), "Incompatibilism, Sin, and Free Will in Heaven," *Faith and Philosophy*, 26 (4), 398–419.

Timpe, K. (2007), "Source Incompatibilism and its Alternatives," *American Philosophical Quarterly*, 44 (2): 143–55.

Turner, Jr., J. T. (2020), "Perfect Obedience, Perfect Love, and the (So-Called) Problem of Heavenly Freedom," in O. D. Crisp, J. M. Arcadi, and J. Wessling (eds.), *Love: Divine and Human*, 235–53, London: T&T Clark.

Van Inwagen, P. (1989), "When Is the Will Free?" *Philosophical Perspectives*, 3: 399–422.

White, T. (2008): "Dyothelitism and the Instrumental Human Consciousness of Jesus," *Pro Ecclesia*, 17 (4): 396–422.

CHAPTER SEVENTEEN

Philosophical Issues in the Atonement

WILLIAM LANE CRAIG

I. INTRODUCTION

Many Christian philosophers have taken up the task of helping systematic theologians to formulate and defend coherent statements of Christian doctrine. So philosophers have been actively engaged in discussion of the doctrines of the Trinity, Incarnation, and Atonement, which might be called "the big three" of peculiarly Christian doctrines.[1] The activity of Anglo-American Christian philosophers in the field of systematic theology has even come to the attention of German theologians. In the standard German reference work in theology, the *Theologische Realenzyklopädie* (TRE), Christoph Gestrich draws attention to the contribution of Anglo-American analytic philosophy to the subject of the incarnation and its possible relevance for the subject of the atonement:

> In Great Britain there was already during the 19th century a widespread and growing *atonement-literature* spanning theological lines and confessions and a nearly general consensus concerning Christ's substitutionary atonement. It was extensively debated, for example, whether one should speak of the "objective" validity of this atonement or the necessity of a "subjective" realization in faith and morals. By the 20th century this topic had for the most part been exhausted in the English-speaking realm—until during the '70s a lively discussion about the historicity of the incarnation of the Son of God, stimulated by analytic philosophy, was kindled. Is the atoning descent of the heavenly Son of God to earthly flesh "only" a metaphor—and thus by no means a part of objective history? Chiefly related to this question there was once more in the '80s and '90s of the 20th century a whole series of English-language theological investigations concerning the "problem" of the *atonement*. The predominant result: the admittedly metaphorical talk of the incarnation of the Son of God in the Christian confession remains now as always indispensable and refers to an actual event. Nevertheless, one must consider anew *in what way* it leads to the divine *atonement*. (Gestrich 2001, s.v.)[2]

---

[1] See, e.g., Murray and Rea (2012), which singles out for discussion the doctrines of the Trinity, Incarnation, and Atonement. It is surprising that this article includes no discussion of penal substitutionary theories in distinction from satisfaction theories.
[2] A list of references to English language resources by Christian philosophers and theologians then follows. The nineteenth-century British literature alluded to by Gestrich is still worth reading and is, sadly, largely overlooked by Christian philosophers today. Standouts include Smeaton ([1870] 1957), Dale (1884), and a bit later Denney (1907).

It is the purpose of this chapter to advance the discussion by looking more closely at certain philosophical problems involved in the classic doctrine of Christ's substitutionary atonement.

Although a bewildering variety of atonement theories have been proposed over the centuries,[3] at the heart of any biblical theory of the atonement lies the notion of penal substitution. Penal substitution is rooted biblically in the vicarious suffering of the Servant of the Lord described in Isaiah 53 and in its New Testament application to Jesus. The suffering of the Servant is agreed on all hands to be punitive. What is remarkable, even startling, about the Servant is that he suffers substitutionally for the sins of others. The substitutionary as well as punitive nature of the Servant's suffering is expressed in phrases like "he was wounded for our transgressions," "crushed for our iniquities," "upon him was the punishment that made us whole," "the Lord has laid on him the iniquity of us all," and "stricken for the transgression of my people" (vv. 5, 6, 8).[4] According to Otfried Hofius ([1996] 2004), substitutionary punishment "is expressed several times in the passage and should undoubtedly be seen as its dominant and central theme" (164). New Testament authors took Jesus to be the sin-bearing Servant of Isaiah 53. For example, 1 Pet. 2:24-25 states, "He himself bore our sins in his body on the tree, that we might die to sin and live to righteousness. By his wounds you have been healed."

Ever since the time of Faustus Socinus (1539–1604), the doctrine of penal substitution has faced formidable, and some would say insuperable, philosophical challenges. A discussion of such challenges takes us into lively debates over questions in the philosophy of law, the field of philosophy where the theory of punishment is most thoroughly discussed.

A theory of punishment should offer both a *definition of punishment* and a *justification of punishment*. Challenges to penal substitution arise with respect to both. Thus philosophical objections to penal substitution have been lodged concerning both the *coherence* of penal substitution and the *justice* of penal substitution. In addition, there are objections to the *satisfactoriness* of penal substitution.

II. COHERENCE OF PENAL SUBSTITUTION

With respect to the *coherence* of penal substitution, some critics have claimed, on the basis of an expressivist theory of punishment, that it is conceptually impossible that God punish Christ for our sins. For according to an expressivist theory of punishment, for an act to count as punishment, it must send "a message of condemnation or censure for what is believed to be a wrongful act or omission" (Walen 2014). Some critics have argued that God could not condemn or censure Christ, since he was sinless (e.g., Murphy 2009: 255–9). Therefore, God could not have punished Christ for our sins.

The crucial premises of this argument seem to be the following:

1. If Christ was sinless, God could not have condemned Christ.
2. If God could not have condemned Christ, God could not have punished Christ.
3. If God could not have punished Christ, penal substitution is false.

Thus, it follows from the sinlessness of Christ that penal substitution is false.

---

[3] For a good survey see Rivière (1909).
[4] Biblical quotations in this chapter are taken from the Revised Standard Version of the Bible.

To mention but one of the many shortcomings of this argument, it seems to be based upon a fundamental misunderstanding of the expressivist theory of punishment. An expressivist theory does *not* require that the person punished is condemned or censured for the act or omission believed to be wrong. Censure could be either of the person who did the act or of the act itself. It is no part of expressivism that the censure expressed by punishment target a particular person. Expressivist theories of punishment, as typically formulated, are thus perfectly consistent with penal substitution. Thus, premise (2) of the argument is undercut.

III. JUSTICE OF PENAL SUBSTITUTION

Although a few critics have objected to the *coherence* of penal substitution, by far and away the most common objection is to the *justice* of penal substitution. Critics of penal substitution frequently assert that God's punishing Christ in our place would be an injustice on God's part.[5] For it is an axiom of retributive justice that it is unjust to punish an innocent person. But Christ was an innocent person. Since God is perfectly just, He cannot therefore have punished Christ.

The crucial premises and inferences of this objection appear to be the following:

1. God is perfectly just.
2. If God is perfectly just, He cannot punish an innocent person.
3. Therefore, God cannot punish an innocent person.
4. Christ was an innocent person.
5. Therefore, God cannot punish Christ.
6. If God cannot punish Christ, penal substitution is false.

It follows that if God is perfectly just, then penal substitution is false.

III.1 Retributive Justice: Positive and Negative

Despite the popularity of this objection, it is far from insuperable: first, the objection does not sufficiently differentiate various versions of a retributivism. Premise (2) presupposes a retributive theory of justice, since, on consequentialist theories, punishment of the innocent may be just. But while a so-called *negative retributivism* holds that the innocent should not be punished because they do not deserve it, the essence of retributive justice lies in so-called *positive retributivism*, which holds that the guilty should be punished because they deserve it. What distinguishes retributivism as a theory of justice is the positive thesis that punishment of the guilty is an intrinsic good because the guilty deserve it. God is a positive retributivist "who will by no means clear the guilty" (Exod. 34:7). But the penal substitution theorist may maintain that God is only qualifiedly a negative retributivist, since even if He has prohibited human beings from punishing innocent persons, and even if He is too good to Himself punish innocent human persons, still He reserves the prerogative to punish an innocent divine person, namely, Christ, in the place of the guilty. This extraordinary exception is a result of His goodness, not a defect in His justice. Premise (2) is therefore undercut.

---

[5] E.g., Stump (2018: 124).

III.2 Imputation of Sins

Second, suppose that the *prima facie* demands of negative retributive justice are essential to God and could not be overridden. Would God be unjust to punish Christ? Not necessarily. For consider premise 4:

4. Christ was an innocent person.

For penal substitution theorists like the Protestant Reformers, who affirm the imputation of our sins to Christ, there is no question in Christ's case of God's punishing the innocent and so violating even the *prima facie* demands of negative retributive justice. For Christ, in virtue of the imputation of our sins to him, was legally guilty before God. Of course, because our sins were merely *imputed* to Christ and not *infused* in him, Christ was, as always, personally virtuous, a paradigm of compassion, selflessness, purity, and courage; but he was declared legally guilty before God. Therefore, he was legally liable to punishment. Thus, given the doctrine of the imputation of sins, the moral objection to penal substitutionary theories is a nonstarter, being based on the false assumption of premise (4).

Of course, critics of penal substitution are apt to be unsympathetic to the claim that our sins were imputed to Christ. Whether one holds that our sins, that is to say, our wrongful acts, were imputed to Christ, or one that holds that our guilt for our wrongful acts was imputed to Christ, the complaint in both cases is the same: we have no experience of the *transfer* either of moral responsibility for actions or of guilt in isolation from actions from one person to another (Murphy 2009: 259).[6]

But are we so utterly bereft of analogies to imputation as critics allege? It seems not.

III.2a Legal Fictions

Consider first the idea that our wrongful acts were imputed to Christ. On this view, although Christ did not himself commit the sins in question, God chooses to treat Christ *as if* he had done those acts. Such language is formulaic for the expression of legal fictions.[7] The nearly universal understanding of a legal fiction is that it is something that the court consciously knows to be false but treats as if it were true for sake of a particular action. The use of legal fictions is a long established, widespread, and indispensable feature of systems of law.

Penal substitution theorists have typically been understandably leery of talk of legal fictions in connection with their views, lest our redemption be thought to be something unreal, a mere pretense.[8] But such a fear is misplaced. The claim is not that penal substitution is a fiction, for Christ was really and truly punished on such a view. Nor is his expiation of sin or propitiation of God's wrath a fiction, for his being punished for our sins removed our liability to punishment and satisfied God's justice. All these things are real. What is fictitious is that Christ himself did the wrongful acts for which he was punished. Most orthodox Christian believe that Christ did not and could not commit sins,

---

[6] This complaint is very common, both among philosophers (e.g., Quinn 1986: 445, 456; Purtill 1990: 38; Stump 2003: 432) and theologians (Hofius [1996] 2004: 168).
[7] The seminal treatment of contemporary discussions is Fuller (1930: 363–99; 1931a: 513–46; 1931b: 877–910). The more distant progenitor is Vaihinger ([1911] n.d.).
[8] As charged by Borg and Crossan (2009: 165). By contrast, see O'Collins (2012: 127).

but on the present view, God adopts for the administration of justice the legal fiction that Christ did such deeds.

Penal substitution theorists will sometimes object to the employment of legal fictions in the doctrine of the atonement because God's legally justifying us has real, objective results. Someone whose debt has been legally remitted, for example, really becomes free of the burden of financial obligation to his former creditor. But such an objection is based upon a misunderstanding of the role of legal fictions in the achievement of justice. A legal fiction is a device that is adopted precisely in order to bring about real and objective differences in the world.

Take, for example, the classic case of a legal fiction employed in *Mostyn v. Fabrigas* (1774). Mr. Fabrigas sued the governor of the Mediterranean island of Minorca, then under British control, for trespass and false imprisonment. Since such a suit could not proceed in Minorca without the approval of the governor himself, Mr. Fabrigas filed suit in the Court of Common Pleas in London. Unfortunately, that court had jurisdiction only in cases brought by residents of London. Lord Mansfield, recognizing that a denial of jurisdiction in this case would leave someone who was plainly wronged without a legal remedy, declared that for the purposes of the action Minorca was part of London! Frederick Schauer observes, "That conclusion was plainly false and equally plainly produced a just result, and thus *Mostyn v. Fabrigas* represents the paradigmatic example of using a fiction to achieve what might in earlier days have been done through the vehicle of equity" (2015: 122).[9]

Or consider the legal fiction that a ship is a person.[10] The adoption of this fiction by US federal courts in the early nineteenth century came about because of the efforts of shipowners to evade responsibility for violating embargo laws and carrying unlawful cargo, including slaves. When the ships were seized, the captains and crews passed on legal responsibility to the shipowners, who in turn produced innocent manifests while denying any knowledge of the illegal activity of the captains and crews. The courts responded by making the ship itself (herself?) the person against whom charges were brought. By the end of the century, this fiction became the settled view of ships in maritime law, so that the "offending ship is considered as herself the wrongdoer, and as herself bound to make compensation for the wrong done" (Lind 2015: 95).[11] According to Douglas Lind, the "ontologically wild" fiction of ship personification had profound and beneficial results, facilitating the condemnation and forfeiture of offending vessels and producing a more just, coherent, and workable admiralty jurisprudence (96).

Holding that God, in His role as supreme Judge, adopts for the purposes of our redemption the legal fiction that Christ himself had done the deeds in question in no way implies that our forensic justification before His bar is unreal. Thus, through the device of legal fictions we do, indeed, have some experience of how legal responsibility for acts can be imputed to another person who did not really do the actions, thereby producing real differences in the world outside the fiction.

---

[9]By "equity," Schauer has reference to recourse to "an elaborate series of Chancellor's courts known as courts of equity, in order to gain equitable relief from the rigidity of law."
[10]Described colorfully by Lind (2015: 95–6).
[11]Citing *The John G. Stevens* 170 U.S. 113 (1898: 122).

III.2b Vicarious Liability

Consider now the second alternative, that God imputes to Christ the guilt of our wrongdoing.[12] It is worth noting that the question does not concern the *transfer* of guilt from one person to another, in the sense that guilt is removed from one person and placed on another. For the defender of the doctrine of imputation does not hold that when my guilt is imputed to Christ, it is thereby removed from me. Guilt is merely replicated in Christ, just as, according to the doctrine of original sin, Adam's guilt was replicated in me, not transferred from Adam to me. Adam remains guilty, as do I when my guilt is imputed to Christ. The entire rationale of penal substitution is, after all, the removal of guilt by punishment.

What is at issue, then, is whether we have any experience of the *replication* of guilt in a person different than the person who did the act. The question is not the removal of the primary actor's guilt but the imputation of guilt for his wrongdoing to another as well. So understood, we are not wholly without analogies in our justice system.

In civil law there are cases involving what is called vicarious liability. In such cases, the principle of *respondeat superior* (roughly, the Master is answerable) is invoked in order to impute the liability of a subordinate to his superior, for example, a master's being held liable for acts done by his servant. On the contemporary scene, this principle has given rise to a widespread and largely uncontroversial principle of vicarious liability of employers. An employer may be held liable for acts done by his employee in his role as employee, even though the employer did not do these acts himself. Cases typically involve employers' being held liable for the illegal sale of items by employees but may also include torts like assault and battery, fraud, manslaughter, and so on. It needs to be emphasized that in such cases the employer is not being held liable for other acts, such as complicity or negligence in, for instance, failing to supervise the employee. Indeed, he may be utterly blameless in the matter. Rather, the liability incurred by his employee for certain acts is imputed to him in virtue of his relationship with the employee, even though he did not himself do the acts in question. The liability is not thereby transferred from the employee to the employer; rather the liability of the employee is replicated in the employer. In cases of vicarious liability, then, we have the responsibility for an act imputed to another person than the actor.

It might be said that in such civil cases guilt is not imputed to another person but mere liability. This claim may be left moot, for vicarious liability also makes an appearance in criminal law as well as civil law (Leigh 1982). There are criminal as well as civil applications of *respondeat superior*. The liability for crimes committed by a subordinate in the discharge of his duties can also be imputed to his superior. Both the employer and

---

[12] What follows could have also been said with respect to the vicarious liability of corporations as persons in the eyes of the law. David Ormerod explains, "Corporations have a separate legal identity. They are treated in law as having a legal personality distinct from the natural persons—members, directors, employees, etc.—who make up the corporation. That presents the opportunity, in theory, of imposing criminal liability on the corporation separately from any liability which might be imposed on the individual members for any criminal wrongdoing" (2018: 245). But because corporate persons might be thought by some to be legal fictions, I leave them aside to focus on the vicarious liability of human beings. It is also worth noting that vicarious liability may also, via the so-called delegation principle and the attribution principle, involve the imputation of acts and not just guilt to innocent persons (269–73). In that case, appeal to legal fictions as an analogy to imputation of sins becomes superfluous.

the employee may be found guilty for crimes which only the employee committed.[13] For example, in *Allen v. Whitehead* (1930), the owner of a café was found to be guilty because his employee, to whom management of the café had been delegated, allowed prostitutes to congregate there in violation of the law. In *Sherras v. De Rutzen* (1895) a bartender's criminal liability for selling alcohol to a constable on duty was imputed to the licensed owner of the bar. In such cases, we have the guilt of one person imputed to another person, who did not do the act. Interestingly, vicarious liability is a case of strict liability, where the superior is held to be guilty without being blameworthy.[14] He is thus guilty and liable to punishment even though he is not culpable.

Thus, the vicarious liability that exists in the law suffices to show that the imputation of our guilt to Christ is not wholly without parallel in our experience.[15] In the law's imputation of guilt to another person than the actor, we actually have a very close analogy to the doctrine of the imputation of our guilt to Christ.[16]

Imputation of wrongdoing or guilt to a blameless party is thus a widely accepted feature of our justice system. Now sometimes the ascription of vicarious liability is denounced as unjust, though tolerated as a sort of necessary evil due to practical considerations arising from the human impossibility of administering a system of pure justice. But when would the imposition of vicarious liability be even *prima facie* unjust? Arguably, it could be only in cases in which it is nonvoluntary. Ormerod notes that in cases of corporate vicarious liability it is unclear whether it is necessary for a conviction that an individual controlling mind of the company be identifiable. This leads him to ask, "Can a company waive the need to establish that fact by pleading guilty on the basis that, although no controller was identifiable, the corporation is prepared to accept liability? There would seem no reason in principle why not" (2018: 255). Similarly, if an employer knows that the exaction of justice's demands from his employee would ruin him and out of compassion for his employee and his family wishes to act mercifully by voluntarily being held vicariously liable for his employee's wrongdoing, how is that unjust or immoral? In the same way, if Christ voluntarily invites our sins to be imputed to him for the sake of our salvation, what injustice is there in this? Who is to gainsay him?

---

[13] Leigh (1982: 1) notes that vicarious liability takes two forms. In one, a person is held liable for the acts of another who has a *mens rea*, while in the other, more typical case, a person is held liable for the act of another where the act of the other person amounts to an offense of strict liability.

[14] Indeed, the superior is entirely innocent, having neither an *actus reus* nor a *mens rea*, but is declared guilty by imputation.

[15] Mark Murphy might complain that our experiences of imputation involve only a legal and not a moral transaction. But it is characteristic of the Reformation doctrine of salvation that "justification" and "condemnation" are precisely forensic terms and that imputation is a legal transaction. Indeed, the forensic nature of justification is Pauline. Michael Horton (2011b: 93) reports that there is now a "considerable" and "settled" "scholarly consensus," including advocates of the new perspective on Paul and Roman Catholic exegetes such as Joseph Fitzmeyer, Raymond Brown, and Karl Rahner, that "justification is a declarative, judicial verdict" (see also Horton 2011a: 293. Cf. the verdicts of Dunn (2011: 118) and Bird (2011: 296)).

[16] Intriguingly, a necessary condition of a finding of vicarious liability is that the superior be so related to the subordinate as to have either the right, the power, or the duty to prevent the subordinate's wrongdoing. Christ, of course, stands in such a relationship to us, since he possesses both the power and the right to prevent our sinning, even if he has no duty to do so. Equally intriguing is the fact that a delegation of authority by the superior to the subordinate can be crucial. In *Vane v. Yiannopoullos* (1965), the licensed owner of a restaurant was initially found vicariously liable for a sale in breach of license by a waitress. The House of Lords reversed the decision on the grounds that the waitress had not been left in charge of the premises and all the effective management handed over to her. A striking feature of the Genesis creation story is that God gives to the man and woman authority over creation to act on His behalf and delegates to them the responsibility of managing creation (Gen. 1:27-28).

In sum, the objection to penal substitution based on the justification of punishment is no more successful than the objection to penal substitution based on the definition of punishment.

IV. SATISFACTORINESS OF PENAL SUBSTITUTION

A third sort of objection to penal substitution concerns what we might call its *satisfactoriness*. Some critics have objected that punishing Christ in our place could not possibly meet the demands of divine retributive justice (Gomes 1990: III.3).[17] For punishing another person for my crimes would not serve to remove my liability to punishment. So how can penal substitution satisfy God's justice? We can formulate this objection as follows:

1. Unless the person who committed a wrong is punished for that wrong, divine justice is not satisfied.
2. If God practices penal substitution, then the person who committed a wrong is not punished for that wrong.
3. Therefore, if God practices penal substitution, divine justice is not satisfied.

It follows that penal substitution is thus unsatisfactory.

IV.1 Legal Analogies to Penal Substitution

Now perhaps some progress can be made toward answering this question by considering how penal substitution is regarded in our secular justice system. After all, if we are talking about retributive justice as we know and understand it, then divine justice must be significantly analogous to enlightened human justice systems. If something like penal substitution appears in our justice system, that would lend credibility to the claim that it can be satisfactory of divine justice's demands.

David Lewis claims our Anglo-American system of justice, in point of fact, does countenance cases that are significantly analogous to penal substitution. For although we do not think that a criminal offender's friend can serve his prison sentence or death sentence, we do believe that a friend can pay a criminal's fine if both agree to the arrangement. "Yet this is just as much a case of penal substitution as the others" (Lewis 1997: 207). If we were single-mindedly against penal substitution, Lewis says, then we should conclude that fines are an *unsatisfactory* form of punishment, that such punishment, in other words, fails to satisfy justice's demands. But we do not.[18] Lewis draws the lesson that both secularists and Christians agree that "penal substitution sometimes makes sense after all, even if none can say how it makes sense. And if both sides agreed to that, that is some evidence that somehow they might both be right" (Lewis 1997: 209).

---

[17]For contemporary statements of the objection, see, e.g., Quinn (1986: 440–52); Stump (2003: 436). Socinus presses other objections as well to Christ's satisfaction of divine justice, especially that satisfaction is logically incompatible with God's remitting our sins (Gomes 1990: III.2), an objection that is still repeated today (e.g., by Stump 2018: chapter 3). Hugo Grotius responded ably to Socinus on this score in his work ([1617] 1889: VI).

[18]In response to Lewis, Quinn (2004: 722–30) makes the interesting observation that courts have sometimes expressed diffidence about allowing companies to purchase insurance policies to cover possible penalties. For in such cases the insurance company pays the penalty demanded by the law rather than the guilty party. But such cases do not show that penal substitution is unsatisfactory; quite the contrary, in fact. Rather, such cases furnish a good example of the way in which *ultima facie* considerations can justify penal substitution, thereby meeting justice's demands in a specific action.

We can press the analogy even further. For consider cases involving vicarious liability for criminal acts. In *Allen v. Whitehead*, "the acts of the manager and his mens rea (knowing that the women present were prostitutes) were both to be imputed to his employer, not simply because he was an employee, but because the management of the house had been delegated to him" (Omerod 2018: 270). In *Sherras v. De Rutzen*, even though the bartender poured the drinks and collected the money, the *actus reus* (wrongful act) of the bartender was attributed to the person holding the license to sell alcohol in the bar, since only the licensee can be the seller.

The lesson to be learned from cases of vicarious liability is that what is required for the satisfaction of justice is that only persons who are *liable* for a wrong are to be punished for that wrong. Accordingly, premise (1) should be revised to the following:

1*. Unless a person who is liable for a wrong is punished for that wrong, divine justice is not satisfied.

That person might be the wrongdoer himself or someone vicariously liable for that wrong.

Now in affirming that justice is satisfied only if a person who is liable for a crime is punished for that crime, we have not yet arrived at an analogy to penal substitution. For in a case involving vicarious liability both parties, the subordinate who did the wrong and the blameless superior to whom the wrong is imputed, may be found guilty and punished for the crime.

Intriguingly, however, it is sometimes the case that only the vicariously liable superior is prosecuted and punished. In cases involving the illegal sale of items, only the licensee may be prosecuted as the principal in the crime. Even in cases of delegated responsibility, the state may forgo prosecution of the subordinate or forgo exacting a penalty at his hand in favor of the employer's satisfying justice's demands. In cases where a corporation is held vicariously liable for crimes committed by employees, the corporation alone might be prosecuted. In cases in which the demands of justice are too heavy for individuals to bear, the corporation may be held solely responsible for satisfying justice's demands. Such a case seems to be as much an instance of penal substitution as Lewis's example of fines' being paid by a third party. Sometimes the demands of justice are met not by the wrongdoer himself but by someone held vicariously liable for that wrong. We do seem to have some analogy in our justice system to penal substitution.

We can think of the imputation of our sins to Christ on the analogy of the vicarious liability of a superior for his subordinate. Just as in civil and criminal law a superior can be held vicariously liable for the wrongdoing of his subordinate, so God held Christ vicariously liable for our sins. As in cases in which only the vicariously liable superior is convicted and punished, so God may be satisfied with the infinite penalty paid by Christ for our sins.

IV.2 Inclusionary Place-Taking

But now consider as well:

2. If God practices penal substitution, then the person who committed a wrong is not punished for that wrong.

In cases of penal substitution, is it always the case that the person who did the wrong is not punished for that wrong?

Contemporary theologians have disputed the point by distinguishing between exclusionary place-taking (*exkludierende Stellvertretung*) and inclusionary place-taking (*inkludierende Stellvertretung*).[19] This important distinction requires a word of explanation about substitution and representation respectively. In cases of simple substitution, someone takes the place of another person but does not represent that person. For example, a pinch hitter in baseball enters the lineup to bat in the place of another player. He is a substitute for that player but in no sense represents that other player. That is why the batting average of the player whom he replaces is not affected by the pinch hitter's performance. On the other hand, a simple representative acts on behalf of another person and serves as his spokesman but is not a substitute for that person. For example, the baseball player has an agent who represents him in contract negotiations with the team. The representative does not replace the player but merely advocates for him.

These roles can be combined, in which case we have neither simple substitution nor simple representation but rather substitutional representation (or representative substitution). A good illustration of this combination of substitution and representation is to be found in the role of a proxy at a shareholders' meeting. If we cannot attend the meeting ourselves, we may sign an agreement authorizing someone else to serve as our proxy at the meeting. He votes for us, and because he has been authorized to do so, his votes are our votes: we have voted via proxy at the meeting of shareholders. The proxy is a substitute in that he attends the meeting in our place, but he is also our representative in that he does not vote instead of us but on our behalf, so that we vote. This combination is an inclusionary place-taking.

Swiss Reformed theologian Francis Turretin believes that Christ, in bearing our punishment, was both our substitute and our representative before God. He states, "The curse and punishment of sin which he received upon himself in our stead secures to us blessing and righteousness with God in virtue of that most strict union between us and him by which, as our sins are imputed to him, so in turn his obedience and righteousness are imputed to us" (Turretin 1992: 2.16.3). This relation is not one of simple substitution; there is an inclusive union here which is the basis of the imputation of our sins to Christ and his righteousness to us. According to Turretin, so long as Christ is outside of us and we are out of Christ we can receive no benefit from his righteousness. But God has united us with Christ by means of a twofold bond, one natural (namely, communion of nature by the incarnation), the other mystical (namely, the communion of grace by Christ's mediation), in virtue of which our sins might be imputed to Christ and his righteousness imputed to us. Christ was punished in our place and bore the suffering we deserved, but he also represented us before God, so that his punishment was our punishment. Christ was not merely punished instead of us; rather, we were punished by proxy.[20] For that reason, divine justice is satisfied.

Herein we see the organic connection between Christ's incarnation, death, and resurrection. God's raising Jesus from the dead is not only a ratification to us of the efficacy of Christ's atoning death; it is a necessary consequence of it. For by his substitutionary

---

[19]Alternatively, *ausschliessende vs. einschliessende Stellvertretung*. See, e.g., the influential work of Gese (1981: 106) and Hofius (1994: 41).
[20]Atonement theorists have identified examples of such punishment by proxy even in human affairs, such as a team captain's being punished for his team's failings or a squad leader's being punished for his troops' failings (Porter 2004: 236–7). Of course, Christ has been uniquely appointed by God to be our proxy, which may make his case *sui generis*.

death Christ fully satisfied divine justice. The penalty of death having been fully paid, Christ can no more remain dead than a criminal who has fully served his sentence can remain imprisoned. Punishment cannot justly continue; justice demands his release. Thus, Christ's resurrection is both a necessary consequence and a ratification of his satisfaction of divine justice.

V. CONCLUSION

There remains vastly more to be said about the rich and variegated doctrine of the atonement. But so far forth we have encountered nothing that would rationally undermine the doctrine of penal substitution as a central facet of a biblically adequate theory of the atonement.

References

Bird, M. F. (2011), "Roman Catholic View: Progressive Reformed Response," in J. Beilby and P. R. Eddy (eds.), *Justification: Five Views*, 296–300, Downers Grove, IL: IVP Academic.

Borg, M. J., and J. D. Crossan (2009), *The First Paul: Reclaiming the Radical Visionary behind the Church's Conservative Icon*, San Francisco: HarperOne.

Dale, R. W. (1884), *The Atonement*, 9th ed., London: Hodder & Stoughton.

Denney, J. (1907), *The Death of Christ: Its Place and Interpretation in the New Testament*, London: Hodder & Stoughton.

Dunn, J. D. G. (2011), "Traditional Reformed View: New Perspective Response," in J. Beilby and P. R. Eddy (eds.), *Justification: Five Views*, 117–21, Downers Grove, IL: IVP Academic.

Fuller, L. L. (1930), "Legal Fictions," *Illinois Law Review*, 25 (4): 363–99.

Fuller, L. L. (1931a), "Legal Fictions," *Illinois Law Review*, 25 (5): 513–46.

Fuller, L. L. (1931b). "Legal Fictions," *Illinois Law Review*, 25 (8): 877–910.

Gese, H. (1981), "The Atonement," in *Essays on Biblical Theology*, trans. Keith Crim, Minneapolis: Augsburg.

Gestrich, C. (2001), "Sühne V: Kirchengeschichtlich und Dogmatisch," in G. Müller (ed.), *Theologische Realenzyklopädie*, vol. 32: *Spurgeon-Taylor*, Berlin: Walter de Gruyter.

Gomes, A. (1990), "Faustus Socinus' '*De Jesu Christo Servatore*', Part III: Historical Introduction, Translation and Critical Notes," PhD diss., Fuller Theological Seminary, Pasadena.

Grotius, H. (1889), *A Defence of the Catholic Faith concerning the Satisfaction of Christ, against Faustus Socinus*, trans. Frank Hugh Foster, Andover: Warren F. Draper.

Hofius, O. (1994), "Sühne und Versöhnung: Zum paulinischen Verständnis des Kreuzestodes Jesu," in *Paulusstudien*, 2nd rev. ed., WUNT 51, Tübingen: J.C.B. Mohr [Paul Siebeck].

Hofius, O. ([1996] 2004), "The Fourth Servant Song in the New Testament Letters," in B. Janowski and P. Stuhlmacher (eds.), *The Suffering Servant: Isaiah 53 in Jewish and Christian Sources*, 163–88, Grand Rapids, MI: Eerdmans.

Horton, M. S. (2011a), "Roman Catholic View: Traditional Reformed Response," in J. Beilby and P. R. Eddy (eds.), *Justification: Five Views*, 291–5, Downers Grove, MI: IVP Academic.

Horton, M. S. (2011b), "Traditional Reformed View," in J. Beilby and P. R. Eddy (eds.), *Justification: Five Views*, 83–111, Downers Grove, IL: IVP Academic.

Leigh, L. H. (1982), *Strict and Vicarious Liability: A Study in Administrative Criminal Law*, Modern Legal Studies, London: Sweet and Maxwell.

Lewis, D. (1997), "Do We Believe in Penal Substitution?," *Philosophical Papers*, 26 (3): 203–9.

Lind, D. (2015), "The Pragmatic Value of Legal Fictions," in M. Del Mar and W. Twining (eds.), *Legal Fictions in Theory and Practice*, Law and Philosophy Library 110, 83–109, Switzerland: Springer Verlag.

Murphy, M. C. (2009), "Not Penal Substitution but Vicarious Punishment," *Faith and Philosophy*, 26 (3): 253–73.

Murray, M. J., and M. C. Rea (2012), "Philosophy and Christian Theology," in E. N. Zalta (ed.), *Stanford Encyclopedia of Philosophy*. Available online: https://plato.stanford.edu/entries/christiantheology-philosophy/.

O'Collins, G. (2012), "Roman Catholic Response," in J. K. Beilby and P. R. Eddy (eds.), *Justification: Five Views*, 127–30, Downers Grove, IL: IVP Academic.

Ormerod, D. (2018), *Smith, Hogan, and Ormerod's Criminal Law*, 15th ed., Oxford: Oxford University Press.

Porter, S. J. (2004), "Swinburnian Atonement and the Doctrine of Penal Substitution," *Faith and Philosophy*, 21 (2): 228–41.

Purtill, R. (1990), "Justice, Mercy, Supererogation, and Atonement," in T. P. Flint (ed.), *Christian Philosophy*, Notre Dame, IN: University of Notre Dame Press.

Quinn, P. L. (1986), "Christian Atonement and Kantian Justification," *Faith and Philosophy*, 3 (4): 440–62.

Quinn, P. L. (2004), "Review of *Papers in Ethics and Social Philosophy* by David Lewis," *Noûs*, 38 (4): 711–30.

Rivière, J. (1909), *The Doctrine of the Atonement: A Historical Essay*, vol. 1, trans. Luigi Cappadelta, London: Kegan Paul, Trench, Trübner.

Schauer, F. (2015), "Legal Fictions Revisited," in M. Del Mar and W. Twining (eds.), *Legal Fictions in Theory and Practice*, Law and Philosophy Library 110, 113–30, Switzerland: Springer Verlag.

Smeaton, G. ([1870] 1957), *The Apostles' Doctrine of the Atonement*, rep. ed., Grand Rapids: Zondervan.

Stump, E. (2003), *Aquinas*, New York: Routledge.

Stump, E. (2018), *Atonement*, Oxford: Oxford University Press.

Turretin, F. (1992), *Institutes of Elenctic Theology*, 3 vols., trans. G. Musgrave Giger, ed. J. T. Dennison, Phillipsburg: Presbyterian and Reformed.

Vaihinger, H. ([1911] n. d.), *The Philosophy of 'As if'*, trans. C. K. Ogden, 2nd ed., International Library of Psychology, Philosophy, and Scientific Method, London: Kegan, Paul, Treach, Trubner.

Walen, A. (2014), "Retributive Justice, in E. N. Zalta (ed.), *Stanford Encyclopedia of Philosophy*. Available online: http://plato.stanford.edu/entries/justice-retributive/.

CHAPTER EIGHTEEN

Election, Grace, and Justice: Analyzing an Aporetic Tetrad

JAMES N. ANDERSON

The doctrine of election is frequently—but mistakenly—thought to be the exclusive property of Calvinists. In fact, the New Testament speaks explicitly of God's "election," "choosing," and "calling" of believers. Jesus spoke of "the elect," and the apostle Paul wrote directly about divine predestination. The doctrine of election is thus like the doctrine of creation: the question is not whether Christianity *has* such a doctrine, but *how* that doctrine should be understood. Not surprisingly, there have been sharp disagreements among Christians concerning the doctrine of election. What exactly does it mean to say that God *chooses* people? What are these people chosen *for*? Does God choose individuals or groups? On what basis does God choose? Do those chosen have any say in their election?

As an exercise in analytic dogmatic theology, in the spirit of "faith seeking understanding," we will focus our attention on a philosophical puzzle regarding election. We will reflect upon an *aporetic tetrad*: four theological claims to which Christians seem committed on the basis of divine revelation but which appear to form an inconsistent set.[1] We will then survey four ways of resolving the puzzle by modifying one or more of the limbs of the tetrad. Finally, a defense of one of these options will be briefly explored.

I. THE TETRAD

Consider the following claims that, on the face of it, command the assent of Christians:

E1: God chooses that some individuals will be saved.
E2: Salvation is by divine grace alone.
E3: God is essentially just.
E4: Some individuals will not be saved.

---

[1] The word *aporia* (from the Greek *aporos*: lit. "impassable") means "an irresolvable internal contradiction or logical disjunction in a text, argument, or theory" (OxfordDictionaries.com).

E1 expresses a basic doctrine of election. "God" refers to the transcendent creator of heaven and earth, understood by Christians to be a personal spiritual being and the possessor of all perfections. "Individuals" refers to particular human beings. "Saved" is a catch-all term for final deliverance from the consequences of sin: enmity with God, physical and spiritual corruption, death, and divine judgment. Salvation thus includes "the forgiveness of sins, the resurrection of the body, and the life everlasting" (Apostles' Creed). Note that E1 doesn't specify how or on what basis God chooses, only *that* he chooses.

E2 expresses the distinctively Christian conviction that salvation is entirely the gift of God. Salvation isn't merited in any respect by those who receive it; if it were, there would be grounds for the saved to take at least some credit for their salvation. Thus, we contribute nothing to our salvation that we do not graciously receive from God.

E3 expresses the idea that God is *by nature* perfectly just and therefore *cannot* act unjustly. God's justness isn't a contingent property like (say) Solomon's justness. Rather, God is *necessarily* just: justness is an essential attribute of God.

E4 should be straightforward to understand, since "individuals" and "saved" carry the same senses as in E1.

Why should Christians be inclined to affirm these four claims? In short, because they're warranted by divine revelation; more specifically, they're asserted or implied by Scripture, which Christians have traditionally held to be the inspired Word of God. Consider each claim in turn.

E1 is an explicit teaching of Scripture. No Christian doubts that some will be saved, but the Bible goes further and affirms that those who are saved have been *chosen* by God (Jn 6:37-44, 10:25-30; Rom. 8:28-30, 9:1-24, 11:5; Eph. 1:3-14; 2 Thess. 2:13; 2 Pet. 1:10). The doctrine of divine election is also supported by *a priori* intuitions about God's sovereignty motivated by perfect being theology. If God is perfect in knowledge and power, it would seem to follow that God's will cannot be frustrated or defied by anything within his creation. Thus, all events in the creation (including the salvation of his creatures) take place according to the will of God in some robust sense. If any creature is saved, God *willed* it to be so, which is equivalent to saying that God *decided* that it should be so. If God had decided otherwise, it would *not* have been so. Given that some will be saved, divine perfection implies divine election.

E2 finds strong support in the Pauline epistles (Rom. 4:4-5, 6:23, 11:6; 1 Cor. 1:26-31; Eph. 2:8-9; Tit. 3:5). In these texts the apostle frequently draws a sharp contrast between salvation *by grace* and salvation *by meritorious works*. Eternal life is the free gift of God as opposed to a reward earned by good deeds. For that very reason, he argues, the saved have no basis for pride or boasting in their salvation.

While E3 could be defended from specific biblical texts (Gen. 18:25; Pss. 7:11, 50:6, 145:17; Isa. 5:16; Jer. 11:20; Rom. 3:26), it would be no exaggeration to say the essential justness of God is presupposed by the entire biblical narrative. Moreover, as with E1, perfect being theology offers confirmatory warrant for E3. One who possesses all perfections would be not only just but also *essentially* just. A perfect being simply *could not fail* to act justly.

Finally, E4 is supported by various biblical texts depicting a final judgment where some are delivered and others condemned (Mt. 8:11-12, 22:11-13, 25:31-46; Jn 5:28-29; Rom. 9:22; 2 Thess. 1:9-10; Rev. 20:11-15). That some will be eternally lost is far from a happy thought, but it is nevertheless a teaching that finds considerable warrant in the Christian scriptures and subsequent church tradition.

II. THE APORIA

Christians have good reason to affirm all four limbs of the tetrad. But there's a problem: it looks like the conjunction of the first three propositions implies the negation of the fourth. Consider the following reasoning.

E1 asserts that God chooses that some individuals will be saved. But on what basis does God choose? E2 places constraints on our answer to that question. Consider some elect individual S. There are two possible cases: either (A) God's choice of S is conditioned upon some property or activity of S—some conditioning factor that we'll simply call X—or (B) God's choice is not so conditioned. (Candidates for X might include faith, repentance, obedience, a compliant will, an openness to the divine, or some combination of these.) The first case can be subdivided: either (A_1) S's having X is entirely the product of divine grace or (A_2) it isn't.

Now consider the implications of each of these options. If A_2 is the case, it looks like E2 has been compromised, because S can take at least *some* credit for having X and thus for being chosen by God for salvation. S would have *some* ground for boasting (contrary to Paul's assertions in 1 Cor. 1:28-29 and Eph. 2:8-9). A_1 preserves E2 but implies that S's having X is entirely up to God, in which case (to generalize) it's entirely up to God who will or won't be saved. The same is trivially true in case B. Thus, E2 requires that God's election be *ultimately* unconditional in this sense: it doesn't depend on factors that the elect contribute by their own power, apart from divine grace.

Now add E3 to the mix. It's widely held that justice requires fairness and impartiality. If God is essentially just, he must treat people fairly and impartially. God mustn't "play favorites" or give advantages to some that he withholds from others. E2 implies that no one *deserves* to be saved; indeed, all are equally *unworthy* of salvation. Hence it would appear that if God chooses *any* for salvation, justice demands that he choose *all* for salvation. Choosing some over others would be fundamentally unjust (unless some are more worthy than others, which E2 excludes).[2]

E3 thus seemingly requires that God choose either *all* or *none* for salvation. Since E1 entails that God chooses *some* for salvation, it follows from our reasoning that God must choose *all* for salvation. But obviously that contradicts E4.[3]

The conundrum may be approached from the opposite end. Start by supposing E4 to be true. It follows that God has not chosen some to be saved. If E1 and E3 are also true, presumably there must be some equitable basis on which God discriminates between the elect and the non-elect. There must be something about the elect—the "X factor" mentioned above—that provides *just grounds* for their being chosen over others. While that might be consistent with divine grace, it doesn't seem consistent with the idea of salvation *by grace alone*. E2 is cast into doubt.

Arguably most of the tension is generated by the conjunction of E2 and E3. E3 requires that any discrimination be *just* discrimination: there must be some *morally relevant* basis for choosing some over others. Yet E2 pushes us away from any virtue-based divine election.

---

[2] Notably, the apostle Paul acknowledged (Rom. 9:14) that his teaching on grace and election raised questions about God's justice.
[3] Assuming divine infallibility: if God chooses that S will be saved, then S will be saved.

III. FOUR RESOLUTIONS

In this section, we will survey four prominent positions taken by Christian thinkers on the question of divine election, each of which suggests a different resolution of our aporetic tetrad. These four positions will be labeled Augustinianism, Molinism, Ockhamism, and Universalism.[4]

III.1 Augustinianism

Augustinianism can be taken either broadly, as a view of divine providence, or more narrowly, as a view of divine predestination. On the broad view, Augustinianism holds that God has an eternal decree by which he infallibly ordains whatsoever comes to pass. Thus, whatever takes place in the creation does so ultimately because God willed it. Augustinianism places a premium on divine sovereignty and independence; God's decree isn't contingent upon or conditioned by factors beyond his control. For the Augustinian, God's knowledge of events within the creation is grounded solely in his decree: God *foreknows* because God *foreordains*.

This strong view of providence leads to a distinctive view of predestination. Augustinianism holds that election is *sovereign*, *unconditional*, and *particularist*. Simply put, there are individuals whom God chooses to save, and individuals whom God chooses *not* to save, and the ultimate explanation for why any particular individual is saved is that God was pleased for it to be so. Hence, divine election is *unconditional* in the sense that it isn't conditioned upon any virtuous attributes or actions found in the creature.[5]

Augustinians are typically concerned to preserve not only the sovereignty and independence of God, but also the essentially gracious nature of salvation. They worry that if election were conditioned upon foreseen faith, obedience, compliance, virtue, or the like, salvation couldn't be credited to divine grace alone. Augustinians regard E2 as sacrosanct and therefore strive to understand E1 in a fashion entirely consistent with E2.

How would an Augustinian resolve our aporetic tetrad? Certainly not by rejecting E1 or E2. Abandoning E4 would be one option, since the Augustinian maintains that it is within God's power to ensure that all are saved (Crisp 2003). That's an escape route few Augustinians have been willing to embrace, mainly because of the biblical texts that provide strong *prima facie* support for E4. Besides, for the purposes of this discussion we have simply stipulated that Augustinianism is particularistic rather than universalistic. The position that rejects E4 will be treated separately under the heading of Universalism.

All this to say, Augustinians will be most inclined to focus attention on E3. Since Augustinians typically hold that God possesses all perfections essentially, rejecting E3 is not an option. Rather, the Augustinian will seek to show that unconditional divine election violates no essential principles of justice, even if God chooses only *some* for salvation. This avenue will be further explored in the final section.

---

[4]Although three of these labels are associated with specific thinkers—Augustine of Hippo (354–430), Luis de Molina (1535–1600), and William of Ockham (c. 1280–1349)—no claims are made here about whether those individuals actually held the positions described. The labels are adopted purely for convenience.

[5]For a classic statement of the Augustinian position, see chapter 3 of the Westminster Confession of Faith (1646).

III.2 Molinism

Molinism is primarily a theory of divine providence that seeks to reconcile the idea of an eternal, immutable, infallible divine decree with a libertarian (incompatibilist) view of human freedom. On the one hand, Molinists want to join with Augustinians in affirming that God foreordains all things in some robust sense. On the other hand, Molinists are uncomfortable with the idea that God *determines* all events in the creation, including human free choices. Convinced that determinism is incompatible with freedom and moral responsibility, Molinists insist that God is able to *foreordain* our free choices without *determining* those choices.

How is this possible? Molinists offer an ingenious solution based on the idea of God's *middle knowledge*. Prior to his decision to create, God has two kinds of knowledge: necessary knowledge and middle knowledge. The former includes all *necessary* truths about God's nature and creative powers. The latter consists of God's exhaustive knowledge of *counterfactual* truths about what any possible creature *would* freely choose in any possible set of circumstances. These "counterfactuals of creaturely freedom" (CCFs) take the form of subjunctive conditionals:

(CCF) If S were in circumstances C, S would freely choose A.

Such truths are contingent because S has indeterministic free will. Nothing in circumstances C *necessitates* or *determines* that S chooses A. It's entirely possible for S *not* to choose A in C. Thus, CCFs do not fall under God's necessary knowledge. But neither do these truths depend on God's will. They aren't "made true" by God's decree, because they're logically prior to God's decree. They are, as most Molinists concede, brute facts about which free choices particular agents would make in different circumstances were God to create them.

Given that God has such knowledge, Molinists argue that it's within God's power not only to create a world with libertarian-free agents but also to foreordain—infallibly yet non-deterministically—every event within that world, including the free choices of those agents. Since God knows what choices S *would* make if God were to create S and arrange for S to be in particular circumstances, God can choose to create S and then arrange for S to be in those exact circumstances, thereby guaranteeing that S *will* make the expected choices, even though S isn't determined to do so.

Consequently, God is able to foreordain the entire history of his creation. On the basis of his necessary knowledge, God knows the set of all *possible* worlds, and on the basis of his middle knowledge, God knows the subset of those possible worlds he could *actually* bring about by creating some combination of (1) libertarian-free agents and (2) circumstances in which those agents make choices. It's then entirely up to God *which* world in that subset to actualize. Once God has freely decided (i.e., decreed) which possible world to actualize, he infallibly foreknows everything that will take place in his creation (this is God's *free* knowledge, according to the standard Molinist scheme).

What does this mean for divine election? On the Molinist view, divine election isn't unconditional in the way Augustinians take it to be. Instead, predestination is an indirect consequence of providence in general—that is, God's decree to actualize a specific possible world—and it is partly conditioned on human free choices. In short, God decides which possible world to actualize, and thereby decides (1) which possible creatures will be created and (2) which of those creatures will be finally saved. However, God doesn't have absolute freedom regarding *which* possible world to actualize, because he doesn't choose which CCFs are true, and thus he doesn't choose which possible worlds he *could* actualize. Insofar as the CCFs are dependent upon free choices, they're *human* rather than *divine* choices (Craig 1989: 148).

Thus, whether any individual S is predestined to salvation is ultimately determined by a combination of God's choices and S's choices. William Lane Craig puts the point succinctly:

> In Molina's view, we might say that it is *up to God* whether we find ourselves in a world in which we are predestined, but that it is *up to us* whether we are predestined in the world in which we find ourselves. (Craig 1989: 157, emphasis added)

How would a Molinist resolve our aporetic tetrad? In essence, the Molinist will argue that E1 can be suitably interpreted so as to leave intact the other three propositions. E1 is true precisely because God chooses which possible world will be actualized, and thus which individuals will be created, and which of those will be saved. No one is saved on the basis of their good works, and no one can be saved apart from divine grace. Whether any individual is finally saved depends only on their free response to God's gracious offer of the gift of salvation. God isn't unjust or unfair regarding who is or isn't saved because grace is equally available to all, and thus all have equal opportunity to be saved. Craig again:

> Persons in the world order that God has chosen to create who are not predestined to salvation cannot complain of injustice on God's part, because God in his goodness provides sufficient grace for salvation to all people in the world, and the only reason they are not predestined is that they freely ignore or reject the divine helps that God provides. Their damnation is therefore entirely their own fault. (Craig 1989: 156)

Thus, the Molinist argues, both E2 and E3 are preserved. Furthermore, the Molinist has a ready explanation for why E4 is true. Although there are some (perhaps many) possible worlds in which everyone is saved, God's creative options are constrained by the CCFs. Maybe none of these universalistic worlds are actualizable for God. Or maybe the only actualizable universalistic worlds are sparsely populated ones, and God deemed it better overall to actualize a world in which a multitude enjoy eternal life, even though some do not, compared with a world in which only a small number enjoy eternal life. In other words, the *optimal actualizable* world—given God's overall goals—is one in which E4 is true.

Concerns remain, however, about whether this resolution really does save E2 and E3. As we've noted, for Molinists, election is partly conditioned on the libertarian-free response of the individual: whether S is saved *in this world* is determined by S and not by God. Thus, it still looks as though S is contributing *something* to S's own salvation in addition to the grace God provides to S. Consider two individuals, Elly Elect and Robby Reprobate, who receive the same divine grace and have equal opportunity to respond in faith. Elly responds positively and receives eternal life, while Robby does not; thus, Elly is elect and Robby is not. Is it not the case that whatever distinguishes Elly and Robby with respect to their election (or otherwise) is attributable to them rather than to God? In that case, why shouldn't Elly take at least some of the credit for her election? It was up to her, and she had the "X factor." E2 now seems less pristine.

Furthermore, it's not so clear that Molinism leaves E3 unscathed. The Molinist claims that God's essential justice is preserved because God provides sufficient grace for all to be saved. All sinners are treated fairly and whether they embrace God's saving grace is entirely up to them. But consider again the difference between Elly and Robby. In this world, Robby makes free choices that result in his damnation. Yet, the Molinist must concede that in *other* possible worlds God could have actualized, Robby makes different choices, ones that result in his salvation. God *could* have actualized a world in which Robby is elect, but God chose otherwise. Indeed, if God *had* actualized such a world, Robby *would* have been elect. Yet that decision was entirely up to God. Robby had no say in the matter.

Presumably, God made that call on the basis of some greater-good principle: God was committed to actualizing a possible world with an optimum balance of saved and unsaved. Still, Robby might justifiably see himself as the unwilling and unwitting victim of a cosmic trade-off: God actualized *this* world, a world in which Robby is reprobate rather than elect, so that others could be elect rather than reprobate. Robby took one for the team. Perhaps there's nothing ultimately unjust about this, but arguably the Molinist story needs to be filled out further if we're to be satisfied that E3 has been preserved.

III.3 Ockhamism

Ockhamism represents a weaker view of providence than Augustinianism and Molinism, and thus a weaker view of election. On the Ockhamist view, God doesn't infallibly *foreordain* every event within his creation, although he does infallibly *foreknow* every event. Simply put, God decides to create a particular cosmos and to populate it with creatures possessing libertarian free will.[6] Prior to this decision, God doesn't know how things will eventually turn out because at that point *there's nothing to know*.[7] Only once God has made his decision—or perhaps only once he has executed it—does God foreknow how things will turn out. Rather than exercising meticulous providential control over his creation, God directs events in more general terms through his initial act of creation and subsequent actions within the world (e.g., the calling of Abraham). The exact course of events is determined "in real time" by the free decisions of his creatures. Nevertheless, the Ockhamist insists, God infallibly foreknows all these free decisions.

Inevitably this leads the Ockhamist to understand election in *conditional* terms. God foreknows that humans will fall into sin, but in his grace and mercy God decides to offer a way of salvation. No one *deserves* this salvation: God is under no obligation to make it available to anyone. Thus, salvation is entirely the free, gracious gift of God. However, because God has also bestowed the gift of libertarian freedom, and is loath to override or circumvent that freedom, God leaves it entirely up to each individual whether to accept the free gift of salvation.

Suppose then that S freely accepts the gift and is consequently saved. In what sense did God *choose* S for salvation? Only in a conditional sense: S's election is conditioned on S's free choices. In effect, God chooses S for salvation *because* God foresees S's positive response to the offer of salvation. Only in a very generic sense is election unconditional: without regard to any *actual* creaturely choices, God freely chooses a particular *class* of individuals to save (e.g., believers) or a particular set of *conditions* for salvation (e.g., faith and repentance).

---

[6] Strictly speaking, God doesn't decide which, or how many, libertarian-free creatures will populate the universe; that's partly left up to the creatures themselves in the free use of their procreative capacities.
[7] "Prior" is used here in a logical or explanatory rather than temporal sense.

The Ockhamist view of election may be expressed by way of a medieval distinction between God's *antecedent* and *consequent* will (Ockham 1983: 13–16). Antecedently—that is, prior to his foreknowledge of human choices—God wills the salvation of all (i.e., that all respond positively to the offer of salvation). Consequently—that is, considering his foreknowledge of human choices—God wills only the salvation of believers. The decree of election is thus a function of God's *consequent* will.

In sum, whereas the Molinist makes election conditional on God's *middle knowledge* of human free choices, the Ockhamist makes election conditional on God's *foreknowledge* of human free choices.

Despite the differences between the Molinist and Ockhamist positions on divine providence and predestination, the Ockhamist's resolution of the aporetic tetrad will be similar to the Molinist's: both will appeal to the conditionality of election, which places the determinative "X factor" squarely on the shoulders of the creature. On the Ockhamist view, God doesn't have an infallible pre-creational plan that entails the salvation of specific individuals (and the non-salvation of others). Instead, God creates a world that establishes certain general parameters for the course of events, without specifying the events themselves. It's entirely up to God *whether* salvation is made available, *what form* that salvation will take, and *upon what conditions* that salvation will be obtained. But it isn't up to God *which* individuals will obtain salvation. In short, God makes salvation available to all on an equal basis, and it's entirely up to the creatures themselves, exercising their libertarian free choices, whether or not they are saved. The Ockhamist will argue that God cannot be charged with unjust discrimination regarding his election of some to salvation, because God's choices are, in effect, merely the rubber-stamping of the choices of the elect themselves.

To the extent that the Ockhamist's resolution shares ground with the Molinist's solution, it carries the same baggage. The Ockhamist strategy is to preserve E3 by qualifying E1: divine election is conditioned on foreseen human free choices. Likewise, E4 is protected because, given how divine election operates, it's not up to God who is saved and who isn't. But as with the Molinist resolution, concerns remain as to whether E2 has really been preserved. Consider again our friends Elly and Robby. The Ockhamist will insist that neither can be saved *apart* from grace and both receive *sufficient* grace in the sense that both have it within their power to respond freely to the offer of salvation and to receive it. Yet if Elly responds positively while Robby does not, such that Elly is elect and Robby is not, it's hard to see why Elly shouldn't claim some of the credit for having that determinative "X factor."

III.4 Universalism

Universalism, as we will define it here, is the view that everyone will be finally saved. Universalists need not take a position on the nature of human free will, although a compatibilist view arguably fits better with their other commitments. For the Universalist wants to affirm that, in normal circumstances, S will be saved only if S freely responds to the offer of salvation. Thus, for God to secure the salvation of all, it must be within God's power to ensure that every individual freely responds to the offer of salvation. It's hard to see how God could possess that power if humans have libertarian free will (Crisp 2003: 140).

In any event, whatever position is taken on the nature of human free will and the means by which God accomplishes universal salvation, the Universalist's resolution of our aporetic tetrad is simple: deny E4. For the Universalist, *everyone* is elect, since everyone is saved in the end. If God decrees that *all* individuals will be saved, E1 follows by trivial entailment. Since no one deserves to be saved, and election isn't conditioned on anything found in some individuals but not others, E2 is safeguarded. Moreover, there's no threat to E3 because God treats everyone equally, inasmuch as God doesn't choose some for salvation but not others.

Of course, this resolution still exacts a cost. The significant support for E4 in both Scripture and Christian tradition cannot be easily dismissed. The Christian doctrine of the final judgment, and the many warning passages in the New Testament, look rather blunted if not altogether redundant on the supposition of universal salvation.

It's also questionable whether E2 is adequately preserved on the Universalist view. One of the characteristics of grace is that it must be *freely* bestowed; it cannot be necessitated or obligated. If E3 commits God to ensuring the salvation of all, how could that salvation also be regarded as a free act of grace? If the Universalist replies that God didn't *have* to elect everyone to salvation, even though he freely chose to do so, that's tantamount to saying that the aporetic tetrad presents no logical problem in the first place. And if there's no problem, there's nothing for the Universalist—or anyone else—to solve.

IV. TOWARD A DEFENSE OF AUGUSTINIANISM

In this final section, let us revisit the Augustinian position and consider how it might be further defended. This resolution invites a closer look at E3 and its entailments. Augustinians don't want to deny that God is essentially just, only to question whether divine justice requires that God treat people equally in this specific respect: if God unconditionally elects *some* individuals to salvation, then God must unconditionally elect *all* individuals to salvation.

Some Augustinians have invoked the so-called *ex lex* defense, according to which God is literally "above the law" (Clark 1995: 240–2). On this view, God's essential justness entails only that he judges *his creatures' actions* fairly and impartially; it imposes no constraints God's own actions, including election. To ask whether such-and-such a divine action would be just is either to commit a category mistake or to invite a logically trivial answer. Although this approach dissolves the problem quite effectively, few Augustinians have found it attractive, because it suggests that principles of justice "float free" of God's nature and requires us to sacrifice any analogical relationship between divine justice and human justice. Would E3 even be an intelligible claim on this view?

A more promising approach for the Augustinian will be point out that justice is not a monotonic concept. There are competing conceptions of justice and its demands (Miller 2017). Precisely which principle of justice would be violated by God on the Augustinian view? Let's review six candidates and consider how the Augustinian might respond in each case, starting with the classical conception of justice reflected in *The Institutes of Justinian* (AD 533):

J1: Justice requires giving people what they deserve.[8]

Clearly on the Augustinian view the elect do not get what they deserve. As sinners and rebels against God, they (along with the non-elect) deserve damnation, but they receive

---

[8]"Justice is the constant and perpetual wish to render every one his due" (Sandars 1865: 77).

salvation instead. Yet the same is true for all four positions surveyed above. Divine mercy *entails* that some people will not receive the punishment they deserve. There's nothing distinctive to Augustinianism that presents a problem here, if indeed there is a problem. Furthermore, Augustinians can argue on the basis of a penal substitutionary theory of the atonement that the demands of justice are satisfied *even in the case of the elect*: their sins are imputed to Christ, who bears the penalty on their behalf as a vicarious sacrifice (Craig 2018: 37–48).

J2: Justice requires treating people equally.

Egalitarian conceptions of justice are all the rage today, but more precision is needed here. We must ask *in what respect* people should receive equal treatment. Does justice require equality of *outcome*? Universalism alone could satisfy J2 in that respect, but we've already noted the problems that raises for E2, and the idea that justice demands equal *outcomes* is highly suspect. What about equality of *opportunity*? Augustinians can argue that with regard to circumstances and capacities the non-elect have the same opportunities as the elect.[9] Equality of *standards*? Again, Augustinians will observe that no double standards are deployed here: the sins of the elect and the non-elect are judged by the same measure. In short, there's no obvious interpretation of J2 that singles out Augustinianism as peculiarly problematic.

J3: Justice requires treating people impartially.

The relationship between justice and impartiality is much debated among ethicists (Feltham and Cottingham 2010). The notion that justice excludes *any and all* partiality is morally counterintuitive. (Is it inherently unjust to show special favor towards one's family and friends?) Again, more precision is needed. What *kind* of impartiality is relevant here? If J3 means only that everyone should be judged by the same standards, such that no class of people (e.g., the wealthy or the powerful) receive special exemptions from the demands of justice, the Augustinian position is entirely consistent with J3, since it doesn't entail that the elect are treated with different *standards* of justice than the non-elect.[10] In fact, one could argue that J3 is better satisfied by unconditional election than conditional election, for on the first view God pays no heed to the specific traits of S when choosing S for salvation.

J4: Justice requires treating people indiscriminately.

Since non-universal election *entails* discrimination, Augustinians can observe again that Molinists and Ockhamists face the same challenge. In any case, justice itself *requires* certain kinds of discrimination, for example, between the guilty and the innocent. The question is whether unconditional election involves *unjust* discrimination. If J4 is reduced to the tautological principle that justice requires treating people justly, that hardly presents a challenge to Augustinians or to anyone else.

J5: Justice requires treating people non-coercively.

The concern here is that it's unjust to force people to do things against their will or to subject people to painful experiences without their consent. On the Augustinian view, it

---

[9] We should resist the temptation to argue, in a tight circle, that *being chosen by God* is an opportunity the elect alone enjoy.
[10] At most J3 would require God to elect at least *some* people from every relevant class.

could be argued, election isn't conditioned on human free choices, and thus individuals are saved or damned *without their consent*—and that's an injustice.

In response, Augustinians can point out that unconditional election doesn't entail coercion. The Augustinian position is consistent with the claim that the elect are those, and only those, who *will* to be saved—who freely respond to God's offer of salvation. Although *election* is unconditional, *salvation* (obtaining eternal life) is conditional on the responses of the creatures. What God's decree of election does, in effect, is determine which creatures will respond positively. Only someone committed to libertarian free will would consider that a violation of J5. But the Augustinian is not so committed. Whether the Augustinian position is consistent with J5 thus reduces to the question of whether compatibilism is true. Compatibilism may not be the majority view among Christian philosophers, but neither is it a position easily refuted (Cowan and Welty 2015; Welty and Cowan 2015; Bignon 2018).

J6: Justice requires treating people non-arbitrarily.

Finally, one might think that God violates J6 on the Augustinian view. Unconditional election implies that God arbitrarily picks some people over others, with no reference to the individuals themselves, like the shopper who randomly pulls a packet of Oreos off the shelf simply because she wants some Oreos. The shopper's choice is arbitrary insofar as she has no reason to take one packet rather than another. Any packet will do! Wouldn't it be unjust to treat *people* in that way?

Augustinians can point out that unconditional election doesn't entail that God has *no reasons at all* for his choices, only that those reasons don't terminate in commendable actions or attributes of the elect, such as favorable responses to divine grace, that obtain independently of God's will. The Augustinian can affirm that God has reasons for his decree of election, while insisting that those reasons do not include any considerations that conflict with E2. For example, God might choose S not because of anything about S *per se* but rather because S's conversion has ramifications for other people and subsequent events. In other words, S's salvation plays a role in a larger plan for which God has good and wise reasons.

Whether the Augustinian resolution of our aporetic tetrad can be finally vindicated is hardly a question to be settled in such a brief treatment. But at least our discussion has exposed the tight connections between the doctrine of election and other central Christian doctrines. Analytical reflection upon these inter-doctrinal relationships can challenge and enrich our understanding of the Christian faith—indeed, of the One on whom that faith depends.

References

Bignon, G. (2018), *Excusing Sinners and Blaming God: A Calvinist Assessment of Determinism, Moral Responsibility, and Divine Involvement in Evil*, Eugene, OR: Pickwick Publications.

Clark, G. H. (1995), *Religion, Reason, and Revelation*, 2nd ed., Hobbs, NM: The Trinity Foundation.

Cowan, S. B., and G. A. Welty (2015), "Pharaoh's Magicians Redivivus: A Response to Jerry Walls on Christian Compatibilism," *Philosophia Christi*, 17 (1): 151–73.

Craig, W. L. (1989), "Middle Knowledge, a Calvinist-Arminian Rapprochement?," in C. H. Pinnock (ed.), *The Grace of God, the Will of Man*, 141–64. Grand Rapids, MI: Zondervan.

Craig, W. L. (2018), *The Atonement*, Cambridge: Cambridge University Press.

Crisp, O. D. (2003), "Augustinian Universalism," *International Journal for Philosophy of Religion*, 53 (3): 127–45.

Feltham, B., and J. Cottingham, eds. (2010), *Partiality and Impartiality: Morality, Special Relationships, and the Wider World*, Oxford: Oxford University Press.

Miller, D. (2017), "Justice," in E. N. Zalta (ed.), *The Stanford Encyclopedia of Philosophy*. Available online: https://plato.stanford.edu/archives/fall2017/entries/justice/.

Ockham, W. of. (1983), *Predestination, God's Foreknowledge, And Future Contingents*, trans. M. M. Adams and N. Kretzmann, 2nd ed., Indianapolis, IN: Hackett.

Sandars, T. C. (1865), *The Institutes of Justinian with English Introduction, Translation, and Notes*, 3rd ed., London: Longmans, Green.

Welty, G. A., and S. B. Cowan (2015), "Won't Get Foiled Again: A Rejoinder to Jerry Walls," *Philosophia Christi*, 17 (2): 427–42.

PART IV
Pneumatology

CHAPTER NINETEEN

The Indwelling of the Holy Spirit

ADONIS VIDU

The coming of the Holy Spirit to indwell believers (Rom. 5:5, 8:9, 11; 1 Cor. 3:16; Jn 14:17, 23) poses a number of conceptual problems for theologians and philosophers. Within the space allotted, I will only focus on a single issue, namely, what the Catholic tradition calls the *formality* of the indwelling: What form does the coming of the Spirit into a human person take?

It must not be assumed that the notion of "indwelling" is conceptually transparent. Before any explanatory account can be given (which is what I take a discussion of the formality to be), we have to agree on the description itself. I will therefore start with a clarification of the vocabulary and then move to a clarification of the grammatical rules governing the use of indwelling language. Note that while issues of definition (meaning) are necessarily entangled with issues of explanation (truth), they should nonetheless be distinguished. We start from meaning and then proceed to ask questions of truth.

I. PRELIMINARY CONSIDERATIONS

First, some vocabulary definitions. Let us define indwelling as a relation between the Spirit (S) and a human person (P) that bears the following characteristics:

(V1): Both S and P retain their personal and substantial identities. That is, the terms of the relation remain the persons that they are, and they do not undergo substantial changes. If, say, S were to undergo a substantial change, it would not be indwelling P but would be dissolved in her. The stipulation that P retains her personal identity indicates that what makes P a person, the person that she is, is and remains some intrinsic quality in P. Any relationship in which either P or S undergo such changes would no longer be recognizably a relationship of indwelling. Note that I am not suggesting that such changes are impossible, only that, were they to occur, they would characterize a different kind of relation.

(V2): P can be said to have, or to possess, S. While "having" and "possessing" are not yet defined, at a *prima facie* level a relationship of indwelling should be characterized in this way, with certain stipulations later to be discussed. This vocabulary stipulation simply indicates that indwelling is also a relationship of inclusion, where P includes S in some sense. Or, to put it differently, S must be in some sense intrinsic to P, in the sense that either S or a certain relationship to S becomes constitutive for P. While it is true that P also exists in S (Rom. 8:9; Gal. 5:16, 25; Rev. 1:10), it does not "indwell" S.

(V3): In virtue of this relationship, and given certain conditions, P acquires capacities that may only be had as a result of such a relationship. It is recognized as axiomatic in the community of authorized users of this language that the indwelling of the Holy Spirit is ordered to an end that concerns the sanctification of the human being. However, to say that P is in a relationship of indwelling is not synonymous with saying that P is actively exercising the capacities that are thereby acquired. It only indicates that P has those capacities, whether or not she is using them.

Now that we have clarified what we mean by indwelling, we are closer to understanding the formality of the indwelling, but not before setting out a number of grammatical rules that govern such an inquiry in the community of Christian theologians.

(G1): Both P and S must retain genuine control of their agency in some way sufficient for her personal integrity. This rule stipulates not that every one of P's actions must be under her exclusive control, but that a sufficient number of such operations must be agented by her in order to safeguard her freedom. It can also be said that P must not be understood to be passive, on the whole, during the exercise of those capacities that have been acquired as a result of the indwelling. Let us call this stipulation, following Adams (2013), the Genuine Agency Problem.

(G2): The relationship of indwelling must be sufficiently distinct from other relationships whereby S is present to P, or whereby S is present to other objects. Christian theology recognizes several forms of divine presence: by immensity or omnipresence whereby God is present to all reality in virtue of his being its creator and sustainer; by intensity, whereby God is taken to be present through special action; by incarnation, which is the presence of God in the hypostatic union; and, to keep the alliteration, by impanation, which is the Eucharistic presence of God. It is readily recognized that all of these are different modalities of divine presence. The indwelling must be sufficiently distinguished from all of these, on pain of massive theological failure. Failure to distinguish it from divine presence by immensity entails that all people are indwelt by the Spirit, which is explicitly denied by Scripture (Jn 7:39; Rom. 8:9). Failure to distinguish it from presence by intensity similarly confuses the operation of the Spirit in the lives of many people, not all of whom can be said to belong to him. Crucially, a failure to distinguish the indwelling from the hypostatic union (leaving aside the question whether Christ was also indwelt by the Spirit) sacrifices the uniqueness of the incarnation. Let us call this the Special Connection Problem.

(G3): Given the particular correlation of unity and diversity, and of persons and essence, in trinitarian theology, any account of the indwelling of the Holy Spirit must respect such trinitarian grammar. For the purposes of this chapter, I will assume the classic trinitarian doctrine of inseparable operations, which stipulates that the divine persons act indivisibly *ad extra* in virtue of their common essence and of their one will, one intellect, one power. Let us call this the Trinitarian Distribution Rule.

Whatever explanatory account is provided, it must conform to these grammatical rules. It goes without saying that these rules do not prejudge the outcome of our conversation, but they set the boundaries for both meaningful and truthful theological speech. With that, we are now in a position to survey the field.

II. THREE HISTORIC POSITIONS

I will identify three broad historic positions on the question of the formality of indwelling. Two of these positions are specific to Catholic theology, where the conversation about the formality of the indwelling has been—by far—the most active. A third position will be identified as the Eastern Orthodox position. For the reader who is wondering if there is no Protestant contribution to this discussion, it has to be said that it may be understood as a synthesis of one of the Catholic positions and the Orthodox position. More on this in the last section of the chapter, though. In what follows I will have to be schematic, trying to distill the essence of the most important positions, although there is much variation in details and much diversity between the authors of even a single school of thought. I will also proceed in an approximate historical order.

But what is the conversation fundamentally about? The stage has to be set before we understand the plot. We have defined indwelling as a particular kind of relation between S and P, having certain characteristics and being governed by certain rules. The fundamental reason we have such an array of views is because the ontological difference between S and P poses a particular dilemma. Given this ontological difference, any relation raises certain issues. As the literature demonstrates, any of the accounts of divine presence creates special problems. No less does the presence of God by indwelling.

Take the incredibly suggestive and insightful *Flatland*, by Edwin Abbott (1992), which is an exploration of the possible relations between uni-, bi-, and tridimensional objects. A sphere passing through a two-dimensional space will have a certain form in that space: it will be a circle. We might say that the presence of the sphere in two-dimensional space takes the form of a circle (or, tangentially, of a single, ideal point). Given that the concept of indwelling does not simply identify a bare relation, but a relation in which S becomes intrinsic to P (per V2), and given that S and P belong to two fundamentally different realms of being and, moreover, that both S and P must not be understood to change substantially (V1), it is not difficult to sense the difficulty. A circle is substantially not a sphere. Yet, to put it somewhat loosely, it is all that a sphere can be in such a dimension of space. A sphere cannot be present as itself, that is, as spherical, inside a two-dimensional space. It can certainly be related to two-dimensional space, as spherical, but it cannot become intrinsic to it, as spherical.

We thus have our problem: Given the ontological difference between God and finite human persons, can the Holy Spirit, as the third person of the Trinity, eternal, uncreated, and transcendent, be intrinsically present as himself in a human being, created, temporal, finite? Now, on to the various positions.

II.1 Uncreated Grace Model

The first school originates with Peter Lombard, who takes a position on the question of whether in being united with the Holy Spirit we are principally united with his gifts, or with his person. Lombard (2007: 97) argues that we are primarily united with the Holy Spirit himself, who acts in the human person directly, perfecting her operations. Therefore, P's new operation, love, is newly created in him by a direct action of the Holy Spirit. Thus, P's charity is the Holy Spirit himself and not merely S's gift to P. The

Holy Spirit, Lombard holds, is given to us when the Holy Spirit makes us love God. Note that, on this position, it is the Holy Spirit as himself, and through himself, which becomes intrinsic to P. It is as if the sphere is indwelling two-dimensional space precisely as a sphere.

Much about this position is appealing. From a Protestant perspective, it supports a soteriology that prioritizes God's unilateral and omnipotent action (uncreated grace) over any created habit, or infused virtues. Neither Lombard nor many of the Reformers would deny the necessity for sanctification of those infused virtues, yet both would hold that their infusion follows as an effect from the presence of the Spirit himself. For them the Spirit indwells through himself and not through any created intermediaries or forms.

Despite having suffered, as we shall see, heavy blows at the hands of Bonaventure and Thomas Aquinas, this position has seen something of a resurgence in the work of Petavius (1865), Scheeben (2008), and a number of post-Vatican II theologians (Donnelly 1947; Rahner 1961, 1970; Coffey 2005; etc.), owing not to a small extent to G3, the Trinitarian Distribution Rule. The argument of this later group goes something like this: unless the Spirit is given to us as himself, not as some created form (created charity), we cannot experience him in his hypostatic particularity. If the Spirit's indwelling is through some created form, then, given the doctrine of inseparable operations, according to which anything created or acted through the divine efficient causality is common to the three persons, the personal reality of the Spirit will be obscured from the life of the believer.

However, as Adams (2013: 27) suggests, Lombard's proposal struggles with G1, the Genuine Agency requirement. If the love in our soul *just is* the Holy Spirit, it follows that P's love for God is not genuinely P's. One might also argue that the Uncreated Grace Model, in assigning an external operation exclusively to the Holy Spirit, flaunts the inseparable operations doctrine (under G3). If the Spirit is present by direct action and the indwelling must be proper to the Spirit, then this direct action must be exclusively the Spirit's. To prevent this implication, it has been suggested that the operation of the Spirit upon the believer is not in the order of efficient causality but of a quasi-formal nature (Rahner 1961: 330). By this is meant that the Spirit becomes the quasi-form of the believer's love, which is to say that P's love is S. However, since it would appear to make God, or one of the trinitarian persons, the form of a created reality, quasi-formal causation has been vehemently opposed by a number of Thomists (Congar 1983: 88; Hill 1983: 293; Emery 2007: 348; Levering 2016: 251).

II.2 Created Grace Model

The second solution to this issue insists that the formality by which S indwells P is not S itself but some created form, specifically, the habit of charity, which is a gift received in the soul and which perfects the operation of P.

In his *Commentary on the Sentences*, Aquinas argues that

> whatever is received into a thing is received according to the recipient's mode. But uncreated love, which is the Holy Spirit, is participated in by the creature; therefore he must be participated in according to the creature's mode. But the creature's mode is finite; thus what is received into the creature must be some finite love. But every finite thing is created. Therefore in the soul having the Holy Spirit, there is a created charity. (Aquinas 2008: 10)

Aquinas in fact is speaking of an "assimilation of one thing into another" (Aquinas 2008: 10), which conforms to V2: S does not remain extrinsic to P but is assimilated into P through some form that bears the likeness of S, in this case, created love. This way Aquinas can say that the efficient cause behind the indwelling is the whole Trinity (G3), while the Holy Spirit is, distinctly, the exemplary cause of the indwelling—given that created loved is patterned after uncreated love (the Spirit himself). Similarly, the Genuine Agency test (G1) is passed, given that the love which the habit of charity perfects is still genuinely P's love.

Finally, as far as G2 is concerned, the relation of P to S is not simply in terms of God's omnipresence, which is in fact presupposed. Rather, it is in terms of an operational change brought about in P by divine grace. As an operational change brought about through an infused habit that perfects P's operation, this is not a substantial change (V1). P remains who she always was, but now an infused capacity disposes her to love God.

To summarize, the created grace model claims that the formality by which the Holy Spirit indwells a human being is a created, finite charity, brought about by the whole trinity, and which disposes the person to love God. Against this model converge the objections of both the Uncreated Grace Model as well as those of the next model. Since I hold to a version of the present model, I will seek to respond to the most significant of these objections in the final section of the chapter.

II.3 Uncreated Energies Model

The Eastern Orthodox approach, generically more Platonist than Aristotelian, puts the matter in an entirely different way. Eastern Orthodoxy eschews a strict demarcation between uncreated and created reality, a binary that commits the Western tradition to a doctrine of pure act, whereby God's being is identical to his actions. Such an approach seems to inhibit a real communion between God and creation, thus preventing the ultimate finality of the Orthodox understanding of salvation, viz. deification. To preserve both divine aseity and eternity, Eastern theologians introduce an ontological distinction between the essence and the energies of God. The energies of God are God's activity and God's life, which are distinct from the essence (contra pure act), yet naturally flow from it. The energies flow from the common essence of the persons and so inseparably belong to all the divine persons.

Orthodoxy stresses to a greater extent the mysterious character of the indwelling union, and it refuses to explore further the formality of this communication. At the same time, it stresses that the gifts that are consequent upon the indwelling are nothing else but the uncreated energies of God himself. Given that the energies function as a sort of intermediary between the "superessential" being of God and creation, no additional calculus of the formality of the indwelling is necessary.

It is somewhat unfair to evaluate this model in such a space, given that, as we have seen, the justification of punctual theological claims presupposes the acceptance of a common language and conceptual framework. The Orthodox model of indwelling can only be judged together with an evaluation of the conceptual framework in which it is lodged, as a whole. I will therefore restrict myself to a number of modest observations.

First, as far as G1 goes, since the energies belong to the Trinity as a whole, and not specifically to a trinitarian person, P's faculties do not appear to be in danger of being en-hypostasized in a divine person. On the contrary, an insistence on the mysterious character of the indwelling leads Vladimir Lossky to make much of the anonymity of the indwelling Spirit: "The Holy Spirit in His coming, while He manifests the common nature of the Trinity, leaves His own Person concealed beneath His Godhead. He remains unrevealed, hidden, so to speak, by the gift in order that this gift which He imparts may be fully ours, adapted to our persons" (Lossky 1976: 168).

The gift of the energies common to the whole Trinity obscures the personality of the Spirit. In this, there is a real distinction established with regards to the incarnation (G2, the Special Connection Problem). Lossky writes that the work of Christ includes in itself the human nature, while the Spirit's work includes the human person: "The one lends His hypostasis to the nature, the other gives His divinity to the persons. Thus, the work of Christ unifies; the work of the Holy Spirit diversifies" (Lossky 1976: 167). There is no thought here of any actuation or information of any human attributes by the person of the Spirit —as in the case of the incarnation, where one might be able to speak of an actuation of the human nature by the person of the Logos (De la Taille 1952). Rather, P receives not the identity of S but its "divinity." Admittedly, one strength of the Orthodox position is that it appears to account for the reality of the deification: the human person participates not in a created gift but directly and mysteriously in the common uncreated energies of the Trinity.

This brings us to the third grammatical rule (G3), the Trinitarian Distribution Rule. While the orthodox model is to be commended for its observance of the rule of inseparability, in my view at least, it makes it difficult to understand in just what way the indwelling is proper to the Holy Spirit. The uncreated grace model tends to highlight the very personal presence of the Spirit himself, either through an exclusive operation of the Spirit or through an exclusive quasi-formal causality upon P's will. The Orthodox model, on the contrary, embraces the Spirit's anonymity. However, in doing so, and given the inseparability of the energies themselves, it struggles to account for just in what way the indwelling belongs to the Spirit himself.

In my judgment, the Created Grace Model does have the resources to account for a distinct relation to the indwelling Spirit, while also observing the classic doctrine of inseparability. I will now turn to two significant and powerful objections to the Created Grace Model.

III. OBJECTION I: EXTRINSICISM

In the *Summa Theologica* I.Q43.a2, Aquinas (1981) gives what has been called an "operational" account of the indwelling. Whereas in his commentary on the Lombardian *Sentences* his analysis was ontological, proceeding from above, as it were, in the *Summa Theologica*, he proceeds from below. Aquinas argues that the Holy Spirit is present in the believer in the manner in which the object known is present in the knower and the object loved is present in the lover. Since in the indwelling God does not change, the change that takes place is in the operations of the believer.

This analysis of the divine presence raises the critique that God's presence to the indwelt is rather extrinsic (thus failing V2). S is not intrinsic to P but is only present in P in the semblance of a form, created charity, which is intrinsic to P. But if S really remains extrinsic, the goal of indwelling cannot possibly be reached, as Donnelly (1947: 452) fears: "How can a created, physical accident make us truly sharers of the divine nature, and how can uncreated grace, which surely does not inform the soul, truly sanctify?"

William Alston (1988: 140–1) formulates a similar criticism of what he calls the "fiat" model of indwelling: "My objection to this account is that it leaves God too external and so fails to account for the distinctive sort of internality we are seeking to understand. God is present within us only as something known and loved." Alston takes Aquinas to be saying that sharing

> in the divine life amounts to no more than my having, in infinitely lesser measure, a knowledge and love of God of the same sort as that possessed by God himself. What is shared are attributes, features, aspects. On this account I do not share in the divine life in any way other than that in which I share in your life when you and I know and love something (perhaps you) in the same way. (Alston 1988: 141)

Alston also rejects what he has called the "interpersonal model," which I have not included in this historical survey, despite a notable recent defense by Steven Porter and Brandon Rickabaugh (Porter and Rickabaugh 2018). This leads to Alston's own explanatory account of indwelling: "there is a literal merging or mutual interpenetration of the life of the individual and the divine life, a breaking down of the barriers that normally separate one life from another." We each conduct our lives separately, even if we share much of the same kind of reactions, experiences, and so on.

> If we can now imagine some breakdown of those barriers, perhaps by a neural wiring hookup, so that your reactions, feelings, thoughts, and attitudes, or some of them, are as immediately available to me as my own, and so that they influence my further thinking and feeling and behavior in just the same way that my own do, there would have occurred a partial merging of our hitherto insulated lives. (Alston 1988: 141–2)

Alston in fact suggests that, in the indwelling, the Spirit allows part of his life to be shared with us, and shares in our own life, after the manner in which two people might experience a neural wiring hookup, or after the manner of two people sharing a common experience.

Alston does not, in fact, appreciate that for Aquinas it is truly the Holy Spirit that becomes intrinsic in the believer, even if this only takes place according to a created form. Many theologians fail to understand that Aquinas is not interjecting an alien intermediary between us and the Spirit. What he has in mind is the Spirit all along, only through a particular relation with its finite *terminus*. In Dist 17.2 of his commentary on the *Sentences*, he uses the distinction between light as regarded in itself, or "as it is in the extremity of a limited diaphanous" (Aquinas 2008: 11) where it is called color. Color is nothing but light, received in something as color. To say that color is the form of light is not to say that there is an extrinsic relation between the two. Rather, color *just is* light in this particular medium. In the same way, Thomas explains, "the Holy Spirit considered in Himself is called Holy Spirit and God; but considered as existing in the soul that he moves to the act of charity is called charity" (Aquinas 2008: 11).

Eleonore Stump's recent work has paid much attention to the notion of union with God, and hence to indwelling. Drawing on recent work in neuroscience, especially the phenomenon of mirror neurons, she argues that we can understand the relationship of indwelling as a sharing of thoughts and emotions between two persons. Such a relationship exceeds the manner in which the loved one is in the lover. In love there is a second-personal presence of one to the other. In the Spirit's indwelling "an even more powerful second-personal presence of shared love is possible for God in the indwelling of the HS, where what is united is not just thoughts and feelings but persons themselves" (Stump 2018: 139).

Stump does not appear to reject Aquinas's account. In fact, she thinks that "Aquinas makes a roughly analogous point" with the neuroscience on shared attention "about the mechanisms of cognition for perception" (Stump 2018: 137). She does think, however, that there is a quantitative difference between indwelling and this presence of the beloved in the lover. For present purposes, it is enough to say that, in my view, Aquinas does account for that quantitative superiority precisely because he is offering not just an operational analysis of indwelling, where the analogy of the beloved's presence in the lover belongs, but also a metaphysical one, where he clarifies that this is an aspect of the proper mission of the Holy Spirit.

It must also be added that only an operational analysis can do justice to G3. Both Alston and Stump give an analysis of the indwelling in terms that appeal to God's essential acts: sharing a life (Alston), mind reading and sharing of thoughts, emotions, persons (Stump). But, as we have seen, such an appeal to divine operations that are essential and thus inseparable cannot get us to what is truly proper to the Spirit in the indwelling. An operational account of indwelling, where the presence of the Spirit is regarded from the perspective of the elevation of P's charity through the infusion of love can illuminate that which is distinctively the Spirit's in the indwelling, namely, love. Here the Spirit is not simply part of the common efficient causality behind mind reading and sharing of life but the exclusive exemplary cause of created charity. Finally, this exemplary charity is not extrinsic to either S or P but intrinsic to both.

IV. OBJECTION 2: THE PROTESTANT OBJECTION

The position I am taking in this chapter appears to conflict with instincts close to the heart of Protestant theology. To introduce a created intrinsic form into the analysis of the indwelling appears to make salvation, and union with God, depend upon a human operation. In reacting against the perceived "synergism" of the Roman Catholic doctrines of grace, the Reformers tended to retrieve the Lombardian view. As Charles Moeller and Gérard Philips argue, "their practically exclusive emphasis on 'uncreated' source of justification and sanctification is close to the Eastern tradition, or to that of Peter Lombard" (Moeller and Philips 1961: 40). Other researchers have also noted Martin Luther's and John Calvin's preference for Lombard's view (Billings 2008: 49, 105). Without denying the necessity of infused habits in process of sanctification, post-Reformation theologians such as John Owen insist on a clear distinction between the gifts and the Giver himself: "All gracious habits are effects of the operation of the Spirit, but not the well itself" (Owen 1965: 327). Herman Bavinck (2008: 94), too, notes that the habits that are infused "are distinguished [...] from the Holy Spirit, who effects them but does not coincide with them." Contemporary Reformed theologian Michael Horton, for instance, does not hide his admiration for the Eastern Orthodox identification of the gifts with the uncreated energies of God himself: we have the gifts because we have the Spirit (Horton 2007: 213–4).

I have to admit, as a Protestant theologian, that any account of a salvific action, such as I take the indwelling to be, which makes it contingent upon a human activity, is deficient. However, upon a fair inspection of what the Thomistic tradition holds, making a divine mission contingent upon a created reality is quite adamantly what Aquinas is not doing! It is in fact quite the opposite. The apparent priority that is awarded to created grace over uncreated grace is carefully circumscribed within an epistemological account, having to do with the order of knowledge, not of being.

Charles Cardinal Journet explains that both created and uncreated grace are primordial (Journet 2004: 79–80). Their "order" depends on the angle from which one analyzes the indwelling. In fact, it is better to call them "correlative" concepts. In the order of knowledge, we know the Spirit's indwelling in the form of created love. Ontologically speaking, or in the order of being, created charity is consequent upon uncreated love, or love proceeding, which is the Spirit himself. The *habitus* of love is not a form that preexists the indwelling but simply the resulting form of the indwelling Spirit. Much like the two-dimensional circle does not *enable* the three-dimensional sphere to be present in the two-dimensional realm but is only the consequent condition of its presence therein, created grace does not make possible the creature's reception of the Spirit but is its consequent condition. In this context, a consequent condition refers to the second half of a proposition of implication, *if p then q*.

Thus, to speak of uncreated grace and created grace as correlative is to pay attention to the "intricacies of contingent predication," as Robert Doran (2012: 30) puts it. Commenting on Bernard Lonergan's (2009: Assertions 15, 16, pp. 439–46) substantive labor in this area, he explains that "whatever is predicated contingently of God is true through extrinsic denomination, and requires a created consequent condition if the predication itself is to be true" (Doran 2012: 31). For instance, the ascription of creation to God is a contingent predication, since God did not create out of necessity. But that means that any such predication has to be with reference to a term that is external to God. To say that God is Creator, then, is to denominate (designate) God in relation to something that is not God. Now, this something is necessary for this denomination to be true, but only as a consequent condition. The condition does not enter into what Lonergan calls the immanent constitution of the thing itself.

In my view, the Protestant objection, much like Peter Lombard, struggles to account for G2, which is the Special Connection Problem. If the Spirit's presence is understood in terms of his *acta*, that is, as efficient causation (given that Protestant thinkers did not quite commit to the notion of Spirit as quasi-formal cause), in what way is this activity of the Spirit different from other operations of the Spirit in the life of, say, nonbelievers, or nonhuman things? Regarded simply in terms of activity, without a proper attention paid to the consequent formality on the part of P, the Protestant position on the indwelling fails to differentiate it from presence by immensity or by intensity. As we have seen in the case of Orthodoxy, without such an "operational" account, the special activity of indwelling blends in with the rest of the uncreated energies.

The Thomist-Catholic appeal to a created formality, then, is in consequence of observing the demanding grammar of God-talk, in this case, contingent predication. The consequent condition does not enter into the constituent structure of the act any more than the circle enters into the structure of the sphere. The habit of charity does not enable the Spirit to indwell; rather, it disposes the creature to receive his indwelling, in the very act of receiving it.

Further rapprochement between the "created grace" approach and Protestant sensibilities is possible if one understands the sending of the Spirit to be the work of Christ's humanity as well, and not of his divinity exclusively. As Ray Yeo demonstrates, indwelling can be understood as an infusion of Christ's human disposition, which is "a certain motivation for union with God and a good-seeing tendency towards God" (Yeo

2014: 225). Pending additional Christological clarifications (Yeo 2014: 230), it could be said that this human love of Christ is the created consequent condition of the uncreated divine love, which is the Holy Spirit.

V. CONCLUSION

In this chapter, I have surveyed some of the literature on the nature of the indwelling, historic and recent. I have distinguished between three broad approaches and taken a stand with one of these, before responding to two significant objections against it. The present discussion attests to how the vocabulary and grammar of Christian confession regulate the conversation. The reality of the indwelling is ultimately a supernatural reality, which will remain a mystery as far as its innermost reality is concerned. We may observe its manifestation, phenomenologically, so to speak. But there is no exhaustive explanation of the "causal joint" between the Creator and creature. In the end, and in this case as well, theology must proceed by paying close attention to the grammar of Christian faith.

References

Abbott, E. A. (1992), *Flatland: A Romance of Many Dimensions*, New York: Dover.
Adams, M. M. (2013), "Genuine Agency Somehow Shared? The Holy Spirit and Other Gifts," in Robert Pasnau (ed.), *Oxford Studies in Medieval Philosophy*, vol. 1, Oxford: Oxford University Press.
Alston, W. (1988), "The Indwelling of the Holy Spirit," in T. V. Morris (ed.), *Philosophy and the Christian Faith*, 121–50, Notre Dame: University of Notre Dame Press.
Aquinas, T. (1981), *Summa Theologica*, trans. Fathers of the English Dominican Province, Westminster, MD: Christian Classics.
Aquinas, T. (2008), *Aquinas: On Love and Charity: Readings from the Commentary on the Sentences of Peter Lombard*, Washington, DC: Catholic University of America.
Bavinck, H. (2008), *Reformed Dogmatics. Volume 4: Holy Spirit, Church, and New Creation*, trans. John Vriend, Grand Rapids, MI: Baker Academic.
Billings, J. T. (2008), *Calvin, Participation, and the Gift: The Activity of Believers in Union with Christ*, Oxford: Oxford University Press.
Coffey, D. (2005), *Did You Receive the Holy Spirit When You Believed?* Milwaukee: Marquette University Press.
Congar, Y. (1983), *I Believe in the Holy Spirit*, trans. David Smith, New York: Crossroad and Herder.
De la Taille, M. (1952), *The Hypostatic Union and Created Actuation by Uncreated Act*, West Baden Springs: West Baden College.
Donnelly, M. J. (1947), "The Inhabitation of the Holy Spirit: A Solution according to De La Taille," *Theological Studies*, 3: 445–70.
Doran, R. M. (2012), *The Trinity in History: A Theology of the Divine Missions. Volume 1: Missions and Processions*, Toronto: University of Toronto Press.
Emery, G. (2007), *The Trinitarian Theology of St. Thomas Aquinas*, trans. F. A. Murphy, Oxford: Oxford University Press.
Hill, W. (1983), *The Three-Personed God*, Washington, DC: Catholic University of America Press.
Horton, M. (2007), *Covenant and Salvation: Union with Christ*, Philadelphia: Westminster John Knox.

Journet, C. (2004), *The Theology of the Church*, trans. V. Sczczurek, San Francisco: Ignatius.
Levering, M. (2016), *Engaging the Doctrine of the Holy Spirit: Love and Gift in the Trinity and the Church*, Grand Rapids, MI: Baker Academic.
Lombard, P. (2007), *Sentences*, trans. G. Silano, Toronto: Pontifical Institute of Medieval Studies.
Lonergan, B. (2009), *The Triune God: Systematics*, in *The Collected Works of Bernard Lonergan*, vol. 12, Toronto: University of Toronto Press.
Lossky, V. (1976), *The Mystical Theology of the Eastern Church*, Crestwood, NY: St. Vladimir's Seminary Press.
Moeller, C., and G. Philips, (1961), *The Theology of Grace and the Ecumenical Movement*, London: Mowbray.
Owen, J. (1965), *Pneumatologia*, in *The Works of John Owen*, vol. 3, Edinburgh: Banner of Truth Trust.
Petavius, D. (1865), *Dogmata Theologica*, Paris: Vives.
Porter, S. L., and B. Rickabaugh, (2018), "The Sanctifying Work of the Holy Spirit: Revisiting Alston's Interpersonal Model," *Journal of Analytic Theology*, 6: 112–30.
Rahner, K. (1961), "Some Implications of the Scholastic Concept of Uncreated Grace," in K. Rahner, *Theological Investigations*, vol. 1, trans. C. Ernst, O.P., Baltimore: Helicon Press.
Rahner, K. (1970), *The Trinity*, trans. Josef Donceel, Tunbridge Wells: Burns and Oates.
Scheeben, M. (2008), *The Mysteries of Christianity*, New York: Crossroad.
Stump, E. (2018), *Atonement*, Oxford: Oxford University Press.
Yeo, R. S. (2014), "Towards a Model of Indwelling: A Conversation with Jonathan Edwards and William Alston," *Journal of Analytic Theology*, 4: 210–37.

CHAPTER TWENTY

Deification and Union with God

CARL MOSSER

The second-century church fathers first described the telos of Christian redemption as deification. Nineteenth-century scholars portrayed deification as a distinctively Greek patristic and Eastern Orthodox doctrine incompatible with the mainstream Western theological tradition. Increasingly deification is instead seen as an ecumenical doctrine native to all three branches of Christendom (Ortiz 2019; Mosser 2020). Unfortunately, the notion is often touted in the current theological literature but seldom analyzed with the sort of care it warrants (Crisp 2018: 85). The concept of deification may be particularly amenable to clarification and new insight by means of analytic theology.

Prior to the twentieth century, deification was an important theological theme but did not constitute a clear doctrinal locus for either Eastern or Western Christianity. It emerged as a distinct doctrine within systematic theology for the first time in the twentieth century. Only recently have theologians begun to broaden the conversation in a constructive mode that draws upon the resources of analytic philosophy. This chapter will survey the doctrine's biblical and patristic foundation, traditional ways the creator-creature distinction has been maintained, and some contemporary models analytic theologians have proposed to elucidate the doctrine.

I. BIBLICAL AND PATRISTIC FOUNDATION

It commonly is assumed that deification derives from 2 Pet. 1:4, which speaks of becoming "partakers of the divine nature."[1] In fact, this verse played almost no role in the doctrine's early development and is never cited by some of its most well-known expositors. Rather, the doctrine's "fundamental tenet" is the principle that the Son of God became as we are that we might become as he is (Russell 2004: 321). This idea is captured in the patristic exchange formula. Irenaeus provides the most well-known example:

> But [we follow] the only true and steadfast Teacher, the Word of God, our Lord Jesus Christ, who did, through his transcendent love, become what we are, that he might bring us to be even what he is Himself. (Irenaeus 1885: 526)

---

[1] Biblical quotations in this chapter are from the English Standard Version of the Bible.

Prior to Irenaeus, the apostle Paul succinctly expressed the notion of saving exchange in several passages (2 Cor. 5:21, 8:9; Gal. 3:13; Phil 2:7-9). In longer form, it undergirds Paul's conviction that God sent his Son in the likeness of sinful flesh (Rom. 8:3) that we might be adopted as sons conformed to his image (Rom. 8:3, 15, 29; cf. Gal. 4:4-7; 1 Cor. 15:48-49; 2 Cor. 3:18). Passages like these have led New Testament scholars to publish detailed studies of deification as an aspect of Paul's theology (esp. Blackwell 2011; Litwa 2012). After Irenaeus, variations on the exchange formula appear across the patristic traditions. For example, Athanasius: "For he was incarnate that we might be made God. ... He endured the insults of human beings, that we might inherit incorruptibility" (2011: 167). Hilary of Poitiers: "For when God was born to be man the purpose was not that the Godhead should be lost, but that, the Godhead remaining, man should be borne to be God" (1899: 183–4). Ephrem the Syrian: "Since he gave divinity to us, we have given humanity to him" (2015: 87). Cyril of Alexandria: "Since he became like us (that is, a human being) in order that we might become like him (I mean gods and sons), he receives our properties into himself and he gives us his own in return" (2015: 363). The exchange formula affirms that Christ took on our humanity in order to heal and elevate it so that we may become divine in some qualified but real sense. The relevant sense is grounded in the broad semantic range of the ancient Greek word *theos*.

Theos most frequently refers to deities, but it is also used with an attributive sense. Anything immortal, incorruptible, glorious, or sublimely beautiful—hallmarks of the divine in antiquity—can be described as *theos* without implying the referent is a deity. This is somewhat like describing an accomplished singer's performance as divine or even referring to her as a "diva." Both senses of *theos* can be employed in close proximity and authors can play on those senses with little risk of misunderstanding, just as native English speakers do with polysemes like *love*, *stock*, and *bank*. That is what occurs in versions of the formula that speak of God becoming man in order for men to become "God" or "gods."

If we examine the New Testament in this light, it is easy to see why Christians summarized the goal of redemption this way. Jesus taught that "the righteous will shine like the sun in their Father's Kingdom" (Mt. 13:43; cf. Dan. 12:3; Mt. 17:2). Paul says the resurrected body will be immortal, incorruptible, and glorious (1 Cor. 15:35-54). When Christ returns, he will "transform our lowly body to be like his glorious body (Phil. 3:21). In Hebrews we are told Jesus was made like us (except sin) in order to "bring many sons to glory" (2:10, 17, 4:15). According to 1 Peter, the resurrection of Jesus secures "an inheritance that is imperishable, undefiled, and unfading" (1:4). By ancient standards, to obtain immortal life in resplendent glory is to be made *theos*.

New Testament writers insist on three things that ensure Christian redemption cannot be equated with Greco-Roman apotheosis. First, it is axiomatic that there is but one true God (Jn 17:3; 1 Cor. 8:4-6; Gal. 3:20; Eph. 4:6; Jas. 2:19). Second, God "alone has immortality" (1 Tim. 6:16). Third, believers are called to *God's* own glory (1 Thess. 2:12; 1 Pet. 5:10; 2 Pet. 1:3). The church fathers inferred that redeemed persons will be united to God in such a manner that they will share his immortal, incorruptible, and glorious life. Scriptural warrant for referring to them specifically as *theoi* (pl.) came from an ancient Jewish interpretation of Ps. 82:6 that understood it to refer to God's promise of immortality to Adam and Israel. The church fathers saw that promise fulfilled in the adoption of believers as God's sons, initially at baptism but fully realized in the resurrection (see further Mosser 2005).

Paul says Christians "participate" in the body of Christ and are "members" of it (1 Cor. 10:16, 12:27). This relationship is more profound than the marital bond (Eph. 5:29-32). Just as coitus makes a man and woman "one flesh," the person who "cleaves to the Lord" is "one spirit" with him (1 Cor. 6:17). Paul also frequently speaks of being "in Christ" and the indwelling of God's Spirit. He goes so far as to say, "It is no longer I who live, but Christ who lives in me" (Gal. 2:20). In John's gospel, union with Christ is described by means of the organic metaphor of a vine and its branches (Jn 15:5). Jesus prays that his followers "may all be one, just as you, Father, are in me, and I in you, that they also may be in us" (Jn 17:21). Yet, their union cannot be metaphysically identical to Jesus's since he is the incarnate Word who was "in the bosom of the Father" in the beginning (Jn 1:1-3, 18). His union with the Father is natural, necessary, and everlasting; theirs is contingent and entered into at a point in time.

Early Christians used a variety of quasi-technical terms as shorthand for our concept (Russell 2004: 333–44). *Theopoiēsis*, otherwise used for the manufacture of idols, was most popular into the sixth century. Gregory Nazianzus coined the term *theōsis*, but it was not much used until Pseudo-Dionysius and Maximus Confessor. Thereafter it became the term of choice in Byzantine theology. Maslov observes that *theopoiēsis* "appears to put emphasis on the benevolent activity of God by whose grace, through the incarnation of the Logos, the human has already, in some sense, been made divine" (2012: 452). As introduced by Gregory, *theōsis* "posits the attainment of the divine as ethical process, which can never be brought to completion" (Maslov 2012: 452). The latter was attractive because it lent itself to the ascription of monastic ascetic ideals. Late patristic and early Byzantine writers also placed increasing emphasis on union with God as mystical experience. *Theōsis* provided Byzantine writers a way to speak about union with God distinct from the Neoplatonic concept of *henōsis*, union with the One.

II. DEIFYING UNION AND THE CREATOR-CREATURE DISTINCTION

Critics sometimes allege that deification violates the creator-creature distinction. In actuality, it is almost always affirmed in ways that guarantee it. The most common way of doing so is to say that we become *by grace* or *by adoption* what Christ is by nature. To be *theos* by adoption or by grace is to be divine in a fundamentally different manner than God is. Deification also is commonly affirmed as participation in God. By definition, participation (*methexis*) is a relation that obtains between ontologically diverse entities. Moreover, that which is participated in is ontologically superior to the participant.

Two traditional analogies attempt to capture the reality of union with God and transfiguration of human nature in a way that preserves the metaphysical distinction between God and creation. The analogy of the sunbeam and mirror builds on the idea that we will share God's own glory. If somebody positions a mirror to reflect a sunbeam into your eyes, you see the sun's light. The mirror has not become the sun. It retains all its essential properties, one of which is the ability to reflect light. It was designed to do that. Like a mirror, deified human beings will reflect God's glory within creation by design. The analogy of the iron in a fire helps us think about the indwelling of the Spirit. Presupposing ancient ontology, fire is conceived as an element that comes to inhere in the iron. As a result, the iron acquires new characteristics such as luminosity (it glows red), flexibility, and heat. Yet, it loses none of the essential properties of iron. Just as iron can be fired, created beings can be divinized in ways appropriate to their natures.

Another traditional way to maintain the creator-creature distinction is to adapt Plato's concept of conformity to God (*homoiōsis*). Plato says we should escape from the evils of this world in order to "become like God" in righteousness, holiness, and wisdom "so far as this is possible" (1921: 129). Early Christians readily embraced moral similitude with God as the ethical ideal (e.g., Eph. 4:24, 5:1). There is also a long tradition of adapting Plato's formula as an ontological claim about union with God. Theologians as different as Pseudo-Dionysius and John Calvin have found this language helpful because it resonates with the creation narrative (Gen. 1:26-27), likeness is not identity, and "as far as possible" indicates limitation. The Areopagite defines *theōsis* as "being as much as possible like and in union with God" (Pseudo-Dionysius 1987: 198). Calvin identifies deification as the telos of the gospel and then states, "When we have put off all the vices of the flesh we shall be partakers of divine immortality and the glory of blessedness, and thus we shall be in a way one with God so far as our capacity allows" (Calvin 1963: 330). The obvious question is, just how far can we be made one with God?

1 John 3:2 ties our eschatological transformation with seeing Christ "as he is" when he returns. Jesus promises that the pure in heart will "see God" (Mt. 5:8). But in what sense and by what faculties will the redeemed see God? A series of biblical antinomies make this a challenging question. Scripture testifies that God dwells both in "thick darkness" (Exod. 20:21; Deut. 5:22; 1 Kgs 8:12) and "in unapproachable light, whom no one has ever seen or can see" (1 Tim. 6:16; cf. Jn 1:18, 4:12). Yet, numerous times the Lord "appeared" to the patriarchs and prophets. The angel of the Lord appeared to Moses in the burning bush (Exod. 3:2) but Moses later asked to see God. He was told, "You cannot see my face, for man shall not see me and live" (Exod. 33:20). Moses was permitted to see only the "backside" of God's glory. Isaiah records a vision of the Lord on his throne but expresses woe because "my eyes have seen the King, the Lord of hosts!" (Isa. 6:5). Ezekiel also had a vision of the divine throne. Instead of saying he saw God, he says he saw the "appearance of the likeness" of his glory (Ezek. 1:28). Complicating matters further, Paul says God's invisible characteristics can be intellectually perceived from the things that are made, including his eternal power and divinity (Rom. 1:20) but goes on to speak of the inscrutability and unsearchable depths of God's wisdom and knowledge (Rom. 11:33). Elsewhere he says we presently "know in part" as if looking into a dim mirror (1 Cor. 13:12a), but when the perfect comes we will see "face to face" and "know fully" as we have been fully known (1 Cor. 13:12b).

Juxtaposed in this way, these passages invite distinctions to be drawn between the ways in which God can and cannot be seen and the ways in which he can and cannot be known. Because metaphors about light, darkness, and so forth are more suggestive than denotative, consideration of the issues generates competing accounts of the intelligibility of God, limits of human reason, and the ways in which God can be experienced. These issues and their bearing on deification became the subject of intense debate in the fourteenth-century Hesychast controversy. In that controversy, Gregory Palamas defended the possibility of experiencing *theōsis* and the uncreated divine light by appeal to a distinction between God's imparticipatable essence and his participatable energies.

Apologists for and against Orthodoxy have portrayed the Hesychast controversy as the archetypical clash between theological traditions and methods that supposedly separate the Christian East and West. In reality it was a conflict between two philosophical and theological traditions within Orthodoxy that had to that point peacefully coexisted. Norman Russell describes the differences as follows:

> One tradition conceived of divine–human communion in ontological terms. For the Palamites participation in God implied a real transformation, a change in human nature that could begin even in this life through contemplation, prayer, and sharing in the Eucharist. The other tradition understood divine–human communion mainly in analogical terms. For the antiPalamites it was only in a manner of speaking that a human being could become divine. For them deification was the eschatological goal of the Christian life, not a reality attainable in this world. Both traditions had ample patristic support, which is why it was so difficult to resolve the conflict. (Russell 2017: 507–8)

The exact nature of the Palamite distinction remains a topic of scholarly discussion. It is much easier to describe the work it is intended to do than say what it actually affirms. Interpreters have long debated whether it corresponds to a Thomistic real minor distinction, a Thomistic rational distinction, a Scotistic formal distinction, or something else. Moreover, fourteenth-century Palamites construed it in different ways, some compromising Palamas's distinction in a way that he would hardly have approved (Demetracopoulos 2011). Modern Orthodox theologians also seem to understand it in different ways.

David Bradshaw concludes that the Scotistic formal distinction is the nearest correlative among scholastic options. However, he observes that Palamas operates with a very different conceptual framework than Scotus. We should therefore try to understand his thought on its own terms as a multiform concept (Bradshaw 2019: 35). According to Bradshaw,

> The best general description of the essence-energies distinction remains that which is implied by the meaning of the word *energeia* itself: it is the distinction between an agent and that agent's activity. In the case of God, however, we must recognize that the range of His *energeiai* is extremely diverse. As I have pointed out elsewhere, some are eternal and others temporal; some are contingent and others necessary; some are best conceived as "realities" or "energies," others as activities or operations, and yet others as attributes.

Bradshaw's description is informed by detailed work on the history of *energeia* from Aristotle to Palamas (Bradshaw 2004, 2006a). Moreover, he ably argues in favor of a distinction between God's essence and energies from scripture (Bradshaw 2006b,c). However, some of Palamas's opponents, most notably Gregory Akindynos, would probably accept Bradshaw's general description as far as it goes (compare Kapriev 2011: 438). Nonetheless, they accused Palamas with hypostatizing the divine energies, positing a lesser mediatorial deity akin to Plato's demiurge, and polytheism. Bradshaw does not discuss many of the passages that led to these charges (Bradshaw 2004: 234–42). It may be best to see Bradshaw's exposition as a chastened recasting of the essence-energies distinction that draws from across the philosophical and patristic traditions. In any case, as the most philosophically astute account available, analytic theologians do well to carefully consider Bradshaw's arguments.

III. TWO ANALYTIC APPROACHES

William Alston's "The Indwelling of the Holy Spirit" is the earliest discussion of deification that might be considered an example of analytic theology, though he did not set out to discuss deification as such. Alston distinguishes between fiat, interpersonal, and sharing models of indwelling. What follows will begin with an overview of Alston's sharing model. Eleonore Stump's account of union with God will be discussed as an example of the interpersonal model. The divine fiat model will be passed over for lack of representation in the literature. For our purposes, these "models" are better thought of as meta-models, broad types under which various models of union with God and deification can be usefully classified. It will then be suggested that Alston's basic approach is correct but needs to be filled out with more metaphysically robust models. Several mutually complimentary candidates will be briefly sketched.

To begin, Alston sets out to give an account of how the Spirit works to regenerate and sanctify Christians. He focuses on ways the Spirit "modifies the character of the person, her values, tendencies, attitudes, priorities, and so on" (Alston 1988: 122). He finds the fiat and interpersonal models inadequate because they do not embody "the special mode of internality" characteristic of the Spirit's work in scripture. On the fiat model, God simply wills certain changes to be brought about as he might with a rock or tree. The interpersonal model is better but does not "represent God as more internal to the believer than one human person is internal to another when they are related as intimately as possible" (Alston 1988: 137). He mentions the Aristotelian-Thomist account of sanctifying grace as an exemplar. On this view, God can be within us only as something known and loved. "God is not present to me in any different, any more intimate way than that in which my wife is present to me as an object of knowledge and love." Participation in divine life, then, "amounts to no more than my having, in infinitely lesser measure, a knowledge and love of God of the same sort as that possessed by God himself. What is shared are attributes, features, aspects." Alston proposes "a stronger, more literal, construal of the sharing notion" (141). His proposal is basically the early patristic doctrine of deification, though he does not show much awareness of the church fathers' teaching.

"God's basic intention for us is that we should become like him, insofar as in us lies, and should thereby be in a position to enter into a community of love with him and with our fellow creatures" (Alston 1988: 123). The Spirit indwells believers to carry out this intention by regenerating and sanctifying them. "Being filled with the Spirit," Alston says, "is like being plugged into a source of electricity, or being permeated by fog, or, closer to the etymology, being inflated by air pressure, or being filled with a liquid" (138). These material analogies are inadequate since indwelling is a personal relationship with the Spirit. But they helpfully show that indwelling is of a fundamentally different character than even the most intimate relationship between two human beings.

The internal character of the indwelling relationship is explained as participating in the divine nature (cf. 2 Pet. 1:4). It is to be drawn into the divine life "and living it, to the extent our limited nature permits." It is to "realize in our life and, to some extent, in our consciousness, the very life of God himself." This is the fulfillment of Jesus's prayer in John 17 that, Alston contends, "can be understood fairly literally as asking God to bring it about that believers may share, in the measure of which they are capable, in the same divine life that is his by nature" (Alston 1988: 139). Taking this further, he says talk of being filled, permeated, and pervaded by the Spirit and the Spirit's being poured into our hearts "strongly suggests that there is a literal merging or mutual interpenetration of the life of the individual and the divine life, a breaking down of the barriers that normally separate one life from another" (141). There are, after all, none of the physical or psychological barriers that separate two human persons.

Alston goes on to develop a cognitive and conative picture to illustrate how the Spirit's indwelling may result in character change. The further details continue to be assessed, modified, and defended (e.g., Yeo 2014; Porter and Rickabaugh 2018; Kroll 2019). For our purposes, the significance of Alston's proposal lies elsewhere. First, Alston's analysis leads him to develop a model of indwelling that is clearly a form of Christian deification. He finds the Thomistic account inadequate at precisely the same point Eastern theologians do. Yet, Alston did not sense any need to posit something akin to the essence-energies distinction. Second, Alston's analysis is immune to some common criticisms leveled against analytic theology. For example, typical of the analytic method, Alston identifies and assesses competing models but is attentive also to the teaching of scripture and Christian experience of the Spirit. Just as importantly, he is not interested in speculative theology. Alston wants to clarify the Spirit's sanctifying work to help believers more fully experience divine life in the present. The downside of this practical focus, however, is that Alston does little to fill out the metaphysical picture.

Stump has also developed an account of union with God in terms of mutual indwelling. In contrast to Alston, she embraces the interpersonal model and develops Aquinas's thought in interesting ways. Her account is detailed and nuanced, but, with respect to deification, underdeveloped. "To be united with something is to be made one with it, in some sense. To be made one with God in any sense, however, is deification, at least in some analogous sense" (Stump 2010: 387; Stump 2018: 41). Her account of indwelling is parsed out primarily in terms of love, will, desire for the good of the other, and shared attention. She insists union with God is "ontologically greater than any union possible between two human persons" (Stump 2018: 166). On her account, it is. But is it enough to account for all that scripture indicates about union with God?

Stump claims that the "implicit understanding of deity in discussions of deification sometimes highlights standard divine attributes, which can characterize one individual taken in isolation." In contrast, her account of mutual indwelling "implies that there is a different understanding of deification provided by the Christian doctrine that the deity is triune." She goes on to assert that to be made like God "requires not a particular set of unusually excellent intrinsic attributes on the part of an individual. Rather, it requires a particularly powerful metaphysical mutuality of indwelling among persons." Because God is triune, deification cannot be anything an individual could have in isolation (Stump 2018: 167).

The first understanding of deification is attributed to Orthodox theologians, but it is doubtful any would concede Stump's dichotomy. Many theologians (Protestant as well as Orthodox) certainly understand deification in terms of obtaining certain attributes but not as an alternative to a "powerful metaphysical mutuality of indwelling among persons." To the contrary, properly divine attributes such as immortality and incorruption can be manifest in the redeemed only by virtue of such indwelling. Deification is consistently understood in terms of adoption, sharing in Christ's own Sonship and hence in the love between him and the Father and Spirit. The "metaphysical mutuality of indwelling" is so powerful on this account that it does not simply transform a person's will, dispositions, affections, openness to others, and so forth; it transforms the totality of their being, body as well as soul. The believer's life is so hidden with Christ in God that when he returns, they "will appear with him in glory" (Col. 3:3-4) because he "will transform our lowly body to be like his glorious body, by the power that enables him even to subject all things to himself" (Phil. 3:21).

Stump's exposition of union with God is impressively rich and nuanced. Nonetheless, it is inadequate as an account of deification. As with all interpersonal accounts of indwelling, it "leaves the parties involved external to each other in a fundamental way; they are separate, distinct persons, each with his or her own autonomy and integrity" (Alston 1988: 137). As such, it does not sufficiently account for the scriptural data and patristic teaching surveyed earlier. More metaphysically robust accounts of union as sharing in divine life are needed that are congruent with Stump's many insights. Here are a few possibilities.

IV. FURTHER ANALYTIC MODELS

In their article (1998), Andy Clark and David Chalmers argue for an active externalism about the mind and cognition that implies that selves extend beyond boundaries of consciousness or even one's own skin. The way in which we use technological aids to remember, analyze, compute, and act in the world suggests that selves can be regarded not so much as individual, autonomous organisms but as an extended system in which a biological organism is coupled with external resources. This becomes easy to illustrate when we think about the way in which people use smartphones connected to the servers of Google. John Jefferson Davis has put this line of thinking to theological use. He suggests that from the moment a believer is converted and baptized into Christ, he or she "is metaphysically 'coupled' or 'bonded' with Christ by the Holy Spirit, as really and truly as a Verizon customer is networked or connected to others in the Verizon network" (Davis 2012: 57–8). Similarly, our Facebook pages extend our molecular selves into cyberspace to represent ourselves to others. The New Testament's teachings about believers united in the body of Christ by the Spirit, Davis says, require "the enlarged notion of a *hybrid self* or 'complex self'" (58). The believing Christian "is no longer an empirical, visible, molecular self, but in fact, an extended *complex* self, metaphysically linked in the body of Christ by the Holy Spirit of Christ, the head of the body" (58). This "Head-body-Spirit-believer" connection, he insists, "is not just a metaphor but an ontological reality, inaugurated by the resurrection of Jesus Christ, his ascension to heaven, the outpouring of the Holy Spirit, and the incorporation of the believer into the body of Christ by the Holy Spirit at conversion" (58).

Davis's analogy can be extended to account for some aspects of the transformative element in deification. The capacities of a personal computer are limited by the speed of its processor, the size of its memory, and the data and software installed on it. Connected to the internet, however, its capacities are greatly enhanced. It can use the computational power, software, and data of Google's much more powerful computers. Updates to the operating system can be downloaded that make it function more efficiently while new software can be installed that give it new abilities altogether. In similar fashion, in union with God, resurrected Christians may have vastly increased capacities and abilities. If, for no other reason, their "operating systems" will be updated and fixed, their "hardware" will be reengineered for optimal performance, and they will have access to the mind of Christ. Moreover, an implication of this model is that God becomes a proper part of the human person.

J. T. Turner presents an interesting model that also has the implication that God becomes a proper part of the human person. Turner defends the idea that "the human mind, at least in the resurrected human, is in a part-whole relationship with the Holy

Spirit" (2019: 172). He calls that relationship "mental saturation." Drawing on Peter van Inwagen's mereological account of living things, Turner first asks us to consider a household sponge. The telos of a sponge is to be saturated and put to certain uses. He argues that when the sponge is saturated, "the saturating liquid becomes a proper part of the sponge" (Turner 2019: 174). To be full of the saturating liquid does not obliterate the sponge's distinct identity or turn it into a numerically distinct entity from what existed before saturation occurred. Rather, the sponge more fully exemplifies what it is by virtue of fulfilling its telos. In similar fashion, Turner thinks the indwelling relationship allows the mind of the Spirit to become a proper part of the human organism. The model he proposes "means to suggest that through mental saturation the Spirit maximizes, *in a way proper to human nature*, the attributes of being wise, being just, being holy, and so on" (Turner 2019: 177).

There is no obvious reason why Turner's operative notions of fullness and saturation cannot also be used as a heuristic device to explain metaphysical attributes like immortality, glory, and incorruption. Furthermore, it provides an analogy that may also account for the phenomenology of the mystical experience of union with God. Mystics often report a sense of being completely filled with God, swallowed up in him, being lost in the ocean of God's love, and so forth. This sensation leads some of them to describe their ecstatic experience and/or eschatological union with God as an undifferentiated union in which personal identity is lost. However, if a sponge is thrown into the ocean, on Turner's view, "the water filling the sponge is a part of the sponge, but the sponge is not part of the ocean (since, minimally, it is not caught up into the non-biological 'life' of the ocean)" (Turner 2019: 182). In a real sense, the sponge is completely filled with the ocean and lost within the enormity of its vastness, but it retains its distinct ontological identity and does not become something other than a sponge. The sponge can still be pulled out of the ocean and wrung. The fact that mystics leave their ecstatic states proves they did not merge with God and literally lose their identity. Thus, a sponge saturated in the ocean is a better analogy for mystical experience than the well-known drop of rain that falls into the ocean. The extended mind and saturation models comport well with more traditional accounts of deification. Deification entails that human nature is not fully realized apart from union with God. Just as an acorn may be totally oak in nature, it is not fully an oak tree until it germinates and grows from sapling to tree. The apostle Paul intimates there is a similar relationship between our pre- and post-resurrection selves (1 Cor. 15:37, 42-44). There is a sense in which our humanity is not fully realized apart from deification. This leads some Orthodox theologians to speak of a "theological structure" and "openness to God" that is constitutive of human persons. Drawing on the work of such theologians, Jonathan Jacobs argues for the idea that human beings should be understood as the union of soul and body *with* God (2009: 615). This seems equivalent to saying God is a proper part of fully realized human nature. On this view, "when we are distant from God, the result is not merely psychological. It is ontological. Absent from God, the claim is, we are not fully human" (Jacobs 2009: 622).

Analytic theologians have proposed other interesting models of union with God or deification that can only be mentioned due to space. In dialogue with transhumanism, I suggest a model of instrumental union with God as a way of accounting for a number of things scripture says about the eschatological state related to being enthroned and ruling with Christ (Mosser 2018: 271–7). In passing, I also suggest other potential models that draw upon the resources of analytic philosophy such as a mutual manifestation of powers account, hypostatic inherence, and something analogous to an emergent superorganism or holobiont.

The most controversial model that has been proposed is Thomas Flint's theory of final assumptions. He suggests that the ultimate end of all human beings who attain salvation is to be assumed by the Son in a manner closely analogous but not quite identical to the way in which the Son assumed his human nature (Flint 2011: 198). Ryan Mullins contends that Flint's proposal is too radical and questions its orthodoxy (Mullins 2015; Mullins 2017; cf. Flint 2016). Oliver Crisp finds it intriguing but demurs from endorsement because he thinks it creates more problems than it solves (Crisp 2018: 97).

V. CONCLUSION

Analytic theology is a mode of constructive theology that seeks to present contemporary models for elucidating and extending our understanding of historic Christian doctrine. Analytic models of deification should seek to account for the full range of biblical data in a manner consistent with the consensus of patristic teaching. They do well to be informed about medieval debates regarding the intelligibility of God, limits of human reason, and religious experience that led to competing ways of understanding deification. However, discussion of the doctrine's relevant metaphysical and epistemological commitments should not be confined to the mode of historical theology or intellectual history. This chapter has attempted to identify some of the biblical desiderata for an adequate model, describe traditional ways its metaphysical parameters have been maintained, and illustrate that contemporary philosophical tools can be employed to move discussion forward in interesting and fruitful ways.

References

Alston, W. (1988), "The Indwelling of the Holy Spirit," in T. Morris (ed.), *Philosophy and the Christian Faith*, 121–50, Notre Dame: University of Notre Dame Press.

Athanasius (2011), *On the Incarnation*, trans. J. Behr, Yonkers: St Vladimir's Seminary Press.

Blackwell, B. C. (2011), *Christosis: Pauline Soteriology in Light of Deification in Irenaeus and Cyril of Alexandria*, Tübingen: Mohr Siebeck.

Bradshaw, D. (2004), *Aristotle East and West: Metaphysics and the Division of Christendom*, Cambridge: Cambridge University Press.

Bradshaw, D. (2006a), "The Concept of the Divine Energies," *Philosophy & Theology*, 18 (1): 93–120.

Bradshaw, D. (2006b), "The Divine Energies in the New Testament," *St. Vladimir's Theological Quarterly*, 50 (3): 189–223.

Bradshaw, D. (2006c), "The Divine Glory and the Divine Energies," *Faith and Philosophy*, 23 (3): 279–98.

Bradshaw, D. (2019), "Essence and Energies: What Kind of Distinction?," *Analogia*, 6: 5–35.

Calvin, J. (1963), *The Epistle of Paul the Apostle to the Hebrews and The First and Second Epistles of St Peter*, trans. W. Johnston, Grand Rapids, MI: Eerdmans.

Clark, A., and D. Chalmers (1998), "The Extended Mind," *Analysis*, 58 (1): 7–19.

Crisp, O. D. (2018), "Theosis and Participation," in M. Cortez, J. R. Farris, and S. M. Hamilton (eds.), *Being Saved: Explorations in Human Salvation*, 85–101, London: SCM.

Cyril of Alexandria (2015), *Commentary on John*, volume 2, trans. D. R. Maxwell, Downers Grove, IL: IVP Academic.

Davis, J. J. (2012), *Mediation and Communion with God: Contemplating Scripture in an Age of Distraction*, Downers Grove, IL: IVP Academic.

Demetracopoulos, J. A. (2011), "Palamas Transformed: Palamite Interpretations of the Distinction Between God's 'Essence' and 'Energies' in Late Byzantium," in M. Hinterberger and C. Schabel (eds.), *Greeks, Latins, and Intellectual History 1204–1500*, 263–372, Leuven: Peeters.

Flint, T. P. (2011), "Molinism and Incarnation," in K. Perszyk (ed.), *Molinism: The Contemporary Debate*, 187–207, New York: Oxford University Press.

Flint, T. P. (2016), "Orthodoxy and Incarnation: A Reply to Mullins," *Journal of Analytic Theology*, 4: 180–92.

Hilary of Portiers (1899), *On the Trinity*, in Watson, E. W. and L. Pullan, *Nicene and Post-Nicene Fathers, Second Series*, volume 9, New York: Christian Literature.

Irenaeus (1885), *Against Heresies*, in Roberts, A., J. Donaldson, and A. C. Coxe, *The Ante-Nicene Fathers*, volume 1, Buffalo: Christian Literature.

Jacobs, J. D. (2009), "An Eastern Orthodox Conception of Theosis and Human Nature," *Faith and Philosophy*, 26 (5): 615–27.

Kapriev, G. (2011), "Gregory Akindynos," in H. Lagerlund (ed.), *Encyclopedia of Medieval Philosophy: Philosophy between 500 and 1500*, 437–39, Dordrecht: Springer.

Kroll, K. (2019), "Indwelling without the Indwelling Holy Spirit: A Critique of Ray Yeo's Modified Account," *Journal of Analytic Theology*, 7: 124–41.

Litwa, M. D. (2012), *We Are Being Transformed: Deification in Paul's Soteriology*, Berlin: Walter de Gruyter.

Maslov, B. (2012), "The Limits of Platonism: Gregory Nazianzus and the Invention of *theōsis*," *Greek, Roman, and Byzantine Studies* 52: 440–6.

Mosser, C. (2005), "The Earliest Patristic Interpretations of Psalm 82, Jewish Antecedents, and the Origin of Christian Deification," *Journal of Theological Studies*, 56 (1): 30–74.

Mosser, C. (2018), "Two Visions of Being Saved as Deiform Perfectibility," in M. Cortez, J. R. Farris, and S. M. Hamilton (eds.), *Being Saved: Explorations in Human Salvation*, 265–80, London: SCM.

Mosser, C. (2020), "Recovering the Reformation's Ecumenical Vision of Redemption as Deification and Beatific Vision," *Perichoresis*, 18 (1): 3–24.

Mullins, R. T. (2015), "Flint's Molinism and the Incarnation is too Radical," *Journal of Analytic Theology*, 3: 1–15.

Mullins, R. T. (2017), "Flint's "Molinism and the Incarnation" is Still Too Radical—A Rejoinder to Flint," *Journal of Analytic Theology*, 5: 515–32.

Ortiz, J., ed. (2019), *Deification in the Latin Patristic Tradition*, Washington, DC: Catholic University of America Press.

Plato (1921): *Theaetetus; Sophist*, trans. H. N. Fowler, Cambridge, MA: Harvard University Press.

Porter, S. L., and B. Rickabaugh (2018), "The Sanctifying Work of the Holy Spirit: Revisiting Alston's Interpersonal Model," *Journal of Analytic Theology*, 6: 112–30.

Pseudo-Dionysius (1987), *Pseudo-Dionysius: The Complete Works*, trans. C. Luibheid, New York: Paulist.

Russell, N. (2004), *The Doctrine of Deification in the Greek Patristic Tradition*, Oxford: Oxford University Press.

Russell, N. (2017), "The Hesychast Controversy," in A. Kaldellis and N. Siniossoglou (eds.), *The Cambridge Intellectual History of Byzantium*, 494–508, Cambridge: Cambridge University Press.

St. Ephrem the Syrian (2015), *The Hymns on Faith*, trans. J. T. Wickes, Washington, DC: Catholic University of America Press.

Stump, E. (2010), *Wandering in Darkness*, Oxford: Oxford University Press.
Stump, E. (2018), *Atonement*, Oxford: Oxford University Press.
Turner, J. T. (2019), "The Mind of the Spirit in the Resurrected Human: A Mereological Model of Mental Saturation," *Philosophia Christi*, 21 (1): 167–86.
Yeo, R. S. (2014), "Towards a Model of Indwelling: A Conversation with Jonathan Edwards and William Alston," *Journal of Analytic Theology*, 2: 210–37.

CHAPTER TWENTY-ONE

Toward an Analytic Theology of Charismatic Gifts: Preliminary Questions

JOANNA LEIDENHAG

I. INTRODUCTION

An analytic theology of charismatic gifts would be a beneficial and timely task for analytic theologians to pursue in the service of the contemporary church. In 2011, the Pew Research Center reported over 584 million Pentecostal and Charismatic Christians, making up over a quarter of the global church and this number continues to rise rapidly. What unites these diverse groups of Christians is the centrality of the experience of the Holy Spirit through the practice of charismatic gifts (Barrett and Johnson 2002: 23–5). In addition to this important new tradition within contemporary Christianity, almost every other theological sub-tradition (Roman Catholic, Orthodox, mainline Protestants) of Christianity has something to say about charismatic gifts. Since I know of no work already published within analytic theology on charismatic gifts, this chapter demonstrates the possibility for analytic theology "to be stretched and expanded" into this area (McCall 2015: 124). This demonstration is accomplished by exploring nine preliminary questions that an analytic theology of charismatic gifts might ask. This chapter is split into questions of definition and ontology and questions regarding epistemology. The result is a rough map for how one might construct an analytic theology of charismatic gifts, one that will hopefully serve as a springboard for new research.

II. QUESTIONS OF DEFINITION AND ONTOLOGY

Analytic theologians value clear, working definitions of the key terms under discussion. One common way to achieve this is by outlining the necessary and/or sufficient conditions to a phenomenon or concept. The first question for an analytic theology of charismatic gifts is likely to be the hardest:

1. How should we define "charismatic gifts"?

Identifying a charismatic gift is not a straightforward matter. Some theologians have limited the list of charismatic gifts to the most spectacular and miraculous activities (exclusively healing, prophecy, and speaking in tongues), whilst others broaden the definition to include any and every event that is normative for a Christian life (Turner 1996: 181–2; cf. Congar 2003: 162–5; Moltmann 2001: 181–6).[1] Even when we start with the Pauline literature, from whence we get the category χάρισμα, we find no clear statement for defining "charismatic gifts."[2] The term χαρίσματα (often translated as "spiritual gifts" despite having no semantic reference to the Spirit without additional context or explicit qualifiers) comes from the root χάρις (grace) and so indicates "a concrete expression of grace, thus a 'gracious bestowment'" (Fee 1994: 33).[3] The colloquial Christian usage of this term often refers to the activities of the Holy Spirit listed in 1 Corinthians 12–14.[4] Even here χαρίσματα seems to be very loosely applied in a nontechnical fashion to the miraculous (prophecy, healing, etc.), to the unusual (tongues), and to more mundane activities (teaching, exhortation, generous giving, words of encouragement, administration, leadership, discernment, faith, etc.) and it is strongly implied that these are representative, such that there is no fixed number of gifts (Fee 1994: 158–60; Turner 1996: 262–3; Snyder 2010: 329–30). In addition, it is not immediately clear which New Testament texts and individual terms (beyond, χαρίσματα) refer to charismatic gifts, and which should be categorized under a different heading, for example, graces, ecclesial offices, natural gifts, or fruits of the Spirit.

I do not claim to have overcome these substantial exegetical difficulties but offer the following criteria as a provisional, working definition of charismatic gifts:

(CG1). A phenomenon is a charismatic gift only if it is a gift of grace.

(CG2). A phenomenon is a charismatic gift only if the Holy Spirit is the primary, but not the sole, agent.

(CG3). A phenomenon is a charismatic gift only if it or its effects are concretely perceivable.

(CG4). A phenomenon is a charismatic gift only if it builds up the Christian community.

(CG5). A phenomenon is a charismatic gift only if it is realized in the context of eschatological expectation.

As the most direct translation of χαρίσματα and as a central part of Paul's overall argument in 1 Corinthians, (CG1) is a necessary but insufficient condition for defining a charismatic gift. Together, (CG1) and (CG2) rule out any phenomenon that comes exhaustively from the natural powers of the recipient, and so a person cannot deserve a charismatic gift or gain merit from receiving one. Similarly, (CG5) denotes a posture of receptivity and an openness to being surprised as the human person cooperates with, but cannot conjure, the activity of the Holy Spirit (Blankenhorn 2014: 376). However, in contrast to other miracles, a gift to a creature involves the cooperation of the recipient, such that the Holy

---

[1]Mark Stibbe critiques Moltmann in his review, as promoting "anonymous Charismatics" (Stibbe 1994: 14).

[2]Sixteen out of the seventeen New Testament instances of χάρισμα (or χαρίσματα) occur in Pauline texts, the exception being 1 Pet. 4:10. Since Paul does not define or explain the term for his readers, it is unlikely he coined it himself. However, we have no textually secure pre-Pauline instance of the term to aid us (Fee 1994: 32–3; Turner 1996: 262).

[3]Fee doubts that χάρισμα should be translated as, "gift *of the Spirit*" or "spiritual gifts," since it is only in 1 Cor. 12:8-10 that the χαρίσματα are explicitly tied by Paul to the concrete manifestations of the Spirit in the community. Instead, Fee argues that χάρισμα is a broader category for "graces" such as eternal life (Rom. 6:23), the privileges given to Israel (Rom. 11:29), celibacy and marriage (1 Cor. 7:7), and deliverance from deadly peril (2 Cor. 1:10) (Fee 1994: 33–5).

[4]See, Rom. 1:11 where χάρισμα is qualified by the noun πνευματικόν and 1 Cor. 12:7 where the χαρίσματα are described as "manifestations of the Spirit" (Fee 1994: 33).

Spirit may be the primary but not strictly speaking the sole agent of the phenomenon. Since there is a human agent involved in the reception and performance of a charismatic gift it seems fair to say, as in (CG3), that these will be concretely perceivable in some way. This is not to say that charismatic gifts are always publicly self-evident, nor transparent in nature, but only that there is something to remark upon. How this cooperation between the agency of the Holy Spirit and the human person is best articulated would be a fruitful area for further research.

(CG4) is probably the most emphasized criteria for charismatic gifts within the literature, and it places at least two constraints and one implication upon any theology of charismatic gifts. The first constraint is that in service of the Body of Christ, a charismatic gift must, directly or indirectly, declare the lordship of Jesus Christ. This is closely connected to (CG5), where eschatological expectation anticipates the glorious return of Jesus Christ (Smith 2010: 44; Albrecht and Howard 2014: 244).[5] The second constraint is that virtues, such as hope, faith, and love (1 Corinthians 13), must remain at the center of the practice of charismatic gifts. In light of these criteria, some scholars go so far as to define the church as "essentially charismatic" and "a charismatic organism" (Snyder 2010: 328; cf. Küng 1965: 41–61). An important area for further research is how far charismatic gifts may be given primarily to congregations, rather than individuals, and considered a group liturgical action (Leidenhag 2020). This may have interesting implications for questions of discernment, authority, and church unity.

2. What type of thing is a charismatic gift?

The above five criteria have not settled the question as to what type of thing a charismatic gift is: an act, a quality, a disposition, a habit, or a power? This is not a question that has been given much attention, at least not since medieval scholasticism (Blankenhorn 2014: 376). This modern lacuna is unfortunate since differing answers to hotly disputed pastoral questions (such as how charismatic gifts relate to ecclesial authority, personal identity, or whether they endure over time) assume different ontologies of charismatic gifts. By briefly considering Thomas Aquinas's discussion of this question, I echo the thesis of Bernhard Blankenhorn, OP (2014), that charismatic gifts have a twofold metaphysic, as actions of the Holy Spirit for which a person can also acquire a receptive *habitus* or sensitivity.

Aquinas (1920) distinguishes between gratuitous grace (*gratia gratis data*), which he associates with the list of phenomena in 1 Corinthians 12, and sanctifying grace that is a direct effect of the indwelling of the Holy Spirit that produces the spiritual gifts that perfect the virtues, which he associates with the list of phenomena in Isa. 11:2-3 (I-II. Q111.a1). The latter, the spiritual gifts (sanctifying grace), are an active *habitus* resulting from infused grace and a disposition to be acted upon by the Holy Spirit (I-II.Q55.a2, Q68.aa1&3). By contrast, Aquinas denies that charismatic gifts (gratuitous grace), such as prophecy, are an active *habitus*, similar to natural agential cognition, since charismatic gifts surpass natural capacities and are not at the disposal of the human to actualize (II-II.Q171.a2; cf. Blankenhorn 2014: 387–90). Instead, Aquinas writes, the "principle of things that pertains to supernatural knowledge, which are manifest through prophecy, is God himself," and not primarily the human agent, to whom a charismatic gift is only a

---

[5] 1 Cor. 1:6-7, provides a clear link between the charismata and eschatological expectation. See also, Rom. 8:23, 2 Cor. 1:22, 5:5; Eph. 1:13-14, and Heb. 6:4-5.

"passion" or "disposition for being acted upon" (II-II.Q171.a2 *sed contra*).⁶ This concurs with CG1 and CG2 above.

However, this neither helps to explain why it is that some individuals seem to have a greater receptivity for these actions, which charismatic and Pentecostal communities often refer to as a special anointing, nor why eschatological expectation is necessary, nor what role free human action plays in the manifestation of a charismatic gift. Thus, one might justifiably complement this view of a charismatic gift as an act of the Holy Spirit, with a receptive *habitius* such that the human agent has an "increased sensitivity, receptivity, and docility" to the Spirit's actions (Yong 2005: 293–4).⁷ This inner receptivity to the Spirit will itself be an act of the Spirit, but one that the person can resist or receive with hopeful expectation for its future operation. A role of a *habitus* could provide a link between charismatic gifts and sanctification, as is common in notions of charismatic gifts as a sign of the Spirit's indwelling or evidence of salvation. However, it does not entail this link, which Thomas objected to on the grounds that charismatic gifts were exclusively for evangelism and not for the perfection of the recipient themselves (Blankenhorn 2014: 407–9, 418).⁸

3. Are charismatic gifts supernatural or natural phenomena?

Since Christians view "nature" as a creation sustained, providentially ordered, and intimately related to God, it makes little sense to view the ordinary processes of the natural world as autonomous from or in competition with God. As a result of this doctrine of creation, the definition and even validity of the category of the supernatural has undergone substantial debate in recent decades. In a discussion of charismatic gifts, Amos Yong (2005) argues that the "early modern distinction between 'natural' and 'supernatural' should be abandoned when one talks about the *charismata*" (294). Leading analytic theologian, Michael Rea, characterizes the visions and voices reported within the Vineyard movement, and even the most paradigmatic examples of special revelation (i.e., Moses and the burning bush), as "purely natural" requiring no "special causal contact" between God and humanity (2018: 98, 101–2, 106–7).

Should one use Rea's model to develop an account of charismatic gifts as purely natural phenomena? Although retaining a role for the human agent is important, a purely natural account of charismatic gifts will struggle to satisfy (CG1) and (CG2). Rea denies that God is the "immediate stimulus" or "direct cause" for these events and uses an ambiguous appeal to providence to maintain their divine origin (2018: 107). This approach might be metaphysically possible, but it does not seem theologically beneficial. The providence of God may arrange events to occur solely through the powers that are created as proper to the nature of a thing, but to claim that something is "of grace" or a (sometimes, temporary) "gift" is to claim that a particular event exceeds the powers of a natural agent.

---

⁶This is true even for Christ's humanity, see Aquinas (III.Q13.a2; II-II.Q171.a2; QQ.176–8); Blankenhorn (2014: 394–5).

⁷For example, Aquinas describes that "a certain disposition (*habilitas*) to be acted upon again" or "illuminated again more easily" remains in the prophet, after the Holy Spirit has acted to provide supernatural knowledge. (1920: II-II.Q171.a2.ad2). Blankenhorn (2014) refers to this as a "quasi-natural after-effect of a supernaturally received cognition" (399).

⁸However, Aquinas does not exclude the possibility that the gift of tongues may be habitual (1920:II-II.Q176. a2.ad3) and implies the Christ had such a habitual gift of xenoglossia (1920: III.Q7.a7.ad.3); Blankenhorn (2014: 398).

I see no reason why one cannot hold divine activity to work in a diversity of ways. God might both create and uphold the ordinary powers of nature as described by the natural sciences or the doctrine of providence, and God might perform actions that empower creatures beyond (hence, "super-") these ordinary powers (hence, "-natural") to achieve some surprising and, scientifically inexplicable, outcome. Rather than collapsing all of God's activities into one paradigm, it seems far more theologically beneficial to mark the different ways in which God's agency manifests in and through creation (Abraham 2017). If one accepts this view of what is meant by "natural" and "supernatural," then it seems clear that charismatic gifts, and indeed all forms of grace that go beyond the powers granted to the essence of a creature, should be considered supernatural.

To be clear, since there is so much confusion on this topic, to say that charismatic gifts extend the powers that human beings have in and of themselves is not to say that human agency must be suspended or violated in some way. Thus, a charismatic gift may not be self-evidently or transparently supernatural, even to the recipient. Despite the primary agency and empowerment of the Spirit, the cooperation of fallen agents means that the gifts remain vulnerable to misinterpretation and misuse in certain ways. To affirm the supernatural quality of charismatic gifts is not to deny this but simply to maintain (CG1) that these are instances of grace, and (CG2) that the primary (but not sole) agent is a supernatural (uncreated) one.

4. Can charismatic gifts be learned or practiced?

Sarah Coakley has emphasized that liturgical learning is not like immediate perception, but a "complex means of *training* the mind and senses, over time, in order to come into a right relation with God" (Coakley 2013: 137–8). Is the same true of charismatic gifts? Are the gifts more like liturgical learning or immediate perception? On the one hand, the idea of learning a charismatic gift seems contrary to the gratuitous and coming-from-without nature of these phenomena (CG1). Additionally, training may allow for the possibility of a new spiritual elite and undermine the equalizing potential of charismatic gifts within the church. On the other hand, the intentional pursuit of God in contemplative prayer and ascetic practices is clearly a part of charismatic spirituality, often as a means of expectant and preparatory waiting for the Spirit (CG5) (Albrecht and Howard 2014: 240). Yong (2005) affirms that "the *charismata* can be cultivated and developed" through practice and mentorship (295). How are we to make sense of this tension?

In her influential study, *When God Speaks Back*, T. M. Luhrmann emphasizes this knowledge-how aspect of how charismatic gifts function within the Vineyard Church. She writes that, for the Christians she encountered, coming to know God personally "was more like learning *to do* something than *to think* something. I would describe what I saw as a theory of attentional learning," whereby members of the church learned to pay attention to God in certain ways and learned "to identify some thoughts as God's voice, some images as God's suggestions, some sensations as God's touch or the response to his nearness" (2012: xxi, see also 40–1, 60, 371–2). Luhrmann calls this "new Christian theory of mind" a "participatory theory of mind," because it teaches participants that the barrier between their own mind and God's is porous in certain ways (Luhrmann 2012: 40; cf. Rea 2018: 93–6, 106–7). In this, Luhrmann describes the learning to perceive God's presence, to receive a word of prophecy, or be "nudged" to act in a certain way (all activities that may be categorized as charismatic gifts, although Luhrmann never uses the term), as akin to learning to read a sonogram or become a professional sommelier. Charismatic gifts may then be a learnt form of perception. What this indicates is that, the Spirit's appearance, movement, or communication must remain gratuitous, uncontrollable, and beyond any human capacity to "conjure up," but that humans can still learn to perceive, sense, or be correctly attuned to such movements of the Spirit, and they can do so to greater or lesser degrees. This seems to fit with the twofold metaphysic argued for above whereby the charismatic gifts are actions of the Spirit mediated through the receptive *habitus* of the human, the latter of which may be developed and honed but remains useless without the former. The unearned nature of charismatic gifts does not entail that they are also unlearned.

III. EPISTEMOLOGICAL QUESTIONS

The first epistemological question for any community where a charismatic gift is reported is:

5. How does a community know that a reported charismatic gift is the work of the Holy Spirit, and not another spirit—supernatural, demonic, psychological, alcoholic, or other—that may explain the phenomena?

The literature in analytic epistemology of religion cannot exhaustively adjudicate this important area of spiritual discernment, but it may offer some aid. Let us accept the classic definition of knowledge as a justified true belief. Whether the belief that it is the Holy Spirit who is the primary agent behind a phenomenon is a *true* belief seems beyond our capacity to be certain about, although one might build a cumulative case to assess the probability of the claim (Middlemiss 1996: 194–236). Thus, any report of a charismatic gift will always remain provisional. Focusing instead on the issue of epistemic justification, we might rephrase this question to:

5a. When is the community, justified in believing that a charismatic gift is authentically the work of the Holy Spirit?

As Estrelda Alexander describes, it is important that this act of discernment "is a corporate responsibility," and not the responsibility of any one individual (2015: 143). When a person perceives themselves to have received a charismatic gift that does not immediately manifest in any other publicly discernible way, it is likely that she will report this experience verbally. Thus, we move into the epistemology of religious testimony. In believing the speaker who claims to have a charismatic gift, the community is authorizing the activity of the speaker, as well as ascribing justification, warrant, and possibly authority to her assertions. Should the standards for presumptive credulity remain the same as in more mundane testimonial interactions? As with all accounts of testimony, the speaker is capable of deception and error, and second-personal knowledge or the standing of the person within the community may play an important role in the community's discernment process.

Whilst there are likely to be additional sources of justification, such as the public manifestation of the gift, a memory of such events previously in the life of the community, or corroboration with other accepted authorities (e.g., scripture), I do not think that these are taken as necessary within many epistemic communities accustomed to discerning the presence of a charismatic gift. Instead, such communities often practice a Reidian non-reductionist account of testimony where, as with children, there are presumptions of veracity and credulity (Reid 1997: 6.24; cf. Wolterstorff 2000: 163–84). Indeed, charismatic theologians often give a normative role to children, childlikeness, and playfulness in their accounts of testimony and charismatic gifts. But is this doxastic practice justified? According to Reid, both of these principles are implanted as innate mental faculties by God in order that "we should be social creatures, and that we should receive the greatest and most important part of our knowledge by the information of others" (1997: 193–4). This approach not only provides an externalist justification of testimony but also suggests that the social benefits of testimony make it a preferable form of knowledge acquisition. In the case of charismatic gifts, which by definition builds up the community, it seems preferential then that not all members of the community receive all the gifts, but that they must trust one another's testimony at various points.[9] For this line of inquiry to be developed further analytic theologians may need more robust accounts of epistemic communities, in which testimonials about charismatic gifts can be appropriately discerned (Hankinson Nelson 2013).

However, before a testimony of a charismatic gift can be made, a person themselves needs to believe that they have received a specific gift. Therefore, the related question is:

5b. When is an individual justified in believing that she is a recipient of a charismatic gift?

Authentic charismatic gifts are probably best categorized, from the perspective of the recipient, as a religious experience. More controversially, many recipients of charismatic gifts take this to be a *perceptual* religious experience. That is, charismatic gifts are a religious experience whereby the subject encounters the Holy Spirit or perceives a communication from God. William P. Alston (1991) has argued that, in a way parallel to how physical sense perception justifies beliefs about ordinary objects, a person is rationally justified in believing that their apparent non-sensory perception of God's presence is veridical and the beliefs resulting from this perception are also justified. There is substantial overlap between Alston's way of justifying belief in mystical perception and how many recipients of charismatic gifts describe their religious experience, as a non-inferential doxastic practice arising directly from spiritual perception. Analytic theologians could, therefore, employ Alston's work on religious experience to argue that a person is justified in believing that she has received a charismatic gift just in the case that she perceives this to be so. In addition, however, it must be remembered that charismatic gifts are given for the good of a community and so it may well be that the community has epistemic authority in this case of discernment. This may entail that the individual is justified in offering her testimony/interpretation of the phenomenon but withholds judgment until the community discerns whether or not her prophecy, word of knowledge/wisdom, healing, tongues and interpretation, is a special act of the Holy Spirit in their midst.

6. What type of knowledge can be obtained from a charismatic gift?

What makes charismatic gifts frightful to some and exciting to others is the claim that new or confirmatory religious knowledge can be gained from a charismatic gift. Some gifts, such as words of knowledge, words of wisdom, prophecy, and speaking in tongues with interpretation, seem to be a form of special revelation. The reception of these charismatic gifts involves the use of the recipient's cognitive faculties as a belief-forming process. Moreover, this special revelation or insight to an individual does not appear to be a mere commentary on God's activity, but often functions as a herald or even means by which

---

[9] There is some irony in the epistemic fit between a Reidian account of testimony with charismatic gifts since, as Jon Ruthven has argued, B. B. Warfield's cessationism is also heavily reliant upon Reid's Scottish common-sense philosophy (1993: 44–52).

the Spirit achieves God's purposes at a specific time and place. It is these further claims, that beliefs obtained from a charismatic gift have warrant, can be taken as evidence, hold authority, and even release divine power, which makes careful discernment of whether a reported charismatic gift is truly the work of the Holy Spirit so important.

Above, I claimed that from the perspective of the recipient charismatic gifts are a type of religious experience in which a person claims to have an experience of encounter with the Holy Spirit. As Michael Sudduth notes, this is in contrast to the post-Kantian liberal Protestant trend to view religious experiences as mystical, apophatic, and non-cognitive natural phenomena interpreted as religiously significant only for the individual recipient (2009: 220–1). The only charismatic gift that could match this form of religious experience is a sub-type of glossolalia reserved for private prayer and emotional expression, which cannot be articulated or even interpreted into semantic content.[10] Apart from this phenomenon, charismatic gifts seem to be a thoroughly cognitive form of religious experience that generates, or at least claims to generate, a variety of types of knowledge about God or to receive knowledge about the world from God. Happily, the latter half of the twentieth century has seen an increasing number of theologians and philosophers maintain that religious experience can also be cognitive, often as a form of perception (e.g., Ballie 1939: 166–77; Hick 1971: chapter 7; Alston 1991; Swinburne 2013: chapter 13).

Intuitive perception is commonly described as analogous to when we perceive the presence of another mind and obtain knowledge by acquaintance, rather than through propositions. This second-personal knowledge appears to be of immediate advantage to theology, since it suggests that God can be known not merely as an object of perception but as a person with whom humans can engage in an inter-personal relationship. As such, second-personal accounts of religious experience have become popular among analytic theologians (e.g., Stump and Pinsent 2013). This area of research could be particularly helpful in providing a fuller account of charismatic gifts.

Second-personal accounts of knowledge of God and religious experience tend to rely upon recent psychological research on shared or joint attention, sometimes called "intersubjective perception" (Hobson 2005: 190). Joint attention occurs when two or more participants are aware of the other's awareness and are introspectively aware of the others awareness of their own awareness (Green 2009: 459–60). This can be dyadic, where both parties attend to the other as in reciprocal smiling, or triadic, where both parties attend to the same object, often coordinating by pointing or by some other physical gesture. Importantly, shared attention gives a "heightened opportunity for the communication of affect," so that learning how the other participant feels is essential to the overall communicative experience (461).

In the case of charismatic gifts, attention may be shared dyadically with the Holy Spirit, such that the congregation become aware of the Spirit's presence, love, or voice, or triadically as the Spirit may prompt a person's attention toward a third object, such as, a person in need, the persistence of a certain sin in one's life, or a passage of scripture.[11] The strength of the paradigm of joint attention as an account of charismatic gifts is that it allows for substantial similarities to other forms of religious experience and it has traction with the descriptions from Charismatic and Pentecostal communities of the gifts as including

---

[10]Tongues (glossolalia) seem to come in a variety of forms and can refer to speaking in unknown or angelic languages, speaking in another known language (xenolalia), a language of private prayer, and free doxological speech among the congregation that functions as a herald of the Spirit's presence, and simultaneously symbolizes humanity's remaining distance from God and the promise of eschatological renewal (Turner 1996: 312–13).

[11]Green (2009) describes "a triadic experience, for example, by the divine showing a prophet the fate of a nation, and so on" (462).

a distinctive type of intuitive, sensitive, and receptive "attention" given to the Holy Spirit (Albrecht and Howard 2014: 241). In particular, as a situationally irreducible form of interpersonal knowledge, testimony regarding joint attention lends itself to social cohesion (CG4) and the kinds of narratives that are common within charismatic communities as a way of scrutinizing and transmitting beliefs formed on the basis of charismatic gifts.

Whilst knowledge by acquaintance appears to be a central and essential form of knowledge obtained through charismatic gifts, it should not exhaust the forms of knowledge obtained through the gifts. Instead, a place needs to be maintained for propositional knowledge and knowledge-how to hear or encounter the Spirit (see question 4 above). In what follows, I will focus on propositional knowledge and explore the questions of warrant, evidence, and authority that quickly arise.

7. Do beliefs obtained from charismatic gifts have warrant?

The concept of warrant, as developed by Alvin Plantinga, is that which turns mere belief into knowledge, but unlike justification it is conferred upon the beliefs directly, rather than upon the subject of those beliefs. An extension of Plantinga's defense of the rationality of "the great things of the gospel" to beliefs held on the basis of charismatic gifts would be no insignificant task (Plantinga 2000: 244). Plantinga argues that a person can rationally hold beliefs by appealing to a belief-producing process of a special kind, namely, the "inner testimony" or "inner instigation" of the Holy Spirit as "a supernatural gift" (245–6, 251). Such beliefs, according to Plantinga, are "properly basic" and require neither argument nor evidential basis from other propositions, nor even an argument from religious experience although they are formed on the occasion of a religious experience (259). I see no reason why Plantinga's model, which he applies to the gift of faith, could not be extended to include other doxastic charismatic gifts.

The first question facing a Reformed Epistemologist's account of charismatic gifts is:

7a. When beliefs are obtained by means of a charismatic gift, are these beliefs produced by cognitive processes functioning properly?

An affirmative answer to this question would be a direct refutation of characterizations of charismatic gifts as sheer irrationality (a symptom of madness, mass hysteria, the manipulation of a malevolent spirit, or deceptive self-aggrandizement), all of which assume that charismatic gifting is not what proper function looks like. Regardless of what one thinks about Reformed Epistemology overall, this is surely an important theological question regarding the relationship of charismatic gifts to the *imago Dei* and God's providential plan for humanity. If charismatic gifts are representative of regenerated and eschatological proper cognitive functioning, then an important second question may be:

7b. What is the proper cognitive environment for which this particular cognitive process was designed?

It may well be that, unlike other cognitive processes that God has designed for human beings to obtain knowledge, the gathered congregation is the primary or even the only appropriate environment in this case.

8. Can charismatic gifts be rightly treated as evidence?

One of the most striking and controversial aspects of charismatic gifts arises from their employment as evidence for other beliefs or states of affairs, such as the existence of God, the recipients own state of salvation, or a Spirit-baptism distinct from water-baptism.

John Locke (1975, book 4, chapter 19) argued that the doxastic gifts (e.g., prophecy, dreams, visions, words of knowledge and wisdom) required further evidence from publicly available gifts (healings, miracles). The idea that publicly available charismatic gifts provide evidence for the credibility of new religious knowledge, also lies at the heart of B. B. Warfield's cessationist argument against the existence of charismatic gifts since the closing of the biblical cannon (Ruthven 1993: 43). This history of correlating charismatic gifts with evidence provides a surprising point of contact with analytic philosophy of science that, through the historic influence of positivism and evidentialism, has been highly invested in the concept of evidence (most often) as that which justifies belief. It is perhaps also one of the main reasons that charismatic gifts such as *glossolalia* (speaking in tongues) have been a major focus of empirical research into religious phenomena (Mill 1986; Newberg et al. 2006; Newberg and Waldman 2009).

The correspondence between charismatic gifts and evidence may be surprising because evidence is often closely related to objectivity; where a person is objective if their beliefs are determined by evidence and not, for example, texts or teaching whose authority is obtained through tradition, personal attachment, or conviction. There seems to be a tension in the notion that charismatic gifts are a form of evidence defined and constrained by reports of their existence in scriptural texts, arising in the context of community-building and religious conviction.

8a. What form of evidence are charismatic gifts?

There is a wide range of definitions of "evidence" from physical objects (a bloody knife at a crime scene) to perceptual experiences (seeing the murderer stab the victim). Trent Dougherty argues that at the bottom of any account of evidence is an experience, perhaps even a mental event generated by the imagination in response to certain stimuli (2017: 241–2). Charismatic gifts, following Dougherty's definition of evidence, may be characterized as testimonial evidence (237). Similarly, Paul K. Moser (although he never mentions charismatic gifts) describes the experiential aspect of the inner witness of the Holy Spirit as not only "experiential evidence of God's intervention for a recipient" but also the "sole evidential foundation for believing in God and for believing that God exists" (2017: 119, 121). The debates within analytic philosophy regarding what kinds of things count as evidence and how evidence relates to belief would be a fruitful area for an analytic theology of charismatic gifts to pursue.

And yet another question emerges:

8b. What are charismatic gifts evidence for?

Again, there is a wide variety of philosophical accounts of the relationship between evidence and hypotheses, but it is the narrative account that seems best suited to the case of charismatic gifts (Dougherty 2017: 242). We see this narrative relationship between evidence and hypothesis in the interweaving of scripture within contemporary testimonies regarding charismatic gifts to generate new "narrative knowledge" (Smith 2017: 610). In Charismatic and Pentecostal communities, this is captured by the hermeneutical slogan "this-is-that," which frames contemporary events as an echo or fulfilment of promises from scripture (McPherson 1923; Stibbe 1998). Scripture then provides the best story about the contemporary phenomena and the contemporary phenomena function as evidence for the propositions of scripture (Smith 2010: 23). In this way, charismatic gifts can function as a form of evidence, without jettisoning the authority of scripture, personal attachment, or conviction.

9. What type of epistemic authority do charismatic gifts carry or bestow upon the recipient?

The question of epistemic authority lies at the heart of a great many disputes regarding charismatic gifts.[12] As mentioned above, Protestant cessationism reduces to a concern that a charismatic gift challenges the sufficiency of scripture and some wings of the Roman Catholic Church worry that charismatic gifts undermine ecclesial hierarchy.[13] This is largely because the claims of direct inspiration or anointing by the Holy Spirit in the case of a charismatic gift appear indistinguishable from many Protestant articulations of the authorship of scripture and many Roman Catholic notions of the power granted by ordination. This has given charismatic gifts great potential to be employed and abused by anti-establishment, self-autonomous movements, and by those in authority throughout the church's history (Tanner 2006). It is unsurprising, then, that arguments have not often revolved around what authority a charismatic gift bestows, since this is assumed on both sides, but instead have revolved upon whether a charismatic gift is authentically present (question 5).

The power of charismatic gifts to grant spiritual authority to the socially disenfranchised or economically oppressed margins of society is, and will likely remain, a central part of their importance and appeal across the globe. As Albrecht and Howard describe in the context of Pentecostalism, "leadership in a congregation may arise at any moment as one sister or brother becomes the vehicle for the authoritative word or touch of God in the midst of a gathering" (2014: 244). Whilst, as Smith notes, the Pentecostal epistemological testimonial claim, "I know that I know that I know," prioritizes narrative and allows space for testimony and witness within a community's doxastic practices, it may also be used as a claim for the authority of introspection and a defense against skeptical attacks or critical reflection (2010: 50, 62–71). However, it would be a mistake to conclude that charismatic gifts, even when authentic, grant absolute authority to an autonomous individual over and against all other socially agreed forms of epistemic and religious authority. Since a charismatic gift is (by definition) given for the edification of the church and the community is where an individual learns to receive charismatic gifts, she has good preemptive reasons to submit herself to the authority of the community in discerning and interpreting the gift. Insofar as this community has submitted itself to the authority of scripture and to certain appointed leaders, it has preemptive reasons to submit any prophetic word or new propositional knowledge to these other authoritative sources. Questions of epistemic authority clearly abound in the context of charismatic giftings and are essential to the communal practice of such phenomena.

---

[12]There is a great deal of literature dealing with political/social authority, rather than epistemic authority, of charisms arising out of Max Weber's sociological description of charisms as a form of domination and the "the routinization of charisma" in the early church (1964: 363–73).

[13]Thus, Warfield writes that the actions of the Holy Spirit cannot function as rational evidence themselves but can only be a feeling that accompanies the evidence of scripture (Ruthven 1993: 14–15, 53). This seems approximately in line with Moser's (2017) work on the testimony of the Holy Spirit as "epistemically *confirming* God's reality and work" (114). In *Counterfeit Miracles*, Warfield also wrote that the gifts were given "to authenticate the Apostles as the authoritative founders of the church" (cited in Ruthven 1993: 72). As D. A. Carson concludes, Warfield's "argument stands up *only* if such miraculous gifts are theologically tied *exclusively* to a role attestation; and this is demonstrably not so" (1987: 156). For an overview of the Roman Catholic/Pentecostal dialogue over the authority that charismatic gifts, see Kärkäinen (2001).

IV. CONCLUSION

This chapter has shown that analytic theology holds fruitful resources for answering some of the urgent questions facing the church on the matter of charismatic gifts. Further topics of investigation still remain, such as, what doctrine of God is implicit within the theology and practice of charismatic gifts; this could pertain to the Trinity of God, the personhood of the Holy Spirit, the metaphysics of indwelling, the hiddenness of God, and countless other areas. There is also good reason to think that analytic theology itself will benefit from giving greater attention to charismatic gifts, as these gifts are a central part—perhaps even the spiritual foundation—of the church's worship and knowledge of God. Charismatic gifts should then provide resources that constrain, modify, and breathe life into the models constructed by analytic theologians.

References

Abraham, W. J. (2017), *Divine Agency and Divine Action: Exploring and Evaluating the Debate*, Oxford: Oxford University Press.

Albrecht, D. E., and E. B. Howard (2014), "Pentecostal Spirituality," in C. M. Rodeck and A. Yong (eds.), *The Cambridge Companion to Pentecostalism*, 235–53, Cambridge: Cambridge University Press.

Alexander, E. Y. (2015), "The Spirit of God: Christian Renewal in African American Pentecostalism," in J. W. Barbeau and B. F. Jones (eds.), *Spirit of God: Christian Renewal in the Community of Faith*, 128–46, Downers Grove, IL: InterVarsity Press.

Alston, W. (1991), *Perceiving God*, Ithaca, NY: Cornell University Press.

Aquinas, T. (1920), *Summa Theologica,* 2nd ed., trans. Fathers of the English Dominican Province. Available online: http://www.newadvent.org/summa/2001.htm.

Ballie, J. (1939), *Our Knowledge of God*, New York: Charles Scribner's Sons.

Barrett, D. B., and T. M. Johnson (2002), "Annual Statistical Table on Global Mission: 2002," *International Bulletin of Missionary Research*, 26 (1): 23–5.

Blankenhorn, B. (2014), "The Metaphysics of Charisms: Thomas Aquinas, Biblical Exegesis and Pentecostal Theology," *Angelicum*, 91 (3): 373–424.

Carson, D. A. (1987), *Showing the Spirit: Theological Exposition of 1 Corinthians 12–14*, Grand Rapids, MI: Baker Academic.

Coakely, S. (2013), "Beyond 'Belief': Liturgy and the Cognitive Apprehension of God," in T. Greggs, R. Muers, and S. Zahl (eds.), *The Vocation of Theology Today*, 130–45, Eugene OR: Wipf and Stock.

Congar, Y. (2003), *He Is Lord and Giver of Life: I Believe in the Holy Spirit,* vol. 2, trans. D. Smith, New York: Crossroad.

Dougherty, T. (2017), "Evidence and Theology," in W. J. Abraham and F. D. Aquino (eds.), *The Oxford Handbook of the Epistemology of Theology*, 236–52, Oxford: Oxford University Press.

Fee, G. (1994), *Empowering Presence: The Holy Spirit in the Letter of Paul*, Peabody: Hendrickson.

Green, A. (2009), "Reading the Mind of God (without Hebrew Lessons): Alston, Shared Attention, and Mystical Experience," *Religious Studies*, 45: 455–79.

Hankinson Nelson, L. (2013), "Epistemic Communities," in L. Alcoff and E. Potter (eds.), *Feminist Epistemologies*, 121–60, New York: Routledge.

Hick, J. (1971), *Arguments for the Existence of God*, New York: Herder & Herder.

Hobson, P. R. (2005), "What Puts the Jointness in Joint Attention?' in N. Elian, C. Hoerl, T. McCormack, and J. Roessler (eds.), *Joint Attention: Communication and Other Minds*, 185–204. Oxford: Oxford University Press.

Kärkäinen, V. (2001), "Church as Charismatic Fellowship: Ecclesiological Reflections from the Pentecostal-Roman Catholic Dialogue," *Journal of Pentecostal Theology*, 9 (1): 100–21.

Küng, H. (1965), "The Charismatic Structure of the Church," *Concilium*, 4: 41–61.

Leidenhag, J. (2020), "For We All Share in One Spirit: Charismatic Gifts as Liturgical Group Actions," *TheoLogica: An International Journal for Philosophy of Religion and Philosophical Theology*, 4 (1): 64–87.

Locke, J. (1975), *The Clarendon Edition of the Works of John Locke: An Essay Concerning Human Understanding*, ed. P. Nidditch, Oxford: Oxford University Press.

Luhrmann, T. M. (2012), *When God Talks Back: Understanding the American Evangelical Relationship with God*, New York: Random House.

McCall, T. H. (2015), *An Invitation to Analytic Christian Theology*, Downers Grove, IL: IVP Academic.

McPherson, A. S. (1923), *This is That: Personal Experiences, Sermons, and Writings of Aimee Semple McPherson,* Los Angeles: Echo Park Evangelistic Association.

Middlemiss, D. (1996), *Interpreting Charismatic Experience*, London: SCM Press.

Mills, W. E. (1986), *Speaking Tongues: A Guide to Research on Glossolalia*. Grand Rapids, MI: Eerdmans.

Moltmann, J. (2001), *The Spirit of Life: A Universal Affirmation*, Minneapolis: Fortress Press.

Moser, P. (2017), "The Inner Witness of the Holy Spirit," in W. J. Abraham and F. D. Aquino (eds.), *The Oxford Handbook of the Epistemology of Theology*, 111–25, Oxford: Oxford University Press.

Newberg, A., and M. R. Waldman (2009), *How God Changes Your Brain*, New York: Ballantine Books.

Newberg, A. B., N A. Wintering, D. Morgan, and M .E. Waldman (2006), "The Measurement of Regional Cerebral Blood Flow during Glossolalia: A Preliminary SPECT Study," *Psychiatry Research: Neuroimaging*, 148: 67–71.

Pew Research Center (2011), "Global Christianity – A Report on the Size and Distribution of the World's Christian Population," accessed June 30, 2019. Available online: https://www.pewforum.org/2011/12/19/global-christianity-exec/.

Plantinga, A. (2000), *Warranted Christian Belief*, Oxford: Oxford University Press.

Rea, M. (2018), *The Hiddenness of God*, Oxford: Oxford University Press.

Reid, T. (1997), *An Inquiry into the Human Mind on the Principles of Common Sense*, ed. D. R. Brookes, Edinburgh: Edinburgh University Press.

Ruthven, J. (1993), *On the Cessation of the Charismata: The Protestant Polemic on Postbiblical Miracles*, Sheffield: Sheffield Academic Press.

Smith, J. K. A. (2010), *Thinking in Tongues: Pentecostal Contributions to Christian Philosophy*. Grand Rapids, MI: Eerdmans.

Smith, J. K. A. (2017), "Pentecostalism," in W. J. Abraham and F. D. Aquina (eds.), *The Oxford Handbook of the Epistemology of Theology*, 606–18, Oxford: Oxford University Press.

Stibbe, M. (1994), "A British Appraisal," *Journal of Pentecostal Theology*, 4: 5–16.

Stibbe, M. (1998), "This Is That: Some Thoughts Concerning Charismatic Hermeneutics," *Anvil: An Anglican Evangelical Journal for Theology and Mission*, 15 (3): 181–93.

Stump, E., and A. Pinsent (2013), "The Second-Personal in Philosophy of Religion," [Special Issue] *European Journal for Philosophy of Religion*, 5 (4).

Sudduth, M. (2009), "The Contribution of Religious Experience to Dogmatic Theology," in O. D. Crisp and M. C. Rea (eds.), *Analytic Theology: New Essays in the Philosophy of Theology*, 214–32, Oxford: Oxford University Press.

Swinburne, R. (2013), *The Existence of God*, Oxford: Clarendon Press.

Snyder, H. (2010), "Spiritual Gifts," in G. R. McDermott (ed.) *The Oxford Handbook of Evangelical Theology*, 325–37, Oxford: Oxford University Press.

Tanner, K. (2006), "Workings of the Spirit: Simplicity or Complexity?," in M. Welker (ed.), *The Work of the Spirit: Pneumatology and Pentecostalism*, 87–105. Grand Rapids, MI: Eerdmans.

Turner, M. (1996), *The Holy Spirit and Spiritual Gifts: Then and Now*, Carlisle: Paternoster Press.

Weber, M. (1964), *The Theory of Social and Economic Organization*, trans. A. M. Henderson and T. Parsons. New York: Free Press.

Wolterstorff, N. (2000), *Thomas Reid and the Story of Epistemology*, Cambridge: Cambridge University Press.

Yong, A. (2005), *The Spirit Poured Out on All Flesh: Pentecostalism and the Possibility of Global Theology*, Grand Rapids, MI: Baker Academic.

PART V

Creation and Humans

CHAPTER TWENTY-TWO

Creatio Ex Nihilo

ANDREW TER ERN LOKE

I. INTRODUCTION

The doctrine of *creatio ex nihilo* (Latin for "creation from nothing") refers to the view that the world is created by a free act of God out of nothing (Ward 2003: 184).[1] This doctrine is affirmed by many adherents of the Abrahamic religions (Burrell et al. 2010).[2] In this chapter, I focus on assessing the controversies involving the Christian tradition in response to those who advocate creation out of an eternal preexisting entity (e.g., Mormons and Process Theologians who claim a coeternal interdependent relationship between God and world), and those who advocate creation out of divine substance. I shall assess the controversies in relation to scripture, the history of Christian theology, and contemporary science and religion discussions that have largely been stimulated by recent advances in Big Bang Cosmology. I shall then explain how the arguments of analytic philosophy—in particular, the philosophical version of the Kalam Cosmological Argument and the *modus tollens* argument for the Causal Principle—can assist the constructive task of the theologian.

II. THE DOCTRINE IN SCRIPTURE AND HISTORY OF CHRISTIAN THEOLOGY

In an influential study, which is cited by almost all scholars who object to *creatio ex nihilo*, Gerhard May (1994) argues that the doctrine is not found in scripture at all but arose in the second century ce where it emerged as the standard teaching of the church against Greek views of the eternity of matter and gnostic accounts of emanation. May claims that many early Christians (e.g., Justin, Athenagoras, Hermogenes, and Clement of Alexandria) believed that God initially created out of something rather than nothing.

Others observe that May's argument suffers from a failure to distinguish between words and concepts; in particular, the concept of creation from nothing can be present without the terminology, and vice versa (Osborn 2001: 66). While the concept may not have been clearly articulated, clearly understood, or widely held earlier on, this does not imply that it was not present earlier. On the contrary, it can be argued that "the meaning and substance of the doctrine, though not the terminology, is firmly rooted in scripture and pre-Christian Jewish literature" (Bockmuehl 2012).

---

[1] Whether abstract entities are also created by God is discussed in Lindsay Cleveland's essay in this volume.
[2] There is dispute concerning whether it is also found in other religions (Ge 2018).

Nevertheless, the demonstration of this conclusion is not as straightforward as some may think. While many throughout history have understood the majestic opening verse of the Bible "In the beginning God created the heavens and the earth" (Gen. 1:1) as affirming *creatio ex nihilo*, others have disputed this interpretation by claiming that it affirms the ordering of preexisting thing(s) (e.g., Keller 2003; Walton 2009; van Wolde 2010; for response, see Collins 2018).[3] Genesis was understood even in antiquity to be somewhat ambiguous on this point (Bockmuehl 2012). In any case, unlike other ancient cosmologies, the opening to Genesis does not affirm the eternity of preexisting matter and thus does not preclude the possibility of an earlier *creatio ex nihilo* event (Arnold 2009: 36). The narrative that portrays God using preexistent material to create entities, such as letting the earth bring forth living creatures (Gen 1:24), does not imply that this material (e.g., the earth) had existed from eternity; on the contrary, the narrative is compatible with the idea that God had earlier created all matter from nothing prior to creating living creatures.

Already in the pre-Christian Dead Sea Scrolls, we see an affirmation of God's free creation of the world without recourse to preexisting matter (Bockmuehl 2012). While the first century Philo was not entirely consistent in his thinking about this topic, the basic tenets of *creatio ex nihilo* are already present in his writings (Soskice 2010: 33–4, citing *Legum Allegoriae* iii; *De Fuga et Inventione*, 46; *De Vita Mosis* ii, 267).

In the New Testament, Paul affirms that all things come from "God" (1 Cor. 8:6; Rom. 11:36) and not from "God and another pre-existent entity." Moreover, the implication of saying in Col. 1:16–17 that Christ is prior to all things is that there was a state of being in which Christ existed and all other things did not (Copan and Craig 2004: 85). While Oord (2015: 110) objects by claiming that 2 Pet. 3:5 implies *creatio ex materia* ("… long ago by God's word the heavens came into being and the earth was formed out of water and by water"), Copan (2005: 47–8) replies that Peter is probably describing a two-stage creation in which God first created the "waters" out of which He subsequently formed the world; this does not imply that the waters were eternal or made out of eternal matter.

In conclusion, passages such as 1 Cor. 8:6, Rom. 11:36, and Col. 1:16-17 taken together imply that God did not create out of an eternal preexisting entity.[4] Against those who advocate creation out of divine substance (Zbaraschuk 2015), traditional Christian theology affirm a fundamental ontological discontinuity between Creator and creature (McFarland 2014: xii). This is rooted in scripture which affirms a strict Creator-creature divide (e.g., Rom. 1:18-25), and which "enables the Bible to depict God's transcendence and otherness from creaturely reality, while at the same time stressing the significance of a relationship that can be characterized by the language of covenant and fellowship" (Fergusson 2007: 77).

By affirming *creatio ex nihilo* and the goodness of the material world as a creation of a good God, early Christians objected to Gnostics who claimed that the material world is inherently evil. Against this affirmation, some have claimed that those who affirm *creatio ex nihilo* cannot offer a satisfying account for why a good God capable of total control

---

[3]Biblical quotations in this chapter are taken from the New American Standard Bible.
[4]Other passages which are often cited are not so compelling. For example, phrases such as "God did not make them out of things that existed [*ouk ex ontōn*]" (2 Macc. 7:28) and "calls into existence the things that do not exist [*ta mē onta*]" (Rom. 4:17) can be explained as a Greek idiom used for the coming into being of anything new, without any implication for whether or not this new thing is derived from any preexisting substance (McFarland 2014: 4–5). "Not made out of things that are visible" (Heb. 1:2) does not rule out "made out of invisible things" (https://www.fairmormon.org/archive/publications/reviews-of-the-new-mormon-challenge).

does not prevent genuine evils when they arise (Oord 2015: 112). Others do not find this objection convincing and have offered various theodicies in response (Meister 2018).

Creatio ex nihilo has also been criticized for its claim that God's creative activity is a unilateral, controlling use of power, and that such a one-sided power relationship is difficult to reconcile with the dynamics of a love relationship which is supposed to exist between God and creatures and which takes the other into account (Vail 2015: 58). However, it can be replied that God uses his power in accordance with his character of love and justice and that he created the word in accordance with his middle knowledge which takes the other into account (Loke 2013).

Against *creatio ex nihilo*, it has been argued that, unless the world exists necessarily, God does not essentially love creation, which goes against the intuition that "God will always love me because to stop loving me would mean that God isn't acting like God" (Oord 2015: 118–20). However, this intuition only requires that God continuously love a created person once he/she exists, it does not require that he/she or the world exists necessarily. Rice (2015: 94–5) explains that

> the notion of a world whose very existence is contingent argues for, rather than against, divine love. Although creation is a choice, not a necessity, for God, this does not lessen the world's value to God. Instead, voluntary creation shows its importance. After all, a freely chosen commitment can express one's deepest character just as much as one that is inevitable. For many people, having children is a choice, not a necessity, but this hardly makes their children incidental to their identity.

While some have reasoned that, if God is essentially characterized by self-giving love, creation becomes necessary, and William Lane Craig and J. P. Moreland (2003: 560–1) observe that

> the Christian doctrine of the Trinity suggests another possibility. Insofar as he exists without creation, God is not, on the Christian conception, a lonely monad, but in the tri-unity of his own being, God enjoys the full and unchanging love relationships among the persons of the Trinity. Creation is thus unnecessary for God and is sheer gift, bestowed for the sake of creatures, that we might experience the joy and fulfillment of knowing God. He invites us, as it were, into the intratrinitarian love relationship as his adopted children. Thus creation, as well as salvation, is sola gratia.

III. CONTEMPORARY SCIENCE AND RELIGION DISCUSSIONS

The astonishing discovery of the expansion of the universe in the twentieth century and the formulation of the Hawking-Penrose theorems which postulate a cosmic singularity as an initial boundary to space-time have led many scientists to speak excitedly about the creation of the universe *ex nihilo*. For example, physicists John Barrow and Frank Tipler (1986: 442) state, "At this singularity, space and time came into existence; literally nothing existed before the singularity, so, if the Universe originated at such a singularity, we would truly have a creation ex nihilo."

Others cautiously note that, while there is no longer any significant doubt that our universe had an explosive beginning about fourteen billion years ago, this conclusion does not imply that there was a beginning to all physical things. As Barr explains, our universe is not necessarily the totality of all physical things, but a "space-time manifold" that possess some well-defined geometrical properties. He notes that, over the years, a number of speculative cosmological scenarios have been proposed in which the Big Bang was not the beginning (Barr 2012: 179–83). Nevertheless, there are also cosmological models (e.g., Vilenkin 2006) in which there was a beginning to all physical things. Many physicists of various persuasions (theists, atheists) have argued that cosmological models that attempt to avoid a beginning face various technical difficulties related to the Second Law of Thermodynamics, acausal fine-tuning, or having an unstable or a metastable state with a finite lifetime. Models that attempt to avoid a beginning by postulating a reversal of the arrow of time nevertheless have a type of "thermodynamic beginning," which still requires an explanation (Craig and Sinclair 2009: 179–82; Bussey 2013; Wall 2014; Chan forthcoming). It is noteworthy that an eminent and highly motivated opponent of Craig (a well-known proponent of the Kalam Cosmological Argument, see below), such as atheist cosmologist Laurence Krauss, was willing to agree with Craig in public debate that it is likely that there was such a beginning (Krauss and Craig 2013).[5]

Against the conclusion that "the physical sciences seem therefore to warrant theology," Carlo Cogliati (2010: 9–10) objects that "there is a misunderstanding of the very terms in play. Creation accounts for the existence of things, not for the beginning of things." In reply, while it is true that creation "is not the same thing as the Big Bang theory" (Soskice 2010: 24), providing evidence for the beginning of all physical things does support one of the premises of the Kalam Cosmological Argument (KCA) for a Creator (see below). Following Thomas Aquinas (*Summa Theologiae* Ia.Q46.aa1–2), Cogliati (2010: 9–10) asserts that reason is only able to demonstrate that there is creation, but whether the created world began to exist or that it has always existed cannot be resolved demonstratively (Aquinas held the view that it has a beginning on the basis of faith in the church's teachings). However, a defense of the soundness of the KCA would show that such a beginning can in fact be demonstrated.

IV. THE KALAM COSMOLOGICAL ARGUMENT

The KCA is a version of the Cosmological Argument.[6] Bruce Reichenbach (2016) notes that, in Western philosophy, the earliest formulation of the Cosmological Argument is found in Plato's *Laws* (893–96), and took its classical expression in Aristotle's *Physics* (VIII: 4–6) and *Metaphysics* (XII: 1–6). From this, Islamic philosophy developed two types of arguments: an atemporal version from contingency which was later taken up by Aquinas (1225–1274) in his *Summa Theologica* (Ia.Q2.a3) and his *Summa Contra Gentiles* (I.13), and a temporal version known as the Kalam. Traces of the Kalam can be found earlier in the writings of the Christian philosopher John Philoponus (*c*.490–*c*.570), before the Muslim *mutakallimūm* (theologians who used argumentation to support their beliefs) such as al-Ghāzāli (1058–1111) developed it. From an overview of its history, three types of Cosmological Arguments can be distinguished:

1. The Thomist (named after Aquinas; this version attempts to show that the world has a First Sustaining Cause).

---

[5] Krauss emphasizes that we nevertheless cannot know with certainty, while Craig argues that in this case reasonableness of belief does not require certainty but likelihood.
[6] Some theologians have claimed that the task of offering the arguments of Natural Theology is inconsistent with scripture. For response, see Loke (2019).

2. The Leibnizian (named after Gottfried Wilhelm Leibniz (1646–1716)); see his *Monadology*: §32, this version attempts to ground the existence of the contingent realm of things in a necessarily existent being).
3. The KCA that, in distinction from the Thomist and Leibnizian versions, focuses on the issue of the *beginning of existence* (Craig 1980).

The KCA is an *a posteriori* argument that reasons from the observable aspects of the cosmos to deduce its ultimate Cause. It is formulated by Craig as follows:

1. Whatever begins to exist has a cause (Causal Principle)
2. The universe began to exist (note: in the context of Craig's formulation, universe refers to all physical things, not merely a "space-time manifold").
3. Therefore, the universe has a cause.

A more rigorous formulation of the philosophical version of this argument that demonstrates the properties of the cause of the universe is as follows:

1. There exists a series of causes-and-effects and changes (= events), and the number of earlier entities is either actually infinite or finite.
2. If the number of earlier entities is finite, then either earlier and later entities are joined together like a loop such that there is no first member in the series, or the series has a first member, that is, a First Cause and a first change (= first event).
3. It is not the case that the number of earlier entities is actually infinite.
4. It is not the case that earlier and later entities are joined together like a loop.
5. Therefore, there exists a First Cause and a first change (= first event).
6. Since the First Cause is the first, it must be uncaused.
7. Since everything that begins to exist has a cause (Causal Principle), the First Cause must be beginningless.
8. Since the first change (= first event) did not began to exist uncaused (because of the Causal Principle), the first change (= first event) must have been caused by a First Cause which was initially changeless.
9. In order to cause the first event from an initial changeless state, the First Cause must have
    9.1. The capacity to be the originator of the first event in a way that is un-determined by prior event, since the First Cause is the first, and
    9.2. The capacity to prevent itself from changing, for otherwise the First Cause would not have been initially changeless.
    9.1. and 9.2. imply that the First Cause has libertarian freedom.
10. In order to bring about the entire universe, the First Cause must be enormously powerful.
11. A First Cause that is uncaused, beginningless, initially changeless, has libertarian freedom, and enormously powerful is a Creator of the Universe.
12. Therefore, a Creator of the universe exists.

In Loke (2017), I have defended the crucial steps of the more rigorously formulated argument, viz., establishing premises 3 (ruling out an actual infinite regress), 4 (ruling out a loop), 7 (the Causal Principle), and 9 (the First Cause must have libertarian free will). In particular, I defend three philosophical arguments for premise 3, viz., the argument for the impossibility of concrete actual infinities, the argument for the impossibility of traversing an actual infinite, and the argument from the lack of capacity to begin to exist.

(Others have defended additional arguments formulated in terms of paradoxes, such as the Methuselah diary (Waters 2013) and Grim Reaper paradoxes (Koons 2014; Pruss 2018)). The third argument is particularly interesting. Aquinas objects to Bonaventure's attempt to prove that the world had a temporal beginning. However, the third argument shows that insights from the Thomist tradition concerning the impossibility of an essentially ordered infinite regress can (contra Aquinas) also be used to demonstrate the impossibility of a temporal infinite regress (for details, see Loke 2017: chapter 3). This argument assumes a relational view of time, according to which time is regarded as an ordered series of changes/events. The alternative substantival view of time affirms that time is substance-like (e.g., space-time is like a container) that can exist independently of the entities/events in them. Regardless of which view of time is true, the above arguments demonstrate that there must exist an initially changeless First Cause with free will (i.e., a Creator God) who freely brought about the first event, and who is distinct from the world which had a temporal beginning at the first event.

To elaborate, the above arguments imply that there must be a first change/event requiring a beginningless First Cause which must therefore have been either (1) an initially changeless-in-timeless state causally antecedent to the first change/event, or (2) an initially changeless state with an actual infinite past extension on a substantive view of time, causally and temporally antecedent to the first change/event.[7] On either view, it seems that "when the universe came into existence out of nothing God began to stand in a new causal relation that He did not previously stand in" (Mullins 2016: 101), and "for God to actively use His capacities to create would involve Him undergoing some kind of change. He would go from a state of not actualizing His capacity to create, to a state of actively creating" (112). While this poses a problem for Classical Theism's view of a strong version of divine immutability and essential atemporality, many theologians would be untroubled by this given their arguments that a strong version of divine immutability and essential atemporality are unwarranted scripturally and philosophically (see Loke 2014 and the chapter by R. T. Mullins in this volume).

In his discussion of the First Antinomy in *Critique of Pure Reason*, Immanuel Kant (1965: A466/B494) claims that, if time has a beginning, there will be an empty time before the first moment of time, and no coming to be of a thing is possible in an empty time. Craig has replied that this problem can be resolved by postulating the existence of an initially timeless First Cause with free will, and that such an entity freely brought the first event (and with it, the first moment of time) into existence (Craig 1979). In Loke (2017: chapter 6), I argue that, among various problems with Stephen Hawking's no-boundary proposal, which postulates an initial timeless state (Hawking and Mlodinow 2010), is its inability to account for the origin of the first event, which requires a First Cause with free will as explained by premises 8 and 9 above.

V. *EX NIHILO NIHIL FIT*

A key premise of the KCA is the Causal Principle that whatever begins to exist has a cause. A key motivation for this principle is the conviction that "from nothing, nothing comes." This conviction led Aristotle to insist that every state of the world must have come from

---

[7]This view is proposed by Alan Padgett (1992); according to this view, God exists before creation in an undifferentiated, nonmetric time.

a previous state of the world and hence the world must be everlasting (Cogliati 2010: 7). However, this conclusion is unwarranted given the distinction between efficient cause and material cause. *Creatio ex nihilo* only denies that the world has a material cause; it does not deny that the world has an efficient cause. On the contrary, *creatio* implies that the Creator is the efficient cause; in this sense, the world is from God and not from nothing.

Aristotle might object that "from nothing, nothing comes" applies to material cause as well, and insists that "from no material cause, nothing comes." He might appeal to our daily experiences, which seem to support the inductive generalization that whatever begins to exist has a material cause. Craig replies that such an inductive generalization can be treated merely as an accidental generalization, "akin to human beings have always lived on the Earth, which was true until 1968. The univocal concept of 'cause' is the concept of something which brings its effects, and whether it involves transformation of already existing materials or creation out of nothing is an incidental question" (Craig and Sinclair 2009: 188–9, 195). On the one hand, there has been no compelling argument offered to show that causes must involve the transformation of already existing materials. On the other hand, God as a causal agent could have causal powers that other entities (e.g., humans) do not have. While humans, for example, require preexisting materials to work from in order to create (say) a table, God does not require that.[8] Moreover, there are independent arguments for the Causal Principle (Loke 2017: chapter 5). Note, in particular, that the *modus tollens* argument for this principle (see below) is not dependent on inductive considerations, and, because of this additional deductive argument, the Causal Principle enjoys greater support than the principle that "whatever begins to exist has a material cause," which, in any case, can be regarded as an accidental generalization, as Craig argues.

The Causal Principle has been rejected in recent years by some philosophers due to considerations from quantum-mechanical indeterminacy (Grünbaum 2009: 15). However, others have responded that quantum particles emerge from the quantum vacuum which is not nonbeing but something with vacuum fields (quantum particles are manifestations of fields) and can be acted on by the relevant laws of nature (Bussey 2013: 33). Moreover, many different interpretations of quantum physics exist, and some of them, such as Everett's Many World's interpretation and de Broglie-Bohm's pilot-wave model (Bricmont 2016), are perfectly deterministic. The Heisenberg uncertainty principle does not imply that it is possible that energy comes from absolutely nothing; it just means that the pre-existing energy (i.e., the vacuum energy which is already present) can (unpredictably) have a very high value in a very short period of time. Our inability to predict the appearance of the quantum particles in quantum vacuum may be due to our epistemological limitation. Physicist John Wheeler notes that our current understanding of quantum mechanics is provisional. Some deeper theory, waiting to be discovered, would explain in a clear and rational way all the oddities of the quantum world, and would, in turn explain the apparent fuzziness in the quantum classical boundary (Ford 2011: 263).

While some scientists have claimed that the universe could have begun to exist from "nothing" (e.g., Vilenkin 2006; Krauss 2012), what they mean by "nothing" is not the absence of anything; rather, it is something that can behave according to the equations of quantum physics. Cosmologist George Ellis observes that the efforts by these scientists

---

[8] I thank Fr. Michael Dodds for this point.

cannot truly "solve" the issue of creation, "for they rely on some structures or other (e.g. the elaborate framework of quantum field theory and much of the standard model of particle physics) pre-existing the origin of the universe, and hence themselves requiring explanation" (Ellis 2007: section 2.7). Even if it is the case that the negative gravitational energy of our universe exactly cancels the positive energy represented by matter so that the total energy of the universe is zero, as portrayed in some cosmological scenarios (Stenger 2007: 116–17), this does not imply that the positive and negative energy arose uncaused from zero energy. One can still ask what made the energy in the quantum vacuum as well as the laws of physics to be the way they are (consider this analogy: the fact that a company's total expenses cancel the total revenue, such that the net profit is zero, does not imply that the expenses and revenue occurred uncaused! One can still ask what made the expenses and revenue the way they are).

In summary, no compelling scientific evidence has been offered against the Causal Principle. On the other hand, the following *modus tollens* argument can be offered for the Causal Principle (for details, see Loke 2017: chapter 5):

1. If something x begins to exist uncaused, then some other particular things/events (y, z, ...) that begin to exist would also begin to exist uncaused.
2. It is not the case that y begins to exist uncaused.
3. Therefore, it is not the case that x begins to exist uncaused.

Very briefly, the justification for premise 1 is that, if x begins to exist uncaused, then (1.1) there would not be any causally antecedent condition which would make it the case that only x rather than y, z, ... begin to exist uncaused; (1.2) the properties of x and the properties of y, z, ...that differentiate between them would be had by them only when they had already begun to exist; and (1.3) the circumstance is compatible with the beginning of existence of y and z. (1.1), (1.2), and (1.3) jointly imply that there would be no essential difference between x and some other particular things y and z where beginning to exist uncaused is concerned.

Thus, if the universe, space-time itself or the initial state of reality, begins to exist without any antecedent condition whatsoever, then there would not be any antecedent condition which would make it the case that only these rather than other particular things/events (e.g., the beginning of a rapid increasing in strength of electric fields around me) begin to exist uncaused. Moreover, the properties of these and the properties of other things/events that differentiate between them would be had by them only when they had already begun to exist, and the present circumstance is compatible with those other things/events beginning. This implies that there would be no essential difference between them where beginning to exist uncaused is concerned. Thus, if the universe, space-time itself or the initial state of reality, begins to exist uncaused, then it cannot be the case that only these begin to exist uncaused. In that case, the beginning of other things/events (say, a rapid increasing in strength of electric fields around me) would also be uncaused. But this is contrary to my experience. I (thankfully!) do not experience such events happening without causally antecedent conditions such as (say) having to switch on the electric field generator. Therefore, it is not the case that something begins to exist uncaused.[9]

In his review of my work, Joshua Rasmussen (2018) suggests a number of potential countermoves to my argument. My responses are as follows.

---

[9] For replies to objections, see Loke (2017: chapter 5).

First, Rasmussen suggests "a Platonist might suppose that there are brute necessary truths about uninstantiated properties, including truths about which properties can begin to be instantiated uncaused. On this theory, perhaps (contra Loke) there are things—abstract things—prior to an uncaused beginning that could explain why that beginning has its particular properties" (2018: 190).

The problem with this suggestion that abstract things can make a difference as to which metaphysically possible set of properties are instantiated in the concrete world is that it requires abstract things to have causal powers. But abstract things are supposed to be causally inert. A Platonist who raises the objection is thinking about noncausal explanation. However, in order for an explanation to make a difference as to which metaphysically possible set of properties are instantiated in the concrete world—which the Platonist hopes the explanation would do in this case—such an explanation would have to be causal, contrary to what the Platonist supposes.

Second, Rasmussen suggests "one might decline to accept that there needs to be any explanation of why only certain things, such as our universe, can begin uncaused. Perhaps it is just brute" (2018: 190).

In response, as argued in Loke (2017: 146), the postulation that only certain things can begin to exist uncaused requires a relevant difference between these things and other kinds of things—one cannot simply assert that it is brute. However, as explained above, there cannot be any relevant difference. Given that there is no relevant difference between (say) X, Y, and Z, this implies that the postulation that "only X (rather than Y or Z) begin to exist uncaused" is meaningless, since (given the absence of relevant difference) X, Y, and Z would be the same where beginning to exist uncaused is concerned.

It might be objected that what follows from this is that Y and Z *could* pop into existence uncaused, not that they *would*.[10] In reply, "could" concerns possibility; but, I am not referring to possible events here. Rather, I am referring to actual events, and arguing that there would be no difference between them where beginning to exist uncaused is concerned. For example, consider the scenario in which something (say) the universe began to exist and there was also a rapid increasing in strength of electric fields around me. In this scenario these are not just possible events (i.e., it is not merely the case that the universe *could* begin to exist and electric fields *could* increase in strength), but actual events, that is, the universe did begin to exist and electric fields did increase in strength. Since (as explained above) there would be no difference between these events where beginning to exist uncaused is concerned, if the universe did begin to exist *uncaused*, the increasing in strength of the electric fields around me would also began to exist uncaused (e.g., without being preceded by the switching on of an electric field generator).

Third, Rasmussen (2018: 190) suggests that perhaps one can develop further hypotheses about how existing things place causal conditions with respect to any new state of affairs; then, only a first state could begin without a causal condition. I responded to this in Loke (2017: 144–5) by explaining that "Y begins to exist uncaused" would mean "Y begins to exist without any causal antecedents such as, say, without having to switch on the electric field generator under certain circumstances." There can be no further hypotheses about how existing things would place causal conditions with respect to increasing in strength in electric field in this case, given that I define uncaused in this case as "without having to switch on the electric field generator under certain circumstances."

In conclusion, the potential countermoves suggested by Rasmussen are unsuccessful.

---

[10] I thank J. T. Turner for raising this objection.

VI. *CREATIO ORIGINANS* AND *CREATIO CONTINUANS*

Creatio ex nihilo traditionally has been thought to involve two subdivisions: *creatio originans* (God's creation at the beginning of the world) and *creatio continuans* (God's ongoing conservation of the world in existence) (Craig and Moreland 2003: 555).[11] Thus it is not just a onetime act of origination in the past, but rather an enduring bond of intimate and complete dependence on God (McFarland 2014: 58).

The core concepts are God's bestowal of being on the world and the dependence of the world on God, such that, without God, the world would fall back to nothing (Soskice 2010: 24, noting that Aquinas thought that God could have created, *ex nihilo*, a world without beginning). Because of this, some have concluded that *creatio ex nihilo* is a metaphysical position that is completely unaffected by the scientific question of whether or not the world had a temporal beginning (McFarland 2014: xv). This conclusion is unjustified, for while science may not falsify the core concept, as explained previously, providing scientific evidence for the beginning of all physical things does support one of the premises of the KCA for a Creator. Moreover, Aquinas himself believed, on the basis of scripture, that the world in fact had a beginning (*Summa Theologiae* Ia.Q46.a2). As argued previously, contra May et al., the scripture does in fact imply this, and most theologians throughout history have concluded this as well. A full-bodied doctrine of *creatio ex nihilo* that is consistent with scripture and tradition therefore cannot ignore the issue of temporal origin.

The neglect of this issue by many modern theologians may be related to fear of potential conflict with science (Craig and Moreland 2003: 558). For instance, Soskice (2010: 38–9) claims that "*creatio ex nihilo* is a metaphysical claim, not an empirical one, and does not dictate a particular cosmology. It is thus not in competition with scientific explanation, nor potentially defeasible by it." However, this fear is unwarranted, for the conclusion of the KCA is not based on ignorance that can be replaced by scientific explanations. The KCA does not say "because we still do not know how to explain the origin of the universe, therefore there must be a Creator." Rather, it is because there are reasons (mentioned above) for thinking that an actual infinite causal regress is metaphysically impossible and that the regress could not be terminated by a causal loop that there must be a First Cause. It is because there are reasons for thinking that everything that begins to exist has a cause that this First Cause must be beginningless. The rest of the properties—initially changeless, has free will, and enormously powerful—are likewise derived on the basis of reasons rather than ignorance, as shown above.

Nor is the conclusion of KCA merely based on current scientific explanations that are defeasible by future scientific explanations. Rather, it is based on the above reasons as formulated by the philosophical version of KCA, which are independent of scientific explanations, and which are already sufficient to warrant its conclusion. Current scientific explanations that indicate that there was a beginning to all physical things make the argument even more powerful, but they are not required by the argument. Moreover, while "laws of nature" may vary from one possible world to another and different possible worlds may have different "laws" (Sidelle 2002), logically and metaphysically necessary truths such as "shapeless cubes cannot exist" and the premises of the philosophical version of KCA such as "an actual infinite regress of causes cannot

---

[11] There is ongoing debate concerning whether creation and conservation are to be conceived as distinct kinds of actions (Vander Laan 2017).

exist" are true in all possible worlds. This implies that the philosophical version of KCA is more powerful than the conclusions of science (Loke 2017: chapter 6). Therefore, while the progress of science could generate newer explanations to replace other explanations for the phenomena we observe—and even if our current understanding of Big Bang cosmology were to be replaced one day—it would never replace a First Cause (Creator) as the explanation for the existence of all things, including the laws of nature themselves which must have come from this First Cause. Thus, the conclusion of the KCA cannot in principle be overturned by future scientific discoveries. Rather future scientific discoveries would only enhance our understanding of the world which the Creator had created *ex nihilo*.

References

Aquinas, T. (1920), *Summa Theologiae*, New York: Benziger Brothers.
Aquinas, T. (1975), *Summa Contra Gentiles*, trans. A. C. Pegis, Notre Dame: University of Notre Dame Press
Arnold, B. (2009), *Genesis*, Cambridge: Cambridge University Press.
Barrow, J. D., and F. J. Tipler. (1986), *The Anthropic Cosmological Principle*, Oxford: Clarendon.
Barr, S. (2012), "Modern Cosmology and Christian Theology," in A. G Padgett and J. B. Stump (eds.), *The Blackwell Companion to Science and Christianity*, Chichester: Wiley-Blackwell.
Bockmuehl, M. (2012), "Creatio Ex Nihilo in Palestinian Judaism and Early Christianity," *Scottish Journal of Theology*, 65 (3): 253–70.
Bricmont, J. (2016), *Making Sense of Quantum Mechanics*, Cham: Springer Nature.
Bussey, P. (2013), "God as First Cause – a Review of the Kalam Argument," *Science & Christian Belief*, 25: 17–35.
Chan, M. H. (forthcoming), "Is the History of Our Universe Finite?," *Theology and Science*.
Cogliati, C. (2010), "Introduction," in D. B. Burrell, C. Cogliati, J. M. Soskice, and W. R. Stoeger (eds.), *Creation and the God of Abraham*, Cambridge: Cambridge University Press.
Collins, C. J. (2018), *Reading Genesis Well: Navigating History, Science, Poetry, and Truth in Genesis 1–11*, Grand Rapids, MI: Zondervan.
Copan, P. (2005), "Creation Ex Nihilo or Ex Materia? A Critique of the Mormon Doctrine of Creation," *Southern Baptist Journal of Theology*, 9 (2): 32–54.
Copan, P., and W. L. Craig. (2004), *Creation Out of Nothing: A Biblical, Philosophical and Scientific Exploration*, Leicester: Apollos.
Craig, W. L. (1979), "Kant's First Antinomy and the Beginning of the Universe," *Zeitschrift. für Philosophische Forschung*, 33: 553–67.
Craig, W. L. (1980), *The Cosmological Argument from Plato to Leibniz*, London: Macmillan.
Craig, W. L., and J. P. Moreland (2003), *Philosophical Foundations for a Christian Worldview*, Downers Grove, IL: InterVarsity Press.
Craig, W. L., and J. Sinclair (2009), "The Kalam Cosmological Argument," in W. L. Craig and J. P. Moreland (eds.), *The Blackwell Companion to Natural Theology*, Chichester: Wiley-Blackwell.
Ellis, G. (2007), "Issues in the Philosophy of Cosmology," in J. Butterfield and J. Earman (eds.), *Philosophy of Physics*, Amsterdam: Elsevier.
Fergusson, D. (2007), "Creation," in J. Webster, K. Tanner, and I. Torrance (eds.), *The Oxford Handbook of Systematic Theology*, Oxford: Oxford University Press.
Ford, K. (2011), *101 Quantum Questions: What You Need to Know About the World You Can't See*, Cambridge, MA: Harvard University Press.

Ge, Y. (2018), "Creatio Ex Nihilo and Ancient Chinese Philosophy: A Revisiting of Robert Neville's Thesis," *Philosophy East and West*, 68 (2): 352–70.
Grünbaum, A. (2009), "Why Is There a Universe *At All*, Rather Than Just Nothing?," *Ontology Studies*, 9: 7–19.
Hawking, S., and L. Mlodinow (2010), *The Grand Design*, New York: Bantam. Books.
Kant, I. (1965), *Critique of Pure Reason*, trans. N. Kemp-Smith, London: Macmillan.
Keller, C. (2003), *Face of the Deep: A Theology of Becoming*, London: Routledge.
Koons, R. (2014), "A New Kalam Argument: Revenge of the Grim Reaper," *Noûs*, 48: 256–67.
Krauss, L. (2012), *A Universe from Nothing: Why There Is Something Rather Than Nothing*, New York: Free Press.
Krauss, L., and W. L. Craig. (2013), *Life, the Universe, and Nothing (III): Is It. Reasonable to Believe There Is a God?* Available online: http://www.reasonablefaith.org/life-the-universe-and-nothing-is-it-reasonable-to-believe-there-is-a-go#ixzz4WHegKUWq (accessed January 20, 2017).
Leibniz, G. (1979), *Monadology*, in P. P. Weiner (ed.), *Leibniz Selections*, New York: Charles Scribner's Sons.
Loke, A. (2013), "Is the Saving Grace of God Resistible?," *European Journal of Theology*, 22: 28–37.
Loke, A. (2014), *A Kryptic Model of the Incarnation*, London: Routledge.
Loke, A. (2017), *God and Ultimate Origins: A Novel Cosmological Argument*, Cham: Springer Nature.
Loke, A. (2019), "Theological Critiques of Natural Theology: A Reply to Andrew Moore," *Neue Zeitschrift für Systematische Theologie und Religionsphilosophie*, 61: 1–16.
May, G. (1994), *Creatio ex Nihilo: The Doctrine of "Creation out of Nothing" in Early. Christian Thought*, Edinburgh: T&T Clark.
McFarland, I. (2014), *From Nothing: A Theology of Creation*, Westminster: John Knox Press.
Meister, C. (2018), *Evil: A Guide for the Perplexed*, London: Bloomsbury.
Mullins, R. T. (2016), *The End of a Timeless God*, Oxford: Oxford University Press.
Oord, Thomas (2015), "God Always Creates out of Creation in Love: Creatio ex Creatione a. Natura Amoris," in Thomas Oord (ed.), *Theologies of Creation: Creation Ex Nihilo and Its New Rivals*, London: Routledge.
Osborn, E. (2001), *Irenaeus of Lyons*, Cambridge: Cambridge University Press.
Pruss, A. (2018), *Infinity, Causation, and Paradox*, Oxford: Oxford University Press.
Padgett, A. (1992), *God, Eternity, and the Nature of Time*, New York: St. Martin's.
Rasmussen, J. (2018), "Review of God and Ultimate Origins," *European Journal for Philosophy of Religion*, 10 (1): 189–94.
Reichenbach, B. (2016), "Cosmological Argument," in E. N. Zalta (ed.), *The Stanford Encyclopedia of Philosophy* (einter 2016 edition). Available online: https://plato.stanford.edu/archives/win2016/entries/cosmological-argument/ (accessed January 13, 2017).
Rice, R.. (2015), "Creatio ex Nihilo: It's Not about Nothing," in T. Oord (ed.), *Theologies of Creation: Creation Ex Nihilo and Its New Rivals*, London: Routledge.
Sidelle, A. (2002), "On the Metaphysical Contingency of Laws of Nature," in T. Gendler and J. Hawthorne (eds.), *Conceivability and Possibility*, Oxford: Oxford University Press.
Soskice, J. M. (2010), "Creatio Ex Nihilo: Jewish and Christian Foundations," in D. B. Burrell, C. Cogliati, J. M. Soskice, and W. R. Stoeger (eds.), *Creation and the God of Abraham*, Cambridge: Cambridge University Press.
Stenger, V. (2007), *God: The Failed Hypothesis*, Amherst, NY: Prometheus Books.

Stoeger, W. (2001), "Epistemological and Ontological Issues Arising from Quantum Theory", in Robert J. Russell, Philip Clayton, Kirk Wegter-McNelly, and John Polkinghorne (eds.), *Quantum Mechanics: Scientific Perspectives on Divine Action*, Vatican City State: Vatican Observatory.

Vail, E. (2015), "Creation out of Nothing Remodeled," in T. Oord (ed.), *Theologies of Creation: Creation Ex Nihilo and Its New Rivals*, London: Routledge.

Vander Laan, D. (2017), "Creation and Conservation," in E. N. Zalta (ed.), *The Stanford Encyclopedia of Philosophy*. Available online: https://plato.stanford.edu/archives/win2017/entries/creation-conservation/.

Van Wolde, E. (2010), "Why the Verb ברא Does Not Mean 'to Create' in Genesis 1.1-2.4a," *Journal for the Study of the Old Testament*, 34 (1): 3–23.

Vilenkin, A. (2006), *Many Worlds in One*, New York: Hill and Wang.

Wall, A. (2014), "Did the Universe Begin? X: Recapitulation," Undivided Looking. Available online: http://www.wall.org/~aron/blog/did-the-universe-begin-x-recap/ (accessed January 20, 2017).

Walton, J. (2009), *The Lost World of Genesis One: Ancient Cosmology and the Origins. Debate*, Downers Grove, IL: IVP Academic.

Ward, K. (2003), "Creatio Ex Nihilo," in J. W. V. van Huyssteen, N. H. Gregersen, N. B. Howell, W. J. Wildman (eds.), *Encyclopedia of Science and Religion*, New York: Macmillan Reference.

Waters, B. (2013), "Methuselah's Diary and the Finitude of the Past," *Philosophia Christi*, 15: 463–9.

Zbaraschuk, M. (2015), "Creatio Ex Deo: Incarnation, Spirituality, Creation," in T. Oord (ed.), *Theologies of Creation: Creation Ex Nihilo and Its New Rivals*, London: Routledge.

CHAPTER TWENTY-THREE

The Soul as *Imago Dei*: Modernizing Traditional Theological Anthropology

JOSHUA R. FARRIS

> After God had made all other creatures, he created man, male and female, with reasonable and immortal souls, endued with knowledge, righteousness, and true holiness, after his own image.
>
> —The Westminster Confession of Faith

Imagine the process of painting a portrait. During this process the portrait depends on the raw materials (e.g., a paint brush, a canvass, a board). The process of painting begins with the outline and structure of the image. Over time, the "flesh" of the portrait slowly takes shape. By the time the process culminates, we have a clear and discernable portrait. Unlike stick figure drawings, portraits depicting flesh and blood persons give us a story and point us to a perspective on reality. The *imago Dei* is something like that of a portrait. It too has raw materials, comes to exist through a process, and when it is complete it reflects the generalities and contingencies of human nature. At least this is my view and what I will argue in what follows. I have two objectives in the present chapter. First, upon surveying common models of the *imago Dei*, I show that an immaterialist conception of the *imago Dei* is part of the dogmatic core—or an implication from the dogmatics—of Catholic and Reformed orthodoxy.[1] Second, I recommend my own constructive interpretation of the Tradition that best accounts for uniqueness. Elsewhere, I have called my view an immaterial substance with rich-property view (hereafter ISRP) (Farris 2017a). My general pattern, which I use here, is to begin with scripture read through the lens of Tradition (by Tradition I am referring to the broad ecumenical and conciliar consensus among all the sub-traditions, which includes in particular Roman Catholicism, Eastern Orthodoxy, Anglicanism, and Reformed orthodoxy rather than on their idiosyncratic differences, primarily codified in conciliar, catechetical and confessional statements), then move to reason and experience.[2] But first I survey some the standard models as exemplified in contemporary analytic theology.

---

[1] What I will term the Tradition to comprise the dogmatic teachings held by the broad ecumenical Christian Church.

[2] A brief word about method is in order. I arrive at dogma through explicit statements found in authoritative symbols of the Tradition. In the case of the soul, there are several explicit statements that identify the image with the soul or they come very close to it; yet with others we have good reason to think that it is presupposed. More

I. THE MODELS

Before addressing the dogmatic material and my own constructive interpretation of it, we should consider some of the common models of the *imago Dei* on offer in the recent analytic theology literature.

I.1 The Structural Model

The hallmark of the structural model is that it highlights the capacities that purportedly distinguish humans from other creatures, namely, the intellect and the will. Its perceived weaknesses are well documented in the contemporary literature, including its lack of biblical support, its propensity toward marred individualism, and its isolating of one capacity over others (Cortez 2010: 19–20). Arguably, the structural model has an advantage if we understand humans as having some similarity to God that makes them suitable for ruling over the creation, as we find in Gen. 1:26-28. One promising analytic option is the structural, or substantive, model that remains faithful to the wider tradition avoiding the criticisms above, and, arguably, coheres with my own constructive option.

Mark Spencer develops an account of the *imago Dei*, which describes the whole human person as the image. In other words, human persons, not just one aspect of the human, are images of God. Motivated by Thomas Aquinas, Spencer develops an account that gives primacy to the soul and its faculties, particularly those faculties that relate to knowledge and righteousness. As God is an immaterial being, so are we immaterial beings with capacities that reflect God. However, on Aquinas's account, the image includes the body as a second image not because God is or has a body, but because the body participates in the "image" by way of the soul. The body is a lesser image in the sense that it has traces that point to the Divine. The body too shares in the image and, through phenomenology, Spencer is able to harmonize the body and soul as one functional whole (Spencer 2018).[3]

Lawrence Feingold builds on Spencer's account by extending the notion of "second image." Feingold describes the view in this way:

> The extension of the image goes upwards as well as downwards … the primary image is elevated upwards by grace and glory, and is extended downwards analogically into the bodily realm through our bodily nature, thereby elevating and ennobling the physical order. I will also reflect on how the image of God in man and angels is alike with regard to openness to grace and glory, but complementary insofar as it extends into the bodily realm in man, which makes possible distinct ways that the image of God can exist uniquely in man. (Feingold 2018: 43)

For Feingold, humans are at the center of creaturely reality, serving as both the pointers upward to God and as the "microcosm" of the natural realm (with Psalm 8 as the guiding text). In this way, not only do humans image God internally as spiritual beings with the capacity for reflection, but their bodies image God as second images. Feingold sees the image as extending itself through the "unitive" and "procreative" function of humans. This reflective capacity is twofold. One its creative capacity reflects God's power. Two, the act of procreation conjoins similarity and difference, plurality in unity as a reflection

---

modestly, when we consider the coherence of the anthropological package, from creation to eschatology, the soul is a necessary piece of the package or it is implied as a doctrinal essential.
[3]Here he points us to a key text in Thomas Aquinas ST I. Q. 93.

of the Trinitarian being. Consistent with the relational account of sexual differentiation of male and female, humans reflect a deep mystery that points us to the Divine reality of Christ and his Church (John Paul II 2006: 14 and 163).[4] The danger with using the language of primary image and secondary image is that it suggests a splitting of images when, in fact, it might be better to speak of different levels of imaging.

I.2 The Relational Model

The hallmark of a relational view is the participation in Divine attributes. An alternative to a Thomistic understanding of human nature, Mark S. McLeod-Harrison emphasizes the uniqueness of humanity in its diversity. McLeod-Harrison (2014) states, "So we should celebrate our commonalities. They bind us together in our lives. But we should equally celebrate our uniqueness and our diversity for that is, indeed, the way the image of God is" (159). Referring to Christ as the image, he claims that rather than following a classical focus on the image as a common set of properties, we should focus on the portrait like portrayal of God through individual distinctions (159). McLeod-Harrison highlights the personal dimension of the image as the medium for our commonalities. What is original about McLeod-Harrison's account is his identifying the image with personal uniqueness, and it is in this way that his view might be understood along relational lines because it is through our individual uniqueness as humans that we reflect God. While there is something insightful about McLeod-Harrison's modern move toward the individual, it lacks the ontological grounding that is otherwise provided in a view like Thomas's as expressed by Spencer and Feingold. As I argue below, both accounts have strengths and can be accommodated in my account of the ISRP. What is foundational to our "uniqueness," I suggest, is our individuality as one of the common features of all humans.

I.3 The Functional Model

While it is arguable that the relational and functional models could be conflated, the hallmark of the functional model is the endorsement of some specified human activity or behavior reflecting Divine activity. Some take the image as described in Gen. 2:16-28 to refer to a physical representation of God (Feinberg 1972: 235–46; for explicit accounts, see: Gottstein 1994; Costa 2010; for a global materialist account, see: Webb 2011). Others not quite identifying the image with the physical, identify representation with the physical and external and not an internal capacity of the soul. Additionally, given the nature of the image as contrasted with idols of pagan religions and the function it plays in God's temple, some suggest that it is *in fact* on exhibit for the world to see (see Beale 2008 and Lints 2015). Old Testament scholar and specialist in theological anthropology, J. Richard Middleton, develops what he sees as the commonly accepted view in Old Testament studies, namely, the royal-functional view of the image. As he understands it, the image is characteristically the function of "humanity's office and role as God's earthly delegates" (Middleton 2005: 18; also see Arcadi 2020). Middleton distinguishes this from a classical understanding of the image when he says, "The vast majority of interpreters right up to recent times have understood the meaning of the image in terms of a metaphysical analogy or similarity between the human soul and the being of God,

---

[4]For an exposition of this through Thomistic personalism, see: John Paul II: 9:3, 163 and 14. See also the following passages of scripture: Eph. 5:32 in conjunction with Gen. 2:23-24.

in categories not likely to have occurred to the author of Genesis" (Middleton 2005: 18 and 60).

There is another promising option within the analytic theology literature. James T. Turner, Jr. (2018) takes his cues from a sampling of recent biblical scholarship as the appropriate starting point for constructing an analytically sophisticated account of the *imago Dei*. Consistent with much of the Old Testament scholarship, Turner argues neither for an immaterialist substance account nor a substantive account more broadly. Instead, he opts for a functional account of the *imago Dei* that depends on a specific kind of substance—yet is not identical to it. By describing the image through an eschatological lens, Turner offers what he believes is a way to arrive at an appropriate understanding of the *imago Dei*. If you agree with Turner, then you think that this entails that we are "essentially embodied," but it is not clear to me that this is the case. As I have suggested already, the scriptural material leaves open conceptual space for an immaterial image and is not sufficiently captured in an external, physical image, but there are other reasons to prefer an immaterialist conception of the image, which we will consider in a moment.

I.4 The Christological Model

The Christological model avoids some of the challenges found in the three most common models by affirming that humans are not strictly speaking images of God, but that there is one image of God, namely the concrete person Jesus Christ. Evidence for this view comes from several important New Testament paradigm passages (e.g., 2 Cor. 4:4; Col. 1:16; Heb. 1:3) (see Tanner 2010; Cortez 2016, 2018; Crisp 2017). Rather than individual humans existing as individually distinct images, humans *participate* in the image. There are at least two advantages of this view. First, the view has clear scriptural support. Second, the model avoids the various challenges found in the previous models (e.g., from the propensity to individualism, isolated capacities concern, and the uniqueness challenge) by locating the "image" not in individual humans but in Christ.

There are also two weaknesses of a Christological model. First, it fails to account for all the scriptural data that highlights humanity as an image. Second, this view fails to preserve the creational integrity of the image by eclipsing it with an eschatological image because it falters when describing initial humanity in addition to non-redeemed humans.

There is another way to articulate the image, and it favors a version of the structural model, but unlike most structural views it is not beholden to an individualist understanding of humanity nor does it rely on one isolated capacity to do all the work necessary. Instead, it resembles the "multi-faceted" interpretation by making room for the diverse features described of the image in scripture (Cortez 2010: 29), but unlike the "multi-faceted" interpretation my view unifies all the facets in an immaterial substance.

II. IMMATERIAL SUBSTANCE WITH A RICH-PROPERTY VIEW (ISRP)

On the ISRP view, I take my cues from John Calvin and the Reformed theological tradition that the image is found primarily in the soul with all of its capacities, and that the image is traceable in the body and perfected in union with Christ. Hence, the image is a rich-property. A rich-property is a complex property that depends on a particular kind of substance with a *telos*. This complex property is a cluster of teleologically related properties that depend on a substance with capacities that provide necessary conditions for actualizing the potential of the substance. And, the potency of this substance is only fully seen once its rich-property has been actualized. In making this move, I have argued elsewhere (Farris 2017a,b,c) that a substantial rich-property view captures the full picture of scripture as discussed in the Old Testament and their varied and complex teaching on the *imago Dei* (e.g., Gen. 1:26-28, 5:1-3, 9:6; 1 Cor. 11:7; Jas. 3:9—in fact these New Testament passages come close to explicit statements for an "essentialist" understanding of the image from creation; contrast with 2 Cor. 4:4; Col. 1:15-16; Heb. 1:3).

In keeping with an open-textured reading of scripture that begins in the creational narrative, yet continues to unfold in the redemptive narrative, the present view is also dependent on the received wisdom and collective consensus of ecumenical reflections. On this account, the image is a property of the soul, but the actualization of that image awaits full manifestation in the eschaton as it is revealed in Christ. Going back to the original analogy, the "image" is like the process of a painting in that it has features of all the models. Consider the structural capacities (like intellect and will) as the raw materials spoken of earlier and the form of the painting, which is dependent on a particular substance (more on that below). But these raw materials are not the complete story of the painting. Like the painting, the "image" as it is captured in each individual tells a story of persons in relation. These persons have what some philosophers have called teleo-functions, and they find completion not in creation but in redemption. In this way, the view presented here is holistic, but, at its heart, humans have a substantial soul in keeping with the Tradition. What is clear in the Tradition is that the "image" is an immaterial substance primarily. In short, there are three aspects of the "image" that are described in the Tradition, namely, that: (1) the image is an immaterial substance, (2) that the image has specified capacities (i.e., the structural aspect), and (3) that the image is fulfilled in relation to Christ (i.e., the Christological aspect).

III. THE UNIQUENESS OF THE *IMAGO DEI* IN SCRIPTURE AND TRADITION

Let me offer just one biblical-theological reason to consider a substantive, even immaterial view of the *imago Dei*. Biblical scholars like Middleton prefer a functional interpretation of the Gen. 1:26-28 passage because of the Ancient Near East background of images as idols. Given the prominence of this passage in theological reflections on the image and its order in scripture as the first passage to make explicit mention of the "image", it makes sense that we should cite it in whole. It states,

> Then God said, "Let us make man in our image, after our likeness. And let them have dominion over the fish of the sea and over the birds of the heavens and over the livestock and over all the earth and over every creeping thing that creeps on the earth." So God created man in his own image, in the image of God he created him; male and female he created them. And God blessed them. And God said to them, "Be fruitful and multiply and fill the earth and subdue it, and have dominion over the fish of the sea and over the birds of the heavens and over every living thing that moves on the earth." (Gen. 1:26-28)[5]

---

[5] Biblical quotations are taken from the English Standard Version of the Bible.

As is clear, Gen. 1:26-28 gives us some information in the context of God's creation of humankind. Humans are described as representing God (v. 26). Ruling is significant to the role God gives to his human creatures over all other creatures (v. 26). Creation of the image includes both male and female (v. 27). Finally, the content and blessing of the image is expressed in the acts of procreation and dominion (v. 28). However, beyond this, the passage does not explicitly tell us what the image is, and passages of scripture that occur later in Genesis and elsewhere inform the Gen. 1:26-28 image concept. Theologian Nico Vorster argues that the Genesis notion of the *imago Dei* is "open-textured" (Vorster 2011: 12). The "image" meaning is underdetermined in the Gen. 1:26-28 passage and requires additional information to fill out its meaning. Systematic theologian Stephen Wellum and Old Testament scholar Peter Gentry argue that Gen. 1:28 actually provides us with an ontological understanding of the image as that which is *presupposed* in the covenantal representation function rather than being *equivalent* to the covenantal representation function (Gentry and Wellum 2012: 186, 200–1; also see Mangano 2008). In fact, they argue that grammatically the covenantal representation spoken of in Gen. 1:26 presupposes an *image*, which I suggest creates conceptual space for a traditional understanding. The grammatical construction of imaging the royal "we" (which is either a reference to the heavenly court or specifically the Trinity) includes a cohortative subjunctive and should be translated literally "so that" they may rule or take dominion. Now, presumably, "dominion" means stewardship of the earth that God has entrusted to his covenantal representatives whom are to function as rulers and priests. Beyond this meaning, it is arguable that there is some semantic latitude in the rest of Genesis, not to mention the rest of the Old and New Testament teaching on the "image."

When scripture's voice presents what appears to be different understandings of the "image" or different "images," and so forth, where does one turn next? One could appeal to Tradition. The challenge is that we lack a creedal (i.e., ecumenical) statement on the "image," which speaks clearly and definitively on the nature and content of the "image." With that said, the Tradition presumes that the image is an immaterial substance, given that God himself is an immaterial substance, and this is reflected in several Catholic symbols (Helm 2005: 132; commenting on Calvin who reflects Plato and Augustine, specifically, but Aquinas broadly). By selecting some of the most important theological authorities and confessions, I will show that, through the Church's reflections and ruminations, there is a long and sustained commitment to a dogmatic package that ties the *imago Dei* to the soul (for more on this, see Farris 2020). For, as Lewis Ayers has stated, it is the soul that furnishes the "anthropological context within which the structure of traditional discussions of grace and sanctification and the restoration of the *imago Dei* can be articulated" (Ayers 2008: 183 n. 22).

One of the common reasons that it is traditionally presumed that humans image God as immaterial beings has to do with the fact that God is a pure immaterial substance that thinks, makes choices, and has powers. In a world where the highest being is God and we are the highest earthly created entities that mediate Divine reality, the Tradition has it in mind that God's nature implies that his image bearers will be immaterial as well (i.e., the similarity thesis). A related reason is given and presumes the ontology of similarity, namely the fact that immateriality is necessary to know God (the epistemic thesis). Terence Nichols summarizes this traditional argument, when he comments on the inability of material things to know God: "then even in heaven we could not know God directly, through intuition; for that to happen, we would need a spiritual receptor, a faculty by which we could perceive the spiritual God …Without such a faculty, we can know God only indirectly" (Nichols 2010: 123; also see Helm 2005: 371).

The capacities of the soul are certainly a part of the conceptual background of the dogmatic tradition. In ancient thought, the images of God were often described with the rich property of "rationality" (see Mangano 2008: 5; cf. 2 En. 65:1-2). This understanding was commonly assumed in ancient depictions (Runia 2005: 69). It is also common to an Augustinian understanding of humans (Haddan 1887: 1.1). Highlighting this property of the soul did not mitigate the role that the physical earth and the body play in the image, but these were understood in a larger ontological framework where God created the world according to a rational order of which humans are reflections.

In the Western tradition, several symbols support not only a substantive view of the image, but an *immaterial* substance view of the image. The Roman Catholic Catechism tells us, "The divine image is present in every man" (1702). In the context of discussing the *imago Dei*, the Catechism states, "Endowed with 'a spiritual and immortal' soul, the human person is 'the only creature that God has willed for its own sake.' From his conception, he is destined for eternal beatitude" (1703). It also gives special place to Christ as the image when it states, "Christ … In the very revelation of the mystery of the Father and of his love, makes man fully manifest to himself and brings to light his exalted vocation" (1701). In summary, the Roman Catholic Catechism systematically ties the image to human beings generally, as ensouled bodies (following both Augustine and Aquinas) with particular emphasis on the soul, who are by nature teleologically oriented toward "beatitude" (i.e., blessedness), most clearly revealed in the person and work of Christ.[6]

Consistent with the Roman Catholic Catechism, there are Reformed symbols that bear out essentially the same understanding of the image. While the unity of the Reformed tradition is not found in a centralized authority, as with Roman Catholicism, it finds a unity in its confessions, and I would argue that these confessions reflect the conciliar consensus distilled along with other features which reflect their own contingent circumstances, and is the same essential Catholic anthropology (van den Brink and Goudriaan 2016). The Reformed theologians agreed. The Reformed confessions highlight the following attributes: immortal, holy, righteous, and wise (and, correspondingly, souls, with rational intellect and will), which makes them fitting agents to rule over creation. It is also worth noting that in keeping with Eastern and Western Christianity these structural capacities presumed a substantial ontology (see Helm 2005: 70, 129–57; 2010: 277; 2018: chapter 7).

The *Large Emden Catechism* (1551) supports this claim and given that the philosophical ruminations of the Reformed (once again see Helm 2018) presumed an immaterialist substantial ontology when describing the *imago Dei* attributes: "This image of God was in Adam in the beginning, by virtue of which he was immortal, holy, wise, and lord of the entire world, and thus was endowed with the freedom and ability to completely execute or disregard the commandment of God." While the catechism does not explicitly state that the image is the immaterial substance, it is presumed in the ancient connotation of substance (see Helm 2005: 135), which means not just any substance but a substance that is *immortal*, and this entails immateriality (Helm 2005: 132). Further, not only is

---

[6]There is a conciliar consensus understanding in Anglicanism as well, arguably, see: http://www.anglicanlibrary.org/homilies/bk2hom02.htm.

it the case that the structural approach is highlighted in the descriptive content of being "immortal, holy, wise, and lord" but also the soul as substance is implied by the fact that the image is immortal because material things like bodies die and cease to exist (Helm 2005: 135). The *Heidelberg Confession* (1563) concurs with the basic understanding of the image in ancient thought that humans are unique via some rational property and with the thought that the image is intimately tied to the soul. "The Westminster Confession of Faith" (1647) offers one of the most explicit support from the Reformed heritage for the immateriality of the image along with the capacities necessary for achieving God's purposes for humanity. It states, "After God had made all other creatures, he created man, male and female, with reasonable and immortal souls, endued with knowledge, righteousness, and true holiness, after his own image" (Dennison 2014: 502). Hence, we see the attributes as tied to immortal souls as descriptive of our similarity to and imaging of God. Consistent with the *Westminster* symbol, the framers of the *Synopsis purioris theologiae,* often called the Leiden Synopsis, intend it to provide a summary of Reformed orthodoxy according to the theological faculty of Leiden University and is recognized as an authority that has influenced the Dutch Reformed tradition that followed—including Reformed theologian Herman Bavinck. It affirms that the soul is central to the Reformed definition of the image, yet the body has a role to a lesser degree as it is ruled by the soul and points to the soul's attributes (Burman 1671; for commentary, see van den Brink and Goudriaan 2016: 83–7). In other words, humans are created "with reasonable and immortal souls" and it is this package (along with the properties of knowledge, righteousness, and holiness and their corresponding faculties) that is what reflects or represents God.

Additional support for the close connection between the soul and the image is found in the ecumenical teaching on "immortality." Particularly, a Christological argument from the doctrine of the intermediate state, presumes that Christ is the normative and prescriptive reflection of humanity. Here's the basic argument: If humans persist during the intermediate state, then they persist either as image bearers or not as image bearers. Humans persist during the intermediate state as image bearers, if Christ persists as an image bearer during the intermediate state. Christ persists as an image bearer during the intermediate state. Thus, humans persist during the intermediate state as image bearers.

The Catholic teaching on the intermediate state is that humans will persist during a unique state between somatic death and somatic resurrection during which the saints will be grafted immediately into the presence of God and others will either experience punishment or the refining fire of purgatory (Farris 2017d). The important fact of the intermediate state is that it requires that something persist, and if it is the earthly body that does not persist, then the person persists in virtue of some other part (Farris 2017c). That other part according to Catholic anthropology is the immaterial and spiritual soul. The intermediate state with disembodied soul is an essential dogmatic teaching in Catholic anthropology manifest in Christ's representative work of descent into hell for humanity (Levering 2012: 19–22). To suggest that one could conceptually divorce the "image" from the disembodied soul would not only be odd (see Helm 2010: 275), but it would render the doctrine of Christ's human representation as a fellow image bearer null and void during the intermediate state. In other words, the body is nonessential for the image to persist because the image persists disembodied. Unless we take it that the intermediate state includes a new, yet temporary, body, it follows that the body is not an essential part of the image, but I know of no Reformed theologian who takes a bodily intermediate state position seriously prior to contemporary discussions (e.g., Corcoran 2006: 140–2, 144). It is not the understanding of the dogmatic tradition. Further, it would render an excessive number of bodily resurrections. As shown earlier, several Catholic symbols support the dependence of the *imago Dei* on the soul and the intimate link between the *imago Dei* and the soul.[7]

That the image is intimately tied to the substantial soul is not really a matter of debate within this tradition. Instead, the question within the Tradition has to do with what kind of immaterial ontology of the image we should presume. And, it is on this point that there is a plurality of orthodoxy, not over the immateriality of the substantial soul; for, again, that it is the ground for the nurturing of the image (for this feature of the Tradition is stable), but over whether to follow Plato or Aristotle on the soul-body arrangement (Helm 2010: 40–64, 2018: 80). Aquinas and much of the scholastic tradition follow Aristotle. Calvin and others follow Plato. It is on this point that, in a moment, I will recommend that we follow Plato, with the help of the modern philosopher René Descartes, to the view that individual humans are essentially souls by considering some contemporary challenges to ISRP.

IV. THREE CONTEMPORARY CHALLENGES TO AN IMMATERIAL SUBSTANCE VIEW

As we take a modern turn from the Tradition, there are several notable trends that can be accounted for in my constructive interpretation of the Tradition, but it seems to presuppose a Cartesian view of human beings. Let us consider three contemporary challenges to the sort of view I advance here.

IV.1 The Demarcation Challenge or Creaturely Uniqueness

A common problem is raised in the contemporary scientific and theological literature against a substantive model, namely, that there is nothing *significant* or *unique* about human substances from mere animal substances. Taking this as a point of departure, some have argued for a relational view of the image not dependent on or inherent in substance ontology (Dalferth 2016: 18–43 and 73–4).[8] Others have opted, once again, for an eschatological or Christological orientation as a way out (Tanner 2010). The advantage of ISRP is that it incorporates the insights of these models.

Joshua Moritz takes us through a series of reasons from contemporary science for thinking that there is a unique difference between *Homo sapiens* in recent history and other *Homo sapiens*, and for that matter that there is not much of distinction in kind between higher level animals and humans (Moritz 2017: 52). The problem, according to Moritz, is that there is no empirically verifiable distinction between present humans and the oldest *Homo sapiens*.

On the view of human ontology I advance, humans are essentially kind-natured (i.e., the common nature, or the generables/determinables) souls that require *de novo* Divine creation. This view is distinguished by a particular mental substance. It is in this way that my preferred view is similar to McCleod-Harrison's.

Rather than arrive at the generalities/determinables of human nature by empirical means, it seems that we can arrive at it from particular minds. When I consider my own

---

[7]What would it mean if Christ did not persist as the image during the disembodied state? And, as our representative both normatively and prescriptively, it would be the same for us.
[8]Dalferth gives a sophisticated constructive Lutheran account.

consciousness, I arrive at it through an *inside perspective*. That inside perspective seems to depend on some fact of the matter. A fact of the matter that makes me *me* and distinguishes my*self* from *your*self. The distinguishing feature that makes me *me* is not dependent on my properties or relations, since both of which can be shared with or exemplified by others; rather, it is dependent on some primitive fact of the matter precisely because *I*, as a conscious observer with a particular inside perspective, contribute something novel to the world that is non-multiply exemplifiable. This is what some philosophers call a haecceity (i.e., an individual thisness), which makes all persons unique from other higher-level animals. If it were multiply-exemplifiable, then presumably I could be someone else, but that would be foolish. Or, alternatively, there could exist a self that was my duplicate; but if there is no primitive feature that *that* self has that I don't have, then there would be no fact of the matter that grants us the ability to make a distinction between whether the two *selves* are duplicates or identicals.

What does this tell us about the uniqueness thesis? It tells us how it is that we can arrive at the generables/determinables of those essential properties that comprise individual human beings through the primitive particular consciousness. It also tells us something about the creaturely distinctiveness of humans as image bearers—that they are created by God directly and immediately so that they may know God (Farrow 2019: 43). In this way, the model I put forward integrates the "personal" or relational view (see again Mcleod-Harrison 2014) with the structural view in a novel way, but this not only depends on but begins with an unpopular understanding of human nature—something like a Cartesian soul.[9] Cartesianism, while a minority report in Reformed orthodoxy, is not without its support in the Reformed tradition (Helm 2005, 2010; Farris 2017c). That said, where the Reformed tradition highlighted the nature and content of the image as soulish, I emphasis something native to modern theology—namely, the primitive particularity of personhood.

IV.2 *The Representational Challenge*

As noted earlier, a functional/representational challenge comes from the view that we are physically and externally representations of deity as is common to the ancient near east, but I will argue that the kind of representation present in scripture and Tradition is one that is internal as well. The first response is to suggest that human images depend upon a substance of a particular kind that presumes an in-built design with the capacities and powers necessary to perform the representative-function that God gives to humans in creation. A simple retort is to say that functional-relations depend on *relata*, that is, substances. And, assuming there is a *telos* to those functional-relations, then that would depend upon particular kinds of substances with particular capacities and powers to perform those functions. Both Jerry Walls and Richard Mouw have taken this line in arguing that the image could be understood in a relational/functional way, but that a substantial ontology is required (Walls 2002: 109; Mouw 2012).

One might take this further suggesting that the relational/functional account not only depends on a substantial ontology, but in requiring it the image itself is something intrinsic to the individual. In fact, Mouw leans in this direction when he considers the image in light of personal eschatology (i.e., the study of the afterlife for humans).

---

[9]Alternatively, it depends on a Cartesian understanding of the soul and how we should understand the body along immaterialist or materialist lines is open to discussion.

Mouw argues that personal eschatology is both heavenly and earthly, that is, "theocentric" and "anthropocentric." In summarizing a Calvinian interpretation, Mouw takes it that the image is conceived along the lines that both an intellectual and embodied experience of God is required, which appropriately details for us the eschatological lens of the image and should point to the fact that it is not merely our bodies that represent God as images, but our souls internally (Mouw 2018: 68).

On this understanding of human purpose, we are neither simply bodies nor simply souls, but the imaging capacity begins in the soul. We look to both the intellectual vision of God and the physical resurrection of our bodies. The image capacity is not simply an external or physical representation as some suggest, but one where we represent God in the internal life. For it is in the life of the soul that we find the development of virtue. All of this depends on the eschatological view of humans.

IV.3 Eschatological Challenge

In keeping with Middleton's understanding of *imago Dei*, Turner (2018), argues that an appropriate interpretation of scripture on personal eschatology entails an essentially embodied understanding of the *imago Dei*. In analytic form, he lays out his argument that the eschatological world (W), that is, God's temple, will be inhabited by essentially embodied humans:

1. W's telos is to be YHWH's temple, the place in which YHWH dwells with and is worshipped by his creation.
2. W's telos will be completed at the eschaton.
3. At the eschaton, W will be YHWH's temple, the place in which YHWH dwells with and is worshipped by his creation. (From 1 and 2)
4. An essential property of W is that it contains YHWH's image bearers.
5. The conjunction <IG_{OT} is true and it's true that human beings are IG_{OT} [image of God from Old Testament]> is true.
6. EI is true. (i.e., Embodied image)
7. Therefore, at the eschaton, W will contain embodied human beings. (From 3 to 6)
8. The eschatological bodily resurrection furnishes W, at the eschaton, with embodied human beings.
9. Therefore, at the eschaton, W will contain resurrected human beings (Turner 2018, my inserts).

While a sustained and careful response to Turner's argument will not occur here, there are several lines of response that need stating. Turner's argument hinges on premise 5, which follows from the image bearers inhabiting YHWH's temple in the eschaton, and, in keeping with the Old Testament, according to Turner and the Old Testament scholars he follows, this requires an embodied image. First, it is not clear from Turner's argument that one could not simply replace the word "essential" with "functionally necessary" in some sense. For essential, I do not mean to suggest that one's identity is essentially embodied or that embodiment is essential to personal persistence, but it could mean that the body is functionally necessary for a flourishing human life. If persons are carriers of the image and cannot lose that image, then it does not follow that the body is essential either to personhood or the image. However, the body may be functionally necessary in some senses. Further, the body could be a second image similar to Spencer's approach. The body may be necessary to flourish as a human being or to perform all the tasks identified in the

Old Testament as God's covenantal representative. Additionally, there may be necessary conditions for my origins, such as causally necessary conditions. Second, it is not clear from what Turner states that simply because an embodied image will inhabit YHWH's temple at the end of time that entails that embodiment is essential to the constitution of the first image or the image that takes priority. It depends on the further assumption that the Old Testament yields an understanding of the image as embodied. Third, even if the image is descriptive of an external temple that we (i.e., the image bearers) comprise, it does not follow that the image is essentially embodied—if by embodied what is meant is material. Fourth, it is not clear that such an argument excludes an additional stage in the eschatological process, namely, a disembodied intermediate state of existence where we experience the presence of YHWH in anticipation of the final resurrected state, and as argued earlier from Christology, it would seem to follow that if Christ was an image disembodied then so are we.

Following the Tradition (along with several passages of scripture like 2 Cor. 5:1-10), there is an eschatological step missing in Turner's account that requires not only a substantial soul, but that the image persists from one state of glory to the next. The question is: are we image bearers during the intermediate state of disembodied existence, if Catholic Christianity is right that there is in fact an intermediate state? It would seem that we are, with most of Catholic Christianity, soul-body compounds, and souls are naturally or contingently immortal. This raises a further question about the nature of image bearers: What is the primary end or telos of human beings? Is it a vision of God (with its theocentric focus), the physical resurrection (with its anthropocentric focus), or some combination of both? With Calvin and the Reformers, I contend that it is both, but an exploration of the specifics must wait. Assuming this is the case, the fact that the image is intimately tied to the soul and its capacities, if not dogmatic, is an entailment from dogmatic eschatology.

V. CONCLUSION

While recognizing the validity of particularity, the significance of relationality, and the importance of rigorous biblical scholarship, the cost of stepping outside of essential dogmatic tradition is too high. Recognizing a plurality of orthodoxy within Reformed thought does not require that we sacrifice what is central to the Tradition, namely, the theological centrality of the image bearing capacity to the soul as having a similarity relation to God, albeit metaphysically analogous. To do so, might mean sacrificing the Tradition for traditions. My advice is to stay close to the Tradition. Catholic anthropology, here I stand.

References

Arcadi J. M. (2020), "*Homo adorans: Exitus et Reditus* in Theological Anthropology," *Scottish Journal of Theology* 73 (1): 1–12.

Ayers, L. (2008), "The Soul and the Reading of Scripture: A Note on Henri D Lubac," *Scottish Journal of Theology*, 61: 173–90.

Beale, G. K. (2008), *We Become What We Worship: A Biblical Theology of Idolatry*, Downers Grove, IL: IVP Academic.

Beveridge H. and J. Bonnett, eds. (1983), *Selected Works of John Calvin: Tracts and Letters*, reprint. Grand Rapids, MI: Baker.

Burman, F. (1671), *Synopsis theologiae, et speciatim oeconomiae foederum Dei, ab in- itio saeculorum usque ad consummationem eorum*, vol. 1., Utrecht: Cornelius Jacobus Noenard.
Calvin, J. (1948), *Institutes of the Christian Religion*, trans. J. T. McNeil, Philadelphia: Westminster Press.
Corcoran, K. (2006), *Rethinking Human Nature: A Christian Materialist Alternative to the Soul*, Grand Rapids, MI: Baker Academic.
Cortez, M. (2010), *Theological Anthropology: A Guide for the Perplexed*, London: T&T Clark.
Cortez, M. (2016), *Christological Anthropology in Historical Perspective*, Grand Rapids, MI: Zondervan.
Cortez, M. (2018), *Resourcing Theological Anthropology: A Constructive Account of Humanity in Light of Christ*, Grand Rapids: Zondervan.
Costa, J. (2010), "The Body of God in Ancient Rabbinic Judaism: Problems of Interpretation," *Revue De L'Histoire Des Religions*, 227 (3): 283–316.
Crisp, O. D. (2017), "The Christological Model of the *Imago Dei*," in J. R. Farris and C. Taliaferro (eds.), *The Ashgate Research Companion to Theological Anthropology*, 217–29, New York: Routledge.
Dalferth, I. (2016), *Creatures of Possibility: The Theological Basis of Human Freedom*, Grand Rapids, MI: Baker Academic.
Dennison, J. T. (2014), *Reformed Confessions of the 16th and 17th Centuries*, vol. 4, Grand Rapids, MI: Reformed Heritage Books.
Farris, J. R. (2017a), "An Immaterial Substance View: *Imago Dei* in Creation and Redemption," *The Heythrop Journal*, 58 (1): 108–23.
Farris, J. R. (2017b), "A Substantive (Soul) View of the Imago Dei: A Rich Property View," in J. R. Farris and C. Taliaferro (eds.), *The Ashgate Research Companion to Theological Anthropology*, 165–78, New York: Routledge.
Farris, J. R. (2017c), *The Soul of Theological Anthropology*, New York: Routledge.
Farris, J. R. (2017d), "Christianity," in Y. Nagasawa and B. Matthewson (eds.), *The Palgrave Handbook of the Afterlife*, 129–52, London: Palgrave Macmillan.
Farris, J. R. (2020), *An Introduction to Theological Anthropology: Humans, Both Creaturely and Divine*, Grand Rapids, MI: Baker Academic.
Farrow, D. (2019), *Theological Negotiations*, Grand Rapids, MI: Baker Academic.
Feinberg, P. (1972), "Humanity in God's Image," *Journal of the Evangelical Theological Society*, 53 (3): 601–17.
Feingold, L. (2018), "The Image of God in Man Extended Upwards and Downwards Through Grace and our Bodily Nature," *The Saint Anselm Journal*, 13 (2): 42–59.
Gentry, P., and S. Wellum (2012), *Kingdom through Covenant: A Biblical-Theological Understanding of the Covenants*, Wheaton: Crossway.
Gottstein, A. G. (1994), "The Body as Image of God in Rabbinic Literature," *Harvard Theological Review*, 87 (2): 171–95.
Haddan, A. W. (1887), in P. Schaff (ed.), *From Nicene and Post-Nicene Fathers*, First Series, vol. 3, Buffalo, NY: Christian Literature. Available online: http://www.newadvent.org/fathers/130101.htm (accessed April 14, 2020).
Helm, P. (2005), *John Calvin's Ideas*, Oxford: Oxford University Press.
Helm, P. (2010), *Calvin at the Centre*, Oxford: Oxford University Press.
Helm, P. (2018), *Human Nature from Calvin to Edwards*, Oxford: Oxford University Press.
Levering, M. (2012), *Jesus and the Demise of Death*, Waco: Baylor University Press.
Lints, R. (2015), *Identity and Idolatry: The Image of God and its Inversion*, Downers Grove, IL: IVP Academic.

Mangano, M. J. (2008), *The Image of God*, Lanham: University Press of America.
McLeod-Harrison, M. S. (2014), "On Being the Literal Image of God," *Journal of Analytic Theology*, 2: 140–59.
Middleton, J. R. (2005), *The Liberating Image: The Imago Dei in Genesis 1*, Grand Rapids, MI: Brazos Press.
Moritz, J. (2017), "Evolutionary Biology and Theological Anthropology," in J. R. Farris and C. Taliaferro (eds.), *The Ashgate Research Companion to Theological Anthropology*, 45–56, New York: Routledge.
Mouw, R. (2012), "The Imago Dei and Philosophical Anthropology," *Christian Scholars Review*, 41 (3): 253–66.
Mouw, R. (2018), "The Relevance of Biblical Eschatology for Philosophical Anthropology," in O. D. Crisp and F. Sanders (eds.), *The Christian Doctrine of humanity: Explorations in Constructive Dogmatics*, 61–9, Grand Rapids, MI: Zondervan.
Nichols, T. (2010), *Death and Afterlife: A Theological Introduction*, Grand Rapids, MI: Brazos.
Pope John Paul II (2006), *Man and Women He Created Them*, New York: Pauline Books & Media.
Ratzinger, J., ed. (1995), *Catechism of the Catholic Church*, 2nd ed., New York: Doubleday.
Runia, D.T. (2005), *On the Creation of the Cosmos According to Moses*, Atlanta: SBL Press.
Spencer, M. (2018), "Perceiving the Image of God in the Whole Human Person," *St. Anselm Journal* 13 (2): 1–18.
Tanner, K. (2010), *Christ the Key*, Cambridge: Cambridge University Press.
Turner, J. T. (2018), "Temple Theology, Holistic Eschatology, and the Imago Dei: An Analytic Prolegomenon," *Theologica*, 2 (1): 95–114.
van den Brink, G., and A. Goudriaan (2016), "The Image of God in Reformed Orthodoxy: Soundings in the Development of an Anthropological Key Concept," *Perichoresis*, 14 (3): 81–96.
Vorster, N. (2011), *Created in the Image of God: Understanding God's Relationship with Humanity*, Eugene, OR: Pickwick Publications.
Walls, J. (2002), *Heaven: The Logic of Eternal Joy*, Oxford: Oxford University Press.
Webb, S. (2011), *Jesus Christ, Eternal God: Heavenly Flesh and the Metaphysics of Matter*, Oxford: Oxford University Press.

CHAPTER TWENTY-FOUR

The Fall and Original Sin

OLLI-PEKKA VAINIO

Curiously, the doctrine of original sin has been called both "the most vulnerable part of the whole Christian account" and "the only part of Christian theology which can really be proved" (Chesterton 2006: 24; Madueme 2014). Underlying this paradox seems to be our simultaneous experience of the universality of sinfulness and our capacity to imagine a world without sin.[1] However, the Christian account of this duality seems, at least to some extent, to contain elements that make it scientifically and philosophically difficult to accept.

The Fall, more specifically, is central in the Christian narrative, as it explains the meaning behind the economy of salvation. According to a standard version of this narrative, humans were created in an original state, which was pure and free from sin or death, but this state was disturbed by the Fall, that is, the moment at which human rebellion against God began. Consequently, to return humankind to a prelapsarian state, God established a covenant with the Patriarchs, Israel, and, ultimately, assumed a human nature in the man Jesus Christ, this final act purifying humankind of sin. The whole narrative plays out like traditional theater: set–upset–reset.

The doctrine of the Fall (DOF) is indispensable to Christian theology, as, first, it offers an account of human history in which God is not the originator of sin, and, second, it argues that humankind's current state is degraded and that Christ will save humanity, thus giving a reason for the economy of salvation. However, there are several ways of considering the Fall: Is it historical or ahistorical? Is it momentary, protracted, or eternal? Is it particular to an original human couple or relevant to a wider group of people? Does the Fall happen downward or upward (Smith 2016)?

In any case, the result of the Fall is original sin. All Christian churches subscribe to some version of the doctrine of original sin (DOS), which serves two functions. First, DOS enables a distinction between the status of humans as we are now are (sinners) and how we should be (righteous). Second, it is linked with the doctrine of atonement and the gift of grace merited by Christ: as we are all sinful in Adam, we are all saved in Christ (Rom. 5:12-21). Here, DOS functions as an ultimate equalizer, making everyone equally far from God and paving the way for unmerited redemption through grace. Some further issues also arise from DOS—namely, what was transmitted to us from the original couple and how did this transmission take place?

---

[1] It is often easier for us to imagine things that are evil than things that are perfectly good. Recent, impactful artistic expressions of the effect of sin on all are Steve McQueen's *Widows* (2018) or David Simon's classic *The Wire* (2002–8). Depictions of goodness, on the other hand, are often bland or static. C. S. Lewis's *Ransom* trilogy seems, however, to offer a believable illustration of societies that have not fallen into sin.

There are both scientific and philosophical objections to the DOF and DOS as traditionally conceived. The following chapters explore objections to both doctrines. First, I will discuss various interpretations of the Fall. Then I will offer a brief sketch of the challenges facing the theories regarding the transmission of original guilt.

I. THE DOCTRINE OF THE FALL

When the world was believed to have only been a few thousand years old, and Adam and Eve were believed to be our not-so-distant relatives, it made sense to believe that when Genesis (ch. 3) and Paul (Rom. 5: 12-22; 1 Cor 15: 21-22, 44-49) spoke of the Fall of Adam, they were speaking about (1) a momentary event and (2) a single person (or couple), (3) whose act of disobedience caused their progeny, to lose their original righteousness. The biblical proof text for this view was Rom. 5:12: "Therefore, just as sin entered the world through one man, and death through sin, and in this way death came to all people, because all sinned."

There has always been some ambiguity about the exact nature and the effects of the Fall. For example, Roman Catholic theology has traditionally taught that the Fall merely removed original righteousness, while some Protestants have taught that the Fall corrupted human nature.[2] The Fall has also sometimes been described as a fall "downwards," from a pure original state to one of sin, while others have interpreted it as a fall "upwards," toward greater self-consciousness, moral responsibility, and consequently a sense of guilt (Wiley 1989: 40–2).

When the world was discovered to be significantly older than previously thought, however, and when modern genetics offered an empirical method for tracing out humankind's past, it became virtually impossible to believe in this traditional historical account of the Fall. As a result, recent discussion has mostly focused on the question of whether the fall into sin could have taken place without an original individual or couple and without the Fall having to have been a single event in time. That is, can one still today subscribe to DOF and DOS without a literal interpretation of an Edenic state?[3]

The following offers a summary of the possible options for understanding the Fall:

HFS: Historic Fall of a single couple
HFG: Historic Fall of a group of hominids, either in
    (1) a single moment of time or
    (2) over a period of time
AF: Ahistoric Fall
FH: Fall in Hypertime

The adherent of HFS must decide whether the original couple were our biological ancestors or our spiritual ancestors, since the interpretation of the original couple as both our biological and spiritual ancestors does not seem plausible in light of contemporary science. A literal reading of Genesis, accompanied by a particular kind of interpretation of the various family trees supplied in the Bible, put Adam and Eve at about 6,000 years in

---

[2]On Protestant views, see Batka (2016) and Calvin (2008: 2.1.8); on how Augustine's doctrine of sin can be interpreted in different ways, see Nisula (2012). On the Catholic doctrine, see Anselm (2000); cf. Aquinas (n. d: ST II.I.Q82.a2). Some magisterial documents discussing the theme include the Lutheran *Formula of Concord*, §1, *The Heidelberg Catechism*, §4–11, and *The Catechism of the Catholic Church*, §385–421.
[3]For a longer survey of Christian options on the issue, see Barrett and Caneday (2013).

the past, some place in Mesopotamia. According to modern biology, at that time, human population had already spread across the globe and would have comprised between 1 and 15 million individuals (Stone 2014; Falk 2017).

In this case, one might still argue that Adam and Eve were our spiritual ancestors, but it becomes harder still to argue that they could also have been our biological ancestors. Even pushing the original couple further back into the past (approx. 1.8 million years bc) does not seem to resolve the issue (Stone 2014). While we can trace our ancestry back to a mitochondrial Eve and a Y-chromosomal Adam (who were the individuals from whom our X and Y genes originate), these individuals seem not to have lived at the same time. This version would also require a nonliteral reading of the biblical family trees and other stories that describe the beginning of the human race.

However, it is still possible to claim that Adam and Eve were a historical couple whom God chose among the nations at a point in time when there were already millions of people wandering the earth. By this act of election, the couple became our spiritual ancestors, even if we are not direct biological descendants from this couple.[4] This interpretation is typically coupled with that of *federalism*, which tries to explain how the Fall of two individuals can affect the whole of the human race. According to this interpretation, Adam became the federal head of the human race, and everything he did affected all his subjects, much like everything a king or queen does would affect everyone in his/her realm. Federalism is discussed in further detail below.

The momentary HFG shares similar problems with HFS. It is hard to imagine an act that all human individuals around the globe could have participated in at one moment of time. This is not a problem for the protracted HFG, but this seems to break the one-Adam-one-Christ analogy in Rom. 5:18-19: "Consequently, just as one trespass resulted in condemnation for all people, so also one righteous act resulted in justification and life for all people. For just as through the disobedience of the one man the many were made sinners, so also through the obedience of the one man the many will be made righteous." Nevertheless, "one Adam, one Christ" need not be the only way to understand this passage (Williams 1927; Enns 2012: 119–35).

Many modern theologians and philosophers who wish to remain within the boundaries of the classical Christian tradition, while accounting seriously for advances in scientific study, often opt for a protracted HFG. For example, C. S. Lewis writes,

> We do not know how many of these creatures God made, nor how long they continued in the Paradisal state. But sooner or later they fell. Someone or something whispered that they could become as gods—that they could cease directing their lives to their Creator and taking all their delights as uncovenanted mercies … They wanted some corner in the universe of which they could say to God, "This is our business, not yours."

---

[4]The encyclical *Humani Generis* (1950: §37) seems to require the faithful to believe in the principle of monogenism, according to which

> the faithful cannot embrace that opinion which maintains that either after Adam there existed on this earth true men who did not take their origin through natural generation from him as from the first parent of all, or that Adam represents a certain number of first parents. Now it is in no way apparent how such an opinion can be reconciled with that which the sources of revealed truth and the documents of the Teaching Authority of the Church propose with regard to original sin, which proceeds from a sin actually committed by an individual Adam and which, through generation, is passed on to all and is in everyone as his own.

For a discussion, see Levering (2017: 231–3). Levering suggests that the magisterium could allow for abandoning monogenism, if one could explain how polygenism could be reconciled with the conciliar documents.

… We have no idea in what particular act, or series of acts, the self-contradictory, impossible wish found expression. For all I can see, it might have concerned the literal eating of a fruit, but the question is of no consequence. (Lewis 2015: chapter 5)[5]

HFG theories wish to retain some link to actual human history and ancestry, but some theologians think this is unnecessary or even harmful. AF theories either entirely abandon the historic Fall or treat the actuality of the Fall as unknowable. An example of the former approach is Friedrich Schleiermacher's (1999) reinterpretation of the Fall and original sin as a natural corruption of our self-consciousness. The latter approach, on the other hand, can be found, for example, in Søren Kierkegaard's work (1981). While Kierkegaard does not deny that some event in the past might have taken place, he thinks that starting from a historical perspective prevents us from really seeing ourselves in Adam's shoes, and a focus on historicity will subsequently preclude our attempts to understand the weight of *our* sin. The problem with this stronger version of AF, however, is that it seems to equate original creation with the Fall. This in turn contradicts at least some of the original intentions that drove the first theologians to develop DOF and DOS in the first place (Trueman 2014).

The most recent theory for understanding the Fall is Hud Hudson's (2014) account of the Fall in hypertime. Hudson asks us to imagine the world as a block that grows by one slice every moment in time. We can imagine a world that was literally like Genesis 1, and it is in this world that the Fall takes place. Banishment from paradise then involves the actual termination of this world. However, God preserves one time-slice from this Genesis Fall-world and appends it into our current world's past, into a moment when hominids were just developing consciousness and moral sense. If God indeed is an omnipotent being, God would be capable of such a deed, and there would be nothing related to the philosophy of time that would prevent this sequence of actions from having taken place. According to Hudson, this imaginative proposal enables one to hold on to both a literal reading of Genesis and a modern scientific reading of our evolutionary past.[6] However, Hudson does not insist that this is how history actually unfolded, since the point of this theory for Hudson is to make a more general argument about the compatibility of philosophy, theology, and science, according to which our convictions about the alleged conflicts of science and theology are largely based on existing philosophical presuppositions (Hudson 2014: 1–11, 41).

II. THE DOCTRINE OF ORIGINAL SIN

It is sometimes erroneously argued that St. Augustine invented DOS. However, many church fathers before him had already formed the notion, following St. Paul, that Adam's fall somehow affected human nature as a whole (Wiley 1989: 13–55). While Augustine certainly offered the first rigid definition of DOS, later approved at the councils of Carthage (AD 418) and Orange (AD 529), there is an ongoing debate about to what Augustine's DOS essentially amounts (Couenhoven 2005; Nisula 2012; Sanlon 2014).

---

[5]For similar accounts, see also Jenson (1999); van Inwagen (2006); Smith (2016).
[6]A similar proposition involving other realms has been explored by Chinese science fiction author Cixin Liu in his *The Three-Body Problem* trilogy (Liu 2016). The universe itself undergoes a Fall, from a ten-dimensional Edenic State to the four-dimensional experience with which we are familiar. Liu does not give reasons behind what ultimately causes the Fall in the higher dimensions, but his novels hint toward a theory according to which universe is a "dark forest," where it is always safer for an individual to eliminate others before they can eliminate that individual. This is the cosmic original sin, which corrupts all existence. This pertains not only to humans but also affects the higher-dimensional life forms, whose actions transfer the pattern of elimination to the lower dimensions, just as the Fall in the angelic world affects the human world in the Christian narrative.

Michael Rea (2007) argues that the traditional DOS comprises the three following claims:

1. All human beings suffer from a kind of corruption that makes it very likely that they will fall into sin.
2. All human beings suffer from a kind of corruption that makes it inevitable that they will fall into sin, and this corruption is a consequence of the first sin of the first man.
3. All human beings are guilty from birth in the eyes of God, and this guilt is a consequence of the first sin of the first man.

Let us make the following distinction: the *moderate* version of DOS includes only claims 1 and 2, while the *strong* version includes all three claims (Crisp 2015). Following this definition, many Reformed, Lutheran, and other Protestant churches have traditionally adopted the strong version of DOS, while Orthodox churches have adopted the moderate version (Louth 2013: 68–78). While Catholic tradition once maintained the strong claim, the recent *Catechism of the Catholic Church* seems to have moved the faith toward the moderate version of DOS (CCC §405). I will first look at the philosophical defenses of the strong DOS then assess whether the moderate DOS can fulfill the traditional desiderata of DOS.

II.1 Strong DOS

Rea (2007: 320) notes that the strong DOS seems to be in conflict with the following two theses concerning moral responsibility and our inability to have prevented the first sin.

4. A person P is morally responsible for the obtaining of a state of affairs S only if S obtains (or obtained) and P could have prevented S from obtaining.
5. No human being who was born after Adam's first sin could have done anything to prevent Adam's first sin; and no human being who is born corrupt could have done anything to prevent her own corruption.

The guilt that is transmitted to us can be understood as Alien Guilt or Personal Guilt. Alien Guilt theories suggest that the progeny of Adam participates in the guilt of Adam and thereby share his guilt, even if we have not committed any actual sins. *Federalism* explains how this take place: since he specifically was addressed by God, Adam was given a special role in the human race and became our "head"; thus, everything the head does affects his dominion, just as, when a king goes to war with another nation, all the king's subjects are therefore at war with that nation (Blocher 1997; Walton 2013).

Indeed, federalism seems to capture some of the intentions of the biblical texts and accurately describes shared decision making in this fallen world. For example, following the attack on Pearl Harbor, some 100,000 Japanese residing in the USA were interned in concentration camps, many of which were US citizens. While only perhaps a tiny fraction of them had been involved in military affairs and espionage, the whole group was subjected to punishment because of their relation to their federal head, Emperor Hirohito. From the viewpoint of political pragmatism, the decision seems to make sense; but, from the viewpoint of the individual, this was a tragedy and took little, if any, consideration of justice. In sum, accepting Alien Guilt theories requires abandoning claims 4 and 5, as some theologians, such as St. Anselm and Jonathan Edwards, appear to do.[7]

---

[7] Rea (2007: 322), however, points out that, while Edwards abandons these moral maxims, his own theory in fact offers a way of sustaining them, unbeknownst to him.

Personal Guilt theories try to offer ways to subscribe to all five claims. Instead of Adam's sin and guilt being considered alien, they are understood somehow to be universal, though this connection requires a complicated theory of the metaphysics of persons. In his thorough article, Rea (2007) distinguishes several theories, but I note here only those that Rea considers to be the most cogent accounts of DOS: Fission Theory and Conditional Transworld Depravity.

Fission Theory is a theological counterpart to a physicalist theory of persistence, explaining that the human stages x, y, and z of Adam that led him to the first sin are similar to us in that Adam and I share the same or similar human stages x, y, and z. In the same way that two copies of *War and Peace* can be said to be the same book, God treats the human race as the same human individual. How then does this theory join claims 4 and 5? In this metaphysical construction, I could have prevented Adam's sin because *I was Adam* (Rom. 5:12); therefore, claim 5 is refuted. But how plausible is this account of personhood, given that it requires us to think that, while Adam and I did not share spatial stages, we nonetheless shared a temporal stage? Fission Theory does well to explain situations concerning, for example, Siamese twins, who before separation shared the same spatiotemporal stages; but removing spatiality from human constitution creates additional problems that are hard to solve (Hudson 2014: 77).

The Conditional Transworld Depravity solution requires that one commit to the existence of true counterfactuals of freedom, which can have false antecedents, and that we are free to decide which counterfactuals of freedom are true of us. This means that we possess the sort of freedom by which we could have prevented the first sin, if we would have been there, but we did not do so. Effectively, this requires that I would have had to have power to decide whether or not Conditional Transworld Depravity pertained to me. The challenge this view faces is that is it subject to all the standard objections to Molinism and therefore dependent on the plausibility of God having middle knowledge and the possibility of backward causation (Laing 2019).

This discussion shows that it is possible to defend strong DOS, but making it philosophically plausible requires extensive metaphysical explanations, which makes the approach unpalatable to laypeople as well as to many philosophers. Whether or not this lack of credulity is actually relevant to these constructions is uncertain, since all philosophical theories share more or less the same fate: pushed to extremes, problems always arise.

II.2 Moderate DOS

The moderate DOS attempts to dodge the problematic claim that has to do with the imputation of the guilt of the original couple to their progeny, which many contemporary theologians think is morally and philosophically unsustainable.[8] According to the moderate DOS, we are responsible only for our own personal and actual sins, not for the sins of the original couple. Nonetheless, we are affected by their sin such that we are destined to live in a world where we, too, will inevitably fall.

Does this mean that the game is rigged? It was not our fault that we were born into this wretched human race. Maybe if we would have had a say, we would have chosen some other, less sinful world to inhabit. Our situation is somewhat analogous to those

---

[8]For a discussion, see, e.g., Crisp (2015); Kärkkäinen (2015); McFarland (2010); Swinburne (1989: 141–3).

who lived in Nazi Germany. Everyone at the time was indoctrinated and expected to participate in various levels of fascist acts, starting from the Hitler Youth and culminating in an active role in the National Socialist German Workers' Party. Even if we could say that a young German boy, Hans, would not be fully culpable for joining the Hitler Youth, because there was no option for him to do otherwise, we might still say that it was not right for him to have done so.[9] Consequently, Hans and his parents are to some extent blameworthy for not standing up to the Nazis. Nevertheless, we would ultimately judge Hans's character based on his actions, not merely on his membership, for which he was not responsible. In fact, we might even think that, if Hans did good in this situation, this is especially laudatory because of his membership in a community that had done everything in their power to limit moral behavior. Paradoxically, then, being born in a sinful state appears to be a merit for some—namely, to those who resist this condition.

If the moderate DOS is to escape the philosophical problems outlined above, however, it needs to explain why being born in a corrupt state does not mean that the game has been rigged against Hans. To offer another analogy, our fallen situation resembles a poker game, where players are playing with decks lacking odd-numbered cards but are nevertheless expected to play a straight flush in every single game. In this scenario, the similar faults of players are not imputed to others, and each individual player is judged by her own merits or lack thereof. But the situation is hardly any fairer than in the strong DOS.

One way the moderate and strong versions differ from one another is in their account of moral responsibility, with the moderate version emphasizing the individual in reckoning moral responsibility. That is, individuals are never responsible for their actions when there is nothing that they could have done to prevent being in that state, a condition present also in the strong DOS. It might be possible to rescue the moderate view by claiming that moral responsibility must only require that the actions performed by an individual genuinely reflect the kind of person that an individual is. In other words, people must recognize their actions as *their* actions. However, in the literature on moral responsibility, this requirement is often coupled with additional desiderata, which includes, among other things, the absence of manipulation. If Hans were, before his birth, subjected to the experiments of an evil Nazi scientist whom altered his DNA to create a perfect national socialist, we would not blame Hans; instead, we would attribute the evil Hans commits to the scientist.[10]

If this question could be answered, we still might ask whether the moderate view is able to do justice to the traditional function of DOS. I think it can. The moderate version attributes to all humans a state where they will inevitably fall into sin and from which they are unable to save themselves. The moderate DOS might also have advantages over the strong version, which seems to trivialize the notion of actual sin. Namely, even if one draws a distinction between the original sin and actual sins, it is ultimately the original guilt that damns a person, not his or her actual sins. Thus, there seems effectively to be no difference between jaywalking and committing genocide (McFarland 2007: 146–7, 155–6).

---

[9]The membership of the Hitler Youth was optional until 1936, when it became compulsory for all the children born in Germany.
[10]For a discussion on why the postlapsarian condition is not a manipulated state, see Bignon (2017).

III. CONCLUSION

To conclude, one's interpretation of DOF is, to a great extent, governed by biblical hermeneutics and more specifically on the reliability of the Bible with regard to genealogies and history. Another important issue is one's interpretation of Romans 5. Nonetheless, it seems that, as there are no strong conciliar claims to be made on these issues, churches are relatively free to construct various interpretations of the Fall.

As for DOS, the strong version is justifiable, if one accepts the metaphysical constructions that enables the treatment of Adam and his progeny as one person. The obvious downside is that these constructions are so delicate that, for most people, it is easier simply to dismiss the notion of inherited guilt. The moderate version somewhat reduces the burden, but its challenge is to account for moral responsibility in light of an inherited corrupt nature.

LITERATURE SURVEY

A thematic introduction to original sin is Jacobs (2008) and a good historical survey is Wiley (1989). Three edited collections that cover a good amount of various related topics are Madueme and Reeves (2014), Smith (2016), and Burdett (2018). Different viewpoints on the question of the historicity of Adam are offered in Barrett and Caneday (2013). Books that engage with biblical material include Blocher (1997), Enns (2012), and McFarland (2010). A cogent philosophical defense of the strong version of DOS is Rea (2007). Hudson (2014) offers a broad discussion of various perspectives.

References

Anselm (2000), *The Virgin Conception and Original Sin*, trans. J. Hopkins, Minneapolis: The Arthur J. Banning Press.
Aquinas, T., (n. d.), *Summa Theologiae*, trans. Fathers of the English Dominican Province Translation. Available online: http://www.documentacatholicaomnia.eu/03d/1225-1274,_Thomas_Aquinas,_Summa_Theologiae_%5B1%5D,_EN.pdf.
Barrett, M., and A. B. Caneday, eds. (2013), *Four Views on the Historical Adam*, Grand Rapids, MI: Zondervan.
Batka, L. (2016), "Martin Luther's Teaching on Sin," in D. Nelson and P. Hinlicky (eds.), *Oxford Encyclopedia of Martin Luther*, Oxford: Oxford University Press.
Bignon, G. (2017), *Excusing Sinners and Blaming God: A Calvinist Assessment of Determinism, Moral Responsibility, and Divine Involvement in Evil*, Eugene, OR: Pickwick Publications.
Blocher, H. (1997), *Original Sin*. Downers Grove, IL: IVP Academic.
Burdett, M., ed. (2018), *Finding Ourselves after Darwin: Conversations on the Image of God, Original Sin, and the Problem of Evil*, Grand Rapids, MI: Baker Academic.
Calvin, J. (2008), *Institutes of the Christian Religion*, Peabody: Hendrickson.
Chesterton, G. K. (2006), *Orthodoxy*, Peabody: Hendrickson.
Couenhoven, J. (2005), "St. Augustine's Doctrine of Original Sin," *Augustinian Studies*, 36 (2): 359–96.
Crisp, O. D. (2015), "On Original Sin," *International Journal of Systematic Theology*, 17 (1): 252–66.
Enns, P. (2012), *The Evolution of Adam: What the Bible Does and Doesn't Say about Human Origins*, Grand Rapids, MI: Brazos.

Falk, D. R. (2017). "Human Origins. The Scientific Story," in W. T. Cavanaugh and J. K. A. Smith (eds.), *Evolution and the Fall*, 3–22, Grand Rapids, MI: Eerdmans.
Hudson, H. (2014), *The Fall and Hypertime*, Oxford: Oxford University Press.
Jacobs, A. (2008), *Original Sin*, New York: HarperOne.
Jenson, R. W. (1999), *Systematic Theology, Vol 2. The Works of God*, New York: Oxford University Press.
Kärkkäinen, V-M. (2015), *Creation and Humanity: A Constructive Christian Theology for the Pluralistic World, Vol. 3*, Grand Rapids, MI: Eerdmans.
Kierkegaard, S. (1981), *The Concept of Anxiety: A Simple Psychologically Orienting Deliberation on the Dogmatic Issue of Hereditary Sin*, Princeton: Princeton University Press.
Laing, J. D. (2019), "Middle Knowledge," *Internet Encyclopedia of Philosophy*. Available online: https://www.iep.utm.edu/middlekn/.
Levering, M. (2017), *Engaging the Doctrine of Creation*, Grand Rapids, MI: Baker Academic.
Lewis, C. S. (2015), *The Problem of Pain*, New York: Harper.
Liu, C. (2016), *The Three-Body Problem*, New York: Tor Books.
Louth, A. (2013), *Introducing Eastern Orthodox Theology*, Downers Grove: IVP Academic.
Madueme, H. (2014), "'Most Vulnerable Part of the Whole Christian Account' Original Sin and Modern Science," in H. Madueme and M. Reeves (eds.), *Adam, the Fall and Original Sin*, 225–50, Grand Rapids, MI: Baker Academic.
Madueme, H., and M. Reeves, eds. (2014), *Adam, the Fall and Original Sin*, Grand Rapids, MI: Baker Academic.
McFarland, I. (2007), "The Fall and Sin," in J. Webster, K. Tanner, and I. Torrance (eds.), *The Oxford Handbook of Systematic Theology*, 140–59, Oxford: Oxford University Press.
McFarland, I. A. (2010), *In Adam's Fall: A Meditation on the Christian Doctrine of Original Sin*, Oxford: Wiley-Blackwell.
Nisula, T. (2012), *Augustine and the Functions of Concupiscence*, Leiden: Brill.
Rea, M. C. (2007), "Metaphysics of Original Sin," in P. van Inwagen and D. Zimmerman (eds.), *Persons. Human and Divine*, 319–57, Oxford: Clarendon.
Sanlon, P. (2014), "Original Sin in Patristic Theology," in H. Madueme and M. Reeves (eds.), *Adam, the Fall and Original Sin*, 85–108, Grand Rapids, MI: Baker Academic.
Schleiermacher, F. (1999), *The Christian Faith*, Edinburgh: T&T Clark.
Smith, J. K. A. (2016), "What Stands on the Fall? A Philosophical Reflection," in W. T. Cavanaugh and J. K. A. Smith (eds.), *Evolution and the Fall*, 48–66. Grand Rapids, MI: Eerdmans.
Stone, W. (2014), "Adam and Modern Science," in H. Madueme and M. Reeves (eds.), *Adam, the Fall and Original Sin*, 53–84. Grand Rapids, MI: Baker Academic.
Swinburne, R. (1989), *Responsibility and Atonement*, Oxford: Clarendon Press.
Trueman, C. (2014), "Original Sin and Modern Theology," in H. Madueme and M. Reeves (eds.), *Adam, the Fall and Original Sin*, 167–88. Grand Rapids, MI: Baker Academic.
van Inwagen, P. (2006), *The Problem of Evil*, Oxford: Oxford University Press.
Walton, J. (2013), "A Historical Adam: Archetypal Creation View," in A. B. Canedy (ed.), *Four Views on the Historical Adam*, 89–118. Grand Rapids, MI: Zondervan.
Wiley, T. (1989), *Original Sin: Origins, Developments, Contemporary Meanings*, New York: Paulist Press.
Williams, N. P. (1927), *The Ideas of the Fall and Original Sin*, London: Longmans.

CHAPTER TWENTY-FIVE

Sin as Self-Deception

WILLIAM WOOD

The language of "sin" is explicitly religious, and, as I understand it in this chapter, explicitly Christian. Whatever else Christians may mean by "sin," the doctrines of sin and salvation are correlative, and so we can formally define sin as that from which we are saved by the power of Christ. Moreover, to say that Christ is the remedy is to say something about the disease: sin is a failure or fault with respect to the divine, whether we understand that as estrangement in some general sense, as failing to love God properly, or as violating a specific divine command. Theologians typically distinguish (1) "the fall," understood as the first human sin, (2) "original sin," understood as the human condition after the fall, or our present fallen state, and (3) "personal" or "individual" sin, the ubiquitous sinful thoughts and actions that we all know from our own lives. This chapter focuses on (3). The doctrines of the fall and original sin have been a fertile ground for analytic theorizing, because they present so many tricky conceptual problems.[1] By contrast, analytic theologians and philosophers of religion have paid comparatively little attention to personal sin. We therefore have an opportunity for constructive reflection: sin may be morally dreadful, but it is also philosophically interesting.

In this chapter, after briefly discussing some definitional matters, I explore the relationship between sin and self-deception. I begin with Augustine of Hippo's definition of sin as "turning away from God" ("To Simplician" 1.2.18, in Burleigh 1953). Augustine's definition is a valuable beginning, but it leaves crucial questions unanswered. Although the theological rhetoric around the concept of sin is filled with language of "turning away from," "rejecting," and even "rebelling against" God, most of us—even those of us who are very sinful—usually do not explicitly think of our sinful actions as a kind of open rebellion. Indeed, we rarely even think of them as sinful, at least not while we are still engaged in them. Indeed, it almost seems as though we must hide the sinful character of our actions, from ourselves and others, in order to pursue those sinful actions at all. In other words, sin—the turn away from God—typically presupposes a parallel act of self-deception—a turn away from truth. I pursue that suggestion at some length, using an extended (and mostly imagined) story built around the biblical narrative of King David and Uriah the Hittite (2 Sam. 11–12). I develop a short account of the form of self-deception that is most likely to enable sinful behavior and then use that account of self-deception to shed further light on the nature of sin.

---

[1] See the chapter "Fall and Original Sin" by Olli-Pekka Vainio in this volume.

I. ON NOT DEFINING SIN

One might think that analytic theological work on sin should begin with a rigorous definition of sin, perhaps even an attempt to specify its necessary and sufficient conditions. I very much doubt that this level of precision is really possible when describing a complex, socially expressed phenomenon like sin, however. Perhaps scripture can help. Christians should certainly turn to the Bible to learn more about how to understand sin, but as with other major Christian doctrines, we quickly find that scripture does not present us with clearly defined propositions or perspicuous arguments about exactly what sin is. Instead, we find a range of images and metaphors. The idea of sin as "missing the mark" or failing to reach a target is especially prominent. On this understanding, sin "is not a thing, but a moving away from. It is a missing, a falling short, a deviating" (Nelson 2011: 29; see, e.g., Gen. 20:9; Num. 14:41; Ps. 58.3; Ez. 44.10; Rom. 5:12, 6:20). We also find sin presented as rebellion (Isa. 1:2; Hos. 7:13), as debt (Mt. 6:12; Lk. 11:4, 13:4), and as a kind of enslaving power (Rom. 6:12, 14, 7:4-8). In summary, although this heterogeneous biblical material can form the basis of a more systematic account, it is not a systematic account by itself.

Even if a full-blown analysis of sin is not available, there are two definitional issues that are especially pressing for any constructive account of sin:

1. How should we understand the distinction (if any) between sin and moral wrongdoing?
2. Is pride the basic form of sin?

I.1 Sin and Moral Wrongdoing

Much of the analytic philosophical reflection on personal sin focuses on the relationship between sin and moral wrongdoing (Dalferth 1984; Mitchell 1984; Adams 1991; Couenhoven 2009). At first blush, this initial question may not seem like a difficult one. Sinful acts and morally wrong acts seem obviously coextensive. Certainly some actions—like murder, for example—seem both immoral and sinful. On the other hand, certain forms of distinctively religious wrongdoing such as idolatry, blasphemy, or other failures of worship are certainly sinful, but they are not obviously immoral (Adams 1991: 2). More controversially, there may also be actions that are immoral but not sinful. Perhaps at least some people are morally obliged to vote, for instance, but it seems strange to say that not voting is a sin. And when considering the relationship between sin and moral wrongdoing, perhaps "actions" are not the right unit of analysis in the first place. Perhaps even personal sin is properly understood as a state of being, or a breach in one's relationship with God, or as something otherwise not reducible to discrete actions at all (Mitchell 1984: 169–70).

In my view, questions about how to distinguish sin from moral wrongdoing depend more on one's account of moral wrongdoing than on one's account of sin, and as such, are beyond the scope of this chapter. Someone who holds that moral obligations only apply among human beings will hold that sin and moral wrongdoing are disjunct (Adams 1991: 2). By contrast, someone who agrees that we can have moral obligations to God, or someone who thinks that our moral obligations to other humans are also moral obligations to God, will more closely associate sin and moral wrongdoing (Dalferth 1984). On this understanding, "distinctively religious" wrongful actions can still be immoral: human beings may be morally obligated to avoid idolatry, or to engage in ritual actions appropriately, for example. Similarly, with respect to more strictly relational understandings of sin—such as "failing to love God properly" or "maintaining the right relationship with God"—we could simply say that God morally obligates us to love and relate to him properly. But, again, the way we answer these questions will depend more on our underlying account of moral obligations than on any account of sin.

I.2 Is There a Basic Form of Sin?

The Christian tradition has long regarded pride as the basic form of sin. Yet "pride" in the Christian lexicon does not mean general self-regard or self-esteem. Rather, pride is a sin of disordered, excessive self-love (Timpe and Tognazzini 2017). In *The City of God*, Augustine opposes the earthly city, characterized by unconstrained self-love (*amor sui*), to the heavenly city, characterized by the love for God (*amor dei*): "the earthly city was created by self-love, reaching the point of contempt for God," he writes (14.27; see also 14.28, 12.1, 12.6, 14.3 [in Bettenson 1984]). The tradition has followed his lead. On a common construal, pride is the sin of excessive self-love, because the prideful sinner treats his own self and his own desires as the final, ultimate good and loves them inordinately (Niebuhr 1941; Pannenberg 1991). Pride so defined entails denying that God is the ultimate good and refusing to love God above all things.

Sometimes, the claim that pride is the basic form of sin is understood as a historical claim: the first sin is a sin of pride, and all subsequent sins derive from the fall effected by this first sin. It is relatively easy to map the suggestion that the primal sin is a sin of pride onto the traditional story of the fall of Adam and Eve (Genesis 3) or the fall of Satan (Isa. 14:12-15, according to premodern exegetes). These first sins arise when creatures reject their divinely given limitations and pursue their own forbidden desires, which does seem like a form of prideful self-love. Alternatively, the suggestion that pride is the basic form of sin is sometimes understood as a universal claim about all personal sin: that every sin reduces to the sin of pride, or at least includes some element of pride. On this construal, every sin without exception is fundamentally an act of excessive self-love.

The claim that every sin reduces to the sin of pride has been the target of considerable criticism from contemporary theologians (Plaskow 1980; Outka, Santurri, and Werpehowski 1992; McFadyen 2000). They argue that prideful self-assertion—loving the self too much—is not a characteristic sin of those who are systematically oppressed. Instead, as a consequence of their oppression, the oppressed often understand themselves to be of too little worth. Their characteristic sin is not excessive self-love, but excessive self-abasement. An adequate account of sin also needs to be able to speak to those who love themselves too little.

Despite its venerable pedigree, then, it seems unhelpful to say that pride is the basic form of sin, such that all sins exemplify excessive self-love. Sins of self-abasement do not seem to flow from pride, and human beings can also love many things other than the *self* with an excessive and sinful love: nation, race, wealth, power, and so forth. Sometimes we might love such other things as a function of a more primordial self-love (loving one's nation because one sees it as an extension of oneself, for example), but I see no reason in principle why the causality could not run the other way (loving oneself because of one's prior love of the nation). In short, instead of saying that all sins exhibit pride, understood as excessive *self*-love, it seems more plausible to say that all sins exhibit some form of disordered love, without assuming that the disorder is tied to the self. We should love things to the degree that they are lovable, and to the degree that God wants us to love them. If there is a basic form of sin, it seems to be disordered love as such, not any particular species of disordered love.

II. AUGUSTINE ON SIN AS TURNING AWAY FROM GOD

After the Bible, the best place to look for an initial account of sin is Augustine of Hippo. By any measure, Augustine is one of the primary architects of the Western Christian understanding of sin, and his influence on subsequent Protestant and Roman Catholic thought is unparalleled. In an essay written just before his famous *Confessions*, Augustine defines sin as "perversity and lack of order, that is, a turning away from the Creator who is more excellent, and a turning to the creatures which are inferior to him" ("To Simplician" 1.2.18, in Burleigh 1953). This definition expresses the Augustinian understanding of sin in its most compact form: sin is a kind of "turning," away from God and toward other things that are, necessarily, inferior to God. The turn away from God is a movement of the will, and since the will always moves toward an object of delight, the turn itself is sinful because it displays disordered—perverse—forms of desire and attraction. Although original sin is not the focus of this chapter, Augustine's definition of sin can also be extended to capture the state of original sin: to be in the state of original sin is to be constitutively turned away from God in the relevant sense.

This definition of sin, as a turn away from "the Creator who is more excellent" and toward "creatures which are inferior," helpfully reveals some important aspects of what it is to sin. To sin is to prefer the lesser good over the greater, by definition. Yet this choice is not relevantly similar to other (secular) examples of moral weakness. The excellence of the Creator unimaginably surpasses the excellence of any created thing, and yet the sinner chooses the created thing over the perfectly good Creator. How could a rational agent ever make such a choice? Furthermore, on the Christian story, God is not just intrinsically good in some abstract way but also (as it were) instrumentally *good for us*. Human beings find their deepest happiness in loving and enjoying God. It follows that they cannot be fully, completely happy while also turning away from God. And yet the sinner turns away from God, and in so doing, turns away from his or her own happiness. This turn is a performative contradiction: the sinner pursues happiness by rejecting the very source of happiness. It is easy to see why Augustine resorts to the language of "perversity" and "lack of order" here: given the goodness of God, there is a sense in which any sin, even the most trivial, is inexplicable, even incoherent.

There is something deeply, profoundly true in this Augustinian insight, but at the same time, it cannot be the whole story. All human beings are sinners, but when we sin, we do not avowedly, explicitly turn away from God and goodness as such—at least not usually. We are not like Milton's Satan, cursing God and declaring openly that we choose evil over good. In fact, for most of us, most of the time, sin is not really open rebellion against God but something far more subtle and insidious. We sin only because we successfully avoid thinking about our actions as sinful in the first place.

Consider the biblical story of King David and Uriah the Hittite (2 Samuel 11–12).[2] David desires Bathsheba, the wife of Uriah, and contrives to ensure that Uriah is killed in

---

[2] Although I discuss this story at some length later, it should be clear that I am treating it as an imaginative illustration of self-deception. I am not actually doing biblical exegesis as such. For an authoritative commentary on 2 Samuel, see McCarter (1984); see also Alter (1999).

battle so that he can marry Bathsheba himself. The scriptural narrative does not provide much detail about David's mental states during this episode, but it seems clear that David only admits the wrongness of his actions much later, when he is confronted by the Prophet Nathan. In fact, Nathan tells David a parallel story, about some other man, who does something equally bad, and David is outraged at *that* man's behavior but does not initially recognize it as equivalent to his own. Only when Nathan dramatically proclaims "You are that man!" does David recognize what he has done and conclude "I have sinned against the Lord" (2 Sam. 12:13).[3] Until Nathan rebukes him, David does not reflect on the wrongness of his actions at all.

III. SIN AND SELF-DECEPTION

Most of us are like David in this story.[4] We do not attend to the wrongness of our sinful actions while we are doing them, let alone attend to the fact that we are turning away from God. More prosaically: in order to sin, we need to divert our attention from the fact that we are sinning. This claim is not an exceptionless generalization. I would not want to assert that "clear-eyed" sinning is impossible. But I do not think it is the norm. The norm seems to involve things like diverting our attention from the wrongness of our actions, rationalizing and justifying them to ourselves and others, and persuading ourselves that they are good rather than bad. Speaking summarily, I would call such behaviors "self-deceptive." Sinners are typically also self-deceivers, because sinful acts typically presuppose some form of self-deception.

"Self-deception" is a notoriously tricky concept, one that is the subject of a lively and ongoing philosophical debate in its own right. Taken literally, in its strongest form—successfully lying to oneself—self-deception seems quite paradoxical (Mele 2001). How can the same agent be both deceiver and deceived? So appealing to self-deception in order to understand sin might seem like explaining one mystery by appealing to another, deeper mystery. I have argued elsewhere that even very strong forms of self-deception are possible (Wood 2013: 179–208), but one does not have to endorse this view to agree that sinful acts typically presuppose self-deceptive behaviors of some kind. So my question now is: suppose that sinning typically requires some form of self-deception. What can we learn about sin?

To say only that sinning requires "some form of self-deception" is too vague. But any substantive account of self-deception will be highly controversial, and so there is a danger that further precision will derail the central focus on sin. Even so, I will briefly lay out my own account of self-deception as intentional self-persuasion, before returning to the main topic of sin. This account of self-deception is not meant to be a general model, applicable to everything we might call "self-deception" in ordinary language. Rather, it is intended to capture a form of self-deception that is likely to arise in morally and religiously salient situations—in other words, the kind of self-deception we should associate with sinful behavior.

For the sake of ease of exposition, I will continue use as my example David's decision to arrange for Uriah to die in battle, adding in my own (hopefully plausible) psychological

---

[3] Biblical quotations in this chapter are taken from the New Revised Standard Version Bible.
[4] The early modern moral philosopher Joseph Butler (1729) also discusses this narrative as an example of sinful self-deception in his sermon "Upon Self-Deceit."

details as needed. Recall that, according to the biblical narrative, by the time that he sends Uriah out to die in battle, David knows that Bathsheba is pregnant with his child and knows that Uriah will soon be aware of this fact. David himself wrote the letter to his military commander, Joab, ordering Uriah to the front and ordering the rest of the troops to retreat, leaving Uriah exposed.

We can be confident that David knows, in general, that the decisions he makes in this incident are examples of sinful behavior. Before the incident, David would assent to the general claim: *It is sinful to put an innocent man in a position where he is highly likely to be killed in order to marry that man's wife after he is dead*. Even the biblical narrative makes it clear that David's problem is not general moral ignorance: he does not lack the requisite grasp of the relevant moral standards. His story is also not presented as one in which he learns, in general, that behavior that he previously regarded as licit is in fact illicit. (His reaction to the confrontation with the prophet Nathan is not "Oh! Sorry! I didn't realize that was wrong ....")

It is also clear that David's own behavior throughout the incident is broadly intentional, meaning that he is not under any sort of compulsion or external influence that would prevent him from recognizing and avowing his actions as his own. So he "knows what he has done" in at least the minimal sense that he is capable of assenting to the claim: *I, David, ordered Uriah to the front*. He can also assent to the claim: *I, David, ordered the other troops to withdraw from Uriah leaving him exposed*. Suppose that when he received David's letter, Joab worriedly asked himself "Did David really write this? I'd better double-check with him personally." Presumably David would agree that he wrote the letter. Alternatively, if he denied writing it, that denial would be a lie, not a sincere denial. Depending on how we continue the story, that lie could itself be the moment at which David recognizes the wrongness of his prior actions and repents, or it could further entrench him in his sinful pattern of behavior.

What David does not do is explicitly connect his own concrete and avowed actions with the general moral norms that he also avows. He does not describe his own actions, to himself or others, as *putting an innocent man in a position where he is highly likely to be killed in order to marry that man's wife after he is dead*. My all-too-brief story about self-deception is a story about how he can avoid making this connection explicit, in full awareness, until he is confronted by Nathan.

Again, the biblical narrative does not tell us any more about David's thought processes, so we have to fill out the story for ourselves. As I see it, when David learns that Uriah is dead, we can correctly ascribe to him the following belief: *I, David, am culpable for Uriah's death*. Like any case of belief-attribution, we attribute this belief to David on the basis of his own behavior. His behavior seems to express what we might call a guilty conscience. Presumably, when he learns that Uriah is dead, David doesn't say things like "I had Uriah killed! I'm the King and I can do what I want!" Instead, (let's suppose) he lets people think that Uriah just happened to die in a particularly heated battle. To other people, he expresses sorrow that Uriah has died. To himself, he tries not to think about Uriah at all, and when he does, he exploits the intrinsic ambiguity of the situation to make himself seem blameless. He says things like: *I didn't really do anything other than order one of my best fighters to the front, where he was most needed; I didn't really know what would happen; he might have triumphed; in fact, I expected him to! If God had wanted him to live, he would have lived*. These kinds of behaviors—a pattern of very specific actions and omissions—suggest that David does know that he has done something wrong.

At the same time, while he continues his project of self-deception, David is "divided against himself." This is metaphorical language, but it is easy to spell out the metaphor. First, at the cognitive and epistemic level, David needs to police his own consciousness to ensure that he does not explicitly attend to his own culpability. He therefore has to treat himself as an object, and engage in strategies designed to cause himself to think (or prevent himself from thinking) certain thoughts. Yet (obviously) it is he himself who engages in these strategies, which implies that he is both agent and patient—divided against himself. At the psychological level, this project is bound to cause David to experience additional psychic tension, because the threat of self-lucidity and exposure persists throughout. Furthermore, David must constantly present a specific image of himself to the external world: the social persona of someone who is innocent. This persona is itself a kind of socially performed fiction, like an actor playing a role, and is another way that he is divided against himself.

We can also infer that other people tacitly collude with David to help him avoid confronting the truth about his culpability. This kind of social collusion is a feature of most forms of self-deception, but it is especially easy to posit in the case of David, who is, after all, the King. Besides Nathan the prophet, who is likely to present the King with evidence that he is a murderer? No one. Instead, we can easily imagine that those around David would agree with him when he expresses sorrow that Uriah has died. They are careful to avoid the subject at all when speaking to David, and when it does arise, they are more than happy to agree with David's suggestion that the decision to send Uriah to the front was a sound military decision that had nothing to do with his desire for Bathsheba. In the face of such constant flattery and reinforcement, it is even easier for David to avoid attending to his own belief that he is guilty.

In summary, these are the elements of David's project of self-deception. The project stretches from the time of his decision to send Uriah to the front to be killed, to the time that he acknowledges his culpability after he is confronted by Nathan. Let p be the proposition: *I, David, am culpable for the death of Uriah*.

1. David knows that p.
2. When he entertains either p or not–p, David attempts to persuade himself and others that not–p.
3. To the people around him, David acts as if not–p.
4. When the people around David entertain p or not–p, they also attempt to persuade David that not–p.
5. David consistently diverts his attention from p.
6. Minimally, David accepts not–p. Maximally, he believes not–p.[5]

Two further comments. First, the point of filling out David's story as I did above, rather than simply listing the bare conditions, is to focus our own attention on the fact that projects of persuasion—including projects of self-persuasion—are often quite subtle and indirect. The best way for someone else to persuade David that he is not culpable for the death of Uriah is usually not going to involve, for example, frequently and openly

---

[5]One might think that the maximal construal is logically impossible, given condition 1. Not so. While the contradiction "p and not–p" cannot be true, there is no contradiction in asserting both "David knows that p" and "David believes not–p." Knowledge is factive, but belief is not. Furthermore, "David believes not–p" is logically distinct from "It is not the case that David believes p." Whether or not it is psychologically impossible, it is not logically impossible to believe contradictory propositions at the same time.

asserting: "King David, one thing is sure: you are definitely not guilty of murdering Uriah! Nope, definitely not!" Real-world persuasion does not really work like that, at least not most of the time. Similarly, the best way for David to persuade himself that he is not culpable might well be to persuade others that he is not culpable, which might involve sincere expressions of sorrow that Uriah is dead rather than dogmatic assertions of his own innocence. Second, condition 5 expresses the distinction between "acceptance" and "belief." (For more on that distinction, see Cohen 1992.) The idea is that *accepting that p* is a weaker epistemic state than *believing that p*, more like "acting as if *p*," which is compatible with, but does not entail, full-blown belief. In this sense, a good defense attorney can accept that his client is innocent, even though he knows that he is guilty. Whether self-deceivers can believe contradictory propositions is a controversial question that I need not address here. But immoral self-deceivers, including David in the story above, seem to be aware of their guilt at times (they know exactly what conversations and situations to avoid, for example) but seem not to be aware of their guilt at other times (they sincerely act as if they are innocent). We need to posit some kind of conflicting epistemic states to explain this mix of behavior. We can explain David's behavior by saying: he acts guilty because he knows that p, yet he acts innocent because accepts that not–p.

What really matters, for the mini-account of self-deception I am presenting here, is that David recognizes the truth about his culpability but tries to prevent himself from explicitly attending to that truth. In other words, in terms of the elements above, what really matters is the combination of conditions 1 and 4. The key element in David's project of self-deception is his act of recognizing and then rejecting, his own culpability. Just like the sinner turns away from God, the self-deceiver turns away from truth. The self-deceiver needs to hide the truth about his sinful actions from himself and others in order to preserve his own flattering self-image. Crucially, other people are likely to collude in this project by flattering the self-deceiver, distracting him, or otherwise helping the self-deceiver divert his attention from his own sinful behavior.

IV. WHAT CAN WE LEARN ABOUT SIN?

We can now return to the central question: What can we learn about sin from this account of self-deception? First, the fact that we typically hide our sins from ourselves is actually good news. There is something monstrous about people who can openly, avowedly, and explicitly turn away from God and sin in full awareness of the fact that they are sinning. It is when we sin openly and uncaringly that we are truly spiritually dead. Happily, for most of us, most of the time, sinning is not like that. We need to hide our sinfulness from ourselves and others, because we want to think of ourselves as good, and we want others to think of us as good too. This desire for self-esteem and the esteem of others is a form of self-love, and perhaps even a form of pride, but it is also a sign that in some fundamental sense we remain centrally oriented toward God and the Good. Augustine famously argues that evil is a privation of goodness. He intends this as an ontological claim, about the nature of reality, but it is also a moral and epistemological claim. Even as we sin, we remain fundamentally oriented toward God and therefore toward goodness; how could it be otherwise, if God is both our origin and our end, our creator and our *telos*? Sin and self-deception go hand in hand because as sinners, we can never utterly reject this fundamental orientation; all we can ever do is try to distract ourselves from attending to it. So, in a way, the self-deception that accompanies our sinful behavior shows that we still love God and goodness.

Second, although self-deception makes sinning easier, there is good reason to think that self-deception is also sinful itself, at least in the form presented here. The turn away from truth that we find in self-deception is itself a sin, because, like every sin, it expresses the turn away from God. When we deceive ourselves as part of a pattern of sinful behavior, we turn away from the truth about our own culpability. But this is also a turn away from God as the source of all goodness. Sin is recursive. Behaviors intended to facilitate sin are themselves sinful. So when someone engages in a project of self-deception in order to continue sinning or avoid repentance, that project of self-deception is not neutral. It is sinful in itself. So, for example, theft is sinful, but the self-deception that supports an act of theft is also sinful. It follows that the scope of sin and guilt are wider than we might have thought. There is an epistemic dimension to sin.

Third, sin and self-deception are complex social actions that are best seen as ongoing projects that extend through time, not just discrete acts of moral wrongdoing. It is a mistake to sharply distinguish the social aspects of sin from individual sinful acts. Too often, we tend to assimilate the social aspects of sin to the human condition of original sin, and we tend to use the language of social sin only to describe something like structural evil or ideology—the social sins of patriarchy, racism, or economic oppression, for instance. But human beings are social animals and so all sins are social in the relevant sense. In the story above, David's courtiers enable him to continue to divert his attention from his own guilt. Looking at sin and self-deception together reminds us that we all have our courtiers, and we are all courtiers for someone else. We are socialized into a sinful world that shapes us into sinful agents. Sin is always both personal and social.

Fourth, an account of sin as self-deception offers a productive way of understanding the cognitive consequences of the fall and the noetic effects of sin. The traditional doctrine of the fall and original sin teach that, somehow, all human beings inherit the guilt of our first parents. But we have also "inherited"—whatever we mean by that word—an aversion toward truth and a disposition to deceive ourselves and others. Precisely because we are sinful agents in a sinful world, self-deception comes easily and automatically, which means that sinning comes easily and automatically. On the other hand, we can only know and love God with great difficulty, and with the help of God's grace. An account of self-deception helps shed light on why that might be: after the fall, we have an aversion to the truth about God and our sinful natures, which is just to say that our intellects are darkened and our wills are oriented away from goodness.

V. CONCLUSION

This account is only a sketch, but it suggests that sin and self-deception go hand in hand. At the start of the chapter, I noted that the doctrine of sin and the doctrine of salvation are correlative: sin is that from which Christ saves us. The problem of sin is not purely cognitive or epistemic, and so sin cannot be *reduced* to false believing, or even to self-deceptive believing. Although the Gospel is good news, Christ does not save us only by providing us with new information or greater self-lucidity. Yet it should be clear even from the brief sketch above that sinful self-deception is also not just a matter of false believing. Instead, self-deception and sin are both complex social phenomena that involve not only the way we understand ourselves but also the way we want to be perceived by others. At root, however, the turn away from God characterizes all sin, and since nothing is more fundamental to the human person than his or her relationship with God, it is unsurprising that the turn away from God would also have cognitive and epistemic consequences.

LITERATURE SURVEY

For an extended version of the main argument of this chapter, see Wood (2013). There has been comparatively little analytic philosophical theology on individual or personal sin. On the question of defining sin, and the relationship between sin and moral wrongdoing, see Mitchell (1984), Dalferth (1984), and Adams (1991). On the noetic effects of sin, see Plantinga (2000: 199–240). Two valuable treatments of sin are Couenhoven (2009 and 2013). By contrast with analytic philosophical thought, the contemporary theological literature on sin is vast. A useful overview of recent theology on sin is Nelson (2011). Joseph Pieper's *The Concept of Sin* ([1977] 2001) remains a powerful statement from a Roman Catholic perspective. Key contemporary works include McFadyen (2001 and Peters (1994). Philosophical work on self-deception is similarly vast. See Fingarette (1969, Martin (1969), McLaughlin and Rorty (1988), and Mele (2001) for a way into the literature.

References

Adams, M. M. (1991), "Sin as Uncleanness," *Philosophical Perspectives, Philosophy of Religion* 5: 1–27.
Alter, R. (1999), *The David Story: A Translation with Commentary of 1 and 2 Samuel*, New York: Norton.
Augustine ([426] 1984), *The City of God*, trans. H. Bettenson, New York: Penguin.
Augustine ([397] 1953), 'To Simplician', in J. H. S. Burleigh (ed.), *Augustine: Earlier Writings*, Philadelphia: The Westminster Press.
Burleigh, J. H. S., ed. (1953), *Augustine: Earlier Writings*. Philadelphia: The Westminster Press.
Butler, J. (1729 [2017]), "Upon Self-Deceit," in D. M. McNAughton (ed.), *Joseph Butler: Fifteen Sermons & Other Writings on Ethics*, 84–92, New York: Oxford University Press.
Cohen, L. J. (1992), *An Essay on Belief and Acceptance*, New York: Oxford University Press.
Couenhoven, J. (2009), "What Sin Is: A Differential Analysis," *Modern Theology*, 25: 563–87.
Couenhoven, J. (2013), *Stricken by Sin, Cured By Christ: Agency, Necessity, and Culpability in Augustinian Theology*, New York: Oxford University Press.
Dalferth, I. (1984), "How Is the Concept of Sin Related to the Concept of Moral Wrongdoing?," *Religious Studies*, 20: 175–89.
Fingarette, H. ([1969] 2001), *Self-Deception*, Berkeley: University of California Press.
McCarter, Jr., P. K., (1984), *II Samuel: A New Translation with Introduction and Commentary*, The Anchor Bible 9, New York: Doubleday.
McFadyen, A. I. (2000), *Bound to Sin: Abuse, Holocaust and the Christian Doctrine of Sin*, New York: Cambridge University Press.
McLaughlin, B. P., and A. O. Rorty, eds. (1988), *Perspectives on Self-Deception*, Berkeley: University of California Press.
Martin, M. W. (1969), *Self-Deception and Morality*, Lawrence: University Press of Kansas.
Mele, A. (2001), *Self-Deception Unmasked*, Princeton: Princeton University Press.

Mitchell, B. (1984), "How Is the Concept of Sin Related to the Concept of Moral Wrongdoing?," *Religious Studies*, 20: 165–73.
Nelson, D. (2011), *Sin: A Guide for the Perplexed*, New York: T&T Clark.
Niebuhr, R. (1941), *The Nature and Destiny of Man: A Christian Interpretation*, vol. 1, New York: Charles Scribner's Sons.
Outka, G. H., E. N. Santurri, and W. Werpehowski (1992), *The Love Commandments: Essays in Christian Ethics and Moral Philosophy*, Washington, DC: Georgetown University Press.
Pannenberg, W. (1991), *Systematic Theology*, vol. 2, Grand Rapids, MI: Eerdmans.
Peters, T. (1994), *Sin: Radical Evil in Self and Society*, Grand Rapids, MI: Eerdmans.
Pieper, J. ([1977] 2001), *The Concept of Sin*, South Bend: St Augustine's Press.
Plaskow, J. (1980), *Sex, Sin, and Grace: Women's Experience and the Theologies of Reinhold Niebuhr and Paul Tillich*, New York: University Press of America.
Timpe, K., and N. A. Tognazzini (2017), "Pride in Christian Philosophy and Theology," in J. A. Carter and E. C. Gordon (eds.), *The Moral Psychology of Pride*, 211–34, New York: Rowman & Littlefield.
Wood, W. (2013), *Blaise Pascal on Duplicity, Sin, and the Fall: The Secret Instinct*, New York: Oxford University Press.

CHAPTER TWENTY-SIX

Analytic Theological Ethics

KENT DUNNINGTON

I aim to provide an overview of the field of theological ethics today and propose a way forward for analytic theologians interested in contributing to the field. I offer no history of the field of theological ethics. For that, see Sam Wells and Ben Quash (2010). Instead, I begin by trotting out some basic typologies, in order then to step back and note what I consider important and surprising features of the contemporary state of the field. I use "theological ethics" synonymously with "moral theology" (the preferred Roman Catholic nomenclature) to mean ethics done in a way dependent to some extent on claims from the Abrahamic traditions. We could also call it "theistic ethics." Theological ethics is thus distinguishable from philosophical ethics on the one hand (e.g., the ethics of Plato or Aristotle) and non-Abrahamic religious ethics on the other (Buddhist ethics, Hindu ethics, etc.). Theological ethics can be further subdivided into Christian, Jewish, and Muslim ethics. Christian ethics is ethics done in a way dependent to some extent on claims specific to Christian traditions, similarly for Jewish and Muslim ethics. I focus on theological ethics and Christian ethics because analytic theology (AT), despite a few recent Jewish and Islamic contributions, is similarly focused.

But what do I mean by ethics? The field of ethics is usually subdivided into metaethics, normative ethics, and applied ethics. Metaethics asks about the semantic, epistemic, and metaphysical status of moral claims. Semantic: What does "good" mean and are moral claims even the sort of claim that could be true or false? Epistemic: If moral truths aren't perceptual truths ("This is a chair.") or self-evident truths ("I'm hungry.") or analytic truths ("Bachelors are unmarried."), how do we come to know them at all (assuming they exist)? Metaphysical: Supposing there are moral truths, are they made true by facts about the natural order (say, what maximizes human pleasure) or are they the sorts of claims that could only be grounded in nonnatural facts (say, what God wills)?

Normative ethics overlaps this last question since normative ethics is interested in discovering the actual fact or facts—whether natural or nonnatural—that give rise to the range of moral properties, concepts, and judgments that we employ. The "big three" normative theories taught in most contemporary university ethics classes are utilitarianism (Mill), deontological ethics (Kant), and virtue ethics (Aristotle). Utilitarianism: moral facts reduce to facts about whatever maximizes overall pleasure. Deontological ethics: moral facts reduce to facts about what is required to respect the absolute dignity of persons. Virtue ethics: moral facts reduce to facts about the character traits that best promote personal flourishing, with "flourishing" typically understood in a perfectionistic way.

Finally, applied ethics focuses on specific issues. Is it permissible to eat animals? Is it permissible to kill noncombatants in war? Applied ethics can be done from the perspective of a specific normative theory, but it need not be. It can also proceed by moving from more certain to less certain cases by way of analogy. "Even though I don't know which, if any, normative theory is true, I know that x ought not to be done and I know that y is like x in the relevant respects, so I conclude that y ought not to be done."

What has been said to this point is crude in the way all typologies are. I've provided a rudimentary topography of the field of ethics, about as helpful for making sense of contemporary philosophical ethics as a map of the United States would be for getting around in Los Angeles. For a more sophisticated topography of the contemporary terrain, told as a brief history of analytic philosophical ethics, see Stephen Darwall, Alan Gibbard, and Peter Railton (1992).

However, what I've given is sufficient to allow us to step back and note some patterns in theological ethics and Christian ethics. The patterns are generalities, too, and like my typological categories, open to endless qualification and exception. Nevertheless, the following holds true generally: *Contemporary Christian analytic philosophers who do ethics do theological ethics, but rarely Christian ethics. They have a predilection for metaethical puzzles and rarely do sustained applied ethics. By contrast, theological ethicists (those who are trained in theology PhD programs) do mostly Christian ethics and are wary of the universalistic aspirations of theistic ethics. They tend, as well, to focus on applied ethical issues, especially those concerned with marginalized people groups and ecological disaster.*

I support this claim by briefly examining prominent movements among, on the one hand, Christian analytic philosophers doing ethics, and, on the other hand, theologically trained Christian ethicists.

I. CHRISTIAN ANALYTIC PHILOSOPHERS DOING ETHICS

The central debate among Christian analytic philosophers interested in ethics concerns the merits of natural law theories of ethics versus divine command theories of ethics. Representative presentations of the natural law tradition among Christian analytic philosophers are offered by Alasdair MacIntyre (1999), Mark Murphy (2001), Jean Porter (2005), and most notably John Finnis (1980). Representative presentations of the divine command tradition are offered by Philip Quinn (1978), C. Stephen Evans (2013), John Hare (2015), and most notably Robert Adams (1999). The back-and-forth between these alternatives constitutes the bulk of the conversation about ethics among Christian analytic philosophers. The conversation illustrates my claim that metaethical questions predominate and that specifically Christian themes are ancillary to the discussion.

Anything that deserves to be called a natural law theory of ethics builds on the moral thought of Thomas Aquinas (Murphy 2011a). Natural law theories share in common the following metaethical theses: (1) The rightness or wrongness of specific acts is to be explained in terms of facts about what goods are fundamental to the perfection of human nature and facts about how it is appropriate to pursue such goods; (2) Given that such facts are about human nature in general, the natural law is universally binding and universally knowable.

Agreement stops there. Natural law theorists disagree about several important questions. At the normative level, they disagree about what goods actually *are* fundamental to the perfection of human beings. Finnis lists life, knowledge, aesthetic appreciation, play, friendship, practical reasonableness, religion, and "the marital good." Murphy lists life, knowledge, aesthetic experience, excellence in work and play, excellence in agency, inner peace, friendship and community, religion, and happiness. And so on. Natural law theorists also disagree about how to determine when such goods are pursued defectively. It is obviously wrong to steal a painting in order to enjoy it aesthetically, just as it is wrong to prioritize play over religion, but why? Is there a master rule that explains what is defective in such cases (as Finnis argues), or is there a checklist of rules that specify all the different ways in which an action can go bad (as Murphy argues), or does right choice ultimately depend on something not formulable in terms of rules, like the operation of an agent's virtue (as MacIntyre argues)?

Most of the discussion about natural law theory, however, is at the metaethical level, where two interrelated questions are debated. First, can natural law theories actually explain the bindingness of morality, the way in which morality *obligates* us to act or refrain from acting in certain ways? After all, why should one's acknowledgment that pursuit of some basic good is practically rational entail any *obligation*? It is not clear how a theory of practical rationality can double as a theory of moral obligation. And second, does natural law theory require theism to play any explanatory role? One might think a positive answer to this latter question can help with the former; one might think that if *God* has created human nature, then human beings are not merely being practically rational in striving to perfect those natures, they are also fulfilling an obligation (to God) by conforming to God's law. But why think that? Can't I acknowledge that God has given me a nature that is perfectible in certain ways without concluding that I'm obligated so to perfect myself? Murphy (2011b: 97–9) argues compellingly that natural law theories are barred by their very form from giving any prominent explanatory role to God, because they attempt to explain moral properties (rightness, obligation, etc.) by strict appeal to natural and naturally knowable goods. So it should be no surprise that nontheists like Michael Moore (1996) can espouse natural law theory. In short, one of the two prominent moral theories under consideration by Christian analytic philosophers appears to establish no connection between theism and morality (let alone Christianity and morality).

Divine command theories are attractive because they clearly *do* give pride of place to God in explaining some, if not all, of our moral notions. What all divine command theories share in common is the view that God's will is somehow relevant to determining the moral status of some kinds of things (e.g., acts, states of affairs, character traits, intentions, etc.) The moniker "divine command theory" is misleading since some proponents of this type of theory deny that it is God's *command* that is the morally relevant feature of God's will. Murphy (2012) helpfully suggests such theories be classified as versions of theological voluntarism.

Nearly all of the discussion about theological voluntarism takes place at the metaethical level, too. Debate swirls around which aspect of the divine will is supposed to be morally relevant (God's command? God's will? God's desire?), which moral concepts are supposed to be explained by appeal to the divine will (just the obligation concepts or all the moral concepts?), and what the explanatory relation is supposed to be between the relevant feature of the divine will and the relevant moral concepts (is it a causal relation or a supervenience relation or an identity relation, etc.?) There are many different versions of theological voluntarism because there are many possible combinations here. But these are all decidedly metaethical alternatives. No answer to these questions could be action-guiding.

Perhaps it is not surprising that all of the debate about theological voluntarism among analytic philosophers is at the metaethical level. Even philosophers who think that what is morally right and wrong depends on what God wills might think that it belongs to the theologian or the bible scholar, but not to the philosopher, to discover what God does in fact will and how that translates into moral obligations or permissions for human beings. In any event, only the barest theism is relevant to these discussions among Christian analytic philosophers. It matters not that God is believed by Christians to have elected Israel from all the peoples of the earth, nor that God is believed to be Triune, nor that Jesus is believed to have been incarnate as very God and very man.

Jesus is, occasionally, mentioned in these discussions. For example, Adams explains why Jesus is not a counterexample to his claim that there is no such thing as complete human virtue (1999: 56–8), cites Jesus as commending love of God as the ideal ethical motive (1999: 179), and says that Jesus as well as Francis of Assisi and Mohandas Gandhi exemplify special possibilities of goodness that could not otherwise be known (1999: 368). However, Adams's theory is not substantively affected by the doctrine of the incarnation or the person and work of Jesus. The same could be said about other defining Christian doctrines; they make no difference to the ethical theories under consideration by the vast majority of Christian analytic philosophers.

Exceptions to this pattern are usually merely apparent. Take, for example, Nicholas Wolterstorff's acclaimed *Justice* (2010). He argues that justice (which comprises most, though not all, of our moral obligations) consists of the honoring of others' rights. The rights of others are grounded in their worth, and the worth of others is conferred by God's loving them. So here we have a theistic grounding of morality that is neither a version of theological voluntarism (because it is not God's commands but others' God-conferred worth that explains moral notions) nor natural law (because natural law's eudaimonism is too agent-centered to account for the way others' rights can make demands upon me that come apart from my personal flourishing). What's more, Wolterstorff claims that this vision is a distinctively biblical one, and he spends chapters on justice in the Old Testament, justice in the New Testament, and justice in the Gospels specifically. So you might think that his is a view of ethics not easily abstracted from peculiarly Christian commitments. This is not so, however. Justice as characterized by Wolterstorff clearly depends on God, the theistic God who is an omnibenevolent and loving person, but not in any obvious way on the God who is Trinity, who brought Israel out of Egypt and raised Jesus from the dead. Wolterstorff's, too, is an example of theistic ethics, but not of Christian ethics.

The clearest exception to this pattern among Christian analytic philosophers, I think, is Linda Zagzebski's distinctive blend of virtue ethics and theological voluntarism, called "divine motivation theory." Zagzebski writes,

> It seems to me that a moral theory that is Christian in any important way should refer to the person of Jesus Christ and the stories about his life, particularly as they are found in the Gospels. The reference to Christ ought to be an essential aspect of the theory. Christ is not just the instantiation of a set of virtues, and his life is not just an illustration of a set of general principles. (2004: 231)

Zagzebski makes the incarnation central to her moral theory by arguing that moral concepts should be defined in terms of the motivations of paradigmatically good persons. For Christians, Jesus is the paradigmatically good person, but as the doctrine of the incarnation teaches, Jesus is God. Thus, Zagzebski arrives at a kind of divine command metaethics whereby God's motives determine all the moral concepts, combined with a normative virtue ethics centered on the *imitatio Christi*, especially imitation of the motivational profile of Jesus.

Zagzebski acknowledges that this theory remains thin on specifics, but she claims that is the nature of moral theory. "The purpose of theory is not moral training. Rather, the philosophical theorist's aim is to satisfy a purely intellectual desire, the desire to understand" (2002: 315). She has in mind here a sort of division of labor wherein the philosopher does moral theory and someone else does what she calls "narrative ethics," the work of displaying in narrative form the character of the moral exemplar, in this case, Jesus. But who is to do the narrative ethics? She cites Stanley Hauerwas, a theologian to whom I'll turn in the next section, as a narrative ethicist; so perhaps her answer is that theologians are supposed to do the work of "narrative ethics." But why should that be? Her only answer is that "philosophers do not tell stories—at least not good ones" (2004: 251), but I suspect this is just a dodge. Narrative ethics, whatever it is, is not the telling of stories. Presumably it is critical reflection on stories, and there is no reason to think philosophers cannot be helpful with that. See Eleonore Stump (2012) for an example of how analytic philosophy can illuminate narratives.

So, Zagzebski is an exception to my claim that Christian analytic philosophers working in ethics do only theistic ethics, never Christian ethics, but she further illustrates my claim that Christian analytic philosophers prefer to stay on lofty metaethical terrain. There are exceptions to this latter claim as well. A collection on the ethics of food and eating by Andrew Chignell, Terence Cuneo, and Matthew Halteman (2015) comes to mind. But, characteristically, it is not clear what Christianity has to do with the arguments under consideration. In general, the pattern is fixed. Christian analytic philosophers rarely think *as Christians* about the whole field of ethics.

II. CHRISTIAN THEOLOGIANS DOING ETHICS

This pattern does not hold for contemporary theologians who do ethics. There are, of course, theological ethicists who have been more interested in theistic ethics than Christian ethics, but among Protestants since the rise of postliberal theology, that has been a minority trend. Most theological ethicists have been wary of what Wells and Quash (2010) call "universal ethics," ethics pursued in such a way that its claims might appeal to just anyone, or at least just anyone with a vaguely "Judeo-Christian" heritage. Instead, the trend in theological ethics has been a focus on the difference that Christian doctrine and scripture make to the moral life.

The preeminent representative of this trend is Hauerwas. Hauerwas claims, perhaps truthfully, to be a derivative thinker, but his has unquestionably been the dominant voice in theological ethics for the last forty years. He combines MacIntyre's historicism, John Howard Yoder's ecclesiocentrism, and the later Wittgenstein's attention to ordinary language into an ethical approach that treats the church as primary for Christian ethical reflection. Only after Hauerwas did it begin to seem odd that most earlier "Christian ethics" was primarily addressed to America rather than the church. The church is primary for Hauerwas in several senses. First, it is the church's resources—her scripture, doctrine, liturgy, saints, and so on—from which the moral theologian sets out, as opposed to common sense morality or supposedly universal intuitions about cases. Second, the church is primary in that Christian ethics is only intelligible as that of a distinctive community living according to a distinctive vision of the way the world is and will be.

There is no expectation that Christian ethics should appeal to a non-Christian. Third, the church is primary in that its moral success or failure—or as Hauerwas would say, its holiness or lack thereof—is not to be measured by whether or not it makes the world a better, or even more just, place. Rather, "the first social task of the church is to be the church" (1983: xviii), to exist as a contrast-society to the world. Theology and ethics are not separable for Hauerwas; theology has "an inherently practical character" because "Christian convictions are by nature meant to form and illumine lives" (1983: xvi–xvii). The faithful church displays the meaning of Christian grammar.

I have summarized Hauerwas's approach in a manner that I think he would approve and other theologically trained ethicists would recognize. However, analytic philosophers will find this summary opaque. It is just not clear whether Hauerwas is a cognitivist or noncognitivist about moral semantics, or a naturalist or nonnaturalist about what grounds moral facts. It is not clear whether he is making metaethical or normative claims. And so on. Hauerwas could make all this clearer. He is, after all, well versed in analytic philosophical ethics. The Oxford ordinary language philosophers, especially G. E. M. Anscombe and J. L. Austin, were hugely influential on the development of Hauerwas's thinking. Yet he appears to see the kind of clarity sought by analytic philosophers as a temptation. He observes that it became hard for theologians to be thought of as doing ethics once "the carefully wrought articles by analytic philosophers became the model for how to 'do ethics'." "I do not wish to be misunderstood," he continues, "I am deeply indebted to the analytic tradition, but it is nonetheless true that the analytic style can become an end in itself in a way that inhibits richer forms of discourse" (1997: 74).

What exactly is the claim here? Is it just a stylistic claim about how analytic philosophers' penchant for symbolic logic and thorough precisification of definitions makes tedious what should be exciting? I am not sure, but I suspect Hauerwas is worried about something more substantive, namely, about the way that analytic philosophy is perpetually pulled away from the particular to the abstract. It is not the case, as is sometimes alleged, that he is anti-theory. He is too astute to think that one can simply leave theory behind. But he is wary of the trend among Christian analytic philosophers to remain at the level of theory construction and avoid the rough ground of particulars. He, by contrast, has written extensively on so-called applied ethics, focusing particularly on the ethics of disability (1986) and the ethics of war (2011). When writing on these issues, however, his focus remains on the difference Christianity makes to the way the issue is framed.

The same is true of arguably the second-most prominent contemporary theological ethicist, Oliver O'Donovan. He also is engaged in what Wells and Quash call "ecclesial ethics" (2010) insofar as he too thinks that Christians have privileged epistemic access to moral truth. "Christian ethics must arise from the gospel of Jesus Christ. Otherwise it could not be *Christian* ethics" (1986: 11). And like Hauerwas, he has written much on applied ethical issues including war (2003) and the ethics of procreation (1984). There are clear differences between O'Donovan and Hauerwas—creation and resurrection are the central categories for O'Donovan whereas the cross is central to Hauerwas, the role of the Holy Spirit in moral psychology is more pronounced in O'Donovan, and so on—but from the perspective of Christian analytic approaches to ethics, their similarities are far more striking. Both write as though the category of "Christian ethics" is not only intelligible but also required by the Christian proclamation.

The other major trend in contemporary theological ethics is what Wells and Quash (2010) call "subversive ethics." Such ethics combines the Hegelian and Marxist view that oppressed social locations provide privileged access to moral truth with the prophetic strand of Christian scripture that indicates God's special concern for the poor, the widow, and other socially marginalized groups. Subversive ethics among contemporary theological ethicists is indebted to liberation theology, a movement that sought to free Christian theology from its captivity to colonialist, racist, and patriarchal "logics." Major forerunners of contemporary subversive ethics are Gustavo Gutiérrez's (1988) class-based liberation theology, James Cone's (1986) race-based liberation theology, and Mary Daly's (1985) and Rosemary Radford Ruether's (1993) gender-based liberation theologies. Current trends in subversive ethics focus in addition on the marginalization of a broad array of gender, sexual orientation, and disability identities and on the perceived anthropocentrism driving the ecological crisis.

A glance at the table of contents of either *Studies in Christian Ethics* or the *Journal of Religious Ethics*—the two leading outlets for theological ethics scholarship—will confirm that this trend is now dominant. Most of the articles deal with some form of marginalization or with the ecological crisis. This shared concern, however, masks some fundamental differences in approach. Consider, for example, the difference between Cone's black liberation theology and what Jonathan Tran (2012) calls "the new black theology." For Cone, the theological tradition as a whole and even large swaths of scripture (like Paul) are disposable since they are insufficiently attuned to the suffering of the oppressed. Black liberation theology therefore must look beyond scripture and the Christian tradition to find resources for displaying the black experience of God. For Cone, this means relying heavily on the blues and the African-American literary tradition. By contrast, the new black theology—notably Jay Cameron Carter (2008) and Willie Jennings (2010)—attempts to display how a recovery of scripture and premodern Christian tradition exposes the heretical nature of supposedly mainstream Christian theology. In other words, within subversive ethics there are opposed views about whether and to what extent Christian orthodoxy should be centered. Still, what the movement shares in common is a penchant for on-the-ground applied ethical thinking with particular concern for the damage done to the earth and its creatures by Christianity's modern captivity to straight, white, colonizing, European men.

III. ANALYTIC THEOLOGICAL ETHICS

To this point AT has been focused predominantly on theological metaphysics. For evidence in support of that claim, peruse the table of contents of this volume or of any issue to date of the *Journal of Analytic Theology*. Perhaps this is due to a prejudice that continues to view theological ethics as downstream from true theology. Or perhaps the explanation is that analytic philosophy itself came to ethics late. Analytic philosophy begins with Bertrand Russell and G. E. Moore at Cambridge at the beginning of the twentieth century; however, despite G. E. Moore's 1903 *Principia Ethica*, ethics was out of the mainstream of analytic philosophy until the 1960s (Schwartz 2012: xii). Although ethics is now a vibrant subfield within analytic philosophy, it continues to be thought of as less definitive of the ethos of analytic philosophy than are metaphysics and epistemology.

However, AT could provide opportunities for Christian analytic philosophers or for analytically minded Christian theologians to do ethics as Christians and for Christians. I am attracted to the minimalist definition of AT given by Michael Rea, for whom AT is "just the activity of approaching theological topics with the ambitions of an analytic philosopher and in a style that conforms to the prescriptions that are distinctive of analytic philosophical discourse" (2009: 7). If AT is to be distinguishable from analytic philosophy of religion, a good bit of weight will need to be put on what counts as a theological topic. The survey I have offered of contemporary ethics done by Christians has directed attention to the fact that theologically trained ethicists do ethics in a way clearly oriented by Christian theology. Moreover, theologically trained ethicists frequently do ethics in a manner that could actually be action-guiding for Christians. But these deeply theological approaches to ethics are rarely characterized by the kind of precision and rigor that analytically minded philosophers and theologians can bring. It would be a good thing, I believe, if analytically minded philosophers and theologians took up the tasks of what I have called, following Wells and Quash, ecclesial ethics and subversive ethics.

This is beginning to happen already. In "Toward an Analytic Theology of Liberation," a chapter of an edited collection entitled *Voices from the Edge: Centering Marginalized Perspectives in Analytic Theology*, Sameer Yadav observes that there is "no discernible strand of AT that contributes centrally to the current state of black or womanist theologies, more critical and revisionary feminist theologies, queer theologies, or any other radical social and political theologies." He proposes that this is because proponents of AT see liberation theology as "an enterprise aimed at the moral or ethical consequences of Christian theology rather than as theology per se." He argues, however, that this is precisely to miss liberation theology's challenge to mainstream theology. Liberation theology is not merely suggesting that theologians should *also* be concerned about matters of oppression. Rather, liberation theology reveals the impoverishment of the vision of human flourishing that lies back of the theory construction typical of mainstream theology. In any discipline, even the so-called hard sciences, what demands theorization and what theories get constructed and chosen are matters that are responsive to concerns about the human good. In other words, Yadav argues that the continuing dismissal of liberation theology is emblematic of the continuing inability to see that there is no distinction between theology and ethics.

In the same volume, Kevin Timpe has a chapter entitled "Defiant Afterlife," in which he develops a Christian ethics of disability by thinking through eschatological questions about perfected human bodies. His is an applied ethics of disability that is dependent upon Christian theology for its intelligibility. *Voices from the Edge*, along with another edited collection entitled *The Lost Sheep in Philosophy of Religion* (Timpe and Hereth 2019) together mark the beginning of a welcome movement within AT to engage in subversive ethics from a distinctively Christian perspective.

Thomas Crisp provides another example of the kind of theological ethics that should take place under the banner of AT. He describes his forthcoming book, *Into Shalom: An Ethics of Radical Discipleship*, as analytic Anabaptist ethics. Chapters of the book include "Jesus and Affluence," "Love and Borders," and "Jesus and Markets." He describes the chapters of his book as a mixture of analytic philosophy, scripture exegesis, and biblical theology, and he wonders whether such a strange combination can find a readership. I think, however, that people who want to do Christian ethics analytically will have to cross such disciplinary boundaries in just this way. Theologically trained ethicists borrow freely from philosophy (usually Continental philosophy), cultural studies, biblical studies, and so on. It is time that analytic philosophers begin to return the favor and adopt a more courageous attitude toward interacting with other disciplines.

Finally, my book in the Oxford Studies in Analytic Theology series, entitled *Humility, Pride, and Christian Virtue Theory* (2019), is an attempt to display how analytic philosophers could think more theologically about the virtues. I provide an account of the virtue of humility, and the vice of pride, that makes no sense abstracted from a set of Christian theological claims about the doctrine of the Trinity and the meaning of the cross and resurrection of Jesus. Whether or not the argument is successful, it displays, I hope, how *any* rich account of the virtues depends upon assumptions about human nature and destiny that are typically suppressed. I question why the best contemporary virtue theorists, many of whom are Christian, continue to offer accounts of the virtues that would be acceptable to just anyone. Remember that early Christian virtue was offensive to pagan moral sensibilities, depending as it did on a story about a crucified and resurrected peasant. I challenge Christian virtue theorists to reclaim earlier modes of Christian moral thought in which the virtues were windows into the peculiarity of what Christians believe about the crucified and resurrected Lord.

That such projects are happening under the auspices of AT is, I think, an exciting sign. Although the first decade of AT was devoted largely to theological metaphysics, perhaps the next decade will see a flowering of theological ethics done in a manner that can help Christians identify the difference Christ makes to the way they may live.

References

Adams, R. (1999), *Finite and Infinite Goods*, Oxford: Oxford University Press.
Carter, J. C. (2008), *Race*, Oxford: Oxford University Press.
Chignell, A., T. Cuneo, and M. Halteman, eds. (2015), *Philosophy Comes to Dinner*, New York: Routledge.
Crisp, T. (unpublished), *Into Shalom: An Ethics of Radical Discipleship*.
Cone, J. (1986), *A Black Theology of Liberation*, Maryknoll, NY: Orbis Books.
Daly, M. (1985), *Beyond God the Father*, Boston: Beacon Press.
Darwall, S., A. Gibbard, and P. Railton (1992), "Toward Fin de siècle Ethics: Some Trends," *Philosophical Review*, 101 (1): 115–89.
Dunnington, K. (2019), *Humility, Pride, and Christian Virtue Theory*, Oxford: Oxford University Press.
Evans, C. S. (2013), *God and Moral Obligation*, Oxford: Oxford University Press.
Finnis, J. (1980), *Natural Law and Natural Rights*, Oxford: Oxford University Press.
Gutiérrez, G. (1988), *A Theology of Liberation*, London: SCM Press.
Hare, J. (2015), *God's Command*, Oxford: Oxford University Press.
Hauerwas, S. (1983), *The Peaceable Kingdom*, Notre Dame, IN: Notre Dame University Press.
Hauerwas, S. (1986), *Suffering Presence*, Notre Dame, IN: Notre Dame University Press.
Hauerwas, S. (1997), "Christian Ethics in America (and the JRE): A Report on a Book I Will Not Write," *Journal of Religious Ethics*, 25 (3): 57–76.
Hauerwas, S. (2011), *War and the American Difference*, Grand Rapids, MI: Baker Academic.
Jennings, W. (2010), *The Christian Imagination*, New Haven: Yale University Press.
MacIntyre, A. (1999), *Dependent Rational Animals*, Peru, IL: Open Court.
Moore, M. (1996), "Good without God," in R. George (ed.), *Natural Law, Liberalism, and Morality*, Oxford: Oxford University Press.
Murphy, M. (2001), *Natural Law and Practical Rationality*, New York: Cambridge University Press.
Murphy, M. (2011a), "The Natural Law Tradition in Ethics," in *The Stanford Encyclopedia of Philosophy*. Available online: https://plato.stanford.edu/entries/natural-law-ethics/.
Murphy, M. (2011b), *God and Moral Law*, Oxford: Oxford University Press.

Murphy, M. (2012), "Theological Voluntarism," in *The Stanford Encyclopedia of Philosophy*. Available online: https://plato.stanford.edu/entries/voluntarism-theological/.
O'Donovan, O. (1984), *Begotten or Made?*, Oxford: Oxford University Press.
O'Donovan, O. (1986), *Resurrection and the Moral Order*, Grand Rapids: Eerdmans.
O'Donovan, O. (2003), *The Just War Revisited*, Cambridge: Cambridge University Press.
Porter, J. (2005), *Nature as Reason*, Grand Rapids: Eerdmans.
Quinn, P. (1978), *Divine Commands and Moral Requirements*, Oxford: Oxford University Press.
Rea, M. (2009), "Introduction," in O. D. Crisp and M. Rea (eds.), *Analytic Theology*, Oxford: Oxford University Press.
Ruether, R. (1993), *Sexism and God Talk*, Boston: Beacon Press.
Schwartz, S. (2012), *A Brief History of Analytic Philosophy*, West Sussex: Wiley-Blackwell.
Stump, E. (2012), *Wandering in Darkness*, Oxford: Oxford University Press.
Timpe, K. (2020), "Defiant Afterlife: Disability and Uniting Ourself to God," in M. Panchuk and M. Rea (eds.), *Voices from the Edge: Centering Marginalized Perspectives in Analytic Theology*, Oxford: Oxford University Press.
Timpe, K., and B. Hereth, eds. (2019), *The Lost Sheep in Philosophy of Religion*, New York: Routledge.
Tran, J. (2012), "The New Black Theology: Retrieving Ancient Sources to Challenge Racism," *The Christian Century*, January 26. Available online: https://www.christiancentury.org/article/2012-01/new-black-theology.
Wells, S. and Quash, B. (2010), *Introducing Christian Ethics*, West Sussex: Wiley-Blackwell.
Wolterstorff, N. (2010), *Justice*, Princeton: Princeton University Press.
Yadav, S. (2020), "Toward an Analytic Theology of Liberation," in M. Panchuk and M. Rea (eds.), *Voices from the Edge: Centering Marginalized Perspectives in Analytic Theology*, Oxford: Oxford University Press.
Zagzebski, L. (2002), "The Incarnation and Virtue Ethics," in S. Davis, D. Kendall S.J., and G. O'Collins S.J. (eds.), *The Incarnation*, Oxford: Oxford University Press.
Zagzebski, L. (2004), *Divine Motivation Theory*, Cambridge: Cambridge University Press.

CHAPTER TWENTY-SEVEN

Willie Jennings on the Supersessionist Pathology of Race: A Differential Diagnosis

SAMEER YADAV

I. RACISM: A THEOLOGICAL DIAGNOSIS

Few Christian theologians, I suspect, would deny that American (and more broadly Western European) Christianity has in the past had a race problem consisting in race-based advantages and disadvantages favoring whites over non-whites. Nor would most deny that despite civil rights legislation and attempts at church reforms our race problem lingers and remains "unfixed"—the life of the church still exhibits phenomena of racial segregation, race-based hierarchy, and implicit bias that are similar (and in some cases worse) to that found in wider secular society (Emerson and Smith 2001; Hawkins 2013; Blum and Harvey 2014; Hill-Fletcher 2017). The more difficult question is just how to theologically analyze and explain our race problem. What do we Christians suppose explains the manifestations of racism that infect, disease, and disfigure the body of Christ? While a theological diagnosis of our malady might easily take us to a doctrine of sin, we confront several further questions. Are the various manifestations of racism in Christian social life extrinsic or intrinsic to that life? That is, do such manifestations arise more basically from influences internal to Christian community that define it as such (i.e., *endogenous* influences), or from influences external and incidental to its form of life (i.e. from *exogenous* influences)? Should we diagnose the sin of racism as more fundamentally personal or social, that is, does it reduce more basically to a problem with the configuration of the dispositions of individuals, or the configuration of our social arrangements (whether secular or ecclesial)? Finally, there remains a question about how Christians should theologically characterize the wrong-making features of racism in virtue of which we ought to regard it a sin. Is the wrong-making feature of racism most fundamentally practical—a matter of some (exogenous or endogenous) influences uniquely deforming us personally through corrupting our wills or socially through corrupting our social structures and practices? Or, are the wrong-making features of racism also ineliminably noetic and doxastic, a matter of deformity in either individual mental function or the collective acceptances and rationales inherent in our social arrangements?

When theologians relegate questions of race and racism to matters of applied ethics—far downstream of the tasks of doctrinal formulation belonging to topics like the Trinity, Incarnation, or Atonement in the order of theological explanation—this is because they either explicitly or implicitly diagnose racism as either exogenous to Christian social life (and hence not a proper topic for theological reflection on Christianity *per se*) or, if endogenous to it, merely as a matter of practical rather than doctrinal reform. Thus, it may indeed be that European and American Christianity have a race problem, and further perhaps that problem indeed imposes upon us demands of theological reasoning not only about the dangers of secular malformation but also about some uniquely Christian malformations. Even so, the relevant kind of reasoning is not an inquiry into what we ought to believe *qua* Christian but rather an inquiry into what we ought to think, say, and do in virtue of what we believe *qua* Christian. On a theologically practical conception of racism, our reasoning about the personal or social sins of racism moves outward from strictly doctrinal commitments that can be (or already have been) worked out by Christian theologians independently of any considerations about race or racism. In that case, any diagnosis of our race problem is consistent with a perfectly well-formed theological anthropology. If, for example, the various forms of racism that we Christians perpetuate among ourselves are explicable in terms of personal sin, then our remediation is a matter of determining how some particularly racist dispositions violate the practical demands of our doctrine of the *imago Dei*,[1] which we can take to imply human equality and dignity whether racism existed or not as one particular way of falling afoul of that doctrine.

If our manifestations of racism are, on the other hand, more fundamentally explicable in terms of social sin, then the nature of that sin and its remedy will likewise derive from a doctrine of ecclesial or more broadly human peoplehood that of itself makes no essential reference to race or racism. The sin of racism is just one way of violating an ecclesiological doctrine of Christians as a kind of renewed human community that promotes and exhibits the joining together of all peoples in the one social body of the church. A theologically social diagnosis and remediation of racism would consist in a practical outworking of, for example, an inaugurated eschatology in which church-as-multicultural community strives to become in the present a foretaste of the future reconciliation of "every tribe, tongue and nation" (Rev. 7:9) with racism as one contingently identifiable obstacle to that outworking in our context. In neither case, however, is a personal or social diagnosis and proposed path of remediation for Christian racism a task for systematic or dogmatic theologians as such. Rather, it can only appear to be a matter for Christian ethicists, as well as pastors and laity concerned with anti-racism in spiritual formation and church governance.

It might be, however, that the symptoms of racism manifest in Christian communities and institutions are not only endogenous and practical but also noetic and doxastic. More specifically, it might be that the disease of racism that infects Christian social reality stems from a doctrinal rather than merely a practical infection. While mainstream liberation theologies and recent work being dubbed the "new black theology" (Tran 2012; Teel 2017)

---

[1] It remains a popular Christian stance to suppose racism is merely a failure to practically live out the scope of ethical demand already implied in a traditional doctrine of the *imago Dei*. For a paradigmatic example of how this reasoning goes, see, e.g., Archbishop Harry Flynn's pastoral letter on racism to the St. Paul diocese, "In God's Image: Pastoral Letter on Racism" (Flynn 2003).

have argued for precisely this view, it has not received any critical attention from analytic theologians.[2] Rather than speculating about why that is so, this chapter will focus on Willie James Jennings's recent influential doctrinal account of Christian racism. In *The Christian Imagination: Theology and the Origins of Race*, Jennings argues that contemporary Christian and secular racism alike in our society originate in—and continue to be sustained by—distorted notions of peoplehood and group belonging that are deeply endogenous to the social vision of Christian ecclesiology in the European theological tradition.[3] The primary locus of doctrinal malformation that Jennings diagnoses as the source of this "diseased Christian social imagination" is our implicit and explicit collective acceptance of "supersessionism" (Jennings 2010: 7):[4] the view that one people (Christians) have in some way superseded, replaced or supplanted another (Israel) as God's chosen race to bring salvation to the world. The supersessionist conception of Christian supremacy and privilege nurtured within European social and political life developed into a naturalized and biologized conception of white supremacy during the period of Christian Europe's colonial expansion in the sixteenth to nineteenth centuries. The various forms of white privilege that continue to predominate in secular and Christian social life remain infected with the racializing (and racist) inner logic of Christian supersessionism (Jennings 2010).[5] Jennings's point is not that racism is *exclusively* a doctrinal problem. His claim is rather that supersessionist doctrinal commitments are a necessary constituent in an explanation of the racism exhibited in our society, not that supersessionism is of itself sufficient for such an explanation. Jennings's prescribed remedy for the symptoms of racism in the church, therefore, necessarily includes the work of uprooting its *doctrinal* dependence on the offending supersessionist disease afflicting our theological anthropology (Jennings 2010: 36).

My aim in this chapter shall not be to assess whether Jennings's diagnosis and remedy are correct. Instead, my argument will be that his proposed doctrinal diagnosis and remedy for racism remain insufficiently specific to be properly assessed for their correctness. Jennings's diagnosis of a problematic doctrine of Christian supersession hides many distinct possible diagnoses and remedies that are in some ways mutually incompatible pathologies. Compare: "autoimmune arthritis" does not name any one single pathology. Instead, it is an umbrella term for many, each of which might exhibit similar symptoms that result from different biological mechanisms and accordingly respond to different treatments. To be told that the inflammatory pain in one's connective tissue is due to (some sort of) immune system dysfunction and is best treated with (some sort of) anti-inflammatory medication is insufficient in its specificity; it is a merely *differential* diagnosis. Properly understanding and treating one's disease is better served knowing precisely *which* autoimmune arthritis one has (rheumatoid arthritis? ankylosing spondylitis?). A rheumatologist's ability to identify and target a more specific disease pathology in order to commend suitable treatment, moreover, owes in large measure to the diagnostic

---

[2] For an analysis of and critique of the failure of analytic theology to take up an engagement with liberation theology, see Yadav (2020).
[3] There have also been important accounts of racism as doctrinally rooted in malformations of Christian teaching about the *imago*. See Teel (2010).
[4] J. Kameron Carter (2008) likewise focuses on supersessionism as a ground of modern racism and racial identity.
[5] As Vincent Lloyd and Andrew Prevot rightly suggest: "If the problem is fundamentally about theology infected by supersessionist heresy, then fixing theology should fix anti-blackness, but of course that is too simple" (2017: xxiii).

tools available to pinpoint more specific mechanisms of disease: sophisticated blood tests, radiographic imaging, and so on.

Similarly, in what follows, I draw on the tools developed by recent analytic philosophical work on social group ontology that can help us to differentiate within Jennings's proposal many more specific and incompatible diagnoses of Christian supersessionism, and many correspondingly different sorts of remedies for rehabilitating an appropriately anti-racist Christian doctrine of peoplehood. In the next section, I will offer a brief elaboration of Jennings's thesis about the racializing problem of supersessionism and his proposed amelioration of that problem. I will then go on to identify three distinct ways of construing the racializing mechanism he finds in supersessionism. More carefully refining Jennings's diagnosis by way of these distinctions places important constraints on the task of revising a Christian doctrine of peoplehood in the direction of an anti-racist theological anthropology. Future work on diagnosing and treating "the" problem of supersessionism, therefore, can proceed by first seeking to establish *which* sort of supersessionism is at issue.

II. JENNINGS ON SUPERSESSIONISM AS THE RACIST PATHOLOGY OF WESTERN CHRISTIANITY

Construed in the most general way, a doctrine of Christian supersession or "replacement theology" just claims that the church in some sense supersedes (i.e., replaces, supplants) Israel as the elect people of God in the divine economy of redemption (Caird 1994: 55; Soulen 1996: 1–2). A careful reading of Jennings suggests that he does not take Christian supersessionism *per se* to be a (proto)racist doctrine. There is, Jennings acknowledges, at least some sense in which Jesus's reimagining of Israel as a shared community of Jew and Gentile gathered around himself as Israel's Messiah—what came to be called "church"— does indeed supersede previous conceptions of who and what Israel is. God chose the people of Israel to embody and mediate God's offer of redemption to the non-Israelite (i.e., Gentile) world. As such, Israel is a representation of "humanity in the presence of God" (Jennings 2010: 256). Jesus as Israel's Messiah gives us a normative conception of the true purpose of Israel, insofar as his life, death and resurrection embodies or "incarnates" the Torah and reveals Israel's vision of redeemed human life in God's presence (Jennings 2010: 256). The intended aim of a reimagined Israel formed around Jesus at its center is a renewed human community: the joining together of Jewish and Gentile life in one new social body called "church" that exists to fulfill God's original redemptive purpose for Israel. The church Jesus envisions and over which Jesus presides post ascension and Pentecost is thus a new humanity gathered around his embodiment of Torah, reconciled to one another, embodying new life together in shared space and in the presence of God through the work of the Spirit. According to Jennings, therefore, Christians *qua* Christian hold that in the church the old enmity between Jewish and Gentile peoples is superseded by their joining a single community of both Jew and Gentile around the living work and word of Jesus as Israel's Messiah. "If there is a moment at the heart of Christianity in which something is superseded," he thus concedes, "it may be found precisely here" (Jennings 2010: 272).

If this proposed healthy form of Christian supersessionism consists in the replacement of Jewish/Gentile division with a reconciled joining of peoples, then what does Jennings identify as a supersessionist *pathology*—the doctrinal malignancy that he takes to have metastasized into European and American white supremacy? Jennings diagnoses a malformed supersessionist doctrine according to at least three characteristic symptoms. First, it conceives of Jewish ethnic particularity as a natural and fixed aboriginal human kind distinguished from other human kinds by ancestry and place. Non-Christian Gentiles are likewise conceived of on analogy from Jews as naturally distinct kinds of peoples delimited and individuated by place. A pathological supersessionism not only conceives of the Jew/Gentile distinction in terms of natural human kinds divided by geography and ancestry, but conceives of the non-Christian ethnic particularities of Jewish and Gentile life as *ideologically* limited in time and place, and as such *inferior* to a more universal social vision (Jennings 2010: 96–7). A second complementary feature of a pathological supersessionism is to regard Christian social existence as a kind of ethnic universality that supersedes these undesirable limits of non-Christian Jewish and Gentile ethnic particularity. Christian peoplehood is superior to non-Christian peoplehood because Christians embody a form of life that "travels" and can—and ought to be—realized everywhere by everyone. This universal way of life prized by Christians may be recognized as always only imperfectly and partially realized by actual Christian communities, but the abstract ideal of Christian universality in faith and practice is nevertheless a largely established or already-achieved Christian possession, capable of translation or discovery among any given people (Jennings 2010: 165–6). Third, since the "church has replaced Israel as the bearer of the true vision of the true God, and all those outside the church are pagan" (Jennings 2010: 97), the Christian task of mediating redemption to non-Christian peoples becomes the task of displacing and alienating the particularity of non-Christian indigenous ways of life. The church thus seeks to supersede the "merely localized" social imaginations and forms of life exhibited by non-Christians by assimilating peoples and places into the maps and ways of life countenanced in and by the church, thus extending its own universalized social imagination. By assimilation into the universal form of human life preached (according to already-established theological canons of correctness) and embodied (albeit imperfectly) by the church, non-Christians may join (or be joined to) the kingdom of God. The supersessionist disease Jennings diagnoses can thus be summarized as consisting in the naturalizing of non-Christian Jewish and Gentile ethnic identity, the universalizing of Christian ethnic identity, and an assimilative model of communal joining.

Construed in this way, Jennings's interpretation of a pathological Christian supersessionism names a naturalized sort of religious ethnocentrism in which the Jew/Gentile/Christian distinction carves human social reality at the joints and privileges Christian over non-Christian groups as a paradigm of human being and belonging. As a matter of historical accident, the Gentile-dominated Christian church that nurtured a supersessionist ecclesiology and social vision happened to find dominant expression in imperial Roman and then Western European societies. Biological and pseudoscientific taxonomies of bodies and bloodlines subsequently became convenient vehicles for the supersessionist impetus to naturalize inferior Jewish and non-Christian ethnic identities in terms of "races" (Jennings 2010: 36).[6] Whiteness—consisting not in any bare facts about skin color but rather as a socially recognized complex of meanings tied to skin color—accordingly emerged as the universalizing lens of a supersessionist Christian

---

[6]The idea that Christianity played a defining role in the invention of racial identity in the Western world does not originate with Jennings. For some historical treatments defending that claim, see, e.g., Buell (2009) and Heng (2018). For a brief summary of recent scholarship suggesting the Christian social and historical contribution to racism along with an assessment of the philosophical and theological implications of a religious genealogy of race, see Yadav (2019).

human social ideal that arrogates to itself the vocation of mediating God's rule and redemptive incorporation into the church via its established (white) Christian cultural norms (Jennings 2010: 59).[7] The colonial project of abstracting people from place and assimilating non-European others into Christian society by exploitatively incorporating them into the European social order was the historically contingent means by which European Christians executed their supersessionist vision of communal joining. On Jennings's diagnosis, however, the disease of whiteness and its "mangling" of human intimacy by imposition of a racial scale on human belonging is like the diseased flesh deadened by leprosy. Just as the leprous flesh is merely the contingent "facilitating reality" or medium through which a mycobacterium has managed to manifest itself, so too white supremacy—whether in its colonial or contemporary forms—is the medium through which an underlying Christian logic of supersessionism has managed to infect our societies (Jennings 2010: 275).

Jennings concludes that the contemporary Western church's infection with a (white) racialized ethnocentrism is thus reducible to a distorted conception of the kind of union between Jew and Gentile accomplished by Jesus. Jesus's proposal about who is host and who is guest have become reversed, such that a traditionally white Gentile Christianity no longer needed to rely on Jesus as the facilitator for their "overhearing" the conversation between God and Israel (Jennings 2010: 263). Rather than retaining their role as *invited guest* at Israel's table, the Gentile church has racialized Israel, colonized her as rightful heir of her heritage, strip-mined her scriptures and ways of life, appropriated her divine promises as ours by divine right, and left her behind in unilaterally setting the terms for redemptive relationship with her God as a divinely appointed gatekeeper for all peoples— Jew and Gentile. The proposed remedy that Jennings recommends for Christians who continue to harbor this diseased social vision is a "return to the original relationship of Jews and Gentiles blocked by the advent of whiteness" (Jennings 2010: 275). This includes a return of white Gentile Christianity to a posture of vulnerable dependence upon Jesus to turn us toward not only biblical but also *living* Israel—contemporary Jewish life in all its diversity and complexity insofar as "the church is always turned toward Israel by its very life" (Jennings 2010: 274). All Gentile forms of life—all our national, ethnic, religious or racial projects and strivings—are subject to reconciled and redeemed relationship to God only insofar as they are brought into relationship with Jewish life by the living appeal to Jesus as Jew who mediates the terms of joining. Jesus brings us to Israel conceived as a people whose relationship to their God both *represents* Gentile ethnic striving for identity and belonging, and *ruptures* all Gentile forms of ethnic striving in order to bring about "church" as a form of Gentile incorporation into Israel—the people of God. A Christian form of union between Jew and Gentile does not occur by way of imposing the demand to assimilate to any already-achieved and settled form of life, but by a negotiation of identity defined by mutual submission and the desire for shared belonging (Jennings 2010: 273). Jennings finds a modern social performance of this "new cultural politic" in the relationship of the Gentile and Jewish life represented in the history of sociopolitical, literary, and exilic kinship between Jewish and black life

---

[7]There is a large body of philosophical literature debating the question of whether racial identity constitutes a natural kind or a social kind, but the latter is by far the more dominant position, both in the philosophy of race and in sociological theories of race and racism (Taylor 2013). For the two most prominent sociological frameworks for defining "whiteness" as a social construct, see Feagin's "framing" analysis (2013) and Omi and Winant's "racial formation theory" (2015).

in America (Jennings 2010: 275–86). Modeling the faith and practices of the church upon this alternative vision of Jewish/Gentile union that Jesus mediates, Jennings claims, is the only treatment with which the church can stave off the supersessionist disease of whiteness that afflicts it.

On Jennings's diagnosis, a modern colonialist doctrine of Christian supersessionism forms a theological, doxastic, and constitutive ground of a contemporary racist social imagination. Supersessionism is a *theological* ground insofar as it expresses the structure of God's relationship to humanity. It is a *doxastic* ground insofar as it names a set of belief-forming practices relative to Christian thinking about God's relation to human peoples, as well as the outputs of those practices. Those outputs include not only beliefs about what sorts of peoples there are and how they relate to one another and to God, but also what Tamar Gendler has called *aliefs*—implicit dispositional attitudes that are belief-like but automatic and that can even exist in tension with explicitly held beliefs (Gendler 2008). Jennings appeals to Bourdieu on "disposition" and "*habitus*" to suggest that he regards supersessionism as shaping not only officially held theological views but also—and perhaps even more fundamentally—racist doctrinal alief commitments or acceptances in Gendler's sense, even when these are held in tension with avowedly anti-racist beliefs (Jennings 2010: 7, 104, 313 n. 100).[8] Finally, by framing his argument with his own experiences of the failure of contemporary attempts at Christian cross-racial intimacy (in the introduction) and a proposal for revising contemporary Christian ecclesiology to ameliorate its infection with a colonialist supersessionism (in the final chapter), Jennings suggests that the significance of a colonial supersessionist disease is not merely historical. It is not just that a colonialist understanding of Jewish/Gentile union historically *prompted* the creation of hierarchical racial identities and their distorted relations of intimacy and belonging. Rather, he takes that colonialist understanding to *constitute* or *figure into* our contemporary ecclesiological beliefs and aliefs.[9]

III. SUPERSESSIONISM: A DIFFERENTIAL DIAGNOSIS

But even if one agrees with Jennings's diagnosis of supersessionism as a theological, doxastic, and constitutive ground of our racially diseased Christian social imagination, this is insufficient to constitute an identification of the disease-mechanism that afflicts us. The wrong-making features of racism conveyed by supersessionism are features of social kinds or categories—features of human groupings and relations that in some way depend on human subject attitudes, rather than nonsocial natural kinds or categories like chemical elements, which do not (Mason 2016). Still, there are several distinct ways for subject attitudes to figure into the construction of human social groups, and if we seek to ameliorate some subset of these attitudes as undesirable features of our social arrangements, then we will need to know *which* among these possible ways the offending

---

[8]Gendler's notion offers one way of analyzing Jennings's appropriation of Bourdieu on the "scholastic disposition" as a feature of supersessionist ideology.
[9]My distinguishing between X as a non-constitutive historical ground of some social artifact Y and X as a constitutive ground of that artifact is another way of negotiating the kind of distinction that Brian Epstein has in mind when he distinguishes between the social history that puts in place the identity conditions constitutive of a social group (its "anchors"), and those identity conditions themselves (its "grounds"). See Epstein (2016). Epstein seems to strictly distinguish between anchoring and grounding, while others identify anchors as a species of grounds (Shaffer forthcoming).

attitudes actually figure into the construction of the relevant groups. Thus, if Jennings is correct in holding that supersessionist belief or alief attitudes continue to plague contemporary Christian social arrangements as the wrong-making features of the racist divisions in the church, then a clear diagnosis will need to specify precisely in what sort of way those attitudes infect the relevant social bodies.

Muhammad Ali Khalidi (2015) has recently offered a taxonomy of "three kinds of social kinds" according to the different ways that subject attitudes might figure in the constitution of a social kind or category. Khalidi distinguishes between types of social categories depending on how they answer to two determinations: (a) Does the category's *existence* depend on any subjective attitudes? (b) Does *belonging* to the category depend on any subjective attitudes? Type 1 social categories answer "no" to both (while nevertheless depending on subjective attitudes toward other things). Type 2 answers "yes" to (a) and "no" to (b), and Type 3 answers "yes" to both (Khalidi 2015: 103–4) If Christians ought to regard the wrong-making feature of the racism that infects our communities as a matter of exemplifying the social property of "being supersessionist" and thus falling under that social category, then what sort of social category is it, on the Khalidi scale? Analyzing our supersessionism in terms of one type rather than another has some important consequences not only for the kind of social reality "supersessionism" names, but also for how we ought to go about uprooting it or ameliorating its symptoms in our communities. But while contending for a theory of supersessionism as one type of social disease rather than another is therefore an important task for theologians to take up, in what follows I will only offer a differential diagnosis, sketching one possible way that we might respectively characterize supersessionism as a Type 3, 2, or 1 ecclesiological infection of the Christian social body.

On a Type 3 conception, a white colonial supersessionism refers to supersessionist *subject attitudes* among Western (?) Christians as a characteristic feature of their Christian identity or self-understanding. In that case, an accurate diagnosis of the manifestations of racism in Christian community as grounded in supersessionism would require showing that, for some individual S, the racist dispositions, attitudes or behavior exhibited by S is grounded in S's supersessionist belief or alief attitudes. For example, Ásta (2018) articulates a Type 3 account according to which for any person S to exhibit the social property of being raced just is for some persons, groups or entities with institutional authority or communal standing—under some contextually appropriate circumstances—to implicitly or explicitly *confer* a given racial status on S by way of some publicly expressed act, attitude, or behavior, in an attempt to perceptually track some set of base properties (such as bodily appearance, ancestry, culture, experience, etc.), resulting in some corresponding determination of S's agency, including their enablements, obligations, and permissions (21–2, 104).[10]

If, therefore, we wish to show on this account that supersessionism is constituent in the wrong-making meaning and effects of possessing a racial social status within a particular Christian context, then we would have to show that such a supersessionism is constituent in the perceptions or judgments of the relevant institutional and communal authorities for that context—in this case, Christian or ecclesial authorities. Making a diagnosis of a Type 3 infection of Christian community with a theological and doxastic commitment to

---

[10]Epstein (2017: 28) construes the characteristic forms of agency essential to membership in a social group as "added essentials" distinct from the identity conditions or criteria of individuation for that group.

supersessionism must therefore appeal to an evidence base consisting entirely of individual subject attitudes comprising particular institutional and communal Christian authorities and their impacts on the collective acceptance of Christians in some particular context. Likewise, the amelioration of a Type 3 supersessionist infection would reduce to the task of targeting the beliefs or aliefs of the relevant authorities in order to bring about a change in their conferral of social statuses grounded in their supersessionism and a corresponding change in the collective acceptances of those conferrals on the part of Christians.

It is also possible, however, to analyze a supersessionism as a Type 2 social property on the Khalidi scale, and hence as a feature of Christian identity that *exists* in virtue of the supersessionist beliefs and aliefs of some collection of individuals, but which may nevertheless be *instantiated* by individuals in a social group independently of whether everyone (or perhaps everyone) in that group holds supersessionist beliefs or aliefs (Khalidi 2015: 100–1). For example, on Haslanger's analysis of race as a social category, the property of being raced is a social status one exhibits in virtue of the *social position* one occupies in a complex set of social arrangements (Haslanger 2012: 235–8). The wrong-making features of the racism that essentially characterize modern racial identities are, or necessarily include, the hierarchical structures of society as a whole that configure advantages and disadvantages along racial lines whether or not any of the individuals with institutional authority or communal standing hold any racist aliefs or beliefs (Haslanger 2017). On the contrary, whereas on Ásta's Type 3 theory structural features of racism must be reducible to the individual subject attitudes of individuals who confer social statuses (2018: 28), Haslanger's Type 2 theory seems to reverse the explanatory direction. Individuals may exhibit a racist social status in the absence of any racist attitudes held by individuals in virtue of taking up positions in hierarchical social arrangements, but it might also be that those social arrangements inculcate racist aliefs and beliefs in the individuals who inhabit those arrangements (Haslanger 2017: 17).

In other words, social structures are put in place by the collective efforts of individual agents operating out of some particular set of aliefs and beliefs, but once erected, the structure of those arrangements can continue to exemplify social meanings and generate social effects that are not reducible to the collective beliefs or aliefs of the individuals responsible for putting those arrangements in place (Barnes 2017). If, therefore we wish to diagnose supersessionism as a Type 2 ground of the wrong-making feature of racism inherent in our racial categories, we should go looking not primarily at the alief and belief attitudes of Christian individuals to find the inner logic of, for example, white Gentile "hubris" (Jennings 2010: 167), assimilationist demands, and so on but rather to the structure of Christian social arrangements, the relative race-based social positions occupied by Christians, seeking to determine what it might mean for those features to be exemplified structurally by Christian communities and/or inculcated in individuals in virtue of some such structural feature. It might accordingly make more sense to target structural change as the means of ameliorating the racism of a supersessionist ecclesiology.[11]

Finally, on a Type 1 diagnosis, supersessionism is most fundamentally *neither* a matter of diseased Christian subject attitudes nor diseased Christian social arrangements erected by those who have held such attitudes (Khalidi 2015: 101–2). Rather, both the coming into being and the instantiation of supersessionism in our midst might be explicable

---

[11]This is one way to interpret Jennifer Harvey's insistence on reparations as a perquisite for "racial reconciliation" in the church (Harvey 2014).

apart from anyone's holding supersessionist beliefs or aliefs. Theodore Bach has been a prominent advocate for an analysis of social categories as Type 1 kinds modeled on the biological concept of phylogeny (Bach 2016). What defines social categories like gender or race, according to Bach, is not "phenetic"—a matter of any set of observable features held in common by raced and gendered individuals, whether features of some determinate kind of social structure or set of individual belief or alief attitudes. Instead, in much the same way that biological kinds are defined by an evolutionary mechanism—a unified lineage of replication and reproduction that can produce various organisms that in fact display different features across time, rather than by any discrete set of shared characteristics organisms have in common—so too we might regard social categories as natural kinds with a historical essence (Bach 2016: 196). But rather than having a historical essence defined by a unified lineage of *biological* replication and reproduction, social categories according to Bach have a historical essence defined by a unified lineage of *social* replication and reproduction.[12]

On a Bachian analysis, racial identities and their inherent racism in our society would most fundamentally refer not to whatever "race" means or does in virtue of any social arrangements or subject attitudes at any given period in Western history, but to an identifiable social function that explains the development of racial identity and its racist character across that history, including all the varying and mutually contrasting social meanings and effects race-thinking has exhibited over the course of that history. If we analyze a theological diagnosis of racism as supersessionist to mean that it is a Type 1 supersessionism of a Bachian sort, then we must be able to identify what it is about the wrong-making features of supersessionism that enables it to be socially replicated or reproduced in our society and Christian communities as white supremacy. A significant task for an explanation of this sort would be figuring out how to carve out the explanatory unity of Christian supersessionism that explains its manifestation as white supremacy from features belonging specifically to the white supremacist manifestation of supersessionism.[13] Just as gene therapy seeks to target the replicative mechanism for disease rather than treating the symptoms manifest in the body, so too a Bachian amelioration of Christian supersessionism would attempt to isolate and revise the supersessionist DNA of our race-based social arrangements and subject attitudes, rather than those arrangements and attitudes themselves.

IV. CONCLUSION

Each of the three ways of parsing out Jennings's supersessionist diagnosis implies a distinct kind of project of theologically analyzing, explaining, and combatting racism as grounded in a Christian doctrine of peoplehood.[14] The difference between each type of diagnosis, moreover, is not that each recognizes only one of three kinds of social phenomena—subject attitudes, structures, and social replication. Rather, they differ in the ontological and explanatory framework they employ to account for the kinds of mutual relations exhibited by all three sorts of phenomena—conferralists seeking to explain,

---

[12]For Bach's application of this view to the category of gender, see Bach (2012).
[13]For example, Hage (2017) identifies the notion of "generalized domestication" as a unified ideological principle that explains a coincidence in the historical trajectories of racial and ecological injustice.
[14]For a fuller account of the desiderata and complications of working out a theory of race and religion, see Yadav (2019).

analyze, and ameliorate supersessionist structures and patterns of development in terms of subject attitudes; structuralists seeking to do so in terms of social arrangements; and phylogenists in terms of socially replicative and reproductive processes. Of course, we might well suppose that Jennings is incorrect in diagnosing Western racism as a fundamentally theological and doxastic pathology grounded in Christian supersessionism. Still, for critics no less than advocates of his diagnosis, assessing its correctness depends on grasping its truth-conditions. Engaging with that project to either rule out or narrow down a differential diagnosis of the sort I've suggested above is just one way that analytic theologians might connect with a large and growing literature that uniquely links Western race-thinking to Christian theology.

References

Ásta (2018), *Categories We Live By: The Construction of Sex, Gender, Race and Other Social Categories*, New York: Oxford University Press.

Bach, T. (2012), "Gender is a Natural Kind with a Historical Essence," *Ethics*, 122: 231–72.

Bach, T. (2016), "Social Categories are Natural Kinds, not Objective Types (and Why it Matters Politically)," *Journal of Social Ontology*, 2 (2): 177–201.

Barnes, E. (2017), "Realism and Social Structure," *Philosophical Studies*, 174: 2417–33.

Blum, E., and P. Harvey (2014), *The Color of Christ: The Son of God and the Saga of Race in America*, Chapel Hill: UNC Press.

Buell, D. K. (2009), "Early Christian Universalism and Modern Racism," in M. Eliav-Feldon, B. Isaac, and J. Ziegler (eds.), *The Origins of Racism in the West*, 109–31, New York: Cambridge University Press.

Caird, G. B. (1994), *New Testament Theology*, Oxford: Clarendon.

Carter, J. K. (2008), *Race: A Theological Account*, New York: Oxford University Press.

Emerson, M., and C. Smith (2001), *Divided by Faith: Evangelical Religion and the Problem of Race in America*, New York: Oxford University Press.

Epstein, B. (2016), "A Framework for Social Ontology," *Philosophy of the Social Sciences*, 46 (2): 147–67.

Epstein, B. (2017), "What Are Social Groups? Their Metaphysics and How to Classify Them," *Synthese*, 196: 1–34.

Feagin, J. R. (2013), *The White Racial Frame: Centuries of Framing and Counter-Framing*, 2nd ed., New York: Routledge.

Flynn, H. J. (2003), "In God's Image: Pastoral Letter on Racism," Archdiocese of St. Paul and Minneapolis. Available online: http://www.archspm.org/pastoral_letters/gods-image-pastoral-letter-racism/.

Gendler, T. S. (2008), "Alief and Belief," *Journal of Philosophy*, 105 (10): 634–63.

Hage, G. (2017), *Is Racism an Environmental Threat?*, Malden, MA: Polity Press.

Harvey, J. (2014), *Dear White Christians: For Those Still Longing for Racial Reconciliation*, Grand Rapids, MI: Eerdmans.

Haslanger, S. (2012), *Resisting Reality*, New York: Oxford University Press.

Haslanger, S. (2017), "Race, Ideology and Social Movements," *Res Philosophica*, 94 (1): 1–22.

Hawkins, J. R., ed. (2013), *Christians and the Color Line: Race and Religion after Divided by Faith*, New York: Oxford University Press.

Heng, G. (2018), *The Invention of Race in the European Middle Ages*, Cambridge: Cambridge University Press.

Hill-Fletcher, J. (2017), *The Sin of White Supremacy: Christianity, Racism and Religious Diversity in America*, New York: Orbis.
Jennings, W. J. (2010), *The Christian Imagination: Theology and the Origins of Race*, New Haven: Yale University Press.
Khalidi, M. A. (2015), "Three Kinds of Social Kinds," *Philosophy and Phenomenological Research*, 90 (1): 96–112.
Lloyd, V., and A. Prevot, eds. (2017), *Anti-Blackness and Christian Ethics*, New York: Orbis.
Mason, R. (2016), "The Metaphysics of Social Kinds," *Philosophy Compass*, 11: 841–50.
Omi, M., and H. Winant (2015), *Racial Formation in the United States*, 3rd ed., New York: Routledge.
Shaffer, J. (forthcoming), "Anchoring as Grounding: On Epstein's The Ant Trap," *Philosophy and Phenomenological Research*.
Soulen, R. K. (1996), *The God of Israel and Christian Theology*, Minneapolis: Fortress Press.
Taylor, P. (2013), *Race: A Philosophical Introduction*, 2nd ed., Malden, MA: Polity.
Teel, K. (2010), *Racism and the Image of God*, New York: Palgrave-Macmillan.
Teel, K. (2017), "The New Black Theology and the Dream of Post-Racialization," *Black Theology*, 15 (1): 3–20.
Tran, J. (2012). "The New Black Theology: Retrieving Ancient Sources to Challenge Racism," *Christian Century*. Available online: https://www.christiancentury.org/article/2012-01/new-black-theology.
Yadav, S. (2020), "Toward an Analytic Theology of Liberation," in M. Panchuk and M. C. Rea (eds.), *Voices from the Edge: Centering Marginalized Perspectives in Analytic Theology*, 47–74, Oxford: Oxford University Press, forthcoming.
Yadav, S. (2019), "Religious Racial Formation Theory and its Metaphysics: A Research Program in the Philosophy of Religion," in B. Hereth and K. Timpe (eds.), *The Lost Sheep in Philosophy of Religion*, 365–90, New York: Routledge Press.

CHAPTER TWENTY-EIGHT

Goodness, Embodiment, and Disability: Lessons from Then for Now

HILARY YANCEY

I. INTRODUCTION

In the Gospels, Jesus heals individuals on numerous occasions, often, though not always, from conditions we might today describe as physical or cognitive disability or illness. In both the philosophy and theology of disability and illness, these narratives raise rich but complex questions. Do such acts of healing—often connected to the proclamation and welcome of the kingdom of God—indicate the normative status of the conditions themselves? Does Jesus heal these individuals because their conditions are intrinsically bad? Will there be such conditions in the afterlife, if Jesus heals people in the here and now?

Such speculative reflection about afterlife embodiment might be fruitless. As Paul notes in 1 Corinthians, the bodies that will be raised will be remarkably different from our current bodies. One might argue that there is such a substantial gap between a current and a resurrected body that conclusions drawn about the one have little import for the other. Having a particular bodily condition—blindness or lower leg paralysis, cystic fibrosis (CF) or Charge syndrome—says nothing about the body that is to come. Indeed, we might even be inclined to think that the vision of the new heaven and new earth in Revelation 21 suggests that, the old one having "passed away," *would not* include such conditions. The one seated on the throne in this vision says, "I will make all things new"; we are often inclined to think that newness naturally includes some physical perfection that would exclude these conditions.

But we should not be so quick to draw those conclusions; richer reflection about resurrected embodiment—particularly so-called "impaired" resurrected bodies—is needed. Not only can such reflection help us reason about the relationship of bodies to personal identity (both identity persistence and broader self-understanding[1]), but it

---

[1] My idea here is that questions about resurrection identity can touch on both specific persistence conditions—what properties can a person gain or lose while remaining the same person—and broader self-understanding, such as what Amos Yong (2012) seems to refer to when he says that, what should persist in resurrected persons are "features that emerge from and express human identities across the lifespan" (5).

also reveals important truths about doing justice in our present, earthly communities. If Christians are called to proclaim, by word and deed, the kingdom of God, then our communities ought to reflect truths about that kingdom. As we think about Jesus's healing activities in conjunction with making sense of, and then ourselves enacting, these kingdom realities, reflection on the nature and normativity of what Richard Cross (2016) calls "bodily configurations"[2] is both natural and important.

A number of philosophers and theologians have written extensively on disability in relation to both its normative status (e.g., Nancy Eiesland (1994), Ron Amundson (2000), Anita Silvers (2003), Elizabeth Barnes (2016), and many others) and its persistence in the afterlife (e.g., Amos Yong (2009, 2012), Richard Cross (2017a,b), Kevin Timpe (2018, 2019), and others). However, a closely related concept—that of illness[3]—has not enjoyed the same kind of attention or speculation. One reason for this is that many disabled groups and individuals strongly resist being classified as "sick." Susan Wendell (2001) points out that this resistance has had strong reasons behind it: "this identification," she writes, "contributes to the medicalization of disability, in which disability is regarded as an individual misfortune, and people with disabilities are assumed to suffer primarily from physical and/or mental abnormalities that medicine can and should treat, cure or at least prevent" (17). Disability activism has, to avoid some of these problematic views, focused on the people who are what Wendell calls "healthy disabled" (19).[4]

More recently, some disability scholars have suggested that the "social model" of disability—wherein disability is exclusively a matter of how one's body interacts with social oppression and/or exclusion, rather than a particular bodily condition (typically called an *impairment*) in itself—has been criticized as separating disability from embodiment too much. As Elizabeth Barnes (2016) writes, "though disability doesn't seem to be entirely explained by what disabled bodies are like, it's also not entirely separate from what disabled bodies are like … We may not be able to give an account of disability based on objective similarities shared by disabled bodies. And yet what your body is like *matters* to whether you are disabled" (36–7).

Could it be that the experiences of both illness and disability are at the intersection of the body and society, neither exclusively a matter of medical condition nor of social situation? To be disabled and to be ill involve a particular bodily state that influences, and sometimes determines, one's social and political context, how one can act, and how one is perceived. And while there are conceptual distinctions to be made between disability and illness, attending to their similarities is valuable, particularly in theological reflection.

---

[2] See Richard Cross (2016), who originated this term as a referent for disabilities. I apply it to disease/illness as well in this chapter.

[3] As I will note later on, many following Christopher Boorse (1977, 1997) will distinguish illness as a subset of disease. I think the two concepts are related but distinct, though probably not along the exact dimensions Boorse suggests. My primary concern in this paper is with what Boorse would call "illness," insofar as it is a certain kind of bodily condition (more often) characterized by the acute onset of symptoms, the need/want for medical intervention or close medical supervision, etc. I do think that there is room to question the distinction that Boorse draws between the non-normativity of disease and the normativity of illness; but for my purposes I will focus on the bodily condition and lived experience of what most of us would refer to as "illness" rather than the particular presence/absence of a pathology.

[4] Perhaps similarly, disability discussions in the past have sometimes focused on physical disabilities rather than cognitive ones, arguing that they might differ substantially enough from physical disabilities to warrant separate treatment. But understanding disability, I think, means engaging with the wide variety of ways individuals experience disability.

The philosophy of both illness and disability suggests that these concepts are only fully understood in the light of social and communal contexts. Thus, when we consider instances of healing in the Gospel narratives, insights from the philosophy of disability can help to illuminate previously neglected components of these passages. In particular, new attention to the social and communal dimensions of these narratives reveals Jesus as particularly concerned with the *person's own* interaction with their disability (asking what they want, or whether they want to be healed) and their communal situation. With this in mind, we can widen our imagination as to how disabled or ill-embodiment relates to resurrection identity and, vitally, to life in our existing theological communities.

Drawing upon literature about the definition of illness as distinct from (or related to) disability, I will argue that both illness[5] and disability have too often been treated as primarily medical conditions of individuals that have negative normative value. This, I think, eclipses the broader social context that plays a role in how individuals experience illness and disability and its overall value in their lives. I will argue that existing work on disability and theodicy enables us to see not merely painless physical conditions (blindness, etc.) as possibly compatible with persistence in the afterlife, but also more complex conditions, perhaps even what we might consider "sick" bodies. Finally, I argue that there is good reason for us to think that the possible (and perhaps probable) persistence of these forms of embodiment give us compelling moral reasons to begin transforming our current communities.

II. THE NORMATIVE VALUE OF ILLNESS, DISEASE, AND DISABILITY

Contemporary philosophical writing on the concept of "disease" has centered largely on whether a disease can be objectively identified, the boundaries between a state of health and a state of disease, and if (or how) the concept is normatively laden. As Elselijn Kingma (2010) notes, a major division in the literature is between those who think disease is a *naturalistic* concept and those who think disease is a *normative* one (242). Christopher Boorse (1977, 1997) offers perhaps the most often cited theory of health and disease that relates both concepts to biostatisical norms for a given reference class of a species (typically these reference classes are constrained by biological sex and age). Importantly, Boorse claims that his view of disease as a theoretical concept, distinct from the *practical* concept of a "treatable illness" makes his view value-neutral. "If diseases are deviations from the species biological design, their recognition is a matter of natural science, not evaluative decision" (1977: 543). According to Boorse's biostatistical theory (BST), one can determine the presence or absence of a disease without making any normative judgments about the condition or the individual. And Julian Savulescu (2009) takes on board the heart of Boorse's BST (61), arguing that on a BST view of these matters, "disease is a value-free scientific concept and illness is a value-laden (normative) concept" (61).

Similarly, Savulescu distinguishes between value-neutral "disease" and value-laden "disability." He reasons that deviation from a biological or statistical norm is not intrinsically significant, whereas disability, which involves questions about how well our lives have gone, must be value-laden in some way. Savulescu's own "welfarist account" (63) of some bodily or psychological condition counts as a disability "in circumstances

---

[5] And disease.

C if and only if X tends to reduce the amount of well-being that this person will enjoy in C" (63). For Savulescu, disability is context-dependent. Having a certain bodily configuration may or may not count as a disability in some context, depending on the relationship between the context and the configuration. More particularly, Savulescu's view implies that being *disabled* is inherently negative for one's well-being. He says expressly, "Disease is a disability to the extent it reduces a person's well-being" (64). A given bodily configuration (whether involving a Boorsian-defined disease or not) may or may not be a disability, depending on context. But it is not possible for Savulescu to claim that the same bodily configuration is *both* a disability *and* an overall good to the person's well-being, a view that is echoed in other writings on disability.[6]

Thus we can see that, while the concept of a disease is not always (at least ostensibly) a value-laden concept, disability almost always is, because, on these views, disability involves the effect of a bodily state on one's overall well-being in (presumably) a negative direction. And, as noted, these treatments of disability resemble Boorse's own treatment of illness as a normatively substantive subset of "disease," one that requires or provides reasons for treatment and is related to a reduction of overall well-being.

For this reason, many disability advocates have resisted linking (or even associating) disability and illness. If disability is seen as similar to illness, it can reinforce this negative normative judgment about the relationship between a disability and a person's well-being, something that many disability activists seek to resist. In some versions of the social model of disability, these individuals would claim that a bodily state previously considered disabled is *not* a disability, and that disability is purely a result of unjust or problematic social structures and inaccessibility. On these views, disease and illness could still be intrinsically bad for an individual, while a "disability" would be exonerated.

But a number of philosophers have recently argued that even the concept of a "disease" is not value-neutral. For example, Rogers and Walker (2017) insist that there is persistent vagueness between health and disease. "It is, however, unclear as to what feature some level of dysfunction should have that makes it pathological rather than normal, especially if a statistical definition of abnormality is recognized to be arbitrary" (407). Rogers and Walker argue further that "if statistical frequency is determinative in the way Boorse seems to suggest, then whether or not I have a disease depends on facts about other people, rather than just on facts about my own condition" (408).[7] The upshot of these discussions is that it is unclear how to identify a state of disease as opposed to a state of health without invoking normative concepts.

Acknowledging that even the concept of disease may not be value neutral, I will stipulate that the main concepts we want to investigate are disability and illness, and particularly how they relate to personal and social context. I will argue that *both* illnesses and disabilities have inextricably personal and social dimensions, the consideration of which is necessary to fully understand how those conditions are experienced and their overall normative value within a given human life. With this in mind, I will now turn to some examples of healing narratives in scripture and argue that fully understanding these

---

[6]See Harris (1992), McMahan (2005), and Kahane (2009).
[7]Explicitly against a "dysfunction" view of disease, Rogers and Walker argue that there are a range of conditions where dysfunction "cannot provide a categorical boundary between disease and non-disease" (414), for example, the line between prehypertension and hypertension, the presence and behavior of abnormal (cancerous) cells, and certain infectious disease such as syphilis, mumps or smallpox (see section III starting on p. 410).

instances of healing require attending to the personal and social context of the individual being healed.

III. SOCIAL AND PERSONAL CONTEXTS OF HEALING IN THE GOSPEL OF LUKE

In this section, I argue that attending to the personal and social contexts of Jesus's healing narratives in the Gospels illuminates a fuller picture of what it means (and does not mean) for those individuals to be healed. For the sake of brevity, I focus on two passages from Luke's Gospel, not because narratives do not exist elsewhere, but because Luke evinces a particular concern for those with disabilities/illnesses in his Gospel. In addition to the numerous accounts of Jesus's interaction with persons who are ill/disabled, Luke is also the only Gospel that records the parable of the wedding banquet in which persons with disabilities are considered honored guests.[8]

Consider first the woman who has been bent over for eighteen years, whom Jesus heals in the synagogue in Luke 13. When Jesus notices her, it is important to note that she has not sought him out for healing. Rather, he notices her in the context of her worship in the synagogue alongside him. "Now he was teaching in one of the synagogues on the sabbath. And just then there appeared a woman with a spirit that had crippled her for eighteen years. She was bent over and was quite unable to stand up straight. When Jesus saw her, he called her over and said, 'Woman you are set free from your ailment'" (Lk. 13:10-12).[9]

One might be tempted to assume that Jesus heals her because her disability is intrinsically bad rather than out of her expressed personal desire, given that Luke does not record her seeking Jesus out for healing nor expressing a desire to be healed. But this is too quick. What Jesus notices is that she has been "bound" by her condition and he expressly rebukes the Pharisees who criticize his healing on the sabbath. "You hypocrites!" Jesus says, "Does not each of you on the sabbath untie his ox or his donkey from the manger, and lead it away to give it water? And ought not this woman, a daughter of Abraham whom Satan bound for eighteen long years, be set free from this bondage on the sabbath day?" (Lk. 13:15-16). This woman's condition involves her experiencing a lack of freedom, which the Pharisees are not concerned with alleviating. Part of their hypocrisy in criticizing Jesus's activity is that they are more than willing to "work" on the sabbath for the sake of tending to the needs of their livestock, but not attending to the needs of this daughter of Abraham. Healing her offers her freedom, yes, but her experience of being "bound" is compounded by the uncaring Pharisees who fail to see, honor, and acknowledge her needs. In other words, understanding this woman's condition fully—how her physical condition is experienced—is not complete until we see how her social context has failed to work toward freeing her (even if some dimensions of that freedom could not be achieved by purely social means).

---

[8] He said also to the one who had invited him, "When you give a luncheon or a dinner, do not invite your friends or your brothers or your relatives or rich neighbors, in case they may invite you in return, and you would be repaid. But when you give a banquet, invite the poor, the crippled, the lame and the blind. And you will be blessed, because they cannot repay you, for you will be paid at the resurrection of the righteous." (Lk. 14:12-14)
[9] Unless otherwise specified, all biblical citations come from the New Revised Standard Version of the Bible.

It seems clear that this woman's body is in a condition where she cannot stand up straight. This runs independent from the way that she is treated. But Jesus's rebuke to the Pharisees when they question his freeing her does suggest that we can more fully understand her situation by attending to how her community failed her. The way that the Pharisees notice, *not* the woman experiencing both suffering and (later) freedom, but rather the act of healing as in conflict with the prescriptions for the Sabbath, shows that they were not (and perhaps still are not) attuned to this woman. They do not notice her. And this failure to notice is a kind of situation all too common for many with disabilities and illnesses.

Consider, too, the woman in Luke 8 who touches the hem of Jesus's robe (Lk. 8:43-44). This woman has been suffering for years, and has, in solidarity with many of those who experience chronic illness and/or disability, extended herself financially and socially. She is following Jesus with a desire to be healed, by touching the fringe of his clothes. It strikes me as particularly powerful here that this woman clearly does not lack agency or autonomy in the midst of her bodily situation. She seeks for herself this healing and relief from her suffering. Healing is not something Jesus bestows on her, but rather something she reaches out for and receives.

As Luke's narrative continues, "Then Jesus asked, 'Who touched me?' ... When the woman saw that she could not remain hidden, she came trembling, and falling down before him, she declared in the presence of all the people why she had touched him, and how she had been immediately healed" (Lk. 8:43-47). The woman is now at the center of the narrative, rather than on the fringes. She is drawn into conversation with Jesus; the crowds hear her story her account both of being healed immediately *and* of seeking healing in the first place. I. Howard Marshall (1978), in his commentary on this passage, notes that "the cure wrought in this manner extends beyond healing of the body; for the woman it involves a personal confrontation with Jesus" (342). And Joel Green (1997) observes that in revealing his ministry, "Jesus indicates his refusal to recognize these socially determined boundaries, asserting instead that even these 'outsiders' are the objects of divine grace" (211).[10] Both commentators note that there is *more* to the discussions of this physical healing than the mere change in bodily condition, and both observe, though do not discuss in great depth, how this woman experiences personal and social change.

The woman's agency as displayed here echoes Wendell's (2001) recommendation to widen the scope of disability activism to including listening to individuals' experiences of their bodily conditions. "Knowing more about how people experience, live with, and think about their own impairments could contribute to an appreciation of disability as a valuable difference from the medical norms of body and mind" (23). Jesus does not merely heal the woman with hemorrhages; he engages her whole person and seeks her out. In doing so, he provides an opportunity for the woman to be heard and seen even in the midst of a pressing crowd. This woman's illness—and more particularly, the suffering it caused—is part of a broader narrative that she is invited to share.

There are a number of other passages in Luke we could consider, such as the blind man (identified in Mark 5 as Bartimaeus) begging on the side of the road, or the man suffering

---

[10] Immediately after this, Green goes on to discuss (briefly) Jesus's ministry as one of "release," which can connect us to the woman bent over in the synagogue discussed above. Indeed, Green observes in this context that "healing is not only physical but also signifies wholeness, freedom from both diabolic and social restrictions" (1997: 212).

from dropsy. Biblical commentary on these passages suggests that these narratives are consistently part of a broader revelation about Jesus's ministry as one that upends contemporary social norms. For example, the pairing of the healing of the man with dropsy (commentators note that this is edema) is in the context of a social gathering, a Sabbath meal with the Pharisees. James Edwards (2015) observes, "It would seem abnormal for such an individual [suffering from edema] to be included in a Sabbath meal in a Pharisee's house, for rabbinic discussions (although somewhat later than Luke's day) associate edema with vice ... Furthermore, an edematous man would seem to compromise Torah rules related to bodily discharges, or offend guests, or both" (348). He concludes that it is probable that this person's presence was meant to "test or trap Jesus on matters related to Sabbath observance" (348). Edwards notes that, while the Pharisee is passive and silent, "Jesus initiated and engaged with human need" (348) by healing the man and sending him on his way. While Jesus does not engage directly with this man (similar to his healing of the woman in the preceding chapter), he does engage directly with the human being's need and immediately follows the healing itself with a parable about the guests one should invite to a feast. These guests include, surprisingly, individuals like the man who has just been healed. Thus while the Pharisees see the man with edema as a useful object with which to test Jesus, Jesus sees both a particular human need in this individual and offers a broader perspective on seeing individuals such as this man as meriting invitation to the banquet.

The nature of the bodily conditions we consider, whether instances of illness or disability, then, seem neither uniformly good nor uniformly bad; different individuals will have different embodied experiences. The healing narratives do not suggest that there is *never* a need for physical changes nor that there is *always* such a need. These seems to accord with what Elizabeth Barnes (2016) describes as a value-neutral model of disability, "The mere-difference view isn't committed to the idea that disability is just a big, grand party, nor to the idea that everyone would experience it as such if we could only eliminate social prejudice. So the goal ... is to develop an account of disability that both counts as a mere-difference view and accommodates the many-splendored, Janus-faced nature of disability" (78–9). A mere-difference view of disability/illness can embrace that the man here desires the restoration of his sight, without being committed to the claim that he desires that restoration because *being blind* is always intrinsically, on the whole, bad for a person. Jesus affirms the importance of listening to the stories of disability and illness, what Wendell calls the "phenomenology of impairment" (2001: 23) and Barnes calls "first-person testimony about disability" (2016: see chapters 2 and 3 in particular). I don't mean to claim here that a person's own perception or first-person experience *wholly or infallibly* determines whether or not they are suffering or whether there are components of suffering in a given bodily situation. Rather, I think the recent philosophical work on disability, disease and illness suggests that we lack a full picture of these conditions when we fail to incorporate (and take seriously) how these conditions interact with an individual's lived experience and in some cases their sense of identity.[11]

---

[11]Importantly, I do not mean here to imply something like an individual's metaphysical identity (that disability or illness is a feature without which the individual cannot persist as the numerically same individual). Rather, I mean to talk about broader psychological identity, a person's sense of themselves.

IV. DISABLED AND ILL BODIES IN THE RESURRECTION

Thus far I have suggested that fully understanding what it is to have a disability or an illness requires understanding about that individual's lived experience and social context. It is possible that an individual has some bodily condition C—an illness or a disability—that is overall beneficial to her life, given her particular circumstances and experiences. In considering how condition C interacts with this person's overall identity, both now and in the resurrection, it is insufficient to know that she has C; more information is required. Thus, the question in this section follows reflections like those of Kevin Timpe (2019) about disability and beatitude: Is it possible that there will be bodies with those conditions we now identify as ill or disabled in the resurrection?[12] If so, how does that reconcile with our understanding of the resurrection as ushering in a kingdom with no pain or suffering?

Indeed, it does seem that it is more difficult to justify the persistence of diseases or illnesses in the resurrection in part because these conditions seem more closely associated with pain and suffering. But, as I argued in sections I and II, perhaps this association needs to be reconsidered. It is not true that *by definition* being ill or disabled means that one's life is on the whole worse off; thus, it is not a foregone conclusion that for any individual who is ill or disabled that person would be better off without that bodily condition, or that it must be removed in the afterlife. Wendell points us toward looking at illness as a way to widen our definitions of these terms to include, without stigmatizing, the bodily realities. Illness, like disability, Wendell (2001) argues, is not merely the suffering even though the suffering might be inextricable to it: "Like living with cerebral palsy or blindness, living with pain, fatigue, nausea, unpredictable abilities, and/or the imminent threat of death creates different ways of being that give valuable perspectives on life and the world. Thus, although most of us want to avoid suffering if possible, suffering is part of some valuable ways of being" (31). Similarly, Aas and Howard (2018) suggest that "a model of disability that is affirmational must make room for us to view the physical state itself associated with a given disability (e.g., blindness, paraplegia, etc.) as a constituent component of a person's distinctive form of flourishing" (1126).

Where does this leave us when thinking about resurrected bodies? It does seem incompatible with the given picture of the resurrected life that there be pain and suffering in heaven. Indeed, the vision offered in Revelation 21 says, "Death will be no more; mourning and crying and pain will be no more, for the first things have passed away" (Rev. 21:4). But is it possible that there can be a decoupling of some bodily conditions and the pain that they entail, without the loss of the condition itself? It is possible that one's body be shaped in fundamental ways by an experience of suffering without the suffering itself needing to persist. Indeed, Marilyn McCord Adams sketches a model of theodicy for horrendous evils wherein suffering is not merely *ended* but *integrated* into the meaning of that person's relationship with God.[13] The experience of a profound, chronic illness such as what Wendell describes might shape the body in particular ways such that, while the pain and its immediate causes no longer exist, the body *as shaped by those things* remains—the suffering becomes integrated in some profound way in the person's afterlife experience. This is not to say that all disabilities are *by themselves* intrinsically instances of suffering or bad for you; rather I want to suggest that there is room to think that even bodies with complex conditions may persist in bearing marks of those conditions. Perhaps

---

[12] See also Timpe (2018).
[13] See Adams and Sutherland (1989).

an individual who gradually loses her vision does not regain it, though the pain associated with the vision loss (headaches, dizziness, etc.) does not persist. Or perhaps an individual with scoliosis has a skeletal structure shaped by scoliosis without the occurrent back and nerve pain. These are possibilities, certainly not givens. It is possible that a person with multiple sclerosis (MS) might be, in heaven, moving with the aid of a mobility device or with some limits in his or her upper mobility, because that is part of what it means for that person to experience the world and experience others, him or herself, and God. It is equally possible that a different person with MS does not have the same limits in upper mobility. To make the persistence of bodies marked by disability and/or illness possible is not to be prescriptive.

Amos Yong (2012) describes something similar in his description of the marks that he thinks disabled/impaired bodies will bear in the resurrection: "My claim is that what persists is at minimal the marks of our present disabilities and impairments. Such marks would include, but not be limited to, phenotypical appearances, mental capacities, behavioral expressions, and verbal, emotional, and interpersonal traits" (5). And while Yong does not make clear whether he thinks such marks are involved in metaphysical identity (and the persistence of a person between earthly and heavenly life), he *does* suggest that these marks emerge and express our identity, broadly understood, across our lifespan. They become part of how we understand ourselves, how we tell our stories.

Indeed, Christ's wounds and scars persist in his resurrected body. This body bears not only scars but also open wounds, as he invites Thomas: "put your finger here and see my hands. Reach out your hand and put it in my side. Do not doubt but believe" (Jn 20:27). Jesus's body in its glorious resurrected state is not absent these marks of a disabled, suffering condition. Of this Thomas Aquinas quotes Augustine in the *Tertia Pars* of the *Summa Theologiae*, saying, "So will He show His wounds to His enemies, so that He who is the Truth may convict them, saying 'Behold the man whom you crucified; see the wounds you inflicted; recognize the side you pierced'" (1920: III.54.4 *respondeo*). As Nancy Eiesland describes so powerfully in *The Disabled God*, "In presenting his impaired body to his startled friends, the resurrected Jesus is revealed as the disabled God" (1994: 311). Jesus does not merely "happen to" keep his open wounds and the marks in his hands and feet. These are marks of resurrection and marks of glory. Jesus's body, though profoundly transformed, is not made more glorious by their erasure. Might we also maintain in our resurrected bodies the same marks and the meaning they bear for our lives?

V. TRANSFORMING OUR COMMUNITIES

We confront facts about individual bodily conditions often. "S is blind," or "S has MS"; "S is in a wheelchair," "S uses a speaking device to communicate." These facts have often been taken to have straightforward (and overwhelmingly negative) normative meanings. But, as I've argued, understanding what it is for someone to experience life as disabled or ill requires understanding other facts about their personal and social context. And more specifically, I've argued, such facts also do not tell us what that person's resurrected body will necessarily look like. Imagining what a resurrected, glorified life might contain, we make room in our imagination to see those same conditions differently here and now. In this last section, I argue that reflection on what may or may not persist in the resurrection has implications for the kind of communities that we create here and now.

Amos Yong (2012) argues, "The 'normal' logic is that if heaven will be a certain way—i.e., one in which there are no disabilities, or their marks thereof—then so should we work in this life to eliminate them. This is precisely the kind of logic that leads at best to churches devoid of people with disabilities" (9–10). At worst, Yong warns, it leads to the active oppression and marginalization of individuals with different bodily configurations. By assuming that disability is incompatible with beatitude or the life to come, we fail to do justice to those with disabilities now.

But if the kingdom of heaven will be a place that is inclusive of a wide variety of bodily configurations—even bodies that are marked in important ways by traits we associate with being ill or disabled now[14]—then we have a moral reason to reflect that kind of celebration here and now. The church is meant to be the reflection of the heavenly kingdom, as Jesus says in Luke that the kingdom of God is amongst you, within your midst (17:21). Jesus, as we noted briefly above, includes those who are disabled/ill in the parable of the heavenly banquet. As Yong observes, "Jesus' parable of the eschatological banquet included the blind, lame, and crippled (Lk. 14:13, 21), just as they were, rather than only after they had been healed" (2012: 69). I do not mean to suggest here that the church should practice a certain form of pity or compassion towards these individuals (though there may be dimensions of care and compassion that are needed). Rather, I claim that the church must do *justice* to these individuals by welcoming them into their midst as presently full members of the kingdom and reflections of the body of Christ.

Second, I want to suggest that the church has an obligation to listen to the voices of those who have disabilities and illnesses. The church ought to adopt the same kind of posture Jesus evokes when he invites individuals into the midst of the crowd, and engages them in dialogue. This posture is one where we do not rush to any kind of conclusion about a particular bodily configuration, whether positive or negative. Instead, we listen to the ways in which the individual experiences his or her body, its limitations and its actions. As both Wendell and Barnes observe, it can be tempting to move immediately from a disability-negative view to a disability-positive one, assuming in the latter that all disabilities are merely matters of injustice or social exclusion, and that there is nothing harmful or bad about having a disability or being ill save those extrinsic features. Rather than jump to this conclusion, we are invited to learn from those with a wide range of bodily experiences, both positive and negative, both socially mediated and not. Kevin Timpe (2018) counsels this approach, writing, "Christians should default to listening to the oppressed" and "we should make sure our priorities reflect the Kingdom initiated by our Christ ... We need to work to realize a new vision of community, one grounded in the vision of the Kingdom of God" (57–8).

VI. CONCLUSION

In this chapter, I have argued that disability and illness are only fully understood in light of how that bodily condition interacts with an individual's personal and communal contexts. To understand whether or not having a disability or being ill is, on the whole, good or bad for the person requires us to understand how that person views her own life and how he

---

[14]This does not mean to suggest that all disabilities or illnesses persist, or all instances or dimensions of a given condition persist. The debilitating pain of MS or CF does not seem compatible with beatific life. However, there is room for bodies marked by those conditions in other ways, as well as bodies marked by other kinds of conditions we consider as being disabled, such as Down syndrome or deafness.

or she has related to others, and how others (personally and structurally) have related to him or her. I have further argued that we can see Jesus, in many of his healing narratives, interact with just these social and personal dimensions, both when he inquires whether or not individuals want to be healed and when he reverses dominant social understandings of particular conditions as linked to sinfulness. Thus, I have suggested, we have room to reflect on how disabled or ill bodies may persist in key ways in the resurrection, even in light of scriptural evidence that pain and occurrent suffering do not persist. Finally, I have argued that this should have real implications for how we structure our communities to be inclusive, because these bodily conditions are not merely temporal and earthly, but perhaps essential in the broad sense, and perfectly compatible with that person's resurrected identity in Christ.

References

Aas, S., and D. Howard (2018), "On Valuing Impairment," *Philosophical Studies*, 175: 1113–33.

Adams, M., and S. Sutherland (1989), "Horrendous Evils and the Goodness of God" *Proceedings of the Aristotelian Society*, supplementary volumes, 63: 297–323.

Amundson, R. (2000), "Against Normal Function," *Studies in History and Philosophy of Science Part C: Studies in History and Philosophy of Biological and Biomedical Sciences*, 31: 33–53.

Aquinas, T. (1920), *Summa Theologica*, trans. Fathers of the English Dominican Province, London: Burns, Oates and Washbourne.

Barnes, E. (2016), *The Minority Body: A Theory of Disability*, Oxford: Oxford University Press.

Barnes, E. (2018), "Against Impairment: Replies to Aas, Howard and Francis," *Philosophical Studies*, 175: 1151–62.

Boorse, C. (1977), "Health as a Theoretical Concept," *Philosophy of Science*, 44: 542–73.

Boorse, C. (1997), "A Rebuttal on Health," in J. M. Humber and R. F. Almeder (eds.), *What Is Disease?*, 3–34, Totowa: Humana Press.

Correia, J. (2016), "Flourishing and Freedom: Exploring Their Tensions and Their Relevance to Chronic Disease," *Health Care Analysis*, 24 (2): 148–60.

Cross, R. (2016), "Impairment, Normalcy, and a Social Theory of Disability," *Res Philosophica*, 93: 693–714.

Cross, R. (2017a), "Aquinas on Physical Impairment: Human Nature and Original Sin," *Harvard Theological Review*, 110 (3): 317–38.

Cross, R. (2017b), 'Duns Scotus on Disability: Teleology, Divine Willing, and Pure Nature', *Theological Studies*, 78 (1): 72–95.

Edwards, J. R. (2015), *The Gospel According to Luke*. Retrieved from https://ebookcentral.proquest.com.

Eiesland, N. (1994), *The Disabled God. Toward a Liberatory Theology of Disability*, Nashville: Abingdon Press.

Green, J. B. (1997), *The Gospel of Luke*, Grand Rapids, MI: Eerdmans.

Harris, J. (1992), *Wonderwoman and Superman: The Ethics of Human Biotechnology*, Oxford: Oxford University Press.

Kahane, G., and J. Savulescu (2009), "The Moral Obligation to Create Children with the Best Chance of the Best Life," *Bioethics*, 23 (5): 274–90.

Kingma, E. (2007), "What Is It to Be Healthy?," *Analysis*, 67 (2): 128–33.

Kingma, E. (2010), "Paracetamol, Poison, and Polio: Why Boorse's Account of Function Fails to Distinguish Health and Disease," *British Journal for the Philosophy of Science*, 61 (2): 241–64.

Marshall, I. H. (1978), *The Gospel of Luke: A Commentary on the Greek Text*, Grand Rapids, MI: Eerdmans.

Moss, C. R. (2011), "Heavenly Healing: Eschatological Cleansing and the Resurrection of the Dead in the Early Church," *Journal of the American Academy of Religion*, 79 (4): 991–1017.

Rogers, W., and M. J. Walker (2017), "The Line-Drawing Problem in Disease Definition," *Journal of Medicine and Philosophy*, 42: 405–23.

Rogers, W., and M. J. Walker (2018), "A New Approach to Defining Disease," *Journal of Medicine and Philosophy*, 43: 402–20.

Savulescu, J. (2009), "Autonomy, Well-Being, Disease, and Disability," *Philosophy, Psychiatry, & Psychology*, 16 (1): 59–65.

Schiffman, L. H. (1985), "Exclusion from the Sanctuary and the City of the Sanctuary in the Temple Scroll," *Hebrew Annual Review* (9): 301–20.

Schwartz, P. H. (2007), "Decision and Discovery in Defining Disease," in H. Kincaid and J. McKitrick (eds.), *Establishing Medical Reality*, 47–63, Dordrecht: Springer.

Shemesh, A. (1997), "'The Holy Angels Are in Their Council': The Exclusion of Deformed Person from Holy Places in Qumranic and Rabbinic Literature," *Dead Sea Discoveries*, 4 (2): 179–206.

Silvers, A. (2003), "On the Possibility and Desirability of Constructing a Neutral Conception of Disability," *Theoretical Medicine and Bioethics*, 24: 471–87.

Timpe, K. (2018), *Disability and Inclusive Communities*, Grand Rapids, MI: Calvin College Press.

Timpe, K. (2019), "Disabled Beatitude," in K. Timpe and B. Hereth (eds.), *The Lost Sheep in Philosophy of Religion: New Perspectives on Disability, Gender, Race and Animals*, 241–64, New York: Routledge.

Wendell, S. (2001), "Unhealthy Disabled: Treating Chronic Illnesses as Disabilities," *Hypatia*, 16 (4): 17–33.

Yong, A. (2012), "Disability Theology of the Resurrection: Persisting Questions and Additional Considerations," *Ars Disputandi*, 12 (1): 4–10.

Yong, A. (2009), "Disability and the Love of Wisdom," *Ars Disputandi* 9: 54–71.

CHAPTER TWENTY-NINE

Gender and Justice: Human and Divine Gender in Analytic Theology

MICHELLE PANCHUK

Gender is everywhere. It shapes everything from our "feminine" pastel or "manly" grey personal hygiene items to our linguistic interactions with complete strangers. And, yet, we rarely give it much thought unless our expectations are violated. Then gender becomes overwhelmingly salient as we cope with our surprise. This is true in theological discourse as elsewhere. Consider the following passage:

> The Second Person of the Trinity is our Mother in Nature ... And He is our Mother in Mercy ... For in our Mother Christ we profit and increase. (Julian of Norwich 2016: 145)

See? Julian's use of gendered language violates our expectations and renders assumptions about the nature of both God and humans starkly visible—and disrupted. In this chapter, I suggest that analytic theology (AT) would benefit from more such disruption, so that we are forced to see and to question gender's role in our practices and our theories. Despite gender's centrality to our experience, and despite the robust literatures on the topic in feminist theology and analytic philosophy, little has been written on the topic within AT or its disciplinary cousin, analytic philosophy of religion (APR).[1] Because there is so little analytic theological landscape to sketch, in this chapter I reach beyond AT to describe the theories and questions regarding gender developing in neighboring fields which are directly relevant to those addressed in AT and to which I believe that AT is well-situated to contribute. In so reaching, the extant literature goes from being vanishingly small to overwhelmingly large, so I limit my consideration to three pertinent topics: (1) the role of gender in the practice of AT, (2) divine gender, and (3) human gender and soteriology. In each section, I demonstrate how attention to gender and the voices of those who have been historically marginalized would contribute to greater justice within our discipline and open the door to fruitful new topics in AT.

---

[1] In 2002, Sarah Coakley wrote that APR "has to date shown a marked (if largely silent) resistance to feminist reflection of any sort" (98), and dishearteningly little has changed in the nearly two intervening decades. Indeed, more recently, she writes that if AT were a club, "it might be one for Men Only [sic]" (2013: 601).

Throughout this chapter, I assume a (not uncontroversial) distinction between sex and gender, according to which sex is related to features of bodies such as genitalia and chromosomes, while "gender" refers to features of social selves.[2] I use the terms "woman," "man," "masculine," "feminine," "non-binary," and "transgender" (or "trans") to refer to people's gender identities and expression, and the terms "male," "female," and "intersex" to refer to sex.

I. GENDER IN THE PRACTICE OF ANALYTIC THEOLOGY

Two themes in feminist epistemology have emerged over the past several decades that provide helpful resources for analytic theologians wanting to think about the significance of gender in our practices as a discipline: standpoint epistemology and theories of epistemic injustice and oppression.

Standpoint epistemology makes explicit the ways that both knowers and the knowledge they can gain are at least partially socially constructed. Almost everyone acknowledges that one's social role is relevant to what one knows (e.g., people who have uteruses are better positioned to gain phenomenal knowledge of pregnancy and childbirth). Standpoint epistemology goes a step further, claiming that differences in access to knowledge are not simply accidental differences in what individuals *happen* to be in a position to come to know but a central epistemic feature of social contexts defined by inequality and oppression. Among other things, standpoint theorists seek to demonstrate that marginalized members of society are better positioned to understand reality in important ways because they must understand not only their own lives but also the perspectives of their oppressors in order to navigate an often-hostile world. The privileged, in contrast, may ignore the lived-experience of those less privileged than themselves, and may even have a vested interest in maintaining their ignorance of it (Mills 2007; Medina 2013). If this is true, then those marginalized within religious communities—including people marginalized on the basis of their gender identities, such as women, non-binary, and trans individuals—should be expected to have insight into theological realities that are unavailable to their relatively privileged counterparts. If the ultimate aim of AT is truth, AT will be worse off to the degree that it lacks contributions from those people.

There are at least two reasons analytic theologians might be skeptical of standpoint theory. First, they might understand standpoint theory as a form of relativism according to which there is no Truth, only true-for-you and true-for-me. But relativism is not a fundamental feature of standpoint theory (Harding 1993; Anderson 2001; Fricker 2006).[3] In fact, a central tenet of realist standpoint epistemologies is that some standpoints are *better* than others at getting at certain truths (Harding 1993), and the critical engagement of individuals thinking from multiple marginalized standpoints is better still (Anderson 2001). As Pamela Sue Anderson puts it,

> We must be able to make true claims ... but our perception of what there is is potentially distorted or obscured by actual states of oppression, and these states of oppression can only be discerned by thinking from the lives of marginalized others ... The role of

---

[2]This should not be taken as an endorsement of the distinction. Rather, it is simply a fairly familiar way to quickly divide up the space of possibility. For a critique of the distinction, see Mikkola (2011). For a critique of the notion that sex is an entirely biological category, see Fausto-Sterling (2000).
[3]Some versions of standpoint theory do endorse it.

standpoint, then, is to enable less partial thinking that, ultimately, seeks to transform unjust power relations. (2001: 145–6)

A second concern might be that standpoint theory advocates the uncritical acceptance of any claim expressed by members of marginalized groups. Yet it seems clear that not every claim made by a woman, non-binary, or trans person should be taken to be true, even when those claims are about gender or gendered experience. No one is epistemically perfect, and the uncritical acceptance of views expressed by marginalized individuals would require endorsement of a plethora of contradictions, since people who share gendered social identities do not agree on everything or even on the issues most central to their experience. Furthermore, it would be a mistake to ignore the ways in which the experience of oppression can distort one's self-understanding and limit one's knowledge (Nelson 2001; Tessman 2005: 11–52; Fricker 2007; Dotson 2011, 2014). Internalized sexism or transphobia—the well-documented phenomena of coming to endorse or unconsciously accept oppressive prejudices and biases about one's own gender (Bartky 1990; Nelson 2001; David 2013: 8)—are clear examples of how oppression can distort one's thinking.

Fortunately, standpoint theory is not committed to accepting every claim made by a member of an oppressed social group. A privileged standpoint, for many theorists, is not one that an individual occupies just in virtue of their group membership; it is one that their group membership *situates them to develop* given appropriate critical engagement with their experiences and the broader social world. While marginalized individuals are more likely and better positioned to develop such a standpoint, their status as marginalized hardly guarantees that they will. In addition, people who are relatively privileged can also work to think about the world through the lens of the testimony of those more marginalized than themselves.

Closely related to the epistemic benefits that marginalization creates are the epistemic injustices to which it renders one vulnerable. The term "epistemic injustice" denotes the ways in which people can, in virtue of their social identities, be unjustly harmed in their capacities as knowers—most often, by being unjustly prevented from participating in knowledge production and communication. Kristie Dotson and Miranda Fricker identify three orders of epistemic injustice that the marginalized may encounter (Fricker 2007; Dotson 2011, 2012). At the first-order level, an agent may suffer from a credibility deficit due to social stereotypes regarding one or more aspects of their identity. Despite being a reliable and competent witness, for instance, a trans woman of color claiming to have been harassed may be seen as a less reliable source than her cis, white counterparts, simply because of her race and gender identity. This is *testimonial injustice*. At the second-order level, an agent may struggle to make certain experiences intelligible because those members of society who occupy the positions and structures that contribute most to shaping the hermeneutical resources available within the community tend not to have similar experiences and often have little interest in understanding them. Prior to the women's movement, a woman being harassed was likely to lack the terminology or conceptual resources adequately to describe the harassment or its harm to herself or to others (Fricker 2007: 149–50). This is *hermeneutical injustice*— "the injustice of having some significant area of one's social experience obscured from collective understanding owing to a structural identity prejudice in the collective hermeneutical resource" (155). At the third-order level, members of marginalized groups may have already developed the conceptual resources needed to make their experience communicatively intelligible, but privileged members of society fail to attend to or make use of those resources. When women activists developed the notion of sexual harassment, for instance, many in society initially resisted the concept, preferring to view unwanted sexual attention as harmless flirting or teasing. This is *contributory injustice* (Dotson 2012: 31–5).

These conceptual resources from feminist epistemology can both help AT to diagnose weaknesses and injustices within the discipline and point the way toward greater epistemic health (Anderson 2001, 2004, 2012; Coakley 2002; Kidd 2017; Merrick 2020; Panchuk 2020; Pogin 2020a, 2020b). The kinds of social conditions that contribute to epistemic injustice have been as present within the Christian tradition (which is the tradition that dominates AT and APR) as elsewhere in society. Women and LBGTQ individuals have had markedly less opportunity to contribute to the development of theology and tend not to be viewed as authorities on theological issues. Their voices are less often invited, present, attended to, respected, or cited within AT than their non-marginalized counterparts. In addition to unjustly disadvantaging women, non-binary, and trans scholars, these circumstances also appear to make the discipline worse off, epistemically speaking.

The dearth of people with marginalized gender identities in AT also has a skewing effect on the range of questions addressed and the shape of dominant responses. For example, why has perfect being theology assumed that independence is greater than dependence, impassibility more perfect than passion, immutability better than responsive change? Many feminists have argued that this is, at least partially, because the former of each of these pairs has historically been understood as a masculine trait, and there are implicit biases that favor the "masculine" virtues. God is constructed in the image of the powerful ruling male (Johnson [1992] 2015: 247). In similar vein, Jewish theologian, Melissa Raphael, argues that standard free-will defenses of God's non-intervention in Auschwitz depend in problematic ways on patriarchal norms (2004). First, they adopt an ideal of human autonomy that has been largely inaccessible to women. Second, they propose that the value of this masculine autonomy outweighs the disproportionate suffering of women and children in the camps and throughout history: "Here both the covenant, and women, children and men feminized by their powerlessness, pay the price for masculine becoming" (146). Finally, it assumes that masculine autonomy depends for its existence on divine hiddenness, but "if the patriarchal aspiration of omnipotence is not attributed to God, she can be present to humanity without disabling their humanity" (146). Others have argued that the existence of pervasive epistemic injustice is grounds for non-deference to religious authority (Merrick 2020), and that diverse voices from the religious margins can contribute to the epistemic health of theological reflection (Dormandy 2018; De Cruz 2020).

A central theme in emerging work on epistemic justice and standpoint epistemology within AT and APR is that we should welcome the disruption of our gendered assumptions and systems—and that doing so is likely to make our practices both morally and epistemically better.

II. DIVINE GENDER

A few years ago, Owen Strachan tweeted that referring to God using feminine pronouns, as Julian of Norwich (following a robust Christian tradition)[4] and Melissa Raphael do

---

[4] See Bynum (1984).

above, is "heresy, straight up" (2014). Perhaps few Christians would go quite as far as an accusation of heresy, but there *is* a pervasive assumption in the history of Christian theology and philosophy that God is masculine. This assumption has been criticized by feminist theologians for decades (e.g., Daly [1973] 1985; Reuther [1983] 1993; Johnson [1992] 2015), but it is only within the past few years that analytic theologians have joined the conversation (Rea 2016, 2020; Pogin 2020a). In this section I consider the reasons one might have for thinking that God is masculine and consider two arguments to the contrary offered by analytic theologians.

Given the definitions I offered in the introduction and the commitments of classical theism, it should be clear that, apart from the incarnation, God lacks *sex*. However, it is often assumed that God nonetheless has a masculine *gender*. There are a number of factors that might help explain this assumption. First, the social contexts in which classical monotheism developed as the dominant religion have been largely patriarchal and have tended to assume that properties understood as *masculine*—like strength, intelligence, self-sufficiency, and impassibility—are superior to those understood as *feminine* (e.g., weakness, intuition, receptivity, dependence, and emotionality). From this, it is easy to infer that the "being greater than which cannot be thought" must be masculine. But this hardly seems like a sufficient explanation of the tendency, since patriarchal cultures have sometimes embraced feminine deities and patriarchal norms are often supported *by* theological commitments (Daly [1973] 1985: 13; Johnson [1992] 2015: 5, 23), rather than (or in addition to) causing them. So these social facts should be considered in conjunction with a second reason: the Christian, Jewish, and Muslim scriptures frequently refer to God using masculine pronouns and more frequently represent God using masculine metaphors than feminine ones. The third reason people tend to assume that God is masculine is that the monotheistic traditions, likely influenced by the previous two points, tend to endorse divine masculinity (although not exclusively, as we have seen above). Take the Christian theological tradition. Thomas Aquinas follows Aristotle in arguing that, although she is not defective in virtue of her *human* nature, in her *individual* female nature woman is defective and instantiates a misbegotten nature (Aquinas 2009: 334). If being feminine is a defect, and God is that greater than which cannot be thought, it follows that God cannot be feminine. Such considerations lead Aquinas to conclude that masculine terminology is more appropriate for referring to God. He argues that because the female principle is passive in generation while the male is active, and the Son is begotten by the self-contemplation of the Father, who is active, "Father" is a more appropriate term than "Mother" for describing the relationship between the first and second persons of the trinity (Aquinas 1975: 90).

Proponents of exclusively masculine speech about and pronouns referring to God (henceforth "exclusivists," in contrast to those who oppose requirements of exclusively masculine language, "inclusivists"), fall into two main camps. First, one might claim that God is *literally* masculine. Second, one could take the weaker position that God is metaphorically or analogically more masculine than feminine. In what follows, I describe and evaluate two arguments against these views that have recently emerged in AT: the argument from the *imago Dei* and the argument from injustice.[5]

---

[5] A third approach, popular among feminist theologians, is what we might call the argument from transcendence. I take it to be implicit in Johnson ([1992] 2015), for example.

II.1 The Argument from the Imago Dei

The *imago Dei* is often invoked in arguments against exclusively masculine speech about God, but it often plays only a peripheral role. In contrast, Michael Rea makes the human possession of the divine image central in this (2016) argument:[6]

1. God is most accurately characterized as masculine only if God is masculine and God is not equally feminine.
2. If God is masculine and not equally feminine, then masculine people are more like God than feminine people.
3. Men and women are equally made in the image of God, so masculine people are not more like God than feminine people.
4. It is not the case that God is masculine and not equally feminine.
5. God is masculine or feminine only if God is equally masculine and feminine.
6. Therefore, God is not most accurately characterized as masculine.

For the sake of brevity, I set aside exegetical arguments against premises (1) and (3).[7] Premise (2) seems plausible, but a detractor might object in the following way: while it is true that if God is literally masculine and not equally feminine, then masculine people (particularly men) share an attribute with God that feminine and non-binary people do not, it would be a mistake to think that this single attribute automatically makes men *more like* God than others. One might think that women can be just as much like God as men can, simply in different ways than men. Karen Swallow Prior (2014) points out that while she is a woman and her father is a man, she is much more like her father than her brother is.

It is true that merely being masculine will not make some masculine person, x, more God-like than some non-masculine person, y. It may be that y is more God-like than x in virtue of having fostered various God-like virtues. Perhaps y is more merciful, kinder, and more knowledgeable than x. Nonetheless, all other things being equal, x will have *the potential* to share more attributes with God than y. Prior may indeed share more attributes with her dad than her brother, but if her brother were equally like their dad in every other way, he would end up being more like him than she, simply in virtue of their shared gender-identity.

This is especially problematic because of the long tradition in monotheism of associating God with goodness. Things have value in virtue of the relation in which they stand to God. To be God-like is a *value-conferring* status. To be more masculine is to be more God-like, and to be more God-like is to be *better* in both a metaphysically and morally significant sense.

The exclusivist could, of course, argue that while being masculine does make men more like God than others, and while this is indeed a value-conferring status, there are perhaps other properties that feminine and non-binary people can share with God that men cannot, such that masculine and non-masculine people are equally like God, just in different ways. If this is true, though, the burden of proof will be on the exclusivist to say how, if feminine and non-binary people share just as many properties with God as

---

[6]While there is significant debate one what it means to be an image of God, and exactly what bearing it entails, I take it that the arguments offered here are compatible with most, if not all, of the prominent views.
[7]Rea addresses some of these arguments (2016, 2020).

masculine people, God is not as feminine as masculine or as appropriately described with feminine and non-binary language as with masculine.

II.2 The Argument from Injustice

Most feminist theologians who criticize exclusivism take as their starting point the belief that it harms women and gender minorities when God is spoken of in exclusively masculine ways, and that believing the truth about God cannot promote injustice. Kathryn Pogin introduces this style of argument into AT and APR (2020a). She points out that "gendered associations make a difference not just in how we conceptualize God, but in how we conceptualize ourselves and our relationships to one another. If maleness is, in general, understood to involve a normative superiority, talent and intelligence in women is no longer strictly a gift, but an aberration" (304).

We can follow Rea (2020: 310) in reconstructing Pogin's argument in the following way:

1. If God exists and is (exclusively) masculine, believing the truth about God would promote injustice and harm—especially to women, but also to men.
2. If God exists, believing the truth about God would not promote injustice.
3. Therefore, if God exists, God is not (exclusively) masculine.

Pogin supports point (2) by claiming that "justice and truth are ineluctably related" (2020a: 302). That is, it should not be the case that in virtue of believing true things about God, we obtain theoretical grounds for committing injustice. The corollary is also true. If we find that some purported truth about God *does* justify harming others, then we have a *prima facie* reason to reject that purported truth about God.

There are two potential difficulties with this argument. First, not all harms are injustices. If the purported belief about God provides theoretical justification for some harm, then the proponent of that view of God has provided themselves with grounds for claiming that the harm is not, in fact, an injustice. Here the proponent of Pogin's argument will be forced to depend on the weight of our moral intuitions and broader moral values (presumably informed by other religious commitments, such as love of neighbor and care for the oppressed), which may have little effect on the person whose moral intuitions and values entail that the harm done to women and gender minorities is neither an injustice nor a failure of love. In other words, while this argument may provide a theoretical justification for inclusivists like Pogin and Rea, it is unlikely to persuade the theologian who does not already share their values.

The second difficulty lies in showing that any particular belief about God logically entails the permissibility of some apparently unjust harm. How would such a demonstration go? Returning to the argument in the previous section, if we assume that God-likeness is a normative, value-laden property, then if God is masculine, men are superior to women in some significant ways. And, if men are superior, one is (likely) justified in treating them *as superior*. Indeed, even if people don't come to consciously endorse the view that men are superior to women, one might still think that the linguistic association of God with masculinity is likely to contribute to systemic injustice (by promoting implicit biases and the like). As Pogin puts it,

> How we put concepts to work ... may ultimately shape the content we take them to have. Likewise, when we take God to be appropriately represented as masculine but not feminine, and when we repeatedly associate divinity with masculinity, something is communicated not just about divinity, but about masculinity itself. (307)

If either of these arguments is successful, they provide grounds for changing not only the language used to refer to God in AT and our assumptions about the relationship between God and gender.

III. HUMAN GENDER

I have so far discussed how gender relates to the practice of AT and to the nature of God. There are also a number of questions that analytic theologians might seek to answer regarding gender and human experience. For example, which contemporary theories of gender are most compatible with biblical theology (Peeler 2020), with particular theological traditions (Potter 2020), or with transphobes and misogynists making morally appropriate amends in the afterlife to the people they have harmed on earth (Hereth 2020; Yancey 2020)? Does recent work in analytic theology on the incarnation offer any insight for the question of the ordination of women (Coakley 2004)? In what follows, I examine a question that has loomed large in feminist theological discussions of human gender: Can a Male Savior Save Women (Reuther [1983] 1993: 116–38)?[8] Throughout, I assume, for the sake of argument, that Jesus was, in fact, male and that the answer to the question of whether he can save women is "yes."[9]

Answering the question requires careful attention to (at least) three different theoretical issues. The references to a "male" savior and "women," for instance, suggest that the answer will depend on what theories of gender and sex (and their relationship) that one adopts.[10] Given that within traditional Christian theology this male savior is understood to be God incarnate, an adequate answer must also consider the metaphysical relationship between Jesus and his human nature. Finally, because what is at stake is the efficacy of Christ's salvific work, both of these metaphysical theories will need to be considered in conversation with theories of the atonement. Given the rich work on the metaphysics of gender being done within analytic feminism and of the incarnation within analytic theology, this question is ripe for analytic theological consideration. In what remains of this chapter I can only offer the broadest strokes of how that conversation might go, considering just two (very broad) theories of gender—gender essentialism and social constructivism—and sketching the questions that one might ask about the incarnation and the atonement with relation to them.

III.1 Gender Essentialism

Gender essentialism, as I will be using the term here, identifies or closely associates gender with a natural, biological kind—in particular, one's biological sex, narrowly understood as a dimorphic biological category. On this view, humans (with the possible exception of

---

[8]To the best of my knowledge, only one paper has been published in analytic theology on this topic (do Vale 2019). As I became aware of its publication only after I wrote the present article, I do not engage with its arguments here.
[9]To the best of my knowledge, no major theologian in the history of Christian theology has defended a "no" answer.
[10]At the time Ruether posed the question, it was not quite as standard to use "male" to refer to sex and "women" to refer to gender, so I don't think she intended to highlight issues about the relationship between gender and sex. They nonetheless arise when we start to think carefully through the issue. I thank Michael Rea for pressing me to clarify this issue.

intersex individuals) are either male or female, and being male or female entails that one should exemplify certain masculine or feminine traits.

This form of gender essentialism seems implicit in many important documents of the Roman Catholic Church and is explicitly taught in many branches of evangelical Protestantism. For example, in *Mulieris Dignitatem*, Pope John Paul II describes virginity and motherhood as two special dimensions of the character of women, suggests that God has entrusted *care* for human persons to women in a special way, and describes *sensitivity* as part of the "genius" of women (1988). Throughout the letter these qualities are described as *essential* and *central* to what it means to be a woman. Evangelical pastor, John Piper, claims that "when the Bible teaches that men and women fulfill different roles in relation to each other, charging man with a unique leadership role, it bases this differentiation not on temporary cultural norms but on permanent facts of creation" (1991: 28). Being male, and thus masculine, entails that one has a sense of responsibility to lead, provide for, and protect women (29), while being female, and thus feminine, entails that one have a disposition to affirm, receive, and nurture the strength of worthy men (37).

On this view, gender is metaphysically basic and essential to who one is and how one lives. If Jesus's human nature was both male and masculine, it was essentially so. This does not initially seem like a problem, since on most popular views of the atonement, Jesus came to redeem fallen *humanity*, and all men and women are equally *human*. However, a popular early Christian aphorism says that "whatever was not assumed was not redeemed." Jesus can only redeem humanity because he assumed human nature. Does this entail that because Jesus didn't assume *feminine* humanity that feminine humans are not redeemed, or that only their humanity is redeemed but not their femininity?

One way to avoid this problem is to argue that Jesus's masculinity is of *no* significance to his atoning purposes (Johnson 1991). That is, Jesus is male only because in becoming human, Jesus must exemplify some determinate of the determinables of sex and gender. In terms of his atoning work, Jesus could have just as well taken on a female and feminine nature. Thus, in virtue of assuming *human* nature, Jesus redeems all humans. This view would need some further metaphysical explanation to work out some possible objections, but assuming those could be addressed, it seems like a reasonable view. Yet a significant number of the Christians who are inclined toward biological determinist gender essentialism—and who, therefore, need to deny that Jesus's maleness plays a salvific role if women are to enjoy redemption in the same way and to the same degree as men—are the very ones most likely to see human representation of Jesus's maleness as necessary to symbolic representation in the Eucharist.[11] As Reuther puts it, "The Vatican Declaration in 1976 against women's ordination sums up this Christological masculinism with the statement that 'there must be a physical resemblance between the priest and Christ.' The possession of male genitalia becomes the essential prerequisite for representing Christ, who is the disclosure of the male God" (126). It becomes difficult to explain why *this* and only this bodily feature, which is inessential to Christ's salvific work, is crucial for representation, but not other, equally inessential bodily features such as ethnicity, race, height, hair color, or eye color. It seems as though one must say either that a male savior cannot save women, or that women can represent the savior just as well as men. Explaining

---

[11] This is primarily true of Roman Catholics, although this argument does have varying degrees of influence in the Anglican and Orthodox communities.

why this is a false dichotomy is one of the challenges left facing gender essentialists who endorse an all-male priesthood on these grounds.

III.2 Social Constructivism

Social constructivists about gender see gender as created by social relations, rather than being something metaphysically or biologically basic. Gender exists, on this view, the same way that presidents and paper money exist. Paper money has no inherent value, but our social arrangements invest it with great power and significance.[12] Gender isn't an inherent property people have, but one constructed by our social conventions, and the way our societies function give gender great power and significance. There are a number of different social constructivist accounts of gender. One well-known example is Sally Haslanger's:

> S *is a woman* if [by definition] S is systematically subordinated along some dimension (economic, political, legal, social, etc.), and S is "marked" as a target for this treatment by observed or imagined bodily features presumed to be evidence of a female's biological role in reproduction. (2003: 6).

It is tempting to assume that the worry about redemption falls away for social constructivists. If gender is not something metaphysically deep, then it is not something that Jesus assumes just in virtue of the incarnation. His gender arises from the social conditions in which he lives. If one's theory of the atonement only requires that Jesus assumes the metaphysically basic "stuff" of human nature in the incarnation, then this might be sufficient. After all, few think that Jesus has to take on all of the social roles that humans can occupy. He does not have to have been a president to redeem presidents.

But theories of the atonement that take *metaphysical* commonality between redeemer and redeemed as essential are not the only theories. Moral exemplarist views and the Christology and soteriology of liberation theologies take Jesus's *social* identity to be morally significant, even central, to his Christological role. These theories might face problems when endorsing social constructivism about gender because the historical Jesus apparently does not share the social positions occupied by women or gender minorities of his time or ours. Does Jesus fail to save women, non-binary, and trans people?

This is why liberation and postcolonial theologians have often construed Christ as black, as the Corn Mother of Native American mythology, or as a queer person (Cone [1986] 2018; Tinker 1998; Bahoche 2008; Pui-lan 2005). "The black community is an oppressed community primarily because of its blackness; hence the christological importance of Jesus must be found in his blackness. If he is not black as we are, then the resurrection has little significance for our time," declares James Cone ([1986] 2018: 126; see also Douglas 1993). Of course, neither James Cone nor Kelly Brown Douglas believe that the historical Jesus was actually of African descent. Rather, what they seem to suggest is that in his role as the *Christ*, as one who entered into the reality of unjust human suffering and oppression, who died and yet liberates, we can interpret his social

---

[12]Social constructivists need not be committed to any particular view of properties in general for this view to be available to them. They could be realists, nominalists, or fictionalists. Just as Peter van Inwagen is a realist about abstract properties who thinks there are no tables, only particles arranged table-wise, a social constructivist might be a realist about properties but think there are no genders in a metaphysical deep sense, just people acting gender-wise.

identity through the lens of contemporary oppressed social identities. Jesus, like us, was oppressed, and so is a member of our social group. "Our being with him is dependent on his being with us in the oppressed ... condition" (Cone [1986] 2018: 127) So, perhaps, the social constructivist with moral exemplarist or liberationist leanings can say that while the historical Jesus may not have been a woman or trans, Christ our Mother and Queer Christ are with us in our oppressed condition as women and gender minorities, as well as in our identities as racialized, disabled, lower-class, or religious minorities. This is the message one might see in Harmonia Rosales's breathtaking painting *I Exist*, which features a crucified black woman surrounded by mourning black women, with a skull lying at the foot of the cross—a painting that disrupts and reforms our expectations about the intersection of gender, race, divinity and redemption.

Contemporary conversations surrounding gender, both in popular culture and in theology and philosophy, are complex and quickly evolving. It might be tempting for analytic theologians to ignore them in favor of what they take to be more "perennial" questions. However, I have demonstrated in this paper that we do so to our detriment. Gender is deeply relevant to the social health of our discipline and to the way we think about God and ourselves. Behold, the fields are white for the harvest of analytic theology of gender.

References

Anderson, P. S. (2001), "'Standpoint': Its Rightful Place in a Realist Epistemology," *Journal of Philosophical Research*, 26: 131–53.

Anderson, P. S. (2004), "An Epistemological-Ethical Approach," in P. S. Anderson and B. Clack (eds.), *Feminist Philosophy of Religion: Critical Readings*, 87–102, New York: Routledge.

Anderson, P. S. (2012), *Re-Visioning Gender in Philosophy of Religion: Reason, Love, and Epistemic Locatedness*, Surrey: Ashgate.

Aquinas, St. T. (1975), *Summa Contra Gentiles*, Book Four: Salvation, trans. C. J. O'Neil, Notre Dame, IN: University of Notre Dame Press.

Aquinas. St. T. (2009), *The Summa Theologiae of Saint Thomas Aquinas: Latin-English Edition*, vol. II, Ypsilanti: NovAntiqua.

Bahoche, T. (2008), *Christology from the Margins*, London: SCM Press.

Bartky, S. (1990), *Femininity and Domination: Studies in the Phenomenology of Oppression*, New York: Routledge.

Bynum, C. W. (1984), *Jesus as Mother: Studies in the Spirituality of the High Middle Ages*, Berkeley: University of California Press.

Coakley, S. (2002), *Powers and Submissions: Spirituality, Philosophy and Gender*, Oxford: Blackwell.

Coakley, S. (2004), "The Woman at the Altar: Cosmological Disturbance or Gender Fluidity?," *Anglican Theological Review*, 86: 75–93.

Coakley, S. (2013), "On Why Analytic Theology Is Not a Club," *Journal of the American Academy of Religion*, 81 (3): 601–8.

Cone, J. (2018), *A Black Theology of Liberation*, fortieth anniversary edition, Maryknoll: Orbis Books.

Daly, M. ([1973] 1985), *Beyond God the Father: Toward a Philosophy of Women's Liberation*, Boston: Beacon Press.

David, E. J. R. (2013), *Internalized Oppression: The Psychology of Marginalized Groups*, New York: Springer.

De Cruz, H. (2020), "Seeking out Epistemic Friction in the Philosophy of Religion," in M. Panchuk and M. Rea (eds.), *Voices from the Edge: Centering Marginalized Perspectives in Analytic Theology*, 23–46, Oxford: Oxford University Press.

Dormandy, K. (2018), "Disagreement from the Religious Margins," *Res Philosophica*, 95 (3): 371–95.

Dotson, K. (2011), "Tracking Epistemic Violence; Tracking Practices of Silencing," *Hypatia*, 26: 236–57.

Dotson, K. (2012), "A Cautionary Tale: On Limiting Epistemic Oppression," *Frontiers: A Journal of Women Studies*, 33 (1): 24–47.

Dotson, K. (2014), "Conceptualizing Epistemic Oppression," *Social Epistemology: A Journal of Knowledge, Culture and Policy*, 28 (2): 115–38.

Douglas, K. B., (1993), *The Black Christ*, Maryknoll: Orbis Books.

Do Vale, F. (2019), "Can a Male Savior Save Women? The Metaphysics of Gender and Christ's Ability to Save," *Philosophia Christi*, 21 (2): 309–24.

Fausto-Sterling, A. (2000), *Sexing the Body: Gender Politics and the Construction of Sexuality*, New York: Basic Books.

Fricker, M. (2006), "Feminism in Epistemology: Pluralism without Postmodernism," in M. Fricker and J. Hornsby (eds.), *The Cambridge Companion to Feminist Philosophy*, 146–65, Cambridge: Cambridge University Press.

Fricker, M. (2007), *Epistemic Injustice: Power and the Ethics of Knowing*, Oxford: Oxford University Press.

Harding, S. (1993), "Rethinking Standpoint Epistemology: What is Strong Objectivity?," in L. Alcoff and E. Potter (eds.), *Feminist Epistemologies*, 49–82, New York: Routledge.

Haslanger, S. (2003), "Future Genders? Future Races?," *Philosophic Exchange*, 34: 4–27.

Hereth, B. (2020), "The Shape of Trans Afterlife Justice," in M. Panchuk and M. Rea (eds.), *Voices from the Edge: Centering Marginalized Perspectives in Analytic Theology*, 186–205, Oxford: Oxford University Press.

Johnson, E. A. (1991), "The Maleness of Christ," *Concilium*, 6: 75–93.

Johnson, E. A. ([1992] 2015), *She Who Is: The Mystery of God in Feminist Theological Discourse*, New York: Herder and Herder.

Julian of Norwich (2016), *Revelations of Divine Love Recorded by Julian, Anchoress at Norwich*, trans. Grace Warrack, The Project Gutenberg. Available online: http://www.gutenberg.org/files/52958/52958-h/52958-h.htm.

Kidd, I. (2017), "Epistemic Injustice and Religion," in I. J. Kidd Jr., J. Medina, and G. Pahlhouse (eds.), *The Routledge Handbook to Epistemic Injustice*, 386–96, London: Routledge.

Medina, J. (2013), *The Epistemology of Resistance: Gender and Racial Oppression, Epistemic Injustice, and Resistant Imaginations*, Oxford: Oxford University Press.

Merrick, T. (2020), "Non-Deference to Religious Authority: Epistemic Arrogance or Justice?," in M. Panchuk and M. Rea (eds.), *Voices from the Edge: Centering Marginalized Perspectives in Analytic Theology*, 97–118, Oxford: Oxford University Press.

Mikkola, M. (2011), "Ontological Commitments, Sex and Gender," in C. Witt (ed.), *Feminist Metaphysics: Explorations in the Ontology of Sex, Gender and the Self*, 67–84, Dordrecht: Springer.

Mills, C. (2007), "White Ignorance," in S. Sullivan and N. Tuana (eds.), *Race and Epistemologies of Ignorance*, 11–38, Albany: State University of New York Press.

Nelson, H. L. (2001), *Damaged Identities, Narrative Repair*, Ithaca, NY: Cornell University Press.

Panchuk, M. (2020), "That We May be Whole: Doing Philosophy of Religion with the Whole Self," in B. Hereth and K. Timpe (eds.), *The Lost Sheep in Philosophy of Religion: New Perspectives on Disability, Gender, Race, and Animals*, 55–76, New York: Routledge.

Peeler, A. (2020), "Mary as Mediator," in M. Panchuk and M. Rea (eds.), *Voices from the Edge: Centering Marginalized Perspectives in Analytic Theology*, 75–93, Oxford: Oxford University Press.

Piper, J. (1991), "A Vision of Biblical Complementarity: Manhood and Womanhood Defined According to the Bible," in J. Piper and W. Grudem (eds.), *Recovering Biblical Manhood and Womanhood: A Response to Evangelical Feminism*, 25–57, Wheaton: Crossway Books.

Pogin, K. (2020a), "God is not a Man," in M. Peterson and R. VanArragon (eds.), *Contemporary Debates in Philosophy of Religion*, 2nd ed., 302–9, Oxford: Wiley Blackwell.

Pogin, K. (2020b), "Conceptualizing the Atonement," in M. Panchuk and M. Rea (eds.), *Voices from the Edge: Centering Marginalized Perspectives in Analytic Theology*, 166–82, Oxford: Oxford University Press.

Pope John Paul II, (1988), *Apostolic Letter Mulieris Dignitatem of the Supreme Pontiff John Paul II on the Diginity and Vocation of Woman on the Occasion of the Marian Year*. Available online: http://w2.vatican.va/content/john-paul-ii/en/apost_letters/1988/documents/hf_jp-ii_apl_19880815_mulieris-dignitatem.html.

Potter, K. D. (2020), "A Transfeminist Critique of Mormon Theologies of Gender," in B. Hereth and K. Timpe (eds.), *The Lost Sheep In Philosophy of Religion: New Perspectives on Disability, Gender, Race, and Animals*, 312–27, New York: Routledge.

Prior, K. S. (2014), "Female and Made in My Father's Image," Women (blog), Christianity Today. Available online: https://www.christianitytoday.com/women/2014/may/female-and-made-in-my-fathers-image.html.

Pui-lan, K. (2005), *Postcolonial Imagination and Feminist Theology*, Louisville: WJK Press.

Raphael, M. (2004), "The Price of (Masculine) Freedom and Becoming: A Jewish Feminist Response to Eliezer Berkovits's Post-Holocaust Free-will Defense of God's Non-Intervention in Auschwitz," in P. S. Anderson and B. Clack (eds.), *Feminist Philosophy of Religion: Critical Readings*, 136–50, New York: Routledge.

Reuther, R. R. ([1983] 1993), *Sexism and God-Talk: Toward a Feminist Theology*, Boston: Beacon Press.

Rea, M. (2016), "Gender as a Divine Attribute," *Religious Studies*, 52: 97–115.

Rea, M. (2020), "Is God a Man?," in M. Peterson and R. VanArragon (eds.), *Contemporary Debates in Philosophy of Religion*, 2nd ed., 293–301, Oxford: Wiley Blackwell.

Strachan, O. (2014), Twitter post. May 16, 11:58 am. Available online: https://twitter.com/ostrachan.

Tessman, L. (2005), *Burdened Virtues: Virtue Ethics for Liberatory Struggle*, Oxford: Oxford University Press.

Tinker, G. (1998), "Jesus, Corn Mother, and Conquest: Christology and Colonialism," in J. Weaver (ed.), *Native American Religious Identity: Unforgotten Gods*, 134–54, Maryknoll: Orbis Books.

Witt, C. (2011), *The Metaphysics of Gender*, New York: Oxford University Press.

Yancey, H. (2020), "Heavenly (Gendered) Bodies? Gender Persistence in the Resurrection and Its Implications," in B. Hereth and K. Timpe (eds.), *The Lost Sheep in Philosophy of Religion: New Perspectives on Disability, Gender, Race, and Animals*, 328–46, New York: Routledge.

CHAPTER THIRTY

Analytic Theology and Animals

FAITH GLAVEY PAWL

I. INTRODUCTION

With several notable exceptions, theologians and analytic philosophers of religion giving attention to animals in their work do so in a piecemeal fashion. Given the fragmentary nature of most theological reflection on animals and the amorphous boundary conditions for analytic theology, the job of canvasing the field of analytic theology of animals is simple. The field is empty. But while there may not be a comprehensive analytic theology of animals yet, there are many opportunities for engagement with excellent work on animals from other quarters of theology and related disciplines.

In this chapter, I critically engage the work of David Clough, whose exemplary systematic theology of animals stands out for, among other things, its comprehensiveness. I focus on what he has to say about the nature of animal agency and sin, as many of the pressing questions about the place of animals in salvation history hang in one way or another on what we have to say about animals as agents. By exploring Clough's understanding of animal sin, I hope to show a way analytic theology can bring a bit more clarity to a lively and important debate.

II. CLOUGH AND THE LANDSCAPE OF THEOLOGICAL REFLECTION ON ANIMALS

Among theologians and analytic philosophers of religion who give consideration to animals—what sort of creatures they are, how they are like and unlike us, how they fit into the Christian story of salvation—their chief priorities center around three questions. The first is practical, the second two theoretical. How should we understand our moral obligations to animals in light of Christian theological commitments? Second, what can we say about the amount, variety, and intensity of animal suffering we see throughout the long history of the world, and do such phenomena constitute evidence against Christian theism? The stories Christians have told through the ages about why a perfect God would allow human beings to suffer do not seem to go very far toward explaining why God would allow animals to suffer, at least at first glance. The third locus of theological attention to animals is closely related to but broader than the project of theodicy. The problem of animal suffering is just one of a larger set of questions about animals raised by evolutionary theory, and theologians working in the science and religion dialogue have turned their attention to the implications of evolutionary theory for various Christian doctrines in connection with animals, especially questions about human uniqueness and the *imago Dei*.[1] One theologian's work spans all three of these areas of focus and goes beyond. David Clough's (2012, 2018) magisterial two-volume work of systematic and practical theology of animals takes the welcome step of treating a whole host of questions about animals as theologically interesting in their own right.

Clough identifies a series of errors common to most theological reflection on animals. For the most part, we have left animals out of the stories we tell about God's involvement in the world. We have focused too narrowly on the human experience and have consequently mischaracterized the kind of dignity animals have. Likewise, we have misidentified what is unique and important about our own place in the created order. We have ignored the relevant empirical data showing that animal behavior is far more sophisticated than we would have imagined, and that many facets of human behavior aren't quite as sophisticated as we thought. I find his assessment very convincing, and would add to this litany of errors that we speak about animals as if there were this one, monolithic group, "animals," concerning which we can coherently theorize—the "them" we contrast with "us"—rather than millions of species of creatures whose ways of life are incredibly diverse.

The primary strategy theologians like Clough have taken to correct for these errors has been to emphasize continuities between humans and animals, and to question whether the human attributes we take to be difference-makers in our moral and theological reasoning really do carry the weight we take them to. In particular, the weight placed on rationality in theological and philosophical anthropology has come under fire. Clough goes so far as to charge that traditions of explaining human superiority in terms of rationality express little more than arbitrary preferences driven by self-interested bias. He says, "We must recognize that the human/animal difference is being used as a trope for discussion of the authors' preferred features of human beings" (2012: 72). He thus rejects the "routine and thoughtless, the logical or philosophical, drawing up of a list of attributes supposedly possessed by all human beings, and excluding all non-human beings" (72). Clough is right to put pressure on an overly narrow understanding of rationality. In what follows, I will critically examine just how far we should go in deconstructing narratives about the role of rationality in what sets humans apart, especially when it comes to moral agency. In our attempts to include animals in the narrative of salvation history, we should be careful to attend not only to the continuities Clough rightly stresses, but to the important differences between humans and animals as well, lest we collapse animal stories into human ones. What I wish to call attention to in the arguments below may just identify a difference in emphasis, and not in any substantive conclusions to be drawn about animals in theology across the board. But if analytic theology is good for anything, it is useful for clearing up surface disagreements and mapping out the conceptual space of a given dialectic. So in that spirit, I wish to illustrate a helpful way to advance theologizing about animals by taking a close look at what Clough has to say about animal agency and sin.

---

[1] See, e.g., Deanne-Drummond (2009), Creegan (2013), and Sollereder (2018).

III. CLOUGH ON ANIMALS AND SIN

Clough condemns the tendency in theology to leave animals (and the rest of nonhuman creation) out of the stories we tell about salvation history. His resistance to this tendency is rooted in conviction that the Bible expresses a much more inclusive vision. Among other passages, he cites the first chapters of both Colossians and Ephesians, where Paul writes that Christ's cross and resurrection express the mystery of God's will to reconcile all things to Godself through Christ, and to bring unity to all things under heaven and earth (2013: 87). Clough's whole project can be seen through the lens of this concern. I will dub a principle Clough does not explicitly articulate, but consistently employs through his work, the "Inclusion Principle."

> **Inclusion Principle:** Whatever we can say about God's involvement with history should be able to apply to animals, unless we have principled reasons to exclude animals from the relevant narratives.

Like, Clough, I think that if we are to take Paul's words seriously, we should adopt something like the Inclusion Principle, though there will be a variety of options for how to do so.

To see the Inclusion Principle in action, consider Clough's view of the Incarnation. He argues that Christ became incarnate not just for humankind, but for all living things. We cannot argue from the particularity of Christ's humanity that he became incarnate just for the sake of humans any more than we can argue from the particularity of Christ's maleness or Jewishness that he became incarnate just for the sake of males or Jews (2013: 84). In assuming a human nature, Christ was also simultaneously assuming an animal nature, bringing all living things into God's plan for the restoration of the world and extending eschatological hope to all creatures.

After arguing that Christ became incarnate for animals as well as humans, Clough goes on to say that the atoning work of Christ's death and resurrection is for the sake of animals as well. He charges that if we fail to take this possibility seriously, we risk implying a "drastic narrowing of God's interests to the fate of a single species. If Anselm is right that the motivation of the incarnation is a response to human sinfulness, other creatures are mere bystanders" (104). He likewise claims that if we "retain the cosmic scope of the incarnation while making the atonement a species-specific event, we seem to be left with a very unattractive asymmetry and separation between Christmas, Easter, and Ascension. Christmas and Ascension on this account seem to be for all creation; Easter for just one kind of creature that has been badly behaved" (105). One solution to these dilemmas is to attribute sin to animals, so they too can be included in the work of the atonement.

There are two issues at stake here. The first is whether or not the atonement is for animals, and the second is whether animals can be considered sinful. The first, Clough argues, has strong scriptural support, and on that score, I think he is right. For the second, Clough takes there to be good evidence that animals are sinful, independent of considerations of the atonement, but he also motivates his claim that animals can be sinful by framing the broader issue in light of what I am calling his Inclusion Principle. This is my attempt to reconstruct his framing argument:

1. Christ's atoning work is meant to be the solution for the problem of sin. (Assumption)
2. Whatever we can say about God's involvement with history should be able to apply to animals, unless we have principled reasons to exclude animals from the relevant narratives. (Inclusion Principle)

3. Animals are not left out of the work of the atonement. (1, Inclusion Principle)
4. If animals are not left out of the work of the atonement, it is because they are implicated in the problem of sin.
5. Therefore, animals are implicated in the problem of sin. (2,3 MP)

Premise (1) is an assumption Clough attributes to Anselm. I think the best way to characterize Clough's strategy in employing this assumption is exploratory. He sets aside debates about the adequacy of Anselmian accounts of the atonement in order to see what would follow about animals if Anselmian accounts were true, but does not wed himself to the Anslem's particular version of the assumption. As I will argue below, the lesson to be drawn from Clough's work might be that Anselmian accounts of the atonement are non-starters for models that aspire to a cosmic scope. However, it is not necessary to interpret premise (1) in an Anselmian manner. Other models of the atonement hold that Christ's death and resurrection are meant to be the solution to problem of sin, but do not conceive of the problem *or* the solution in the same way that Anselm does. Premise (1) has broad support from various corners of the Christian tradition.

Premise (2) states the Inclusion Principle, and premise (3) is its application to the doctrine of the atonement. I built an exception clause into the Inclusion principle, so it is fair to ask whether the doctrine of the atonement might be one place where we could find principled reasons to exclude animals from the narrative. However, since the scriptural passages Clough gives for his general strategy of inclusion refer to the cosmic scope of what Christ accomplished specifically through the cross, premise (3) seems as good a candidate for application of the Inclusion Principle as any.

The most difficult premise to defend in the argument then is premise (4). It would certainly be true that if animals were implicated in the problem of sin, we could see a way they could be the beneficiaries of the work of the atonement. But *need* it be the case that they are implicated in the problem of sin in order for them to be beneficiaries? More would need to be said about what is meant by "sin" and "being implicated in the problem of sin" in order to make a good case for premise (4).

Clough canvasses a number of possibilities for conceptualizing sin. He considers sin as violating a covenant with God (2013: 109), missing the mark (115), forgetting the ways of God (116), and "a power under which people are universally bound, and from which they need salvation" (116). We might also think of sin as corruption or contagion (108), being caught up in harmful structures (121), or a kind of failure to satisfy some purity standard. I will treat these as a cluster of normative concepts, some of which overlap, and all of which share a family resemblance having to do with a suboptimal relationship to God.

Most strikingly, Clough also talks about sin as provoking of God's wrath, which renders agents guilty (108). I will dub this conception "sin_{mr}." By "sin_{mr}" I mean any bad action or bad attitude for which it is appropriate to hold an agent *morally* responsible. It may very well be that instances of any of the conceptions of sin canvassed here can count as sin_{mr}. Likewise, it is possible that there are instances of sin conforming to the other conceptions but not counting as sin_{mr}.[2] We should ask, are any animals themselves guilty

---

[2] Some philosophers argue that even *humans* can never be morally responsible for their actions or attitudes. Derk Pereboom, a skeptic about free will, thinks that moral responsibility does not actually attach to human agency. Nevertheless, Pereboom (2009) thinks that even in the absence of moral responsibility, agents can be called to give account for their actions, and certain reactive attitudes toward agents might be appropriate (just not ones of strict praise or blame).

of sin_{mr}? Or are they in some other sense sinful but not blameworthy for being in that state? Or are they merely adversely affected by human or angelic sin? As I argue in section IV, the plausibility of premises (4) and (5) depends on how we answer these questions.

Clough's arguments for attributing sin to animals seem to trade primarily in sin_{mr}. This makes sense, given that he is exploring the possibility of applying an Anselmian account of the atonement to animals. In that tradition, satisfaction models of the atonement hold that God's justice requires the debt of sin to be repaid, and Christ dies on the cross to satisfy divine justice in the place of guilty humanity. Relatedly, penal substitution models hold that Christ bears the penalty for sin. The concepts of debt, blame, and punishment are most appropriate, one could argue *only* appropriate, in connection with sin_{mr}.

Since I have insufficient space and no expertise, I will set aside Clough's biblical arguments for attributing sin_{mr} to animals and focus instead on what he says about animal behavior and human moral responsibility. Clough begins by making the case that animals are not mere slaves to instinct. They have some control of over how they act and can exhibit moral emotions like empathy and shame.[3]

He then goes on to cite examples from ethological studies where animals engage in behaviors that are hard to dismiss as entirely innocent. Jane Goodall recounts aggressive, violent chimpanzee behavior that shocked her in her early days of field work. Chimpanzees would engage in what looked like warfare and brutally retaliate against opposing factions by killing rival offspring. Infanticide is in fact very common across primate species, and we need not look very far to find instances of brutal or cruel behavioral tendencies in other species. Clough argues that it will not do to write off these behaviors as innocent just because they enhance the evolutionary fitness of individual animals or groups. We generally do not take facts about what human behaviors enhance fitness to be exculpatory for selfish human behavior.

I think Clough is right that there are clear examples of animals acting in ways that are inimical to their own flourishing or to the flourishing of their group, and they have the ability not to perform those actions. There is something undeniably suboptimal about the exercise of animal agency in these cases, and I am fine with calling these instances of animal sin. At the same time, whether these count as instances of animal sin_{mr} depends on what we take moral responsibility to consist in.

Here Clough argues that we routinely hold humans morally responsible for the things they do, but humans are, like animals, very compromised in their agency. He is right on this score. Humans are subject to constitutive and antecedent moral luck, as our temperaments and upbringing determine our character but are largely out of our control. We act in ways that are partly determined by our deliberate choices and partly determined by external influences. Our behavior is highly susceptible to situational variants, and our characters far more fragile than we care to imagine. Human moral responsibility is a messy, mixed bag.

So why, Clough asks, do we rule out the possibility that animals are morally responsible for who they are and what they do on the grounds that they act from a mixture of deliberate and nondeliberate factors when we are perfectly happy to attribute moral responsibility to humans who are in more or less the same position? He asks for a principled reason to attribute a difference in kind as opposed to a difference in degree between human an animal agency. In what follows, I make the case for such a reason.

---

[3] See in connection here Deane-Drummond (2009).

IV. ANIMAL AGENCY AND MORAL RESPONSIBILITY

I will now argue that if animals are implicated in the problem of sin, sin_{mr} is the wrong type to attribute to them.[4] Whether or not any agent is capable of acting morally or immorally will depend on what conception of what morality one begins with. Philosopher Grace Clement gives a helpful genealogy of views of animal agency and morality, classifying them as broadly Rationalist or Empiricist. Rationalists theories, in the traditions of Aristotle and Kant, say moral agency depends on the ability to act for the right sorts of reasons. Though moral emotions play a crucial role in many Rationalist theories, views in this camp contend that animals cannot be moral agents because they are not able to take any kind of evaluative stance toward the reasons and/or motivations they have for acting (Clement 2013: 2).

Empiricists like Hume, however, think morality is a matter of having the right kind of moral sentiments. There is good empirical evidence that many mammals, especially primates, have rich emotional lives and are able to share a basic level of empathy with others (de Waal 2008). Since animals arguably have moral sentiments like empathy (or something in the neighborhood), they may have a certain kind of moral agency on Empiricist theories. But as Clement explains, even Hume doubted that animals participate in morality in a way relevantly similar to what humans do, since animals are unable to judge the deliverances of their moral sentiments as right or wrong, or to transcend their natural, sentimental biases in a way that allows them to follow impartial norms of justice. By a large majority, philosophers have denied that animals are the kinds of agents who can be held morally responsible for what they do (Clement 2013). While there are some detractors, this view comes close to something like philosophical orthodoxy, and if true it precludes the possibility that sin_{mr} is attributable to animals.

Are these philosophers right to rule out the possibility that animals are morally responsible agents? In my view, Clough is right to affirm the great dignity of animal agency, and I wish to go as far as possible with him in crediting many species of animals with significant agency. Danger lurks though in how we raise or lower the bar for what makes an agent count as morally responsible. If we fail to get the criteria correct, we will make errors not just in whether we give appropriate moral praise or blame to animals, but also in whether we get the human cases correct.

The expansive contemporary literature on moral responsibility in philosophy is full of complication and nuance in order to account for the messiness of human agency to which Clough's arguments appeal. Though no philosophical account of moral responsibility is without controversy, one influential distinction made early on by Harry Frankfurt offers a helpful point of entry. Frankfurt distinguishes between an agent's having free will and having freedom of the will. Free will consists in the ability to act such that one can choose either to perform an action or not to perform that action. Freedom of the will, on the other hand, consists in being able to endorse or repudiate one's action and attitudes as one's own. Animals, Frankfurt readily admits, have free will in many instances. They are not mere creatures of instinct. In Frankfurt's assessment though, animals do not have freedom of the will (Frankfurt 1971).

---

[4] I will limit my reflections here to highly intelligent animals like primates, corvids, elephants, and cetaceans. If the considerations I bring to bear on animals in these species rule out the possibility that sin_{mr} is attributable to them, it will follow that sin is likewise not attributable to less intelligent species either.

Frankfurt explains freedom of the will in terms of a hierarchical understanding of the will. A person has first-order desires, and then higher-order desires about those first-order desires. To illustrate, I may want to point out a colleague's flaws, but I also wish I did not have such a desire, as I do not want to be the kind of person who is quick to point out the flaws of others. What is important about higher-order desires is that they express the kind of person an individual wants to be. An individual's sense of who they are, according to Frankfurt, is rooted in this ability to endorse or repudiate their lower-order desires. This is what allows a person to have a say in who she is and who she becomes.

Frankfurt's idea of a hierarchically structured will is just a heuristic, the adequacy of which is debated by philosophers. But what he thinks a person's higher-order desires express maps onto what some philosophers call the "deep self." Another influential view, David Shoemaker's, contends that the deep self is made up of a cluster of cares and commitment. Caring, he says, is "emotionally dispositive" (Shoemaker 2015: 25). If I care about someone or something, I will be disposed to have positive emotional reactions when things go well for the object of my care and negative ones when things go poorly for them. Commitments are more like evaluative stances that spell out what matters to a person. According to Shoemaker, moral responsibility is attributable to an agent only if her actions or attitudes express the care-commitment cluster compromising her deep self (48). The intuitive idea here is that we hold agents accountable for what their actions and attitudes show us about who they really are.

Does it make any sense to attribute moral responsibility to an animal in virtue of its deep self? It is not clear to me in what sense an animal could *have* what Shoemaker calls a deep self. Now, I should say that the language of "deep self" is somewhat misleading. It would seem to connote a lack of a meaningful subjectivity, or the absence of a seat of thought and feeling. I would not want to deny such meaningful subjectivity to animals, or to humans whose agency is impaired such that they do not have the kind of care/commitment clusters Shoemaker is talking about. But if we limit the meaning of "deep self" to the rather technical sense explained above, I find it empirically implausible that any animals would have one.

Animals likely do not have higher-order desires or commitments. Having such mental states would require fairly sophisticated skills for meta-cognition and executive functioning. While there is some empirical evidence that some primates, for example, do have *some* skills in those domains, they are rather limited.[5] Perhaps some animals have cares in the sense of relatively stable dispositions to respond emotionally to the things that matter to them. But how would it be that they would "own" or identify with those cares? What could unify or harmonize the competing cares an animal might have? And most importantly, how could those cares allow them to be in the driver seat, determining what sort of animals they become? Shoemaker himself denies that moral responsibility is attributable to animals (2015: 25), and I am inclined to think both he and Frankfurt are right.[6]

The most generous estimate in my view would be that some highly intelligent animals with limited forms of self-awareness fare as well as human children do when it comes to agency. That is, we do not hold them morally responsible for their actions and attitudes,

---

[5] See Smith and Beran (2013) and Chudasama (2011) for a helpful summaries of meta-cognition and executive function research in primates.
[6] Shoemaker's work is expressly concerned with clarifying what is going on with cases of marginal agency. While I focus on what Shoemaker says about attributability here, it would be interesting to look at the applicability of the other facets of responsibility in his taxonomy—answerability and accountability—though I think the case is even stronger against applying those categories to animals.

but there is something in the neighborhood of moral responsibility that we can assign to them in virtue of which they can be the appropriate targets of our admiration or disdain. Bringing children into the conversations should illustrate that there is much at stake in where we locate the standards for moral responsibility. Such distinctions are not, as Clough charges, mere artifacts of anthropocentric bias favoring traits allegedly possessed by only humans. They are necessary considerations for making proper judgments about human cases.

For Roman Catholics, children must reach what's dubbed "the age of reason" before they go to the sacrament of reconciliation. Before reaching that age, children cannot actually perform any actions or hold any attitudes that count as sin_{mr}.[7] It is hard, perhaps impossible, to nail down when individual children cross the relevant threshold of maturity, but some threshold is nevertheless very helpful. The age specified as the age of reason is currently seven. In my view, just as it is wrong to attribute sin_{mr} to children, it would be wrong to attribute sin_{mr} to animals. We might express reactive attitudes of praise or blame toward children, but we do so just in anticipation of the kind of agents we hope they will become. The same cannot be said for animals.

I think a helpful way to think about this is to consider the difference between a rebellious toddler and rebellious teenager. There are similar psychological phenomena in play in both the toddler and teenage years. In both phases of development, children try to differentiate themselves from their caregivers and resist the guidance of authorities in order to assert their independence. In both stages they are going through rapid brain development. But when we say that a teen is rebelling, we mean something quite different than what we mean when we say that a toddler is rebelling.

Teens have some ability to take ownership of their choices, to reflect on whether the ways they act out express who they want to be. They will get much better at making good decisions as their prefrontal cortices develop, but this second developmental pass at individuation is very different than the first pass they had in toddlerhood, even if the tantrums look the same. The point here is not that the rebelliousness of teens is always bad—it is in very many cases just a healthy part of their development. The point is rather that an agent's increased abilities in executive functioning and reflection make a huge difference in whether attitudes of praise or blame will be appropriate in many cases.

Now let's bring these considerations back to the version of the atonement we are considering. Since Anselmian models of the atonement make weighty claims about dessert of debt or punishment, we should ask if the story we tell about the wages of sin makes any sense at all if the agents in question are toddlers or the agential equivalent. If the rebellion in the Garden (or wherever) was like the rebellion of a toddler, the Anselmian way of conceiving of the problem of sin looks highly unpalatable, insofar as it supposes that the sinners in question deserve death. Whatever sense we make of Rom. 6:23, the attribution of this debt to children should, at the very least, make us stop and think.

Philosopher Mark Rowlands makes a similar point about the relationship between whatever kind of responsibility we can attribute to animals and what sorts of punishments would be appropriate to dole out to them. He says,

---

[7] Part of what is in play in the Roman Catholic tradition is the distinction between mortal and venial sins. I have bracketed off discussion of this distinction as it is not shared across Christian traditions. However, I think the case against attributing mortal sin_{mr} to animals would be quite easy to make.

It is not helpful, in this context, to talk of degrees of responsibility. Suppose a pig—let us call her "Babe"—has been tried and is to be executed for the heinous crime of stealing the neighboring farmer's turnips. Babe, the court has decided, is a moral agent and so is responsible for what she does. This does seem silly. But the attempt to save the idea of moral agency by invoking the idea of degrees of responsibility scarcely redeems it. To claim that Babe is less responsible for what she does—less than, say, an average adult human—seems to imply that the punishment should be mitigated. Instead of death, perhaps a good flogging would be appropriate. This punishment is as silly as the original. (2013: 19)

I share Rowland's intuition here. When it comes to evaluating the fittingness of punishment to crime, especially on a retributive theory of justice, the fact that an agent's moral responsibility is highly mitigated does not just mean we ought to dial down the intensity of the punishment we assign. It means that what is needed *instead* is some way to correct or restore what is broken or underdeveloped in that agent. Attributing damnable sin_{mr} to animals makes Anselm's story awfully ugly.

There is one additional theoretical cost to attributing sin_{mr} to animals I wish to mention. In some ways, attributing moral responsibility to animals makes the problem of evil (as it applies to animals, at least) a bit thornier. What if the phenomenon of predation, or at least certain instances of predation, were attributable to animal sin_{mr}? Killing seems to be a pretty good candidate for what would count as sinful action. If it is the case that animals sin_{mr} when they prey upon other animals, then the world contains the following states of affairs: (a) prey animals suffer what are in millions of instances slow, painful deaths, and (b) predators are worse off for having been the cause of those instances of suffering. State (a) seems to be a datum that is already hard enough to explain. Is the theist stuck with state (b) as well? She would be if the predators' causal connection to suffering is of the sort for which they were morally responsible.[8]

To sum up this section, I want to return to the framing argument I formulated above. I said that whether or not the premises would be plausible would depend on what is meant by "sin" and "implicated in the problem of sin." As I have argued now, I find it very difficult to make sense of attributing sin_{mr} to animals. The conclusion of the framing argument states that animals are implicated in the problem of sin. But if what is meant by sin is sin_{mr}, the conclusion strikes me as false. The most likely premise to question then in order to see how the argument misfires is premise (4). That premise is conditional and states that if animals are not left out of the work of the atonement, it is because they are implicated in the problem of sin. If the antecedent here is true, like Clough argues from Pauline texts, we should think of some other way to explain how it is that the atonement applies to animals that does not implicate them in being blameworthy for sin.

---

[8] Now, one could object that one way to deal with the badness of (a) would be to attribute those deaths not to God's design for the world, but to the exercise of animal agency. In this way, we could explain predation much in the same way various philosophical defenses and theodicies explain instances of human suffering—as the collateral damage of the great good of free will. But given that animal agency is much more limited than human agency, it is arguably not as weighty a good as is human free will. And since animals would seem to have rather limited control as to whether they preyed on others, it is hard to see how God would be off the hook for leaving such consequential matters up to animal choice. In this way, the objection is vulnerable to the kinds of criticism Marilyn McCord Adams raises about the adequacy of free will defenses with her famous stove analogy. See Adams (1999: 38).

As far as I can see, Anselmian models depend on sin_{mr} as the target notion of sin. The lesson to be drawn is that whatever advantages Anselmian models have, they cannot tell the whole story of the atonement if the scope of the atonement is supposed to be cosmic. This may not trouble many, as it is now commonplace to argue that one need not wed themselves to one model of the atonement in hopes that it will offer a grand theory of everything. But one area where analytic theologians could advance this dialectic is to explore other notions of sin and models of the atonement that might apply to animals.

V. CONCLUSION

If these criticisms of Clough's view of animal agency suggest anything other than admiration for his work, I hereby cancel any such implication. I intend this kind of critical attention as the greatest kind of compliment an analytic theologian can pay. In my view, analytic theologians can find no better place to enter into dialogue with theology of animals than in Clough's work. In particular, the provocative questions he raises about the nature of animal agency have far reaching implications for theological matters, both systematic and practical, and ought to be explored in more detail.

In one sense, the nature of animal agency might not matter much for baseline discussions about the moral status of animals, as most defenders of animal rights and animal welfare have argued that patienthood should not depend on moral agency. (And the same point can and should be made about humans with marginal agency.) However, there are other important ethical questions about animals that might depend on what we say out about their agency. What forms of paternalism, if any, are acceptable in our interactions with animals? This question might be of particular interest to theologians who conceive of our obligations to animals in terms of dominion or stewardship. Additionally, we can ask whether working animals or companion animals have special rights or responsibilities in virtue of what they contribute to our communities, whether deliberations about keeping animals in captivity depend on what sort of agency those animals have, and so on.

There are likewise a whole host of important questions in systematic theology that might be at stake here too. We ought to have something to say about the value of animal agency in our theodicies and defenses for animal suffering. Considerations of animal agency might shape how we think about animals in the afterlife. The evolutionary emergence of moral responsibility has implications for accounts of the fall, as our pre-hominid ancestors might have been marginal agents *par excellence*. And as I hope to have shown in this chapter, figuring out how the atonement might apply to animals, at least on some models, requires careful attention to the nature of animal agency. These would all be very excellent candidates for analytic attention.[9]

References

Adams, M. M. (1999), *Horrendous Evils and the Goodness of God*, Ithaca, NY: Cornell University Press.

Anselm, St. (1969), *Why God Became Man, and The Virgin Conception and Original Sin*, trans. J. M. Colleran, Albany: Magi Books.

---

[9] I am grateful to Alicia Finch, Christa McKirkland, Davis Meadors, Tim Pawl, James Arcadi, J. T. Turner, Jr., and especially Jonathan Rutledge for generous and insightful advice on this chapter.

Bauckham, R. (2011), *Living with Other Cretaures: Green Exegesis and Theology*, Waco: Baylor University Press.
Bekoff, M. (2004), "Wild Justice and Fair Play: Cooperation, Forgiveness, and Morality in Animals," *Biology and Philosophy*, 19 (4): 489–520.
Berkman, J. (2009), "Towards a Thomistic Theology of Animality," in C. Deane-Drummond and D. Clough (eds.), *Creaturely Theology: On God, Humans and Other Animals*, 21–40, London: Hymns Ancient and Modern.
Camosy, C. C. (2013), *For Love of Animals: Christian Ethics, Consistent Action*, Cincinnati: Franciscan Media.
Chignell, A., T. Cuneo, and M. C. Halteman, eds. (2015), *Philosophy Comes to Dinner*, London: Routledge.
Chudasama, Y. (2011), "Animal Models of Prefrontal-Executive Function," *Behavioral Neuroscience*, 125 (3): 327–43.
Clement, G. (2013), "Animals and Moral Agency: The Recent Debate and Its Implications," *Journal of Animal Ethics*, 3(1): 1–14.
Clough, D. (2012), *On Animals. Vol. 1: Systematic Theology*, London: T&T Clark.
Clough, D. (2013), "Putting Animals in Their Place: On the Theological Classification of Animals," in C. Deane-Drummond, R. Artinian-Kaiser, and D. L. Clough (eds.), *Animals as Religious Subjects*, New York: T&T Clark.
Clough, D. (2018), *On Animals, Vol. 2: Theological Ethics*, London: T&T Clark.
Creegan, N. H. (2013), *Animal Suffering and the Problem of Evil*, Oxford: Oxford University Press.
Crummett, D. (2017), "The Problem of Evil and the Suffering of Creeping Things," *International Journal for Philosophy of Religion*, 82 (1): 71–88.
Crummett, D. (2019), "Eschatology for Creeping things (and Other Animals)," in B. Hereth and K. Timpe (eds.), *The Lost Sheep in Philosophy of Religion: New Perspectives on Disability, Gender, Race, and Animals*, London: Routledge.
Deane-Drummond, C. and D. Clough, eds. (2009), *Creaturely Theology: On God, Humans and Other Animals*, London: Hymns Ancient and Modern.
Deane-Drummond, C. (2009), "Are Animals Moral? Taking Soundings through Vice, Virtue, and Imago Dei," in C. Deane-Drummond and D. Clough (eds.), *Creaturely Theology: On God, Humans, and Other Animals*, 190–210, London: Hymns Ancient and Modern.
de Waal, F. B. M. (2008), "Putting the Altruism Back into Altruism: The Evolution of Empathy," *Annual Review of Psychology*, 59 (1): 279–300.
Dougherty, T. (2014), *The Problem of Animal Pain: A Theodicy for All Creatures Great and Small*, New York: Palgrave Macmillan.
Frankfurt, H. G. (1971), "Freedom of the Will and the Concept of a Person," *Journal of Philosophy*, 68 (1): 5–20.
George, M. I. (2003), "Thomas Aquinas Meets Nim Chimpsky: On the Debate about Humans Nature and the Nature of Other Animals," *The Aquinas Review*, 10: 1–5.
George, M. I. (2009), "Descartes's Language Test for Rationality," *American Catholic Philosophical Quarterly*, 83 (1): 107–25.
Halteman, M.C. (2009), "Compassionate Eating as Care of Creation," *Between the Species: A Journal of Ethics*, 13 (9): 1–15.
Hasker, W. (2008), *The Triumph of God over Evil: Theodicy for a World of Suffering*, Downers Grove, IL: IVP Academic.
Hauerwas, S., and J. Berkman (1992), "The Chief End of All Flesh," *Theology Today*, 49 (2): 196–208.
Hearne, V. (2007), *Adam's Task: Calling Animals by Name*, New York: Skyhorse.

Hereth, B. (2019), "Animal Gods," in B. Hereth and K. Timpe (eds.), *The Lost Sheep in Philosophy of Religion: New Perspectives on Disability, Gender, Race, and Animals*, London: Routledge.

Linzey, A. (1976), *Animal Rights: A Christian Assessment of Man's Treatment of Animals*, London: SCM Press.

Linzey, A., and T. Regan, eds. (2007), *Animals and Christianity: A Book of Readings*, Cascade: Wipf and Stock.

Linzey, A., and D. Yamamoto, eds. (1998), *Animals on the Agenda: Questions about Animals for Theology and Ethics*, London: SCM Press.

Murray, M. (2011), *Nature Red in Tooth and Claw: Theism and the Problem of Animal Suffering*, Oxford: Oxford University Press.

Pawl, F. G. (2016), "Suffering and Flourishing in Social Animals," in D. V. Meconi, SJ (ed.), *On Earth as It Is in Heaven: Cultivating a Contemporary Theology of Creation*, 159–73, Grand Rapids, MI: Eerdmans.

Pawl, F. G. (2018), "Human Superiority, Divine Providence, and the Animal Good: A Thomistic Defense of Creaturely Hierarchy," in O. D. Crisp and F. Sanders (eds.), *The Christian Doctrine of Humanity*, 41–60, Grand Rapids, MI: Zondervan.

Pawl, F. G. (2019), "Exploring Theological Zoology: Might Animals be Spiritual but not Religious?," in B. Hereth and K. Timpe (eds.), *The Lost Sheep in Philosophy of Religion: New Perspectives on Disability, Gender, Race, and Animals*, 163–82, London: Routledge.

Pereboom, D. (2009), "Hard Incompatibilism," in Fischer, J. M., R. Kane, D. Pereboom, and M. Vargas, *Four Views on Free Will*, 85–125, Malden, MA: Blackwell (2007, print).

Regan, T. (2004), *The Case for Animal Rights: Updated with a New Preface*, 1st ed., revised, Berkeley: University of California Press.

Rowlands, M. (2013). "Animals and Moral Motivation: A Response to Clement," *Journal of Animal Ethics*, 3(1): 15–24.

Seacord, B. (2011), "Animals, Phenomenal Consciousness, and Higher-Order Theories of Mind," *Philo: A Journal of Philosophy*, 14 (2): 201–22.

Shoemaker, D. (2015), *Responsibility from the Margins*, Oxford: Oxford University Press.

Singer, P. (2009), *Animal Liberation: The Definitive Classic of the Animal Movement*, reissue, New York: Harper Perennial Modern Classics.

Smith, J. D., and M. Beran (2013), "The Highs and Lows of Theoretical Interpretation in Animals Meta-Cognition Research," *Philosophical Transactions of the Royal Society B: Biological Sciences*, 367 (1594): 1297–309.

Sollereder, B. (2018), *God, Evolution, and Animal Suffering: Theodicy without a Fall*, London: Routledge.

Southgate, C. (2008), *The Groaning of Creation: God, Evolution, and the Problem of Evil*, Louisville: Westminster John Knox Press.

Tardiff, A. (1998), "A Catholic Case for Vegetarianism," *Faith and Philosophy*, 15 (2): 210–22.

van Inwagen, P. (2008), *The Problem of Evil*, Oxford: Oxford University Press.

Visala, A. (2018), "Human Cognition and the Image of God', in O. D. Crisp and F. Sanders (eds.), *The Christian Doctrine of Humanity*, 91–109, Grand Rapids: Zondervan.

CHAPTER THIRTY-ONE

Analytic Theology and the Sciences

AKU VISALA

The question of how analytic theology is related to the sciences can be taken in two ways. On the one hand, we can ask whether analytic theology qualifies as a science or science-like discipline. Are its methods and results such that they would satisfy the criteria of science? Should analytic theology justify its project by adopting scientific methods and results? On the other hand, we can ask how analytic theology has engaged and could possibly engage with the sciences, like biology, psychology, or physics. While acknowledging the importance of the former, this chapter will focus on the latter set of questions.[1] More specifically, I will suggest some motivations for analytic theologians to think carefully about their relationship to the sciences and examine cases where analytic theologians have in fact engaged with the sciences.[2] I will conclude the chapter by looking at how analytic theology might contribute to the more general religion and science dialogue and point to untapped potential for future engagement.

I. WHY THINK ABOUT SCIENCE AND THEOLOGY?

When discussing methodological issues, the focus of analytic theologians so far has been on making sense of their relationship to analytic philosophy. Because of this, direct engagement with the sciences has been relegated to the background. A brief look into a recent bibliography of analytic theology (Abraham 2012) reveals only a handful of articles even mentioning the sciences. Similarly, analytic theology handbooks and readers (e.g., Crisp 2009) offer little to no articles on these themes.[3] This lack of systematic engagement is understandable. If one's central aim is to formulate a coherent account of the metaphysics of the incarnation, for instance, it seems that the results of physics and neuroscience are mostly irrelevant for this task. This explains why analytic theology has yet to develop a systematic form of engagement with the sciences. There are, however, a number of reasons why analytic theologians should carefully consider this issue.

First, analytic philosophers themselves are engaged in an extensive debate over the relationship between analytic philosophy and the sciences (Haug 2014). These debates

---

[1] Regarding the former set of questions, see Benedikt Göcke's chapter in this volume.
[2] I take "the sciences" rather broadly as natural and behavioral sciences. Biology, physics, psychology and neuroscience are instances of science whereas most humanities, like history, are not.
[3] The two exceptions are Ratzsch (2009) and Murray (2009), as well as the present volume.

often culminate in the question of whether metaphysics is possible and, if it is, how it is related to the sciences (Tahko 2015; Kornblith 2016). Analytic theologians have large stakes in the debate. If it turns out, for instance, that the naturalists insisting on the continuity of science and metaphysics are correct, some analytic theologians would take this to undermine the whole theological project, since theology often relies on general metaphysical categories.

Second, the relationship of theological commitment to "the scientific worldview" is very much a popular topic of discussion in Western societies. This is especially the case in politically loaded controversies over creationism, theistic evolutionism, the so-called New Atheism, and secularization, for instance. Religious and nonreligious people ask whether and how the scientific picture of the natural world might be reconciled with traditional religious views. Given the pressing need for clear and sophisticated analyses, analytic theologians would do well to apply their expertise to this subject. Although it has multiple other functions as well, analytic theology could also perform an *apologetic function* in this specific context. There are arguments suggesting that large-scale scientific results, evolutionary biology and cosmology, for instance, undermine the Christian theological project in some way or another. It is often argued that Darwinist evolutionary biology undercuts reasons to believe in God. The challenge is not restricted to the results of the sciences. Rather, the progress and trustworthiness of the sciences raises epistemological challenges to the rationality of religious beliefs and commitments. Herman Philipse (2012), for instance, has argued that the ways in which religious beliefs are formed (claims about revelations, testimony, etc.) are epistemically inferior to scientific ways of forming beliefs. He concludes that, for this reason, one should take science as having superior authority over less reliably produced religious beliefs.

Third, it would be easy to divide up the domains of the sciences and analytic theology by invoking the distinction between metaphysics and empirical study. This would not, however, do justice to the richness of the Christian theological tradition and ways of speaking. As a distinctively theological project, analytic theology is mostly focused on core theological doctrines. But these do not exhaust the domain of theology: scriptures and the theological tradition are hardly devoid of empirical claims. Theologians make empirical claims when they discuss theological anthropology, natural history, creation, eschatology, theological ethics, and many other such topics. Sometimes, such claims are not even clearly identified and empirically assessed. This is where engaging with contemporary sciences might help analytic theology. Furthermore, even while the sciences cannot directly approach the metaphysics of theism, they can approach how people reason about such things and the moral psychology assumed by various theological doctrines, for instance.

Finally, the overall integrative aim of analytic theology should give ample motivation for analytic theologians to incorporate as much science as they can into Christian theology. It is clear that theologians of the past have used and sought to integrate Christian theology and the best available scientific knowledge. If analytic theologians only engage with the best of what analytic epistemology and metaphysics have to offer, they will, arguably, fail in the project of formulating, clarifying, and defending the overall Christian worldview.

In the following sections, I will briefly examine some cases in which analytic theologians engage with the sciences. I will begin from epistemology and move towards issues revolving around evolution, theodicy, and the emergence of religion.

II. WAYS OF KNOWING PERSONS

In her extensive theodicy, Eleonore Stump (2010: chapter 3) uses results in neuroscience and cognitive science to support her epistemological stance. When arguing for the centrality of narrative and personal knowledge in Christian philosophy, she draws a distinction between Dominican and Franciscan knowledge. By "Dominican knowledge," she refers to propositional knowledge that analytic philosophers usually work with. This leaves analytic theodicies and their background theories too "rationalistic" and such that they do not connect with the human experience of pain, love, and suffering. Stump contrasts this with "Franciscan knowledge," which is very difficult to form in propositional terms. This form of knowledge is obtained through narrative and direct personal interaction. For the purposes of theology, it is especially this intimate knowledge of persons that is at stake, since God, the object of theological knowledge, is a personal agent.

In defense of Franciscan knowledge, Stump then invokes a number of scientific results. She refers to studies of autism, where it has become standard to take autism as a failure of human social cognition. Those with autism do have *knowledge that*, Dominican knowledge, but they have great difficulties in attending to persons and relating to them, Franciscan knowledge (*knowledge of*). One possible explanation is that their social cognition, which allows for relatively direct and nonconceptual forms of knowledge of the other person, is impaired. There is discussion about whether the neural mechanisms of this type of cognition operate on mirror neurons. Recently discovered mirror neurons, which fire both when an action is done and when it is perceived to be done by someone else, give humans the ability to "perceive" emotions, intentions and actions of others. These results point to the existence of a neural and cognitive mechanism specialized in knowledge of persons (especially their intentions and emotions) and also that this mechanism works somewhat independently from other systems, like those specialized in processing propositional knowledge (Stump 2010: 64–75).

Stump also discusses other results concerning autism and social cognition, namely, those that pertain to a phenomenon called *joint attention*. Developmental evidence suggests that even young children have a unique ability to share attention with one another. Babies are able to direct their gazes where the caregiver is looking, and children carefully attend to whatever others are pointing towards. Again, joint attention is often lacking in autistic children.[4] Stump subsequently uses the notion of joint attention to develop a novel notion of omnipresence: it is not enough that God has unmediated causal and cognitive contact with the creation; God must be personally present by being available for shared attention with creatures. This is what proper personal intimacy requires. Stump then uses joint attention as a springboard to develop notions of love and personal closeness (Stump 2010: 109–18).

Mirror neurons and joint attention provide scientific evidence for a specialized form of knowledge about persons that is neither first-person knowledge nor third-person knowledge. Stump calls this *second-person knowledge* (Stump 2010: 75–80). Second-person knowledge is direct knowledge about another person's experience, a form of intimately sharing another person's experience via empathy. It is not first-person knowledge, where the subject knows her own experience, nor is it third-person knowledge, where the

---

[4]Primatologist Michael Tomasello (2014) has suggested that the basic abilities of joint attention and shared intentionality are prior to language and are the key cognitive features that make human social and cultural life possible.

subject reports another person's properties or experiences. Second-person knowledge is best approached via closeness to other people and, crucially, through narrative and storytelling, which cannot be reduced or translated into propositional knowledge.

III. EVOLUTION, SIN, AND THEODICY

Consider another case: the evolutionary account of human origins and uniqueness (or the lack thereof). Here we have two forms of engagement intertwined. On the one hand, there is an apologetic issue of whether Christian theological anthropology is compatible with the Darwinian evolutionary account. On the other hand, there is also the possibility of scientific contribution to theological anthropology in a constructive sense. Theologically, there are a number of overlapping questions here: what it means to be created in the image of God, the nature of original sin, human uniqueness and basic abilities, the notion of human nature, the nature of biblical accounts of creation and fall, just to mention a few.

Thomas McCall seeks to demonstrate the usefulness of analytic theology for complex theological and scientific debates (2015: 124–52). He examines the recent debate on revisionist accounts of the fall. Traditional accounts posit the existence of an original couple of humans, whose disobedience introduces sin in the world. From this moral failure, various other evils follow: death, decay, and widespread corruption. Because of this, God must put a plan of salvation in motion that reaches its high point in Christ.[5] This basic story is the reason why so much ink has been spilled over the "evolution versus creation" controversy. People on both sides see the traditional story in contradiction with the scientific story of human origins, which involves millions of years of gradual evolution, where death and moral evil are already present. Given the evolutionary evidence, it is very difficult to see how *Homo sapiens* could be the progenitors of one, single human pair that were uniquely created.

One solution to this problem is to formulate a revisionist account of sin and human origins that takes the scientific evidence seriously. The revisionist account, motivated by contemporary evolutionary biology, maintains that the Genesis account of Adam and Eve is a literary creation, not meant to be taken as a history as modern scholarship understands it. Death, decay, and immoral behavior do not exist because of the fall. They exist because humans have inherited certain behaviors (some good, others bad) from their nonhuman ancestors. From this, the revisionist account draws the conclusion that sin, decay, and death were part of God's original plan, not forces of evil that were unleashed in the world because of the disobedience of humans.

McCall suggests that analytic theologians would do well to get involved in such debates (2015: 136–8). First and foremost, they can clarify the central concepts being used. McCall points out that the debate is somewhat unclear as to what evolutionary biology and related disciplines actually entail and on what basis. If there is to be a conflict between evolution and creation, we must carefully distinguish different meanings of "evolution" and "creation." The revisionists often take "evolution" as a package deal including the old age of the Earth, natural selection as the central mechanisms of change, and the common origins of all biological life. All these claims can come apart and each requires different evidence in support. Similarly, Creationists not only take "evolution" as a package deal, they also take

---

[5]For an inventive defense of the traditional account, see Hudson (2014).

"creation" to refer simultaneously to a number of claims, including the claims that God created everything *ex nihilo* and that God created the first human pair as images of God.

McCall does not want to argue for a specific solution to these challenges. Instead, he points out how analytic work could help to map out possible answers. First, he sees no necessary contradiction between creation and evolution, since theists are well within their rights to reject naturalism as a metaphysical thesis. Similarly, there is no contradiction between creation out of nothing and biological organisms emerging slowly over time. Moreover, there is no contradiction between evolution and God creating Adam and Eve as images of God. Even if Adam and Eve share much of their biology with other species, it does not follow that God could not have created them uniquely. Even if the evolutionary account is accepted, the option of special creation for humanity still remains open. Or there is the possibility of God addressing or "refurbishing" some pair or a group of existing Homo sapiens for his special purposes (McCall 2015: 146). So, McCall concludes that there are plenty of options left and claims that there is a necessary contradiction between Christian and evolutionary accounts of human origins are false.

A related debate revolves around evolution and the goodness of God. McCall highlights this issue but does not deal with it directly. This is crucial for theology, not just in the apologetic sense, because of its picture of how the natural world works. Some have argued that since theology posits the existence of a good and personal creator, it is incompatible with the evolutionary picture of nature, which necessarily involves death and suffering as mechanisms for life. If a good God were to create a world, it seems improbable that God would choose a mechanism, such as evolution by natural selection. This is exactly the problem that vexed Charles Darwin: creation by means of natural selection involves so much death, violence, and senseless suffering that it is difficult to imagine how an omnipotent and good God could not have found another way to create the variety of biological life we now see (Draper 2012). The resulting problem has different names, such as the problem of animal suffering and the problem of evolutionary evil. Given the fact that both Darwin and contemporary critics of religion like Richard Dawkins often argue in this fashion, it is surprising that analytic theologians and philosophers of religion have only recently begun to work on this problem.

Given the restrictions of the present chapter, I cannot offer an overview of recent attempts to answer the problem of animal suffering. Let me instead make a point about how the sciences, especially primatology and the study of non-human animals, have contributed to the discussion. According to Michael Murray, one way to solve the problem is to deny that non-human animals suffer in a morally relevant way (2008: 52–8). Such Neo-Cartesian views would entail that animal consciousness is such that it does not allow for self-reflection or self-understanding. Given this, nonhuman animals can be said to be conscious and feel pain, but they cannot suffer in the moral sense of the word, since they lack the ability to form higher-order representations of themselves. However, Murray is not too optimistic about such views being true, because of other results from the study of animal cognition. Although there are a number of problems in attributing phenomenal consciousness to nonhuman animals (perhaps even humans themselves!), recent studies show that many animals are more like humans than we previously anticipated. These studies suggest that not only do many animals have internal cognitive states, some non-human animals might also have abilities for self-representation and self-consciousness. There is also evidence of non-human animal complex social emotions (Murray 2008: 58–68). Therefore, given our knowledge of animal cognition and neuroscience, the problem of animal suffering is not easily dissolved.

There is also another strand of analytic work related to evolutionary problem of evil. Sarah Coakley has worked closely with mathematician Martin Nowak researching altruism in evolution. Nowak has attempted to demonstrate how the "survival of the fittest" notion of biological evolution is false, or at least partial. Increasing one's fitness does not automatically lead to egoistic behaviors. Developing mathematical tools to analyze the benefits of cooperation, Nowak argues that the biological world is full of cooperation and altruism (sacrificing one's survival for others). An edited volume discussing this work contains essays on cooperation from different perspectives (Nowak and Coakley 2013). For the purposes of this chapter, the most interesting contributions in this volume discuss the theological and ethical aspects of cooperation in nature.

The volume discusses the ethical implications of cooperation and altruism. Should these facts have an impact on theological metaethics? In the case of human moral cognition, there is significant potential for fertile interaction between theology and the sciences. One popular view is that human morality is very much continuous with the social and moral behavior of other social primates, such as orangutans and chimpanzees. The same might apply to our moral judgments and intuitions: moral judgments might be based on our moral and social emotions, which are, in turn, responses to adaptive challenges in our social and natural environments. It has been suggested that humans are equipped with a set of cognitive modules that draw inferences about fairness and justice, for instance, in a way that is mostly insensitive to cultural differences (Hauser 2007).

The fact of widespread cooperation and altruism in the biological world, including human behavior, could be theologically significant. Alexander Pruss (2013) suggests that cooperation and altruism might be taken as evidence for the existence of the Christian God. This is so, because the sciences do not explain very well why moral altruism and biological cooperation coincide so completely. Moreover, Pruss suggests that naturalists have no scientific explanation for excessive or radical moral altruism. A theist could invoke God as the source of saintly moral motivation. Another theological contribution from Coakley (2013) suggests that scientific insights about cooperation and altruism might be relevant for formulating an account of divine providence and human freedom. Instead of predetermining the outcome of the complex process of the development of biological organisms, she suggests that God sets the rules of the development but gives it freedom to run by itself. God will, nevertheless, make sure that God's goals are realized as God can, like a chess-master, anticipate and counter all the moves of a novice player.

Finally, Michael Rota (2013) suggests that the novel view of extensive cooperation in nature might make the evolutionary problem of animal suffering examined above easier to solve. Perhaps the biological world is not simply a machine of competition and death but a source of creativity and cooperation. A theodicist might invoke God's willingness to make humans and other biological organisms co-creators and contributors to the creative process. The aforementioned points are brief but I hope they demonstrate the implications and usefulness of evolutionary considerations in a wide range of theological issues.

IV. RELIGION, EVOLUTION, AND DEBUNKING

I want to mention another case of analytic theology and science that is connected both to evolution and religion. Recently, a number of theologians and philosophers of the analytic mindset have engaged with *cognitive science of religion*. Cognitive science of religion is a multidisciplinary field of research in which theories from cognitive science, evolutionary psychology, and developmental psychology are invoked to explain religious beliefs and behaviors. For the most part, these engagements have been apologetic in nature; that is, their aim has been to diffuse the challenge from naturalistic accounts of religion. As such, the debates have mostly revolved around the issue of *debunking*, namely, whether results of cognitive science of religion undermine the rationality, justification or truth of religious beliefs. In addition to the debunking debate, however, there has been a genuine attempt by analytic theologians to contribute to the scientific study of religion as a whole (Schloss and Murray 2009).

The debate about debunking is not specific to religion only. It also involves our beliefs about values and morality (Joyce 2003; Griffiths and Wilkins 2013). Debunking arguments can be aimed at undermining the truth of these beliefs or the grounds on which we come to believe them. An evolutionary explanation can be counted as evidence against the truth of a religious belief or it can be used to undermine its justification. For the most part, the debate has focused on this latter point: debunking arguments usually target the grounding of a belief rather than its truth. In this case, they seek to undermine the rationality, justification, or otherwise cast doubt upon the belief on the basis of how it is generated (Kahane 2011). Debunking argument aimed against the rationality or justification of Christian theism have created a lively debate revolving around epistemological notions of reliability, evidence and warrant. A considerable body of work exists on this topic already (e.g., Clark and Rabinowitz 2011; Leech and Visala 2011; De Cruz and De Smedt 2014; Jong and Visala 2014; Visala 2014).[6]

In addition to the debunking discussion, there have been attempts to apply cognitive science of religion as a platform for theological theorizing. Justin Barrett and Kelly James Clark (2010), for example, have suggested that cognitive science now offers support for the notion of the natural knowledge of God, or the *sensus divinitatis*. If cognitive science of religion is correct and religion is easy for beings who have brains and bodies like ours, this provides evidence for the theological notion that humans are naturally open to God's revelation. Rather than being a product of very specific religious experiences, cultural contexts or some underlying pathology, the propensity for religion might be a deeply seated feature of panhuman cognition (Barrett 2011).

Finally, let me briefly mention the recent *Ashgate Companion to Theological Anthropology*, which explicitly adopts an analytic approach (Farris and Taliaferro 2015: xiii). This comprehensive volume provides discussions of various forms of *imago Dei*, accounts of person/body relationships and traditional doctrines of sin and grace as they relate to theological anthropology. Interestingly, many chapters either invoke scientific results in support of theological views or address scientifically motivated challenges to theological claims. A number of chapters invoke evolutionary biology in criticizing traditional forms of structural *imago Dei* and the closely associated view of human cognitive uniqueness. Although this line of reasoning is rather popular, there are authors maintaining that there is plenty of evidence that *Homo sapiens* are indeed cognitively unique in ways that coincide nicely with the idea that *imago Dei* refers to some structural features of human minds (Visala 2018; Barrett and Jarvinen 2015). Moreover, some chapters invoke neuroscience and cognitive science as evidence against traditional

---

[6]See also, van Eyghen (2020). Collected volumes include Schloss and Murray (2009) and Trigg and Barrett (2014).

forms of substance dualism. These challenges, by no means, prove human uniqueness or substance dualism false; but they put pressure on these ideas nevertheless.[7]

V. THE "RELIGION AND SCIENCE DIALOGUE" AND ANALYTIC THEOLOGY

We can now ask what analytic theology might contribute to the more general theological discussion on science and theology. Contemporary Christian theologians have had much to say about the relationship of science and theology. Here, I am referring to the enterprise often known as "the religion and science dialogue." For the most part, the religion and science dialogue is distinct from analytic theology. First, the dialogue has distinct theological and scientific roots. It can be traced to the 1960s Britain and United States where a number of scientist/theologians began to reflect systematically upon this topic. Subsequently, a subdiscipline of theology was formed. The normalization of this subfield can be seen in the establishment of institutions, programs, and the proliferation of basic textbooks and handbooks (e.g., Clayton and Simpson 2006). Second, the authors in the religion and science dialogue often represent wildly different methods, approaches, and aims. This is especially evident in epistemology: various non-foundationalist or post-foundationalist epistemologies are popular (e.g., van Huyssteen 2006). Accompanying these epistemological stances, there are forms of non-realism or anti-realism regarding religious language. Also, there is a wide variety of metaphysical views: theologians and scientists in this field have developed versions of panentheism, emergentism, and process philosophy and theology.

Despite the differences, there is clearly much overlap between analytic theology and the religion and science dialogue. Analytic theologians could easily participate in the dialogue, since contributions of analytic philosophy as well as analytic philosophy of religion have already established a foothold there. Alister McGrath (2002), who does not see himself as an analytic theologian, has provided extensive discussions of analytic philosophy of science and its contributions to theology. McGrath (2009) and others have also extensively discussed various theistic arguments, especially those invoking biological or cosmological design. Another example is Mikael Stenmark who has developed an analysis and several criticisms of scientism (2001). Stenmark (2004) has also suggested a detailed model of possible science/religion relationships. Finally, the overall aims of the religion and science dialogue and analytic theology partly overlap: both seek to diffuse the scientific challenge to Christian theology as well as take into account the best available knowledge when formulating theological theories. In other words, both seek to open a gateway through which theologians retain access to scientific results and form a methodology by which systematic theologians could employ in scientific engagement and theorizing.

As we already saw, McCall suggests that analytic theology might have a lot to contribute to theological work, in which complex empirical, philosophical, and theological questions overlap. This might be applicable to the case of the religion and science dialogue as well. Analytic theology can clarify the central questions and provide methods and tools for

---

[7] In Visala (2014), I suggest that there is no necessary contradiction between dualism and evolution. For an extensive discussion of evolutionary challenges to theology (including the image of God and the problem of evil), see Rosenberg (2018).

theologians. One area where these tools could make a significant contribution is that of epistemology. Analytic theologians have offered extensive reflections on Christian epistemology, revelation, and experience that might function as an antidote to the fragmentation of the religion and science dialogue. Of course, there is no overall agreement among analytic theologians as to what the best approach to Christian epistemology ultimately is (Abraham 2006; Diller 2014). Nevertheless, the proposals on the table might help to clarify and present the different approaches in a more rigorous way.

Consider the work of Richard Swinburne as an example. Swinburne has, in his numerous works, sought to defend Christian theism as a metaphysical hypothesis (e.g., 2004). His aim has been to formulate a system of natural theology such that central Christian claims at least would turn out probable given the evidence. Overall, Swinburne rejects the attempts of some theologians to give up on providing an epistemic foundation for theology. Instead, he adopts a scientific-style inference to the best explanation reasoning kind of natural theology. In so doing, Swinburne has pioneered internalist epistemology and Bayesian confirmation theory as tools for analytic theology (2009). According to Swinburne (2004), metaphysical claims, such as the existence of God, can be established with some probability by invoking a large spectrum of empirical evidence. These include the existence and general features of our world, certain historical events, and religious experiences. The theistic hypothesis, according to Swinburne, explains this evidence better than the naturalistic one. Swinburne's work is, thus, characterized by an overarching integrative aim: a defense of Christian theology should be able to take into account all available evidence and subsume the scientific picture of the world as well.

Another contribution to the religion and science dialogue comes from the other end of the epistemological spectrum. Alvin Plantinga's (2011) central contribution to this debate is the way in which he systematically applies his reliabilist epistemology to it. Plantinga and other Reformed Epistemologists differ from Swinburne in maintaining that belief in God and "central truths of the Gospel" are *properly basic*; that is to say, they are warranted without explicit argument if they are formed in the basic way and defeaters are absent. If Christian theism is true, our beliefs about God could be warranted this way and require neither scientific evidence nor philosophical argument. This forms the set up for Plantinga's discussion of scientific challenges: it is enough to defeat the defeaters arising out of natural science; one need not provide a scientifically informed argument for God. This allows Plantinga to draw a distinction between a Christian evidence base and a scientific evidence base. Natural sciences are committed to a methodological naturalism that tends to disregard theistic and other supernatural explanations. A Christian is not obligated to stick to this evidence base: she has warrant to invoke Christian evidence arising out of the tradition and experience.

Plantinga also discusses most of the themes already touched upon in this chapter. Not only does Plantinga think that Christian theology and science are compatible, he argues also that naturalism is actually in conflict with the sciences in a deep sense. There is a superficial conflict between biological evolution and divine action in natural history. The alleged conflict is driven by the purported randomness of natural selection. For Plantinga, theism entails some kind of teleology in nature. Natural selection, however, looks like a random process that is not guided toward any specific end. Plantinga argues that we cannot infer from the results of biology to non-purposiveness, because this requires the naturalistic assumption that the universe is a closed physical system and that it is nonpurposive. The Christian is not obliged to take this assumption on board, so it is always possible for her to believe that God guides evolution in some way or another. So, the core claims of Christian theology are compatible with evolution. Conflicts arise only if one smuggles philosophical assumptions into the interpretation of scientific results. But these commitments are not result of science, but naturalistic philosophy used to interpret the results of the sciences.

Plantinga offers a number of reasons why there is a deep concord between theology and science. Here he invokes the fine-tuning argument for design and also examines the possibilities of a biological design argument. One of Plantinga's contributions is his suggestion that the biological design argument could be repurposed as an argument for the design inference based on ordinary experience. Reformulating the argument this way might save the "design discourse" without committing to notions of design that are incompatible with standard evolutionary explanations. Plantinga also argues that Christian theism is a better fit with science than naturalism, since it offers superior explanations of the preambles of science. The naturalist has no good explanation for why the natural world functions in a law-like way and can be understood by the human mind. Similarly, theism explains why abstract creations of the human mind, like mathematics, are fit to describe and produce predictions of the natural world. These facts can be explained by invoking a rational God that has created humans as rational creatures.

VI. TOWARD AN EXPERIMENTAL ANALYTIC THEOLOGY

To conclude, I want to mention some topics and areas in analytic theology that could benefit from increasing engagement with the sciences. This engagement might not only invoke scientific results in theological theorizing but also contribute to the sciences in terms of new hypotheses and questions. Perhaps analytic theology could be supported by an "experimental analytic theology" very much like analytic philosophy is constantly being expanded by experimental philosophy. Theological anthropology might be the most natural place to start with this kind of work. Above, I make clear how philosophical, theological, and scientific questions overlap in issues such as sin, *imago Dei*, personhood, and morality.

One set of questions revolves around free will and moral responsibility. Not only are these notions crucial for core Christian doctrines of incarnation, sin, grace and salvation, but they are also central for any Christian account of moral agency and personhood, both God's and humans'. Moreover, moral psychology contributes to the theology of spiritual life and development of virtues. Given the fact that psychologists and neuroscientists have had much to say about free will and related matters, it is somewhat surprising that analytic theologians have mostly conducted their investigations in isolation from the sciences.[8]

Analytic theologians have an interest in holding onto free will, because Christian theology, as a whole, takes human beings as moral agents who are responsible for their actions. Thus, they have a motivation to participate in the debate concerning the interpretation of scientific results.[9] However, analytic theologians should not simply restrict themselves to defending the compatibility of free will and neuroscience, for instance. They might enrich the whole debate by bringing insights from the history of theology. Indeed, Jesse Couenhoven (2013) suggests that Augustinian accounts of moral

---

[8] Kevin Timpe's discussion on free will and theology (2014) makes no reference whatsoever to the sciences. Similarly, see essays in Timpe and Speak (2016).
[9] For instance, Daniel Wegner (2002) has argued that scientific evidence is clearly on the side of the impossibility of free will for humans.

responsibility could be developed in such a way that could contribute to contemporary debates about ownership of action, action control, and responsibility. Theologians in the Augustinian tradition, for instance, have developed detailed analyses of these issues that would enrich contemporary compatibilist notions of free will. Couenhoven also invokes psychological and neuroscientific results in support of an Augustinian compatibilist account of free will. Contemporary psychology of decision making suggests that we are sometimes mistaken about the sources of our actions, and our decisions are more deeply conditioned by our background and environment than we ordinarily assume. This, Couenhoven claims (2018: 140–56), puts pressure on the idea that the best account of free will is libertarian in nature.

There is a need for analytic theology to open up towards more political and moral topics. There is already much work on virtues and vices in analytic theology (Boyd and Timpe 2014). This work could be enriched greatly by engagement with recent work in moral and social cognition. Contrary to the traditional picture of clear-cut differences between virtuous and vicious individuals, new empirical work suggests that the picture is rather complex. It seems that our characters are much more dependent on contextual and social factors than previously thought. None of us is simply virtuous or vicious; rather we are virtuous and vicious in certain contexts (Miller 2014; Peterson and Seligman 2004). Analytic theology could contribute to this work by proposing new questions to study: to what extent religious motivations contribute to the formation of virtues and vices, for instance.[10]

There is already some theological work on disagreement that is sensitive to the constraints of our moral and social cognition. As a response to both philosophical debates about disagreement in analytic epistemology and recent results of the cognitive sciences, Olli-Pekka Vainio (2017) has suggested a virtue-based solution to the problem of disagreement. According to Vainio, disagreement will probably be a permanent feature of our epistemic endeavors and, as such, is not a reason to adopt skepticism. However, some of its negative effects might be overcome by developing relevant intellectual virtues. The issue of disagreement is particularly pressing because of impending political and social conflicts where religion seems to play a significant part. Analytic theology could contribute to this research by disentangling the complex issues of violence and religion. In order to combat the simplistic claim that religion causes violence, philosophical tools, social sciences, anthropology, psychology, and history have been used to argue successfully for a more complex picture (Atran 2010; Clarke et al. 2013; Vainio 2017).

VII. CONCLUSION

The cases above make it clear that analytic theology as a whole has taken an open and constructive attitude toward the sciences. While a perusal of the seven volumes of *Journal of Analytic Theology* published so far (2019) reveal only a handful of articles that refer to the sciences, there is a wide variety of themes represented: interpretations of quantum mechanics as they contribute to the debate about personal ontology and randomness; psychology of virtues and biases in moral life; biological and physiological accounts of animal pain as they contribute to the debate about animal theodicy; and, finally, physics and biology of design arguments. In addition, there is an extensive debate on God, sin and

---

[10]Editors' note: see Kent Dunnington's contribution to this volume.

time (Hudson 2014). In most cases, analytic theologians invoke scientific results in order to support or undermine empirical premises in theological theorizing. Although its focus has been elsewhere, analytic theology has acknowledged that the sciences can contribute to many traditional *loci* of theology. These include: accounts of personhood, morality and metaethics, moral psychology and the doctrines of sin and providence. Opening up toward the sciences is also evident in a number of recently finished or ongoing research and training projects where analytic theologians seek closer engagement with behavioral sciences in particular.

So far, analytic theologians have engaged with the sciences in two ways. On the one hand, the apologetic motive is clearly present: analytic theologians engage with the interpretation of scientific results in order to demonstrate the compatibility of Christian theology and scientific results, or the overall scientific worldview. This is often the case with debates about evolution and various Christian doctrines. Apologetic motive also drives much of the work of individuals like Swinburne and Plantinga examined above. On the other hand, many engagements are ultimately driven by theological interest: scientific results are used in theological theorizing. Here, the engagement is mostly *ad hoc*, not aiming toward any kind of deep integration. Consider Stump. Her discussion is driven by her theological project of forming a theodicy. In order to develop relevant epistemological notions, she invokes scientific results about human cognition and its neural implementation. This makes her account of personal knowledge more plausible and practical. Stump feels no need to provide empirical support for all, or even most, of her claims. The program of analytic theology needs no scientific justification as a whole.

For the time being, it seems to me that analytic theology should remain a pluralistic enterprise and analytic theologians should remain open to different aims and theological interests. Thus, it might be best that analytic theology would conduct its engagements with the sciences in an *ad hoc* manner in the future as well. That is to say, analytic theologians should not take deep integration with the sciences as their main goal. The apologetic work as well as the theological theorizing inspired by the sciences requires no commitment to integration or justifying the theological project by scientific means. This *ad hoc* attitude view would avoid the problem of "doormat love" that Michael Murray (2009) identifies. In "doormat love," theologians blindly and uncritically accept and adapt to whatever the scientists are saying. Murray takes some representatives of the religion and science dialogue to be dangerously close to this attitude.[11]

References

Abraham, W. (2012), *Analytic Theology: A Bibliography*, Dallas: Highland Loch Press.
Abraham, W. (2006), *Crossing the Threshold of Divine Revelation*, Grand Rapids, MI: Eerdmans.
Atran, S. (2010), *Talking to the Enemy: Religion, Brotherhood, and the (Un)Making of Terrorists*, London: Allen Lane.
Barrett, J. (2011), *Cognitive Science, Religion and Theology: From Human Minds to Divine Minds*, West Conshohocken: Templeton Press.

---

[11] I want to thank the editors, J. T. Turner, Jr. and James Arcadi, for their comments and corrections to this chapter. I would also like to thank the Finnish Academy for funding the research project that made the writing of this chapter possible.

Barrett, J. L., and M. Jarvinen (2015), "Cognitive Evolution, Human Uniqueness, and the *Imago Dei*," in M. Jeeves (ed.), *The Emergence of Personhood: A Quantum Leap?*, Grand Rapids, MI: Eerdmans, 163–83.
Clark, K. J., and J. Barrett (2010), "Reformed Epistemology and the Cognitive Science of Religion", *Faith and Philosophy*, 27: 174–89.
Clark, K. J., and D. Rabinowitz (2011), "Knowledge and the Objection to Religious Belief from Cognitive Science," *European Journal for Philosophy of Religion*, 3 (1): 67–82.
Clarke, S., R. Powell, and J. Savulescu, eds. (2013), *Religion, Intolerance, and Conflict: A Scientific and Conceptual Investigation*, Oxford: Oxford University Press.
Clayton, P. and Z. Simpson, eds. (2006), *Oxford Handbook of Religion and Science*, Oxford: Oxford University Press.
Coakley, S. (2013), "Evolution, Cooperation, and Divine Providence," in M. Nowak and S. Coakley (eds.), *Evolution, Games, and God: The Principle of Cooperation*, 375–86, Cambridge, MA: Harvard University Press.
Couenhoven, J. (2013), *Stricken by Sin, Cured by Christ: Agency, Necessity, and Culpability in Augustinian Theology*, New York: Oxford University Press.
Couenhoven, J. (2018), *Predestination: A Guide for the Perplexed*, London: T&T Clark.
Crisp, O. D., ed. (2009), *A Reader in Contemporary Philosophical Theology*, London: Routledge.
De Cruz, H., and J. De Smedt (2014), *A Natural History of Natural Theology: The Cognitive Science of Theology and Philosophy of Religion*, Cambridge, MA: MIT Press.
Diller, K. (2014), *Theology's Epistemological Dilemma: How Karl Barth and Alvin Plantinga Provide a Unified Response*, Downers Grove, IL: IVP Academic.
Draper, P. (2012), "Darwin's Argument from Evil," in Y. Nagasawa (ed.), *Scientific Approaches to the Philosophy of Religion*, 49–70, London: Palgrave Macmillan.
Drees, W. (2009), *Religion and Science in Context: A Guide to the Debates*, London: Routledge.
Farris, J., and C. Taliaferro, eds. (2015), *The Ashgate Research Companion to Theological Anthropology*, Abingdon: Routledge.
Griffiths, P. E., and J. E. Wilkins (2013), "Evolutionary Debunking Arguments in Three Domains: Fact Value and Religion," in G. Dawes and J. Maclaurin (eds.), *A New Science of Religion*, 133–46, London: Routledge.
Haug, M., ed. (2014), *Philosophical Methodology: The Armchair or the Laboratory*, Abingdon: Routledge.
Hauser, M. (2007), *Moral Minds: The Nature of Right and Wrong*, New York: Harper Perennial.
Hudson, H. (2014), *The Fall and Hypertime*, New York: Oxford University Press.
Jong, J., and A. Visala (2014), "Evolutionary Debunking Arguments against Theism, Reconsidered," *International Journal for Philosophy of Religion*, 76 (3): 243–58.
Joyce, R. (2003), *Evolution of Morality*, London: MIT Press.
Kahane, G. (2011), "Evolutionary Debunking Arguments," *Nous*, 45: 103–25.
Kornblith, H. (2016), "Philosophical Naturalism," in H. Cappelen, T. Gendler, and J. Hawthorne (eds.), *The Oxford Handbook of Philosophical Methodology*, 147–57, Oxford: Oxford University Press.
Leech, D., and A. Visala (2011), "The Cognitive Science of Religion: Implications for Theism?," *Zygon: Journal of Religion and Science*, 46 (1): 47–64.
Leech, D., and A. Visala (2012), "How the Cognitive Science of Religion might be Relevant for Philosophy of Religion?," in Y. Nagasawa (ed.), *Scientific Approaches to Philosophy of Religion*, 165–83, London: Palgrave.
McCall, T. (2015), *An Invitation to Analytic Christian Theology*, Downers Grove, IL: IVP Academic.

McGrath, A. (2002), *A Scientific Theology, Vol 2: Reality*, London: T&T Clark.
McGrath, A. (2009), *A Fine-Tuned Universe: The Quest for God in Science and Theology*, Louisville: Westminster John Knox Press.
Murray, M. (2008), *Nature, Red in Tooth and Claw: Theism and the Problem of Animal Suffering*, New York: Oxford University Press.
Murray, M. (2009), "Science and Religion in Constructive Engagement," in O. D. Crisp and M. Rea (eds.), *Analytic Theology: New Essays in the Philosophy of Theology*, 233–47, New York: Oxford University Press.
Miller, C. B. (2014), *Character and Moral Psychology*, Oxford: Oxford University Press.
Nagasawa, Y., ed. (2012), *Scientific Approaches to the Philosophy of Religion*, London: Palgrave Macmillan.
Nowak, M., and S. Coakley, eds. (2013), *Evolution, Games, and God: The Principle of Cooperation*, Cambridge, MA: Harvard University Press.
Peterson, C., and M.Seligman (2004), *Character Strengths and Virtues*, Oxford: Oxford University Press.
Philipse, H. (2012), *God in the Age of Science: A Critique of Religious Reason*, Oxford: Oxford University Press.
Plantinga, A. (2011), *Where the Conflict Really Lies: Science, Religion, and Naturalism*, Oxford: Oxford University Press.
Pruss, A. (2013), "Altruism, Normalcy, and God," in M. Nowak and S. Coakley (eds.), *Evolution, Games, and God: The Principle of Cooperation*, 329–42, Cambridge, MA: Harvard University Press.
Ratzsch, D. (2009), "Science and Religion," in T. Flint and M. Rea (eds.), *The Oxford Handbook of Philosophical Theology*, 54–77, New York: Oxford University Press.
Rosenberg, S. ed. (2018), *Finding Ourselves after Darwin: Conversations on the Image of God, Original Sin, and the Problem of Evil*, Grand Rapids, MI: Baker.
Rota, M. (2013), "The Problem of Evil and Cooperation," in M. Nowak and S. Coakley (eds.), *Evolution, Games, and God: The Principle of Cooperation*, 362–74, Cambridge, MA: Harvard University Press.
Schloss, J., and M. Murray, eds. (2009), *The Believing Primate: Scientific, Philosophical, and Theological Reflections on the Origin of Religion*, New York: Oxford University Press.
Stenmark, M. (2001), *Scientism: Science, Ethics, and Religion*, Abingdon: Routledge.
Stenmark, M. (2004), *How to Relate Science and Religion: A Multidimensional Model*, Grand Rapids, MI: Eerdmans.
Stump, E. (2010), *Wandering in Darkness: Narrative and the Problem of Evil*, New York: Oxford University Press.
Swinburne, R. (2004), *The Existence of God*, Oxford: Clarendon Press.
Swinburne, R. (2009), *Epistemic Justification*, Oxford: Clarendon Press.
Tahko, T. (2015), *Introduction to Metametaphysics*, Cambridge: Cambridge University Press.
Timpe, K. (2014), *Free Will in Philosophical Theology*, New York: Bloomsbury.
Timpe, K., and G. Boyd, eds. (2014), *Virtues and Their Vices*, New York: Oxford University Press.
Timpe, K., and D. Speaks, eds. (2016), *Free Will & Theism: Connections, Contingencies, and Concerns*, New York: Oxford University Press.
Tomasello, M. (2014), *A Natural History of Human Thinking*, Cambridge, MA: Harvard University Press.
Trigg, R., and J. Barrett, eds. (2014), *The Roots of Religion: Exploring the Cognitive Science of Religion*, Farnham: Ashgate.

Vainio, O-P. (2017), *Disagreeing Virtuously: Religious Conflict in Interdisciplinary Perspective*, Grand Rapids, MI: Eerdmans.

Visala, A. (2011), *Theism, Naturalism, and the Cognitive Study of Religion*, Farnham: Ashgate.

Visala, A. (2018), "Human Cognition and the Image of God," in O. D. Crisp and F. Sanders (eds.), *The Christian Doctrine of Humanity*, 91–109, Grand Rapids, MI: Zondervan.

Wegner, D. (2002), *The Illusion of Conscious Will*, Cambridge, MA: MIT Press.

Van Eyghen, H. (2020), *Arguing from the Cognitive Science of Religion: Is Religious Belief Debunked?*, London: Bloomsbury.

Van Huyssteen, W. (2006), *Alone in the World? Human Uniqueness in Science and Theology*, Grand Rapids, MI: Eerdmans.

CHAPTER THIRTY-TWO

The *End* of Things: Resurrection and New Creation

JAMES T. TURNER, JR.

In recent academic Christian theological and biblical scholarship, the subject of eschatology—the study of "last things"—has made a substantial turn away from futuristic prognostications concerning the "end of the world" and literal readings of the Book of Revelation toward a renewed emphasis on the *telos* of the created order (e.g., Bauckham 2007: 316; Middleton 2014). That is: instead of understanding the "end of all things" as a synonym for the *destruction* of all things, many now understand such turns of phrase to suggest the *fulfillment* and *bringing to its purpose* of all things. To my mind, this shift is appropriate. If one is rightly to answer questions about the creation and the things in it (particularly humans), one first must discover—in good Aristotelian and Scholastic fashion—the purpose of such things (i.e., a thing's final cause).

What then is the purpose of the created order? What is the purpose of human beings? In this chapter I follow the deliverances of recent biblical theological scholarship to provide a starting place for thinking about the purpose of creation and the purpose of human beings within it. The idea I follow is this: the cosmos is meant to be God's temple and humans are meant to be his temple-dwelling priestly and royal representatives. The fulfillment of these purposes is eschatological, and it results in the establishment of a renewed creation and resurrected human beings (Beale 2004: 137 (and elsewhere); Middleton 2014; Mugg and Turner 2017: 122–4; Mosser 2018). Supposing that this is true generates various conceptual difficulties, not the least of which concerns what resurrection is and whether it is metaphysically possible. So, I will bring analytic insights to bear on competing answers that provide a way forward for thinking through the difficulties.

I proceed as follows: in section I, I provide an overview of the recent literature concerning the telos of the created order and human beings. In section II, I survey attempts to explain the bodily resurrection of humans. In section III, I try and point a way forward for making sense of the deliverances of section I in the face of the difficulties surrounding the models of resurrection in section II.

I. THE *TELĒ* OF THE COSMOS AND ITS STEWARDS

The *Catechism of the Roman Catholic Church* suggests that the purpose of the created order is to communicate and display the glory of God, so that God "may at last become all in all" (RCC: 293 and 294). The *Westminster Confession of Faith* says quite a bit less than the RCC; it says only that the creation is "for the manifestation of the glory of His eternal power, wisdom, and goodness" (WCF: IV.1). These are two important catechetical documents in Western Christianity. Yet, these are vague sentiments, even if true. For it isn't at all clear that this sort of "purpose" is the sort of purpose that is useful for thinking through the definition of what it is to be the creation and what it is to be *this* creation. Compare: the *telos* of a chair is for it to be a thing on which humans reasonably and comfortably can sit. The *telos* of the chair is intrinsic to chairness. We can evaluate objects *as chairs*—both good and bad—effectively because we know this to be constitutive of what it is to be a chair. The way these two catechetical documents spell out the purpose of the cosmos does not seem to suggest a teleology of creation that is constitutive of the creation's definition. For one can imagine any number of things God could have created to communicate his glory; *prima facie* it does not seem to be the case that God had to make *this* world, this *sort* of world, or even a cosmos at all to communicate his glory (arguably God can communicate his glory to Godself in God's intertrinitarian life). So, this way of spelling out the creation's *telos* doesn't seem to explain what it is to be the cosmos.

Enter recent biblical scholarship. If analytic theology truly is to be an interdisciplinary research project—one that takes seriously the deliverances of various academic schools—then it strikes me as obvious that analytic theologians should take seriously what it is that biblical scholarship reports. This is the sort of thing analytic theologians and philosophers do, for example, with the physical sciences.[1] With respect to the purpose of the cosmos, here is what we find if we follow the deliverances of recent biblical scholarship. By the lights of an increasing number of scholars, the *telos* of the cosmos is to be the God of Israel's temple (Levenson 1984; Beale 2004; Walton 2009; Beale and Kim 2014; Middleton 2014; Wright [2017] 2019).[2] Further, reading the Christian scriptures canonically provides the following insight: Genesis 1 and Revelation 22 provide bookending temple imagery. The cosmic temple's creation occurs in Genesis 1 and its consummation occurs in Revelation 22 (complete with cubic Holy of Holies imagery pulling from the temple design in 1 Kings 6) (Beale 2004: 23, 328; Middleton 2014: 170–1). An upshot of this way of thinking about the created order is that one of God's purposes is to live with and in his creation rather than, say, evacuating the inhabitants of his creation *out* of the created order. The idea seems to be this: from the beginning, God intends for the place wherein God dwells—what often is called "Heaven"—to be joined to God's cosmos so that, as it seems in Revelation 22, Heaven comes down to earth. Though the cosmos does not function currently as a place in which God can dwell, marred by sin as it is, the biblical story suggests that God intends to set things right; the creation finally will be brought to shalom (Middleton 2005: 89–99; Middleton 2014: 24).

Immediately one should see that, if this is the way things are designed to be, then understanding the eschatological end of humans as "going to Heaven" is to understand

---

[1] See the chapters by Benedikt Göcke and Aku Visala in this volume.
[2] For an edited volume putting together a number of works that point this direction, see Morales (2014).

things the wrong way around.³ Neither humans nor the creation *go to* God; God comes *to us*. For, as Walton (2015: 47) suggests, the cosmos is designed to be God's *home*.⁴ Doing theology with this biblical theological insight as a "central and load-bearing theme" is what N. T. Wright has come to call "temple theology" (Wright [2017] 2019: 11).

Thinking about the *telos* of the created order in this way impacts also how biblical theologians think about the *telos* of human beings. It is, of course, a well-worn truth of Christian theology that human beings are divine image bearers.⁵ And though the understanding of this image-bearing title/descriptor through history has been understood in various ways, recent biblical theology suggests that understanding the creation as God's temple sheds new light on what it is for humans to be his image bearers. In the first place, "divine image bearer" is not original to Hebrew (let alone Christian) thought. It comes first from older ancient near eastern religions. In the context of the Hebrew Bible, rather than the phrase "divine image" referring to an ontological similarity between the divine One and his images—for example, being immaterial because God is immaterial (e.g., Pelikan 1993: 131)—the phrase points first to a particular *task* or *function*: humans are to be priestly rulers in God's temple (Middleton 2005: 27–8; Gorman 2014: 357; Mosser 2018: 265; Arcadi 2020).⁶ The exegesis biblical scholars use to get here is technical and beyond the scope of this chapter. But, one easy piece of evidence follows from the way in which the writer of Genesis 1 structures the creation narrative: the last thing that God places into his creation are humans. The last things to be placed in temples in the ancient near east: divine images (Middleton 2005: 87).⁷ This is a key insight used both to tell readers that Genesis 1 is a temple building narrative *and* what sort of things humans are. Images in divine temples do one thing: they represent the rule and reign of the deity in the temple. If God's temple is the cosmos, and humans are his image bearers, then humans are to represent the rule and reign of God in the cosmos. This is what it is to be a divine image bearer of the Creator God. And when humans eschatologically are put right, they will fulfill their purpose (Middleton 2005: 89–90).

Elsewhere ([2018] 2019) I argue that the particular sort of task to which humans have been called *does* deliver an important ontological upshot: God's image bearers must be *rational*. They must be the sort of things that have *minds*, that are capable of wisdom, and that are capable of preparing the creation to be habitable for God (28–9). With much of the theological and philosophical tradition, we can call individuals with a rational nature, "persons" (e.g., Boethius n.d.: III.34; Aquinas 1952: Ia.Q29.a1 *respondeo*). If that's a correct way to understand persons, then the task to which God sets his image bearers entails that his images be persons.

There's a further upshot to understanding divine image bearing in this way. Divine images in the ancient near east—the cultural context and language into which Genesis 1 is written—are *embodied* and *localizable* entities (Middleton 2005: 25). That is, contrary to much of Christian tradition, divine image bearing entails *embodiment* rather than

---

[3] If readers have been paying attention to N. T. Wright over the last twenty years, they should be familiar with this line of reasoning. See, e.g., Wright (2008).
[4] See also Walton (2009: 71–6).
[5] See Joshua Farris's chapter in this volume.
[6] Some suggest that humans are social animals because God is social *qua* Trinity. See Grenz (2001).
[7] There is more textual evidence, too, including the ways in which the temple building story in 1 Kings 6 mirrors structurally the Genesis 1 creation story. The similarity between the two has made the dating of the Genesis account vexed; for, it *could be* that the Genesis account was written *after* the building of Solomon's temple (Middleton 2005: 144–5; Enns 2012: chapter 2).

immateriality. Here's another way to put this: one cannot be a divine image if one is disembodied.

This is a cursory survey, of course. But it shines a light on a way to understand the *telos* of the created order, generally, and human beings, specifically, that delivers at least two important points of data:

(A): The creation is God's temple.
(B): God's images are embodied persons.

I suggest that if (A) and (B) are true, then a particular sort of eschatological future follows. I turn now to that discussion.

II. PERSONAL ESCHATOLOGY: THE ESCHATOLOGY OF THE HUMAN PERSON

Personal eschatology deals generally with afterlife. That is, whereas eschatology deals generally with the topic of "last things"—what's going to happen "at the end of the world"—personal eschatology deals with the following question: What's going to happen at the end of *me*? Putting it this way, though, is confused. At least, it's confused if Christian theology is correct. For, given most explications of Christian theism, no one *ends* at death.[8] And that's because Christians typically believe in a life after death.

What's more, Christians have particular thoughts about what life after death will be like. In the place of ultimate importance is the resurrection of the body. That is, according to Christian theology, when Jesus the Messiah returns—the *Parousia*—he will raise from the dead the bodies of (at least) the redeemed. On this way of thinking about life after death, the term "resurrection" carries with it the full semantic weight of its Greek construction, *anastasis*: to stand *again*. According to Wright (2003: 146–50), this is precisely the way first-century Christians and Second Temple Jews would have understood the word/concept. If that's correct, then in more precise philosophical language, the "standing again" of a dead body entails the *numerical identity* of a premortem and post-resurrection body. So, if Jones has a particular body, B1, at the time of her death, then Jones will have that same particular body, B1, at the time of her resurrection. Thus, one can read a presupposed numerical identity between a person's pre-mortem body and post-resurrection body out of the following biblical text:

> What is sown is perishable; what is raised is imperishable. *It* is sown in dishonor; *it* is raised in glory. *It* is sown in weakness; *it* is raised in power. *It* is sown a natural body; *it* is raised a spiritual body ... For *this* perishable body must put on the imperishable, and *this* mortal body must put on immortality. (1 Cor. 15:43–53, emphases added)[9]

Following Paul, the Christian theologian committed to the numerical identity of the premortem and post-resurrection bodies (really: body) will emphasize the *qualitative* difference between the premortem and post-resurrection bodies. The body is, after all,

---

[8] For exceptions, see the recent literature on annihilationism, the thesis that "the damned" are annihilated from existence (Pinnock 1990; Bowles 2014; Wenham 2014; Spiegel 2015).
[9] All biblical quotations in this chapter are taken from the English Standard Version of the Bible.

sown in a perishable state and raised in an imperishable one. And, qualitative difference needn't—so goes the thought—entail numerical difference.

II.1 Numerical Identity and the Resurrection of the Body

Once one commits to the claim that a human's premortem body and her post-resurrection body are numerically the same, one confronts philosophical problems concerning the persistence of objects over time and through change.[10] Here is why: there's a philosophical principle that suggests that identical objects—numerically the same objects—must have all and only the same properties. This principle is called the indiscernibility of identicals.[11] The problem is that, for an object to change, at one time it has to have a certain set of properties and then at another time it has to have another set. This means that a changing object becomes discernibly different from its previous version, thus not the identical object. The resurrection passage quoted above describes an exaggerated instance of change. For, it's obvious that premortem and post-resurrection bodies have different properties. Given the indiscernibility of identicals, then, it seems to follow that premortem and post-resurrection bodies cannot be numerically identical. If so, it's false that a body that dies can come back to life through resurrection.

Notice, though, that this worry about the indiscernibility of identicals and the possibility of change over time generalizes to *all* objects that one normally thinks change. If the indiscernibility of identicals is true, it is not immediately clear how *any* material object both qualitatively changes and remains numerically the same over time. Analytic philosophers have been especially helpful in providing options for how to respond to this problem (see e.g.: van Inwagen 1990; Sider 2001; Dainton 2010; Olson 2019; Hawley 2020). Perhaps, then, one could appeal to a reigning theory of object persistence to account for the numerical identity between the pre-mortem and post-resurrection body.

There is, however, a cluster of further worries nearby. Suppose one could provide an analysis of how material objects, like human bodies, can persist through time and change. What's happening in the case of resurrection, though, is quite a bit different. For, the resurrection of the body seems to require the possibility of the coming back into existence of a thing that has ceased to exist. Consider the body of Moses. Supposing that there was such a person (as I do), it's clear that he's been dead for thousands of years. It's likely that the remains of his body have been absorbed back into the earth, the carbon atoms of which have been absorbed into any number of things, including other living organisms.

This generates at least two further problems. Problem one stems from another intuitively plausible philosophical principle. We can call this Locke's Axiom (LA): that whatever begins to exist and then fails to exist cannot begin again to exist (Locke 1975: 328; Mavrodes 1977; van Inwagen 1978: 116–17; Turner 2018: 78).[12] If LA is true, then it's not possible for a body that begins to exist and then fails to exist to begin again to exist. This seems to rule out the resurrection of bodies that have disintegrated and been absorbed into the ground, have been digested by wild animals and thus absorbed into their bodies, or have been digested by cannibals. (The latter of which generates the so-called cannibal problem for resurrection. If Jones eats and digests the body of Smith,

---

[10] E.g., see Gallois (2016) and Mortenson (2020) for introductions to these issues.
[11] A related axiom, sometimes called "Leibniz's Law," is the identity of indiscernibles that states that no two things have exactly the same properties (Forrest 2016).
[12] But see Haldane (2007: 262–3) and Merricks (2001).

the body of Smith becoming a part of the body of Jones. At the resurrection whose body will be raised (Davis 1993: 100; Bynum 1995; Merricks 2001: 187; Peters 2002: 312; Davis and Yang 2017: 224)?

Fortunately for Christian thinkers committed to LA and the thesis that resurrection requires that the risen body be numerically identical to the body that died, there have been a few models in the analytic philosophy of religion proffered as a way to make sense of the bodily resurrection. The first attempt—the one it seems to me that generated much of the recent literature—was proposed by Peter van Inwagen (1978). His so-called simulacrum thesis suggests the following: first, suppose that one could provide an account of a human organism's identity over time through an analysis of the ways in which the parts of an organism interact to explain the identity of the organism. Second, suppose that, just before the moment of death—the moment at which the processes that provide the conditions of an organism's identity cease—God snatches the body away and preserves its operations in a diminished state until restored fully at the resurrection. In its place, he provides a simulacrum, a look alike. In other words, the thing that comes to be buried, or cremated, or fully digested (or whatever other fate) is a simulacrum of the original body. If one is committed to LA and to the claim that the Christian doctrine of the resurrection requires numerical identity between the pre-mortem and post-resurrection bodies, the simulacrum thesis is a creative attempt to solve the apparent conceptual conflict.

However, I think there are some difficulties for this model of resurrection. Elsewhere (2018), I've provided arguments against it. The sum of which is that what seems to be going on in the simulacrum thesis is divine deception. It looks as though God is guilty of hoodwinking an untold number of people who think they're either burying/cremating their loved one or else their loved one's body. I suppose that God's nature and divine deception are incompatible. As such, I reject the simulacrum thesis. In fact, I know of no philosopher or theologian who thinks it's true. This includes van Inwagen (2018).

But, van Inwagen's (1978) genius proposal—even if false—spawned rival models. Two competing yet related rivals involve thinking about the moment of death as a moment at which the atoms that make up a human body "fission" such that a corpse-full of atoms are left behind and a body-full of atoms jumps to an undetermined location to await final resurrection (Zimmerman 1999; Corcoran 2001). This fission thesis can be imagined by appeal to "the 'physics' of cartoons" such that, in a falling elevator, a character can spring safely from the elevator just before it crashes into the ground (Zimmerman 1999: 196). On this "falling elevator" model of the resurrection, analogically the same could be true of a human body. Where the moment of death is the moment when the elevator hits the ground, so it is that the fissioning of the human's atoms and moving to a waiting location is the cartoon character's jumping to safety.

Here, as one might imagine, there are a host of worries. Again, I've detailed the issues elsewhere (Turner 2018: 89–97; see also Hershenov 2002); but I will summarize two considerable problems presently. The first has to do with the attendant metaphysics of human organisms assumed by the model. Following the analysis of the persistence conditions of human organisms set out in van Inwagen's (1990), both Zimmerman and Corcoran assume (for their models) that jointly necessary and sufficient for a body's persistence through time is a graduated and slow assimilation/losing of a body's parts over time. To count as parts of an organism, parts must establish "immanent causal connections" with the organism (Corcoran 2001: 206–10). In van Inwagen's terminology, parts must be caught up into the "life" of the organism (van Inwagen 1990: 87–97). Parts that are just passing through, one might say, don't count properly as being a part of a whole (94–5). It also is the case, on this view, that an all-at-once switching of parts will not count properly as being caught up into the life of an organism. That is, the immediate loss/switch of the whole compliment of a body's parts would be too quick, resulting in the annihilation of one body and the creation of an entirely new one (Hershenov 2002: 460; Turner 2018: 92–4). And it's just here that falling elevator models run into a significant problem; for, they posit that, at the moment of death, there is an all-at-once part replacement. An entire body of newly generated atoms fissions from the dying atoms.

The second worry concerns the resurrection of Jesus. If fission is the way that resurrection works for humans, then this is the same for the body of Jesus the Messiah. If it's the case that the body on the cross at Golgotha fissioned just before the moment of Christ's death, then it looks like the body that was laid in Jesus's tomb *did not* walk out of the tomb. At best, the living body of Jesus—the one that fissioned off from the body on the cross—"jumped" to the tomb and waited to walk out on Easter Sunday. If so, there would have been two objects in that tomb: the living body of Jesus and his corpse. At worst, the living body "jumped" elsewhere and so did *not* walk out of the tomb (because it was never in it to begin with). According to the gospel stories, though, the tomb is empty precisely because Jesus walked out (Turner 2018: 96–7).[13] Note, too, that there was no corpse left behind (nor, does it seem a leftover corpse was smuggled out) (Harris 1983: 44; Fergusson 1985: 303).[14]

Van Inwagen, Zimmerman, and Corcoran rely on similar analyses of the persistence conditions of organisms; they all rely on a similar set of criteria of identity. In other words, they all suppose that there are informative necessary and sufficient conditions for the persistence of an organism's identity over time. But suppose that there are no criteria of identity; suppose that the diachronic identity of an object is an unanalyzable fact. This is Trenton Merricks's (1998) position on the matter. And, following from that, he argues that the numerical identity of a premortem body and a post-resurrection body becomes a trivial truth: the resurrection body is numerically identical to its premortem body because it is (Merricks 2001: 191–6). Notice here that this fundamentally involves a rejection of LA. Something *can* fail to exist and begin again to exist. That is, on this sort of view, there could be temporally "gappy objects." The analysis of such an occurrence ends up being nothing more than an uninformative tautology: an object O at time T_1 is identical to an object O_2 at time T_2 if and only if O at T_1 is identical to O_2 at T_2 (Merricks 1998: 107).

A problem for Merricks's proposal is that it is counterintuitive. One need only to look at the vast amount of literature in the philosophy of mind, philosophical anthropology, or the philosophy of time to see that philosophers (and theologians!) have been vexed by the question of identity over time. It would be quite remarkable if the explanation—indeed the solution to the millennia-old problem of change—ended up being an uninformative tautology. This, of course, isn't a knockdown argument against it. To my mind, the view merits further consideration.

The same is true for a proposal that is underexplored in the literature. Steven T. Davis (2010) provides a model suggesting that the numerical identity of a premortem and

---

[13] Mt. 28:2-15; Mk 16:2-8; Lk. 24:2-12; Jn 20:2-18.

[14] Another worry: if Jesus's living body fissioned to the tomb, was it hiding somewhere in the shadows of the tomb while the dead body was being placed there by Jesus's disciples? To be frank, this strikes me as silly. There's good news on this score, neither Zimmerman nor Corcoran have proposed (to my knowledge) that this is the case.

post-resurrection body is a matter of the divine will. To this end, Davis and Eric Yang have strengthened this proposal, a proposal that they call a "modified patristic account" (2017: 225). Though they do not commit themselves to the modified patristic account, they suggest that one problem with the views I canvas above is that the models refuse to entertain the sort of resurrection theory that the church fathers assumed, viz., resurrection by reassembly. So goes the argument, resurrection is the bringing together again and back to life of the very material parts that made up a premortem body. One way to make this patristic claim plausible, they say, is to assume that the will of God—or God's willing—is a "crucial feature in both the occurrence of composition and diachronic identity" (222–3). In other words, a necessary condition for an object's being the object that it is, is that God wills for its parts to compose that object (220). It is not the only necessary condition they offer, of course; but it is a necessary condition not elsewhere offered in the contemporary literature.[15]

One problem for this proposal is that it appears too much like a "god of the gaps" argument. In view of a conceptual difficulty and a failure to be able fully to explain an object's identity via intrinsic features of a human organism, Davis and Yang punt to God's will as the glue that holds seemingly incompatible puzzle pieces together. In fairness to their proposal, though, it is not ad hoc. For this proposal suggests that the composition and diachronic identity of *all* objects features, as a necessary condition, God's willing that the objects be composed of the parts that compose them. And, of course, it's also true that, given Christian theism, explanations of various sorts fundamentally bottom out on God as the primary cause of all things (e.g., the existence of contingent beings). So, punting to God's will to solve this puzzle might not be as problematic as it initially may seem.

The proposals I've just surveyed assume that the body that dies is numerically identical to the body that resurrects at the *Parousia*. As we've seen, this generates conceptual difficulties, particularly if one thinks that the indiscernibility of identicals and LA are true. Thus, the above models give resources to help clarify how resurrection is possible. And these aren't the only ones. The views above all are consistent with a particular—and hotly contested—view of time called "presentism." This is a view of time that suggests that all that exists, exists in the present moment. The future and the past do not exist. They're likewise consistent with a particular view of object persistence called "endurantism." This is a view of persistence that suggests that each object that exists is *wholly present* at any individual temporal moment in which it exists. An alternate view of time and persistence called "eternalism" and "perdurantism" respectively have different ways of thinking about resurrection. Space requires that I leave that to the reader for homework.[16] The same is true of the work of Hud Hudson, who offers a "hypertime" theory of resurrection (Hudson 2017; Crisp 2019: 233–5). Again, I leave that to the reader for homework. The important point is that the analytic theologian who reads the Christian scriptures and tradition to support the claim that there's numerical identity between the two bodies have these models to help make sense of Christian doctrine. Yet, each has a set of difficulties, some worse than others.

---

[15] For their detailed account, see Davis and Yang (2017). For another view appealing to the divine will, see Woznicki (2018).
[16] For an excellent resource on the matter, see Dainton (2010) and Le Poidevin (2003).

II.2 Non-Identity and the Resurrection

But what if the Christian doctrine of the resurrection pertains primarily to *persons* rather than bodies? Stewart Goetz (2018) recently has offered such an argument. In response to an argument that Joshua Mugg and I published (2018) advancing the claim that, in part, scripture teaches the numerical identity of pre-mortem and post-resurrection bodies, Goetz suggests that scripture underdetermines the matter (Goetz 2018: 302–6). Additionally, so he thinks, there's no good reason to think that a human's identity is tied up with her body. And this is because he's committed to the claim that a body's identity requires sameness of parts; so, given parts replacement over time, bodies constantly are in numerical flux (303). The upshot is that if a human's ontological identity isn't tied up with a particularly numbered body, then the resurrecting of a particular body adds nothing to the ontological identity of a person. Instead, he thinks that substance dualism is true. That is: humans are identical to immaterial souls/minds. They have bodies; but they are not bodies. So, a person's being resurrected from the dead has nothing to do with the resurrection of a once dead body.

As Joshua Farris (2017) notes, the issue of whether or not resurrection bodies are numerically identical to premortem bodies has been "hotly contested in Ecclesiastical history" (178 n.26). And, so he suggests, if substance dualism is true, then the issue of the numerical identity of the body is much less relevant than it would be if a human person's identity were tied to her body (178 n.26). (This follows now a well-worn path in philosophical theology that is argued famously by John Cooper ([1989] 2000: 139–40).) If scripture underdetermines whether the premortem and post-resurrection bodies are numerically identical, one might wish to opt for a theory of postmortem survival that doesn't run into the sorts of conceptual difficulties generated by requiring the numerical identity of the body.[17]

III. THE *TELĒ* OF THE COSMOS AND ITS STEWARDS: A MODEL FOR MOVING FORWARD

It is true that attempting to explain the numerical identity of the premortem and post-resurrection bodies is fraught with conceptual difficulties. It stands to reason that metaphysicians as sharp as van Inwagen, Zimmerman, Hudson, et. al. are pushed to consider extraordinary solutions (e.g., smuggled in simulacra, fissioning bodies, and hyper-time, respectively). And it sure looks like punting to substance dualism helps make matters simpler. For, if a human person is identical to an immaterial soul that doesn't change its parts, then it seems as though tracking a person's identity is easier.[18] But there's a significant worry here, an exegetical one. If it's the case that the analytic theologian ought to pay careful attention to the deliverances of biblical scholarship, then one must do so here. And many of the exegetes tell us that *resurrection* presupposes that the body

---

[17] A *very* helpful resource on these issues is Farris (2020: 231–52). Though Farris argues against the sort of view that I hold (more about which below), the summary and analysis of the relevant literature is a detailed and helpful starting point for the interested researcher.

[18] I have no space to address this here, but it's not at all clear to me why this should be so widely assumed. Souls change too; their thoughts change. Their properties change, and the like. The problem of persistence is driven by the indiscernibility of identicals. It doesn't say anything about material objects, even if material objects are an obvious example of the problem.

that died is the body that rises again: hence *anastasis* (to stand *again*). To my mind, this is not a point that is easy to eschew.

Moreover, there's a biblical theological point. The promise of Christ's return and the resurrection of the dead is packed with the promise of a renewed creation. It is not a promise that Christ will throw away the present cosmos into the bin of history; rather, it's a promise that he will *heal* what's broken (Middleton 2006; Bauckham 2007; Middleton 2014: 27). God will put "everything to rights" (Wright 2008: 142). This is important to note because, as it turns out, the resurrection of human bodies is a microcosm for the renewal of all things (Pelikan 1993: 10, 121; Johnson 2003: 307; Walton 2015: 123).[19] What's more: *Christ's* resurrection provides an example of resurrection. His crucified body was raised to life. *It* is the body that walked out of the tomb on Easter Sunday. Christ's resurrection is, in Pauline language, the "first-fruits" of the resurrection (1 Cor. 15:20; Harris 1998: 158; Thiselton 2000: 1224; Middleton 2014: 26–7). The argument that Paul makes is that what happened to Christ's body will happen to ours; so too what happened to his body will happen to the entire created order. Our bodies and the cosmos will be brought from death to life (Wolters 2005: 69–86; Wright 2008; Middleton 2014; Mugg and Turner 2017; Turner 2019).

With this in mind, recall the following from Section I:

(A): The creation is God's temple.
(B): God's images are embodied persons.

(A) and (B) are the ends—the *telē*—of creation and humans, respectively. If (A) and (B) are true, then the promise of the new creation, the new heavens and new earth of Revelation 22, is the promise of God finally returning to live in his cosmic temple. Further, if it's the case that all redeemed humans will be made in the exact likeness of Jesus the Son of God, then it follows that all redeemed humans will rule and reign as perfect image bearers of God. For he is, say the scriptures, the perfect image of God (Col. 1:15). And if so, following from (B), we can conclude that humans will be embodied. The embodiment of humans in the eschaton is, of course, straightforward for any orthodox Christian.

I've argued elsewhere that the culmination of what I've said in this section gives good reason to suppose a bodily resurrection rather than a new creation in which God makes entirely new bodies—that is to say, bodies numerically and qualitatively distinct from premortem bodies (Mugg and Turner 2017: 126–8; Turner [2018] 2019: 31–3). But arguing that resurrection of the numerically same bodies is a logical consequence of this sort of biblical theology doesn't explain *how* it's accomplished. It doesn't even begin to explain how it's *possible*. As we saw in Section II, explaining the resurrection of a body that is numerically identical with a body that died (in most cases, many years prior to the general resurrection of the dead) is extremely difficult. And, the views I surveyed in that section—the most popular views in the literature—are not at all immune to critique (perhaps even withering critique).

To begin to assuage these worries, I can offer only an outline of a view I have spelled out more fully elsewhere (2018: chapter 5). There I offer a theory of human persons that trades on a—what I call—broadly Thomistic account of human beings. That is, I think that humans are hylemorphic compounds. Humans are individual organisms that are products of two metaphysical causes, viz., form (*morphe*) and prime matter (*hyle*).

---

[19] This has patristic support, as well (McDonough 2017: 117).

Form and matter on this account are understood respectively to be causal principles that explain the actuality and potentiality of a given substance. Pellucid accounts of this metaphysics in the contemporary literature are offered by thinkers like David Oderberg (2007: 65–85), Christopher Brown (2005: 55–100), and Edward Feser (2014: 164–71). On this sort of view, the informative criterion of identity of a human organism is its form, the metaphysical constituent of a substance that explains what it is, why it is that thing, and why it's not something else. This form cannot exist on its own but can and does exist insofar as it informs a living organism.

I combine this theory of human persons with a particular theory of time that I call Eschatological Presentism (EP) (2018: chaps. 5 and 6). EP borrows both from presentism—the thesis that all that exists, exists in the present—and four-dimensional eternalism, the thesis that the past, present, and future all exist; that time is spread out in a way analogous to space. Briefly, here's how EP works: for any present moment, there exist two temporal locations. There is the *now* present—what you and I intuitively take to be the present—and the time of Christ's return. So, for any given present moment there is a Present (notice the capital 'P') moment that is a compound of, say, *now* and the time of Christ's return. Call the present we experience right now, "T_1". Call the moment of Christ's return, "T_Ω". The Present moment is, on this view, $T_1 + T_\Omega$. T_1 neither exists all by itself nor does T_Ω. Instead, what exists is $T_1 + T_\Omega$. If the *now* time is T_2, then what exists is $T_2 + T_\Omega$. And so on.

On this view, it is not merely the case that time is spread out. Much like a perdurance account of persistence, objects are spread out in time, too. Unlike most accounts of perdurance, though, on EP, objects are spread out over, at most, two times (rather than an infinite amount). So, if it's presently T_1, then a human person, Jones, is spread out over $T_1 + T_\Omega$. Jones neither is wholly in T_1 nor wholly in T_Ω. She has a temporal part in T_1 and a temporal part in T_Ω. She wholly is in $T_1 + T_\Omega$. Compare: I am not located wholly in one portion of my chair. I am located wholly over the total sum of chair parts that my parts overlap. Couple EP with a broadly Thomistic hylemorphism, and one can explain the numerical identity of premortem and post-resurrection bodies. Bodies just are prime matter that have received a particular form; and, on this way of thinking about things, the necessary and sufficient condition of a body's identity is that it is informed by the same form. Now suppose that Jones has a temporal part that dies at T_1 and one that resurrects at T_Ω. If her body has the same form at T_1 and T_Ω, it follows that the body is one and the same. And this makes sense given that it just is the one body spread out over two times.

Though a complicated and admittedly bizarre model of resurrection, it accomplishes at least one important thing that the ones surveyed in Section II do not: it accounts for immediate post-mortem presence in Paradise; for if Jones dies at T_1, she finds herself immediately at T_Ω, the time of the *Parousia*. Now, immediate postmortem presence in Paradise is a condition of personal eschatology assumed in the Christian tradition and arguably taught in Christian scripture (See Turner 2018: chapter 1). And this model explains this by way of resurrection, which is what the eschatological fulfilment of the *telos* of human creatures requires.[20]

---

[20]Thanks to James Arcadi, Roger Turner, Kegan Shaw, Jesse Gentile, and Jordan Wessling for feedback on an original draft of this paper.

References

Aquinas, T. (1952), *Summa Theologica*, in R. M. Hutchins (ed.), Great Books of the Western World, no. 19, trans. Fathers of the English Dominican Province, Chicago: Encyclopedia Britannica.

Arcadi, J. M. (2020), "*Homo Adorans*: *Exitus et Reditus* in Theological Anthropology," *Scottish Journal of Theology*, 73 (1): 1–12.

Bauckham, R. (2007), "Eschatology," in J. Webster, K. Tanner, and I. Torrance (eds.), *The Oxford Handbook of Systematic Theology*, 306–22, Oxford: Oxford University Press.

Beale, G. K. (2004), *The Temple and the Church's Mission: A Biblical Theology of the Dwelling Place of God*, Downers Grove, IL: IVP Academic.

Beale, G. K., and M. Kim (2014), *God Dwells Among Us*, Downers Grove, IL: InterVarsity Press.

Boethius (n.d.), "A Treatise Against Eutyches and Nestorius," in *The Theological Tractates*, trans. H. F. Stewart and E. K. Rand, 30–46, Grand Rapids: Christian Classics Ethereal Library.

Bowles, R. G. (2014), "Does Revelation 14:11 Teach Eternal Torment?," in C. M. Date, G. G. Stump, and J. W. Anderson (eds.), *Rethinking Hell: Readings in Evangelical Conditionalism*, 138–54, Eugene, OR: Cascade Books.

Brown, C. (2005), *Aquinas and the Ship of Theseus*, London: Continuum.

Bynum, C. W. (1995), *Resurrection of the Body in Western Christianity: 200–1336*, New York: Columbia University Press.

Cooper, J. W. ([1989] 2000), *Body, Soul, and Life Everlasting*, Grand Rapids, MI: Eerdmans.

Corcoran, K. J. (2001), "Physicalism and Postmortem Survival without Temporal Gaps," in K. J. Corcoran (ed.), *Soul, Body, and Survival: Essays on the Metaphysics of Human Persons*, 201–17, Ithaca, NY: Cornell University Press.

Crisp, O. D. (2019), *Analyzing Doctrine: Toward a Systematic Theology*, Waco: Baylor University Press.

Dainton, B. (2010), *Time and Space*, 2nd ed., Durham: Acumen.

Davis, S. T. (1993), *Risen Indeed: Making Sense of the Resurrection*, Grand Rapids, MI: Eerdmans.

Davis, S. T. (2010), "Resurrection, Personal Identity, and the Will of God," in G. Gasser (ed.), *Personal Identity and Resurrection*, 19–21, Surrey: Ashgate.

Davis, S. T., and E. T. Yang (2017), "Composition and the Will of God: Reconsidering Resurrection by Reassembly," in T. R. Byerly and E. J. Silverman (eds.), *Paradise Understood: New Philosophical Essays about Heaven*, 213–27, Oxford: Oxford University Press.

Enns, P. (2012), *The Evolution of Adam: What the Bible Does and Doesn't Say About Human Origins*, Grand Rapids, MI: Brazos.

Farris, J. R. (2017), *The Soul of Theological Anthropology: A Cartesian Exploration*, London: Routledge.

Farris, J. R. (2020), *An Introduction to Theological Anthropology: Humans, both Creaturely and Divine*, Grand Rapids, MI: Baker Academic.

Fergusson, D. (1985), "Interpreting the Resurrection," *Scottish Journal of Theology*, 38 (3): 287–305.

Feser, E. (2014), *Scholastic Metaphysics: A Contemporary Introduction*, Heusenstamm: Editiones Scholasticae

Forrest, P. (2016), "The Identity of Indiscernibles," in E. N. Zalta (ed.), *The Stanford Encyclopedia of Philosophy*. Available online: https://plato.stanford.edu/archives/win2016/entries/identity-indiscernible/.

Gallois, A. (2016), "Identity over Time," in E. N. Zalta (ed.), *The Stanford Encyclopedia of Philosophy*. Available online: https://plato.stanford.edu/archives/win2016/entries/identity-time.

Goetz, S. (2018), "On the Nature of Human Persons and the Resurrection of the Body," *Journal of Analytic Theology*, 6: 300–12.

Gorman, F. H. (2014), "Priestly Rituals of Founding: Time, Space, and Status," in L. M. Morales (ed.), *Cult and Cosmos: Tilting Toward a Temple-Centered Theology*, 351–66, Leuven: Peeters.

Grenz, S. J. (2001), *The Social God and the Relational Self*, Louisville: Westminster.

Haldane, J. (2007), "Philosophy, Death and Immortality," *Philosophical Investigations*, 30 (3): 245–65.

Harris, M. J. (1983), *Raised Immortal: The Relation between Resurrection and Immortality in New Testament Teaching*, London: Marshall, Morgan, and Scott.

Hawley, K. (2020), "Temporal Parts," in E. N. Zalta (ed.) *The Stanford Encyclopedia of Philosophy*, Available online: https://plato.stanford.edu/archives/sum2020/entries/temporal-parts/.

Hershenov, D. (2002), "Van Inwagen, Zimmerman, and the Materialist Conception of Resurrection," *Religious Studies*, 38 (4): 451–69.

Hudson, H. (2017), "The Resurrection and Hypertime," in T. R. Byerly and E. J. Silverman (eds.), *Paradise Understood: New Philosophical Essays about Heaven*, 263–72, Oxford: Oxford University Press.

Johnson, A. (2003), "Turning the World Upside Down in 1 Corinthians 15: Apocalyptic Epistemology, the Resurrected Body and the New Creation," *Evangelical Quarterly*, 75: 307.

Le Poidevin, R. (2003), *Travels in Four Dimensions*, Oxford: Oxford University Press.

Levenson, J. D. (1984), "The Temple and the World," *Journal of Religion* 64 (3): 275–98.

Locke, J. (1975), *Essay Concerning Human Understanding*, ed. P. H. Nidditch, Oxford: Clarendon Press.

Mavrodes, G. I. (1977), "The Life Everlasting and the Bodily Criterion of Identity," *Noûs* 11 (1): 27–39.

McDonough, S. M. (2017), *Creation and New Creation: Understanding God's Project*, Peabody: Hendrickson.

Merricks, T. (1998), "There Are No Criteria of Identity Over Time," *Nous* 32 (1): 106–24.

Merricks, T. (2001), 'How to Live Forever without Saving Your Soul', in K. J. Corcoran (ed.), *Soul, Body, and Survival: Essays on the Metaphysics of Human Persons*, 183–200, Ithaca: Cornell University Press.

Middleton, J. R. (2005), *The Liberating Image: The Imago Dei in Genesis 1*, Grand Rapids, MI: Brazos.

Middleton, J. R., (2006), "A New Heaven and a New Earth: The Case for a Holistic Reading of the Biblical Story of Redemption," *Journal for Christian Theological Research*, 11: 73–97.

Middleton, J. R. (2014), *A New Heaven and a New Earth: Reclaiming Biblical Eschatology*, Grand Rapids, MI: Baker Academic.

Morales. L. M., ed. (2014), *Cult and Cosmos: Tilting Toward a Temple-Centered Theology*, Leuven: Peeters.

Mortenson, C. (2020), 'Change and Inconsistency', in E. N. Zalta (ed.), *The Stanford Encyclopedia of Philosophy*, available online: https://plato.stanford.edu/archives/spr2020/entries/change/

Mosser, C. (2018), "Two Visions of Being Saved as Deiform Perfectibility," in M. Cortez, J. R. Farris, and S. M. Hamilton (eds.), *Being Saved: Explorations in Human Salvation*, 265–80, London: SCM.

Mugg, J. and J. T. Turner (2017), "Why a *Bodily* Resurrection?: The Bodily Resurrection and the Mind/Body Relation,' *Journal of Analytic Theology* 5: 121–44.

Oderberg, D. S. (2007), *Real Essentialism*, New York: Routledge.

Olson, E. T. (2019), "Personal Identity," in E. N. Zalta (ed.), *The Stanford Encyclopedia of Philosophy*, available online: https://plato.stanford.edu/archives/fall2019/entries/identity-personal/.

Pelikan, J. (1993), *Christianity and Classical Culture*, New Haven, CT: Yale University Press.

Peters, T. (2002), "Resurrection: The Conceptual Challenge," in T. Peters, R. J. Russell, and M. Welker (eds.), *Resurrection: Theological and Scientific Assessments*, 297–321, Grand Rapids, MI: Eerdmans.

Pinnock, C. (1990), "The Destruction of the Finally Impenitent," *Criswell Theological Review*, 4: 243–59.

Sider, T. (2001), *Four-Dimensionalism: An Ontology of Persistence and Time*, Oxford: Oxford University Press.

Spiegel, J. S. (2015), "Annihilation, Everlasting Torment, and Divine Justice," *International Journal of Philosophy and Theology*, 76 (3): 241–8.

Thiselton, A. (2000), *The First Epistle to the Corinthians: A Commentary on the Greek Text*, Grand Rapids, MI: Eerdmans.

Turner, J. T. (2018), *On the Resurrection of the Dead: A New Metaphysics of Afterlife for Christian Thought*, London: Routledge.

Turner, J. T. ([2018] 2019), "Temple Theology, Holistic Eschatology, and the *Imago Dei*: An Analytic Prolegomenon in Response to N. T. Wright," *Canadian-American Theological Review*, 8 (1): 16–34.

Turner, J. T. (2019), "The Mind of the Spirit in the Resurrected Human: A Mereological Model of Mental Saturation," *Philosophia Christi*, 21 (1): 167–86.

Van Inwagen, P. (1978), "The Possibility of Resurrection," *International Journal for Philosophy of Religion*, 9 (2): 114–21.

Van Inwagen, P. (1990), *Material Beings*, Ithaca, NY: Cornell University Press.

Van Inwagen, P. (2018), "I Look for the Resurrection of the Dead and the Life of the World to Come," in J. Loose, A. Menuge, and J. P. Moreland (eds.), *The Blackwell Companion to Substance Dualism*, 488–500, Oxford: Wiley Blackwell.

Walton, J. H. (2009), *The Lost World of Genesis One: Ancient Cosmology and the Origins Debate*, Downers Grove, IL: IVP Academic.

Walton, J. H. (2015), *The Lost World of Adam and Eve: Genesis 2-3 and the Human Origins Debate*, Downers Grove, IL: IVP Academic.

Wenham, J. (2014), "The Case for Conditional Immortality," in C. M. Date, G. G. Stump, and J. W. Anderson (eds.), *Rethinking Hell: Readings in Evangelical Conditionalism*, 74–98, Eugene, OR: Cascade Books.

Wolters, A. M. (2005), *Creation Regained: Biblical Basics for a Reformational Worldview*, 2nd ed. Grand Rapids, IL: Eerdmans.

Woznicki, C. (2018), "'Thus Sayeth the Lord': Edwardsean Anti-Criterialism and the Physicalist Problem of Resurrection Identity', *TheoLogica*, 2 (1): 115–35.

Wright, N. T. (2003), *The Resurrection of the Son of God*, London: SPCK.

Wright, N. T. (2008), *Surprised by Hope*, New York: HarperOne.

Wright, N. T. ([2017] 2019), "History, Eschatology, and New Creation in the Fourth Gospel: Early Christian Perspectives on God's Action in Jesus, with Special Reference to the Prologue of John," *Canadian-American Theological Review*, 8 (1): 1–15.

Zimmerman, D. W. (1999), "The Compatibility of Materialism and Survival: The 'Falling Elevator' Model," *Faith and Philosophy*, 16 (2): 194–212.

PART VI

Experiences and Practices

CHAPTER THIRTY-THREE

Analytic Spirituality

DAVID EFIRD

Who am I? Why am I here? How do I live a good life? These are some of the existential questions that prompt a spiritual approach to the examined life and the search for meaning. As such, spirituality is not confined to religion, in general, or theism, in particular. For example, Robert C. Solomon, one of the foremost secular philosophers on this topic, takes spirituality to mean "the grand and thoughtful passions of life" and holds that "a life lived in accordance with those passions" entails choosing to see the world as "benign and life [as] meaningful," with the tragic not to be denied but accepted (Solomon 2002: 6, 51). For reasons of space, and because it is the tradition I know best, I will focus on a Christian approach to spirituality. On a Christian approach to spirituality, the goal of the spiritual life is to grow in the knowledge and the love of God. This is (however falteringly) accomplished through inward disciplines such as meditation, prayer, fasting, and study; outward disciplines such as simplicity, solitude, submission, and service; and corporate disciplines such as confession, worship, guidance, and celebration. In this chapter, I will describe how analytic philosophy can help us to clarify the nature and activities of spirituality, something I call "analytic spirituality". As such, analytic spirituality is an instance of conceptual engineering, or so I argue.

To do this, I will give a brief explanation of conceptual engineering and then argue that analytic spirituality is an instance of this by showing how analytic philosophy can help us to clarify the concept of knowing God and how this involves conceptual engineering. Using this same approach, I will then show how analytic philosophy can help clarify how we can know God through an inward discipline, namely, study, and how these clarifications involve conceptual engineering. I conclude by discussing how, using this account of analytic spirituality as conceptual engineering, the field of analytic theology may proceed.

I. CONCEPTUAL ENGINEERING

To argue that analytic spirituality is an instance of conceptual engineering, I first need to explain what conceptual engineering is. Conceptual engineering concerns "the activity of assessing and improving our representational devices" (Cappelen 2020: 1). It sounds a rather technical activity, but it is not; it is something that many, if not most, if not all, of us do regularly when we do philosophy.

Think of it like this.[1] A lot of the time, we do philosophy with words. But we did not create the vast majority of the words we use; moreover, we did not create the

---

[1] In the following, I am indebted to Herman Cappelen's (2020) "master argument" for conceptual engineering.

meanings they have, or the concepts they refer to. Rather, we inherited them. Now, when we do philosophy, we want our words to have the best meanings and refer to the best concepts. But, often, our words do not have the best meanings or refer to the best concepts: they may be theoretically deficient, such as being vague, indeterminate, ambiguous, or inconsistent (either individually or jointly with other meanings or concepts), or be practically deficient, such as being inconsistent with certain social or political aims. And so, often, we have to change the meanings our words have and the concepts they refer to, while preserving sufficient continuity to avoid "changing the subject," in order to do the best philosophy. When we do this, we do conceptual engineering.

Some examples include Rudolf Carnap's ([1947] 1956) method of explication, where he aims to improve the meanings of certain words by removing indeterminacy and vagueness, so that they are a better fit for science,[2] and Sally Haslanger's (2012) work on race and gender, where she aims to improve these concepts for social and political aims.[3] We can see this kind of activity throughout philosophy,[4] and, at least in my view, throughout analytic theology.[5] In this chapter, I suggest that conceptual engineering is also a central activity of analytic spirituality, and, to do this, I provide an example of engineering the concept of personal knowledge so as to allow for personal knowledge of God.

---

[2]Indeed, it was Richard Creath (1991) who coined the term "conceptual engineering" in his edited edition of the correspondence between Carnap and Quine.
Perhaps the best example of explication is the definition of "planet" by the International Astronomical Union (IAU) in 2006 (cf. Murzi 2007). The IAU were moved to define the term more precisely because there had been several discoveries of planet-like bodies, that is, bodies that resembled the then accepted nine planets orbiting the Sun. Because there had, at that point, been no accepted definition of "planet, it was unclear whether these planet-like bodies counted as planets. To remove this unclarity, the IAU stipulated that a planet is "a celestial body that (a) is in orbit around the Sun, (b) has sufficient mass for its self-gravity to overcome rigid body forces so that it assumes a hydrostatic equilibrium (nearly round) shape, and (c) has cleared the neighbourhood around its orbit" (IAU 2006). A consequence of this definition was the ruling out not only of the planet-like bodies recently discovered from being a planet but also Pluto, which had been previously regarded as a planet.
[3]For example, Haslanger takes gender to be "the social meaning of sex" where to have a certain gender is to be taken to have certain bodily features that are presumed to be evidence of a particular role in biological production and, in virtue of that role, to have a specific position in a social hierarchy. Part of the point of this analysis is that it helps to combat gender oppression by understanding gender in terms of social hierarchy.
[4]For example, when a philosopher gives a theory of causation, they are engaged in conceptual engineering in metaphysics, or when a philosopher gives a theory of knowledge, they are engaged in conceptual engineering in epistemology, or when a philosopher gives a theory of moral goodness, they are engaged in conceptual engineering in moral philosophy.
[5]For example, when analytic theologians give a theory of the Trinity, they are engaged in conceptual engineering, at least as I see it. To give a sense of this, consider what it would be for there to be one God existing in three persons. If there is but one God, it seems there is but one instance of divinity, and, if there are three persons, it seems there are three instances of personhood. But how then could all three instances of personhood be divine, since there is but one instance of divinity? This is one of the logical problems of the Trinity. Solving it requires conceptual engineering, at least as I see it. For solving it requires one of the following: revising the concept of truth, so that some contradictions can be true, revising the concept of identity, so that it is relative and not classical, revising the concept of monotheism, so that there being three divinities counts as monotheism, or revising the concept of the Trinity, so that there being just one instance of personhood counts as three persons.

II. KNOWING ANOTHER PERSON

As mentioned above, on a Christian conception of spirituality, the goal of the spiritual life is to grow in the knowledge and the love of God. But what is it to know God personally? Here analytic philosophy can help us to answer this question by helping us to understand what it is to know a person, and then apply that to our knowing God personally. As will become evident, this application will involve some conceptual engineering, as it is not straightforward how we could come to know an incorporeal, eternal, and ineffable being, the kind of being I take God to be. But before we go on to the revisions needed in our concept of knowing someone for our knowing God, let us be clear about just what it is to know someone.

To begin, according to Bonnie M. Talbert, "knowing another person depends on (at least) two things: direct, face-to-face interaction and an understanding of who that person is in the world" (2017: 545).[6] Such knowledge is distinct from first-personal knowledge, for example, knowledge my own occurrent mental states, and from third-personal knowledge, for example, knowledge of facts about the world. It is, rather, second-personal knowledge, that is, knowledge of you, that is, your mental states and who you are in the world. It might seem, though, that this second-personal knowledge is, after all, reducible to third-personal knowledge, since other people are part of the world, and so knowledge of them would be knowledge of facts about the world. Such reasoning, though, is undermined by a thought experiment put forward by Eleonore Stump, which, in turn, derives from Frank Jackson's famous thought experiment about Mary, the color scientist.

> Mary is a brilliant scientist who is, for whatever reason, forced to investigate the world from a black and white room via a black and white television monitor. She specialises in the neurophysiology of vision and acquires, let us suppose, all the physical information there is to obtain about what goes on when we see ripe tomatoes, or the sky, and use terms like "red," "blue," and so on. She discovers, for example, just which wave-length combinations from the sky stimulate the retina, and exactly how this produces via the central nervous system the contraction of the vocal chords and expulsion of air from the lungs that results in the uttering of the sentence "The sky is blue." (It can hardly be denied that it is in principle possible to obtain all this physical information from black and white television, otherwise the Open University would of necessity need to use colour television.)
>
> What will happen when Mary is released from her black and white room or is given a colour television monitor? Will she learn anything or not? It seems just obvious that she will learn something about the world and our visual experience of it. But then it is inescapable that her previous knowledge was incomplete. But she had all the physical information. *Ergo* there is more to have than that, and Physicalism is false. (Jackson 1982: 130)

Innovatively extending this thought experiment, Stump asks us to imagine that Mary is brought up in a room in which she has access to only facts about the world; in particular,

---

[6]Whether such interactions must be face-to-face, a crucial issue for coming to know God personally, is discussed below.

she has never met her mother and never read any stories about her. What would Mary learn, Stump asks, when she encounters her mother for the first time? According to Stump,

> When Mary is first united with her mother, it seems indisputable that Mary will know things she did not know before, even if she knew everything about her mother that could be made available to her in non-narrative propositional form, including her mother's psychological states. Although Mary knew that her mother loved her before she met her, when she is united with her mother, Mary will learn what it is like to be loved ... [W]hat will come as the major revelation to Mary is her mother ... What is new for Mary is a second-person experience. (2010: 52–3)

As Stump's thought experiment seems to indicate, to know a person it does not suffice to know something or even a lot of things about them. Something more is required. That something more includes a second-personal experience.

Generalizing from her thought experiment concerning Mary meeting her mother, Stump claims that Paula has a second-person experience of Jerome only if

- Paula is aware of Jerome as a person (call the relation Paula has to Jerome in this condition "personal interaction"),
- Paula's personal interaction with Jerome is of a direct and immediate sort, and
- Jerome is conscious (2010: 75–6),

and this kind of experience is required in order for Paula to come to know Jerome, that is, for Paula to come to have personal knowledge of Jerome.

It should be noted at this point, that Paula's having a second-personal experience of Jerome is necessary, but not sufficient, for knowing Jerome. For all that is required for a second-personal experience is a kind of awareness. For Paula to come to know Jerome, not only must she be aware of Jerome, but also, she must attend to him, and him to her. This kind of mutual attending psychologists call "joint attention" (cf. Seemann 2012). More specifically, for Paula to come to know Jerome she must engage in dyadic joint attention with him, where dyadic joint attention consists in Paula and Jerome attending to one another. (Triadic joint attention consists in Paula and Jerome attending to a third object while they attend to one another.) The reason dyadic joint attention is required for personal knowledge is that it is only in the context of joint attention that Paula can reveal herself to Jerome and Jerome can accurately perceive what Paula has revealed to him. So, personal knowledge not only requires second-personal experience but also dyadic joint attention.

Now, one of the ways in which personal knowledge is different from propositional knowledge is that personal knowledge comes in degrees. You can know one person better than you know another, and you can come to know a person better than you do now. What Stump has described as knowing someone, namely, having a second-personal experience with someone and sharing attention with them, can be satisfied in a quite minimal way, say after a single conversation. At that point, you know them, but not at all well. What we are interested in, when we think about knowing God in the spiritual life, is knowing him more than minimally, even well. So, we need some further conditions to understand what it is to know God better than minimally, or even well.

III. KNOWING ANOTHER PERSON WELL

According to Talbert, we know someone, A, well, when

(1) we have had a significant number of second-person face-to-face interactions with A, at least some of which have been relatively recent;
(2) the contexts of those interactions were such as to permit A to reveal important aspects of her/himself, and A has done so;
(3) A has not deceived us about him/herself in important respects;
(4) we have succeeded in accurately perceiving what A has revealed, that is, we are not "blinded" by his/her own biases or other impairments. (2015: 194)

These conditions, as Talbert describes them, help us to "map out features of interactions ordinarily necessary to ground claims to know someone well" (2015: 196).

Now these conditions can be satisfied more or less well. That is, Paula can know Jerome, for example, more or less well in virtue of Paula and Jerome having more or fewer second-personal face-to-face interactions, these interactions being in more or less varied contexts, Jerome revealing more or less of himself to Paula, and Paula perceiving more or less accurately what Jerome is revealing of himself to her. Consequently, the more these conditions are satisfied, the "more well" Paula knows Jerome. When she does know Jerome well, her interactions with him create a "shared world," where not only are there a significant number of such interactions (their shared world has a certain breadth) but also at least some of these interactions are meaningful and important (their shared world has a certain depth) (Talbert 2015: 198–200). What makes this shared world possible is, in part, the skill Paula has interacting with Jerome, and the skill Jerome has in interacting with Paula. For, to know someone well, you have to know how to interact with them over time (Talbert 2015: 196–7; 2017; cf. Bergamin 2017).

The skill of interacting with a person over time consists in a complex of skills, which involve at least the following: the skill of recognizing them, the skill of detecting their mental states, and the skill of communicating your own mental states to them. Each of these skills are likely to be particular to that person, for, while a person may have the skill of interacting with some other person, or people, generally, they would need the skill of interacting with a particular person if they are to come to know them over time. For example, the skills involved in interacting with my mother are different from the skills involved in interacting with my father, which are different again from the skills involved in interacting with my partner, even though, underlying all of these particular skills, is a general skill I have in interacting with people.

We acquire these general skills in large part through socialization, where we learn to recognize certain patterns and respond appropriately. We then apply these skills when we come to meet someone new, in order to acquire a related, but new, skill, that of interacting with this particular person, something we acquire over time, through many interactions in various circumstances, and often on a trial-and-error basis. We learn to interpret what they say and what they do, their facial expressions and bodily movements, as clues to their thoughts and emotions, clues we sometimes interpret correctly and sometimes incorrectly. And we learn from our successes and failures, so that, over time, and after many interactions with someone and in a variety of contexts, we effortlessly, and largely unconsciously, interact with them successfully.

This is "the best case," where we do indeed acquire the skill of interacting with a new person, and we have that skill to a high degree. But there are a continuum of cases between this "best case" and "the worst case," where, despite the best intentions on both sides, you never acquire the skill of interacting with them; for whatever reason, you simply cannot come to know them, even though you have tried on many occasions and in many circumstances to learn how to interact with them. And in between "the best case" and "the worst case" are a great many more or less good cases, probably the vast majority of cases in our lives, where we have the skill of interacting with a particular person more or less well.

But even in "the best case," people change, from time to time, and they sometimes do the unexpected. So we cannot ever really "figure someone out" or "master their personality" because people are "moving targets," always subject to change (Talbert 2017).[7] Consequently, knowledge of another person is always open-ended, a continuous process of discovery, and part of the skill of knowing someone over time is adjusting how you interact with them now, in light of who they have become.

IV. KNOWING GOD AND KNOWING HIM WELL

For the purposes of this chapter, I will adopt Stump's analysis of what it is to know a person and Talbert's analysis of what it is to know a person well, and I will now apply it to give an analysis of what it is to know God and know him well. According to Stump, Paula knows God when she interacts with him second-personally, and, in this interaction, shares attention with him. So far so good. There seems to be nothing in Stump's analysis that would prevent Paula from knowing God in just the same way that I, say, know someone I meet for the first time. But things are not so straightforward when we apply Talbert's analysis of what it is to know someone well. If we simply substitute 'Paula' and 'God' in Talbert's conditions at the relevant places, we have the following:

1*. Paula has had a significant number of second-person face-to-face interactions with God, at least some of which have been relatively recent.
2*. The contexts of those interactions were such as to permit God to reveal important aspects of himself, and God has done so.
3*. God has not deceived Paula about himself in important respects.
4*. Paula has succeeded in accurately perceiving what God has revealed, that is, Paula is not "blinded" by her own biases or other impairments.

An obvious difficulty with applying Talbert's analysis to our knowing God well is that her analysis emphasizes that the interactions which ground such knowledge are, at least typically, face-to-face.[8] But, given that God is incorporeal, he does not have a face, at least not in a literal sense.[9] And so it seems hard to see how Talbert's analysis could help us to understand what it is to know God well. To see our way through this, we will need to do

---

[7]Indeed, sometimes such changes are due to our own interactions with them. I thank James Arcadi for this point.
[8]There are other such difficulties, particularly if God is taken to be eternal and ineffable. For it is not clear how we could interact with an eternal God, or how we could know an ineffable God at all, let alone well. But I am not dealing with them here because they have been dealt with elsewhere, using, at least in my view, conceptual engineering. With Norman Kretzmann, Stump (1981) has provided a way for an eternal God to interact with a temporal creation, largely relying on the concept, which they coin, of Eternal-Temporal Simultaneity, where an event or an object can be simultaneous in two modes of existence, one eternal and one temporal. I, with David Worsley, (2017) have addressed how we could know an ineffable God, by distinguishing two concepts of ineffability, one personal and one propositional, such that God is personally effable but propositionally ineffable.
[9]Of course, given that Christ is God, and that Christ has a face, God has a face, too. But for most people most of the time, they don't see Christ physically face-to-face. And so for the purposes of this chapter, I will take it that God does not have a face.

some conceptual engineering, modifying the concept, as Talbert has defined it, of what it is to know someone well.

To begin, let us attend to why Talbert thinks face-to-face interactions are important in coming to know someone well. She writes,

> In face-to-face interaction, we can see, hear, and smell the same things at the same time. The possibilities for joint attention (where two people are paying attention to the same thing, and each is aware of the other's attention) make it possible that not only are we both looking at the same tree, I know you see the tree and you know that I see it, and we both know that we both see the tree. In short, we can jointly attend to objects in our shared environment. (2015: 193)

While we could grant that triadic-shared attention is difficult for us with God for the reasons Talbert gives, and it should be noted that she goes on to say that she does not rule out non-face-to-face triadic-shared attention,[10] I will go on to explain how such shared attention could occur while reading scripture. Concerning dyadic shared-attention, that, too, seems to be difficult with God. For typically we attend to each other's thoughts and emotions (in dyadic shared-attention) by, in part, attending to their faces and other bodily movements. But we cannot do that with God. So how could we perceive his thoughts and emotions if he has neither a face nor a body? It seems that there are two ways we could do this, either by directing our attention inwardly or directing it outwardly.

Directing our attention inwardly, an example of dyadic-shared attention with God might be a model of prayer popular with many Christian traditions but often associated with the Vineyard. As Tanya Luhrmann summarizes it,

> When you attend a church like the Vineyard, you are presented with a theory of mind in which that distinction [the distinction between sounds and sights in the world and thoughts and images in our mind] is all of a sudden no longer straightforward. You are asked to experience some of your thoughts as being more like perceptions. In a church like the Vineyard, God participates in your mind, and you "hear" what he says as if it were external speech. The general model is clear enough, although no one actually presented it to me as a bullet-point list. God wants to be your friend; you develop that relationship through prayer; prayer is hard work and requires effort and training; and when you develop that relationship, God will answer back, through thoughts and mental images he places in your mind, and through sensations he causes in your body. You still experience those thoughts and images and sensations, for the most part, as if they were your own, generated from within your own mind and body. You have learned to experience those you have identified as God's as different. (2012: 41)

---

[10]For further discussion on the epistemology of non-face-to-face interactions, particularly with respect to online technologies such as email, Facebook, Twitter, and Skype, see Talbert (2013), where she argues that face-to-face interaction is the "gold standard" (335) for knowing another's mind

> because face-to-face contexts allow for and promote joint attention (often through the use of such behavioral signals), where perceptions can be shared in a more transparent sense, something Christopher Peacocke has characterized as "open knowledge." A shared perception in face-to-face interaction has an openness that sharing in noninteractive contexts lacks—an openness which creates the possibility of shared meanings, feelings, etc. that are reinforced by the interactive context. (337)

This method, of attending to your thoughts and detecting which ones God has placed in your consciousness, allows you to share attention with God, as by attending to these God-implanted thoughts you attend to God himself.

Directing our attention outwardly, an example of dyadic-shared attention with God might be given by Michael C. Rea's (2018) recent account of religious experiences. On this account, religious experiences are not at all uncommon. He writes,

> It is not uncommon for people to report having a sense of God's presence in the midst of a church service, or around a campfire singing hymns or praise songs; nor is it uncommon for people to experience the love and forgiveness of Christ in the Lord's Supper, or at various other points in a Christian liturgy ... Similarly, people often report apparently non-mystical, non-numinous experiences of God's presence, love, majesty, and the like in nature—out in the woods, on the beach, climbing a mountain, and so on. People sometimes experience God speaking to them through the scriptures, or through a sermon, or through the words of a friend. (2018: 116)

One might go further and say that, given God's omnipresence, it is possible to experience God anytime and anywhere (Stump 2013), such that all experiences could be religious experiences, if we were but attentive enough to recognize God in them and skilled enough to interpret them accurately, that is, as revealing what God intends to reveal of himself.[11]

When we do this, that is, recognize God in an experience and interpret it accurately as revealing what God intends to reveal of himself, we then have a different experience than if we did not. For example, if two people look out across the Grand Canyon, and one recognizes God in the experience and interprets it accurately, perhaps as revealing God's creative work in the sequences of rocks, but the other, say, an atheist, does not, seeing the sequences of rocks as the result of purely naturalistic processes, they experience the mountain top differently—just as an art historian, who knows little of mathematics, will experience a Jackson Pollock "drip painting" differently from a mathematician, who knows little of art history: while the former sees the drips and splashes of paint as direct expressions of the artist's emotions, something new in American art, the latter sees the drips and splashes of paint as fractals, geometric patterns repeated thousands of times. Based on years of training, the art historian and the mathematician have developed different skills in seeing the Pollock painting as something different from what the other sees it as. And both may be correct: for the drips and splashes of paint could be both direct expressions of the artist's emotions and fractals at the same time. However, the theist and the atheist cannot both be correct in how they each see the Grand Canyon. For it is either the result of a process that involves a supernatural element or not. Assuming that it does involve this supernatural element, that is, God's creative input, the theist has developed the skills needed for discerning this element in his experience, that is, of recognizing God in his experience and interpreting it accurately as revealing one of God's mental states, namely what God intends to reveal of himself. On this view, then, religious experiences outside of our own mental lives, such as experiences of participating in corporate worship

---

[11] On this view, then, the so-called problem of divine hiddenness is really the problem of human "willed loneliness" (Stump 2010), where we are unwilling to develop the skill of experiencing God second-personally at all times and in all places.

or of viewing nature from a mountain top, can direct us to God's mental states if we have the knowledge and skills necessary for recognizing him in those experiences and interpreting them as he intends them to be interpreted.

Let us now take stock. If, on a Christian approach to spirituality, the goal of the spiritual life is to grow in the knowledge and the love of God, achieving this goal requires developing the skill of interacting with God second-personally and of sharing attention with him dyadically. Developing these skills, in turn, require developing the skills of accurately recognizing God in our experiences and accurately interpreting those experiences as revealing what God intends to reveal of himself to us, either in our own mental lives, as on the Vineyard model of prayer, or in our experience of the world outside of us, as a world where God is available for second-personal experience anytime and anywhere. Developing these skills, then, is the point of the spiritual disciplines, to which I now turn.

V. DEVELOPING THE SKILLS NEEDED FOR KNOWING GOD THROUGH SPIRITUAL DISCIPLINES

Given that goal of the spiritual life is growth in the knowledge and the love of God, and the skills needed for achieving it, spiritual disciplines are about providing a mode of, and an occasion for, experiencing God second-personally and sharing attention with him, and, through many such experiences, and in many contexts, over a sustained period of time, developing the skills necessary for knowing God, that is, recognizing him in our experiences and interpreting them accurately, that is, as revealing what God intends to reveal of himself in them. To illustrate this, I will begin by outlining how study, an inward discipline, can be a mode of, and an occasion for, second-personal experience of God and of sharing attention with him, and then I will outline how study over a sustained period of time can allow a person to develop the skills needed for knowing God.

Study can take many forms, but I will concentrate on the study of the Christian scriptures. It might seem odd to suggest that, in the study of the scriptures, we can interact with God, since, it seems, our focus will be on the text, which reports other people's experiences of God, and not on God directly. That is, in studying scripture, we might come to know a lot about God, especially as others have experienced with him, but how could we come to experience God ourselves in reading about other's experiences? According to Adam Green and Keith A. Quan (2012), scripture is not merely a record of other's experiences of God; rather, scripture is a mode of, and an occasion for, our experiencing God. Consider the following examples, given by Green and Quan:

Case 1

Becky likes to cook along with the Rachael Ray show. The show is on the Spanish-speaking channel during her dinner hour, and Becky does not speak Spanish, so she follows the English subtitles. When Ray says "Consider the golden brown crust of this zucchini bake" Becky is able to use her abilities to engage in shared attention as mediated by the subtitles to attend to the zucchini bake pictured on the screen. She then imagines what Rachael Ray would say about the zucchini bake that Becky is cooking and is led to look at the crust of her own zucchini bake, pondering whether it is golden brown as it should be.

Case 2

> Alex wins a private cooking lesson with Rachael Ray. He is deaf, so Rachael communicates with him using written notes. At a certain point in the lesson, she hands him a note that reads, "Consider the golden brown crust of this zucchini bake," at which point he attends with Rachael to the crust. He looks back at Rachael who smiles and holds out a note between them that reads, "You done good." (2012: 423)

While Case 1 is not a case of genuine shared attention, since Ray is not present for Becky to share attention with her, Becky still uses the skills needed for sharing attention with another person. However, Case 2 is an example of genuine shared attention, since Alex and Ray share attention triadically mediated by a text, and then dyadically following the Alex's reading of the text. In the same way, because of God's omnipresence, we can share attention with God, mediated by the text of scripture. It can be as if God is speaking directly to us using scripture as his way of sharing attention with us, just as Ray uses a note to share attention with Alex.[12] For example, we might imagine ourselves in a biblical story, such as when we read the Sermon on the Mount, we can imagine Jesus speaking the beatitudes directly to us.[13] Practices of reading scripture, such as *Lectio Divina*, encourage just this sort of imaginative engagement with the text. In this way, reading scripture can be a mode of sharing attention with God.

In addition, we can think of another way that scripture allows us to share attention with God by reflecting on this example, also from Green and Quan:

> If Rachael Ray hands Alex a note that says, "My producer Buddy is in the next room and he wants to give you a new blender," Alex may then be empowered by the note to have dyadic and triadic shared experiences with Buddy, but the note is not part of any cooperative activity shared by Alex and Buddy. The note is only a means of putting Alex in a position to engage in shared attention with Buddy. (2012: 422)

Similarly, scripture can alert to us to God's presence with us. I think we might think of the following passage from Job in that way:

> For I know that my Redeemer lives, and that at the last he will stand upon the earth; and after my skin has been thus destroyed, then in my flesh I shall see God, whom I shall see on my side, and my eyes shall behold, and not another. (19:25-27a)[14]

While this text is sometimes cited as a proof text for the resurrection of the body, I think that is to miss its point. For this text comes after Job has experienced a great deal of suffering, suffering because the point of the pain was opaque to him, but then he comes to realize that in the place of his pain, in the center of his suffering, he will see God, who is with him and for him. That is how I read the text, and, whether or not it is an accurate reading of the text, it serves to alert me to God's presence with and for me, especially in difficult times. In this way, then, reading scripture can be an occasion for sharing attention with God.

---

[12]For this model of engagement, a theory of divine inspiration on which God speaks in and through the text of scripture is required. For such a theory, see Wolterstorff (1995).
[13]This is a hallmark of the Ignatian tradition of the *Lectio Divina* method of reading scripture. For expositions of this method, see Foster (2005) and Johnson (2015).
[14]Biblical quotes in this chapter are taken from the New Revised Standard Version of the Bible.

Now, if reading scripture can be a mode of, and an occasion for, experiencing God second-personally and sharing attention with him, it can be a way of developing the skills necessary for knowing God, namely, recognizing him in our experiences and interpreting them accurately, that is, as revealing what God intends to reveal of himself in them. For, in experiencing God in scripture, we come to know something of who God is and how he reveals himself to us. We can then better recognize God in our own lives and better interpret our experiences as revelatory of God. Over a sustained period of time, we can then develop the skills we need to engage with God not only when we are engaging in spiritual disciplines, such as reading scripture, but also in ordinary, day-to-day lives. In this way, we can come to know God and his love for us, until that time when we "see face to face" and "know fully, even as [we] have been fully known" (1 Cor. 13:12).

VI. CONCLUSION

It is clear that I have only touched the surface of what it is to know God and his love for us. But I hope to have shed some light on how analytic philosophy can help us to understand spirituality and the spiritual life, at least from a Christian perspective. What analytic philosophy helps with is clarification, clarification, that is, through conceptual engineering. For, when we try to understand what it is to know God personally, we cannot take this as simply another case of knowing another person. We have to modify our concept of personal knowledge and the skills necessary for acquiring such knowledge. I have tried to show how we can do this, particularly in the example of the spiritual discipline of study. There is, of course, much more to say about this spiritual discipline, and how this way of understanding spirituality and the spiritual life can be carried through the other eleven spiritual disciplines I have listed. But I hope to have shown how further investigations might proceed, and what analytic philosophy has to contribute to our understanding of spirituality and the spiritual life, namely, clarification by conceptual engineering.[15]

References

Bergamin, J. (2017), "To Know and To Be: Second-Person Knowledge and the Intersubjective Self, A Reply to Talbot," *Social Epistemology Review and Reply Collective*, 6: 43–7.

Cappelen, H. (2020), "Conceptual Engineering: The Master Argument," in A. Burgess, H. Cappelen, and D. Plunkett (eds.), *Conceptual Engineering and Conceptual Ethics*, 132–51, Oxford: Oxford University Press.

Carnap, R. ([1947] 1956), *Meaning and Necessity: A Study in Semantics and Modal Logic*, Chicago: University of Chicago Press.

Creath, R., ed. (1991), *Dear Carnap, Dear Van: The Quine-Carnap Correspondence and Related Work*. Berkeley: University of California Press.

Efird, D., and D. Worsley. (2017), "What an Apophaticist Can Know: Divine Ineffability and the Beatific Vision," *Philosophy and Theology*, 29: 205–19.

Foster, D. (2005), *Reading with God: Lectio Divina*, London: Continuum.

Green, A., and K. A. Quan (2012), "More Than Inspired Propositions," *Faith and Philosophy*, 29: 416–30.

---

[15] I thank James Arcadi and Joshua Cockayne for very helpful comments on a previous draft of this chapter.

Haslanger, S. (2012), *Resisting Reality: Social Construction and Social Critique*, Oxford: Oxford University Press.

International Astronomical Union (IAU) (2006), "IAU 2006 General Assembly: Result of the IAU Resolution Votes," Prague. Available online: https://www.iau.org/news/pressreleases/detail/iau0603/.

Jackson, F. (1982), "Epiphenomenal Qualia," *Philosophical Quarterly*, 32: 127–36.

Johnson, J. (2015), *Meeting God in Scripture: A Hands-On Guide to Lectio Divina*, Downers Grove, IL: IVP Books.

Luhrmann, T. (2012), *When God Talks Back*, New York: Vintage Books.

Murzi, M. (2007), "Changes in a Scientific Concept: What Is a Planet?," PhilSci Archive. Available online: http://philsci-archive.pitt.edu/id/eprint/3418.

Rea, M. C. (2018), *The Hiddenness of God*, Oxford: Oxford University Press.

Seemann, A., ed. (2012), *Joint Attention: New Developments in Psychology, Philosophy of Mind, and Social Neuroscience*, Cambridge, MA: MIT Press.

Solomon, R. C. (2002), *Spirituality for the Skeptic: The Thoughtful Love of Life*, Oxford: Oxford University Press.

Stump, E. (2010), *Wandering in Darkness*, Oxford: Oxford University Press.

Stump, E. (2013), "Omnipresence, Indwelling, and the Second-Personal," *European Journal for Philosophy of Religion*, 5: 29–53.

Stump, E., and N. Kretzmann. (1981), "Eternity," *Journal of Philosophy*, 78: 429–58.

Talbert, B. M. (2013), "Screened Conversations: Technologically Mediated Interactions and Knowledge of Other Minds," *Techné: Research in Philosophy and Technology*, 17: 333–49.

Talbert, B. M. (2015), "Knowing Other People: A Second-Person Framework," *Ratio*, 28: 190–206.

Talbert, B. M. (2017), "Overthinking and Other Minds: The Analysis Paralysis," *Social Epistemology*, 31: 545–56.

Wolterstorff, N. (1995), *Divine Discourse: Philosophical Reflections on the Claim that God Speaks*, Cambridge: Cambridge University Press.

CHAPTER THIRTY-FOUR

Christian Baptism: A Reformed Account

NATHANIEL GRAY SUTANTO

While some analytic treatments on the sacraments in general and the Eucharist in particular do exist, treatises on baptism from an analytic perspective are surprisingly sparse. Terence Cuneo has offered what is thus far the only analytic treatment that focuses on baptism, and he does so from an Eastern Orthodox perspective (Cuneo 2016: 167–203). This is surprising because, though the Eucharist is often considered to be philosophically perplexing enough to be worthy of the sacrifice of many forests for the fodder of metaphysical reflection, the sacrament of baptism is theologically no less significant and arguably no less ripe for analysis and yet enjoys scant attention in the literature. Considered as an initiation rite, the history of theology showcases that baptism is a locus of substantial contention and identity division. Discussions on it debate the agent(s), mode, proper recipients, soteriological efficacy, its signification (if it is to be considered a sign at all), and the simple meaning of *what happens* when a baptism takes place.

In this chapter, I hope to stimulate further philosophical reflection on baptism by presenting an analytically informed Reformed view. The Reformed confessions offer what might be called a pneumatic and covenantal account of baptism. I begin by offering a sketch of baptism from a Reformed perspective in dialogue with current works in analytic theology. I then move on to engage with Cuneo's "intelligibility puzzle," which questions the intelligibility of the seemingly hyperbolic claims surrounding baptism's significance, while assessing his own Eastern Orthodox response to that puzzle. Finally, I close by arguing that a Reformed account, due to a difference in the theology of the efficacy of baptism and the nature of the regenerative states, eludes Cuneo's intelligibility puzzle, and that this is a benefit of that model. I then close with some brief concluding comments.

I. BAPTISM IN REFORMED THEOLOGY

Baptism is a sacrament and is thus a visible sign of an invisible grace (WCF 27:1–2). In Reformed theology, baptism, along with the Lord's Supper, belongs within a pneumatic and covenantal context. Let us begin with the former before moving on to the latter.

Considered pneumatically, God the Spirit is the proper person behind and the efficient cause of the thing signified in baptism.[1] Drawing from James Arcadi's helpful taxonomy, a pneumatic account sits between what he calls "corporeal" and "no non-normal" models of a theology of the sacraments (2018: 15–22). While Arcadi offers these terms specifically to canvas the various views of the Lord's Supper, I suggest that they can also be deployed to display the different views on offer concerning baptism. Let me define these models briefly. In the Lord's Supper, these models denote primarily the *mode* of divine (Christological) presence in the sacramental elements of bread and wine. Corporeal models argue that Christ is corporeally present in the elements. Pneumatic models argue that it is the Spirit of the ascended Christ that is present in the elements, lifting believers to Christ in the heavenly places. A no non-normal model argues that Christ is present in the elements in the same way the divinity of Christ is present everywhere and is thus not an exception to the exemplification of his omnipresence.

If in the Lord's Supper the focus is on the mode of divine presence in the elements, in baptism the focus is on the mode of divine *action*—specifically, God's acting through the elements to transform the recipient.[2] A Reformed model can agree with Cuneo when he writes that in "the eucharistic rite, the emphasis falls on the transformation of the bread and wine- the imposition upon them of a new function. In the baptismal rite, by contrast, the emphasis falls on the transformation of the one baptized" (2016: 169). More questions emerge. Does God act through the water corporeally, pneumatically, or in a way that is not exceptional to God's ordinary way of acting in the world (no non-normally)? Is the relation between divine action and the element physical, relative, or merely preservative? Corporeal accounts uphold a form of baptismal regeneration, according to which the water *effects* an internal cleansing or regeneration unto the recipient in a physical way—it works *ex opere operato*. A no non-normal model argues that God acts in the sacrament in a way that is not exceptional to his providential preserving and ordering of the cosmos. Baptism is thus a pledge, oath, and testimony to the believer's commitment that bears a primarily horizontal function to the witnesses of baptism.

A pneumatic account, however, argues that God acts in baptism not corporeally but metonymically (Fesko 2009: 322). Water baptism represents in visible ways the work of the Spirit in internal cleansing. The recipients of baptism are not only admitted into the membership of the visible church and set apart unto service for God on earth but also receive baptism as a sign of an inward grace. As a *sign*, the water points beyond itself toward the thing signified and the word promised: the inward cleansing of the recipient, regeneration, the remission of sins, union with Christ, resurrection, and so on (WCF 28.1). As a *seal* instituted by God, it is God's authority and name that stamps the validity of the baptismal act, which then initiates the recipient into the covenant community.[3]

Hence, with regard to the question of whether baptism is necessary for salvation, it is worth heeding a distinction drawn by Francis Turretin between two kinds of necessity: the

---

[1] Westminster Larger Catechism, Q&A 161, in *The Confession of Faith and Catechisms* (2005).
[2] This is not to suggest that the divine presence and action can be neatly or metaphysically separated. Indeed, divine action presupposes divine presence. The distinction is meant only to be in focus.
[3] This is one main reason why the majority of Reformed theologians admit the validity of Roman Catholic baptisms. Despite claiming that the Roman Catholic Church has a distorted soteriology and sacramentology, the Reformed hold that the Roman Catholic Church maintains the essence of baptism in the name of the Triune God, and thus their baptisms are not to be rejected. The validity of baptism, then, does not depend on the precise theology or piety of the administrators but rather on the seal of God's triune name (see Calvin 1960: 4. 15.16 and Turretin 1997: 396–8).

absolute and the relative. The former stems from "the simple nature of the thing, which is said to be of means, without which the end cannot be secured," while the latter is "relative from the ordination of God" (Turretin 1997: 387). The absolute means of salvation are due to the internal and intrinsic nature of the thing, "having of themselves a necessary connection with the end so that the end cannot be obtained without them" (387). Turretin lists the examples of faith, repentance, justification, and regeneration as those states that are absolute necessary for salvation. Baptism, however, is considered an "external" mean. These "external means" are "not by themselves connected with the end, but subserving it only from the ordination of God, still not of so great necessity as the end themselves cannot be secured without them" (387). As such, though it is a "heinous crime" to despise the institution of baptism, the sacraments are not absolutely necessary "but only relatively from the force of the divine command and his institution" (387).

The relative necessity of the sign highlights God's freedom to consecrate water in order to signify the invisible graces. As such, though baptism is only relatively necessary and exhibits the benefits of salvation as a sign and seal, the link God establishes between them is not arbitrary, but fitting. Herman Bavinck is typical of Reformed theologians when he argues that water was chosen not "accidentally but in account of its striking resemblance to the thing signified" (2008: 515). The text often pointed to is 1 Pet. 3:21, where a parallel is drawn between water, which washes away physical pollution, and the cleansing of one's conscience before God in baptism (cf. Turretin 1997: 382).

Two things follow from affirming that it is the Spirit's working that is metonymically signified in baptism. First, the evangelical Word preached should always accompany the baptismal act, proclaiming Christ and his benefits as visibly presented in baptism. Baptism communicates nothing new or different from what is conferred in the gospel. Christ has given believers all spiritual and soteric benefits, which believers have received by faith. These benefits are not divided up—it is not as if some graces are bestowed in preaching and others in the sacraments. The Gospel is proclaimed in the word, heard in preaching, and signified in baptism.[4] The same evangelical grace is thus distributed by way of two different means: word and sacrament. Further, just as the preaching of the word can have no automatic efficacy on its listeners inwardly, so does the baptismal act depend on the Spirit through the Word to confer the thing signified (see Kolb and Trueman 2017: 165).

Second, a pneumatic account affirms that the Spirit is free to affect the inward thing signified in a separate moment from the baptismal act (Bavinck 2008: 519). The words of institution do not physically or automatically imbue the water with spiritual power, nor does the water automatically effect the things signified (518). Rather, the inward grace signified is applied by the Spirit to the elect at his appointed time. The Reformed account of baptism is thus inextricable from its doctrine of election, according to which God foreordained beforehand the election of a fixed number of sinners in eternity past and then effectually calls those sinners in a specific appointed time in history. Water baptism applied to those who do not enjoy the thing signified (those who do not enjoy God's

---

[4] The Reformation, by contrast, posited the scriptural principle that the sacrament imparts no other benefit than that which believers already possess by trusting in the Word of God. Faith alone apart any sacrament communicates, and causes believers to enjoy, all the benefits of salvation. Now if baptism presupposes faith, there is no other remaining benefit that could be imparted to believers by baptism. Baptism can only signify and seal the benefits that are received by faith and thereby strengthen that faith. (Bavinck 2008: 515)

election), then, bestows no positive spiritual effect. The key clause is in the Westminster Confession of Faith (WCF) 28:6:

> The efficacy of Baptism is not tied to that moment of time wherein it is administered; yet, notwithstanding, by the right use of this ordinance, the grace promised is not only offered, but really exhibited, and conferred, by the Holy Ghost, to such (whether of age or infants) as that grace belongs unto, according to the counsel of God's own will, in his appointed time.

The "grace promised" is not merely exhibited but also "conferred" to "such as that grace belongs unto" and not, therefore, automatically by virtue of the baptismal act. Hence, the Reformed have differing opinions as to when the inward thing signified is effected by the Spirit: before, during, or after the elect recipient is baptized, as the "efficacy of baptism is not tied to the moment of time where it is administered."[5] The Westminster Larger Catechism Q&A 167 elaborates on this point and argues that a lifetime's walk in newness of life and a profession of faith, as signs of regeneration, form an "improvement" on one's baptism:

> Q. 167. How is our baptism to be improved by us?

> A. The needful but much neglected duty of improving our baptism, is to be performed by us all our life long, especially in the time of temptation, and when we are present at the administration of it to others; by serious and thankful consideration of the nature of it, and of the ends for which Christ instituted it, the privileges and benefits conferred and sealed thereby, and our solemn vow made therein; by being humbled for our sinful defilement, our falling short of, and walking contrary to, the grace of baptism, and our engagements; by growing up to assurance of pardon of sin, and of all other blessings sealed to us in that sacrament; by drawing strength from the death and resurrection of Christ, into whom we are baptized, for the mortifying of sin, and quickening of grace; and by endeavoring to live by faith, to have our conversation in holiness and righteousness, as those that have therein given up their names to Christ; and to walk in brotherly love, as being baptized by the same Spirit into one body.

One ought to clarify the sense of the word "improved" in this context, as it's not used in the ordinary sense of the term. It is not that the recipients of baptism are called to render their baptism more excellent, but they are to recognize that "the great indicatives of baptism" place "imperatives on the one baptized" (Kolb and Trueman 2017: 168). While Robert Kolb and Carl Trueman note that this improvement highlights the existential dimensions of baptism, one ought not to miss that it has this existential implication precisely because it is the Spirit that brings about the things signified in baptism into the elect recipient.

We do well to make explicit here the covenantal backdrop that undergirds Reformed accounts of baptism. The Reformed draw a distinction between a *federal* holiness and an *inherent* holiness (Turretin 1997: 415–18; Witsius 2006: 128–30).[6] A Reformed account of baptism considers the sacrament to be an initiation rite into the visible church—God's covenant people, inhering the promises of God to Abraham. God's covenant community is

---

[5] For a survey of Reformed theologians on whether the elect is regenerated before, during, or after baptism, see Bavinck (2008: 511) and Swain (2015: 369–71). Swain is summarizing the discussion in Witsius (2006: 132–68).
[6] Bavinck names this distinction as between a "theocratic holiness" and a "regenerate holiness" (2008: 529–31).

broader than the elect, for not all who enjoy the covenant benefits are truly regenerate (Rom. 9:6, 13). In the old covenant, circumcision was a sign and seal of spiritual circumcision, and not merely of Israelite ethnic identity. Just as not all who are physically circumcised and included into the covenant community were spiritually circumcised, so not all those who are baptized outwardly receive the thing signified internally. The baptism of infants is located within this covenantal context: (1) the continuity that persists between the old and new covenants, (2) the parity of baptism with circumcision as covenant signs, and (3) the inclusion of the infants into the covenant by virtue of their parents.[7] Citing 1 Cor. 7:14, Turretin argues that infants "are said to be a holy by a federal holiness (i.e. Christians and belonging to the church)" (1997: 418; cf. Witsius 2006: 128–33).

The national citizenship analogy is instructive. Consider citizens of a particular nation—say, the nation of Indonesia. Children born in Indonesia should acquire passports to report their admission into Indonesia by way of their birth, thereby becoming citizens. They might grow up either personally accepting that citizenship, or rejecting it altogether, seeking citizenship elsewhere. Further, not all who grow as citizens within the country, ruled by its laws, enjoying its islands, bearing its national responsibilities, do actually ascribe their loyalties to the principles of its constitution as enshrined in the *Pancasila* or represented by their president. Likewise, the church is called a holy nation (1 Pet. 2:9), and its members are citizens of a new city (Hebrews 13). Its members are made up of citizens from many earthly nations, but the citizenship of the invisible church is elsewhere—a heavenly city. They are called to be ambassadors (2 Corinthians 5) in the present world, bearing witness to the next world, residing in community outposts here that are merely temporary and subject to persecution and tribulation. Not all who enjoy admittance into those outposts, however, bear true loyalty to the principles and ethics of the spiritual kingdom or subscribe to the rule of its King. The mixed nature of the members of the visible church is a function of the church's location within this phase of redemptive history. The new covenant is already inaugurated but not yet consummated, as the need for discipline and a vulnerability to apostasy still characterize the church's members (WCF 25:3–5).[8] Those who belong in the invisible church will persevere on earth as the visible church is subjected to temptation and warfare, but those who fall away never belonged to the number of God's elect and will thus fail to join the triumphant church in heaven.[9]

In this regard, Geerhardus Vos makes the helpful distinction between "*being-under-the-covenant* and *being-in-the-covenant*" (Vos 2013: 109, emphasis mine).[10] The former has to do with the objective covenantal status itself, with its attendant laws, obligations, and privileges. The latter has to do with the actual *fellowship* with God that a member would internally enjoy by way of election, regeneration, and a life of faith. "Every covenant in the first sense looks forward and is intended to become a covenant in this second sense, a living fellowship or a fellowship of life" (105). There is, in other words, an "organic connection" between them (109). In relation to infant baptism and the question

---

[7]Gibson also helpfully highlights that a holistic, covenantal anthropology further grounds the propriety of infant baptism (2015: 14–34).
[8]See also Kline (1968: 76–7).
[9]"Then, indeed, the church includes not only the saints presently living on earth, but all the elect from the beginning of the world" (Calvin 1960: 4.1.7).
[10]Vos applies this distinction after observing that the Reformed tradition has deployed several distinctions to denote the two sides of the covenant of grace: between the external and an internal side, between the essence and administration of the covenant, and between an absolute and conditional covenant of grace (2013: 100–12).

of whether the unregenerate might be under the covenant of grace, this distinction aids the Reformed tradition by (1) alleviating them of the burden of explaining whether or how baptism effects the internal state of the recipient, while (2) maintaining that there remains a real *efficacy* to baptism that is not corporeal, but *covenantal*. Hence, while regeneration is necessary to enter into covenant fellowship with God, those baptized and received as members of the visible church are already being-under-the-covenant and should be roused to be-in-the-covenant, according to God's promise. As Vos puts it,

> The covenant relationship into which a child enters already at birth is the image of the covenant fellowship in which it is expected to live later. And on the basis of that expectation, or more accurately, on the basis of the promise of God that entitles us to that expectation, such a child receives baptism as a seal of the covenant. The child is regarded as being in the covenant. As it matures, it is again and again pointed out how it lives under the promises and how the reasonable expectation is that it will live in the covenant. These promises and this requirement as they apply to the child are precisely the means appointed by God as the way to be traveled, along which the communion of the covenant, the being "in" in a spiritual sense, is reached. Being-under-the-covenant not only precedes, but it is also instrumental. (2013: 109–10)[11]

Hence, as an initiation rite that admits one into covenantal membership, the ordinance of baptism was given not to private individuals but to the representatives of the institution of the church to administer. A precondition for baptism is the recognition of a community and an ordained minister to baptize the recipient into that covenantal community: "no one can meddle with the seals of a king, except he who in a special manner obtains this office and performs the functions of a chancellor" (Turretin 1997: 394).[12]

So, baptism has two connected but distinguished aspects: covenantal and pneumatic. The former happens during the moment of baptism, whereas the latter is dependent upon the free operation of the Spirit that "improves" upon the baptism previously received. The unbeliever only receives the covenantal aspects as a product (thus bearing responsibility for covenantal curses upon his proving disobedient to the covenant sign and seal). One might say that this adds an extra layer of responsibility for those who have undergone baptism, for they have tasted of the Spirit (a typical Reformed reading of Hebrews 5–6). They must not take their baptism lightly and pursue the God that had already marked the recipients by causing them to enjoy the benefits of being inside the covenant community (cf. Fesko 2009: 323).

II. ON THE INTELLIGIBILITY PUZZLE

Now that a sketch of a Reformed account of baptism is in place, let us consider Cuneo's discussion of the intelligibility puzzle before moving on to suggest how a pneumatic view of baptism might elude it.

---

[11] "On this basis, the Reformed churches assumes the salvation of the children of the covenant who die in infancy. Here, too, there could be exceptions, but one may not for this reason allow himself to be robbed of comfort" (Vos 2013: 110).

[12] This covenantal backdrop can be considered as a theological refinement of Arcadi's observation that a linguistic community that accepts a linguistic authority is a precondition for a sacrament to function as an exercitive of renaming (2018: 126). It is precisely the establishment of a covenantal bond between an authority and its people that causes a linguistic agreement to arise.

The sketch above already states a remarkable array of claims concerning the sacrament of baptism. Water somehow enacts divine action, exhibiting a state of affairs of enormous proportions for the recipient: remission of sins, an effectual regeneration, an entrance into God's covenant community, and so on. The remarkability of the significance of baptism is felt all the more acutely by those who affirm a more direct and causal link between the rite of baptism and regeneration itself, along with the benefits thereof. Cuneo, writing from the Eastern Orthodox tradition, refers to these collective results of baptism as "the *regenerate states*" (Cuneo 2016: 168, emphasis original).[13] Cuneo articulates the perplexity one might feel when one encounters the claims being made about this sacramental act. Commenting specifically on the Eastern Orthodox's dogmatic claims concerning baptism, Cuneo writes,

> These [regenerate] states ... are acquired upon and by the performance of the baptismal rite—"by water and the Spirit." But how could that be? How could a person be illumined or enlightened as a result of being baptized? And isn't there good empirical evidence that the imposition of the regenerate states is not in fact accomplished in the vast majority of cases? ... Moreover, when one considers the further fact that the regenerate states are typically predicated of infants and young children who are baptized, the predications are paradoxical, even unintelligible. In what sense could an infant be sanctified, illumined, or enjoy remission of her sins? On a straightforward reading, the text appears to make a series of serious category mistakes. (Cuneo 2016: 168)

Cuneo calls this concern the "Intelligibility Puzzle" (2016: 168). How can the act of baptism somehow confer the regenerate states to the one baptized, especially when the agents baptized are infants, or when those baptized seem not to be morally affected by the reception of baptism? To clarify further, Cuneo suggests that at least one transformative effect of baptism is easier to understand—that of a new normative standing before God. Baptism, he argues, effects the recipient's new "juridical" status before God (170). Much like the legal act of adoption, baptism effects the believer's status vis-à-vis God that puts the recipient under God's fatherly care. The normative transformation also involves "the acquisition of new responsibilities and obligations to God ... and obligations vis-à-vis the church and vice versa" (171).[14]

But this is not the puzzling bit of the intelligibility puzzle, for the confessional texts of the Eastern Orthodox tradition (and, here, one might also add that of the Reformed tradition) seems to communicate much more about the significance of the baptismal rite. Homing in on the puzzle:

> Two alterations, then, appear to lie at the heart of the baptismal rite. One alteration consists in the imposition of a normative standing, the other in the imposition of the regenerate states. If the first alteration is familiar and intelligible in its basic structure, the second—as I noted earlier—is baffling. It generates what I earlier called the *Intelligibility Puzzle*, this puzzle consisting not simply in the concern that it is difficult to see how the regenerate states could be conferred on someone, as opposed to acquired

---

[13]There are salient differences between Eastern Orthodox and Reformed accounts of baptism's relation to the regenerate states, as we shall see, especially as the former seems to tie a stronger causal connection between baptism and the states.

[14]Cuneo includes the right and responsibility of the baptized, no matter the age, to partake of the Eucharist.

over time with effort. It also has an empirical dimension, since the behavior of those baptized rather often strongly indicates that they have not had these states conferred on them. The problem only gets worse, moreover, when we consider the fact that it is often infants and small children who are baptized. (Cuneo 2016: 173)

Baptism, in other words, is said to alter not merely one's status externally before God but also to impose new *internal* states. But how, exactly, could a ceremonial and external rite confer the states of regeneration internally to its recipient? It is not only seemingly empirically obvious that the water or the ceremony cannot effectually bring about those internal states. In fact, there seems to be evidence to the effect that they do *not* in fact bring about real internal changes in the recipients (especially in infants or small children). And this is the crux of the intelligibility puzzle.

After ruling out the appeal to explain the connection the confessional documents make concerning baptism as merely harmless fictions, Cuneo considers an interpretation offered by Alexander Schmemann concerning baptism as participating in some way in the faith of Christ. While granting that this interpretation sheds light on the recipient's desire to obey as Christ obeyed until death, it does little to address the case of infant baptisms and the intelligibility puzzle in particular (Cuneo 2016: 176–7).[15] Cuneo homes in again on the text from the Orthodox service book on the baptismal rite:

> Blessed are you, O Lord God, Source of all good things ... who has given to us, unworthy though we be, blessed purification through hallowed water, and divine sanctification, through life-giving Christmation; who now, also, has been pleased to regenerate your servant that has newly received illumination by water and the Spirit, and granted unto him/her remission of sins, whether voluntary or involuntary.[16]

In what way, precisely, does the water and the Spirit effect illumination, regeneration, and the remission of sins? Cuneo, here, makes the distinction between a *product-interpretation* of this passage, and a *process-interpretation*. A *product* reading of this passage suggests that the recipient of baptism has undergone—in past perfect tense—purification, sanctification, regeneration, and so on. In a *process* reading, however, "the one baptized is now *being* purified, *being* sanctified, *being* regenerated, *being* illumined, and *being* released from sin" (Cuneo 2016: 178, emphases original). Hence, he suggests that baptism confers not the product of the regenerate states but rather instigates the beginning of the process of the regenerate states. Cuneo envisions the process of divine agency fusing into human agency as that which begins during the baptismal rite. Some of these processes are epistemic (illumination), and others are status-states (ritual purification) (Cuneo 2016: 180–1).

This distinction renders the meaning of the baptismal rite more intelligible. Process-states can begin imperfectly, call forth the participation of the recipient in the life of the

---

[15] In a Reformed perspective, to participate into the death and resurrection of Christ in baptism is to communicate that baptism signifies the recipient's transition from a state of spiritual death and alienation from God to a state of life in God's presence. It expresses not primarily the desire of the person to follow Christ's example (though that is indeed a result) but the reception of regeneration by the Spirit. Spiritual resurrection, in regeneration, is necessary to overcome total depravity, and it anticipates the final, physical, resurrection. On this, see R. Gaffin (1987 and 2013).

[16] Cuneo is citing a modernized version of the *Service Book of the Holy Eastern Orthodox Catholic and Apostolic Church According to the Use of the Antiochian Orthodox Christian Archdiocese of North America* (2002), in his work (2016: 168).

community (and vice versa), and encourage the recipient to exercise his or her agency in conformity with the Spirit's agency. While this process reading does not solve all of the intellectual conundrums (what do we do with the clearly punctiliar way in which baptism's benefits are brought about at the moment of administration, according to the liturgical documents?), it does make progress in significant respects in providing clarity regarding the precise effects of the baptismal rite.

III. A PNEUMATIC-REFORMED RESPONSE

In response to Cuneo's discussion of the intelligibility puzzle, one could begin first by admitting that his solution to the problem is not available to adherents of confessional Reformed theology. That is, Reformed theologians cannot admit that regeneration is a *process*, for, in their theologies, regeneration—much like justification—is a punctiliar moment that effects conversion and is the irreversible act of God that makes possible the daily acts of repentance and the moral progress of the believer.[17] Effectual calling decisively calls the sinner from the spiritual darkness into the light. As Q 67 of the Westminster Larger Catechism puts it, the Spirit works by "renewing and powerfully determining their wills" such that sinners who were once incapable of obeying are thus "made willing and able to freely answer this call." Hence, to suggest that regeneration is a process is, according to this confessional document, to commit a category mistake. While sanctification and the continual moral renovation of the regenerated indeed is a process, regeneration is the decisive moment that makes sanctification possible. It follows that answering the intelligibility puzzle by arguing that baptism does not communicate the *product* of the regenerative states but rather only the *process* of those states, is not available to the Reformed.

I suggest, however, that this should not worry those who adhere to a Reformed perspective, for it is unclear to me that the intelligibility puzzle would apply to those who hold the pneumatic account of baptism. That is, I'm suggesting that resolving something like the intelligibility puzzle is the responsibility only of those who hold to a more direct causal link between baptism and regeneration—to those who hold to confessional traditions that claim that baptism causally *effects* regeneration. Note again that Cuneo observed that "these [regenerate] states ... are acquired upon and by the performance of the baptismal rite" (2016: 168).[18] One senses here that something like a corporeal model of baptism is at work, such that it is claimed that the baptismal rite automatically bestows either the *product* of the regenerative states, or begins the *process* of acquiring the regenerative states.

In contrast to Cuneo's claims and the Orthodox documents to which Cuneo refers, the Reformed typically deny that such a causal link exists between baptism and regeneration. Rather, the Reformed argue that the sacraments merely sign and seal the internal graces rather than actually *effecting* these graces (a form of the doctrine of baptismal regeneration), which is the exclusive work of the Holy Spirit (Swain 2015: 366). As a physical and external element, water cannot vivify or renovate the moral nature of the baptized agent. Indeed, "to attribute to the water a spiritual operation is to transfer God's 'incommunicable power to creatures'" (367). It seems that a pneumatic account is more

---

[17]Cuneo agrees that justification marks a punctiliar moment in (2016: 184).
[18]See also Butcher (2015: 330, 336, 341).

modest about the efficacy of the sacraments than Cuneo's and the Eastern Orthodox tradition. Again, their service book reckons it appropriate to pray that the water in baptism "may be sanctified with the power, *and effectual operation and indwelling* of the Holy Spirit" (cited in Cuneo 2016: 178). In this rendering, the water is somehow imbued with the power of the Spirit such that the connection between them is not that of mere signification.

In other words, adherents of Reformed theology would happily agree with the potential objection that the rite of baptism simply does not seem to be able to produce the regenerate states, especially when it comes to the baptism of infants. But there is no discrepancy here, for it has never claimed that baptism *would* cause the acquisition of those states, and certainly not of regeneration itself. The Spirit freely works apart from baptism and can affect the things signified in baptism before, during, or after the baptismal rite itself. Hence, there is no puzzle to be resolved here—or at least *this* puzzle is not one that should trouble the Reformed.

This does not mean, however, that the Reformed can only resort to the legal fiction account of the effects of the baptismal rite, nor does it trivialize its significance. For, the *product* of baptism, whether applied to infants or adults, is the entrance into the covenant community of God by way of membership. There is, again, a *covenantal* efficacy to the baptismal rite. The recipient of baptism is consecrated and become members of a community that anticipates an eschatological kingdom—an entrance into a visible union with Christ (Fesko 2009: 343). Indeed, baptism is a "solvent of *natural* social, ethnic, religious, sexual differences … Baptism does not signify an undifferentiated unity or a chaos of disorder, but a complexly ordered community. As a sign of *this* ecclesial form, it is a sign of inaugurated eschatology. Baptism is a flood (cf. 1 Pet. 3:20-21). When it has washed away the old, what emerges is a new social *cosmos*" (Leithart 2015: 634–5, emphasis original). Whether those who enjoy the physical sign and seal of the covenant would ultimately evidence themselves to be truly benefitting of the new birth of the Spirit is ultimately left to the secret operations of God's electing and sovereign will.

IV. CONCLUSION

In this chapter, I have presented a Reformed account of baptism in conversation with current analytic-theological works on the issue. It presents a Reformed account as a pneumatic and covenantal model. It then suggests that one benefit of this account is that it eludes Terrence Cuneo's "intelligibility puzzle" concerning the efficacy and significance of the baptismal rite. While intelligibility indeed becomes a puzzle for those who embrace a corporeal model, a Reformed account denies a causal link between the baptismal rite and regeneration, even while it retains the significance of the sacrament by virtue of its relative relation to God's word and its signifying and sealing function within the new covenant. Hence, I suggest that a Reformed account of baptism is to be preferred over corporeal models because it eludes the intelligibility puzzle while maintaining a thick theological description of the baptismal rite.[19]

---

[19] I'm grateful to David Gibson, Scott Swain, Sam Simanjuntak, and Greg Parker for their feedback on earlier drafts of this chapter.

References

Arcadi, J. M. (2018), *An Incarnational Model of the Eucharist*, Cambridge: Cambridge University Press.

Bavinck, H. (2008), *Reformed Dogmatics*, vol. 4, *Holy Spirit, Church, and New Creation*, trans. J. Vriend, ed. J. Bolt, Grand Rapids, MI: Baker Academic.

Butcher, B. (2015), "Orthodox Sacramental Theology: Sixteenth-Nineteenth Centuries," in H. Boersma and M. Levering (eds.), *Oxford Handbook of Sacramental Theology*, 329–47, Oxford: Oxford University Press.

Calvin, J. (1960), *Institutes of the Christian Religion*, trans. F. L. Battles, ed. J. McNeill, Louisville: Westminster John Knox.

Cuneo, T. (2016), *Ritualized Faith: Essays in the Philosophy of Liturgy*, Oxford: Oxford University Press.

Fesko, J. (2009), *Word, Water, and Spirit: A Reformed Perspective on Baptism*, Grand Rapids, MI: Reformation Heritage Books.

Gaffin, R. (1987), *Resurrection and Redemption: A Study in Pauline Soteriology*, Philipsburg: Presbyterian & Reformed.

Gaffin, R. (2013), *By Faith, Not By Sight: Paul and the Order of Salvation*, Philipsburg: Presbyterian & Reformed.

Gibson, D. (2015), "'Fathers of Faith, My Fathers Now!': On Abraham, Covenant, and the Theology of Paedobaptism," *Themelios*, 40 (1): 14–34.

Kline, M. (1968), *By Oath Consigned: A Reinterpretation of the Covenant Signs of Circumcision and Baptism*, Grand Rapids, MI: Eerdmans.

Kolb, R., and C. Trueman. (2017), *Between Wittenberg and Geneva: Lutheran and Reformed Theology in Conversation*, Grand Rapids, MI: Baker Academic.

Leithart, P. (2015), "Signs of the Eschatological Ekklesia: The Sacraments, the Church, and Eschatology," in H. Boersma and M. Levering (eds.), *Oxford Handbook of Sacramental Theology*, 631–44, Oxford: Oxford University Press.

Swain, S. (2015), "Lutheran and Reformed Sacramental Theology: Seventeenth-Nineteenth Centuries," in H. Boersma and M. Levering (eds.), *Oxford Handbook of Sacramental Theology*, 362–79, Oxford: Oxford University Press.

Turretin. F. (1997), *Institutes of Elenctic Theology*, vol. 3, *Eighteenth through Twentieth Topics*, Philipsburg: Presbyterian & Reformed.

Vos, G. (2013), *Reformed Dogmatics*, vol. 2, *Anthropology*, Bellingham: Lexham Press.

The Confession of Faith and Catechisms: The Westminster Confession of Faith and Catechisms as used by the Orthodox Presbyterian Church (2005), Willow Grove: Orthodox Presbyterian Church.

Witsius, H. (2006), "On the Efficacy and Utility of Baptism: In the Case of Elect Infants Whose Parents Are Under the Covenant," trans. J. M. Beach, *Mid-America Journal of Theology*, 17: 121–90.

CHAPTER THIRTY-FIVE

On the Intelligibility of Eucharistic Doctrine(s) in Analytic Theology

JAMES M. ARCADI

I. INTRODUCTION

In the essay "The Intelligibility of Eucharistic Doctrine," Michael Dummett writes,

> I propose to understand the doctrine as requiring no more than that the correct and unqualified answer to the question, "What is it?", asked of either of the consecrated elements, is "The Body of Christ" or "The Blood of Christ." (1987: 234)

Despite the singular focus of the title of this important essay, there is no one Eucharistic doctrine about whose intelligibility one might inquire. Rather, a plethora of doctrines, theories, and theologies have emerged in the Christian tradition that all stem from the curious utterances regarding bread and wine which Christ made at his Supper. As is well known, on the night before his crucifixion, Christ took bread and wine and said of each respectively, "This is my body" and "This is my blood."[1] Giving an account of how these utterances can be understood is the task of making intelligible—a project undertaken by theologians since St. Paul. Analytic theologians and philosophers too have commenced with this project. Surveying their work and offering a constructive attempt at intelligibility is the undertaking of this present chapter. In what follows, I sketch a spectrum of views of the Eucharist followed by an explication of points plotted along the spectrum that correspond to instances in analytic theology. I then offer a precis of my own attempt at a constructive account of the intelligibility of Eucharistic doctrine.[2]

---

[1] The New Testament accounts are found in Mt. 26:26-28, Mk 14:22-24, Lk. 22:19-20, and 1 Cor. 11:23-25.
[2] I note that I am here avoiding a multitude of other thorny questions in Eucharistic theology such as who may say these curious utterances, what liturgical form these utterances may take, who may receive the elements, when the consecration (if one thinks there be one) occurs, or a whole host of other worthy questions that have not yet been discussed in the analytic literature.

I.1 A Spectrum of Views

In recent publications, I have described Eucharistic accounts as falling on something of a spectrum.[3] The spectrum motif categorizes the manners in which certain traditions offer attempts at intelligibility. These attempts differ on how they understand the linguistic and metaphysical contours of Christ's utterance.[4] Along this spectrum, I distinguish three main categories or families of views that are joined by what they say about the metaphysical connection (or lack thereof) between the body of Christ and the bread of the Eucharist. These metaphysical conceptions typically accompany more or less literal interpretations of Christ's words. Within each family, I further delineate various species that can be distinguished by their nuanced explications of what this connection is or means regarding either the body of Christ or the bread of the Eucharist.

One can see the Eucharistic spectrum as spanning from more realist perspectives on, say, the left to less realist views on, say, the right.[5] By "realist," I intend to mean a more or less metaphysically robust connection between the elements and the body of Christ, which typically corresponds to more or less literal explications of Christ's predication, "This is my body." Hence, on the left side is what I call the *Corporeal Mode* family of views. These views state that in the Eucharist the bread becomes so connected to the body of Christ that the predication, "This is the body of Christ," is literally true when said of that object. The next family of views along the spectrum toward the right are the *Pneumatic Mode* perspectives. These views hold that Christ is connected in some sort of spiritual fashion. Here, a phrase like "This is the body of Christ" ought to be understood to mean, "This symbolizes the body of Christ" or "This is like the body of Christ in important respects." Finally, on the right side of the spectrum are views that do not hold there to be any connection between the bread and the body of Christ; call this the *Ordinary Mode*. Here, the Biblical/liturgical utterance is to be understood as "there is no metaphysical connection between this object and the body of Christ, but one should think about Jesus Christ when one sees or eats it." I now turn to make a further exposition of these points on the spectrum in reverse order.

II. THE ORDINARY MODE

Perhaps the easiest point on the spectrum to plot is the Ordinary Mode. I have variously designated this the "No special presence Mode" (Arcadi 2016) or the "No non-normal Mode" (Arcadi 2018). The basic idea is that adherents to views in this family do not think that there is any unique or special relationship between the bread of the Eucharist and the body of Christ. This is, of course, not to say that adherents to this family of views necessarily think the Eucharist inconsequential or trivial. Although traditionally there has been a connection between an elevated view of the importance of the Eucharist and one's understanding of the metaphysical connection to Christ's body, this is not a conceptually necessary connection. Likely the most well-known proponent of this view in the tradition

---

[3] My most thorough constructive attempt at intelligibility comes in Arcadi (2018), the seeds of which are sown in Arcadi (2015). Sections of this present chapter owe much to Arcadi (2016).

[4] For the sake of brevity, I will assume that a theological analysis of the meanings of the phrases "This is the body of Christ" and "This is the blood of Christ" when uttered by Christ or ministers in appropriate circumstances are sufficiently similar. I will also tend to focus on the bread/body; I intend a similar analysis *mutatis mutandis* for the wine/blood.

[5] See the chart at the end of the chapter.

is Huldrych Zwingli; those following in his theological lineage likewise endorse such a view.[6]

On this view, the intelligibility of the Eucharist stems from another utterance of Christ's: the mandate to celebrate the Eucharist in remembrance of him. In a manner similar to a good sermon, the Eucharist serves the cognitive function of bringing to mind Christ and his work. As of the publication of this chapter, I know of no analytic attempts to articulate the merits of this view. Yet, there would seem to be much potential for analytics to do so. Whereas most of the analytic work on the doctrine of the Eucharist borrows such philosophical tools as metaphysics and philosophy of language, proponents of this location on the spectrum might be interested in applying the rich literature in analytic epistemology to articulate the benefits of this view. Furthermore, Cuneo (2016) and Wolterstorff (2018) recently have produced analytic treatments of liturgy and ritual, at times venturing into the epistemological.[7] This would also seem to be a fertile avenue to cultivate Eucharistic fruit; I am eager to see work of this nature come to blossom in the future.

III. THE PNEUMATIC MODE

As a midpoint on the spectrum, the Pneumatic Mode is more challenging to characterize than the views on its flanks. I simply categorize views in this family as those that do not posit a metaphysical connection between the elements and the body of Christ, but that also posit more than a cognitive recollection as at the heart of the meaning of Christ's utterance.[8] Oftentimes, this position is defined in opposition to either other extreme. The proponent of this family of views typically wants to say that there is more going on with the elements and the consumer than just a cognitive change, as the Ordinary Mode posits. Yet, the Pneumatic proponent does not want to go so far as to articulate a literal bodily presence, as the Corporeal Mode posits.

Perhaps in a move too clever for my own good, by "pneumatic" here I mean "spirit" both in (a) its Holy Spirit connotation and in (b) its more colloquial "the semblance of" connotation. On (a), at times in the tradition, the "more going on" of the Pneumatic Mode is related to an emphasis on the work of the Holy Spirit. One might find this connotation in Reformed theologies of the Eucharist stemming from Martin Bucer, John Calvin, or Peter Martyr Vermigli—what Brian Gerrish (1966) calls "instrumentalism." Relatedly, the "parallelism" view of Thomas Cranmer would fit in this family as well (Gerrish 1966; Arcadi 2019). On (b), the lower case "s" "semblance of" spirit sense of the Pneumatic Mode is how I characterize views that attempt a literal explication of Christ's words without recourse to an explication of a metaphysical connection to the body of Christ. Typically, in the systematic theological literature, a view like this is referred to as transignification. As there are no—so far as I know—instances of (a)-type Pneumatic

---

[6]For instance, this is typically the view one might find in such Protestant traditions as the Baptistic, Free, Pentecostal, Fundamentalist, nondenominational Evangelical, Salvationist, Adventist, some Reformed, and some Methodist expressions.
[7]See also Joshua Cockayne's chapter in this volume.
[8]One can see views like this in the Patristic period and one is likely to recognize something of Augustine's emphasis on symbolism in this family. In post-Reformation Christianity, the Pneumatic Mode categorizes the views found in the Reformed traditions, some Methodist, and some Anglican expressions.

explications of the Eucharist in the analytic literature, my survey will focus on (b)-type spiritual theories.

III.1 Transignification

It is my contention that the thought of an early-twentieth-century Dominican phenomenologist provides the fertilizer for some of the Eucharistic theories that have sprung up in the analytic orchard. Edward Schillebeeckx attempted to "save the phenomenon" of the traditional Roman Catholic doctrine of transubstantiation but without recourse to the Aristotelian substance metaphysics that had provided the conceptual infrastructure for these explications since the middle ages. The basic idea behind a transignification theory is that questions about what an object is are more properly questions about what an object means. So, if it is determined by Christ, the Church, the Magisterium, or whomever, that the bread of the Eucharist means "the body of Christ," then it is such.

I begin with what I estimate to be the first discussion of the doctrine of the Eucharist in the analytic tradition, that of the renowned G. E. M Anscombe (1974). Her "On Transubstantiation" attempts to express a traditional Roman Catholic view of transubstantiation. Her post-Wittgensteinian model focuses on the manner in which youth should be instructed in ways of speaking about the Eucharistic elements such that they come to treat the consecrated objects as no longer bread and wine, but as the actual body and blood of Christ. She does not stray into metaphysical talk, but instead focuses on a Wittgensteinian way of life motif.

Similarly, another Roman Catholic philosopher, Michael Dummett (1987), proffered a more explicitly Schillebeeckxian model. For instance, Dummett uses a simple example of a Pyrex dish that was probably intended to be used for food, but he uses as an ashtray. Is the object into which Dummett casts his cigarette ashes a dish or an ashtray? He asserts that he has the right to determine the meaning of this object, and since he uses it as an ashtray, it is in fact an ashtray. In application to the Eucharist, the bread of the Eucharist might have been intended to be just ordinary Passover fare, but after Christ deemed the bread his body, it was in fact his body. Dummett places emphasis on the act of "deeming" (250) that Christ performs with respect to the elements. Because Christ is God, his deemings are to be taken as authoritative by any who believe him to be God. He states that taking the bread as Christ's body requires the antecedent belief in the Incarnation, and, thus, those who do not have the requisite antecedent belief cannot be expected to hold the deeming to have obtained.

A similar move is made by H. E. Baber in two articles, one in which she explicitly engages with Dummett (Baber 2013a). By an appeal to recent analytic work in social ontology, Baber construes the change in the elements to be a matter of a change in the institutional conventions respecting the elements. Baber states, "The act of consecration is a conventionally generated action analogous to, for example, the act of writing out a cheque" (2013b: 21). By all empirical counts, a rectangular piece of paper with numbers and letters on it literally is worth no more than a piece of paper. Yet, given certain conditions constituted by particular social and institutional conventions, a check one writes for $200 is, according to social ontology, $200. The meaning of the object goes beyond its metaphysical makeup.

Might one allege that this view is simply subjective, being based on the psychological states of the participants in the liturgy? Baber argues that the presence of the body of Christ *qua* institutional fact is similar to other social conventions,

> But marriage, money, boundaries, and the like are not "subjective". They are the products of collective rather than individual intentionality and the institutions in which it is embodied. An individual cannot by his own initiative, through believing, wishing, or acting as if it were so, enter into or dissolve a marriage, acquire citizenship or increase the value of his portfolio. And, on the account proposed here, the presence of Christ in the Eucharist is likewise secured by the collective intentionality of an institution, viz. the Church. (Baber 2013b: 26)

Like Dummett's view, assenting to the truth of the metaphysical state of affairs that undergirds the liturgical utterance requires the antecedent participation in the relevant institution that sanctions the institutional fact of that object being the body of Christ.

Corporeal Mode theorists tend to hold Christ's body to be present independent of the perceptive experience of anyone, members of the Church, believers in the Incarnation, etc. The body of Christ is present to encounter regardless of one's beliefs or participation in a linguistic community. For (b)-type spiritual or transignification views, the body of Christ does not metaphysically undergird the aptness of the liturgical utterance, rather it is the declaration of the linguistic community that grounds the truth of the phrase "This is the body of Christ." Declaring as, deeming as, designating as, and so on does not bring about a connection between the elements that are perceived and the body of Christ.

Relatedly, then, have Cockayne et al. (2017) pitched their model as akin to a Lutheran, Corporeal Mode expression. However, because they do not posit a metaphysical connection between the bread and the body of Christ, I locate it within the (b)-type Pneumatic family on my Eucharistic spectrum. For this view, the bread of the Eucharist becomes a location whereby a second-personal encounter between Christ and the recipient can occur. They attempt to cut through, what they term, "identity" and "symbolic" explications of the real presence by offering an "iconic" model of the Eucharist (176). In this regard, the emphasis is not so much on Christ's presence in the bread as it is Christ's presence to the consumer. The authors specify that the Eucharistic encounter between Christ and the Christian is not different in kind from what can occur by other means. Moreover, they write that "the presence of Christ is located in the interaction between Christ and the communicant" (192) not connected to the elements *per se*, but only insofar as these serve to facilitate this relational encounter.

III.2 Cross's Action-at-a-Distance

I now offer Richard Cross's (2002) view as something of a transitional one between the Pneumatic and Corporeal Mode theories of the Eucharist. In fact, Cross thinks that closer attention to the nature of action could bring about a unification of the traditionally Calvinist strain of Pneumatic Mode models and Corporeal Mode models, in their Lutheran and Roman Catholic instantiations. In order to pursue this line of rapprochement, one has to accept the notion that immediate causation from a distance is bodily presence, of the sort desired in Eucharistic discussions. Cross argues that the kind of sacramental presence the body of Christ enjoys in the Eucharist is a *definitive* presence, where this kind of presence is like the way immaterial substances are located at places, by causing effects at those locations. Thus, "a substance is definitively present at a place if it directly or immediately causes an effect at that place without being spatially present at that place" (303). The action-at-a-distance motif is to assuage a worry of those Pneumatic Mode theorists in the Reformed tradition that insist Christ currently is sitting bodily at the right hand of the Father. For them, this entails some non-bodily presence of Christ in the Eucharist. But if Cross's definition of bodily presence is granted, than all one has to accept is that Christ performs some immediate action at the location of the elements and this entails his presence, indeed his bodily presence. This would then serve to undergird the aptness of the liturgical utterance. This also, so Cross argues, fits nicely with Calvin's emphasis on Christ being in the Eucharist by his virtue or power despite Calvin's worries about substantial bodily presence.

IV. THE CORPOREAL MODE

Recall that I have lumped those views on the intelligibility of the Eucharist into the Corporeal Mode who posit a robust metaphysical connection between the bread of the Eucharist and the body of Christ.[9] This family of views can be further subdivided into two main lineages: what I call "Roman" and "German" views, respectively. Both have been the subject of recent discussions in analytic theology.

IV.1 Roman Views

Many recent explications of the Eucharist in the analytic literature have been proffered by those attempting to explicate the official teaching of the Roman Catholic Church. Roman views all affirm the following key propositions about the Eucharist once a minister has said the appropriate words in the appropriate context:

(1) Christ's body is substantially present.
(2) The sensible qualities of Christ's body are not present.
(3) The bread is no longer substantially present.
(4) The sensible qualities of the bread are present.

The Roman view has sometimes been referred to as a "real presence/real absence" view,[10] whereby one must assent to the real presence of the body of Christ and the real absence of the bread. However, within the Roman manner, the tradition has distinguished further nuances regarding how the body comes to be present.

Roman-annihilation
Includes the "Roman" (1)–(4) and

(5) The substance of the bread is annihilated when the substance of Christ's body arrives.

Roman-transubstantiation
Includes the "Roman" (1)–(4) and

(6) The substance of the bread is converted into the substance of Christ's body.

The two Roman views share the perspective that Christ's body is substantially present and that the bread no longer is. Where they differ is on how this occurs. Roman-transubstantiation is the official position of the Roman Catholic Church, as noted especially at the Councils of Lateran IV, Constance, and Trent. Roman-annihilation was a position that some medieval commentators entertained as they sought to exposit the Roman Catholic Church's official position. Both of these views entail that there is a

---

[9]Typically this is the family of views found in most Orthodox expressions, including the Oriental and Coptic branches, the Roman Catholic Church, the Lutheran tradition, and some Anglicans.
[10]See Pruss (2011).

separation of substance from sensible qualities that occurs at the Eucharist. Both the body of Christ and the bread are divided along substance/sensible qualities lines. For the body of Christ, the substance arrives at the location of the bread, but none of its sensible qualities do. For the bread, its substance is removed, while all of its sensible qualities remain. Being the official position of such a large segment of Christianity as the Roman Catholic Church, Roman-transubstantiation has received the most discussion in the analytic literature.

IV.1.1 Roman-Transubstantiation

Alexander Pruss (2011) offers one of the more sophisticated metaphysical expressions of the real presence/real absence Roman motif. In his essay, he first surveys a number of options for achieving the real presence of Christ's body at the location of the consecrated bread including a Leibniz-inspired partial presence option, an Aquinas-inspired placeless presence option, and options relating to curved space and bilocation. He then constructively pursues a couple of multi-location strategies for articulating the real presence of the whole of Christ's body in the Eucharist. Here is one such strategy. Suppose

> there is also a primitive relation L that can hold between an extended entity x and a non-empty set P of points in space at any given time. We can read LxP as "x is wholly located at P." Given this, what happens in the real presence on the present model is that the internal causal relations and intrinsic properties of Christ's body remain as they were, but Christ's body comes to be additionally L-related to the area in space to which the bread was previously related. (531)

Thus, Christ is wholly multi-located (in heaven, on various altars, in every morsel of consecrated bread, etc.) by being appropriately related to various locations.

Pruss also wants to account for the real absence of the bread post-consecration and he offers a couple of ways of thinking about this. For instance, suppose the accidents of the bread—the sensible qualities of the bread—are akin to the appearances of, say, the sound of thunder after a lighting strike or the light from a distant star. It could be that the bread itself does not exist at present (but does in the past) while the appearances remain. Similar to how the sound of thunder can reach a human's perceptive sphere well after the lightning strike or how the light from a distant star can appear well after the star has died. In these ways does Pruss defend the intelligibility of Roman-transubstantiation.

Another attempt at intelligibility is offered by Patrick Toner (2011), who wishes to defend Roman-transubstantiation within an essentialist ontology. It might be supposed that if a piece of bread has some cluster of characteristic essential properties, and those properties are instantiated even after the consecration, then so is the bread. But, so Toner argues, it could be simply that God miraculously holds the cluster of characteristic properties together independent of a subject that has those properties. Somewhat similarly for the presence of the body without its sensible properties, Toner appeals to the notion of Christ having a glorified body that, on Thomas Aquinas's explication, has the power to "be visible or invisible, tangible or intangible, at will" (223). Toner's argument runs like this: Christianity teaches that on the third day after his crucifixion, Jesus Christ was brought back to life by the power of the Holy Spirit. However, the body he had post-resurrection, while sufficiently similar to his pre-resurrection body so as to be recognized by his companions, also possessed the ability to enter locked rooms and suddenly vanish. Thus, there may be all kinds of properties that resurrected bodies possess that pre-resurrected bodies do not. So, Christ's being able to multi-locate his body or locate the entirety of his body at the location of the host or other Eucharistic oddities might be no problem for a resurrected body. Hence, it does not necessarily seem unintelligible within an essentialist ontology to suppose that there could be the sensible properties of bread on the altar, but no bread, and the body of Christ, but which is not sensibly perceivable.

Whether time-travel is possible or not has bearing on the next attempt at explicating the intelligibility of Roman-transubstantiation. Martin Pickup (2015) uses this concept to specify further the multi-location component of the Roman view. On this view, not only does the body of Christ need to be in heaven and on an altar, the body of Christ needs to be on multiple altars across the globe, perhaps even simultaneously. If time-travel is possible, then it could be the case that Christ enters a cosmic time-travel machine and simply ports his body to multiple locations throughout time and space (6). Moreover, on the Roman view, not only does Christ need to multi-locate on multiple altars, the body of Christ needs to be wholly in each piece of bread. For Pickup, Christ could just multiply-port his body to the location of each of the particular pieces of the consecrated elements (each morsel of bread, each sip of wine). Thus, the whole of his body is present, via time-travel, at every morsel of bread or sip of wine. Pickup admits this analysis is a bit bizarre and rests on the acceptance of a controversial account of time-travel, but for those for whom that is intelligible, a Roman-transubstantiation doctrine might also be intelligible.

Before leaving the Roman perspective, I must make mention of Marilyn McCord Adams's (2010) study. Although her work is a piece of history of philosophy, her analytic theological prowess is on full display in this volume. It is a careful working through the Eucharistic theologies of such key medieval figures as Thomas Aquinas, Giles of Rome, Duns Scotus, and William Ockham using the tools of contemporary analytic philosophy. The views of these thinkers largely fall into the Roman category, although they entertained German views as well. Adams's text is impressive both in its historical detail and in its philosophical rigor and repays careful study by historians, philosophers, and theologians.

IV.2 German Views

The other family of views within the Corporeal Mode I have termed the "German" view. I use this moniker due to the inspiration from Martin Luther, Andreas Osiander, and other Lutheran theologians who were proponents of Eucharistic views in this conceptual stream during that pivotal sixteenth century.[11] However, the general tenor of this family of views can be found discussed by such medieval theologians as Scotus and Ockham.[12] Hence this is not only a Lutheran view but also does resonate with Eucharistic values from that ecclesial lineage.

As I describe it, the German views affirm these key propositions:

(7) Christ's body is substantially present (NB: identical to the Roman (1)).
(8) The bread continues to be substantially present.
(9) The sensible qualities of the bread are present (NB: identical to the Roman (4)).

---

[11]To be clear, I am not saying that the German views are *the* Lutheran views. Moreover, many Lutherans would balk at such a term in use below as "consubstantiation." I do, however, think the views here are harmonious with broadly Lutheran Eucharistic desiderata.

[12]In Arcadi (2018: chapter 6), I offer a historical survey of views in this family that reaches from the Patristic period to the twentieth century.

In distinction from the Roman view, the German view might be a termed a real presence/real presence category—both the body of Christ and the bread continue to be present. As with the Roman view, the German view can be further subdivided into:

German-consubstantiation
Includes the "German" (7)–(9) and

(10) The sensible qualities of Christ's body are not present (NB: identical to the Roman (2)).
(11) The body of Christ is in, with, and under the bread.

German-impanation
Includes the "German" (7)–(9) and

(12) The sensible qualities of the bread are the sensible qualities of the body of Christ.
(13) A union between the bread and the body of Christ modelled on the Incarnation obtains.

German views hold to the substantial presence of Christ's body and blood as well as the continued existence of the bread and wine. Both the terms "consubstantiation" and "impanation" carry some conceptual and ecumenical baggage; however, I am not here concerned with defending particular terms, I am interested in the states of affairs those terms are supposed to denote. There has not been, so far as I know, an attempt in the analytic literature to advocate for the intelligibility of the German-consubstantiation view. This would be a fruitful endeavor for someone to take on.[13]

IV.2.1 German-Impanation

Despite the lack of an advocate for the German-consubstantiation view, the German-impanation view has received some discussion in the literature. In such, proponents of the intelligibility of this view utilize the metaphysical resources of its near homophone the Incarnation to ground intelligibility. German views hold to the presence of Christ's body without recourse to denying the continued existence of the bread. The German-consubstantiation view says that the bread and the substance of the body of Christ (with none of its sensible qualities) are colocated. Whereas the German-impanation view postulates a union between the elements and Christ that is patterned after the Incarnation.

Adams (2006: 304–7; 2010: 262–5) identifies two main types of impanation as they have been explored in the tradition. The first type posits a union between the bread and the second person of the Trinity. Adams states that, in this model, "the Divine Word assumes the Eucharistic bread the way that He assumes the human nature" (2006: 305). Further, "just as the Divine Word becomes in-carnate (en-fleshed) when it assumes a particular human nature into hypostatic union with itself, so the Divine Word becomes im-panate (em-breaded) when—at the moment of consecration—it hypostatically assumes the Eucharist bread nature on the altar" (296). I denote this model of impanation as "*Type-H Impanation*"[14] (Arcadi 2015: 5) or "Hypostatic Impanation" (Arcadi 2018: 201). A second type of impanation posits that the Incarnation-like union obtains between the body of Christ and the bread.

---

[13]In Arcadi (2018: chapter 6), I make mention of some reservations I have regarding the intelligibility of the German-consubstantiation model.
[14]Where "H" stands in for the kind of union, "hypostatic."

Like a human soul, the human body of Christ is not a complete individual substance, but only part of one. If one allows with Ockham that God could make an individual substance nature depend on a substance part, then one could say that the human body of Christ is the proximate assumer of the bread nature. (Adams 2006: 306)

I term this impanation model *"Type-S Impanation"*[15] (Arcadi 2015: 5) or "Sacramental Impanation" (Arcadi 2018: 209, chapter 7). Where Type-H Impanation posits a union between the person of the Word and the elements, Type-S Impanation posits a union between the human body of Christ and the elements. My 2018 book explores Type-S or Sacramental Impanation as an attractive model of explicating the aptness of Christ's curious utterance. The following is a distillation of some of the main contours of my book-length argument.

V. AN INCARNATIONAL MODEL OF THE EUCHARIST

My own approach at intelligibility has been to proffer a view of the Eucharist in the conceptual stream of German-impanation of the Sacramental or Type-S Impanation variety. The basic idea of German-impanation is to use the Incarnation as a model for the Eucharist. As there has been much recent analytic work on Christology,[16] there is much fertile Christological ground for Eucharistic seeds to be sown. One such seed that has germinated into a sapling is the manner of conceiving of the human nature of Christ as a vehicle or enabling device for the divine Word. By extension, then, to the Eucharist, the bread can be seen in like manner as a vehicle or enabling device for the body of Christ.

V.1 Enabling Externalism and the Incarnation

In their description of the extended mind thesis (Clark and Chalmers 1998), a theory within the analytic philosophy of mind, Andy Clark and David Chalmers offer the Parity Principle to push against the prejudice that all cognitive processes are done in the head. Here I offer that principle as slightly revised by Clark in a subsequent publication:

> If, as we confront some task, a part of the world functions as a process which, were it to go on in the head, we would have no hesitation in accepting as part of the cognitive process, then that part of the world is (for that time) part of the cognitive process. (Clark 2010: 44)

In their article, Clark and Chalmers offer an illustration that has come to be the canonical story of the extended mind thesis in action. An Alzheimer's patient, Otto, uses a notebook to record pieces of information that he wishes to remember. Every time he has information he may want later (say, the address of a museum he will visit later in the day), he writes that down in his notebook. In this way, the notebook has become part of Otto's mind.

Following Susan Hurley (2010), let us refer to the object that is extended as the "extended entity" and the object that is being extended onto as the "enabling entity." Hence, here I make the Parity Principle more generic to cover all instances of, what is called, enabling externalism:[17]

---

[15] Where "S" stands in for the kind of union, "sacramental."
[16] See especially Timothy Pawl's chapter in this volume.
[17] The terms "extended entity" and "enabling entity" are Hurley's, the generic Parity Principle is mine.

If an activity were done by an extended entity alone, we would accept this activity to be an extended entity process. If the activity were done utilizing an enabling entity, then that enabling entity is part of the extended entity process, and, for that time, the enabling entity is part of the extended entity.

We can deploy the framework of an extended entity and an enabling entity to help us imagine better the Incarnational action that is Chalcedonian Christology. And this has been done by Richard Cross in his Scotus-inspired account of Christ's Incarnation (2011). The human nature in Christ enables the Word to act within the created sphere as a human, something the Word as divine cannot do. Because of this efficiently causal or instrumental unity, the human nature in Christ and the Word form one entity, that is, the composite Christ. Here is Cross comparing the Incarnation to the use of a knife by a human (*á la* Otto's use of the notebook):

> By being an instrument of the Word, the human nature and the Word become one subsisting thing ... just as the knife becomes (in effect) a part of the body. The body *extends itself* to include the knife; the Word *extends himself* to include the human substance. (Cross 2011: 190)

The act of extension is the relation of efficient causality obtaining between the agent and the instrument. Just as the knife enables a human's hand to cut in the act of cutting, the human nature in Christ enables the Word to act as a human in the Incarnation; just as in cutting the knife becomes a part of the human's hand, in the Incarnation an instance of human nature becomes a part of Christ. Thus, we can see parallel instances of extension and parallel instances of unities forming for various extended entities and enabling entities in the execution of specific activities.

V.2 *Enabling Externalism and the Eucharist*

The Extended Mind Thesis and its theory of enabling externalism can help us to grasp the intelligibility of the Incarnation. Both, then, can help the analytic theologian add intelligibility to the proposition *that the bread of the Eucharist is the body of Christ*. In fact, to some extent, applying enabling externalism to the Eucharist is easier than it is in the case of the Incarnation, for we have more frequent experience of this sort of phenomena than we do the extension of a divine person into a human nature. Think of the bodily activity of cutting with a knife. I am unable, by my organic hand alone, to slice through a juicy apple. However, an adequately sharp knife enables me to extend my bodily power to perform my desired activity. In the Eucharist, the properly demarcated bread enables Christ to extend his body to be in a location in which he is not organically located. Although he is not organically located, we might say he is artifactually located, located by means of an artefact *qua* enabling device.

But, one might question on what grounds do we say that an artefact actually becomes someone's body such that it would be apt to say, as Christ does of bread, "This is my body"? Suppose we think of a leg amputee who uses a prosthetic device. Call her, "Sue." Upon first receiving her prosthetic leg, Sue might go through a process whereby she considers the prosthesis to be foreign and not her body. But over time, and through the action of repeated use, she may come to see her prosthesis as incorporated into her body. For instance, one prosthesis user remarks, "Within my body schema, my prosthetic is as much a part of my body as my skin, blood, and organs" (Wright 2009: 1). If a prosthetic user personally attests to her prosthesis as being a part of her body, phenomenologically and artefactually, I suggest we ought to be willing to allow for a conception of body that moves beyond the organic to include certain artefacts. And if Christ similarly attests to an artefact as being part of his body, we ought to as well.

VI. CONCLUSION

The doctrine of the Eucharist has been not only one of the most contentious in the history of Christian theological reflection, but also one that has been the location of a wide array of metaphysical and linguistic creativity. Analytic theologians have followed this long history by their creative attempts to offer intelligible explications of Christ's curious predications. In the course of the tradition, too, there has been a diversity of ways of making sense of these utterances. So too, then, has recent analytic work reflected a diverse manner of making these utterances intelligible. It is clear that there are still many potentially fruitful avenues to explore. Although I have offered a thorough defence of one view, my hope is that future analytics will cultivate many other fruit-bearing models.[18]

ADDENDUM: A SPECTRUM OF EUCHARISTIC VIEWS

Mode:	Corporeal				Pneumatic			Ordinary
	Roman		German		spirit (b)	Spirit (a)		(Zwingli)
	Ann.	Tsub	Csub	Impan.	Transfig	Instru.	Parallel.	
Promoter: analytic or (non-analytic)		Pruss		Adams	Anscombe	(Calvin)	(Cranmer)	
		Toner		Arcadi	Dummett			
		Pickup		Sac. Hyp.	Baber			
					Cockayne, et al.			
		Cross						

References

Adams, M. M. (2006), *Christ and Horrors: The Coherence of Christology*, Cambridge: Cambridge University Press.

Adams, M. M. (2010), *Some Later Medieval Theories of the Eucharist Thomas Aquinas, Gilles of Rome, Duns Scotus, and William Ockham*, Oxford: Oxford University Press.

Anscombe, G. E. M. ([1974] 1981), "On Transubstantiation," in *The Collected Philosophical Papers of G.E.M Anscombe*, vol. 3, Oxford: Basil Blackwell.

Arcadi, J. M. (2015), "Impanation, Incarnation, and Enabling Externalism," *Religious Studies* 51 (1): 75–90.

---

[18] For comments and suggestions, I am grateful to J. T. Turner, Jordan Wessling, Jesse Gentile, Christopher Woznicki, David Luy, Kevin Vanhoozer, and Parker Settecase.

Arcadi, J. M. (2016), "Recent Philosophical Work on the Doctrine of the Eucharist," *Philosophy Compass* 11 (7): 402–12.

Arcadi, J. M. (2018), *An Incarnational Model of the Eucharist*, Cambridge: Cambridge University Press.

Arcadi, J. M. (2019), "Discerning the Body of Christ: A Retrieval of Thomas Cranmer's Eucharistic Theology by Way of the Spiritual Senses," *Journal of Anglican Studies* 17 (2): 183–97.

Baber, H. E. (2013a), "Eucharist: Metaphysical Miracle or Institutional Fact?," *International Journal for Philosophy of Religion*, 74 (3): 333–52.

Baber, H. E. (2013b), "The Real Presence," *Religious Studies*, 49 (1): 19–33.

Clark, A. (2010), "Memento's Revenge: The Extended Mind Extended," in R. Menary (ed.), *The Extended Mind*, 43–66, Cambridge, MA: MIT Press.

Clark, A., and D. J. Chalmers (1998), "The Extended Mind," *Analysis*, 58: 7–19.

Cockayne, J., D. Efird, G. Haynes, D. Molto, R. Tamburro, J. Warman, and A. Ludwigs (2017), "Experiencing the Real Presence of Christ in the Eucharist," *Journal of Analytic Theology*, 5: 175–96.

Cross, R. (2002), "Catholic, Calvinist, and Lutheran Doctrines of Eucharistic Presence: A Brief Note towards a Rapprochement," *International Journal of Systematic Theology*, 4 (3): 301–18.

Cross, R. (2011), "Vehicle Externalism and the Metaphysics of the Incarnation: A Medieval Contribution," in A. Marmodoro and J. Hill (eds.), *The Metaphysics of the Incarnation*, 186–204, Oxford: Oxford University Press.

Cuneo, T. (2016), *Ritualized Faith: Essays on the Philosophy of Liturgy*, Oxford: Oxford University Press.

Dummett, M. (1987), "The Intelligibility of Eucharistic Doctrine," in W. J. Abraham and S. W. Holtzer (eds.), *The Rationality of Religious Belief: Essays in Honour of Basil Mitchell*, 231–61, Oxford: Clarendon Press.

Gerrish, B. (1966), "The Lord's Supper in the Reformed Confessions," *Theology Today*, 23 (2): 224–43.

Hurley, S. L. (2010), "Varieties of Externalism," in R. Menary (ed.), *The Extended Mind*, 101–53, Cambridge, MA: MIT Press.

Pickup, M. (2015), "Real Presence in the Eucharist and Time-Travel," *Religious Studies*, 51 (3): 379–89.

Pruss, A. R. (2011), "The Eucharist: Real Presence and Real Absence," in T. P. Flint and M. C. Rea (eds.), *The Oxford Handbook of Philosophical Theology*, 512–40, Oxford: Oxford University Press.

Toner, P. (2011), "Transubstantiation, Essentialism, and Substance," *Religious Studies*, 47 (2): 217–31.

Wolterstorff, N. (2018), *Acting Liturgically: Philosophical Reflections on Religious Practice*, Oxford: Oxford University Press.

Wright, E. (2009), "My Prosthetic and I: Identity Representation in Bodily Extension," *Forum: University of Edinburgh Journal of Culture and the Arts*, 8.

CHAPTER THIRTY-SIX

Analytic Theology and Liturgy

JOSHUA COCKAYNE

I. A LITURGICAL TURN

Analytic theology, in Oliver Crisp's words, involves utilizing the tools of contemporary philosophy to the theological task of

> explicating the conceptual content of the Christian tradition (with the expectation that this is normally done from a position within that tradition, as an adherent of that tradition), using particular religious texts that are part of the Christian tradition, including sacred scripture, as well as human reason, reflection, and praxis (particularly religious practices), as sources for theological judgements. (2017: 160)

The *practice* of the Christian religion is thus central to the task of explicating its content. Yet, it seems this practical component of the Christian life has been largely ignored by thinkers in the analytic tradition. Nicholas Wolterstorff, one of the notable exceptions to this general trend, lamented this lack of focus on liturgy almost thirty years ago in writing,

> Christian existence incorporates Christian belief and Christian ethical action, Christian experience and Christian ritual. In our century we who are Christian philosophers have thought especially about Christian belief and Christian ethics, somewhat about Christian experience. We have thought scarcely at all about Christian liturgy. (1990: 157)

The significant progress that has been made in analytic philosophy of religion, and the emergence of analytic theology as a discipline in its own right, has not entirely redressed this imbalance. This is attested to by Wolterstorff's reiteration of these concerns about the narrowness of analytic theology and philosophy of religion in his address at the 40th Anniversary of the Society of Christian Philosophers. Echoing these words penned nearly thirty years prior, Wolterstorff states,

> In our publications and in our meetings we have paid some attention to ethics, but almost none to liturgy … I am at a loss to understand this inattention to liturgy. In short, I don't understand our lack of interest in liturgy, it baffles me and I lament it. I would love to see a flowering of discussion about liturgy in the next decade or two, perhaps that flowering is beginning. … I have come myself to think that liturgy is

in fact one of the most challenging and fascinating fields for philosophical inquiry. (2018b: 41.00)

There is some sign that analytic theology is beginning to take seriously this lacuna, and, to borrow a phrase from James K. A. Smith, there has been something of a "liturgical turn" (2018: 118) in recent years. This chapter seeks to outline some of the developments that have emerged in this *flowering* of the analytic theology of liturgy and to outline areas in which more development is needed.

I begin by considering the ways in which the term "liturgy" has been used in analytic theology and outline the work that has been done to explain what it is to act liturgically, and what it is to come to know God through liturgy. I then argue that the discussion of liturgical action in analytic theology needs to be connected more carefully with the study of ecclesiology and, in particular, to questions concerning the social reality of the church. It is important to see that to worship God through liturgy is to engage in some kind of group action. While there is some engagement between liturgy and ecclesiology, I argue that for an analytic theology of liturgy to take seriously the task of explicating the conceptual contents of the Christian tradition, more work needs to be done to address the communal dimensions of liturgy.[1]

II. DEFINING LITURGY

First, we should note the complexity of the term "liturgy" as it is used in the philosophical literature. "Liturgy" has been used broadly to denote all goal-orientated practices or rituals in human life, but also much more specifically to refer only to certain practices of the gathered church. *Analytic* theologians have typically used the latter sense of the word, but it will be worth pausing to consider its broader usage before proceeding.

In the broad sense of the word, Bruce Ellis Benson writes that "although 'liturgy' is used almost exclusively today in connection with church services, it originally referred to how people *lived* ... Liturgy was never intended to be something merely done on a Sunday. Instead, liturgy is a way of life" (2013: 24). Similarly, Smith, who has written extensively on the philosophy of liturgy, writes of human persons as *homo liturgicus*, that is, as creatures who are shaped by certain rituals and practices that determine the kind of things they love, and, thus, the kind of people they are. For Smith, this is at the heart of the nature of liturgies, which are, as he defines them, "*rituals of ultimate concern*: rituals that are formative for identity, that inculcate particular visions of the good life, and do so in a way that means to trump other ritual formations" (2009: 86). As he describes it, liturgy is pervasive in all aspects of human life and not restricted merely to the practices of the church.

Yet, there is also a much narrower sense of "liturgy" that is more often discussed by those in the analytic tradition. As Benson notes (borrowing from Charles P. Price and Louis Weil (1979)), we can make a distinction between "intensive liturgy," that is, the worship of a gathered group of religious believers, and "extensive liturgy," that is, how these religious believers act in their daily lives after gathered worship disperses (2013: 128). As Benson is keen to stress, these two kinds of liturgy should not be disconnected—liturgical worship ought not to stop when one leaves a place of worship.

---

[1] Some material in this chapter has been adapted from Cockayne (2018a,b) where I summarize the recent literature on philosophy of liturgy. The material is printed here with permission.

It is this narrower *intensive* use of the term that has so far dominated the analytic discussion of liturgy. As Wolterstorff delineates his focus, "liturgy" refers to the scripted acts of worship usually performed within a Christian community (2018a: 11–12). We might also use the term to refer to a set of act-types within a particular tradition. In my own Anglican tradition, for instance, the liturgy minimally consists of the acts of reading, singing, listening, sitting and standing, and eating and drinking the Eucharistic elements. But it is important to note at the outset that liturgy is not something practiced only in formal or traditional churches. As Wolterstorff observes, even worship with no written script or liturgical text should be considered "liturgical," since there is always a script involved in worship, even if this is implicit (2015: 9). In charismatic and Pentecostal traditions, there are often bodily actions that play an important role in liturgy (such as raising hands during times of sung worship, or audibly responding to the sermon in various ways), which are both spontaneous and scripted (e.g., one has to know when it is appropriate to shout "Amen!" or lift one's hand, and when it is not).[2] In a very basic way, the act of sitting to hear a sermon and standing to sing a hymn can be seen as scripted actions. There are right and wrong ways of worshipping in such contexts, and cultural expectations of how one should act, even if these are as minimal as standing up to sing a hymn, or not heckling when the preacher is speaking. Given the narrowness of scope in the discussion of analytic theology and liturgy so far to consider only *intensive liturgy*, I will restrict my discussion accordingly. Yet, it is worth noting that the connection between extensive and intensive liturgy (a topic typically addressed in continental approaches to liturgy) is an area requiring attention by analytic theology.

III. ACTING LITURGICALLY

What are we doing when we engage in liturgy? This has been a question that has been addressed by many of those writing on the philosophy of liturgy. As Terence Cuneo observes, "to the untrained eye," the liturgies of his own tradition, the Eastern Orthodox Church, appear to be a "jumble of disconnected actions" (2016: 154), such as "kissing, standing, bowing, prostrating, chanting, singing, anointing, processing, praying, kneeling, sensing, reading, listening, eating, washing, vesting ... and even spitting" (2016: 154). With "increased exposure," Cuneo suggests, one would come to see that such actions aren't random, disconnected events; rather, they are scripted actions that form the part of a central pattern of engaging God by blessing, petitioning and offering thanks to God (2016: 156).

Wolterstorff agrees that liturgy primarily has to do with engaging God in important ways. He suggests that, "liturgy is a species of ritual" that "has to do with God. More specifically, when enacting a liturgy the participants *orient* themselves toward God ... When we orient ourselves toward God by enacting a liturgy we engage God directly and explicitly" (2018a: 27). Moreover, while we might use the term "liturgy" to refer to a text used in communal worship, Wolterstorff claims that, "a liturgical text exists not for its own sake but for the sake of enactments of the liturgy" (2015: 4). As he defines it, liturgy is a "universal," that is, something that "can be repeatedly enacted" (2015: 4). More specifically, liturgies are "types of sequences of actions of certain kinds" that always include bodily actions (such as "listening, speaking, singing ... crossing oneself, distributing

---

[2] With thanks to Joanna Leidenhag for this suggestion.

bread and wine...and more besides" (2015: 5)) as well as non-bodily actions such as blessing and thanking. In the context of liturgy, bodily actions "count as performances of actions that are not bodily" (2015: 5). As Cuneo expands this point, bodily acts "do not merely *accompany* the linguistic acts prescribed by the liturgical script," but, in the context of liturgy, (at least some) bodily actions "count as cases of engaging God by blessing, petitioning and thanking God" (2016: 156).[3]

According to Cuneo, successfully thanking God in the liturgy doesn't depend on having a specific mental state: "To thank someone at some time, one needn't be feeling gratitude at that time" (2016: 157) but requires only that the relevant intention is present. If the agent wants to thank God by repeating the words of the liturgical script "thanks be to God," while she doesn't need to *feel* gratitude, she does need to intend that this speech act count as an instance of thanking God. Wolterstorff makes a similar point in his discussion of whether having faith in God is required for successfully performing liturgical actions. Wolterstorff suggests that in the instance of someone who utters, "Thanks be to God," "on the off-chance and in the hope that God does exist and is the sort of being who can be thanked and who is worthy of being thanked" (2018a: 104), if such a God does exist, then this person has thanked God.[4]

While, for Cuneo and Wolterstorff, the success conditions of acting liturgically don't depend on the agent's mental states or beliefs but only their intentions (or absence of negative intentions), liturgical acts can be evaluated in terms of how appropriately they engage God. For instance, in the case of the person who thanks God without having faith in God, Wolterstorff thinks such a person thanks God, but writes that this "is not a well-formed instance of thanking God" (2018a: 104). Cuneo suggests that the liturgical script provides us with the opportunity not only to engage God *simpliciter* but also to engage God appropriately. Just as in ordinary social situations there are apt and inapt ways of expressing thanks (writing a letter as a means of expressing thanks for passing the salt appears to be an inapt way of expressing thanks, for instance (2016: 164)), Cuneo suggests that "the liturgical script ... repeatedly draws attention to the fact that the ways of acting it prescribes are not inapt" (2016: 164).

It is important to see that liturgy as a sequence of act-types requires some kind of script. As Wolterstorff describes it, "those who participate in enacting some liturgy do so by following what I shall call a *script*, the result being *scripted activity*" (2018a: 13). In a number of places, Wolterstorff makes comparisons between the ontology of liturgy and the ontology of music to explain the relation between a script and the performance of some act-type (2015: 5). In the performance of some orchestral symphony, for instance, a musician follows a score to guide her to perform a certain sequence of sounds, and, he argues, "the musical work is the sound sequence type that is instantiated when the correctness-rules that the composer has instantiated are faithfully followed" (2015: 6). Similarly, the liturgical script of a particular tradition "specifies a set of rules for a correct

---

[3] It is important to note that liturgical actions need not only be vertical in direction (i.e., directed toward God), but they might also be horizontal (i.e., directed toward one another). A good example of this (with thanks to Tim Pawl) is in sharing the sign of the peace, which appears to be act of blessing the neighbor. I explore this horizontal direction to liturgical action in Cockayne and Efird (2018).

[4] Wolterstorff even goes as far as to suggest that "if it is the intention of the participant, when performing the prescribed verbal and gestural acts, that he not thereby perform the prescribed acts of worship, then he has not performed them; otherwise he has" (2018a: 108). Implicit in Wolterstorff's account here is a certain view of the nature of faith as non-doxastic (see Howard-Snyder 2016). If one can have a kind of faith even if they lack certain specific beliefs, then it seems plausible that they can successfully thank God without such beliefs.

liturgical enactment" (2015: 7), which, in turn, allows for the performance of certain acts of worship. Wolterstorff notes that scripts can be followed "correctly or incorrectly" (2018a: 15), even if these correctness rules are often "tradition-specific" (2015: 8). Thus, just as a team of football players can execute their game plan correctly or incorrectly, a congregation can follow a liturgical script correctly or incorrectly. To follow a liturgical script correctly requires suspending acting on one's own judgment "as to what would be good to do and instead follow the script" (2018a: 15). This requires a kind of submission to the authorities of one's tradition, Wolterstorff thinks—"to be inducted into the tradition of Catholic liturgical practice is to be confronted with the authority of that tradition" (2018a: 51).

Yet, while a tradition determines the actions one is to perform in engaging God, a script cannot prescribe all the actions that should be performed (2018a: 16)—"the script for enacting a particular liturgy is never fully specified by a text, nor by a text supplemented by oral directives. Always some of the prescriptions constituting the script are embedded within the social practice of that particular religious community for enacting its liturgies" (2018a: 20). As Smith describes, there is a kind of irreducible logic of practice which can only be acquired by being embedded in a liturgical community (2013: 77). Thus, while liturgical scripts prescribe some of the actions involved in engaging God liturgically, some of our liturgical behavior must be learned through experience. Analogously, while a football team may follow a particular routine to execute a defensive set piece, being able to follow this routine effectively can only be learnt through practice. While a newcomer to football might be able to follow a particular scripted action (such as "run from point B to point A"), executing a plan will always require actions that a script cannot fully specify, such as how to time a run to receive the ball from a particular pass.

IV. CORPORATE LITURGICAL ACTION

So far, the discussion of liturgical action has focused on the actions of individuals. But we know that the liturgies of Christian worship are typically corporate acts and not merely individual acts.[5] This can be seen straightforwardly by attending to the fact that most liturgical scripts use the second-personal pronoun throughout. In the Church of England's *Common Worship*, for instance, the congregation confesses their sins together ("*we* have sinned against you and against *our* neighbour in thought and word and deed" (*Common Worship*, Holy Communion, Prayers of Penitence; emphases added)), they share in the breaking of bread together ("Though *we* are many, *we* are one body, because *we* all share in one bread" (*Common Worship*, Holy Communion, Breaking of the Bread; emphases added)), and they typically sing hymns together ("Thee *we* would be always blessing, serve thee as thy hosts above, pray and praise thee without ceasing, glory in thy perfect love" ("Love Divine," Charles Wesley; emphasis added)). This is a point made succinctly by Evelyn Underhill, a twentieth-century Anglo-Catholic theologian, who writes,

> The worshipping life of the Christian whilst profoundly personal, is essentially that of a person who is also a member of a group ... The Christian as such cannot fulfil

---

[5] This does not mean that liturgical actions are not sometimes individual acts too. Confessional liturgy, for instance, often uses the first-person singular pronoun. With thanks to Tim Pawl for raising this point. However, as I will go on to suggest in the conclusion (see Underhill 1936), even these individual liturgical acts should be thought of as corporate in some sense, even if they are not part of a physically copresent joint action.

his spiritual obligations in solitude. He forms part of a social and spiritual complex with a new relation to God; an organism which is quickened and united by that Spirit of supernatural charity which sanctifies the human race from above, and is required to incarnate something of this supernatural charity in the visible world. Therefore even his most lonely contemplations are not merely private matter; but always to be regarded in their relation to the purpose and action of God Who incites them, and to the total life of the Church. (1936: 83)

As Underhill goes on to note, a Christian's relationship to God must be understood through her relationship as a member of a group—the body of Christ. To understand the nature and purpose of liturgy, according to Underhill, we need to see liturgical action as an example of "joint action" (1936: 99), which is, she maintains, the reason why some agreed pattern of liturgy is so vital for Christian worship.[6] Thus, it seems clear that an account of acting liturgically needs to remain sensitive to the communal nature of worship.

There have been some attempts to capture this communal dimension of liturgical action in analytic theology. For instance, as Wolterstorff notes, "the church blesses God, praises God, thanks God, confesses her sins to God, petitions God, listens to God's Word, celebrates the Eucharist. It's not the individual members who do these things simultaneously; it's the assembled body that does these things" (2015: 11). Both Cuneo and Wolterstorff have given accounts of collective intentionality in liturgy to explain the corporate aspect of communal worship. Cuneo draws on work by John Searle (1990, 2010), and Wolterstorff, from Michael Bratman (2009). For Searle, in *joint* actions, the structure of an individual's intentions is different than in individual actions. For instance, if we perform a piano/violin duet (2010: 52), it is not the case that I intend that I play the piano while believing that you play the violin, but instead, Searle thinks, I *"we-intend"* that we perform the duet by means of my performing the piano part and you performing the violin part. Rather referring to mysterious we-intentions, Bratman (2009) prefers to describe individual intentions as meshing or interlocking to perform joint intentions.

Both accounts have been applied to the context of liturgy to explain the nature of collective liturgical action. For instance, drawing from Searle, Cuneo writes,

> Group singing clearly seems to satisfy the criteria for collective action specified above: it requires the requisite "we intentions," that these intentions fit together in the right ways, and awareness of one another's intentions ... to engage in group singing also requires that I adjust my singing to yours and that you adjust your singing to mine in "real time," often in ways that are not dictated by the score that we are following. (2016: 138)

Applying Bratman's account, Wolterstorff suggests that "when the participants in some liturgical enactment come together they don't do any such thing *as come to agreement with each other* over their actions. Joint action automatically results from each participant intending to fill his or her role in together following the script. Shared joint-action

---

[6]J. B. Torrance, in his influential work on worship, *Worship, Community and the Triune God of Grace*, makes a similar point. He states that our theology of worship needs "a better understanding of the person not just as an individual but as someone who finds his or her true being in communion with God and with others ... God ... has created us male and female in his image to find our true humanity in perichoretic unity with him and one another" (1996: 27). Thus, our worship is not done as individuals in response to the work of Christ but as the collective of God's people.

intentions that interlock emerge automatically" (2018a: 63). Yet, while joint intention is necessary for acting together, it's not sufficient, as there must also be the kind of mutual responsiveness Cuneo describes in his account of liturgical singing. Similarly, Wolterstorff observes that "if one person ... says the creed very slowly and another says it very quickly, they are not saying the creed *together*" (2018a: 64; emphasis in the original).

While the application of the material on collective intention has its uses, it also has its shortcomings. It might seem to some to suggest something too homogenous about the nature of corporate liturgical action, particularly to those from less formal liturgical traditions. In recent work, I have argued (2018c) that one limitation of collective intention accounts of group action is that they exclude neuro-atypical individuals from participating in liturgy. Here I point to the psychological literature on autism; many individuals with autism spectrum disorder have difficulty engaging in the kind of intention meshing and mutual responsiveness described in Wolterstorff's and Cuneo's accounts. This is not to say that such accounts have no value, but just that they are limited in what they can explain. Instead, I offer an account of church action based on Christian List and Phillip Pettit's (2011) discussion of group agency, in which there are a number of ways of contributing to the corporate actions of a church's worship other than through the collectively intended liturgical script. Just as a corporation acts by means of committees, subgroups and experts, I argue that we should diversify our understanding of how individuals can contribute to group liturgical acts.[7]

V. KNOWING GOD LITURGICALLY

As we have seen, acting liturgically is primarily aimed at engaging with God through the corporate acts of blessing, thanking, and petitioning God. There are important epistemological implications of this understanding of liturgy.[8] For in engaging in these liturgical acts, one comes not only to know how to read a script or to know what it is like to listen to a piece of music but also to know something in relation to God. Put succinctly, liturgy provides an opportunity for a person to know God. Let's explore how this might be so.

First, it seems clear that there is a kind of practical knowledge that is made possible by participating in liturgy. For as we have already seen, there are ways of participating in liturgy that require repeated exposure to a particular community and way of acting. Yet, if liturgical actions are more than bodily actions, and get also to be counted as instances of engaging God, it seems plausible that one might acquire a knowledge of how to engage God in liturgy. This is precisely what Cuneo argues. Echoing Bonnie M. Talbert's (2015) claim that knowing a person well requires a kind of know-how, Cuneo observes that "knowing God ... consists in (although is not exhausted by) knowing how to engage God" (Cuneo 2016: 149). Liturgy allows a person to gain a kind of knowledge-how to engage God. As Cuneo describes,

> liturgy makes available act-types of a certain range such as chanting, kissing, prostrating, and eating that count in the context of a liturgical performance as cases of blessing, petitioning, and thanking God ... If this is correct, the liturgy provides the materials

---

[7]This is also an important point for more informal traditions in the church. Joanna Leidenhag explores the role of charismatic liturgy in her contribution to this volume.
[8]See David Efird's contribution to this volume ("Analytic Spirituality") for more detail on knowing God personally.

for not only engaging but also knowing how to engage God. Or more, precisely: the liturgy provides the materials by which a person can acquire such knowledge and a context in which she can exercise or enact it. ... [T]o the extent that one grasps and sufficiently understands these ways of acting, one knows how to bless, petition, and thank God in their ritualized forms. One has ritual knowledge. (2016: 163)

Thus, we can see that if bodily liturgical actions should count as instances of blessing God, thanking God, and petitioning God, then repeated engagement in liturgy provides a participant with a kind of personal know-how. Just as repeatedly engaging with another person allows us to know how to engage them better (e.g., we might get better at knowing how to make someone laugh, or feel at ease), repeatedly engaging with God allows us to know how to engage God better.

Second, along with a kind of ritual know-how, it might be argued that liturgy provides an individual with knowledge of what God is like. As Sarah Coakley notes, there are clear parallels between knowledge that is acquired by acquaintance with an object (such as knowing the beauty of a piece of art, for instance) and the knowledge gained through liturgy (2013: 134). However, she suggests that the acquaintance knowledge of God made possible by engagement with liturgy is not like the immediate knowledge that is acquired through perception, as in the case of beautiful art. Rather, acquaintance knowledge of God is acquired slowly through the repetition of certain practices, which train an individual rightly relate to God and to see God. She writes that

the specific, bodily ways in which Christians seek to "perceive" God through liturgy involve a range of ramified practices (including hymnody; or "walking in patterns" ...) that are not merely straightforward analogies of "perception" in "immediate" response to God, but complex means of *training* the mind and senses, over time, in order to come into a right relation with God. (2013: 137–8)

Thus, in coming to see God through repeated exposure to certain kinds of liturgy, one might come to a kind of knowledge of what God is like. One reason why liturgy allows for such knowledge, it might be thought, is because it is a kind of narrative. As Eleonore Stump describes, narrative has an important role to play in the communication of personal knowledge. Exploring the role of narrative in Eucharistic liturgy, she writes,

The moving knowledge of persons with respect to Christ mediated by the story which originally brought Paula to second-person experience of Christ is there again for her in every instance in which Paula participates appropriately in the Eucharist. ... [E]very time she participates in the rite, she will find that, however inclined she is to give up on herself or on God, God is still there, still loving her, still wanting her to come into union with himself. ... [W]ith every participation in the Eucharist, Paula will be strengthened for perseverance, in virtue of growing in love of God and in experience of God's continued love and presence to her. (2015: 223–4)

If liturgy provides a narrative to engage with God, should liturgical actions be thought of as mere reenactments of historical events?[9] How do the actions of the present (e.g., the priest's blessing the elements) relate to the actions of the past (e.g., Christ's blessing

---

[9] Wolterstorff thinks not. Such an approach "displaces the focus from the actuality of what is presently taking place" (1990: 146), he thinks. According to him, "the celebrant actually blesses; he does not play the role of Christ blessing" (1990: 146).

the elements)? Cuneo considers these questions in some depth. For him, liturgical reenactment cannot be thought of as a purely narrative work; instead, it requires an individual "to insert oneself into a complex sequence of scripted action performance" (2016: 82). Thus, he thinks,

> the activity called for is not that of pretending to be a disciple present at the rite or pretending to be present at the rite in one's own person. Rather, what the script calls for is that those assembled attend to and take up a vantage point within the core narrative, screening-off various features of the presentation of this narrative and sometimes certain features of the narrative itself. (2016: 82)

As Cuneo goes on to argue, the purpose of this kind of immersion is for participants to engage with the narrative of the Christian gospel in such a way that their identities are challenged and revised by God through the liturgy (2016: 87).[10] Thus, in entering into the liturgy in this immersive way, one comes to know something of what God is like, which could never be communicated through mere propositions.[11]

Third, along with knowing how to engage God and knowing what God is like, liturgy might also provide a means of knowing *about* God. Coakley (2013), in her short essay on truth in liturgy, briefly suggests some ways in which liturgy might allow us to acquire propositional knowledge. While liturgy's principle aim is not to provide participants with propositional knowledge about God, Coakley argues that "it could in principle also be that liturgy, in virtue of certain repetitive belief-forming practices, could actually mount some kind of 'justification' thereby for beliefs" (2013: 134). Indeed, this provides a helpful summary of one of Wolterstorff's focuses in his discussion of liturgy in *The God We Worship*. As he argues, liturgies typically have an implicit understanding of God; for instance, "Blessing God with explicitly trinitarian language presupposes that God is the sort of being whom it is appropriate to bless" (2015: 17). As Wolterstorff (2016) later argues, repeated exposure to what is theologically implicit in liturgy can play a role in shaping those things an individual takes for granted about God, and thereby in what a person knows about God.

Finally, just as ecclesiology shapes one's understanding of liturgical action, it must also shape one's epistemological understanding of liturgy. For if it is a community that acts in the liturgy, and not just individuals, then it seems pertinent to ask what the community comes to know through liturgy. In a recent paper, David Efird and I (2018) consider how corporate worship might play a role in helping us to know God better. Here, we consider how liturgy can provide an occasion for second-personal experiences of God and how the context of these experiences can be shaped and broadened to provide a variety of shared worlds between a person and God. Rather than thinking only of liturgy as a means of sharing attention with God, we argue that liturgy also provides a means of sharing attention with other congregants, while mutually focusing on God as an object of attention. We suggest two ways in which such experience might improve one's knowledge

---

[10]This account of narrative engagement also comes close to how Smith describes the role of liturgical narrative, which I describe in the next section.
[11]Wolterstorff also has an account of acquiring phenomenal knowledge of what God is like. Instead of focusing on the narratives of Christian liturgy, Wolterstorff focuses on those aspects of God's character that are taken for granted in the repeated practices in which we engage. In taking for granted certain things about God through our use of liturgy, we can come to know that God is a certain way. For example, we can come to know God as being worthy of praise and adoration and as being capable of listening to us (2016: 13).

of God. First, we argue, corporate worship can alter our perception of God—just as experiencing our friends in different social scenarios changes our perception of what they are like, experiencing God alongside other people, with different histories, beliefs, and issues can provide us with a broader and deeper knowledge of what God is like, by allowing us to experience different aspects of God. Second, we suggest, worshipping alongside others plays a causal role in what we attend to—thus, in worshipping alongside another person, we are able to be drawn to aspects of God's character and to come to a broader perception of what God is like than we would by worshipping alone. Elsewhere (2019a), I argue that the discussion of liturgy and know-how needs to take account of the corporate nature of worship, applying recent work on group-know-how to the context of liturgy.

VI. CONCLUSION AND FUTURE DIRECTIONS

These recent developments move in the right direction, but they do not go far enough. Work on the nature of corporate liturgy helps to specify how some participants can act together in preforming a liturgical script and the ways in which their knowledge can be combined and influenced by their corporate setting. Yet, this existing work stops short of showing how an instance of liturgy in a gathered church community can be a part of the life of the mystical body of Christ. For as Underhill describes it, the

> total liturgical life of the *Corpus Christi* is not merely a collective of services, offices, and sacraments. Deeply considered, it is the sacrificial life of Christ Himself; the Word indwelling in His Church, gathering in His enteral priestly action the small Godward movements, sacrifices, and aspirations of "all the broken and the meek", and acting through those ordered signs and sacraments by means of these His members on earth. ... [T]he corporate worship of the Church is not simply that of an assembly of individuals who believe the same things, and therefore unite in doing the same things. It is real in its own right; an action transcending and embracing all the separate souls taking part in it. The individual as such dies to his separate selfhood—even his spiritual selfhood—on entering the Divine Society: is "buried in baptism" and reborn as a living cell of the Mystical Body of Christ. (1936: 86)

If an account of liturgical action and group liturgical knowledge falls short of explaining what it is to participate in the worship of the church and to know God through the liturgy of the church, then such analysis will always fall short of analytic theology's aim to *explicate the conceptual content of the Christian tradition*. Many issues in ecclesiology remain largely unanswered by analytic theology, and I think it is these questions which must be answered to allow liturgical analytic theology to flourish. For if liturgy allows individuals to participate in the worship of the church as a whole, then it seems vital that we can give answers to questions of the following kind: What kind of entity is the church? What relation do its members stand to the whole?[12] Who is authorized to act on its behalf, and when? What role does the Holy Spirit play in the actions of the church? Given the increased attention that group ontology and collective epistemology is currently receiving

---

[12]These are two issues I consider in my recent work (2019b).

in analytic philosophy, these issues of ecclesiology seem to be a ripe and fertile area for those writing in analytic theology to consider.[13]

References

Benson, B. E. (2013), *Liturgy as a Way of Life*, Grand Rapids, MI: Baker Academic.
Bratman, M. (2009), "Shared Agency," in C. Mantzavinos (ed.), *Philosophy of the Social Sciences*, 41–59, Cambridge: Cambridge University Press.
Church of England, Archbishops' Council (2000), *Common Worship: Services and Prayers for the Church of England*. London: Church House.
Coakley, S. (2013), "Beyond 'Belief' Liturgy and the Cognitive Apprehension of God," in T. Greggs. R. Muers, and S. Zahl (eds.), *The Vocation of Theology Today: A Festschrift for David Ford*, 131–45, Portland: Cascade Books.
Cockayne, J. (2018a), "Philosophy and Liturgy Part 1: Liturgy and Philosophy of Action," *Philosophy Compass*, 13 (10).
Cockayne, J. (2018b), "Philosophy and Liturgy Part 2: Liturgy and Epistemology," *Philosophy Compass*, 13 (10).
Cockayne, J. (2018c), "Inclusive Worship and Group Liturgical Action," *Res Philosophica*, 95 (3): 449–76.
Cockayne, J. (2019a), "Common Ritual Knowledge," *Faith and Philosophy*, 36 (1): 33–55.
Cockayne, J. (2019b), "Analytic Ecclesiology: The Social Ontology of the Church," *Journal of Analytic Theology*, 7: 100–23.
Cockayne, J., and D. Efird (2018), "Common Worship," *Faith and Philosophy*, 36 (1): 33–55.
Crisp, O. D. (2017), "Analytic Theology as Systematic Theology," *Open Theology*, 3(1): 156–66.
Cuneo, T. (2016), *Ritualized Faith*, Oxford: Oxford University Press.
Howard-Snyder, D. (2016), "Does Faith Entail Belief?," *Faith and Philosophy*, 33 (2): 142–62.
List, C., and P. Pettit (2011), *Group Agency*, Oxford: Oxford University Press.
Price, C. P., and L. Weil (1979), *Liturgy for Living*, New York: Seabury Press.
Searle, J. (1990), "Collective Intentions and Actions," in P. Cohen, J. Mordan, and M. E. Pollack (eds.), *Consciousness and Language*, 90–106, Cambridge: Cambridge University Press.
Searle, J. (2010), *Making the Social World*, Oxford: Oxford University Press.
Smith, J. K. A. (2009), *Desiring the Kingdom*, Grand Rapids, MI: Baker Academic.
Smith, J. K.A. (2013), *Imagining the Kingdom (Cultural Liturgies): How Worship Works*, Grand Rapids, MI: Baker Books.
Smith, J. K. A. (2018), "Review of Terence Cuneo, Ritualized Faith: Essays on the Philosophy of Liturgy," *Scottish Journal of Theology*, 71 (1): 118–19.
Stump, E. (2015) "Atonement and Eucharist," in O. D. Crisp and F. Sanders (eds.), *Locating Atonement: Explorations in Constructive Dogmatics*, 209–25, Grand Rapids, MI: Zondervan Academic.
Talbert, B. (2015), "Knowing Other People: A Second-Person Framework," *Ratio*, 28: 190–206.
Torrance, J. B. (1996), *Worship, Community and Triune God of Grace*, Downers Grove, IL: InterVarsity Press.
Wolterstorff, N. (1990), "Remembrance of Things (Not) Past," in T. Flint (ed.), *Christian Philosophy*, 118–61, South Bend: Notre Dame University Press.

---

[13] Many thanks to J. T. Turner, Jr., James Arcadi, Tim Pawl, Joanna Leidenhag, and David Efird for their insightful comments on earlier drafts of this chapter.

Wolterstorff, N. (2015), *The God We Worship,* Grand Rapids, MI: Eerdmans.
Wolterstorff, N. (2016), "Knowing God Liturgically," *Journal for Analytic Theology*, 4: 1–16.
Wolterstorff, N. (2018a), *Acting Liturgically*, Oxford: Oxford University Press.
Wolterstorff, N. (2018b), "The SCP, Then, Now and Beyond," *Society of Christian Philosophers 40th Anniversary Conference*, Available online: https://www.youtube.com/watch?v=oYgFX1eN-RE.
Underhill, E. (1936), *Worship*, London: Nisbet.

CHAPTER THIRTY-SEVEN

Prayer

SCOTT A. DAVISON

For some people, prayer is any activity that is somehow directed at the divine, or consciously undertaken in the presence of the divine; this would include prayer as meditation and as contemplation, along with the idea of living life itself as a prayer. I shall refer to this as the "wide sense of prayer." For others, prayer is an attempt to communicate with the divine, usually with a particular purpose in mind. In this sense, to which I shall refer as the "narrow sense of prayer," prayers of gratitude, confession and repentance, adoration and praise, petition and intercession, and lament and complaint all count as examples of prayer. Historically, both senses are important; many religious traditions emphasize not just particular prayers (in the narrow sense) but also prayer as meditation and life attitude (in the wide sense).

Analytic philosophers have focused most of their attention recently upon prayer in the narrow sense, so I will follow their lead and focus only on the narrow sense here. Most of the literature concerns prayers of petition, which involve requesting something from God. (I will treat prayers of intercession as prayers of petition, assuming that intercession involves petitioning on behalf of someone else.) Philosophers have also discussed prayers of praise and gratitude in some detail.

In this chapter, I will explore some of the main philosophical questions that arise in connection with these topics. Along the way, I will indicate related areas of philosophical interest that deserve further attention.

I. PRAISE

It is common for theists to offer prayers of praise to God, highlighting different aspects of God's goodness, holiness, mercy, and so on. But some philosophers (e.g., Howard-Snyder 2008) argue that if someone had no choice about something, then this person does not deserve to be praised for it. Since God had no choice about being perfectly good, one might conclude, God does not deserve to be praised for this. This worry is especially pressing because God's goodness seems essential to God—God cannot be less than perfectly good, or else God would not be God.

In response to this worry, one might challenge the claim that God must have a choice about being perfectly good before it makes sense to praise God. In fact, sometimes it seems that we praise people precisely because they are unable to do anything else. As Daniel Dennett has argued, we find Martin Luther praiseworthy for lodging his protests against clerical abuse by saying, "Here I stand, I can do no other" (see Dennett 1984: 133). There also seems to be an inherent asymmetry between praise and blame: we seem to find it more acceptable to praise people for things beyond their control than to blame them for things beyond their control. (As Peter van Inwagen (1988: 617) says, "You can praise Einstein's genius, but you can't blame a [person of very limited natural intelligence] for being one".) So although it possible to view praise as something one deserves only in virtue of one's free choices, it is also possible to see praise instead as something that is appropriate when it truly tracks excellence, regardless of whether such excellence results from a choice among live options.[1]

II. GRATITUDE

It is very common for theists to offer prayers of thanksgiving and gratitude for particular things in life. One philosophical worry about these prayers of gratitude is closely related to the worry about praise described in the previous section: Does God really have any choice about the good things God does? Simplifying a bit, if God had a choice, then there was some alternative. Either the alternative would be better, worse, or the same as the action God actually took. If the alternative would be better, then God could have been better if God had taken it, which seems impossible. If the alternative would be worse, then God could have been worse by taking it, which also seems impossible. But if the alternative would be the same, and God is not responsible for being in a position to choose between equally good alternatives, then God does not deserve to be praised for doing one of them.[2]

One might respond to this worry in a way that is parallel to the response described above in connection with prayers of praise: one might question whether a benefactor's having a choice is required for gratitude, in general. And one might think that God deserves thanks even if God could not do otherwise, since God's goodness would be the ultimate explanation of God's actions, and we ought to be grateful for good things (see the preface and text of Augustine 1993 and Davison 2012: chapter 7).

A different worry concerning prayers of gratitude involves the idea that since it costs God nothing to benefit us, and God could have just as easily benefited us more (and prevented the evil and suffering we experience), we should not be grateful to God at all—or so argues Nicholas Everett:

> So many lives contain so much pain and suffering—negative features which on the face of it God could have prevented. In such a circumstance, it might well seem that resentment is the more appropriate emotion. Even if God has given something valuable, if he could so easily have given something so very much more valuable, it is less clear that gratitude is the right emotion. The appropriateness of gratitude is a function not just of the benefit that accrues to the beneficiary, but also of the degree of sacrifice which is made by the benefactor. It is far from clear how much gratitude we owe to someone who has brought us a benefit at no cost to himself, and who could, also with no cost to himself, have brought us a very much greater benefit. (Everett 2003: 130)

---

[1] For more on the general question about whether being responsible for something requires alternatives, see Frankfurt (1969), Nagel (1976), van Inwagen (1983), Kane (1985), Adams (1985), Fischer and Ravizza (1998), O'Connor (2000), Clarke (2003), Morriston (2000), and Timpe (2013).
[2] For more on this line of thought, see Howard-Snyder (2008), Rowe (2004), Bergmann and Cover (2006), and Wierenga (2007).

In Everett's defense, we do seem to believe that gratitude for a benefit is more appropriate when a benefactor sacrifices in order to confer it. If someone donates a vital organ, for example, we find ingratitude in the recipient much more puzzling than if a dollar had been donated instead.

But it is not clear that Everett's argument shows that it would be mistaken to be grateful to God to any degree. If a group of very, very wealthy people created a grant program that awarded me 10 percent of my salary to work on a book, I would be very grateful, even if they came out even financially because of some tax loophole. I would be more grateful, of course, to a moderately wealthy person who sacrificed to fund my work, but that seems to be beside the point: I would still be grateful, and appropriately so, for the benefit conferred by the very, very wealthy people. It would be beside the point to note that they could have given me more money instead.[3]

III. PETITION IN GENERAL

Petitionary prayer involves asking God to do something. The practice of asking God to do things seems to have lots of effects on people, some positive and some negative (see the discussions in Phillips 1981, Brümmer 2008, and Davison 2017, for example). But the focus of most philosophical attention in the literature concerns the possibility that such requests might make a difference with respect to what God does. Something counts as a response to a request only if the request plays an important role in bringing about the thing requested. So in order for God's actions to count as answers to our petitionary prayers, the offering of those prayers must play some important role in explaining what God does (see Flint 1998: chapter 10, and Davison 2017: chapter 2). But exactly what role?

Alexander Pruss argues that God is omnirational, which means that God acts on all unexcluded good reasons (see Pruss 2013). If Pruss is right, it seems that when a person prays for something good and it comes to be, then God has answered that prayer—or at least we can say that the offering of the prayer was among God's reasons for bringing about that thing. Others wonder whether this is enough to say that God has actually answered the prayer in question; saying exactly what it means for God to have answered a prayer turns out to be rather complicated.[4]

Traditional theists recognize that God's reasons are limited in various ways—God cannot do what is intrinsically evil, for instance, or what is logically impossible. But they have typically held that there is plenty of room left for God to answer our prayers. Others have argued, though, that if we consider carefully God's attributes, we will realize that petitionary prayers cannot make a difference to God's actions. These arguments are challenges to the efficacy of petitionary prayer.[5] Let's consider some of these, one at a time.

---

[3] For a more detailed discussion of this question, along with a related argument from Everett for the conclusion that we should not be grateful for our own existence, see Everett (2003) and Davison (2012: chapter 7).
[4] For more on this, see the discussion in Rice (2016), Davison (2017: chapter 2), Cohoe (2018), Davison (2018), and DiQuattro (2018).
[5] See Davison (2017: chapter 1) for a longer list of challenges.

IV. PETITION: CHALLENGES AND REPLIES

One kind of challenge comes from the idea that God is either immutable (unable to change) or impassible (unable to be affected by anything external to God), so that no petitionary prayer could make a difference to God. (If God is immutable, then God is impassible, but the converse does not necessarily hold.) One way to respond to this worry would be simply to deny that God is either immutable or impassible. And one reason for doing this would be the idea that God is compassionate and forgiving, which suggests that God is responsive to people in a way that involves God's changing because of external sources (see Wainwright 2017). A very different way to approach this worry would be to provide definitions of immutability and impassibility that do not preclude answered petitionary prayers (see Creel 1985; Leftow 2016; Wainwright 2017).

A different challenge to petitionary prayer involves omniscience, the idea that God knows everything that can be known. If God already knows the future, for instance, how can our prayers make a difference? No matter what we ask for, God knew before we asked whether it is part of the future, so it seems pointless to ask. In order to respond to this worry, we need to consider different views that people have about God's knowledge and providence.

According to Open Theism, some things in the future are not determined yet, such as the free choices of human beings, so not even God can know about them now (see Hasker 1989; Rissler 2017; Borland 2017). This does not contradict God's omniscience, according to Open Theists, because God still knows everything that can be known. They would also say that if our prayers are free, or God's decision whether or not to answer them is free (or both), then those things are undecided, and so petitionary prayer can make all of the difference in the world. Open Theism is controversial because it denies that God knows the future in all of its detail, suggesting that God takes risks.[6]

A different approach involves the Middle Knowledge perspective. According to this approach, God knows the future in all of its detail as a result of knowing both (1) what everyone and everything would do in any possible situation, and (2) which situations everyone and everything will be placed in actually (see Flint 1998 and de Molina 2004). If this is right, then even though God knows what you will do in the future, it is still up to you. In fact, when you make a free choice, you have the ability to do something such that, were you to do it, God would have always known something different from what God knows in fact. This is often described in terms of having "counterfactual power" with respect to the content of God's knowledge (see Flint 1998).

According to the Middle Knowledge approach, petitionary prayer can make a difference because God can consider prayers that will be freely offered in the future when God plans how to create the world. The fact that God knows the future in all of its detail does not mean that this future is determined, according to the Middle Knowledge view, since God's knowledge depends upon what we would choose to do freely. The Middle Knowledge view is controversial too, because people doubt whether there are truths about what everyone and everything would do in every situation, and whether even God could know such things (see Hasker 1989; Davison 1991; Flint 1998; Zagzebski 2014; Borland 2017; and Rissler 2017).

---

[6]For more on this, see Hasker (1989), Flint (1998), Borland (2017), and Rissler (2017).

Finally, defenders of the Timeless Eternity view of God's knowledge and providence think that God knows all of history at once, from a point of view outside of time altogether. Like the Middle Knowledge view, the Timeless Eternity view holds that just because God knows the future, this does not mean that God determines it. Those who defend Timeless Eternity also argue that God's single act of creation from outside of time has many effects that play out in time, including answers to petitionary prayers that God anticipated from the point of view of eternity. Like Open Theism and Middle Knowledge, of course, Timeless Eternity is a controversial view of providence for various reasons (see Hasker 1989; Helm 2014; Zagzebski 2014; Borland 2017; Rissler 2017). Depending on which account of providence one accepts, then, one will have a different reaction to the challenge to petitionary prayer based on God's omniscience.

Yet another challenge starts with something we noted above: If God is perfectly good, then won't God always do what is best for everyone, whether or not anyone ever offers petitionary prayers? If so, wouldn't that make all petitionary prayers pointless?

In response to this worry, some argue that it would be better, in some cases, for God to bring things about in response to petitionary prayers than to bring about those very same things independently. For instance, Eleonore Stump (1979) argues that we could be spoiled by God if all of our prayers were automatically answered, and we could be overwhelmed if God provided everything good for us without waiting for us to ask first. Michael Murray and Kurt Meyers argue that by making some things depend on our offering of petitionary prayers, God helps us to avoid idolatry, that sense of self-sufficiency that fails to recognize God as the source of all good things; they also argue that requiring petitionary prayer in some cases helps us to learn about God's will as we recognize the patterns in prayers answered (Murray and Meyers 1994).[7]

Murray and Meyers also argue that if God makes the provision of certain things for others dependent on our prayers for them, then this can help to build interdependence and community (Murray and Meyers 1994). Richard Swinburne and Daniel and Frances Howard-Snyder argue that by requiring petitionary prayers in some cases, God gives us more responsibility for the well-being of ourselves and others than we would enjoy otherwise (Swinburne 1998; Howard-Snyder and Howard-Snyder 2011). In a similar vein, Nicholas Smith and Andrew Yip argue that petitionary prayer can create a partnership with God, which itself is a great good in the world (Smith and Yip 2010) (for further discussion, see Davison 2017: chapter 7).

Finally, some philosophers (e.g., Basinger 2004) note that there are a number of ways to understand God's obligations (if any) toward created persons, only some of which suggest that God's goodness would be compromised if God withheld things because petitionary prayers were not offered for them. So there are a number of responses that theists can make to the challenge to petitionary prayer that stems from the idea of God's moral perfection.

V. PETITION: EPISTEMOLOGY

As noted above, just because we pray for something and it happens, that alone might not be sufficient for saying that God answered our prayer—it must also be the case that the offering of the prayer played the right kind of role in God's decision to act. One might

---

[7] For more on these defenses, see Davison (2017: chapter 6).

conclude that since we typically would not know God's reasons for acting, we would typically not know whether petitionary prayers have been answered, even when what we request actually come to pass.

But we must be careful here. Consider the following argument:

P1. If God answered my prayer, then the offering of my prayer played a special role among God's reasons for bringing about what I requested.
P2. I don't know whether the offering of my prayer played a special role among God's reasons for bringing about what I requested.
P3. If P implies Q and I don't know that Q, then I don't know that P.
C. I don't know that God answered my prayer.

This argument is valid, but it's not sound, because P3 is false—knowledge is not closed under entailment. Suppose Sue knows that water typically dissolves sugar, but she doesn't know that water is H_2O. "Water typically dissolves sugar" implies that "H_2O typically dissolves sugar;" Sue does not know the latter, but she still knows the former.

Some have argued that given the circumstances of petitionary prayer, it is possible to estimate the likelihood of something happening without petitionary prayer, and to infer from this the likelihood that something is an answer to petitionary prayer, especially in light of teachings from special revelation (see, e.g., Murray and Meyers 1994; Murray 2004; Choi 2016). On the other hand, consider the view popularly known as skeptical theism, which responds to the problem of evil by claiming that we can never know exactly how particular events are connected with each other and with good or bad consequences, some of which may be beyond our understanding (see Wykstra 1984; Bergmann 2009; Howard-Snyder 2010; McBrayer 2010; Dougherty 2014). One might suspect that if this position is correct, then theists are committed to something like agnosticism with regard to God's reasons for bringing about specific contingent events, and this might lead one to be skeptical about claims to know that God has done something specific in response to petitionary prayer.[8]

VI. PETITION DEFENDED

One approach to defending the practice of petitionary prayer is to distinguish different kinds of cases in which such prayers might be offered, and the different kinds of things that might be at stake.[9] For instance, there are some things that only God can provide directly, and God might have very strong reasons for providing some of those things if and only if people ask God to do so. These are the easiest cases to understand. For example, suppose that a person has developed over time a propensity to give in to a certain temptation through a series of free choices, thereby becoming a certain sort of person. If God gives human beings the ability to make free choices so that they can choose what sort of person to become, God might have strong reasons not to change this propensity to give in to temptation unless the person in question asks for it to be removed.[10]

Many defenses of petitionary prayer in the literature try to identify some good thing that would result from God's making the provision of something dependent upon the

---

[8] For on the epistemological issues here, see Davison (2017: chapters 4–5).
[9] For a more detailed discussion in this direction, see Davison (2017: chapter 8) and Cohoe (2018).
[10] For an interesting account of sanctification, choice, and desire, see Stump (1988).

offering of petitionary prayer. A general problem that arises for these defenses is that in some cases, it seems like the good thing identified by the defense, that which would result from God's making provision dependent upon prayer, is not as good as the object of the petitionary prayer in question. In cases like this, it looks like it is more important to provide the good in question than to require petitionary prayers.

For instance, suppose that if God requires Fred to pray for Sue before helping Sue to recover from a severe illness, and Fred does pray for Sue, then Fred will learn from this experience that life is fragile. This might be important for Fred, but what about Sue? Should God let Sue die from the severe illness just because Fred didn't pray for her? A number of authors (for instance, Murray and Meyers 1994: 324–5; Flint 1998: sections 2.3–2.4) have pointed out that if God has middle knowledge, God could also ensure that such cases never arise. This is because God could ensure that significant things depend on petitionary prayers only when the persons in question would offer the relevant prayers (and God could also withhold significant things as a result of a failure to offer petitionary prayers only in cases in which this is an appropriate consequence, all things considered). Of course, not everyone finds it plausible to think that God possesses middle knowledge, as noted above, so this approach will not satisfy everyone.

VII. CONCLUSION

Prayer presents a rich and varied source of philosophical reflection. Current debates have just scratched the surface here. We can expect future work to branch out into the wider sense of prayer, to consider group prayer in addition to the prayer of individuals, to consider how different religious traditions envisage various spiritual goods that might depend on prayer, and to consider other kinds of prayer, such as lamentation.

References

Adams, R. M. (1985), "Involuntary Sins," *The Philosophical Review*, 94 (1): 3–31.
Augustine, St. (1993), *On Free Choice of the Will*, trans. T. Williams, Indianapolis: Hackett.
Basinger, D. (1983), "Why Petition an Omnipotent, Omniscient, Wholly Good God?," *Religious Studies*, 19: 25–42.
Basinger, D. (2004), "God Does Not Necessarily Respond to Prayer," in M. L. Peterson (ed.), *Contemporary Debates in Philosophy of Religion*, 255–64, Malden: Blackwell.
Bergmann, M. (2009), "Skeptical Theism and the Problem of Evil," in T. P. Flint and M. Rea (eds.), *The Oxford Handbook of Philosophical Theology*, 374–99, Oxford: Oxford University Press.
Bergmann, M., and J. Cover (2006), "Divine Responsibility without Divine Freedom," *Faith and Philosophy*, 23 (4): 381–408.
Borland, T. (2017), "Omniscience and Divine Foreknowledge," in E. N. Zalta (ed.) *Internet Encyclopedia of Philosophy*. Available online: http://www.iep.utm.edu/omnisci/.
Brümmer, V. (2008), *What Are We Doing When We Pray? On Prayer and the Nature of Faith*, Farnham: Ashgate.
Choi, I. (2016), "Is Petitionary Prayer Superfluous?," in J. Kvanvig (ed.), *Oxford Studies in Philosophy of Religion*, vol. 7, 32–62, Oxford: Oxford University Press.
Clarke, R. (2003), *Libertarian Accounts of Free Will*, Oxford: Oxford University Press.
Cohoe, C. M. (2018), "How Could Prayer Make a Difference? Discussion of Scott A. Davison, Petitionary Prayer: A Philosophical Investigation," *European Journal for Philosophy of Religion*, 10 (2): 171–85.

Creel, R. (1985), *Divine Impassibility: An Essay in Philosophical Theology*, Cambridge: Cambridge University Press.
Davison, S. A. (1991), "Foreknowledge, Middle Knowledge, and 'Nearby' Worlds," *International Journal for Philosophy of Religion*, 30 (1): 29–44.
Davison, S. A. (2012), *On the Intrinsic Value of Everything*, London: Continuum Press.
Davison, S. A. (2017), *Petitionary Prayer: A Philosophical Investigation*, Oxford: Oxford University Press.
Davison, S. A. (2018), "Requests and Responses: Reply to Cohoe," *European Journal for Philosophy of Religion*, 10 (2): 187–94.
Dennett, D. C. (1984), *Elbow Room: The Varieties of Free Will Worth Wanting*, Cambridge: Cambridge University Press.
DiQuattro, D. (2018), "Review of Petitionary Prayer: A Philosophical Investigation by Scott A. Davison," *International Journal for Philosophy of Religion*, 83 (3): 315–19.
Dougherty, T. (2014), "Skeptical Theism," in E. N. Zalta (ed.), *The Stanford Encyclopedia of Philosophy*. Available online: http://plato.stanford.edu/archives/spr2014/entries/skeptical-theism/.
Everett, N. (2003), *The Non-Existence of God*, London: Routledge.
Fischer, J. M., and M. Ravizza, S.J. (1998), *Responsibility and Control: A Theory of Moral Responsibility*, Cambridge: Cambridge University Press.
Frankfurt, H. G. (1969), "Alternative Possibilities and Moral Responsibility," *Journal of Philosophy*, 66: 829–39.
Flint, T. P. (1998), *Divine Providence: The Molinist Account*, Ithaca: Cornell University Press.
Hasker, W. (1989), *God, Time and Knowledge*, Ithaca: Cornell University Press.
Helm, P. (2014), "Eternity," in E. N. Zalta (ed.), *The Stanford Encyclopedia of Philosophy*. Available online: https://plato.stanford.edu/cgi-bin/encyclopedia/archinfo.cgi?entry=eternity.
Howard-Snyder, D. (2008), "The Puzzle of Prayers of Thanksgiving and Praise," in Y. Nagasawa and E. J. Wielenberg (eds.), *New Waves in Philosophy of Religion*, 125–49, London: Palgrave-Macmillan.
Howard-Snyder, D. (2010), "Epistemic Humility, Arguments from Evil, and Moral Skepticism," in J. L. Kvanvig (ed.), *Oxford Studies in Philosophy of Religion*, vol. 2, 17–57, Oxford: Oxford University Press.
Howard-Snyder, D., and F. Howard-Snyder (2011), "The Puzzle of Petitionary Prayer," *European Journal for Philosophy of Religion*, 2 (2): 43–68.
Kane, R. (1985), *Free Will and Values*, Albany: State University of New York Press.
Leftow, B. (2016), "Immutability," in E. N. Zalta (ed.), *The Stanford Encyclopedia of Philosophy*. Available online: https://plato.stanford.edu/archives/win2016/entries/immutability/.
de Molina, L. (2004), *On Divine Foreknowledge: Part IV of the "Concordia,"* trans. A. J. Freddoso, Ithaca: Cornell University Press.
McBrayer, J. P. (2010), "Skeptical Theism," *Philosophy Compass*, 5 (7): 611–23.
Morriston, W. (2000), "What is So Good about Moral Freedom?," *The Philosophical Quarterly*, 50 (200): 344–58.
Murray, M. (2004), "God Responds to Prayer," in M. L. Peterson (ed.), *Contemporary Debates in Philosophy of Religion*, 242–54, Malden: Blackwell.
Murray, M., and K. Meyers (1994), "Ask and It Will Be Given to You," *Religious Studies*, 30: 311–30.
Nagel, T. (1976), "Moral Luck," *Proceedings of the Aristotelian Society*, 50 (Supplementary Volume): 137–51.
O'Connor, T. (2000), *Persons and Causes*, New York: Oxford University Press.

Phillips, D. Z. (1981), *The Concept of Prayer*, New York: Seabury.
Pruss, A.R. (2013), "Omnirationality," *Res Philosophica*, 90 (1): 1–21.
Rice, R. L. H. (2016), "Reasons and Divine Action: A Dilemma," in K. Timpe and D. Speak (eds.), *Free Will and Theism: Connections, Contingencies, and Concerns*, 258–276, Oxford: Oxford University Press.
Rowe, W. (2004), *Can God Be Free?* Oxford: Oxford University Press.
Rissler, J. (2017), "Open Theism," Internet Encyclopedia of Philosophy. Available online: http://www.iep.utm.edu/o-theism/.
Smith, N. D., and A. C. Yip (2010), "Partnership with God: A Partial Solution to the Problem of Petitionary Prayer," *Religious Studies* 46 (3): 395–410.
Stump, E. (1979), "Petitionary Prayer," *American Philosophical Quarterly*, 16: 81–91.
Stump, E. (1988), "Sanctification, Hardening of the Heart, and Frankfurt's Concept of Free Will," *The Journal of Philosophy*, 85 (8): 395–420.
Swinburne, R. (1998), *Providence and the Problem of Evil*, Oxford: Oxford University Press.
Timpe, K. (2013), *Free Will in Philosophical Theology*, London: Continuum Press.
Van Inwagen, P. (1983), *An Essay on Free Will*, Oxford: Oxford University Press.
Van Inwagen, P. (1988), "Review of Daniel Dennett, *Elbow Room* (MIT Press, 1984)," *Nous*, 22 (4): 609–18.
Wainwright, W. (2017), "Concepts of God," in E. N. Zalta (ed.), *The Stanford Encyclopedia of Philosophy*. Available online: https://plato.stanford.edu/archives/spr2017/entries/concepts-god/.
Wierenga, E. (2007), "Perfect Goodness and Divine Freedom," *Philosophical Books*, 48 (3): 207–16.
Wierenga, E. (2017), "Omniscience," in E. N. Zalta (ed.), *The Stanford Encyclopedia of Philosophy*. Available online: https://plato.stanford.edu/cgi-bin/encyclopedia/archinfo.cgi?entry=free-will-foreknowledge.
Wykstra, S. J. (1984), "The Humean Obstacle to Evidential Arguments from Suffering: On Avoiding the Evils of 'Appearance'," *International Journal for Philosophy of Religion*, 16: 73–93.
Zagzebski, L. (2014), "Foreknowledge and Free Will," in E. N. Zalta (ed.), *The Stanford Encyclopedia of Philosophy*. Available online: https://plato.stanford.edu/cgi-bin/encyclopedia/archinfo.cgi?entry=free-will-foreknowledge.

A COMPREHENSIVE CATEGORIZED BIBLIOGRAPHY OF ANALYTIC THEOLOGY

JESSE GENTILE

Analytic Theology as Theological Method

Abraham, William J. "Systematic Theology as Analytic Theology." In *Analytic Theology: New Essays in the Philosophy of Theology*, edited by Oliver Crisp and Michael C. Rea, 54–69. Oxford: Oxford University Press, 2009.

Abraham, William J. "Turning Philosophical Water into Theological Wine." *Journal of Analytic Theology*, no. 1 (2013): 1–16.

Alston, William P. *Divine Nature and Human Language: Essays in Philosophical Theology*. Ithaca, NY: Cornell University Press, 1989.

Arcadi, James M. "Analytic Theology as Declarative Theology." *TheoLogica: An International Journal for Philosophy of Religion and Philosophical Theology* 1, no. 1 (July 19, 2017): 37–52.

Baker-Hytch, Max. "Analytic Theology and Analytic Philosophy of Religion: What's the Difference?" *Journal of Analytic Theology* 4 (May 2016): 347–61.

Branson, Beau, and Philosophy Documentation Center. "Ahistoricity in Analytic Theology." *American Catholic Philosophical Quarterly* 92, no. 2 (2018): 195–224.

Chignell, Andrew. "As Kant Has Shown." In *Analytic Theology: New Essays in the Philosophy of Theology*, edited by Oliver Crisp and Michael C. Rea, 115–35. Oxford: Oxford University Press, 2009.

Chignell, Andrew. "The Two (or Three) Cultures of Analytic Theology: A Roundtable." *Journal of the American Academy of Religion* 81, no. 3 (September 1, 2013): 569–72.

Coakley, Sarah. "On Why Analytic Theology Is Not a Club." *Journal of the American Academy of Religion* 81, no. 3 (September 1, 2013): 601–8.

Crisp, Oliver. "On Analytic Theology." In *Analytic Theology: New Essays in the Philosophy of Theology*, edited by Oliver Crisp and Michael C. Rea, 33–53. Oxford: Oxford University Press, 2009.

Crisp, Oliver. "Analytic Systematic Theology." In *Analyzing Doctrine: Toward a Systematic Theology*, 15–32. Waco: Baylor University Press, 2019.

Crisp, Oliver, James Arcadi, and Jordan Wessling. *The Nature and Promise of Analytic Theology*. Leiden: Brill, 2019.

Farris, Joshua R., and James M. Arcadi. "Introduction to the Topical Issue 'Analytic Perspectives on Method and Authority in Theology'." *Open Theology* 3, no. 1 (November 27, 2017): 630–2.

Gasser, Georg. "Toward Analytic Theology: An Itinerary." *Scientia et Fides* 3, no. 2 (November 4, 2015): 23–55.

Harrower, Scott. "Analytic Theology as Confessional Theology with a Linguistic Edge." *Open Theology* 3, no. 1 (September 26, 2017): 471–93.

Macdonald, Paul A. "Analytic Theology: A Summary, Evaluation, and Defense." *Modern Theology* 30, no. 1 (January 2014): 32–65.

McCall, Thomas. "Theologians, Philosophers, and the Doctrine of the Trinity." In *Philosophical and Theological Essays on the Trinity*, edited by Thomas McCall and Michael Rea, 336–50. Oxford: Oxford University Press, 2009.

McCall, Thomas. *An Invitation to Analytic Christian Theology*. Downers Grove, IL: IVP Academic, 2015.

Padgett, Alan G. "The Trinity in Theology and Philosophy: Why Jerusalem Should Work with Athens." In *Philosophical and Theological Essays on the Trinity*, edited by Thomas McCall and Michael Rea, 328–35. Oxford: Oxford University Press, 2009.

Rauser, Randal. "Theology as a Bull Session." In *Analytic Theology: New Essays in the Philosophy of Theology*, edited by Oliver Crisp and Michael C. Rea, 70–84. Oxford: Oxford University Press, 2009.

Rea, Michael C. "Introduction." In *Analytic Theology: New Essays in the Philosophy of Theology*, edited by Oliver Crisp and Michael C. Rea, 1–30. Oxford: Oxford University Press, 2009.

Rea, Michael C. "Analytic Theology: Precis." *Journal of the American Academy of Religion* 81, no. 3 (September 1, 2013): 573–7.

Sarisky, Darren. "The Bible and Analytic Reflection." *Journal of Analytic Theology* 6 (July 19, 2018): 162.

Stump, Eleonore. "Athens and Jerusalem: The Relationship of Philosophy and Theology." *Journal of Analytic Theology* 1 (2013): 45–59.

Timpe, Kevin. "On Analytic Theology." *Scientia et Fides* 3, no. 2 (July 10, 2015): 9–21.

Torrance, Andrew. "The Possibility of a Scientific Approach to Analytic Theology." *Journal of Analytic Theology* 7 (July 19, 2019): 178–98.

Westerholm, Martin. "Analytic Theology and Contemporary Inquiry." *International Journal of Philosophy and Theology* 80, no. 3 (May 2019): 230–54.

Wolterstorff, Nicholas. "Is It Possible and Desirable for Theologians to Recover from Kant?" *Modern Theology* 14, no. 1 (January 1998): 1–18.

Wolterstorff, Nicholas. "How Philosophical Theology Became Possible within the Analytic Tradition of Philosophy." In *Analytic Theology: New Essays in the Philosophy of Theology*, edited by Oliver Crisp and Michael C. Rea, 155–68. Oxford: Oxford University Press, 2009.

Wood, William. "Trajectories, Traditions, and Tools in Analytic Theology." *Journal of Analytic Theology* 4 (2016): 254–66.

Yadav, Sameer. "Toward an Analytic Theology of Liberation." In *Voices from the Edge: Centering Marginalized Perspectives in Analytic Theology*, edited by Michael Rea and Michelle Panchuk, 47–74. Oxford: Oxford University Press, 2020.

Theology and Language

Adams, Marilyn McCord. "What's Wrong with the Ontotheological Error?" *Journal of Analytic Theology* 2 (2014): 1–12.

Arcadi, James M. "The Word of God as Truthmaker for Church Proclamation: An Analytic Barthian Approach to the Dogmatic Task." In *The Task of Dogmatics: Explorations in Theological Method*, edited by Oliver Crisp and Fred Sanders, 162–177. Grand Rapids, MI: Zondervan, 2017.

Jacobs, Jonathan D. "The Ineffable, Inconceivable, and Incomprehensible God: Fundamentality and Apophatic Theology." In *Oxford Studies in Philosophy of Religion*, edited by Jonathan L. Kvanvig, 6: 158–76. Oxford: Oxford University Press, 2015.

Keller, John A. "Theological Realism." *Journal of Analytic Theology* 2 (2014): 12–42.

Kvanvig, Jonathan L. "Two Theories of Analogical Predication." In *Oxford Studies in Philosophy of Religion*, edited by Jonathan L. Kvanvig, 4: 20–42. New York: Oxford University Press, 2012.

Wainwright, William J. "Theology and Mystery." In *The Oxford Handbook of Philosophical Theology*, edited by Thomas P. Flint and Michael C. Rea, 78–95. Oxford: Oxford Univeristy Press, 2009.

Yadav, Sameer. "Mystical Experience and the Apophatic Attitude." *Journal of Analytic Theology* 4 (2016): 17.

Scripture and Revelation

Abraham, William J. *Canon and Criterion in Christian Theology: From the Fathers to Feminism*. Oxford: Oxford University Press, 2004.

Abraham, William J. "The Concept of Inspiration." In *Oxford Readings in Philosophical Theology: Volume 2: Providence, Scripture, and Resurrection*, edited by Michael Rea, 144–56. Oxford: Oxford University Press, 2009.

Beilby, James. "Contemporary Religious Epistemology: Some Key Aspects." In *The Enduring Authority of the Christian Scriptures*, edited by D. A. Carson, 795–830. Grand Rapids, MI: William B. Eerdmans, 2016.

Craig, William Lane. "'Men Moved By the Holy Spirit Spoke from God' (2 Peter 1.21): A Middle Knowledge Perspective on Biblical Inspiration." In *Oxford Readings in Philosophical Theology: Volume 2: Providence, Scripture, and Resurrection*, edited by Michael Rea, 157–91. Oxford: Oxford University Press, 2009.

Crisp, Thomas M. "On Believing That the Scriptures Are Divinely Inspired." In *Analytic Theology: New Essays in the Philosophy of Theology*, edited by Oliver Crisp and Michael C. Rea, 171–86. Oxford: Oxford University Press, 2009.

Davis, Stephen T. "Revelation and Inspiration." In *The Oxford Handbook of Philosophical Theology*, edited by Thomas P. Flint and Michael C. Rea, 30–51. Oxford: Oxford Univeristy Press, 2009.

Fales, Evan. "Reformed Epistemology and Biblical Hermeneutics." In *Oxford Readings in Philosophical Theology: Volume 2: Providence, Scripture, and Resurrection*, edited by Michael Rea, 302–17. Oxford: Oxford University Press, 2009.

Green, Adam, and Keith A. Quan. "More than Inspired Propositions: Shared Attention and the Religious Text." *Faith and Philosophy* 29, no. 4 (2012): 416–30.

Helm, Paul. "The Idea of Inerrancy." In *The Enduring Authority of the Christian Scriptures*, edited by D. A. Carson, 899–919. Grand Rapids, MI: William B. Eerdmans, 2016.

Keller, James A. "Accepting the Authority of the Bible: Is It Rationally Justified?" In *Oxford Readings in Philosophical Theology: Volume 2: Providence, Scripture, and Resurrection*, edited by Michael Rea, 192–209. Oxford: Oxford University Press, 2009.

McCall, Thomas H. "On Understanding Scripture as the Word of God." In *Analytic Theology: New Essays in the Philosophy of Theology*, edited by Oliver Crisp and Michael C. Rea, 171–86. Oxford: Oxford University Press, 2009.

Menssen, Sandra, and Thomas Sullivan. "Revelation and Scripture." In *The Oxford Handbook of the Epistemology of Theology*, edited by William J. Abraham and Frederick D. Aquino, 30–44. Oxford: Oxford University Press, 2017.

Pickavance, Timothy H., and Jason McMartin. "The Voice of God In Historical Biblical Criticism." In *The Voice of God in the Text of Scripture: Explorations in Constructive Dogmatics*, edited by Oliver Crisp and Fred Sanders, 127–45. Grand Rapids, MI: Zondervan, 2016.

Plantinga, Alvin. "Two (or More) Kinds of Scripture Scholarship." In *Oxford Readings in Philosophical Theology: Volume 2: Providence, Scripture, and Resurrection*, edited by Michael Rea, 266–301. Oxford: Oxford University Press, 2009.

Rea, Michael C. "Authority and Truth." In *The Enduring Authority of the Christian Scriptures*, edited by D. A. Carson, 872–98. Grand Rapids, MI: William B. Eerdmans, 2016.

Smith, R. Scott. "Non-Foundational Epistemologies and the Truth of Scripture." In *The Enduring Authority of the Christian Scriptures*, edited by D. A. Carson, 831–71. Grand Rapids, MI: William B. Eerdmans, 2016.

Sundberg Jr., Albert C. "The Bible Canon and the Christian Doctrine of Inspiration." In *Oxford Readings in Philosophical Theology: Volume 2: Providence, Scripture, and Resurrection*, edited by Michael Rea, 210–28. Oxford: Oxford University Press, 2009.

Swinburne, Richard. "Revelation." In *Oxford Readings in Philosophical Theology: Volume 2: Providence, Scripture, and Resurrection*, edited by Michael Rea, 127–43. Oxford: Oxford University Press, 2009.

Wahlberg, Mats. *Revelation as Testimony: A Philosophical-Theological Study*. Grand Rapids, MI: William B. Eerdmans, 2014.

Wolterstorff, Nicholas. *Divine Discourse: Philosophical Reflections on the Claim That God Speaks*. Cambridge: Cambridge University Press, 1995.

Wolterstorff, Nicholas. "The Unity Behind the Canon." In *Oxford Readings in Philosophical Theology: Volume 2: Providence, Scripture, and Resurrection*, edited by Michael Rea, 229–41. Oxford: Oxford University Press, 2009.

Worsley, David. "Experiencing the Word of God: Reading as Wrestling." *TheoLogica: An International Journal for Philosophy of Religion and Philosophical Theology* 1, no. 1 (July 19, 2017): 78-93.

Trinity

Adams, Marilyn McCord. "The Metaphysics of the Trinity in Some Fourteenth Century Franciscans." *Franciscan Studies* 66 (2008): 101–68.

Brower, Jeffrey E., and Michael C. Rea. "Material Constitution and the Trinity." *Faith and Philosophy* 22, no. 1 (2005): 57–76.

Cain, James. "On the Geachian Theory of the Trinity And Incarnation." *Faith and Philosophy* 33, no. 4 (2016): 474–86.

Catterson, Troy Thomas. "Indexicality, Phenomenality and the Trinity." *International Journal for Philosophy of Religion* 78, no. 2 (2015): 167–82.

Coakley, Sarah. *God, Sexuality and the Self: An Essay 'On the Trinity'*. Cambridge: Cambridge University Press, 2013.

Cotnoir, A. J. "Mutual Indwelling." *Faith and Philosophy* 34, no. 2 (2017): 123–51.

Craig, William Lane. "Another Glance at Trinity Monotheism." In *Philosophical and Theological Essays on the Trinity*, edited by Thomas McCall and Michael Rea, 126–30. Oxford: Oxford University Press, 2009.

Craig, William Lane. "Toward a Tenable Social Trinitarianism." In *Philosophical and Theological Essays on the Trinity*, edited by Thomas McCall and Michael Rea, 89–99. Oxford: Oxford University Press, 2009.

Craig, William Lane, and James Porter Moreland. "The Trinity." In *Philosophical Foundations for a Christian Worldview*, 575–94. 2nd ed. Downers Grove, IL: IVP Academic, 2017.

Cross, Richard. "Latin Trinitarianism: Some Conceptual and Historical Considerations." In *Philosophical and Theological Essays on the Trinity*, edited by Thomas McCall and Michael Rea, 201–14. Oxford: Oxford University Press, 2009.

Davidson, Matthew. "The Logical Space of Social Trinitarianism." *Faith and Philosophy* 33, no. 3 (2016): 333–57.

Davis, Stephen T., and Eric T. Yang. "Social Trinitarianism Unscathed." *Journal of Analytic Theology* 5, no. 1 (June 2017): 220.

Feenstra, Ronald J. "Trinity." In *The Cambridge Companion to Christian Philosophical Theology*, edited by Charles Taliaferro and Chad Meister, 3–14. Cambridge: Cambridge University Press, 2009.

Goetz, James. "Identical Legal Entities and the Trinity: Relative-Social Trinitarianism." *Journal of Analytic Theology* 4 (2016): 128–46.

Hasker, William. "Can Social Trinitarianism Be Monotheist?" *Faith and Philosophy* 30, no. 4 (2013): 439–43.

Hasker, William. *Metaphysics and the Tri-Personal God*. Oxford: Oxford University Press, 2017.

Hasker, William. "The One Divine Nature." *TheoLogica: An International Journal for Philosophy of Religion and Philosophical Theology* 3, no. 1 (June 19, 2018).

Hughes, Christopher. "Defending the Consistency of the Doctrine of the Trinity." In *Philosophical and Theological Essays on the Trinity*, edited by Thomas McCall and Michael Rea, 293–313. Oxford: Oxford University Press, 2009.

Jedwab, Joseph. "Against the Geachian Theory of the Trinity and Incarnation." *Faith and Philosophy* 32, no. 2 (2015): 125–45.

Leftow, Brian. "Time Travel and the Trinity." *Faith and Philosophy* 29, no. 3 (2012): 313–24.

Leftow, Brian. "The Trinity Is Unconstitutional." *Religious Studies* 54, no. 3 (September 2018): 359–76.

McCall, Thomas H. *Which Trinity? Whose Monotheism? Philosophical and Systematic Theologians on the Metaphysics of Trinitarian Theology*. Grand Rapids, MI: William B. Eerdmans, 2010.

McCall, Thomas H., and Michael C. Rea, eds. *Philosophical and Theological Essays on the Trinity*. Oxford: Oxford University Press, 2009.

Merricks, Trenton. "Split Brains and the Godhead." In *Knowledge and Reality: Essays in Honor of Alvin Plantinga*, edited by Thomas Crisp, David Vander Laan, and Matthew Davidson, 299–326. Dordrecht: Springer, 2006.

Migliorini, Damiano. "Eternal Immolation: Could a Trinitarian Coordinating-Concept for Theistic Metaphysics Solve the Problems of Theodicy?" *International Journal of Philosophy and Theology* 5, no. 1 (2017): 18–35.

Mosser, Carl. "Fully Social Trinitarianism." In *Philosophical and Theological Essays on the Trinity*, edited by Thomas McCall and Michael Rea, 131–50. Oxford: Oxford University Press, 2009.

Mullins, R. T. "Divine Temporality, the Trinity, and the Charge of Arianism." *Journal of Analytic Theology* 4, no. 1 (2016): 267–90.

Mullins, R. T. "Hasker on the Divine Processions of the Trinitarian Persons." *European Journal for Philosophy of Religion* 9, no. 4 (2017): 181–216.

Pickup, Martin. "The Trinity and Extended Simples." *Faith and Philosophy* 33, no. 4 (2016): 414–40.

Pruss, Alexander R. "Brower and Rea's Constitution Account of the Trinity." In *Philosophical and Theological Essays on the Trinity*, edited by Thomas McCall and Michael Rea, 314–25. Oxford: Oxford University Press, 2009.

Rea, Michael C. "The Trinity." In *The Oxford Handbook of Philosophical Theology*, edited by Thomas P. Flint and Michael C. Rea, 403–29. Oxford: Oxford University Press, 2009.

Swinburne, Richard. "The Trinity." In *Philosophical and Theological Essays on the Trinity*, edited by Thomas McCall and Michael Rea, 18–37. Oxford: Oxford University Press, 2009.
Swinburne, Richard. "A Posteriori Arguments for the Trinity." *Studia Neoaristotelica* 10, no. 1 (2013): 13–27.
Tuggy, Dale. "On Positive Mysterianism." *International Journal for Philosophy of Religion* 69, no. 3 (2011): 205–26.
Tuggy, Dale. "Constitution Trinitarianism." *Philosophy and Theology* 25, no. 1 (2013): 129–62.
Tuggy, Dale. "Hasker's Quests for a Viable Social Theory." *Faith and Philosophy* 30, no. 2 (2013): 171–87.
van Inwagen, Peter. "And Yet They Are Not Three Gods But One God." In *Philosophical and Theological Essays on the Trinity*, edited by Thomas McCall and Michael Rea, 216–48. Oxford: Oxford University Press, 2009.
Ward, Keith. *Christ and the Cosmos: A Reformulation of Trinitarian Doctrine*. Cambridge: Cambridge University Press, 2015.
Williams, Scott M. "Indexicals and the Trinity: Two Non-Social Models." *Journal of Analytic Theology* 1, no. 1 (2013): 74–94.
Williams, Scott M. "Unity of Action: A Latin Social Model of the Trinity." *Faith and Philosophy* 34, no. 3 (2017): 321–46.
Yandell, Keith. "How Many Times Does Three Go Into One?" In *Philosophical and Theological Essays on the Trinity*, edited by Thomas McCall and Michael Rea, 151–68. Oxford: Oxford University Press, 2009.

Divine Attributes: General

Crisp, Oliver D. "Incorporeality." In *The Routledge Companion to Philosophy of Religion*, edited by Chad V. Meister and Paul Copan, 2nd ed., 344–55. Abingdon, Oxon: Routledge, 2013.
Göcke, Benedikt Paul, and Christian Tapp, eds. *The Infinity of God: New Perspectives in Theology and Philosophy*. Notre Dame, IN: University of Notre Dame Press, 2019.
Makin, Mark. "God from God: The Essential Dependence Model of Eternal Generation." *Religious Studies* 54, no. 3 (2018): 377–94.
Mawson, T. J. *The Divine Attributes*. Elements in the Philosophy of Religion. Cambridge: Cambridge University Press, 2018.
McCann, Hugh J., ed. *Free Will and Classical Theism: The Significance of Freedom in Perfect Being Theology*. New York: Oxford University Press, 2017.
Morris, Thomas V. *The Concept of God*. New York: Oxford University Press, 1987.
Morris, Thomas V. *Our Idea of God: An Introduction to Philosophical Theology*. Vancouver: Regent College, 2002.
Nagasawa, Yujin. "A New Defence of Anselmian Theism." *Philosophical Quarterly* 58, no. 233 (October 2008): 577–96.
Nagasawa, Yujin. *Maximal God: A New Defence of Perfect Being Theism*. Oxford: Oxford University Press, 2017.
Plantinga, Alvin. *Does God Have a Nature?* The Aquinas Lecture 1980. Milwaukee: Marquette University Press, 1980.
Rea, Michael. "Gender as a Divine Attribute." *Religious Studies* 52, no. 1 (2016): 97–115.
Rea, Michael. *The Hiddenness of God*. Gifford Lectures. Oxford: Oxford University Press, 2018.
Swinburne, Richard. *The Coherence of Theism*. 2nd ed. Oxford: Oxford University Press, 2016.

Wierenga, Edward. "Augustinian Perfect Being Theology and the God of Abraham, Isaac, and Jacob." *International Journal for Philosophy of Religion* 69, no. 2 (April 2011): 139–51.

Divine Attributes: Aseity

Adams, Sarah, and Jon Robson. "Analyzing Aseity." *Canadian Journal of Philosophy* 50, no. 2 (February 2020): 251–67.
Craig, William Lane. "Nominalism and Divine Aseity." In *Oxford Studies in Philosophy of Religion*, edited by Jonathan L. Kvanvig, 4: 43–64. Oxford: Oxford University Press, 2012.
Craig, William Lane. *God over All: Divine Aseity and the Challenge of Platonism*. Oxford: Oxford University Press, 2016.
Craig, William Lane. *God and Abstract Objects: The Coherence of Theism: Aseity*. New York: Springer, 2017.
Gould, Paul M., ed. *Beyond the Control of God? Six Views on the Problem of God and Abstract Objects*. New York: Bloomsbury, 2014.
Gould, Paul M., and Richard Brian Davis. "Where the Bootstrapping Really Lies: A Neo-Aristotelian Reply to Panchuk." *International Philosophical Quarterly* 57, no. 4 (2017): 415–28.
McBrayer, Landon. "Cartesian Aseity in the Third Meditation." *Journal of Analytic Theology* 6, no. 1 (December 22, 2018): 217–33.
McCall, Tom. "Holy Love and Divine Aseity in the Theology of John Zizioulas." *Scottish Journal of Theology* 61, no. 2 (May 2008): 191–205.
Panchuk, Michelle. "Created and Uncreated Things: A Neo-Augustinian Solution to the Bootstrapping Problem." *International Philosophical Quarterly* 56, no. 1 (2016): 99–112.

Divine Attributes: Benevolence

Adams, Marilyn McCord. "Duns Scotus on the Goodness of God." *Faith and Philosophy* 4, no. 4 (1987): 486–505.
Adams, Marilyn McCord. *Horrendous Evils and the Goodness of God*. Ithaca, NY: Cornell University Press, 1999.
Adams, Robert M. "Must God Create the Best." In *The Concept of God*, edited by Thomas V. Morris, 91–106. New York: Oxford University Press, 1987.
Alexander, David E., and Daniel M. Johnson, eds. *Calvinism & the Problem of Evil*. Eugene, OR: Pickwick Publications, 2016.
Arcadi, James, Oliver D. Crisp, and Jordan Wessling, eds. *Love, Divine, and Human: Contemporary Essays in Systematic and Philosophical Theology*. New York: T&T Clark, 2019.
Byerly, T. Ryan. "The All-Powerful, Perfectly Good, and Free God." In *Oxford Studies in Philosophy of Religion*, edited by Jonathan L. Kvanvig, 8: 16–46. Oxford: Oxford University Press, 2017.
Hare, John E. "Goodness." In *The Cambridge Companion to Christian Philosophical Theology*, edited by Charles Taliaferro and Chad Meister, 66–80. Cambridge: Cambridge University Press, 2009.
Morris, Thomas V. "Duty and Divine Goodness." In *The Concept of God*, 107–22. New York: Oxford University Press, 1987.
Murphy, Mark C. "Holy, Holy, Holy: Divine Holiness and Divine Perfection." *Religious Studies* 56, no. 2 (June 2020): 231–55.

Stump, Eleonore. *Wandering in Darkness: Narrative and the Problem of Suffering.* Oxford: Clarendon Press, 2010.
Wessling, Jordan. *Love Divine: A Systematic Account of God's Love for Humanity.* Oxford: Oxford University Press, 2020.

Divine Attributes: Impassibility

Creel, Richard E. *Divine Impassibility: An Essay in Philosophical Theology.* Cambridge: Cambridge University Press, 1986.
Creel, Richard E. "Immutability and Impassibility." In *A Companion to the Philosophy of Religion*, edited by Philip L. Quinn and Charles Taliaferro, 313–22. Cambridge, MA: Blackwell, 1999.
Gavrilyuk, Paul L. *The Suffering of the Impassible God: The Dialectics of Patristic Thought.* New York: Oxford University Press, 2004.
Marshall, Bruce D. "The Dereliction of Christ and the Impassibility of God." In *Divine Impassibility and the Mystery of Human Suffering*, edited by James Keating and Thomas Joseph White, 246–98. Grand Rapids, MI: Eerdmans, 2009.
Mullins, R. T. "Why Can't the Impassible God Suffer? Analytic Reflections on Divine Blessedness." *TheoLogica: An International Journal for Philosophy of Religion and Philosophical Theology* 2, no. 1 (March 27, 2018): 3–22.
Weinandy, Thomas G. *Does God Suffer?* Notre Dame, IN: University of Notre Dame, 2000.

Divine Attributes: Necessity

Leftow, Brian. "Necessity." In *The Cambridge Companion to Christian Philosophical Theology*, edited by Charles Taliaferro and Chad Meister, 15–30. Cambridge: Cambridge University Press, 2009.
Leftow, Brian. *God and Necessity.* Oxford: Oxford University Press, 2012.
Mann, William E. *God, Modality, and Morality.* Oxford; New York: Oxford University Press, 2015.
Pruss, Alexander R., and Joshua L. Rasmussen. *Necessary Existence.* Oxford: Oxford University Press, 2018.

Divine Attributes: Divine Knowledge and Omniscience

Alston, William P. "Divine Foreknowledge and Alternative Conceptions of Human Freedom." In *Divine Nature and Human Language: Essays in Philosophical Theology*, 162–77. Ithaca, NY: Cornell University Press, 1989.
Alston, William P. "Does God Have Beliefs?" In *Divine Nature and Human Language: Essays in Philosophical Theology*, 178–96. Ithaca, NY: Cornell University Press, 1989.
Arbour, Benjamin H. *Philosophical Essays against Open Theism.* New York: Routledge, 2018.
Beilby, James K., Paul R. Eddy, and Gregory A. Boyd, eds. *Divine Foreknowledge: Four Views.* Downers Grove, IL: InterVarsity Press, 2001.
Bignon, Guillame. *Excusing Sinners and Blaming God: A Calvinist Assessment of Determinism, Moral Responsibility, and Divine Involvement in Evil.* Princeton Theological Monograph Series. Eugene, OR: Pickwick Publications, 2018.
Blumenfeld, David. "On the Compossibility of the Divine Attributes." In *The Concept of God*, edited by Thomas V. Morris, 201–16. New York: Oxford University Press, 1987.

Byerly, T. Ryan. "God Knows the Future by Ordering the Times." In *Oxford Studies in Philosophy of Religion*, edited by Jonathan L. Kvanvig, 5: 18–39. Oxford: Oxford University Press, 2014.

Craig, William Lane. *The Only Wise God: The Compatibility of Divine Foreknowledge and Human Freedom*. Reprinted. Eugene, OR: Wipf and Stock, 2000.

Dickinson, Travis M. "God Knows: Acquaintance and the Nature of Divine Knowledge." *Religious Studies* 55, no. 1 (2019): 1–16.

Hasker, William. *God, Time, and Knowledge*. Ithaca, NY: Cornell University Press, 1998.

Laing, John D., Kirk R. MacGregor, and Greg Welty, eds. *Calvinism and Middle Knowledge: A Conversation*. Eugene, OR: Pickwick Publications, 2019.

Peels, Rik. "Can God Repent?" In *Oxford Studies in Philosophy of Religion.*, edited by Jonathan L. Kvanvig, 7: 190–212. New York: Oxford University Press, 2016.

Perszyk, Kenneth J., ed. *Molinism: The Contemporary Debate*. Oxford: Oxford University Press, 2011.

Wierenga, Edward. "Omniscience." In *The Oxford Handbook of Philosophical Theology*, edited by Thomas P. Flint and Michael C. Rea, 129–44. Oxford: Oxford University Press, 2009.

Zagzebski, Linda Trinkaus. *The Dilemma of Freedom and Foreknowledge*. New York: Oxford University Press, 1996.

Zagzebski, Linda Trinkaus. "Omnisubjectivity." In *Oxford Studies in Philosophy of Religion*, edited by Jon Kvanvig, 1: 231–48. Oxford: Oxford University Press, 2008.

Divine Attributes: Omnipresence and Immensity

Arcadi, James M. "God Is Where God Acts: Reconceiving Divine Omnipresence." *Topoi* 36, no. 4 (December 1, 2017): 631–39.

Cross, Richard. "Duns Scotus on Divine Immensity." *Faith and Philosophy* 33, no. 4 (2016): 389–413.

Gasser, Georg. "God's Omnipresence in the World: On Possible Meanings of 'En' in Panentheism." *International Journal for Philosophy of Religion* 85, no. 1 (February 2019): 43–62.

Hudson, Hud. "Omnipresence." In *The Oxford Handbook of Philosophical Theology*, edited by Michael C. Rea and Thomas P. Flint, 199–216. New York: Oxford University Press, 2011.

Inman, Ross D. "Omnipresence and the Location of the Immaterial." In *Oxford Studies in Philosophy of Religion*, edited by Jonathan L. Kvanvig, 8: 168–206. Oxford: Oxford University Press, 2017.

Pruss, Alexander R. "Omnipresence, Multilocation, the Real Presence and Time Travel." *Journal of Analytic Theology* 1, no. 1 (2013): 60–73.

Wainwright, William J. "Omnipotence, Omniscience, and Omnipresence." In *The Cambridge Companion to Christian Philosophical Theology*, edited by Charles Taliaferro and Chad Meister, 46–65. Cambridge: Cambridge University Press, 2009.

Divine Attributes: Divine Power, Providence, and Action

Abraham, William J. *Divine Agency and Divine Action, Volume 1: Exploring and Evaluating the Debate*. New York: Oxford University Press, 2017 (see also Volumes 2 and 3).

Copan, Paul, and William Lane Craig. *Creation Out of Nothing: A Biblical, Philosophical, and Scientific Exploration*. Grand Rapids, MI: Baker Academic Press, 2004.

Craig, William Lane, and James Porter Moreland. "Creation Providence and Miracle." In *Philosophical Foundations for a Christian Worldview*, 556–74. 2nd ed. Downers Grove, IL: IVP Academic, 2017.

Crisp, Oliver D. "Meticulous Providence." In *Divine Action and Providence: Explorations in Constructive Dogmatics*, edited by Oliver D. Crisp and Fred Sanders, 21–39. Grand Rapids, MI: Zondervan, 2019.

Flint, Thomas P. "Divine Providence." In *The Oxford Handbook of Philosophical Theology*, edited by Michael C. Rea and Thomas P. Flint, 262–82. Oxford: Oxford University Press, 2011.

Flint, Thomas P., and Alfred J. Freddoso. "Maximal Power. In *The Concept of God*, edited by Thomas V. Morris, 134–68. New York: Oxford University Press, 1987.

Leftow, Brian. "Omnipotence." In *The Oxford Handbook of Philosophical Theology*, edited by Thomas P. Flint and Michael C. Rea, 167–98. Oxford: Oxford University Press, 2009.

McCann, Hugh J. *Creation and the Sovereignty of God*. Bloomington: Indiana University Press, 2012.

Schneider, Christina. "'God's Acting upon the World' – A Meta-Metaphysical Perspective." *TheoLogica: An International Journal for Philosophy of Religion and Philosophical Theology* 1, no. 1 (July 19, 2017): 171–87.

Spencer, Mark K. "Quantum Randomness, Hylomorphism, and Classical Theism." *Journal of Analytic Theology* 4 (May 6, 2016): 147.

Divine Attributes: Simplicity

Bergmann, Michael, and Jeffrey Brower. "A Theistic Argument against Platonism (and in Support of Truthmakers and Divine Simplicity)." In *Oxford Studies in Metaphysics*, edited by Dean W. Zimmerman, 2: 357–36. Oxford: Oxford University Press, 2006.

Brower, Jeffrey E. "Simplicity and Aseity." In *The Oxford Handbook of Philosophical Theology*, edited by Michael C. Rea and Thomas P. Flint, 105–28. New York: Oxford University Press, 2009.

Crisp, Oliver. "Divine Simplicity." In *Analyzing Doctrine: Toward a Systematic Theology*, 53–75. Waco: Baylor University Press, 2019.

Davies, Brian. "Simplicity." In *The Cambridge Companion to Christian Philosophical Theology*, edited by Charles Taliaferro and Chad Meister, 31–45. Cambridge: Cambridge University Press, 2009.

Dolezal, James E. *God without Parts: Divine Simplicity and the Metaphysics of God's Absoluteness*. Eugene, OR: Pickwick Publications, 2011.

Grant, W. Matthews. "Divine Simplicity, Contingent Truths, and Extrinsic Models of Divine Knowing." *Faith and Philosophy* 29, no. 3 (2012): 254–74.

Long, D. Stephen. "The Logical Question: Analytic Theology." In *The Perfectly Simple Triune God: Aquinas and His Legacy*. Minneapolis: Fortress Press, 2016.

Rogers, Katherin A. *Perfect Being Theology*. Edinburgh: Edinburgh University Press, 2000.

Tomaszewski, Christopher. "Collapsing the Modal Collapse Argument: On an Invalid Argument against Divine Simplicity." *Analysis* 79, no. 2 (April, 2019): 275–84.

Divine Attributes: Eternality and Temporality

Craig, William Lane. *Time and Eternity: Exploring God's Relationship to Time*. Wheaton: Crossway Books, 2001.

Craig, William Lane. "Divine Eternity." In *The Oxford Handbook of Philosophical Theology*, edited by Thomas P. Flint and Michael C. Rea, 145–66. Oxford: Oxford University Press, 2009.
Deng, Natalja. *God and Time*. Cambridge: Cambridge University Press, 2018.
DeWeese, Garrett J. *God and the Nature of Time*. Aldershot: Ashgate, 2004.
Ganssle, Gregory E., and Paul Helm, eds. *God & Time: Four Views*. Downers Grove, IL: InterVarsity Press, 2001.
Ganssle, Gregory E., and David M. Woodruff, eds. *God and Time: Essays on the Divine Nature*. Oxford: Oxford University Press, 2002.
Hasker, William. *God, Time, and Knowledge*. Ithaca, NY: Cornell University Press, 1998.
Hasker, William. "Eternity and Providence." In *The Cambridge Companion to Christian Philosophical Theology*, edited by Charles Taliaferro and Chad Meister, 81–92. Cambridge: Cambridge University Press, 2009.
Helm, Paul. *Eternal God: A Study of God without Time*. 2nd ed. Oxford: Oxford University Press, 2010.
Leftow, Brian. *Time and Eternity*. Ithaca, NY: Cornell University Press, 1991.
Loftin, R. Keith. "On the Metaphysics of Time and Divine Eternality." *Philosophia Christi* 17, no. 1 (2015): 177–87.
Mawson, T. J. "Divine Eternity." *International Journal for Philosophy of Religion* 64, no. 1 (2008): 35–50.
Mullins, R. T. "Doing Hard Time: Is God the Prisoner of the Oldest Dimension?" *Journal of Analytic Theology* 2, no. 1 (2014): 160–85.
Mullins, R. T. *The End of the Timeless God*. Oxford: Oxford University Press, 2016.
Padgett, Alan G. "Eternity." In *The Routledge Companion to Philosophy of Religion*, edited by Chad V. Meister and Paul Copan, 335–43. 2nd ed. Abingdon, Oxon: Routledge, 2013.
Stump, Eleonore, and Norman Kretzmann. "Eternity." In *The Concept of God*, edited by Thomas V. Morris, 219–252. New York: Oxford University Press, 1987.
Tapp, Christian, and Edmund Runggaldier, eds. *God, Eternity, and Time*. Burlington, VT: Ashgate, 2011.

Pneumatology

Abraham, William J. "The Epistemological Significance of the Inner Witness of the Holy Spirit." *Faith and Philosophy* 7, no. 4 (1990): 434–50.
Adams, Marilyn McCord. "The Indwelling of the Holy Spirit: Some Alternative Models." In *The Philosophy of Human Nature in Christian Perspective*, edited by Peter J. Weigel and Joseph Gilbert Prud'homme, 83–100. Washington College Studies in Religion, Politics, and Culture. New York: Peter Lang, 2016.
Alston, William. "The Indwelling of the Holy Spirit." In *Philosophy and the Christian Faith*, edited by Thomas V. Morris, 121–31. Notre Dame, IN: University of Notre Dame Press, 1988.
Kroll, Kimberley. "Indwelling without the Indwelling Holy Spirit: A Critique of Ray Yeo's Modified Account." *Journal of Analytic Theology*, no. 1 (July 19, 2019): 124–41.
Leidenhag, Mikael, and Joanna Leidenhag. "Science and Spirit: A Critical Examination of Amos Yong's Pneumatological Theology of Emergence." *Open Theology* 1, no. 1 (January 27, 2015): 425–35.
Moser, Paul K. "The Inner Witness of the Spirit." In *The Oxford Handbook of the Epistemology of Theology*, edited by William J. Abraham and Frederick D. Aquino, 111–24. Oxford: Oxford University Press, 2017.

Stump, Eleonore. "Omnipresence, Indwelling, and the Second-Personal." *European Journal for Philosophy of Religion* 5, no. 4 (December 22, 2013): 29–53.

Yeo, Ray S. "Towards a Model of Indwelling: A Conversation with Jonathan Edwards and William Alston." *Journal of Analytic Theology* 2 (2014): 210–37.

Christology and Incarnation

Adams, Marilyn McCord. "Christ and Horrors: The Coherence of Christology." *International Journal for Philosophy of Religion* 64, no. 3 (2008): 161–5.

Adams, Marilyn McCord. "Christ as God-Man, Metaphysically Construed." In *Oxford Readings in Philosophical Theology: Volume 1: Trinity, Incarnation, Atonement*, edited by Michael Rea, 239–63. Oxford: Oxford University Press, 2009.

Arcadi, James M. "Impanation, Incarnation, and Enabling Externalism." *Religious Studies* 51, no. 1 (2015): 75–90.

Arcadi, James M. "Kryptic or Cryptic? The Divine Preconscious Model of the Incarnation as a Concrete-Nature Christology." *Neue Zeitschrift für Systematicsche Theologie Und Religionsphilosophie* 58, no. 2 (2016): 229–43.

Arcadi, James M. "Recent Developments in Analytic Christology." *Philosophy Compass* 13, no. 4 (2018): 1–12.

Archer, Joel. "Kenosis, Omniscience, and the Anselmian Concept of Divinity." *Religious Studies* 54, no. 2 (2018): 201–13.

Chan, J. H. W. "A Cartesian Approach to the Incarnation." In *The Ashgate Research Companion to Theological Anthropology*, edited by Joshua R. Farris and Charles Taliaferro, 355–67. New York: Routledge, 2016.

Coakley, Sarah. "What Does Chalcedon Solve and What Does It Not? Some Reflections on the Status and Meaning of the Chalcedonian 'Definition'." In *The Incarnation*, edited by Stephen T. Davis, Daniel Kendall, and Gerald O'Collins, 143–63. Oxford: Oxford University Press, 2004.

Conn, Christopher Hughes. "Relative Identity, Singular Reference, and the Incarnation: A Response to Le Poidevin." *Religious Studies* 48, no. 1 (2012): 61–82.

Craig, William Lane, "Is God the Son Begotten in His Divine Nature?" *TheoLogica: An International Journal for Philosophy of Religion and Philosophical Theology* 2, no. 3 (December 12, 2018): 22–32.

Craig, William Lane, and James Porter Moreland. "The Incarnation." In *Philosophical Foundations for a Christian Worldview*, 595–611. 2nd ed. Downers Grove, IL: IVP Academic, 2017.

Crisp, Oliver. "On the 'Fittingness' of the Virgin Birth." *Heythrop Journal* 49, no. 2 (2008): 197–221.

Crisp, Oliver. *God Incarnate: Explorations in Christology*. London: T&T Clark, 2009.

Crisp, Oliver. "Compositional Christology without Nestorianism." In *The Metaphysics of the Incarnation*, edited by Anna Marmodoro and Jonathan Hill, 45–66. Oxford: Oxford University Press, 2011.

Crisp, Oliver. "A Christological Model of the Imago Dei." In *The Ashgate Research Companion to Theological Anthropology*, edited by Joshua R. Farris and Charles Taliaferro, 217–31. New York: Routledge, 2016.

Crisp, Oliver. *The Word Enfleshed: Exploring the Person and Work of Christ*. Grand Rapids, MI: Baker Academic, 2016.

Davis, Stephen. "The Metaphysics of Kenosis." In *The Metaphysics of the Incarnation*, edited by Anna Marmodoro and Jonathan Hill, 114–33. Oxford: Oxford University Press, 2011.

Deweese, Garrett. "One Person, Two Natures: Two Metaphysical Models of the Incarnation. In *Jesus in Trinitarian Perspective*, edited by Fred Sanders and Klaus Issler, 114–53. Nashville: B&H, 2007.

Evans, C. Stephen. *Exploring Kenotic Christology: The Self-Emptying of God*. Oxford: Oxford University Press, 2006.

Flint, Thomas. "Should Concretists Part with Mereological Models of the Incarnation?" In *The Metaphysics of the Incarnation*, edited by Anna Marmodoro and Jonathan Hill, 67–87. Oxford: Oxford University Press, 2011.

Flint, Thomas. "Molinism and Incarnation." In *Molinism: The Contemporary Debate*, edited by Ken Perszyk, 187–207. Oxford: Oxford University Press, 2012.

Flint, Thomas. "Orthodoxy and Incarnation: A Reply to Mullins." *Journal of Analytic Theology* 4 (2016): 180–92.

Gordon, James R. *The Holy One in Our Midst: An Essay on the Flesh of Christ*. Minneapolis: Fortress Press, 2016.

Guta, Mihretu P. "The Two Natures of the Incarnate Christ and the Bearer Question." *TheoLogica: An International Journal for Philosophy of Religion and Philosophical Theology* 2, no. 3 (January 19, 2019): 113–43.

Hill, Jonathan. "Aquinas and the Unity of Christ: A Defence of Compositionalism." *International Journal for Philosophy of Religion* 71 no. 2 (2012): 117–35.

Holland, Richard A. *God, Time, and the Incarnation*. Eugene, OR: Wipf and Stock, 2012.

Le Poidevin, Robin. "Identity and the Composite Christ: An Incarnational Dilemma." *Religious Studies* 45, no. 2 (2009): 167–86.

Le Poidevin, Robin. "The Incarnation: Divine Embodiment and the Divided Mind." *Royal Institute of Philosophy Supplement* 68 (2011): 269–85.

Leftow, Brian. "Against Materialist Christology." In *Christian Philosophy of Religion: Essays in Honor of Stephen T. Davis*, edited by C. P. Ruloff. Notre Dame, IN: University of Notre Dame Press, 2015.

Leftow, Brian. "Composition and Christology." *Faith and Philosophy* 28, no. 3 (2011): 310–22.

Leftow, Brian. "A Timeless God Incarnate." In *The Incarnation*, edited by Stephen T. Davis, Daniel Kendall, and Gerald O'Collins, 273–99. Oxford: Oxford University Press, 2004.

Loke, Andrew. *A Kryptic Model of the Incarnation*. New York: Routledge, 2016.

Loke, Andrew. "On the Two Consciousnesses Model: An Assessment of James Arcadi's Defense." *Journal of Analytic Theology* 6 (July 19, 2018): 146–50.

McIntosh, Jonathan. "Christ, the Power and Possibility of God in St. Anselm of Canterbury." *TheoLogica: An International Journal for Philosophy of Religion and Philosophical Theology* 2, no. 3 (December 12, 2018): 3–21.

McManus, Skylar D. "Oneness Pentecostalism, the Two-Minds View, and the Problem of Jesus's Prayers." *TheoLogica: An International Journal for Philosophy of Religion and Philosophical Theology* 2, no. 3 (January 14, 2019): 60–87.

Morris, Thomas V. *The Logic of God Incarnate*. Eugene, OR: Wipf and Stock, 2001.

Mullins, R. T. "Flint's Molinism and the Incarnation Is Too Radical." *Journal of Analytic Theology* 3 (May, 2015): 109–23.

Paul, Emily. "Incarnation, Divine Timelessness, and Modality." *TheoLogica: An International Journal for Philosophy of Religion and Philosophical Theology* 2, no. 3 (January 17, 2019): 88–112.

Pawl, Timothy. *In Defense of Conciliar Christology: A Philosophical Essay.* Oxford: Oxford University Press, 2016.
Pawl, Timothy. *In Defense of Extended Conciliar Christology: A Philosophical Essay.* Oxford: Oxford University Press, 2019.
Pawl, Timothy. "A Solution to the Fundamental Philosophical Problem of Christology." *Journal of Analytic Theology* 2 (2014): 61–85.
Rea, Michael C. "Hylomorphism and the Incarnation." In *The Metaphysics of the Incarnation*, edited by Anna Marmodoro and Jonathan Hill, 134–52. Oxford: Oxford University Press, 2011.
Rogers, Katherin A. "The Compositional Account of the Incarnation." *Faith and Philosophy* 24, no. 1 (2007): 52–71.
Rogers, Katherin A. "Christ's Freedom: Anselm vs Molina." *Religious Studies* 52, no. 4 (2016): 497–512.
Swinburne, Richard. "The Coherence of the Chalcedonian Definition of the Incarnation." In *The Metaphysics of the Incarnation*, edited by Anna Marmodoro and Jonathan Hill, 153–67. Oxford: Oxford University Press, 2011.
Turner, James T., Jr. "Hylemorphism, Rigid Designators, and the Disembodied 'Jesus': A Call for Clarification." *Religious Studies* (March 11, 2019): 1–16.
Van Horn, Luke. "Merricks's Soulless Savior." *Faith and Philosophy* 27, no. 3 (2010): 330–41.
Vidu, Adonis. "Trinitarian Inseparable Operations and the Incarnation." *Journal of Analytic Theology* 4, no. 1 (May 6, 2016): 106–27.
Wessling, Jordan. "Christology and Conciliar Authority." In *Christology Ancient and Modern: Explorations in Constructive Dogmatics*, edited by Fred Sanders and Oliver D. Crisp, 151–70. Grand Rapids, MI: Zondervan, 2013.

Soteriology and Atonement

Adams, Marilyn McCord. "Plantinga on 'Felix Culpa'." *Faith and Philosophy* 25, no. 2 (2008): 123–40.
Bayne, Tim, and Greg Restall. "A Participatory Model of the Atonement." In *New Waves in Philosophy of Religion*, edited by Yujin Nagasawa and Erik J. Wielenberg, 150–66. New York: Palgrave-Macmillan, 2009.
Craig, William Lane. *Atonement and the Death of Christ: An Exegetical, Historical, and Philosophical Exploration.* Waco: Baylor University Press, 2020.
Craig, William Lane, and James Porter Moreland. "Atonement." In *Philosophical Foundations for a Christian Worldview*, 612–27. 2nd ed. Downers Grove, IL: IVP Academic, 2017.
Crisp, Oliver. *Approaching the Atonement: The Reconciling Work of Christ.* Downers Grove, IL: Inter Varsity Press, 2020.
Crisp, Oliver. "Is Ransom Enough?" *Journal of Analytic Theology* 3 (2015): 1–16.
Crisp, Oliver. "Original Sin and Atonement." In *The Oxford Handbook of Philosophical Theology*, edited by Thomas P. Flint and Michael C. Rea. Oxford: Oxford University Press, 2008.
Davis, Stephen T, Daniel Kendall, and Gerald O'Collins, eds. *The Redemption: An Interdisciplinary Symposium on Christ as Redeemer.* Oxford: Oxford University Press, 2012.
Evans, Craig A. "Jesus' Self-Designation 'The Son of Man' and the Recognition of His Divinity." In *Oxford Readings in Philosophical Theology: Volume 1: Trinity, Incarnation, and Atonement*, edited by Michael C. Rea, 151–65. Oxford: Oxford University Press, 2009.

Farris, Joshua R., and S. Mark Hamilton. "Reparative Substitution and the 'Efficacy Objection': Toward a Modified Satisfaction Theory of Atonement." *Perichoresis* 15, no. 3 (October 1, 2017): 97–110.
Graham, Gordon. "Atonement." In *The Cambridge Companion to Christian Philosophical Theology*, edited by Charles Taliaferro and Chad V. Meister, 124–35. Cambridge: Cambridge University Press, 2009.
Hare, John E. "Atonement, Justification, and Sanctification." In *A Companion to Philosophy of Religion*. 2nd ed. Malden, MA: Wiley-Blackwell, 2010.
Hill, Daniel J., and Joseph Jedwab. "Atonement and the Concept of Punishment. In *Locating Atonement*, edited by Oliver D. Crisp and Fred Sanders, 139–53. Grand Rapids, MI: Zondervan, 2015.
Moser, Paul K. "Sin and Salvation." In *The Cambridge Companion to Christian Philosophical Theology*, edited by Charles Taliaferro and Chad Meister, 136–51. Cambridge: Cambridge University Press, 2009.
Murphy, Mark C. "Not Penal Substitution but Vicarious Punishment." *Faith and Philosophy* 26, no. 3 (2009): 253–73.
Porter, Steven. "Swinburnian Atonement and the Doctrine of Penal Substitution." *Faith and Philosophy* 21, no. 2 (2004): 228–41.
Strabbing, Jada Twedt. "The Permissibility of the Atonement as Penal Substitution." In *Oxford Studies in Philosophy of Religion*, edited by Jonathan L. Kvanvig, 7: 240–70. Oxford: Oxford University Press, 2016.
Stump, Eleonore. *Atonement*. Oxford: Oxford University Press, 2018.
Swinburne, Richard. *Responsibility and Atonement*. Oxford: Clarendon Press, 1989.
Thurow, Joshua. "Communal Substitutionary Atonement." *Journal of Analytic Theology* 3 (May 4, 2015): 47–65.
Woznicki, Christopher. "Do We Believe in Consequences? Revisiting the 'Incoherence Objection' to Penal Substitution." *Neue Zeitschrift für Systematische Theologie und Religionsphilosophie* 60, no. 2 (2018): 208–28.

Theological Anthropology

Baker, Mark C., and Stewart Goetz, eds. *The Soul Hypothesis: Investigations into the Existence of the Soul*. New York: Continuum, 2011.
Coakley, Sarah. "Analytic Philosophy of Religion in Feminist Perspective: Some Questions." In *Powers and Submissions*, 98–105. Malden, MA: Blackwell, 2002.
Cooper, John W. *Body, Soul, and Life Everlasting: Biblical Anthropology and the Monism-Dualism Debate*. Grand Rapids, MI: Eerdmans, 2000.
Crisp, Thomas M., Steven L. Porter, and Gregg Ten Elshof, eds. *Neuroscience and the Soul: The Human Person in Philosophy, Science, and Theology*. Grand Rapids, MI: William B. Eerdmans, 2016.
Farris, Joshua R. *The Soul of Theological Anthropology: A Cartesian Exploration*. New York: Routledge, 2016.
Farris, Joshua R. "An Immaterial Substance View: Imago Dei in Creation and Redemption." *The Heythrop Journal* 58, no. 1 (2017): 108–23.
Farris, Joshua R., and Charles Taliaferro, eds. *The Ashgate Research Companion to Theological Anthropology*. New York: Routledge, 2016.

Gasser, Georg. *Personal Identity and Resurrection: How Do We Survive Our Death?* New York: Routledge, 2010.

Loftin, R. Keith, Joshua R. Farris, and Thomas H. McCall, eds. *Christian Physicalism? Philosophical Theological Criticisms*. Lanham: Lexington Books, 2018.

McLeod-Harrison, Mark S. "On Being the Literal Image of God." *Journal of Analytic Theology* 2, no. 1 (2014): 140–59.

Moreland, James Porter. *The Recalcitrant Imago Dei: Human Persons and the Failure of Naturalism*. London: SCM Press, 2009.

Moreland, James Porter. *The Soul: How We Know It's Real and Why It Matters*. Chicago: Moody, 2014.

Turner, James T., Jr. "Temple Theology, Holistic Eschatology, and the Imago Dei: An Analytic Prolegomenon." *TheoLogica: An International Journal for Philosophy of Religion and Philosophical Theology* 2, no. 1 (March 27, 2018): 95–114.

Woznicki, Christopher. "The One and the Many: The Metaphysics of Human Nature in T.F. Torrance's Doctrine of Atonement." *Journal of Reformed Theology* 12, no. 2 (August 8, 2018): 103–26.

Anthropology: Disability

Cobb, Aaron D., and Kevin Timpe. "Disability and the Theodicy of Defeat." *Journal of Analytic Theology* 5, no. 1 (April 12, 2017): 100–20.

Mullins, R. T. "Some Difficulties for Amos Yong's Disability Theology of the Resurrection." *Ars Disputandi* 11, no. 1 (January 1, 2011): 24–32.

Timpe, Kevin. "Disabled Beatitude." In *The Lost Sheep in Philosophy of Religion: New Perspectives on Disability, Gender, Race, and Animals*, edited by Blake Hereth and Kevin Timpe, 241–63. New York: Routledge, 2019.

Williams, Scott M., ed. *Disability in Medieval Christian Philosophy and Theology*. New York: Routledge, 2020.

Anthropology: Sin

Adams, Marilyn McCord. "Sin as Uncleanness." *Philosophical Perspectives* 5 (1991): 1–27.

Crisp, Oliver D. "On Original Sin." *International Journal of Systematic Theology* 17, no. 3 (July 2015): 252–66.

Crisp, Oliver D. "Retrieving Zwingli's Doctrine of Original Sin." *Journal of Reformed Theology* 10, no. 4 (January 1, 2016): 340–60.

Franks, W. Paul. "Original Sin and Broad Free-Will Defense." *Philosophia Christi* 14, no. 2 (2012): 353–71.

Hudson, Hud. *The Fall and Hypertime*. Oxford: Oxford University Press, 2014.

McCann, Hugh J. "The Author of Sin?" *Faith and Philosophy* 22, no. 2 (2005): 144–59.

Quinn, Philip L. "Sin and Original Sin." In *A Companion to Philosophy of Religion*, edited by Charles Taliaferro, Paul Draper, and Philip L. Quinn, 614–21. 2nd ed. Malden, MA: Wiley-Blackwell, 2010.

Rea, Michael C. "The Metaphysics of Original Sin." In *Persons: Human and Divine*, edited by Peter Van Inwagen and Dean W. Zimmerman, 319–56. Oxford: Oxford University Press, 2007.

Rogers, Katherin A. "God Is Not the Author of Sin: An Anselmian Response to McCann." *Faith and Philosophy* 24, no. 3 (2007): 300–10.

Rutledge, Jonathan C. "Original Sin, the Fall, and Epistemic Self-Trust." *TheoLogica: An International Journal for Philosophy of Religion and Philosophical Theology* 2, no. 1 (March 27, 2018): 84–94.
Sullivan, Meghan. "Semantics for Blasphemy." In *Oxford Studies in Philosophy of Religion.*, edited by Jonathan L. Kvanvig, 4: 159–72. New York: Oxford University Press, 2012.
Talbott, Thomas. "Why Christians Should Not Be Determinists: Reflections on the Origin of Human Sin." *Faith and Philosophy* 25, no. 3 (2008): 300–16.
Taliaferro, Charles, and Chad V. Meister, eds. "Sin and Salvation." In *The Cambridge Companion to Christian Philosophical Theology*, 136–51. Cambridge: Cambridge University Press, 2010.
Timpe, Kevin. "The Arbitrariness of the Primal Sin." In *Oxford Studies in Philosophy of Religion*, edited by Jonathan L. Kvanvig, 5: 234–58. Oxford: Oxford University Press, 2014.
Vicens, Leigh C. "Sin and Implicit Bias." *Journal of Analytic Theology* 6, no. 1 (July 19, 2018): 100–11.

Anthropology: Free Will

Alexander, David E., and Daniel M. Johnson, eds. *Calvinism and the Problem of Evil*. Eugene, OR: Pickwick Publications, 2016.
Bignon, Guillame. *Excusing Sinners and Blaming God: A Calvinist Assessment of Determinism, Moral Responsibility, and Divine Involvement in Evil*. Princeton Theological Monograph Series. Eugene, OR: Pickwick Publications, 2018.
Couenhoven, Jesse. "The Necessities of Perfect Freedom." *International Journal of Systematic Theology* 14, no. 4 (2012): 396–419.
Kittle, Simon. "Grace and Free Will: Quiescence and Control." *Journal of Analytic Theology* 3 (May 4, 2015): 89–108.
Kittle, Simon. "Some Problems of Heavenly Freedom." *TheoLogica: An International Journal for Philosophy of Religion and Philosophical Theology* 2, no. 2 (May 24, 2018): 97–115.
McCann, Hugh J., ed. *Free Will and Classical Theism: The Significance of Freedom in Perfect Being Theology*. New York: Oxford University Press, 2017.
Timpe, Kevin. *Free Will in Philosophical Theology*. New York: Bloomsbury, 2014.
Timpe, Kevin, and Daniel Speak, eds. *Free Will and Theism: Connections, Contingencies, and Concerns*. New York: Oxford University Press, 2016.
White, Heath. *Fate and Free Will: A Defense of Theological Determinism*. Notre Dame, IN: University of Notre Dame Press, 2019.

Ecclesiology and Liturgy

Abraham, William J. "Church." In *The Cambridge Companion to Christian Philosophical Theology*, edited by Charles Taliaferro and Chad Meister, 170–82. Cambridge: Cambridge University Press, 2009.
Adams, Marilyn McCord. *Some Later Medieval Theories of the Eucharist: Thomas Aquinas, Gilles of Rome, Duns Scotus, and William Ockham*. Oxford: Oxford University Press, 2010.
Arcadi, James M. "Recent Philosophical Work on the Doctrine of the Eucharist." *Philosophy Compass* 11, no. 7 (July 2016): 402–12.
Arcadi, James M. "Idealism and Participating in the Body of Christ." In *Idealism and Christianity*, edited by Joshua Ryan Farris and S. Mark Hamilton, 197–216. New York: Bloomsbury Academic, 2016.

Arcadi, James M. *An Incarnational Model of the Eucharist*. Cambridge : Cambridge University Press, 2018.

Cockayne, Joshua. "Analytic Ecclesiology: The Social Ontology of the Church." *Journal of Analytic Theology* 7 (July 19, 2019): 100–23.

Cockayne, Joshua, and David Efird. "Common Worship." *Faith and Philosophy* 35, no. 3 (2018): 299–325.

Cockayne, Joshua, David Efird, Gordon Haynes, Daniel Molto, Richard Tamburro, Jack Warman, and August Ludwigs. "Experiencing the Real Presence of Christ in the Eucharist." *Journal of Analytic Theology* 5 (April 12, 2017): 175–96.

Cuneo, Terence. "Liturgical Immersion." *Journal of Analytic Theology* 2 (2014): 117–39.

Cuneo, Terence. "Rites of Remission. *Journal of Analytic Theology* 3 (May 4, 2015): 7–88.

Cuneo, Terence. *Ritualized Faith: Essays on the Philosophy of Liturgy*. Oxford: Oxford University Press, 2016.

McGuigan, Colin M., and Brad Kallenberg. "Ecclesial Practices." In *The Oxford Handbook of the Epistemology of Theology*, edited by William J. Abraham and Frederick D. Aquino, 141–56. Oxford: Oxford University Press, 2017.

Pickup, Martin. "Real Presence in the Eucharist and Time-Travel." *Religious Studies* 51, no. 3 (September 2015): 379–89.

Pruss, Alexander R. "The Eucharist: Real Presence and Real Absence." In *The Oxford Handbook of Philosophical Theology*, edited by Michael C. Rea and Thomas P. Flint, 512–37. Oxford: Oxford University Press, 2011.

Pruss, Alexander R. "Omnipresence, Multilocation, the Real Presence and Time Travel." *Journal of Analytic Theology* 1, no. 1 (2013): 60–73.

Taliaferro, Charles. "Religious Rites." In *The Cambridge Companion to Christian Philosophical Theology*, edited by Charles Taliaferro and Chad Meister, 183–200. Cambridge: Cambridge University Press, 2009.

Toner, Patrick. "Transubstantiation, Essentialism, and Substance." *Religious Studies* 47, no. 2 (June 2011): 217–31.

Wolterstorff, Nicholas. "Knowing God Liturgically." *Journal of Analytic Theology* 4 (May 6, 2016): 1–16.

Zagzebski, Linda. "Authority in Religious Communities." In *The Oxford Handbook of the Epistemology of Theology*, edited by William J. Abraham and Frederick D. Aquino, 97–110. Oxford: Oxford University Press, 2017.

Christian Life: Sanctification

Aquino, Frederick D. "Spiritual Formation, Authority, and Discernment." In *The Oxford Handbook of the Epistemology of Theology*, edited by William J. Abraham and Frederick D. Aquino, 157–72. Oxford: Oxford University Press, 2017.

Arcadi, James M. "A Theory of Consecration: A Philosophical Exposition of A Biblical Phenomenon." *The Heythrop Journal* 54, no. 6 (November 2013): 913–25. (Note: this article relates to consecrating objects)

Austin, Michael W. *Humility and Human Flourishing: A Study in Analytic Moral Theology*. Oxford: Oxford University Press, 2018.

Baehr, Jason. "Virtue." In *The Oxford Handbook of the Epistemology of Theology*, edited by William J. Abraham and Frederick D. Aquino, 221–34. Oxford: Oxford University Press, 2017.

Brümmer, Vincent. *The Model of Love: A Study in Philosophical Theology*. Cambridge: Cambridge University Press, 1993.
Coakley, Sarah. "Dark Contemplation and Epistemic Transformation: The Analytic Theologian Re-Meets Teresa of Avila." In *Analytic Theology: New Essays in the Philosophy of Theology*, edited by Oliver Crisp and Michael C. Rea, 280–312. Oxford: Oxford University Press, 2009.
Dunnington, Kent. *Humility, Pride, and Christian Virtue Theory*. New York: Oxford University Press, 2018.
Hector, Kevin. *The Theological Project of Modernism: Faith and the Conditions of Mineness*. Oxford: Oxford University Press, 2015.
Mittleman, Alan. "The Problem of Holiness." *Journal of Analytic Theology* 3 (May 4, 2015): 29–46.
Osmundsen, Gary, "Sanctification as Joint Agency with the Triune God: An Aristotelian Causal Model" *Philosophia Christi* 21, no. 2 (2019): 325–54.
Porter, Steven L., and Brandon Rickabaugh. "The Sanctifying Work of the Holy Spirit: Revisiting Alston's Interpersonal Model." *Journal of Analytic Theology* 6, no. 1 (July 19, 2018): 112–30.
Rickabaugh, Brandon. "Eternal Life as Knowledge of God: An Epistemology of Knowledge by Acquaintance and Spiritual Formation." *Journal of Spiritual Formation & Soul Care* 6, no. 2 (2013): 204–28.
Wessling, Jordan. "Loving Yourself as Your Neighbor: A Critique and Some Friendly Suggestions for Eleonore Stump's Neo-Thomistic Account of Love." *Sophia* 58, no. 3 (March 2019): 493–509.

Christian Life: Prayer

Brümmer, Vincent. *What Are We Doing When We Pray? On Prayer and the Nature of Faith*. Burlington, VT: Ashgate, 2008.
Choi, Isaac. "Is Petitionary Prayer Superfluous?" In *Oxford Studies in Philosophy of Religion*, edited by Jonathan L. Kvanvig, 7: 32–62. New York: Oxford University Press, 2016.
Cohoe, Caleb Murray. "God, Causality, and Petitionary Prayer." *Faith and Philosophy* 31, no. 1 (2014): 24–45.
Collins, Robin. "Prayer and Open Theism: A Participatory, Co-Creator Model." In *God in an Open Universe: Science, Metaphysics, and Open Theism*, edited by William Hasker, Thomas Jay Oord, and Dean W. Zimmerman, 161–86. Eugene, OR: Pickwick Publications, 2011.
Davison, Scott A. "On the Puzzle of Petitionary Prayer. Reply to Daniel and Frances Howard-Snyder." *European Journal for Philosophy of Religion* 3, no. 1 (March 21, 2011): 227–37.
Davison, Scott A. *Petitionary Prayer: A Philosophical Investigation*. Oxford: Oxford University Press, 2017.
Di Muzio, Gianluca. "A Collaborative Model of Petitionary Prayer." *Religious Studies* 54, no. 1 (March 2018): 37–54.
Embry, Brian. "On (Not) Believing That God Has Answered a Prayer." *Faith and Philosophy* 35, no. 1 (2018): 132–41.
Flint, Thomas P. "Unanswered Prayers." In *Divine Providence: The Molinist Account*, 212–28. Ithaca, NY: Cornell University Press, 2006.
Harris, Harriet. "Prayer." In *The Cambridge Companion to Christian Philosophical Theology*, edited by Charles Taliaferro and Chad Meister, 216–37. Cambridge: Cambridge University Press, 2009.

Howard-Snyder, Daniel. "The Puzzle of Prayers of Thanksgiving and Praise." In *New Waves in Philosophy of Religion*, edited by Yujin Nagasawa and Erik J. Wielenberg, 125–49. New York: Palgrave Macmillan, 2009.

Howard-Snyder, Daniel, and Frances Howard-Snyder. "The Puzzle of Petitionary Prayer." *European Journal for Philosophy of Religion* 2, no. 2 (September 23, 2010): 43–68.

Mawson, T. J. "Praying for Known Outcomes." *Religious Studies* 43, no. 1 (March 2007): 71–87.

Pickup, Martin. "Answer to Our Prayers: The Unsolved But Solvable Problem of Petitionary Prayer." *Faith and Philosophy* 35, no. 1 (2018): 84–104.

Taliaferro, Charles. "Prayer." In *The Routledge Companion to Philosophy of Religion*, edited by Chad V. Meister and Paul Copan, 677–85. 2nd ed. New York: Routledge, 2013.

Woznicki, Christopher. "Peter Martyr Vermigli's Account of Petitionary Prayer: A Reformation Alternative to Contemporary Two-Way Contingency Accounts." *Philosophia Christi* 20, no. 1 (2018): 119–37.

Angels, Demons, Satan

Dunnington, Kent. "The Problem with the Satan Hypothesis: Natural Evil and Fallen Angel Theodicies." *Sophia* 57, no. 2 (June 2018): 265–74.

Freeman, Austin M. "Celestial Spheres: Angelic Bodies in Hyperspace." *TheoLogica: An International Journal for Philosophy of Religion and Philosophical Theology* 2, no. 2 (October 9, 2018): 168–86.

Gilhooly, John R. "Angelology and Nonreductive Dualism." *Philosophia Christi* 18, no. 1 (2016): 47–64.

Hart, Matthew J. "Christian Materialism and Demonic Temptation." *Philosophia Christi* 20, no. 2 (2018): 481–96.

McCraw, Benjamin, ed. *Philosophical Approaches to the Devil*. New York: Routledge, 2016.

Eschatology

Baker, Lynn Rudder, and Dean W Zimmerman. "Should Christians Endorse Mind-Body Dualism?" In *Contemporary Debates in Philosophy of Religion*, edited by Michael L. Peterson and Raymond J. VanArragon, Second Edition., 341–68. Hoboken: Wiley, 2019.

Barnard, Justin D. "Purgatory and the Dilemma of Sanctification." *Faith and Philosophy* 24, no. 3 (2007): 311–30.

Buenting, Joel. *The Problem of Hell: A Philosophical Anthology*. Burlington, VT: Ashgate, 2009.

Cockayne, Joshua. "Communal Knowledge and the Beatific Vision." *TheoLogica: An International Journal for Philosophy of Religion and Philosophical Theology* 2, no. 2 (May 8, 2018): 27–46.

Cowan, Steven B. "Compatibilism and the Sinlessness of the Redeemed in Heaven." *Faith and Philosophy* 28, no. 4 (2011): 416–31.

Davis, Stephen T. "Resurrection." In *The Cambridge Companion to Christian Philosophical Theology*, edited by Charles Taliaferro and Chad Meister, 108–23. Cambridge: Cambridge University Press, 2009.

Gaine, Simon Francis. "The Beatific Vision and the Heavenly Mediation of Christ." *TheoLogica: An International Journal for Philosophy of Religion and Philosophical Theology* 2, no. 2 (September 22, 2018): 116–28.

Henderson, Luke. "Character-Development and Heaven." *International Journal for Philosophy of Religion* 76, no. 3 (December 2014): 319–30.

Henderson, Luke. "Impeccability and Perfect Virtue." *Religious Studies* 53, no. 2 (June 2017): 261–80.

Hill, Jonathan. "In Defence of Inactivity: Boredom, Serenity, and Rest in Heaven." *TheoLogica: An International Journal for Philosophy of Religion and Philosophical Theology* 2, no. 2 (May 21, 2018): 3–26.

Holdier, A. G. "Divine Energies: The Consuming Fire and the Beatific Vision." *TheoLogica: An International Journal for Philosophy of Religion and Philosophical Theology* 2, no. 2 (May 24, 2018): 47–59.

Kittle, Simon. "Some Problems of Heavenly Freedom." *TheoLogica: An International Journal for Philosophy of Religion and Philosophical Theology* 2, no. 2 (May 24, 2018): 97–115.

Kvanvig, Jonathan L. *The Problem of Hell*. New York: Oxford University Press, 1993.

Laan, David Vander. "The Sanctification Argument for Purgatory." *Faith and Philosophy* 24, no. 3 (2007): 331–9.

Manis, R. Zachary. "The Doxastic Problem of Hell." In *Oxford Studies in Philosophy of Religion*, edited by Jonathan L. Kvanvig, 6: 203–23. New York: Oxford University Press, 2015.

Merricks, Trenton. "The Resurrection of the Body." In *The Oxford Handbook of Philosophical Theology*, edited by Thomas P. Flint and Michael C. Rea, 476–86. Oxford: Oxford University Press, 2009.

Mugg, Joshua, and James T. Turner, "Why a Bodily Resurrection?: The Bodily Resurrection and the Mind/Body Relation." *Journal of Analytic Theology* 5 (April 12, 2017): 121–44.

Nemes, Steven. "Christian Apokatastasis: Two Paradigmatic Objections." *Journal of Analytic Theology* 4 (May 6, 2016): 66–86.

Pawl, Timothy, and Kevin Timpe. "Incompatibilism, Sin and Free Will in Heaven." *Faith and Philosophy* 26, no. 4 (2009): 398–419.

Rutledge, Jonathan Curtis. "Purgatory, Hypertime, and Temporal Experience." *Journal of Analytic Theology* 6 (July 19, 2018): 151–61.

Sider, Theodore. "Hell and Vagueness." *Faith and Philosophy* 19, no. 1 (2002): 58–68.

Spiegel, James S. "Annihilation, Everlasting Torment, and Divine Justice." *International Journal of Philosophy and Theology* 76, no. 3 (May 27, 2015): 241–48.

Talbott, Thomas. *The Inescapable Love of God*. 2nd ed. Eugene, OR: Cascade Books, 2014.

Timpe, Kevin. "'Upright, Whole, and Free': Eschatological Union with God." *TheoLogica: An International Journal for Philosophy of Religion and Philosophical Theology* 2, no. 2 (May 21, 2018): 60–76.

Turner, James T., Jr. "Purgatory Puzzles: Moral Perfection and the Parousia." *Journal of Analytic Theology* 5, no. 1 (June 14, 2017): 197–219.

Turner, James T., Jr. *On the Resurrection of the Dead: A New Metaphysics of Afterlife for Christian Thought*. New York: Routledge, 2018.

Walls, Jerry L. *Heaven, Hell, and Purgatory: Rethinking the Things That Matter Most*. Grand Rapids, MI: Brazos Press, 2015. (This is a single, newer, more accessible combination of the author's three separate volumes on *Heaven: The Logic of Eternal Joy* (2002), *Hell: The Logic of Damnation* (1993), and *Purgatory: The Logic of Total Transformation* (2012))

Wessling, Jordan. "God Will Wipe Every Tear: Divine Passibility and the Prospects of Heavenly Blissfulness." *Neue Zeitschrift für Systematische Theologie und Religionsphilosophie* 58, no. 4 (January 1, 2016): 505–24.

Worsley, David Andrew. "Could There Be Suffering in Paradise? The Primal Sin, the Beatific Vision, and Suffering in Paradise." *Journal of Analytic Theology* 4 (May 6, 2016): 87–105.

Woznicki, Christopher. "'Thus Saith the Lord': Edwardsean Anti-Criterialism and the Physicalist Problem of Resurrection Identity'. *TheoLogica: An International Journal for Philosophy of Religion and Philosophical Theology* 2, no. 1 (March 27, 2018): 115–35.

Zimmerman, Dean W. "The Compatibility of Materialism and Survival: The 'Falling Elevator' Model." In *Oxford Readings in Philosophical Theology: Volume 2: Providence, Scripture, and Resurrection*, edited by Michael Rea, 321–7. Oxford: Oxford University Press, 2009.

Jewish and Islamic Analytic Theology

Lebens, Samuel. "Hebrew Philosophy or Jewish Theology? A False Dichotomy." *Journal of Analytic Theology* 2, no. 1 (May 8, 2014): 250–60.

Lebens, Samuel. *The Principles of Judaism*. New York: Oxford University Press, 2020.

Nordby, S. N. "Metaphor and the Mind of God in Nevi'im." *TheoLogica: An International Journal for Philosophy of Religion and Philosophical Theology* 2, no. 1 (March 27, 2018): 51–83.

Saeedimehr, Mohammad. "Divine Knowledge and the Doctrine of Badā'." *TheoLogica: An International Journal for Philosophy of Religion and Philosophical Theology* 2, no. 1 (March 27, 2018): 23–36.

Saemi, Amir, and Scott A. Davison. "Salvific Luck in Islamic Theology." *Journal of Analytic Theology* 8 (September 21, 2020): 120–30.

Sztuden, Alex. "Judaism and the Euthyphro Dilemma: Towards A New Approach." *TheoLogica: An International Journal for Philosophy of Religion and Philosophical Theology* 2, no. 1 (March 27, 2018): 37–50.

CONTRIBUTORS

James N. Anderson is Professor of Theology and Philosophy at Reformed Theological Seminary in Charlotte, North Carolina.

Benjamin H. Arbour (1981–2020) was Executive Director of the Institute for Theological and Philosophical Research in Fort Worth, Texas.

James M. Arcadi is Assistant Professor of Biblical and Systematic Theology at Trinity Evangelical Divinity School in Deerfield, Illinois.

Erik Baldwin is Adjunct Assistant Professor at Indiana University Northwest in Gary, Indiana.

Lindsay K. Cleveland received her PhD in Philosophy from Baylor University.

Joshua Cockayne is Lecturer in Analytic and Exegetical Theology at the University of St. Andrews.

William Lane Craig is Professor of Philosophy at Talbot School of Theology in La Mirada, California, and Houston Baptist University in Houston, Texas.

Oliver D. Crisp is Professor of Analytic Theology at the Logos Institute for Analytic and Exegetical Theology at the University of St. Andrews.

Scott A. Davison is Professor of Philosophy at Morehead State University in Morehead, Kentucky.

Kent Dunnington is Associate Professor of Philosophy at Biola University in La Mirada, California.

David Efird (1974–2020) was Senior Lecturer in Philosophy at York University.

Joshua R. Farris is Chester and Margaret Paluch Professor at Mundelein Seminary in Mundelein, Illinois.

David Fergusson is Professor of Divinity at the University of Edinburgh, New College.

Jesse Gentile is a PhD Candidate in Theology at Fuller Theological Seminary in Pasadena, California.

Benedikt Paul Göcke is Research Fellow at the Ian Ramsey Centre for Science and Religion and member of the Faculty of Theology at the University of Oxford.

Adam Green is Associate Professor of Philosophy at Azusa Pacific University in Azusa, California.

Johannes Grössl Assistant Professor for Fundamental Theology and Comparative Studies of Religion at University of Würzburg, Germany.

Daniel Howard-Snyder is Professor of Philosophy at Western Washington University in Bellingham, Washington.

Ross D. Inman is Associate Professor of Philosophy at Southeastern Baptist Theological Seminary in Wake Forest, North Carolina.

Joanna Leidenhag is Lecturer in Theology at the University of St. Andrews.

Andrew Ter Ern Loke is Associate Professor of Religion and Philosophy at Hong Kong Baptist University.

Thomas H. McCall is Professor of Theology and Scholar-in-Residence at Asbury University in Wilmore, Kentucky.

Daniel J. McKaughan is Associate Professor of Philosophy at Boston College in Chestnut Hill, Massachusetts.

Tyler Dalton McNabb is Assistant Professor of Philosophy at the University of St. Joseph (Macau).

Carl Mosser is former Professor of Theology at Gateway Seminary in Ontario, California.

R. T. Mullins is Research Fellow at the Institute for Advance Studies of the Humanities, University of Edinburgh.

Michelle Panchuk is Assistant Professor of Philosophy at Murray State University in Murray, Kentucky.

Faith Glavey Pawl teaches philosophy at the University of St. Thomas in St. Paul, Minnesota.

Timothy Pawl is Professor of Philosophy at the University of St. Thomas in St. Paul, Minnesota.

Katherin Rogers is Professor of Philosophy at the University of Delaware in Newark, Delaware.

R. Lucas Stamps is Associate Professor of Christian Studies at Anderson University in Anderson, South Carolina.

Nathaniel Gray Sutanto is Assistant Professor of Theology at Reformed Theological Seminary in Washington, DC.

James T. Turner, Jr. is Assistant Professor of Philosophy at Anderson University in Anderson, South Carolina.

Olli-Pekka Vainio is University Lecturer of Systematic Theology at the University of Helsinki.

Adonis Vidu is Professor of Theology at Gordon-Conwell Theological Seminary in South Hamilton, Massachusetts.

Aku Visala is Research Fellow of the Finish Academy of Sciences and Docent in Philosophy of Religion at the University of Helsinki.

Jordan Wessling is Assistant Professor of Religion at Lindsey Wilson College in Columbia, Kentucky.

William Wood is George Moody Fellow and Tutor in Theology at Oriel College, Oxford University.

Sameer Yadav is Associate Professor of Religious Studies at Westmont College in Santa Barbara, California.

Hilary Yancey received her PhD in Philosophy from Baylor University.

INDEX

Abbott, Edwin 191, 259
abductive argument 58–64
Abraham, William 2, 5, 46, 51, 162
abstract objects 165–77
Abstracta 105, 107–9, 170–1, 173, 177
accidental properties 88, 93, 96
Ad extra 56, 86, 93, 127–8, 134–6, 184 n.6, 258
Ad intra 56, 127–8, 134–6, 145, 184, 188, 190, 299
Adams, Marilyn McCord 2, 51 n.9, 141–3, 172, 198, 206, 258, 260, 336, 344, 350, 376, 403 n.8, 470, 471–2, 474
adoptionism 216, 225–6
Alston, William 2, 75, 116–17, 121, 263–4, 274–6, 287, 288
analytic philosophy 1–2, 52, 55, 58–9, 115, 125, 133, 161–2, 181, 231, 269, 277, 290, 297, 351–4, 414, 416, 428, 439, 441, 449, 470, 472, 477, 487
animal
  agency 395–6, 399, 400–4
  animal suffering, problem of 395, 403–4
  sin 395–404
Anselm of Canterbury, 50, 90, 101–10, 130 n.8, 133, 136 nn.24–5, 165, 183, 326 n.2, 329, 397–8, 402–4
anti-realism 12–14, 166–7, 173, 189, 414
apotheosis 270
Aquinas, Thomas 1, 14 n.14, 41–2, 50, 51 n.9, 87–9, 102, 104–5, 107–8, 110, 116, 121, 128 n.2, 129 n.5, 131 n.10, 133–4, 136 n.25, 155, 165, 167 n.6, 173–7, 183–4, 198, 222–3, 225, 260–4, 275, 283, 284 nn.6–8, 300, 302, 306, 312, 316–17, 319, 326 n.2, 348, 377, 385, 425, 469–70
Arcadi, James 14 n.15, 15 n.17, 30 n.10, 59 n.13, 133, 199, 202, 206 n.30, 313, 404 n.9, 418 n.11, 425, 433 n.20, 444 n.7, 449 n.15, 452, 456 n.12, 463, 464 n.3, 465, 470 n.12, 471, 471 n.13, 472, 474, 487 n.13
Aristotle 167, 173–4, 177, 198, 273, 300, 302, 303, 319, 347, 385, 400

Arminius, Jacob 88 n.1, 91, 128 n.1, 134
aseity 86, 88, 108, 132 n.14, 165–6, 169–71, 174, 177, 261, 297
Athanasian Creed 49, 127, 181, 201
Athanasius 25, 35, 50, 128 n.2, 270
atonement 47, 218, 231–41, 252, 325, 358, 388–90, 397–9, 402–4
Augustine 1, 47 n.3, 50, 87, 88 n.1, 93, 101 n.1, 102, 104, 107, 110, 128 n.2, 130 n.8, 131, 165, 173–4, 176 n.23, 183, 246 n.4, 316–17, 326 n.2, 328, 335, 337–8, 342, 377, 465 n.8, 490
Augustinianism 246, 249, 251, 252
Austin, J. L. 24, 352

baptism 51, 216, 270, 289, 451–60, 486
Bavinck, Herman 128, 264, 318, 453, 454 nn.5–6
Bayesian probability theorem 35–7, 415
biblical interpretation 22–3, 30, 148, 151, 169, 191, 315, 332
Big Bang Cosmology 297, 300, 307
bootstrapping objection 170–3
Bradshaw, David 273
Bratman, Michael 482
Breck, John 25–6, 29

Calvin, John 34, 50, 155, 158, 160, 264, 272, 314, 316, 319, 322, 326 n.2, 452 n.3, 455 n.9, 465, 468, 474
Calvinist 156, 158, 222, 243, 467
Cartesian 183, 319–20, 411 (*see also* Descartes)
Causal Principle 297, 301–4, 433
Chalmers, David 56 n.1, 276, 472
charismatic gift 281–92
Christology 3, 16, 49 n.7, 52, 191, 198–9, 204, 215–17, 221, 223–4, 226, 322, 390, 472, 473
Classical Theism 3, 15 n.16, 49, 85–95, 118, 136, 157, 159–61, 203, 302, 385
Clough, David 395–6
Coakley, Sarah 2, 192 n.19, 285, 381 n.1, 384, 388, 412, 484–5
cognitive science 409, 412–13, 417

Collins, Kenneth 36–8, 43, 298
community-centered epistemology 42
conceptual framework 9, 14, 17, 61–3, 261, 273, 317
conciliar doctrines 14, 24, 48–9, 51–3, 216, 223–4, 311, 317, 332
constitution relation 15–17, 96, 136, 186, 189, 190
Council of Chalcedon 16, 49, 53, 217
counterfactual of freedom 103, 105, 108, 158, 219–20, 223, 226
Craig, William Lane 25 n.4, 34, 89, 93, 121, 133, 158, 166, 167 n.5, 168–70, 172 n.14, 185, 198 n.5, 200, 202 n.16, 206 nn.29, 30, 224, 227, 248, 252, 298–303, 306
creation *ex nihilo* 85, 92–4, 105–6, 297–307, 411
creator-creature distinction 269, 271–2
Crisp, Oliver 1–2, 4, 14 n.12, n.15, 16 n.20, 46 n.2, 49 nn.5–7, 50 n.8, 51–2, 59 n.13, 64 n.26, 95, 191, 197 n.2, 198 n.4, 199 nn.9–10, 200 n.13, 201, 204 n.23, 206 n.29, 32, 222, 226, 246, 250, 269, 278, 314, 329, 330 n.8, 407, 430, 477
Crisp, Thomas 354
Cross, Richard 47 n.3, 51 n.9, 52, 90, 91 n.4, 133, 136 n.25, 197 n.3, 198, 201, 203, 205 n.28, 206 n.29, 223, 225, 370, 467–8, 473–4
Cuneo, Terence 79 n.3, 351, 451–2, 456–60, 465, 479–80, 482–3, 485

Dead Sea Scrolls 298
deification 142–3, 261–2, 269–78
Descartes, René 109 n.7, 319 (*see also* Cartesian)
disability 352, 353–4, 369–79
divine
 command theory 107, 348, 350
 conceptualism 171–4, 176–7
 hiddenness 114, 141, 152, 292, 384, 446 n.11
 immensity 110, 127–37, 258, 265
 immutability 85–8, 90, 92–3, 96, 202, 221, 223, 302, 384, 492
 impassibility 49, 86, 90–2, 205, 384–5, 492
 knowledge 113–29, 247, 250
 love 141–52, 261–6, 299
 nature 11, 14–16, 85–6, 88, 91–3, 102, 110, 127–8, 132, 141, 184, 190, 199, 203, 215, 223–5, 269

omnipotence 88, 94, 101–9, 114, 133, 134, 185, 188, 202, 221, 384
omnipresence 127–37, 258, 261, 409, 446, 448, 452
omniscience 88, 91, 113–25, 133–4, 145, 145, 159–61, 185, 221, 492–3 (*see also* divine knowledge)
simplicity 15 n.16, 16, 35, 49, 85–8, 90–1, 94–6, 116, 120, 128 n.1, 132 n.14, 135–6, 148, 158, 170–4, 192, 439
timelessness 85–93, 96, 121, 158, 160
wrath 150–2, 234, 398
Dominican knowledge 409
doubt 69, 70, 73–81
Dummett, Michael 463, 466–7, 474

Eastern Orthodoxy 41, 158, 259, 261, 264, 269, 311, 451, 457, 460, 479
Edwards, Johnathan 329, 329 n.7
election 192, 243–53, 327, 453, 454, 455
embodiment 218, 321–2, 360, 369–79, 425, 432
endurantism 89, 90, 430
energeiai 273
Enns, Peter 22–3, 327, 332, 425 n.7
eschatology 161, 312 n.2, 320–2, 358, 408, 423, 426, 433, 460
eternalism 34, 276, 472–4
ethics
 analytic theological ethics 347–55
Eucharist 80, 258, 273, 389, 451–2, 457 n.14, 463–74, 484 (*see also* Lord's Supper)
evidentialism 35, 38, 118–19, 290
evolutionary theory 366, 395–6
extended mind thesis 472–3
externalism 34, 276, 472–3

fallibilism 115, 116
federalism 327, 329
flatland 191, 259
foreknowledge 156, 160–1, 223, 250
Frankfurt, Harry 400–1
free will
 compatibilist view 158, 217–23, 225–7, 250, 253, 417
 libertarian view 103, 107–8, 158–60, 215, 217, 219–27, 247–50, 253, 301, 417

Gettier-style counterexamples 34, 118
great-making properties/attributes 86, 113–14, 146

INDEX

Gregory of Nazianzus 183, 224, 271
Gregory of Nyssa 183

Hasker, William 14, 90, 94, 117 n.3, 123, 159, 161, 186 n.9, 187–8, 190, 198 n.7, 200 n.13, 201, 492–3
Hauerwas, Stanley 351, 352
Heidelberg Confession, the 318
Helm, Paul 46 n.2, 85, 87, 90, 93, 156, 316, 317–20, 493
Homo sapiens 319, 410–11, 413
Hud Hudson 133, 113 n.15, 328, 330, 332, 410 n.5, 418, 430–1
humanity of Scripture 22–3
hylemorphism 432–3
hylomorphism 15
hypostatic union 16, 49, 199, 200–1, 205–6, 222–4, 258, 260, 278, 471

Imago dei 289, 311–19, 358, 386, 396, 413, 416
impeccability 215–27
imputation of sins 234, 236, 237 nn.14, 15, 239–40, 330
incarnation 14–16, 36, 49, 52, 197–206, 225, 231, 240, 262, 271, 388, 390, 397, 467, 471–3
Inclusion principle 397–8
Indiscernibility of identicals 203, 427, 430, 431 n.18
indispensability argument 168–9, 173, 175
inductive argument 36, 58–61, 303
indwelling of the Holy Spirit 257–66, 274, 276–7, 283–4, 292, 460
injustice 233, 237, 248, 253, 366 n.13, 378, 382–5, 387
inspiration of Scripture 21–30, 291, 448 n.12
internalism 34
Irenaeus 47, 222, 269, 270

Jackson, Frank 441
Jennings, Willie James 353, 357, 359, 360–7
Justification Thesis for Authority of Testimony 39

Kalam Cosmological Argument 297, 300
Khalidi, Muhammad Ali 364–5
Kierkegaard, Søren 328

Leftow, Brian 16 n.20, 85, 89, 94, 105 n.4, 113 n.1, 133 n.15, 146, 172, 172 nn.14, 15, 173, 174 n.17, 183, 185–7, 190, 198 n.7, 199, 199 n.10, 200, 200 n.13, 201, 202 n.16, 218, 218 n.4, 219, 492
legal fictions 234–5, 236 n.12, 460
Leibniz, Gottfried Wilhelm 107, 128 n.3, 173–4, 176–7, 301, 427 n.10, 469
liturgy 25, 56, 80, 351, 446, 465–6, 477–87
Locke-persons 183, 186–7
Logos 217, 218 n.4, 219, 221–3
Lombard, Peter 87, 88 n.1, 93, 122, 129, 130 n.8, 135 n.21, 259–60, 262, 264–5
Lord's Supper 446, 451–2
Luther, Martin 50, 264, 470, 489

MacIntyre, Alasdair 33, 41–2, 51, 348–9, 351
Maximal greatness 113–25
McCall, Thomas 1 n.1, 2, 14–15, 16 n.18, 49 n.5, 50–2, 59 n.13, 182 n.2, 184, 186 nn.8, 9, 188, 281, 410–11, 414
Mitchell, Basil 2, 4, 336, 344
mitochondrial Eve 327
modal collapse 85, 94–6
model building 9–17
Molina, Luis de 223, 246 n.4, 248, 492
Molinism 105, 108, 158, 246–9, 330
Molinist 25 n.4, 103, 105, 108, 156, 158, 159, 162, 223, 226, 247–50, 252
monothelitism 217, 224, 226
Mouw, Richard 320–1
Murray, Michael 206 n.32, 231 n.1, 407 n.3, 411, 413, 418, 493–5

natural law 348–50
natural theology 85–6, 162, 415
necessary being 85, 87
necessity
    absolute 94–6, 453
    hypothetical 94, 96
    relative 452–3
neoclassical theism 85
Neoplatonism 1, 105, 157
Newman, John Henry 37–8
Nicene Creed 17, 35, 49, 52
nominalism 167, 172, 176 n.20
norma normans 45, 48, 64
norma normata 45–8, 64

O'Donovan, Oliver 352
Oberman, Heiko 48
occasionalism 157, 172
Ockhamism 223, 246, 249, 250, 252
Open Theism 85, 123, 159–61, 492–3

Oppy, Graham 102, 103, 104
original sin 216 n.3, 325–32, 335, 338, 343, 410

panentheism 85, 92, 414
pantheism 85
papacy 36, 40, 43
Parousia 426, 430, 433
parsimonious agent causation 108
Paul, Apostle 38, 128, 243, 245, 270, 277
Pawl, Timothy 52, 96, 197 nn.1, 3, 472 n.16
Pentecostalism 291
perceptual religious experience 287, 290
perdurantism 430
perfect being theology 15 n.16, 86–8, 90, 104–6, 108, 113–25, 134, 147, 173, 175, 226, 233, 244, 384, 489, 493
perspicuity of Scripture 22, 24, 29–30
petitionary prayer 79, 160, 491–5
Plantinga, Alvin 2, 4, 12 n.7, 33–5, 104 n.2, 118–19, 159, 171–2, 289, 344, 415–16, 418
Plato 105, 165, 168, 173, 272–3, 300, 316, 319, 347
Platonism 165–77
Pogin, Kathryn 384–5, 387
predestination 243, 246, 247, 250
presence
  derivative 132
  fundamental 132–5
presentism 89, 93, 430, 433
prima facie reason to believe that God exists 38, 40–1
principium of theology 46
proper functionalism 34
providence 49, 135 n.23, 155–62, 220, 246–7, 249–50, 284–5, 412, 418, 492–3
Pruss, Alexander 94, 104 n.3, 122, 133, 166 n.4, 174 n.17, 176, 302, 412, 468 n.10, 469, 474, 491
punishment 28, 150–2, 155, 232–41, 252, 318, 329, 399, 402–3

racism 343, 357–67
Rasmussen, Joshua 304–5
Rea, Michael 1, 3, 15, 186, 197 n.2, 284, 329, 353, 386, 388 n.10, 446
realism 3, 12–14, 17, 166–7, 172–3
reformed epistemology 34, 289, 415
Reformed Orthodoxy 156, 311, 318, 320, 322

relativism 382
resurrection of the body 244, 321–2, 376–7, 379, 426–33, 448
Roman Catholic
  Catechism 48, 317, 424,
  Church 46, 48, 326, 452 n.3
Rowlands, Mark 402

Schleiermacher, Friedrich 222, 328
Science
  philosophy of 12, 13 n.10, 26 n.5, 55–65, 290, 414
Searle, John 482
Second Vatican Council 48
self-deception 335, 338 n.2, 339–44
self-love 337, 342
sensus divinitatis 35, 413
sola fide 23
sola gratia 23, 299
sola scriptura 23, 33, 46, 48
Solomon, Robert C. 439
speech act theory 24–25
standpoint epistemology 115, 382, 384
Stump, Eleonore 2, 15 n.16, 28 n.9, 51 n.9, 52, 86, 89, 95, 133 n.16, 141, 143, 145, 162, 198 n.4, 202 n.16, 215, 218, 223, 233 n.5, 234 n.6, 238 n.17, 263–4, 274, 275–6, 288, 351, 409, 418, 441–2, 444, 446, 484, 493, 494 n.10
Summa Contra Gentiles 116
Summa Theologica 105, 262, 300
supersessionism 357, 359–67
Swinburne, Richard 2, 14, 15 n.16, 22, 33, 35–6, 58 n.10, 85–6, 114, 123, 133, 160, 185, 187, 189 n.12, 206 n.32, 221, 225, 288, 330 n.8, 415, 418, 493

Talbert, Bonnie M. 441–5, 483
testimony 21, 29, 33, 35, 38–9, 42–3, 70, 286–7, 289, 291, 375, 383
The Fall 47, 325–32, 337
theistic activism 170–1, 173
theistic concept nominalism 172
theistic conceptual realism 172–3
theistic evolution 408, 415
theological anthropology 49, 311, 313, 318, 322, 358, 359–60, 396, 408, 410, 413, 416
theological methodology 45
theology
  constructive task 4, 9, 297, 463
theotokos 197

Timpe, Kevin 141, 206 n.31, 217, 220, 223, 337, 354, 370, 376, 378, 416 n.8, 417, 490 n.1
Transworld Depravity 330
Trinitarianism
  Anti-Social Trinitarianism 185
  Constitution Theory 186
  Latin Trinitarianism 222 n.5
  mysterianism 191
  relative identity 15, 188–90, 202–3, 205
  Social Trinitarianism 182–3, 221, 222 n.5
Trinity
  economic 190
  immanent 187, 190
  threeness-oneness problem 15, 181, 192
Tuggy, Dale 50, 52, 53, 187–8, 190 n.15
Turner, Jr., James 276–7, 305 n.10, 314, 321–2
Turretin, Francis 128 n.3, 129 n.5, 130, 131, 134, 135 n.21, 136

Underhill, Evelyn 481, 481 n.5, 482, 486
union with God 145, 216, 221
Universalism 38, 40–1, 246, 250, 252
utilitarianism 347

van Inwagen, Peter 15, 52, 56 n.1, 123, 166, 169, 188–90, 202, 202 n.16, 205 n.25, 219, 277, 328 n.5, 390 n.12, 427–9, 431, 490

Vanhoozer, Kevin 23–4, 26, 29–30
vicarious liability 236–7, 239

Walls, Jerry 36, 320
Ward, Keith 187
warrant 33–5, 42–3, 115, 118, 135
Webster, John 46, 50, 128
Welty, Greg 172–3, 253
Wesley, John 45, 136 n.26
Wesleyan 45–6
Wesleyan quadrilateral 45
Wessling, Jordan 2 n.3, 4, 14 n.15, 142–3, 145, 152, 206 n.30, 433 n.20, 474 n.18
Westphal, Merold 22–6
Westminster Confession of Faith 49, 127, 246 n.5, 311, 318, 424, 452 n.1, 454
William of Ockham 51 n.9, 122, 130, 223, 246, 470
Wolterstorff, Nicholas 2, 24–6, 56 n.3, 88, 174, 286, 350, 448 n.12, 465, 477, 479, 480–3, 484 n.9, 485
Wright, N. T. 425–6, 432, 473

Y-chromosomal Adam 327

Zagzebski, Linda 33, 38–43, 91, 122 n.9, 133 n.15, 141, 350–1, 492–3

www.ingramcontent.com/pod-product-compliance
Lightning Source LLC
Chambersburg PA
CBHW080530300426
44111CB00017B/2669